WILLA CATHER
Critical Assessments

Willa Cather outside an ancient Native American cliff-city, New Mexico. By permission of the Nebraska State Historical Society Photograph Collection

WILLA CATHER

Critical Assessments

———◆———

Edited by
Guy Reynolds

VOLUME IV
New Approaches to Willa Cather

HELM INFORMATION

Selection and editorial matter
© 2003 Helm Information Ltd
Helm Information Ltd
The Banks,
Mountfield,
near Robertsbridge,
East Sussex TN32 5JY

ISBN 1-873403-38-0

A CIP catalogue record for this book is available
from the British Library.

All rights reserved. No reproduction, copy or
transmission of this publication may be made
without written permission.

No paragraph of this publication may be
reproduced, copied or transmitted save with written
permission or in accordance with the provisions of
the Copyright Act 1956 (as amended), or under the
terms of any licence permitting limited copying
issued by the Copyright Licensing Agency,
7 Ridgmount Street, London WC1E 7AE.

Any person who does any unauthorised act in
relation to this publication may be
liable to criminal prosecution and civil claims for
damages.

Frontispiece Willa Cather outside an ancient Native American
cliff-city, New Mexico. By permission of the Nebraska State
Historical Society Photograph Collection.

Typeset by Servis Filmsetting Ltd, Manchester
Printed and bound by MPG Books Ltd, Bodmin,
Cornwall

Contents

VOLUME IV:
New Approaches to Willa Cather

Willa Cather and Religion

153. PAUL BORGMAN, 'The Dialectic of Willa Cather's Moral Vision,' *Renascence*, 27, 1975 — 3
154. CATHERINE M. McLAY, 'Religion in the Novels of Willa Cather', *Renascence*, 27, 1975 — 18

Empire and Ethnicity

155. DAVID STOUCK, 'Willa Cather and the Indian Heritage', *Twentieth Century Literature*, 22, 1976 — 41
156. MIKE FISCHER, 'Pastoralism and Its Discontents: Willa Cather and the Burden of Imperialism', *Mosaic*, 23, 1990 — 51

Ideas of History

157. HARRY B. HENDERSON, 'Willa Cather: Idealist Transcendence of Conflict', *Versions of the Past: The Historical Imagination in American Fiction*, Oxford, 1974 — 69
158. PATRICIA LEE YONGUE, 'Search & Research: Willa Cather in Quest of History', *Southwestern American Literature*, 5, 1975 — 72
159. JAMES WOODRESS, 'Willa Cather and History', *Arizona Quarterly*, 34, 1978 — 84
160. DAVID STOUCK, '*The Professor's House* and the Issues of History', *Willa Cather: Family, Community, and History*, ed. John J. Murphy, Provo, UT, 1990 — 95

CONTENTS

Modernism and Modernity

161. PHYLLIS ROSE, 'Modernism: The Case of Willa Cather', *Modernism Reconsidered*, ed. Robert Kieley, Cambridge, MA, 1983 — 109
162. CECELIA TICHI, from *Shifting Gears: Technology, Literature, Culture in Modernist America*, Chapel Hill, NC, 1987 — 127
163. JO ANN MIDDLETON, from 'Fiction's Vacuoles: Tracing What Willa Cather Left Out', *Willa Cather's Modernism: A Study of Style and Technique*, Rutherford, NJ, 1990 — 134
164. KATHLEEN WHEELER, 'Excavating Artistry in Willa Cather's Novels', 1997, Robertsbridge, 2003 — 148

The Literature of Place

165. MARCUS CUNLIFFE, 'The Two or More Worlds of Willa Cather', *The Art of Willa Cather*, eds Bernice Slote and Virginia Faulkner, Lincoln, NE, 1974 — 177
166. SUSAN J. ROSOWSKI, 'Willa Cather and the Fatality of Place: *O Pioneers!*, *My Ántonia*, and *A Lost Lady*', *Geography and Literature: A Meeting of the Disciplines*, eds William Mallory and Paul Simpson-Housley, Syracuse, 1987 — 194
167. DAVID HARRELL, 'The Cliff Dweller Thrill', *From Mesa Verde to The Professor's House*, Albuquerque, 1992 — 206
168. SUSAN J. ROSOWSKI, 'Willa Cather's Ecology of Place', *Western American Literature*, 30, 1995 — 227

Canon Studies

169. DAVID STINEBACK, 'No Stone Unturned: Popular versus Professional Evaluations of Willa Cather', *Prospects*, 7, 1982 — 241
170. SHARON O' BRIEN, 'Becoming Noncanonical: The Case Against Willa Cather', *American Quarterly*, 40, 1988 — 251
171. DEBORAH CARLIN, 'Categorical Cather: Reading the Canon(s)', *Cather, Canon and the Politics of Reading*, Amherst, MA, 1992 — 268

Gender Studies

172. ELLEN MOERS, from 'Performing Heroinism: the Myth of Corinne', *Literary Women*, London, 1978 — 293
173. JANE RULE, 'Willa Cather: 1876–1947' *Lesbian Images*, Trumansburg, NY, 1982 — 301
174. JENNIFER BAILEY, 'The Dangers of Femininity in Willa Cather's Fiction', *Journal of American Studies*, 16, 1982 — 312
175. SHARON O'BRIEN, 'Mothers, Daughters, and the "Art Necessity": Willa Cather and the Creative Process', *American*

Novelists Revisited: Essays in Feminist Criticism, ed. Fritz Fleischmann, Boston, 1982 — 326

176. JOANNA RUSS, 'To Write "Like a Woman": Transformations of Identity in the Work of Willa Cather', *Historical, Literary, and Erotic Aspects of Lesbianism,* ed. Monika Kehoe, New York, 1986 — 359

177. TIMOTHY DOW ADAMS, 'My Gay Ántonia: The Politics of Willa Cather's Lesbianism', *Historical, Literary, and Erotic Aspects of Lesbianism,* ed. Monika Kehoe, New York 1986 — 367

178. SANDRA GILBERT, and SUSAN GUBAR, from 'Lighting Out for the Territories', *No Man's Land,* Vol. II: *Sex Changes,* New Haven, 1989 — 374

179. SUSAN J. ROSOWSKI, 'Writing Against Silences: Female Adolescent Development in the Novels of Willa Cather', *Studies in the Novel,* 21, 1989 — 390

180. JUDITH FETTERLEY, '*My Ántonia,* Jim Burden, and the Dilemma of the Lesbian Writer' *Lesbian Texts and Contexts,* eds Karla Jay and Joanne Glasgow, New York, 1990 — 407

181. KATRINA IRVING, from 'Displacing Homosexuality: The Use of Ethnicity in Willa Cather's *My Ántonia*', *Modern Fiction Studies,* 36, 1990 — 423

182. C. SUSAN WIESENTHAL, 'Female Sexuality in Willa Cather's *O Pioneers!* and the Era of Scientific Sexology: A Dialogue Between Frontiers,' *Ariel,* 21, 1990 — 434

183. JOHN H. FLANNIGAN, 'Thea Kronborg's Vocal Transvestism: Willa Cather and the "Voz Contralto"', *Modern Fiction Studies,* 40, 1994 — 452

Willa Cather and Religion

153
The Dialectic of Willa Cather's Moral Vision

◆

PAUL BORGMAN

> This longing [for God's existence and immortality] begets hope, hope begets faith, and faith and hope beget charity.
>
> Miguel de Unamuno

The tragic sense of life, for both Willa Cather and the Spanish writer Unamuno, is a longing-not-to-die.[1] In a more substantive way, this sense of tragedy is the attempt to deal with an ultimate kind of contradiction; man has a basic instinct to live passionately, to preserve his conscious self; at the same time he has an instinct to know, to perpetuate himself by means of consciousness greater than his own. For Unamuno, this fundamental longing and contradiction can be understood in the metaphor of the heart's diastole and systole. Like the heart, the soul expands and relaxes whenever the instinct of perpetuation settles into a monistic or pantheistic assurance; this diastolic action threatens individual consciousness, however, and so the soul, in an instinctive reaction to preserve, contracts to the separateness of monotheism or egoism. The instinct to perpetuate individual consciousness is the basis for knowing, for the relational impulse which desires absorption into the world; the instinct to preserve individual consciousness is the basis for will, for the solipsistic impulse which desires absorption of the world into self. What interests Unamuno about the Biblical Cain is the outsider's instinct for preservation and his Dionysian 'struggle to survive in God, in the divine memory' (55). Abel represents the Apollonian impulse toward perpetuation and diastolic relaxing of individual consciousness which Cain must slay. For those with the tragic sense of life, however, both must remain alive, as contradictories: Abel-Cain is one person, longing not to die. Cain tends toward hope, Abel toward faith, and a tensioned balance of both tendencies suggests the action of love. A schematic of Miss Cather's moral

SOURCE Paul Borgman, 'The Dialectic of Willa Cather's Moral Vision', *Renascence*, 27, 1975, pp. 145–159

vision, suggested by the dialectic hope-faith-love, will be given first in a prefatory overview which includes a chronological glance at each novel. Because of space limitations, this paper will discuss only the first four and the last of Miss Cather's novels in any detail.[2] The suitability, value, and method of this approach to the author's entire body of novels should be clear from the following examination.

Only in Willa Cather's last novel, *Sapphira and the Slave Girl* (1940), does Abel-Cain live as one person. The book's moral vision is a culmination and synthesis of the longing-not-to-die present in all her novels. Let Cain be hope, an emphasis on Dionysian vitality, a struggle for primordial self-consciousness, and an insistence on sheer possibility and the availability of Time: Miss Cather's first four novels, then, explore the thesis of hope. *Alexander's Bridge* (1912) portrays a successful middle-aged conqueror who needs nonetheless to relearn the value of youth's impetuosity. A vital self-consciousness is preserved, however, at the expense of the perpetuating social self, and the imbalance of selves leads to destruction. *O Pioneers!* (1913) represents a central heroine characterised by vitality, strength, instinct for the Truth, and an ability to look toward the future. Hope is fulfilled in Alexandra Bergson, another conqueror. But Alexandra conquers in the private world of self-preservation rather than in the public world of name, fame, and social obligation. True, all these things are, in a sense, added unto her. But she has sought the first things. Hope is again fulfilled in *The Song Of The Lark* (1915), although the reader has the sense that something besides the split-selves problem of the first novel mitigates against fulfilled hope. As Miss Cather herself points out in an added preface, this problem is fundamental — more basic, I think, than the dramatic collapse of hope in *Alexander's Bridge*. A more cautious and circumspect praise of hope is achieved in the fourth novel, *My Ántonia* (1918), through the dramatic role of the narrator whose deepest instincts are those of faith.

In any dialectical process the movement from one thesis, or basic presupposition, or world-view, to the next is by no means a simple, clear leap. Rather, there appear small signs of stress and inadequacy in the original thesis, and after much living with the original thesis, less and less appropriate, one finally brings to consciousness an antithesis. As a formulation of the thesis deficiencies, this antithesis suggests a stage of disorientation, limbo, or even negativism. Finally a new thesis is brought into being, a synthesis or original thesis and an accomodation based on the antithesis. *One Of Ours* (1922), a seriously flawed work throughout, is the first of two portrayals which examine the insufficiencies of hope. Extrinsic to hope, the world of the common and the trivial is for the first time in the novelist's work triumphant over hope. In *A Lost Lady* (1923), a beautifully sustained work of essentially negative statement, the weakness of hope is intrinsic to hope's own nature. Hope needs help.

Let faith be the will to believe in, or to create, an order of permanence and unity. 'Faith is our longing for the eternal, for God; and hope is God's longing, the longing of the eternal, of the divine in us' (Unamuno, 200). This insight provides an interesting comment on Howard Mumford Jones' response to Miss Cather's earlier fiction, and particularly her treatment of the artist:

> [Henry James] pays homage to Apollo, [Willa Cather] to Dionysius, and though both agree that the artist is possessed of a secret and superior truth, for James the problem is Platonic, whereas Miss Cather narrates the unfolding of her singer in terms of Orphic initiation. Culture, it is James's hope, will eventually lead into that study of perfection which is art; but in Miss Cather's world the initiates already recognise each other by signs too subtle for the multitude. Art for the one is wisdom; for the other it is radiance.[3]

Paying homage to Dionysius is to assume that the overwhelming sense of hope is equivalent to God's longing in us: thus the tendency of the Dionysian toward the independent will and solipsism; faith is man's considered response to the matter of longing, the creation of a permanence and unity: thus the tendency of the Apollonian toward culture. The four novels following *A Lost Lady* imply the expansion and development of Miss Cather's moral vision, and the vision includes, in dialectical fashion, the original thesis and antithesis of her work.

Culture has gone sour in *The Professor's House* (1925), but Professor Godfrey St Peter nearly turns his back on even the culture of sweetness and light; the solitary primitive nearly allows himself to be suffocated to death by both a cardboard culture and a culture of shared truth. But the Professor learns a better way, a compromise between hope and faith. Hope and faith have equal but separate time in the next novel, *My Mortal Enemy* (1926); divided in a startling way, the structure of the book reflects this polarity. The created order and unity of life in Part II is the result of the heroine's careful pruning. Existence has been cleaned of all messy particulars and faith, the will to believe, has produced a sparse but pure essence. So too the effect of the book. *Death Comes For The Archbishop* (1927) is more expansive both in its faith and in its structure. Here faith creates an order and permanence of acceptance rather than negation. No longer eliminated because of their messiness, the particulars of existence have themselves become clean. Essence is a full and beautifully harmonious mosaic.

The contrast between a finely cut diamond, able to refract and play with light and shadows, and a carefully integrated mural, luxuriantly inclusive, is the contrast between *Shadows On The Rock* (1931) and *Death Comes For The Archbishop*. More distant in time and tone, *Shadows On The Rock*, has a shimmering, fragile beauty whose effect, for this reader at least, is more powerfully achieved than the final effect of *Death Comes For The Archbishop*. Less expansive in its created order than the earlier novel, *Shadows On The Rock* portrays a faith with fewer particulars more highly polished.

This precious state of faith gives way, in *Lucy Gayheart* (1935), to a melodramatic and explosive treatment of love. A desperate cry for something beyond the tense paralysis and suffocation of faith can be heard in the story of Lucy; filled with the expectancy and impetuosity of youth, the heroine is in need of a complementary, stabilizing sense of the world outside her. And worldly Harry Gordon filled with faith in the order of existence outside himself, needs the hope of Lucy. The conviction, in this work, that hope and faith cannot possibly work together in producing something finer is shallow, melodramatic, and unconvincing. Yet there is a life — a vitality and promise which had been lessening in the four prior novels of faith. God's longing in us had been progressively unsurped by man's longing for God; the original desire leading to belief now blasts through the will to believe. *Lucy Gayheart* is an antithetical stage in the progress of Willa Cather's moral vision.

A refrain increasingly meaningful to Lucy is sung by Sebastian Clement, her source of dreams and inspiration: 'If with all your heart you truly seek Him, you shall ever surely find Him.' Willa Cather's last novel, *Sapphira And The Slave Girl* (1940), is a subtle and finely wrought dramatisation of love: the integrity and perseverance of Miss Cather's progress as a moral pilgrim is appropriately celebrated only by including this novel among her most important. At times we of the literary establishment too easily find what we too easily look for. That one of Miss Cather's finest novels should be ignored by critics, and out of print, is lamentable. In *Sapphira And the Slave Girl* hope, God's longing within, and faith, man's longing for God, combine in a delicately-drawn but dynamic union. More than even a tensioned balance, this union is the subtle and powerfully achieved dramatisation of love's body.

II. God's Longing In Us: *Alexander's Bridge, O Pioneers!, The Song Of The Lark, My Ántonia*

Cain's strong instinct to preserve himself led him to slay his brother Abel. The younger brother gets along in the world, and enjoys a monistic, pantheistic sense of the divine: Abel perpetuates his consciousness by losing it in the All. But the Cain side of this Abel-Cain person feels his individual consciousness threatened and strikes out in order to retain the distinction between the All and Self; his identity in the divine memory is at stake. Cain seeks the divine through the separateness of monotheism and solipsism: the older brother preserves his consciousness by losing All. Cain's Dionysian struggle becomes a starved hope, for having lost his contradictory, he has indeed lost all and become an outsider. Without the tensioned balance one lives without the tragic sense of life. One lives not really at all.

Bartley Alexander, the hero of Willa Cather's first novel, was born a Cain, gradually becomes a very capable Abel, and finally, as Cain, slays Abel and dies. God's longing in Bartley becomes stronger than Bartley's will to believe, his longing for God. The world of hope destroys the world of faith, and is thereby itself destroyed. All of which Bartley himself explains in an uncharacteristically introspective moment to his mistress. He writes,

> It seems that a man is meant to live only one life in this world. When he tries to live a second, he develops another nature. I feel as if a second man had been grafted into me. At first he seemed only a pleasure-loving simpleton, of whose company I was rather ashamed, and whom I used to hide under my coat when I walked the Embankment, in London. But now he is strong and sullen, and he is fighting for his life at the cost of mine. That is his one activity: to grow strong. No creature ever wanted so much to live. Eventually, I suppose, he will absorb me altogether. (AB 130)

The second man is really the first youth of single purpose, single heart. Earlier in the book, having returned from Europe and reawakened energies, Bartley begins to feel the strangeness and threat of a world which apparently wants his soul. 'He was at home again, among all the dear familiar things that spoke to him of so many happy years.' Charming friends, perfect wife, satisfying pleasures: yet, 'amid this light and warmth and friendliness, he sometimes started and shuddered, as if some one had stepped on his grave. Something had broken loose in him of which he knew nothing except that it was sullen and powerful, and that it wrung and tortured him.'
Bartley is baffled; one imagines Abel among his sheep, facing the suddenly treacherous yet fascinating Cain.

> How could this happen here, in his own house, among the things he loved? What was it that reached in out of the darkness and thrilled him? As he stood there he had a feeling that he would never escape (88).

Bartley has always wanted all the birds in the bushes; hope unqualified is Bartley's dream of sheer possibility (15–16). Even Time will never run out in the Dionysian struggle to absorb the world into one's own consciousness, and this instinct to preserve the individual consciousness amounts to the conviction of immortality. Bartley's source of renewed hope is Hilda, an old acquaintance become mistress. After a long evening in London—which Bartley confesses 'always makes me want to live more than any other city in the world'—Hilda responds to a question about her possible tiredness:

> 'I'm not tired at all. I was just wondering how people can ever die. Why did you remind me of the mummy? Life seems the strongest and most indestructible thing in the world. Do you really believe that all those people rushing about down there, going to good diners and clubs and theaters, will be dead some day, and not care about anything? I don't believe it, and I know I shan't die, ever!' (AB 121)

This longing-not-to-die takes the form of hope, a sense of God's longing within rather than willed creation of, or belief in, ordered permanence. At times Bartley is able to leap free of the struggle between the two poles of tension 'into an overwhelming consciousness of himself. On the instant he [would feel] that marvelous return of the impetuousness, the intense excitement, the increasing expectancy of youth' (99). This instinct to preserve individual consciousness, over-ruling the instinct of perpetuation, leads in Bartley's case to death.

Willa Cather's switch, in *O Pioneers!*, from the tearooms of Boston and the theaters of London to the prairies and early pioneers of mid-America has as much to do, I suspect, with a need to locate hope in a suitable context for survival as with the need for the author to find her real story and style. Much of Miss Cather's 'real story' is, at any rate, a part of the basic structure, style, and implied moral vision of the first novel. Alexandra Bergson, like Bartley Alexander, has tremendous strength and energy, an impulse to always face the future of possibilities and potentialities, and a mind which is subordinate to the instincts of the heart and its truth. Like the other Alexander, she too has a strong instinct to conquer, to absorb the world into her consciousness; but there is at least one important difference:

> For the first time, perhaps, since that land emerged from the waters of geologic ages, a human face was set toward it with love and yearning. It seemed beautiful to her, rich and strong and glorious. Her eyes drank in the breadth of it, until her tears blinded her. Then the Genius of the Divide, the great free spirit which breathes across it, must have bent lower than it ever bent to a human will before. (OP 65)

Alexandra's youthful impetuosity and energies find the soil which will receive her imprint: God's longing in the heart of this woman has an objective correlative.

Another difference between the two central characters is the woman's independent status. Bartley marries young, and loses his Dionysian soul in the kindness and domesticated charm all about him. Revisited by youth, he then loses life. But Alexandra Bergson stays single until, relatively late in life and successful in leaving human landmarks on the barren land, she grants her tired self to an understanding, wise man. What Miss Cather seems to do here is to grant the need of perpetuation's instinct as a balance and salvation to the instinct of preservation. In fact, as Alexandra more or less collapses into the arms of her lover, the story ends; the earth itself receives Alexandra's heart 'into its bosom.' She has been lonely, maintaining her instinct for preservation, and now she will in any case satisfy the longing-not-to-die in perpetuation — in marriage to husband and earth. The two unions are separated by only a few pages at the end of the book. 'Fortunate country, that is one day to receive hearts like Alexandra's into its bosom, to give them out again in the yellow wheat, in the rustling corn, in the shining eyes of youth!' (308-9).

Throughout her Dionysian struggles, this dream has sustained Alexandra with its promise of final rest. Apollo has always been there, at the end of the road. Two of the best pioneers, Emil and Marie, strong in their passion, have been killed by the woman's husband: Alexandra is deeply shaken. Her own essence has been challenged, and she is suddenly tired. 'Longing itself was heavy: she yearned to be free of that.'

> As she lay with her eyes closed, she had again, more vividly than for many years, the old illusion of her girlhood, of being lifted and carried lightly by some one very strong. He was with her a long while this time, and carried her very far, and in his arms she felt free from pain. When he laid her down on her bed again, she opened her eyes, and, for the first time in her life, she saw him clearly, though the room was dark, and his face was covered. He was standing in the doorway of her room. His white cloak was thrown over his face, and his head was bent a little forward. His shoulders seemed as strong as the foundations of the world. His right arm, bared from the elbow, was dark and gleaming, like bronze, and she knew at once that it was the arm of the mightiest of all lovers. She knew at last for whom it was she had waited, and where he would carry her. (OP 282-3)

A life of hope is rescued by a dream of faith. Alexandra's youthful impetuosity and painful struggles have been rewarded, in the end, by the promise of perpetuation.

God's longing in Thea Kronborg, the heroine of *The Song Of The Lark*, does not have any such objective correlative as a barren, exciting prairie awaiting her human landark. In fact, her home town of Moonstone provides only 'the clamour about her' which 'drowned the voice within herself' (SL 73). Thea's instinctive longing to preserve her individual consciousness, described variously as inherent desire (95), a friendly Spirit (100), imagination and stubborn will (122), and instinctive ideals (327), can find in Moonstone no world worthy of absorption into consciousness. This 'hopefulness of first youth' (122) will remain with Thea, forcing her to the city, which is itself described as 'appetent' (244). This city might wish to absorb Thea into its consciousness, but the Dionysian refuses to yield to her individual essence, her ecstasy and majesty. At times Chicago becomes, for the aspiring musical artist, an opposing consciousness which is worthy of her own struggle to dominate:

> All these things and people were no longer remote and negligible; they had to be met, they were lined up against her, they were there to take something from her. Very well; they should never have it. They might trample her to death, but they should never have it. As long as she lived that ecstasy was going to be hers. She would live for it, work for it, die for it; but she was going to have it, time after time, height after height. She could hear the crash of the orchestra again, and she rose on the brasses. She would have it, what the trumpeters were singing! She would have it, have it—it! Under the old cape she pressed her hands upon her heaving bosom, that was a little girl's no longer. (SL 254-5)

Not only the trumpet's voice, but the future as well shall be had, 'time after time, height after height.' Thea's longing-not-to-die takes the form of powerful hope.

But there are only twenty splendid years, says Dr Archie, a life-long friend of Thea's. And 'the main thing is to live those twenty splendid years; to do all we can and enjoy all we can' (175). Some of those years are apparently, for Dr Archie, able to be saved for a second youth; he enjoys his last years with a new youthfulness and undirected impulse (488). Unlike the unfortunate Bartley Alexander, Dr Archie enjoys the freedom with which a dead wife leaves him. But hope needs a sense of the future, and if *The Song Of The Lark* lags some toward the end, the reason is as much the running out of time—those twenty years—as it is the problem that success is less interesting than struggle.

Thea will enjoy perpetuation, however, though not because of any instinct of her own. She herself withers: the tone of Thea's strong impulse to preserve her own artistic consciousness suggests an ultimately withering affair. Life shrinks to that instinct alone. A tragic but vitalizing sense of the contradictory instinct of perpetuation is not a part of Thea's makeup. And yet there is a sense of perpetuation in the novel. Thea lives on in the hearts and smiles of those who hear her. 'If the singer, going home exhausted in her car, was wondering what was the good of it all, that smile [of Spanish Johnny's], could she have seen it, would have answered her' (573). And she lives on, back in Moonstone. Silly Aunt Tillie finds justification for her own meager life. 'Thea Kronborg has given much noble pleasure to a world that needs all it can get,' and Moonstone not least of all (578-81).

There is something conspicuously right—brilliant, integrated, and fitting—about the best of Willa Cather's first four novels, *My Ántonia*. Certainly the prominent place given to Jim Burden, a character-narrator, is a noticeable departure for the author. If these two observations are put together under the rubric of Miss Cather's implied moral vision, we gain at least one perspective for articulating the genius of *My Ántonia*. Bartley Alexander's experience of the God-longing within him was void of any viable faith. His instinct for preservation of individual consciousness overwhelmed any instinct for perpetuation. Solipsism contained its own world, but too great a stress caused this self—like the bridge—to collapse. Yet the author wishes to praise hope, and its inevitable doom is at best not a very rigorously explored idea; at worst, this fissure in the realm of hope is unconvincing melodrama. Alexandra Bergson's vitality comes from a non-introspective heart which humanises the wild prairie with her own landmarks: from such activity, we are told, the histories of lands are made. Alexandra is the subject—a powerful subject—of a history which the author tells. Her Apollonian lover Carl would be an appropriate candidate for writing the history which Alexandra makes. But this instinct for perpetuation is not present, as such, in the novel itself. Miss Cather's own instinct for perpetuation has to rescue Alexandra, and with integrity the author reflects the dilemma by dramatizing this needed complement to hope as a final rest in the arms of a stronger self, in the bosom of a more lasting reality. Missing from the novel, this instinct for perpetuation can only be seen as a collapse of the Dionysian will into the Apollonian consciousness, and this the author faithfully reflects. But the final effect for the reader, as it must have been for the author herself, is less than satisfying. Thea Kronborg is also the appropriate subject for a history. She is a large subject; she has absorbed much of the world into her individual consciousness. Since hope, however, needs the future, and Thea runs out of Time, the reader senses a tone of withering in the last half of the novel. Through an added preface, we know that Miss Cather was herself not satisfied: as she expressed it, success is always less interesting than the struggle. Hope flounders if left to build on its own foundations alone.

My Ántonia has more of Jim Burden than of Ántonia, and an even more important observation is that this is a history which Jim writes. Ántonia is the most important subject of this history, and yet she is just one of 'my country girls,'—the Bohemians and Scandinavians: one of the five chapters is given over exclusively to Lena Lingard. Jim is seeking to capture certain images in the memory, to celebrate his longing for the God of permanence and ordered beauty. 'The pioneer woman's story' (a chapter heading) is suitable for this instinct to perpetuate, because Ántonia provides Jim with a central image, a motif. 'She lent herself to immemorial human attitudes which we recognise by instinct as universal and true' (353). Tony is a strong vital woman: her face, says Jim, was 'the closest, realest face, under all the shadows of women's faces, at the very bottom of my memory' (322). Jim has a heightened consciousness toward all the 'closest, realest' things of this world, while Tony has a heightened consciousness toward her own reality.

Ántonia lives in her skin as a fish lives in his, and yet she is the first of Miss Cather's heroes or heroines of hope to possess an instinct of perpetuation in any marked degree. Her fulfillment does indeed seem to come when she is a living wife and fruitful mother. Jim is able to capture the sense of birth and perpetuation when he visits Tony at the end of his story:

> We turned to leave the cave; Ántonia and I went up the stairs first, and the children waited. We were standing outside talking, when they all came running up the steps together, big and little, tow heads and gold heads and brown, and flashing little naked legs; a veritable explosion of life out of the dark cave into the sunlight (338).

This is appropriate, just as for Alexandra Bergson it was appropriate for the country to reproduce her spirit 'in the yellow wheat, in the rustling corn, in the shining eyes of youth!' One clear difference between the two pioneers is the difference of this suitability. And Ántonia needs Jim as no other of the Dionysians have needed anyone.

But Ántonia's basic instinct and essential reality is that of preservation, and her greatest need for Jim is felt only by the reader. She needs Jim to tell her story, and Jim needs to be a part of the story for that special effect of genius that we feel in *My Ántonia*. And of course a part of this effect is Jim's need for Tony, for a story to tell, for a subject in whom he can believe, and into whom he can let his consciousness be absorbed. From the start Jim has experienced this instinct of perpetuation:

> The earth was warm under me, and warm as I crumbled it through my fingers. Queer little red bugs came out and moved in slow squadrons around me. Their backs were polished vermillion, with black spots. *I kept as still as I could.* Nothing happened. I did not expect anything to happen. I was something that lay under the sun and felt it, like the pumpkins, and I did not want to be anything more. I was entirely happy. Perhaps we feel like that when we die and become a part of something entire, whether it is sun and air, or goodness and knowledge. At any rate, that is happiness; to be dissolved into something complete and great. (MA 18, *italics mine*)

Motion and vitality describe Ántonia, but Jim must keep as still as he can in order to 'become a part of something entire.' The balance achieved between Ántonia and Jim, between hope and faith, is at least a part of this novel's artistic genius.

III. God's Longing In Us and Man's Longing For God: Love's Body in *Sapphira And The Slave Girl*

For Unamuno, the tragic sense of life is understood by viewing Cain and Abel as a contradictory unit, a single person whose instinct to preserve and promote an individual consciousness must live side by side — as diastole and systole of the heart — with its natural enemy, the instinct to perpetuate one's consciousness by means of absorption into a greater Consciousness. Cain has massive hope, and adds to his original bounteous store of talents: he increasingly absorbs the world into his own consciousness. Abel has great faith, and adds to the world's storehouse: he increasingly loses his life to the greater All. Cain-Abel live together as one person, unhappily, for ever and ever (literally for ever and ever) in Unamuno's picture, but what the great Spanish thinker has not emphasised is the Christian mystery of the Body. Together we are Christ's Body, as different and contradictory parts. There are capacities: to hope, adding talents and a sense of individual consciousness; to believe, losing one's life while forfeiting the world. And there is love: the dynamic of contradictories experiencing a common life, as one body.

Marriage is a mystery of union whose dynamic of love resembles the mystery of the Body's union, says St Paul. We begin to understand the nature of God's grace in making the two one flesh. Hope begets faith, and faith and hope beget love. Alone of Willa Cather's novels, *Sapphira And The Slave Girl* has at its dramatic center married love. Bartley Alexander's marriage, and life, are destroyed by excessive hope. Mrs Forrester (*A Lost Lady*) becomes lost by gradually allowing vitality to overshadow her 'other half,' the faith of Captain Forrester. Godfrey St Peter (*The Professor's House*) is reluctant to live in his own house because he can find neither hope nor faith, except, finally, within himself. *My Mortal Enemy* portrays the destructive power of an exclusive and negating faith. But in Miss Cather's last novel we begin and end with a dramatisation of love's body, the union of hope and faith in 'one flesh.'

Delicacy of tone distinguishes what could easily have been a sentimental and melodramatic picture of married love in this novel. Much of its surface has the kind of pleasantness which Sapphira Colbert has—'not very warm' (SSG 16). Only in *My Ántonia*, *My Mortal Enemy*, *Shadows On The Rock*, and possibly *The Professor's House* has the author controlled as well a desired effect, and in no previous novel has the task been as great. This story is, after all, an epiphany of the 'many happy years' which Sapphira claims for her marriage. They have just passed what apparently has been the greatest crisis in their marriage; yet even this drama is not so overblown that the reader has any trouble in understanding the central and abiding reality of their union.

Henry Colbert has been willing to lose his life, rather than win the world. His faith is a humble service to others and a longing after God and His orders and designs. Slavery bothers Henry, terribly; he wrestles with a situation accepted naturally by Sapphira:

> We must rest, he told himself, on our confidence in His design. Design was clear enough in the stars, the seasons, in the woods and fields. But in human affairs—? Perhaps our bewilderment came from a fault in our perceptions: we could never see what was behind the next turn of the road (111).

Henry's longing for God, this will to believe in created orders and permanence, is paralleled by his willingness to serve the world rather than master it, to be absorbed into the great Consciousness rather than to absorb the world into his own consciousness.

This conventional portrait of goodness avoids sentimentality and melodrama into two ways. First of all, Henry's daughter Rachel Blake serves, dramatically, as both a commentator on and an illustration of Henry's goodness. For the most part the reader is not permitted a direct view. From the very first Rachel is a second-hand likeness, an image, of her father. Our first introduction is a decided one: 'She was a woman of thirty-six or -seven, though she looked older—looked so much like Henry Colbert that it was not hard to guess she was his daughter' (11). As commentator, Henry's daughter speaks, early in the novel, with her mother. Rachel thinks the Baptists good people. The high-church Sapphira responds,

> 'So your father thinks. But then he never did mind to forgather with common people. I suppose that goes with a miller's business.'
> 'Yes, the common folks hereabouts have got to have flour and meal, and there's only one mill for them to come to.' (SSG 16)

And a little later the reader encounters Rachel in her role as father's image:

> As she drove along, Mrs Colbert was thinking it was fortunate that for once her daughter had been called to nurse in a prosperous family like the Thatchers

> ... Usually she was called out to some bare mountain cabin where she got nothing but thanks, and likely as not had to take along milk and eggs and her own sheets for the poor creature who was sick. Rachel was poor, and it was not much use to give her things. Whatever she had she took where it was needed most; and Mrs Colbert certainly didn't intend to keep the whole mountain. (SSG 38)

With this delicate distancing the author is able to avoid the unbearable high sheen of goodness viewed in direct and dazzling sunlight. The softness of tone —the 'not very warm' quality of the book's surface—is intentional. The author can then afford to give the reader a few direct observations and glimpses of Henry: hard-working, fair dealing, and completely trustworthy (4–5); acceptance of credit for incurable debtors—the poor which he recognises will always be with him (49); kindness toward Nancy, the slave girl with 'a natural delicacy of feeling' (44); and the maintenance of a difficult self-control (208–11).

The second device Miss Cather uses to avoid a melodramatic characterisation of Henry is suggested indirectly by Rachel and more directly by Henry's own experience. Rachel is a widow, and her obviously incomplete life lacks the gaiety which her husband once provided. Henry needs Sapphira. Without her this good man would be half a person: the reader is convinced not only by viewing Rachel but by the action of the story itself. His need for Sapphira makes Henry's goodness appear as less than the perfect and self-sufficient thing it would have been in a brilliantly layered but garishly ornate cameo. Henry's character, his fundamental instinct to lose himself for a greater whole, is carved into a surface portrait without obvious glitter: his goodness becomes profoundly convincing only in its subtle union with another, contradictory, goodness.

'Whatever [Rachel] had she took where it was needed most; and Mrs Colbert certainly didn't intend to keep the whole mountain.' But Sapphira Colbert keeps her own house beautifully. Like all strong persons of hope, Sapphira has had little time for Henry's kind of reflection. Born with many more talents than most, Sapphira has used them well. She has added to that within her own consciousness and control. Book I, 'Sapphira and Her Household,' concludes with praise: 'It was because she had been so energetic, and such a good manager, that even from an invalid's chair she was still able to keep servants well in hand' (54).

Impervious and reserved, courageous and proud, Sapphira's marital choice has proven an enigma for most of her friends. For these there is an obvious discrepancy: 'his plain manners, his calling, vague ancestry, even his Lutheran connections;' the miller had an 'unbending, somewhat uncouth figure' (25). *Sapphira And The Slave Girl* is a very moving explanation of that enigma. Henry nearly lives at the mill, but only the ignorant and vicious misinterpret the situation. On a late, cold and drizzly spring day Henry is summoned from the mill to the house by Sapphira. The miller is 'glad to escape,' and to take tea with his wife.

> He found his wife dressed for the afternoon, with a lace cap on her head and her rings on her fingers, having her tea by the fire. (When she heard him open the front door she poured his cup, smuggling in a good tot of Jamaica rum, since he didn't take cream.) Before he sat down, he took up a plate of toasted biscuit from the hearth and offered it to his wife. He drank his tea in a few swallows, though it was very hot.
>
> 'Thank you Sapphy. That takes the chill out of a body's bones. It does get damp down there at the mill. Could you spare me another cup?'
>
> Munching his biscuit, he watched her pour the tea. When she reached down for a small red cruet, well concealed on the lower deck of the table, he laughed and rubbed his hands together. 'That's why it tastes so good! I must try to get up here oftener when you're having your tea. But it's just about this time of day the farmers come in. The good ones are at work all morning, and the poor sticks never get around to anything at all till the day's "most gone."'
>
> 'I'm sure the Master would always be very welcome company in the evenings,' replied Mrs Colbert, lifting her eyebrows, whether archly or ironically it would be hard to say.
>
> 'Don't you put on with me, Sapphy.' He reached down to the hearth for another biscuit. 'You're the master here, and I'm the miller. And that's how I like it to be.'
>
> His wife looked at him with an indulgent smile, and shook her head. She stirred her tea gently for a few moments in silence. A log fell apart in the fire and shot up tall flames; the miller put the ends together with tongs. (SSG 49–50)

No scene, excepting that with which the story proper concludes, more delicately and eloquently describes the visible union of their love.

The particular power of this passage is increased by the reader's awareness that Sapphira is deeply concerned about her slave girl, Nancy, and that this concern has something to do with a crisis in the marriage between miller and master. Book I ends on this dramatic note. Sapphira is deeply jealous of the lithe, pretty, well-mannered, and lively mulatto, Nancy. Henry prefers Nancy above all others for the care of his mill. The two are seen by Sapphira in frankly interested and intimate conversation. Henry comes from a family with a reputation for promiscuity. At the deepest core of her being Sapphira is threatened; this is a more unbearable circumstance than her confinement to a wheelchair. Sapphira's essence is to preserve her individual consciousness, to absorb the world into her own controls. And here is a possible, unbearable loss of Henry. What Miss Cather finally reveals to the reader is the inevitability and even appropriateness of this jealousy.

But this complete unwillingness to let the world have any bit of hers lets loose a pandora's box of evil. A perverse and worthless young rascal is encouraged; Nancy experiences a vicious rejection and finally a complete terror; Henry's lusts, dormant at the time of Sapphira's suspicion, are now stirred; Rachel, who aids in Nancy's escape, is sealed off from the Colbert home. And Sapphira has been deeply wounded at her most vulnerable points, her pride and self-esteem. The last book of the story, excluding the epilogue, begins with Sapphira spending most of her time in bed. Finally, concern for her very sick grandchildren rouses Mrs Colbert to her customary action.

The death of little Betty Blake puts in motion the author's crescendo of praise for this union of faith and hope. Love's body has weathered an illness native to its constitution, for love is a dynamic between two contradictories. Sapphira is attempting to comfort Henry, for little Betty was his favorite:

> Mrs Colbert reached out and caught his hand. 'I know, Henry, I know. But these things are beyond us. One shall be left and the other taken. It's beyond us.' She was silent for a moment. Suddenly she gripped his cold fingers and broke out with something of her old masterfulness: 'And, Henry, Mary will get *so much more* out of life!'
> 'More for herself, maybe,' the miller sighed. 'But I doubt if she will be as much comfort to others. The gentle spirit has left us.'
> 'Sit down dear. Get my old hassock yonder and sit low, close to the fire. Your hands are like ice. This is a time when we must both think.' She reached under the tea-table for the red flask and poured the rum into her empty teacup. He drank it obediently. She knew he was too tired to talk, so they sat in silence. (SSG 265-6)

Even the tenderness avoids the wrong kind of softness at this point by the author's gentle reminder that Sapphira is decidedly Sapphira the master, and Henry is Henry the miller: the grand lady takes heart that Mary — so like herself — will get so much more out of life, while Henry, always sympathetic to the gentle, giving spirit, mourns the departure of Betty.

Continuing this exchange, with which their story concludes, Sapphira slowly decides to have Henry invite Rachel and Mary to live with them. Her health is failing, after all . . .

> Colbert felt a chill run through him. Sapphira had never before spoken to him of the possibility that something might happen to her this winter. Though now she mentioned this very casually, it struck terror to his heart. He seemed in a moment to feel sharply so many things he had grown used to and taken for granted: her long illness, with all its discomforts, and the intrepid courage with which she had faced the inevitable. He reached out for her two hands and buried his face in her palms. She felt his tears wet on her skin. For a long while he crouched thus, leaning against her chair, his head on her knee.
> He had never understood his wife very well, but he had always been proud of her. When she was young, she was fearless and independent, she held her head high and made this Mill House a place where town folks liked to come. After she was old and ill, she never lowered her flag; not even now, when she knew the end was not far off. . . . As long as she was conscious, she would be mistress of the situation and of herself. (SSG 267-8)

Henry rouses himself to verbal expression of his admiration. 'She turned it off lightly, tweaking his ear. Stubbornly, the miller follows his train of thought and thanks. 'Sometimes,' he thinks — trying to define this special kind of goodness — 'keeping people in their place is being good to them.' And the scene closes on Sapphira's rejoinder: ' "Perhaps. We would all do better if we had our lives to live over again." She was silent for a moment, then added thoughtfully: "Take it all, though, we have had many happy years here, and we both love the place. Neither of us would be easy anywhere else.'" (269). Indeed. And a final softening touch is added by the author, an epilogue which, with its perspective in time and tone, draws a curtain over the radiance left on stage. And this is the technical genius of the book throughout, the avoidance of sentimentality and melodrama in a surface not too warm.

Longing-not-to-die has two instincts. To preserve is to hope, and to perpetuate is to believe. Hope begets faith, and faith and hope beget love. In the difficult union of contradictories is love's body to be found. From the perspective of the dominant tradition in American letters which emphasises the individual consciousness, and from the perspective of the moral dialectic in Willa Cather's novels, *Sapphira And the Slave Girl* took this author her life time to write. In response to the special achievement of Willa Cather in producing with so much integrity the three things that last, one might wish to sing, or at least hum, Henry Colbert's favorite hymn.

Although Unamuno does not explore the mystery of love's body, he does indicate an insight central to this study. Love seeks to personalise. Love imagines and responds to individual consciousness: it fills the earth with meetings between one center of will and longing and another. St Paul concludes in grand praise of love on a similar note. Love's body, the Body of Christ, allows for and insists on a moral dialectic. From the mind-sets of children we grow, and the dim mirror reflections become gradually more clear. For the Christian, consummation is the clearest moment of all, when 'we shall see face to face' and 'shall know as fully as [we are] known.' Few dramatisations in man's literature suggest so clearly St Paul's meaning as does the final scene between Henry and Sapphira. Face to face, they know and are known in a celebration of mutual recognition.

Notes

1. Miguel de Unamuno, *The Tragic Sense of Life*, trans. J.E. Crawford Flitch (New York: Dover Publications, 1921, 1954), p. 37. The epigraph is p. 185.

2. The following editions of Cather's novels will be cited in the essay with pages noted in parentheses: (AB) *Alexander's Bridge* (N.Y.: Houghton Mifflin Co., 1912); (OP) *O Pioneers!* (Boston: Houghton Mifflin, 1913, 1941); (SL) *The Song of the Lark* (N.Y.: Houghton Mifflin, 1915, 1943); (MA) *My Ántonia* (N.Y.: Houghton Mifflin, 1918, 1954); (SSG) *Sapphira and the Slave Girl* (N.Y.: A. Knopf, 1940).

3. Howard Mumford Jones, *The Bright Medusa;* excerpts reprinted in James Schroeter, ed., *Willa Cather and Her Critics* (Ithaca: Cornell University Press, 1967), p. 248.

154
Religion in the Novels of Willa Cather

◆

CATHERINE M. McLAY

'We approach the world through art and art is our link with it.' In her *Willa Cather: A Memoir*, Elizabeth Shepley Sergeant observes that Willa Cather comes closer to living out this dictum of Goethe's than any other writer she has known.[1] Thus a study of Willa Cather's art involves a study as well of the world as she saw it and recorded it in fiction, and her search for order and meaning, for stability and eternal values in the midst of the flux and change of life itself. For through her art Cather is able, at least temporarily, to bring shape and order to her experience, to record her impressions of life before her materials dissolve and fade. As Cather remarks in 'The Novel Démeublé': 'out of the teaming gleaming stream of the present it [the novel] must select the eternal material of art.'[2]

In her early novels *O Pioneers!* and *My Ántonia* Cather finds a centre of order and meaning in nature and the land, which generate a sense of religious fulfilment. Her middle novels turn for their inspiration to the order of art, an order already treated in the early short stories, the first novel *Alexander's Bridge* and in her novel preceding *My Ántonia*, *The Song of the Lark* which is her 'portrait of the artist.' Although Thea is the only character who finds in art the sense of fulfilment that Jim Burden finds in nature, a discovery which costs her not less than everything, Cather's other protagonists Claude Wheeler, of *One of Ours*, Niel Herbert of *A Lost Lady* and Professor St Peter of *The Professor's House* look to art for their ideals, even their *raison d'être* and their tragedy lies in their recognition that art is no longer possible in America, that the temporal values of post-war America negate the existence of culture and prevent their achieving their quest. And in her late novels *My Mortal Enemy*, *Death Comes for the Archbishop* and *Shadows on the Rock*, Cather attempts to reach the certitude and faith of religion as it is

SOURCE Catherine M. McLay, 'Religion in the Novels of Willa Cather', *Renascence*, 27, 1975, pp. 125–144

expressed in the Catholic church for, as Myra Henshawe says, 'in religion, desire was fulfilment, it was the seeking itself which rewarded' (ME 94).[3] But the order of religion is not the answer either, and in her last works *Lucy Gayheart* and *Sapphira and the Slave Girl*, Cather first returns to the life of the artist to-day, and then begins a fresh direction with a new setting and a new theme: the moral problems of slavery in the South-West. Yet while these three groups of novels seek for fulfilment in different spheres, in nature, art and religion, all three are, in a sense, the quest of the artist, for each protagonist is in a sense Cather herself, and each pursues the ideals which David Daiches describes as 'beauty, order and heroic action.'[4]

The relationship between religion and art has always, for Cather, been close. Long before she commented in the Professor's lecture that art and religion are 'the same thing in the end, of course' (PH 79), she noted the connection between religion and aesthetics. An early article in the *Journal* of 1894 describes God as the supreme artist, the magnification of all earthly artists:

> ... The world was made by an Artist ... of such insatiate love of beauty that He takes all forces, all space, all time to fill them with His universes of beauty; an Artist whose dreams are so intense and real that they, too, love and suffer and have dreams of their own ... this Painter, this Poet, this Musician, this gigantic Artist of all art that is, this God whose spirit moved upon chaos leaving beauty incarnate in its shadow.[5]

Professor St Peter sees the Christian theologians as great artists who revised the books of the Law till they achieved a dramatic effect, and the sculptors, glass-workers and painters of the Renaissance as revealing the truth of the prayer: *'Thy will be done in art, as it is in heaven'* (PH 69). Even the Virgin Mary is seen as an artist, for she composed the poetry of the *Magnificat* (PH 100), and in *Death Comes for the Archbishop* she appears to the missionary priest Juan Diego and paints herself in blue and gold on the coarse material of his mantle.

Cather's late novels still concern the quest of the artist who is not unlike the pioneer. The difference between these and her early works lies in the use of religion as the end of this quest, and as the unifying pattern for the assorted tales, legends, miracles, works of art, and daily experiences of life. Thus even in her religious novels, Cather's viewpoint is consistently that of the artist, not of the theologian.

Cather is not primarily concerned with the material of the more traditional religious novelist: suffering and guilt, the need for redemption, the relationship between man and God, Divine justice. Nor is she concerned with God or the Church as the centre of human existence and she nowhere suggests the need for limitation of individualism. In Cather's novels, God rarely makes an appearance and even Christ, the God-man, is present primarily in paintings, statues, old legends and miracles; once only does he appear in person in the explicitly religious scene which opens *Death Comes for the Archbishop.* The real problem of these novels, as suggested by Maxwell Geismar, is their exclusion of any form of conflict including that between good and evil.[6] Yet Randall Stewart has claimed that *Death Comes for the Archbishop* is 'the outstanding explicitly Christian novel' and Francis Connolly has congratulated Cather on the closeness of her novels to the Catholic view of life.[7] Clearly, then, Cather's interest in her late novels *Death Comes for the Archbishop* and *Shadows on the Rock* is closely allied to some form of religious experience. The elements of this experience remain to be examined.

Cather's own personal spiritual quest, her progression towards the Catholic church as a centre of stability and order, seems almost inevitable, given the conditions of her background and personality. Trilling notes in *After the Genteel Tradition* the psychology which underlies this movement, from the essentially Protestant 'ideal of unremitting search' to the cultural ideal of Catholicism which 'selects what it can make immediate and tangible in symbol,' and which, in the old settled cultures of Europe, 'makes the most of things.'[8] In Cather's own private life, this search was slow and marked by doubt. The affirmation of her Catholic novels *Death Comes for the Archbishop* and *Shadows on the Rock* is not paralleled in her own life, where the shadows are more evident than the rock. 'Faith is a gift,' Cather remarked shortly after the death of her cousin in World War I, and it is a gift that Cather herself seems to have lacked.[9] Even in the records of her childhood Mildred Bennett observes evidence of religious doubt, and in an early oration she subjected mysticism to a scientific investigation (134). She found it 'difficult to believe,' Bennett tells us and quotes Cather's admission to Carrie Miner Sherwood that 'even her Catholic books were written out of admiration for a faith she could not quite accept' (137).

Cather's attitudes to religion in the early books seem to be conditioned by her reaction to the narrow sectarianism of the Protestant churches around Red Cloud. These views are reflected most clearly in *The Song of the Lark* and *One of Ours*, both of which draw on Cather's personal experience through the characterisation of Thea Kronberg, in Part I and II a *persona* for Cather herself, and of Claude Wheeler, modelled in part on George Cather her cousin. In the first of these, Thea is 'perplexed about religion'; an epidemic of typhoid fever which has killed several of her friends has been caused by a social incident, the rejection of a tramp who in revenge commits suicide in the town water-supply. Thea asks Dr Archie:

> That's what I can't understand; do people believe the Bible, or don't they? If the next life is all that matters, and we're put here to get ready for it, then why do we try to make money, or learn things, or have a good time? There's not one person in Moonstone that really lives the way the New Testament says. Does it matter, or doesn't it? (SL 175)

While Thea's query implies Cather's early doubts, Dr Archie's reply is suggestive of Cather's later answer to such problems:

> Every people has had its religion. All religions are good, and all are pretty much alike. But I don't see how we could live up to them in the sense you mean. I've thought about it a good deal, and I can't help feeling that while we are in this world we have to live for the best things of the world, and those things are material and positive. Now most religions are passive, and they tell us chiefly what we should not do. (SL 175)

Cather's condemnation of religious narrowness and parochialism in this novel and *One of Ours* is at times as explicit as Sinclair Lewis' in *Elmer Gantry*. All the characters in Moonstone or Chicago who are involved with religion are Philistines, shallow, worldly, lazy and antithetic to true art. Thea's father Peter Kronberg is a self-important little man who has chosen the Church because it represents an easy form of livelihood and who is admired by the women of the congregation for 'the conventional rhetoric of his sermons' and for his ministerial decorum:

> He did not smoke, he never touched spirits. His indulgence in the pleasures of the table was an endearing bond between him and the women of his congregation. He ate enormously with a zest. (189)

His daughter Ann, considered a devout girl but in truth an ascetic, thinks music is 'nothing very real' (167) and believes in the total depravity of human beings. Rebuked by her mother for attacking Thea's practising on Sunday, Ann revenges herself by praying for Mrs Kronberg's soul. The Reverend Larson, an acquaintance of Kronberg from Divinity School, is even more lazy and self-indulgent, and his father has sent him to the seminary 'to conceal his laziness from the neighbors' (209). He attends symphony concerts, plays his violin at women's culture clubs for 'he could work energetically at any form of play' (210), and he enjoys all the pleasures of a soft existence:

> He slept late in the morning, was fussy about his food, and read a great many novels, preferring sentimental ones. He did not smoke, but he ate a great deal of candy 'for his throat.' (209-10)

Thea is forced by her father to attend prayer-meetings where she must play the organ and lead the singing to 'keep people from talking' (158). She rejects the whole tone of these meetings as narrow and morbid:

> The usual Wednesday night gathering was made up of old women, with perhaps six or eight men; and a few sickly girls who had not much interest in life; two of them, indeed, were already preparing to die.

Thea's reaction is pronounced; she considers these evenings 'a kind of spiritual discipline, like funerals. She always read late after she went home and felt a stronger wish than usual to live and be happy' (160).

Seven years later, in *One of Ours*, Cather's picture of the Church has changed little. Brother Weldon, the sanctimonious little man who influences Mrs Wheeler to send Claude to Temple College, is characterised clearly as he says the blessing over the chicken. Both greedy and unctuous, he sits 'with devout, downcast eyes while the chicken was being dismembered' (OO 30). It is Brother Weldon who influences Enid to marry Claude for 'the most important service devout young girls could perform for the church was to bring young men to its support' (180). The other teachers at Temple College are presented as weak, self-indulgent and shallow, 'preachers who couldn't make a living at preaching' (24) while the students are boys who have failed at the State University, like Edward Chapin, the stupid young man both studious and dull with whom Claude boards. Claude Wheeler finally comes to a decision and rejects conversion, for:

> He did not want to renounce a world he as yet knew nothing of. He would like to go into life with all his vigour, with all his faculties free. (OO 49)

And Claude's rejection of Temple College with its sophistries and evasions is suggestive of Cather's own attitude to Protestantism:

> the noblest could be damned, according to their theory, while almost any mean-spirited parasite could be saved by faith. 'Faith' as he saw it exemplified ... was a substitute for most of the manly qualities he admired (50).

This denunciation of Protestantism, although less evident in the other novels before 1927, is nevertheless present. In *O Pioneers!* where the stress is on Catholicism, the issue appears in the rejection by local society of the ascetic and mystic Crazy Ivar who is condemned by them to a sanitarium because his ways are not their ways. Ivar is ridiculed by a society which has no patience for differences. He says to Alexandra:

> You know that my spells come from God, and that I would not harm any living creature. You believe that every one should worship God in the way revealed to him. But that is not the way of this country. The way here is for all to do alike. I am despised because I do not wear shoes, because I do not cut my hair, and because I have visions. At home, in the old country, there were many like me, who had been touched by God, or who had seen things in the graveyard at night and were different afterward. We thought nothing of it, and let them alone. But here, if a man is different in his feet or in his head, they put him in the asylum. (OP 92-3)

Even in *My Ántonia* where Jim Burden partially accepts the devout Protestantism of Grandfather Burden in Book I, religion in Book II becomes the antithesis of life and vitality. Grandfather does not approve of dancing and prevents Jim from attending the dances at the Fireman's Hall where the hired girls go; as well Jim is barred from Anton Jelinek's saloon because 'your Grandpa has always treated me fine and ... I know he don't like it' (MA 218). The girls tease Jim that his grandmother is making him into a Baptist preacher and remark: 'I guess you'll have to stop dancing and wear a white necktie then' (215). And indeed after Book II religion disappears from the novel. In *The Professor's House*, the Baptist Professor Crane never goes out except to dine once a year at the President's House, for 'music disturbed him too much, dancing shocked him' (141); and, as Mrs St Peter insidiously comments: 'I believe he thinks it's wicked to live with even so plain a woman as Mrs Crane' (141–2). The intellectual concept which lies behind these negations is indicated in Cather's description of Claude's mother:

> She thought dancing and card-playing dangerous pastimes—only rough people did such things . . . and 'worldliness' only another word for wickedness. According to her conception of education, one should learn, not think; and above all, one must not enquire. The history of the human race, as it lay behind one, was already explained; and so was its destiny which lay before. The mind should remain obediently within the theological concept of history. (OO 25)

The most damning portrait of the Protestant ascetic occurs in *One of Ours* in Claude's wife. A fanatic like her mother, Enid serves dinners which are healthful but cold like herself; she leaves Claude temporarily to attend a vegetarian sanatorium with her mother and more permanently, to nurse back to health her missionary sister in China. She is a Prohibitionist, distributing their literature around the country, and finds sex repugnant. She even shuts the rooster away from the hens to keep the eggs fresher. All in all, Enid makes Claude's life 'hideous to him' (210).

In contrast in these early novels, the Catholic church is life-affirming. Consistently, the characters are divided into two groups, the life-affirming Catholic characters with their warmth, simplicity, love of beauty and art, and the Protestant characters, life-denying, cold, sterile, ascetic. The central characters, Alexandra Bergson, Thea Kronberg, Jim Burden, although they are Protestant, are caught between the two. Both Catholics and Protestants are simplified at times, even stereotyped: the Bohemians, French Americans, Mexicans against the solid citizens of Main Street. Ántonia and Marie Shabata are both life-symbols, both Bohemian, Catholic and creative; it is no coincidence that both are fruitful while the marriages of Jim and Alexandra are barren.

In these novels the church itself is the centre of existence for its peoples, the source of their life and warmth as well as their comfort in pain and death. For Emil's friend Amédée the red brick building was 'the scene of his most serious moments and of his happiest hours. He had played and wrestled and sung and courted under its shadow' (OP 252). Here he is married, his son is christened, and here too he is brought to rest. Significantly his funeral on Monday is preceded by a confirmation service on Sunday:

> The Church has always held that life is for the living. On Saturday, while half the village of Sainte-Agnes was mourning for Amédée and preparing the funeral black for his burial on Monday, the other was busy with white dresses and white veils for the great confirmation service tomorrow. . . . Father Duchesne divided his time between the living and the dead. (OP 251)

Here in *O Pioneers!* is the first foreshadowing of the church as refuge in the description of Amédée's death: 'They could not doubt that the invisible arm was still about Amédée; that through the church on earth he had passed to the church triumphant' (252) and in Marie's devotion to her faith during the winter of Emil's absence: 'she found more comfort in her Church that winter than ever before. It seemed to come closer to her, and to fill an emptiness that ached in her heart' (201-2).

Nevertheless, Cather rejects in the end the Catholic mores of love and marriage for Emil's natural passion; ironically it is in the *Ave Maria* of the confirmation service that he finds his emotional release and the ecstasy inspired by the Church ritual leads directly to the triumph of his love over the order of the church, society and the law. And the love affair concludes in a somewhat misty transcendentalism which is a form of natural religion. In the novels after *My Ántonia* this Catholic element disappears; *One of Ours* concentrates on Protestantism and in *A Lost Lady* religion plays no part at all.

With *The Professor's House* and *My Mortal Enemy*, there is a noted change in Cather's direction. There has been a tendency in Cather's fiction to associate religion with death. For both Thea Kronberg and Claude Wheeler, the Church exists for those who have nothing else to live for, the old, the ugly, the poor, for those preparing to die. Cather frequently observed that 'no one under forty could ever really believe in either death or degeneration' and Elizabeth Sergeant adds that Cather herself 'carried that physical nonchalance right on through her fifties' (139). In 1925, the year of publication of *The Professor's House*, Cather was fifty-two, and here for the first time she faces the approach of old age and death. Here Professor St Peter is drawn back from the verge of death by the Catholic seamstress Augusta who reveals to him 'the taste of bitter herbs . . . the bloomless side of life that he had always run away from' (280). Religion becomes necessary to give life any meaning, yet its comfort is essentially negative, static. But the resolution of this crisis, although in terms of life, is actually as John Randall points out, a stoicism which involves a spiritual suicide.[10] The final words of the novel, although they look to the future as opposed to *My Ántonia* which looks to the past, are nevertheless negative for St Peter sees it with fortitude as 'without delight . . . without joy, without passionate griefs' (282-3). In the Middle Ages the Catholic church, with its art and ritual, brought to men a faith in miracles and temptations, in revelations and indeed the drama of their existence. And St Peter concludes: 'that's what makes men happy, believing in the mystery and importance of their own little individual lives' (79). In this novel and the three following, as Elizabeth Sergeant points out (193), Cather comes face to face with death and attempts to come to terms with age and mortality.

Both Myra and the Professor turn to the traditional Catholic church for beauty and for comfort in the alien world of contemporary society. What they seek is clearly expressed by Myra Henshawe:

> Religion is different from everything else; *because in religion seeking is finding.* . . .
> She seemed to say that in other searchings it might be the object of the quest

that brought satisfaction, or it might be something incidental that one got on the way; but in religion, desire was fulfilment, it was the seeking itself that rewarded. (ME 94)

For those weary of the world, the Church provides a sanctuary, a place of rest similar to the peace which Jim Burden found in Nature: 'that is happiness, to be dissolved into something complete and great' (MA 18). In *My Mortal Enemy*, the convent replaces love, age replaces youth; prayers replace parties and religion replaces the comely life. Where Myra once lived her gay social life, where bands played and garden parties followed one another, the Sisters of the Convent walk two by two under the apple trees: 'Since then, chanting and devotions and discipline, and the tinkle of little bells that seemed forever calling the Sisters in to prayers' (17). Myra's end is already foreshadowed in this early passage, an end where even romantic love is viewed as a form of idolatry and replaced by hatred for a 'mortal enemy.' In these novels Cather renounces her artistic code as expressed by Thea Kronberg: 'There is only one big thing—desire' (SL 95) for an illusory tranquility and peace.

Death Comes for the Archbishop and *Shadows on the Rock*, the two Catholic novels, bear the mark of this renunciation. For they not only reject any struggle between the soul and the world; they deny conflict in itself, the first evoking the stylised and abstract mood of the frescoes of Puvis de Chavannes, and the second preferring to concentrate on the 'salad dressing' as the beginning of civilisation rather than the Indian massacres. The Professor and Myra Henshawe pass through Carlyle's 'Everlasting No' but never really achieve his 'Everlasting Yea.' Archbishop Latour and the Auclairs inherit the 'Everlasting Yea' without the struggle that makes it real and convincing, the suffering and pain which man must undergo before he can reach the final affirmation.

The religious texture of these last two works is rich but curiously free of theological or moral issues. There is little concern for God as the centre of order of the universe; although the nuns affirm his role as preserver of order, of night and day, light and darkness, and time (SR 97), elsewhere Cather rarely mentions God. Nor does Christ play a significant role. The meditation of Jean Marie Latour on the Passion of Christ under the cruciform tree in the opening section of *Death Comes for the Archbishop* is unique in Cather's work. The only other references to Jesus in the two novels are the miraculous appearance of the Holy Family to Father Junipero, introduced obtrusively as second-hand narrative into Book IV on Latour's death, the painting of the baby child in the Church of Notre-Dame de la Victoire, and the woodcut of the little Saint-Edmond. The Virgin Mary appears more frequently than Christ in her appearance to Juan Diego, as the centre of Vaillant's May Devotions, as statue or painting, and as doll to be dressed and fondled by the simple Mexican peasants, as well as the ideal of domestic life to which Cécile dedicates herself. But the emphasis on Mary suggests

Cather's real interest, the human rather than the divine, as Latour suggests in his comment on Magdalena's devotion:

> He seemed able to feel all it meant to her to know that there was a Kind Woman in Heaven, though there were such cruel ones on earth. Old people, who have felt blows and toil and known the world's hard hand, need, even more than children do, a woman's tenderness. Only a woman, divine, could know all that a woman can suffer. (DCA 217)

The two priests in *Death Comes for the Archbishop* face no spiritual crisis, as, for example, do the little whiskey priest in Graham Greene's *The Power and the Glory*, or Father Dowling in Callaghan's *Such is My Beloved*. The novels are not religious in this sense. They are rich not in depth but in breadth. For *Death Comes for the Archbishop* reveals not only the central lives of the two bishops, Latour and Vaillant, but also the contrasting lives of the dissolute priests Padre Martínez, Padre Gallegos, Father Lucero, Fray Baltazar and Trinidad, the miracles of the Virgin's appearance to Juan Diego, and the Divine guidance of Father Junipero, the simple faith of the Mexicans, the religious observances and rituals of the Indians, and the practices of the Spanish-American church. Likewise *Shadows on the Rock* incorporates the lives of Mother Catherine and Jeanne le Ber, Father Hector and Noel Chabanel, the decoration of the churches and the pattern of the ecclesiastical year into a novel concerned primarily with the transfer of culture from the Old World to the New through the Church and the domestic life of the salon. Catholicism, in these works, becomes what Josephine Jessup has called the 'aesthetic solvent to unify incidents.'[11] It resolves for Cather the basic antagonism between the Old World and the New, the established culture of Europe and the raw, crude frontier. Here, as Maxwell Geismar notes, she blends together 'her need for spiritual absolution and her craving for worldly comfort and elegance in that final fusion of the Mesa and the Salon' (199).

The sacramental aspect of religion Cather is little concerned with in these novels. The cycle of the Christian year plays little part here as it has had little significance in her earlier fiction. Although Christmas appears in many works, for example *O Pioneers!*, *The Song of the Lark*, *My Ántonia*, *The Professor's House*, *Death Comes for the Archbishop*, *Shadows on the Rock* and 'Neighbour Rosicky,' its significance lies in its human associations rather than in its divine ones. The exceptions to this occur in *My Ántonia* where the Christmas tree is decorated with candles, Nativity figures and even a bleeding heart, and *Shadows on the Rock* where the child Jacques presents to the Christ-Child of the Nativity scene the carved wooden beaver which is his only valued possession. Elsewhere the associations are secular: the preparation of dinner, the memories of the past, the warmth and harmony, even in *Death Comes for the Archbishop* where the central discussion concerns the tradition of the soup and the difficulties of preparing a salad without greens. Easter appears rarely: Leo Cuzack is born on Easter day but this is given no real importance in the novel, and Lent in *Death Comes for the Archbishop* is mentioned only in association with the morbid and even sensual asceticism of Trinidad who scourges himself 'so full of cactus spines that the girls have to pluck him like a chicken' (149) and who hangs all night on a cross, requesting to be scourged with cactus whips until he is made ill by the poison (154-5). The Ascension, Pentecost, the Annunciation do not appear at all, and the only real religious ceremony appears to be Father Vaillant's observance of May as the month of Mary, while the passage is coloured extensively by the natural and fertility associations of the garden (200-01). In *Shadows on the Rock*, recognition is paid to the shape of the church year in All Soul's Day, All Saint's Day and Christmas, yet although these suggest the religious order of life in Quebec, they have little influence on action or character. In short, Cather is almost totally unconcerned with the liturgical cycle of the Catholic Church.

The chief sacraments of the Catholic religion too are given little attention. The sacraments of Baptism, Confirmation, Holy Eucharist, Penance, Extreme Unction, Holy Orders, and Matrimony are mentioned at some point in the Catholic novels, but they rarely form a real pattern or order. In one passage in *Death Comes for the Archbishop*, the four sacraments of marrige, baptism, confession and confirmation are performed in few more words, and the remaining several pages of the incident describe the feasting which follows. None of these sacraments are described. Both Vaillant and Latour have taken Holy Orders many years before; Cécile is married offstage. And despite the predominance of death in these late works, although Myra Henshawe, the Archbishop and count Frontenac all receive extreme unction, all die concerned with personal memories and problems which do not express a confirmed faith in God and an afterlife. Even prayer is not an accepted part of life; in *Death Comes for the Archbishop*, Cather includes the following extraordinary statement:

> [Father Latour] said his prayers before he rolled out of his blankets, remembering Father Vaillant's maxim that if you said your prayers first, you would find plenty of time for other things afterwards (125).

Clearly Cather is concerned with something other than the Church as theological and moral guide, as pattern of everyday life, liturgy or sacrament. In his *Religious Background to Literature* Hall has noted the natural associations of Catholicism with aesthetics which arose in the Middle Ages where 'the whole concept of culture, order, and intelligence was bound up with the Catholic tradition.'[12] As early as her trip to Europe in 1903, Cather felt this attraction of aestheticism in her contrast of London Protestantism, cold, dour and ugly, with Italian Catholicism, warm, full of beauty, colour and order, in the parade for the Feast of Our Lady of Mount Carmel:

> There was scarcely a window that had not a little shrine before it, with a tiny image and burning candles, carefully protected from the rain. The Italian

> quarter here is a poor place enough, and these attempts at ceremonial splendor in spite of time, absence, poverty, and distance, in spite of the oppressive grayness, in spite of the oppressively ugly city, were not a little pathetic. . . . Poor as the people are, nearly every window had a garland or bunch of cut flowers. . . . These poor Latins [were] undoubtedly trying to carry a little of the light and colour and sweet devoutedness of a Latin land into their grey, cold London. . . .[13]

This contrast is born out by the early novels where these stereotypes are again evident, and where again it is predominantly the aestheticism of the Church which appeals to Cather. In *O Pioneers!* the preparations for the confirmation ceremonies coincide with Amédée's death and funeral: the choir rehearses the mass of Rossini, the boys and girls bring flowers, the women decorate the altar, and the remainder of the town prepare the white dresses and veils for the confirmation ceremony or the funeral black for mourning (251). The religious implications of Catholicism are not so clear-cut in *The Song of The Lark*, *My Ántonia* and *One of Ours*, although again it is the Catholic Mexicans, Bohemians and French who counter the sterility of American society in each case, with the richer culture, the love of life, beauty, art and music which for Cather is inseparable from their Catholic roots. While it is in the Methodist church window with its greens and reds and blues that Jim Burden finds the satisfaction of 'a hunger for colour' almost physical like the Laplander's 'craving for sugar and fats' (MA 174), this is the only passage which attributes any beauty to Protestantism. Claude Wheeler finds a similar fulfillment in the Catholic church at Saint Ouen:

> [He] saw far behind him, the rose window, with its purple heart. As he stood staring, hat in hand, as still as the stone figures in the chapels, a great bell, up aloft, began to strike the hour in its deep, melodious throat; eleven beats, measured and far apart, as rich as the colours in the window, then silence. . . . (OO 242)

The attraction of this experience is explained by Professor St Peter who, like Hall, sees Catholicism from the outside as an enriching of life through art and culture, ceremony and ritual, akin in its effect to drama:

> As long as every man and woman who crowded into the Cathedrals on Easter Sunday was a principal in a gorgeous drama with God, glittering angels on one side and the shadows of evil coming and going on the other, life was a rich thing. The king and the beggar had the same chance at miracles and great temptations and revelations. And that's what makes men happy, believing in the mystery and importance of their own little individual lives. It makes us happy to surround our creature needs and bodily instincts with as much pomp and circumstance as possible. Art and religion (they are the same thing in the end, of course) have given man the only happiness he has ever had. (PH 68-9)

This statement reveals Cather's fundamental assumptions with regard to religion. Like drama, it heightens our perception of life, exaggerates the contrast between light and dark, good and evil, and provides richness and colour in lives which are basically dreary. It simplifies issues which are complex in life, in the manner of the morality play, and it provides stability for our faith; we have no need to make perplexing decisions regarding shades of greyness or goodness. Thus it is more satisfying than life and, most important, it creates the illusion of significance for the individual.

My Mortal Enemy treats religion basically from the same angle. Nellie Birdseye recalls the funeral of John Driscoll from the point of view of a six-year-old who sees the Church ritual and order as transcending failure, pettiness, and even death:

> The high altar blazed with hundreds of candles, the choir was entirely filled by the masses of flowers. The bishop was there, and a flock of priests in gorgeous vestments. When the pallbearers arrived, Driscoll did not come to the church; the church went to him. The bishop and clergy went down the nave, . . . preceded by the cross and boys swinging cloudy censers, followed by the choir chanting to the organ. They surrounded, they received, they seemed to assimilate into the body of the church, the body of old John Driscoll. They bore it up to the high altar on a river of colour and incense and organ-tone. . . . I thought of John Driscoll as having escaped the end of all flesh. . . . From the freshness of roses and lilies, he had gone straight to the greatest glory, through smoking censers and candles and stars. (18–19)

Despite the childish viewpoint, this is the vision of John Driscoll which remains, indeed the vision of the Catholic church in Cather's fiction. Although Nellie is grown when Myra Henshawe accepts Catholicism, we see little else of the Church except the ebony crucifix with the ivory Christ which Myra keeps in her hand and dies holding, and the candles which she has burning by her bed to recall the Church and replace the glare of modern electric light bulbs (92, 94). Myra's absolution is achieved not through the last rites of the Church but through the pardoning of nature, which bends with the dawn to receive the sinner into its embrace like the religious houses of old (73).

The aesthetic experience is basic to *Death Comes for the Archbishop* and indeed Cather has told us that one of the inspirations of the novel was her fascination with the old mission churches of the Southwest with their 'moving reality': 'the hand-carved beams and joists, the utterly conventional frescoes, the countless fanciful figures of the saints, no two of them alike, seemed a direct expression of some very real and lively human feeling.'[14] And the replacement of these old images and decorations by factory-made items from Ohio with no such 'definite and historic values' Cather castigates bitterly. The central symbol of the novel is the building of the Cathedral. Father Vaillant is concerned not with the structure itself but with what it points to beyond—'whether it was Midi Romanesque or Ohio German in style, seemed to him of little consequence' (116). But the concern of Latour, the main figure of the novel, is rather different: 'It would be a shame to any man coming from a Seminary that is one of the architectural treasures of France, to make another ugly church on this continent where there are so many already' (244). And indeed the building of this church is Latour's central ambition. He says of the rock of gold from which the stone will be hewn: 'I could hardly have hoped that God would gratify my personal taste, my vanity, if you will, in this way. I tell you, Blanchet, I would rather have found that hill of rock than have come into a fortune to spend in charity' (245). The mission bell, a product of Moorish tradition passed on to Mexico through the Spaniards, is of value to Latour because of its aesthetic characteristics, its silver tone and its transfer of culture from the exotic world of the East to the new frontier. The art of the Mexicans is centered on the decoration of the church, the priest, and the images of the Holy Family. Ultimately Padre Martínez, a licentious priest of scandalous reputation, is allowed to continue at least temporarily with his mission because the Bishop is pleased with his church: 'The building was clean and in good repair, the congregation large and devout. The delicate lace, snowy linen, and burnished brass on the altar told of a devoted Altar Guild,' and Latour compliments Martínez's baritone: 'The Bishop had never heard the Mass more impressively sung' (149–50). Even the Cardinal in Rome, Maria de Allande, is more interested in aesthetics and his family collection of art than in religion and the missions of the New World (11–13).

Shadows on the Rock is much less concerned with Church art, yet here too it is largely an aesthetic appeal which marks religion, and here, the appeal of the art is determined by the child heroine. Thus the works described are the statues of the Holy Family, the child bright and joyful, the mother 'by far the loveliest of all the Virgins in Kébec,' (65–6) the figures of Sainte Genevieve watching her sheep, and Sainte Anne holding the Virgin as a child. The children light candles because 'it was pleasanter, they agreed, when there was enough candles burning before Sainte Anne to show the gold flowers of her cloak' (66). Although Cécile devotedly attends divine service, we are told little of the ritual except on the Christmas eve where the priest sings the Mass and the Monseigneur wears his aube of rich lace, for both Bishop Laval and his successor agree 'the services of the church should be performed in Quebec as elaborately, as splendidly, as anywhere else in the world. For many years, Bishop Laval had kept himself miserably poor to make the altar and the sacristy rich' (113). While church art is not central to the novel, its place is taken not by religious theology but by the efforts of the Auclair family to preserve the flame of French culture in the new World, primarily in the form of the salon and secondarily in the ritual of the church.

But the appeal of the Church for Cather goes beyond the limits of aesthetic experience and illuminates her attraction throughout her career to the figure of the pioneer. For Cather's religious heroes, her saints, reveal the qualities which she has idealised throughout her fiction, the qualities basically associated with the frontier: self-sufficiency, ardour, resolution, optimism, individualism, courage, physical endurance and that dream which inspires the mind of pioneer, artist, or saint: 'A pioneer should have imagination, should be able to enjoy the idea of things more than the things them-

Arizona he took malarial fever from 'exposure and bad water' (200). He finds his real destiny in Pike's Peak, a country crowded with tents and shacks of several thousand miners, and in Denver City where life lacks the essentials of civilised living: not only linens but milk, butter, eggs and fruit (260).

In *Shadows on the Rock* Cécile admires the New World martyrs largely for their courage and for the wonder and terror of their romantic associations: 'To be thrown into the Rhone or the Moselle, to be decapitated at Lyon,— what was that to the tortures the Jesuit missionaries endured at the hands of the Iroquois, in those savage, interminable forests?' (101–2). While Father Hector avows 'Nothing worth while is accomplished except by that last sacrifice, the giving of oneself altogether and finally' (149), his challenge is largely physical, hunger and dirt, solitude, loneliness and isolation. Noel Chabanel is unable to learn the Huron language or communicate with the Indians, is nauseated by the vermin, the mosquitoes, the smell of unwashed bodies and the food of boiled dogs' flesh, by a life without beauty or order, as well as by his inability to pray: 'his martyrdom was his life, not his death' (150). Cather's ideal saint then resembles closely her ideal pioneer, and her ideal artist, a man dedicated to an ideal, courageous, sensitive, capable of physical endurance and mental torture and able to challenge the world which opposes these ideals, whether it be the world of geography and the elements the world of the barbarian or of the philistine. And in her ideal of the saint, Cather reveals the nature of her other religious quest for value in the twentieth century: a quest not essentially Christian or Catholic but aesthetic and philosophical, for something which will recreate the meaning of life which she felt to have been lost with the sunset of the pioneer.

The final appeal of the Catholic Church to Cather as she indicates in *My Mortal Enemy* is as a refuge. Already in 1903, on her trip to Chester Cathedral, she viewed the church as a sanctuary in mediaeval life from the struggles of everyday life, of politics and even existence itself:

> The cloister is perhaps the most beautiful part of the building to one who has never lived in a Catholic country. Its utter peacefulness in the afternoons I spent there, the Norman wall with its half-effaced designs, on which the eyes of faith gaze in bland astonishment after a thousand years, the rain that fell so quietly or the sun that shone so remotely into the green court in the centre, with its old, thick, sod, its pear-tree and its fleur-de-lis—they made the desirableness of the cloister in the stormy years seem not impossible. Without, Norman and Saxon butchered each other, and poachers were flayed alive, and forests planted over the ruins of freeholders' homesteads; but within the cloister the garden court was green, the ale went to the abbot's cellar and venison to his table, and though kings were slain and communities wiped out, the order of prayers and offices and penances were never broken. (*In Europe* 21)

Although the old world is here the villain, born in chaos and struggle, as against the Edenic innocence of the New, we see the cycle which for Cather recurs throughout history, the destruction of grace and culture by the barbarians. Yet the Church is a symbol of this past world, preserving inviolate into the present its past and its culture in the form of the cultivated garden. Alexander Bergson, Thea Kronberg and Jim Burden view religion, when they view it at all, as a negative power encroaching upon creativity, a force which has shaped the narrow morality and materialism of small-town America. By *Death Comes for the Archbishop* and *Shadows on the Rock*, religion has become a refuge from an existence never experienced except perhaps vicariously. When Latour suggests that Magdalena should leave the shelter of the Convent to marry and return to the world, Vaillant protests 'No, no! She has had enough of the storms of this world. Here she is safe and happy' (DCA 210).

While neither the Archbishop nor Cécile reject life for the stability of an ordered ritual existence, nevertheless the Church provides them with sanctuary. Neither face real moral dilemmas. Their religion is straightforward, unequivocal, even childlike. Contradictions are not resolved; they are simply dismissed, as in the Bishop's position in regard to the native Indian religion or to the incumbent padres Martínez or Lucero, in Vaillant's and Auclair's question as to the real value of cultural sacrifice in the missions, or Cécile's disregard of the Harnois' values or Jacques' position as son of the town prostitute. All will be well, for the Church reconciles all opposites and solves all difficulties. Ultimately Cather comes to see sanctuary as the central symbol which unites all human religions:

> These Indians, born in fear and dying by violence for generations, had at last taken this leap away from earth, and on that rock had found the hope of all suffering and tormented creatures—safety.... Sanctuary!... The rock, when one came to think of it, was the utmost expression of human need;... The Hebrews of the Old Testament, always being carried captive into foreign lands,—their rock was an idea of God, the only thing their conquerors could not take from them.... The Ácomas, who must share the universal human yearning for something permanent, enduring, without shadow of change,—they had their idea in substance. They actually lived upon their Rock; were born upon it and died upon it. (DCA 97–8)

In *Shadows on the Rock*, the whole of Quebec is a fortress against the wilderness, the savages, the predators, artificial like the scenes of the Nativity with the Chateau and the convents at the top of the headland. The Church of Notre Dame de la Victoire suggests a 'fortress' with its high narrow windows; it provides shelter from the cold and wind outside, and from the noise and lights of the market-place (62, 49). Even Heaven appears in terms of a fortress, in the painting admired by Cécile and Jacques, of a feudal castle with stone walls, towers and many battlements: 'It was very comforting to them both to know just what heaven looked like,—strong and unassailable, wherever it was set among the stars' (65).

Thus ultimately to Cather, the function of religion is to satisfy this yearning for security, for changelessness, and the Catholic church with its roots in the historic past, its tradition and ritual and cultural richness, fulfills this need more fully than any other.

But despite her temporary refuge in the security of the Catholic church, there is considerable evidence even within these late novels that Cather's personal doubts remain. And this evidence is corroborated by her comment after *Death Comes for the Archbishop*: 'No faith, she feared, could save one from the great spiritual duality of our time—the conflict between the brave ideals of our pioneer ancestors, and the mounting materialism and industrialism of the post-war world' (ser. 238). Cather's personal uncertainty is suggested by the thoughts of Count Frontenac on his deathbed:

> He would die here, in this room, and his spirit would go before God to be judged. He believed this, because he had been taught it in childhood, and because he knew that there was something in himself and in other men that this world did not explain. Even the Indians had to make a story to account for something in their lives that did not come out of their appetites: conceptions of courage, duty, honour. The Indians had these, in their own fashion. These ideas come from some unknown source, and they were not the least part of life. (SR 247)

And the death of Latour in *Death Comes for the Archbishop* implies the direction of Cather's thought during these years. For the death is not really that of a religious figure but of an artist very like Cather, trying to bring meaning to human life and experience not through contemplation of God and the Church but through secular memory:

> During those last weeks of the Bishop's life he thought very little about death; it was the Past he was leaving. The future would take care of itself. But he had an intellectual curiosity about dying; about the changes that took place in a man's beliefs and scale of values. More and more life seemed to him an experience of the Ego, in no sense the Ego itself. This conviction, he believed, was something apart from his religious life; it was an enlightenment that came to him as a man, a human creature. . . . He was soon to have done with calendered time, and it had already ceased to count for him. He sat in the middle of his own consciousness; none of his former states of mind were lost or outgrown. They were all within reach of his hand, and all comprehensible. (DCA 289-90)

This death, apart from religious issues or strife, is an ideal death, as the Bishop's life is an ideal life, and it suggests the closest approach that Cather can make to the comfort and security of religion.

Moreover, Cather's personal doubts underlie the structure of the narratives and undercut the religious beliefs of the central characters who are presented as devout Catholics and indeed frequently as dedicated servants of the Church. One central issue concerns the definition of miracles, and indeed Cather's early scientific investigation of mysticism is apparent in her later attitude. While Vaillant accepts miracles as providential intervention, Archbishop Latour defines them as not opposed to the laws of nature:

> An apparition is human vision, corrected by divine love. I do not see you as you really are, Joseph; I see you through my affection for you. The miracles of the

> Church seem to me to rest not so much upon faces or voices of healing power coming suddenly near to us from afar off, but upon our perceptions being made finer, so that for a moment our eyes can see, and our ears can hear what there is about us always. (DCA 50)

In effect, this negates Divine intervention in human affairs except through a sharpening of human senses. In *Shadows on the Rock* too Cather approaches the miracle cautiously:

> The people have loved miracles for so many hundred years, not as proof or evidence, but because they are the actual flowering of desire. In them the vague worship and devotion of the simple-hearted assumes a form. From being a shapeless longing, it becomes a beautiful image; a dumb rapture becomes a melody that can be remembered and repeated; and the experience of a moment, which might have been a lost ecstasy, is made an actual possession and can be bequeathed to another. (SR 137)

Even this affirmation, which describes the miracle as a symbol or image, is questioned by Auclair's doubts concerning the miracles of the saints' bones which: 'may work cures at the touch, they may be a protection worn about the neck; those things are beyond my knowledge' (127), and by Pierre Charron's scepticism that the Church makes beavers into fish every Friday (224).

More important, these novels question the validity of sacrifice. While Father Hector can say 'Nothing worthwhile is accomplished except by that last sacrifice, the giving of oneself altogether and finally,' Vaillant wonders:

> To man's wisdom it would have seemed that a priest with Father Latour's exceptional qualities would have been better placed in some part of the world where scholarship, a handsome person, and delicate perceptions all have their effect. . . . But God had His reasons. . . . Perhaps it pleased Him to grace the beginning of a new era and a vast new diocese by a fine personality. (DCA 254)

And Auclair questions in similar fashion the sacrifices of Noel Chabanel and Father Hector: '[He wondered] whether there had not been a good deal of misplaced heroism in the Canadian missions,—a waste of rare qualities which did nobody any good,' and ultimately he resolves 'perhaps that is the box of precious ointment which was acceptable to the Saviour' (SR 154–5). Jeanne Le Ber's sacrifice has left her with a voice 'like an old crow's' and a face of stone (180, 182), and Pierre states explicitly that she would have been a happy mother if the Church had not taken her in childhood: 'There are plenty of girls, ugly, poor, stupid, awkward, who are made for such a life' (177–8). And indeed the whole experience of Jeanne Le Ber questions the value of such sacrifice. A recluse who has entombed herself in a cloister, Jeanne even rejects the request of her confessor that she walk in the grounds for air and exercise: 'Ah, mon père, ma chambre est mon paradis terrestre; c'est mon centre, c'est mon élément. . . . Je préfère ma cellule à tout le reste de l'univers' (136). And after suffering every sorrow and every despair, she calls out to the anonymous sinner in the Church who is, in fact, her former lover Pierre, *'God have mercy upon you! I will pray for you. And do you pray for me also'* (183).

While these last novels, then, suggest Cather's underlying doubts, the shadows which obscure the rock of religion, they also reveal her desperate attempt to cling to a faith which will not founder, which outlives nature and art, and is not subject to time and decay. But religion, like writing, provides only a temporary refuge from the human predicament; she finally concludes that when we look up from our faith or our work, we must face again the conflicts of life between the ideal and the real, hope and despair. In her last novels *Lucy Gayheart* and *Sapphira and the Slave Girl*, Cather turns away from the Catholic church and back to the struggle of everyday life. But the fascination remains. Her incomplete work set in Avignon notes the power of Rome which drew her back in space and time, to the Old World of the past and to a traditionalism and ritual which have no place in the modern world of the twentieth century. Her spiritual quest then did not end with *Shadows on the Rock* but continued through the remainder of her life until her death resolved her final doubts concerning the world and her personal quest for order and stability. And on her tombstone in Jaffrey, New Hampshire, are inscribed the words from *My Ántonia*: 'That is happiness; to be dissolved into something complete and great.'

Notes

1. Lincoln: University of Nebraska Press, 1963, p. 2.
2. *Not Under Forty* (N.Y., Knopf, 1964), pp. 48–49.
3. The following editions of Cather's novels will be cited in the essay with text and page noted in parentheses: (ME) *My Mortal Enemy* (N.Y.: Random House, 1961); (PH) *The Professor's House* (N.Y.: Knopf, 1964); (SL) *Song of the Lark* (Boston: Houghton Mifflin, Riverside, 1963); (DCA) *Death Comes For The Archbishop* (N.Y.: Knopf, 1964); (OO) *One of Ours* (N.Y.: Knopf, 1965); (OP) *O Pioneers* (Boston: Houghton Mifflin, Riverside, 1962); (MA) *My Ántonia* (Boston: Houghton Mifflin, Riverside, 1961); (SR) *Shadows on the Rock* (N.Y.: Knopf, 1964); (LL) *A Lost Lady* (N.Y.: Knopf, 1963).
4. *Willa Cather: A Critical Introduction* (N.Y.: Collier, 1972), p. 74.
5. *The Kingdom Of Art*, ed. Bernice Slote (Lincoln: University of Nebraska Press, 1967), p. 178.
6. *The Last of the Provincials* (Boston: Houghton Mifflin, 1949), pp. 199–200.
7. Randall Stewart, *American Literature and Christian Doctrine* (Baton Rouge: Louisiana State University Press, 1961), p. 133; Francis Connolly, *Fifty Years of the American Novel*, pp. 69–87.
8. 'Willa Cather' in Schroeter, ed. *Willa Cather and her Critics* (Ithaca: Cornell University Press, 1967), pp. 152-3.
9. Mildred Bennett, *The World of Willa Cather* (Lincoln: University of Nebraska Press, 1961), p. 137.
10. *The Landscape and the Looking Glass* (Cambridge: Houghton Mifflin, 1960), p. 233.
11. *The Faith of Our Feminists* (N.Y.: Richard R. Smith, 1950), p. 116.
12. N.Y.: Ungar, 1959, p. 112.
13. *Willa Cather In Europe* (N.Y.: A. Knopf, 1956), pp. 61-2.
14. 'On Death Comes For The Archbishop' in *On Writing*. pp. 5–6.
15. *Jesuit Relations*, quoted in Brown, *Willa Cather: A Critical Biography* (N.Y.: Knopf, 1953), p. 272.

Empire and Ethnicity

155
Willa Cather and the Indian Heritage

◆

DAVID STOUCK

In my book-length study of Willa Cather I tried to demonstrate the unusual range and depth of this author's imagination by focusing on the archetypal dimensions of her fictions.[1] *O Pioneers!*, with its tableau of a new land and its heroic settlers, has the qualities of an epic; *My Ántonia*, with its journey into the author's childhood memories, is a pastoral; *The Professor's House*, which tells an ugly story of human greed, is largely satiric; while *My Mortal Enemy*, a tale of self-damnation, *Death Comes for the Archbishop*, a narrative of saintly love and service, and *Shadows on the Rock*, a historical novel of penitence and suffering, form something like a 'mortal comedy,' exploring the whole range of the moral imagination. Willa Cather is viewed in my study as primarily a romantic writer who, like Cooper, Hawthorne, or F. Scott Fitzgerald, gave powerful expression to the American dream of individual freedom and power, and to the artist's struggle to transcend the world through his art. But there is another dimension to Willa Cather's fiction, a strong undercurrent of thought and feeling which turns away from the romantic dreams of selfhood toward the richness and complexity of the perceptual world, and which views art not as the product of self-expression but as a process of sympathy for people, places, and events. Seen from this vantage point Willa Cather belongs with another group of American writers, with the less likely company of Melville, Whitman, Pound, and William Carlos Williams. A clue to this less familiar aspect of Willa Cather's art can be found in her interest in the Indians of the Southwest, for whose various cultures she had such a great affinity. She admired the Indians' communal way of life, their respect for the environment, and the organic forms of their dwellings and their arts. These are attitudes and practices which inform both the shapes and themes of her own art in several places and which make her imaginative world continuous with our own.

SOURCE   David Stouck, 'Willa Cather and the Indian Heritage', *Twentieth Century Literature*, 22, 1976, pp. 433–43

In her Nebraska novels Willa Cather does not describe the Indians who inhabited the plains before the white settlers. Bernice Slote has noted two oblique references to the aboriginal people in Cather's early fiction: there is a description in 'The Treasure of Far Island' of 'the white chalk cliff where the Indians used to run the buffalo over Bison Leap,' and in 'A Wagner Matinee' we are told that the pioneers were often 'at the mercy of bands of roving Indians.'[2] I have found another reference to the Plains Indians in *My Ántonia* when the narrator, Jim Burden, describes the environs of his grandfather's farm:

> Beyond the pond, on the slope that climbed to the cornfield, there was, faintly marked in the grass, a great white circle where the Indians used to ride. Jake and Otto were sure that when they galloped round the ring the Indians tortured prisoners, bound to a stake in the centre; but grandfather thought they merely ran races or trained horses there.[3]

There are probably others, but such references reflect little more than the conventional fear and hostility white settlers felt toward the original inhabitants. Curiously the drama of the Plains Indians did not play a part in Willa Cather's imagination.

However, with the Indians of the Southwest it was quite otherwise. Willa Cather's first trip to Arizona and New Mexico in 1912 was one of the most formative adventures in her imaginative life. Her excitement in part was in discovering an ancient American people and the remains of its civilisation, after having grown up in Nebraska, where there was so little evidence of human time, only geological time. But there was also the intellectual excitement of discovering a completely different kind of existence—a way of life lived in intimate harmony with nature. Unlike the European settlers, with their romantic dreams of individual power and conquest, the Indians adjusted their lives collectively to the natural laws of the universe, never exploiting their environment nor setting themselves against it, but living very much within it. Willa Cather became absorbed in the history and way of life of the Indians of the Southwest, and accordingly in several of her fictions an awareness of Indian culture is crucial to the book's meaning.

Willa Cather described something of her first discovery of the Indians when she wrote *The Song of the Lark*. The heroine, Thea Kronborg, who is an opera singer, goes to Arizona for a rest cure from her work and spends long hours each day in the ruins of an Indian cliff city. There, among other things, she contemplates the fragments of broken pottery that had once been beautifully decorated. Water was life to the Indians of the desert, so that their art, their carefully designed water vessels, was a part of their daily life. Their art moreover was not something which changed or shaped life, but rather contained it. Thea reflects to herself: 'what was any art but an effort to make a sheath, a mould in which to imprison for a moment the shining, elusive element which is life itself.'[4] For the Indians art was a celebration of life's vital essence—water.

In *The Professor's House* Indian life is again observed in the relics of an ancient cliff city, one that Tom Outland finds perched over a mountain canyon.

The beautifully proportioned buildings are arranged together like a beehive, reflecting the close-knit communal nature of the Indians' life. Moreover, they are integrated organically into the setting 'like a bird's nest in the cliff.' The reverence for the ancient people that Tom feels there is not simply for humanity that raised itself out of mere brutality, but for the way the Pueblo Indians lived together in harmony and 'built themselves into the mesa,' not against it. The significance of these communal buildings in natural harmony with their setting emerges in the contrast with other buildings in the novel—the Professor's new house designed to reflect his affluence, the Norwegian manor house being built by the Marselluses, scarcely indigenous to its region and being built as a showcase for personal wealth, or the city of Washington where its petty bureaucrats in their boxlike houses struggle to outdo each other. All the buildings in the novel are places of envy and unhappiness.

Another Indian attitude, what we might call ecological awareness, is presented in living form in *Death Comes for the Archbishop* when Father Latour visits with his friend Eusabio, a leader of the Navahos. As they travel over the desert together Father Latour marvels at his companion's sensitivity to the details of the desert, the rocks, trees, plant life; he thinks to himself that 'travelling with Eusabio was like travelling with the landscape made human.'[5] He sees in Eusabio's activities that the Indian had no desire to master nature, but strove to accommodate himself to the landscape around him, to make his life confluent with his setting. Father Latour notes this particularly after they have broken up camp:

> When they left the rock or tree or sand dune that had sheltered them for the night, the Navajo was careful to obliterate every trace of their temporary occupation. He buried the embers of the fire and the remnants of food, unpiled any stones he had piled together, filled up the holes he had scooped in the sand. Since this was exactly Jacinto's procedure, Father Latour judged that, just as it was the white man's way to assert himself in any landscape, to change it, make it over a little (at least to leave some mark or memorial of his sojourn), it was the Indian's way to pass through a country without disturbing anything; to pass and leave no trace, like fish through water, or birds through the air. (pp. 235-36)

He notes too how the Hopi Indian villages on the rock mesas 'were made to look like the rock on which they sat, were imperceptible at a distance,' and how the Navaho hogans built in the sand and willows 'were made of sand and willows' (p. 236). When the Archbishop comes to build his cathedral, he too wants a building that will be integral with the landscape. The French architect who builds the cathedral strives to retain a kinship between the church and the actual rock from which it is made. When it is finished Father Latour takes great satisfaction in the way the cathedral seems to rise directly out of the hills and to be so much 'of the South.'

Probably the greatest challenge to our experience and understanding of art in the twentieth century has come from those modern artists who reject the romantic drama of the ego as the exclusive subject for art. One thinks here of such American writers as Pound, Stein, Williams, and Charles Olson. Instead of viewing art as autobiographical expression, rooted in the psychology of its author, they see it as a way of exploring the infinite possibilities of the perceptual world. In the visual arts, cubism and its successor movements broke down the traditional idea of perspective so that the eye ('I') is no longer focused, but is directed all over the canvas. In this way the viewer is free to consider form, texture, color, design, the totality of the canvas. The imagination in this kind of art does not impose a static, preconceived notion of form on its subject, but rather finds the form inherent in the subject itself. The practice of much modern art has been (to use Charles Olson's words) 'getting rid of the lyrical interference of the individual as ego, of the "subject" and his soul,' which stand between man and his experience of the world.[6] Ultimately the direction of modern art is away from man's presumptions and dreams of selfhood (he is seen as merely one more dependent in the total environment) and toward the perception of life's natural rhythms and energies.

Willa Cather, who so frequently celebrated the past and the drama of the independent human spirit, might seem remote from these concerns of the modern artist, but at two points during her career—from 1912 to 1915 when she was writing *O Pioneers!* and *The Song of the Lark*, and in the middle 1920s when she wrote *Death Comes for the Archbishop*—she seems to have been moving toward something like the modern writer's stance to his art. That direction is reflected in her concern for organic form in her narratives, her rejection of American materialism, and her fictive renunciation of personal ambitions.

In the early stories and in *Alexander's Bridge* (1912) Willa Cather was learning to write by following literary models, by imposing literary conventions on her material. Sometimes the results were fortunate, as in 'The Sculptor's Funeral' shaped loosely around the formal elements of pastoral elegy; but in other instances such as the imitation of James in 'Eleanor's House' the results were less satisfactory. She eventually rejected her first novel, *Alexander's Bridge*, a story set in Boston and London society, as a contrived novel that followed a fashionable pattern. She relates the change in her writing between *Alexander's Bridge* and *O Pioneers!* to her trip to the Southwest:

> Soon after the book [*Alexander's Bridge*] was published I went for six months to Arizona and New Mexico. The longer I stayed in a country I really did care about, and among people who were a part of the country, the more unnecessary and superficial a book like *Alexander's Bridge* seemed to me. I did no writing down there, but I recovered from the conventional editorial point of view.[7]

O Pioneers! (1913) was put together after she returned from the Southwest. In this novel she said there was no arranging or inventing, rather the subject dictated its own direction. She compared writing *O Pioneers!* to 'taking a ride through a familiar country on a horse that knew the way.'[8] What is especially interesting is her image of the artist yielding herself up to her subject. In another account she says that when a writer begins to work with his real material, 'he has less and less power of choice about the moulding of it. It seems to be there of itself, already moulded.'[9] Form in other words is an extension of content, and to create genuine art the artist must become wholly atuned to the subject. She continues to say of the subject that if the artist tries 'to meddle with its vague outline, to twist it into some categorical shape, above all if he tries to adapt or modify its mood, he destroys its value.'

O Pioneers! in both form and content has qualities that one associates with modern art. Willa Cather admitted to her critics that the form or skeleton of the plot did not stand out boldly, but defended herself saying that the country itself which was her subject had no strong features—no rocks or ridges. The soft, undulating structure of the land itself determined the organic form for the book.[10] *O Pioneers!* actually consists of two stories that were written separately. When they were brought together the author said there was 'a sudden inner explosion and enlightenment.'[11] The form of the novel was both organic and accidental, but Cather clearly felt it was a fortunate accident because she used the five-part structure that resulted (with part four a death or separation sequence) in two more of her novels—*My Ántonia* and *One of Ours*.[12]

The subject of *O Pioneers!* is the struggle of the earliest settlers to wrest a living from the uncultivated prairie. It sets forth in the epic mode (a mode especially congenial to the modern writer's concept of his work) a vision of pioneer community life, focusing on Alexandra Bergson, whose stalwart figure embodies the most heroic gestures of the pioneers. Alexandra is a tall, strong girl who walks 'rapidly and resolutely, as if she knew exactly where she was going and what she was going to do next.'[13] She is not only strong in body (at one point she is described as 'Amazonian'), but her father recognises in her a strength of will and dependability wanting in his sons, and when he dies he turns over the responsibility of the farm and family to her. Alexandra takes up the burden of a man's life, becomes the most successful landowner on the Divide, and the leader in effect of the Swedish pioneer community. But it is especially in her relationship to the land that she acquires her epic stature. The pioneer community suffers through three long years of drought and failure. Many families give up and move away, but Alexandra remains fast. Riding across the prairie she has a vision of doing something big, and the landscape and the heroine merge in identification and purpose:

> For the first time, perhaps, since that land emerged from the waters of geologic ages, a human face was set toward it with love and yearning. It seemed beautiful to her, rich and strong and glorious. Her eyes drank in the breadth of it, until her tears blinded her. Then the Genius of the Divide, the great, free spirit which breathes across it, must have bent lower than it ever bent to a human will before. (p. 65)

Fundamental to the novel is a vision of life's ongoing processes in a vast and fruitful universe. We are told that it fortified Alexandra 'to reflect upon the great operations of nature' (p. 70); she feels one with the land she plows, as if her heart were hidden down in the long grasses with the insects and the plovers. A picture of the people working the rich land and bringing in the harvests is a recurrent leitmotiv which is enhanced throughout the novel by the rhetorical style ('the growing wheat, the growing weeds/the toiling horses, the tired men'). There is no authorial presence in the narration; rather in a sonorous and rhythmic style ('the spring would come again! Oh, it would come again' [p. 202]) the voice of the land and its people can be heard, a voice of celebration first struck by the Whitman title.[14]

The subplot, the story of Emil and Marie, seems to detract from the novel's epic vision—Alexandra's young brother falls in love with a neighbor's wife and both he and the girl are killed by the enraged husband—but we are made to see that these ill-fated lovers are ultimately reabsorbed into the weave of creation. The staining of the white mulberries with the lovers' blood suggests an Ovidian love story, and accordingly, when they die, Cather's lovers are metamorphosed into two white butterflies that flutter over the bodies in the orchard. Alexandra too will become part of the land some day. She says to her friend Carl: '"we come and go, but the land is always here. And the people who love it and understand it are the people who own it for a little while."' The land is a living thing and in its sphere there is no death, rather metamorphoses and rebirth. The novel closes in the rhetorical cadences of a Whitman poem with a vision of life's renewal:

> Fortunate country, that is one day to receive hearts like Alexandra's into its bosom, to give them out again in the yellow wheat, in the rustling corn, and in the shining eyes of youth! (p. 309).

The Song of the Lark (1915) may seem like a novel in the opposite vein, a story of romantic ambitions and an individual's quest for fame and success. But Thea Kronborg does not find the path to her goal as an artist until she abandons the idea of art as self-expression and views her singing as part of 'a long chain of human endeavour' that stretches back to ancient times. Before her vision of art comes to her in the canyon, Thea must shed her individual personality 'of which she was so tired,' and also she must feel 'completely released from the enslaving desire to get on in the world' (pp. 368-69). In the desert she yields herself up for hours to the physical sensations around her:

> She could become a mere receptacle for heat, or become a colour, like the bright lizards that darted about on the hot stones outside her door; or she could become a continuous repetition of sound, like the cicadas (p. 373).

This delving beneath personal identity to something elemental and universal about life prepares Thea for her vision of art as a sacred trust for the whole of mankind, rather than a struggle for individual achievement and recognition.

Thea's understanding of her role as an artist comes one morning when she is bathing in the canyon and sees the broken pieces of Indian pottery in the stream. The Indian water vessels suggest to Thea a meaningful synthesis of art and life. They are functional utensils, serving man's need of water for physical life, but they also give expression in their design and craftsmanship to man's age-old desire to celebrate the joy of existence. The pottery, moreover, reflects the communal aspect of Indian art. For Thea, music had been the essence of her individuality, but in the presence of the ancient pottery and the cliff houses she feels her art no longer alienates her from other men, but connects her vitally to a tradition of human aspiration:

> All these things made one feel that one ought to do one's best, and help to fulfil some desire of the dust that slept there ... These potsherds were like fetters that bound one to a long chain of human endeavour (p. 380).

At the end of the novel Thea, as a great opera singer, appears depersonalised and aloof, callous in the neglect of her family, but perhaps this is not so negative as it first seems. Perhaps instead we are meant to recognise that the artist must shed his personal, appetent self, must extend his family to include ancient ancestors and all men if his art is to be genuinely great. If this was Willa Cather's intention (and I think it was), then her vision of the artist anticipates and is continuous with our own.

In the novels that followed *The Song of the Lark* Willa Cather's personal dilemmas—changes in her relationship with Isabelle McClung, her reaction to the First World War, the disaffection of middle-age—brought forward a romantic, subjective strain in her writing. *My Ántonia* (1918) is a pastoral novel filled with profound nostalgia for a way of life that has vanished. Much like the author, Jim Burden lives in New York and escapes the frustrations of an empty marriage and career by idealizing the period of his childhood. His memories focus on the immigrant girl, Ántonia Shimerda, whose gaiety and impulsive generosity seem to embody everything that he has lost. In the last part of the novel the middle-aged narrator tries to recapture his youth in a visit to Ántonia's farm. One critic sees this as a parallel reenactment of the ancient rites at Eleusis, where a man is initiated into life through the revealed mysteries of the earth mother.[15] But *My Ántonia* remains a romantic novel about the American dream and its failure; Jim Burden does not really affirm life at the book's close, rather he celebrates nostalgically 'the precious, the incommunicable past.'

Willa Cather's disaffection with life marks the novels she wrote in the early 1920s. Her feelings were probably shaped by the upheaval in her friendship with Isabelle McClung, as Leon Edel has suggested; but there was a salutary dimension to this personal crisis, for it brought the author to recognise the limitations that personal ambitions and the quest for power impose on one's life. In the satirical novels Willa Cather wrote in the early

1920s the struggle for power is seen in terms of the quest for material possessions. Willa Cather's rejection of American materialistic society is vividly dramatised in *One of Ours* (1922) by the fact that the hero's death in the war is preferable to his returning home to life in America. In *A Lost Lady* (1923) the heroic generation of pioneers has been succeeded by a class of mean-spirited materialists who exploit the land and its people. Willa Cather's horror at man's lust for wealth reaches a peak in *The Professor's House* (1925), where in the selfless disciplines of religion and art she finds an antidote to man's corrupting material pursuits. In *My Mortal Enemy* (1926) the author denounces individual pride, with all its attendant ambitions and delusions, by reducing her willful heroine to a hell of her own making. In all these novels Willa Cather wrestled with the demon of ambition and the desire for power and wealth; the defeat of the will prepared the way for the writing of *Death Comes for the Archbishop*, probably the author's finest novel.

In *Death Comes for the Archbishop* (1927) Willa Cather created a truly modern work of art which moves beyond the subjectivity and emotional ambiguity of the preceding novels. As in *O Pioneers!* the author, through her gift of sympathy for people and places, gave herself up completely to the landscape, this time the Southwest, and to its history where she found the form for her book in the saint's legend. (She also likens the form of her narrative to two white mules moving slowly forward.[16]) By implication *Death Comes for the Archbishop* repudiates the romantic American dream of heroic destiny. There is no hero in this book; we view instead two priests of the early American church whose lives can never be separated from the land and the people where they work their mission.

There is no plot in *Death Comes for the Archbishop*, no dramatic focus or climax to the story of the two priests' lives, because as a saint's legend all events are simply aspects of a divine drama, the course of which is already known. The events in the book are related in a loose chronological order (from the meeting of the Cardinals in 1848 until the Archbishop's death in 1889), but time is of little significance for the vision informing the narrative is an atemporal one. Like the homogeneous 'all over' style of modern paintings, or the art of painters and poets who work in series, this narrative 'without accent' forms something like a continuum with only the merest formalities marking a beginning or end. The formal character of the narrative is described by the Archbishop himself at the end of the novel:

> He sat in the middle of his own consciousness; none of his former states of mind were lost or outgrown. They were all within reach of his hand, and all comprehensible. (p. 290)

Time is something tactile which the priest can reach for and hold in his hands. Past and future are thus woven together into a continuous present which is informed throughout by the vision of an eternal Present.

In *Death Comes for the Archbishop* Willa Cather did not attempt to present her characters psychologically. Her only concern was to describe their lives in the light of religious faith. The saint's legend form discounts individual personality by eliminating the importance of time and place that put man at the center of phenomena. Instead of man as the pride of creation, we are presented in *Death Comes for the Archbishop* with a vision of man in humility, emulating not Christ as sacrificed god (this would have called for the martyrdom of the priests), but Christ who on the cross experienced doubt before he could utter faith, thus sharing the condition of all men. When the narrative opens, the Bishop, who is riding over the hot desert and has lost his way, is reminded, by the cruciform trees and his thirst, of the cry, 'J'ai soif,' wrung from the Savior on the cross. More important than physical hardship is his experience of an unspoken doubt of survival, which links him, as it does Christ on the cross, to all men. This is the universality of the Bishop's experience in the desert. By contrast a martyrdom would have assumed the romantic dimensions of individual glory achieved through self-sacrifice. Similarly the psychological analysis of character and motives would have detracted from Willa Cather's real subject—the fact of existence itself, inexplicable and inviolable.

The ideal held up in the novel is religious art that is communal and traditional. Throughout the book we are made aware of numerous art objects which the Bishop reflects upon: the wooden figures of the saints fashioned by the Mexicans, the Angelus bell, the wooden parrot of old Padre Jesus de Baca, the Indian blankets, the silver toilet set given the Bishop by Don Olivares. They are not all religious objects, but they are all products of long cultural traditions. They are in the widest sense the work of a people and, though they may have been made by a single artist, they transcend the whole question of private possession and individual ambition. The concern with individual ambition comes to the fore when the Bishop decides to build the cathedral at Santa Fe. When the Bishop discusses architects and styles with Father Vaillant, the latter replies: 'I had no idea you were going in for fine building, when everything about us is so poor—and we ourselves are so poor' (p. 244). This implied criticism brings the Bishop to wonder if he is in fact creating an artifact for selfish and worldly reasons. He admits to Father Vaillant that he preferred to find the yellow rock for his cathedral than to acquire a fortune to spend on charity. But the Bishop's integrity is never really in doubt, and the cathedral stands as the ideal artifact in the book. It is communal in origin, through its relation to European architectural style and through the many hands involved in building it, and it is communally owned in that it belongs to the Mexican people. Moreover, as pointed out before, it is one with its setting: the architect tells the Bishop that the cathedral is part of the place and that 'once that kinship is there, time will only make it stronger' (p. 273).

In her last books Willa Cather turned again to personal memories and stories about artists, but the attitude to life which she observed in the Indians and which likely influenced her art is not wholly abandoned. Lucy Gayheart is an artist, but the lesson she must learn is that living itself is the important thing, that art should enrich life but not supplant it. The lesson that Sapphira Colbert, the slave-owner, must learn is one of humility and compassion. And in some of her late stories like 'Neighbour Rosicky' and 'Before Breakfast' the author endorses, unlike Jim Burden, the rightness and necessity of time and change. I have been suggesting that Willa Cather has a place with a group of writers quite different from the romantic celebrants of the American dream. She belongs with the latter too. But if she is a great artist then she will show a new face to each generation of readers and be rediscovered accordingly as one of the 'moderns.'

Notes

1. *Willa Cather's Imagination* (Lincoln: Univ. of Nebraska Press, 1975).
2. Bernice Slote, 'Willa Cather and the West,' *Persimmon Hill*, IV:4 (Autumn 1974), p. 58.
3. *My Ántonia*, Sentry Edition (Boston: Houghton Mifflin, 1961), p. 62.
4. *The Song of the Lark*, Sentry Edition (Boston: Houghton Mifflin, 1963), p. 378. Further references are to the same text.
5. *Death Comes for the Archbishop* (New York: Knopf, 1927), p. 235. Further references are to the same text.
6. Charles Olson, *Selected Writings*, ed. Robert Creeley (New York: New Directions, 1966), p. 24.
7. *Willa Cather on Writing* (New York: Knopf, 1949), p. 92.
8. *Ibid*, pp. 92–93.
9. 'Preface' to *Alexander's Bridge* (New York: Bantam Books, 1962), p. vii.
10. See James Woodress, *Willa Cather: Her Life and Art* (New York: Pegasus Books, 1970), p. 155.
11. See Woodress, p. 154.
12. Hugh Kenner has frequently observed in lectures that literary forms are accidental in origin and become rigid conventions through borrowing and imitation.
13. *O Pioneers!*, Sentry Edition (Boston: Houghton Mifflin, 1962), p. 6. Further references are to the same text.
14. The oral quality to Willa Cather's prose has been discussed in two recent essays: Richard Giannone's 'Willa Cather and the Human Voice,' *Five Essays on Willa Cather: The Merrimack Symposium*, ed. John J. Murphy (North Andover, Mass.: Merrimack College Press, 1974), pp. 21–49, and Donald Sutherland's 'Willa Cather: The Classic Voice,' *The Art of Willa Cather*, ed. Bernice Slote and Virginia Faulkner (Lincoln: Univ. of Nebraska Press, 1974), pp. 156–79.
15. Evelyn Helmick, 'The Mysteries of Ántonia,' *The Midwest Quarterly*, 17, no. 2 (Winter 1976), pp. 173–85.
16. Letter to Norman Foerster, University of Nebraska Library, dated May 22, 1933.

156
Pastoralism and Its Discontents: Willa Cather and the Burden of Imperialism

◆

MIKE FISCHER

Willa Cather's fiction has recently been subjected to a number of revisionist readings, most notably by feminist critics of *My Ántonia* who have exposed both the various sexist stereotypes that underlie Jim Burden's archetypal eulogizing of 'his' protagonist and the narrative strategies whereby he attempts to expropriate his female muse. Unfortunately, in doing so they have overlooked the fact that it is not only the history of women on the Plains that is being 'rewritten' by Jim but also the conquest of the Plains Indians that is being rewritten by Willa Cather.

Jim initially describes the Nebraskan land upon which he will write his story as 'not a country at all, but the material out of which countries are made' (7); and he imagines himself as writing in the tradition of the *Georgics*, Virgil's pastoral account of the founding of the patria. Factually, however, the history of the Plains has more in common with the brutal imperialism recorded in the *Aeneid*; the development of Nebraska is a pastoral story only in the sense of 'pastor(al)isation.' *My Ántonia* is a story of origins for whites only; its account of conflicts between various selves and their others—an important theme in the novel—ignores the most significant Other in Nebraskan history: the Native Americans whose removal was seen as a *sine qua non* for successful white settlement.

Essential to an 'idyllic' view of Plains history is the premise that what the first settlers had to clear was merely the land, and here one begins to see in a new light Cather's repeated description of the Nebraska which preceded

SOURCE   Mike Fischer, 'Pastoralism and Its Discontents: Willa Cather and the Burden of Imperialism', *Mosaic*, 23, 1990, pp. 31-44.

white settlement as a prairie that was 'empty.' Equally revealing, in turn, is the way Cather's feminist critics have followed her lead. For all her valuable insights into Jim's sexism for example, Jean Schwind describes the Nebraska territory that the Shimmerdas subsequently occupy as 'new virgin land' (61). Similarly, Sharon O'Brien, perhaps Cather's best feminist critic, refers to the Nebraskan landscape into which Cather moved in 1883 as an 'empty world' 'uninscribed in a literary as well as a topographical sense,' a 'new landscape' in which Cather might concern herself 'with the human drive to create culture and civilisation by making marks in a new landscape'—'taming . . . the wild land' (74).

The land on which Cather inscribed her story, however, was not a *tabula rasa*, even if, as in *O Pioneers!*, she conceives of 'the feeble scratches on stone left by prehistoric races [as] so indeterminate that they may, after all, be only the markings of glaciers, and not a record of human strivings' (18–19). In a powerful demonstration of circular logic, Cather's reading of such 'feeble scratches' as 'indeterminate' allows her to relegate the people who made them to a time before writing—to prehistory.

Cather's appropriation of the land's materials for her own purposes—so that she might build a 'country'—required that those contexts and peoples which did not accommodate her textual strategy be marginalised or naturalised so that their stories would not contradict her own. As such, her works confirm what Fredric Jameson has observed with respect to the ideological nature of the esthetic act, which invents 'imaginary or formal "solutions" to unresolvable social contradictions' (79). This is not to accuse Cather of conscious duplicity or racism, any more than it is to indict those feminist critics who ignore her failure to recognise Nebraska's first inhabitants. Instead, the kind of naturalisation of which I speak is indicative of the cultural limitations—Jameson's 'political unconscious'—that condition the historical interpretations of any epoch and which register the blindspots in any period's texts (74–83). Such ways of perceiving result from an individual's incremental and almost unnoticed absorption of the cultural assumptions of his or her particular group or class.

At the same time, however, the 'real' history that such assumptions exclude does not—cannot—just go away. The social contradictions that narrative seeks to resolve, because they are intrinsic to the social infrastructures such narratives depict, have a habit of reappearing at inopportune moments. This 'notion of contradiction,' writes Jameson, 'is central to any Marxist cultural analysis' and it explains why history, in the sense of a grand narrative of human events, will not disappear and cannot be erased; 'it happened' (80). There can be no cultural text, however apparently blind to the political preconditions assuring its provenance, that fails to record the traces of those preconditions, in spite of itself. Any story of the (white) settlement of Nebraska—or 'America'—will inevitably find itself referring to those peoples whose 'removal' preceded that settlement. The function of criticism, accordingly, is to uncover these traces. Or as Tony Bennett argues in corroboration of Jameson's 'notion of contradiction,' an active and critical intervention 'works' upon such texts and serves to expose contradictions that they and their author(s), given their own historical context, could not have seen (141).

While it is true that cultural context inevitably limits the perceptions of any critic, the political struggles of the sixties and seventies—such as the Black Arts and Black Power movements, the American Indian Movement (AIM), and the Chicano Youth Movement's 'Plan of Aztlan'—place us today in an especially advantageous position for 'working' on texts so as to excavate the buried stories in U.S. history. While the most important part of this project must and will remain the recuperation and celebration of these peoples' own texts, a critical explanation of how such stories are embedded within canonical narratives might help us recognise the degree to which suppressed histories are integral not only to the establishment of canons but also to the idea of 'Western Civilisation' that canons celebrate.

Before proceeding, perhaps I can make clearer the nature of the interpretive act with an example. Bernice Slote, trying to explain the absence of non-European ethinc groups in much of Cather's early fiction, offers the following picture of the young Cather's Nebraska: 'She lived in Nebraska in the 1880s and 1890s, when Indians were noticed in the newspapers chiefly as warring tribes with dirty living habits. In any case, they were far from Red Cloud, and Wounded Knee was only a column or so of print. Literary views in Nebraska were composed in highly romanticized legends, some in Hiawatha style . . .' (98-99). Slote's passage underscores an important contradiction in the (white) Nebraskan perceptions it describes. On the one hand, 'columns of print' describing the Indians did in fact exist. On one level, some late-nineteenth-century Nebraskans were still aware of the Indians, as they could not help being, given how recently—as late as the 1870s—much of western Nebraska had still been under Sioux control. On the other hand, the Indians, in Cather's Red Cloud, were reduced from their cultural complexity to 'warring tribes with dirty habits.' As James Olson has demonstrated in his history of Nebraska, early Nebraskan newspapers, often little more than advertising sheets for the companies that owned them, were far more concerned with the price and yield of land than they were with drawing sensitive or accurate portraits of those peoples being thrown off the land (93). As far as such newspapers were concerned, the Wounded Knee massacre had nothing to do with an agrarian Nebraska economy; it, and the Indians who died there, existed 'far away.' They simply did not matter.

They were not so far away, however, either temporally or geographically, as Cather might have wanted—and successfully managed—to believe. Red Cloud itself, established in 1870 as the first permanent town in what had been one of the Indians' last buffalo hunting grounds south of the Platte River, was named after the Sioux chief of that name, who was reputed to have held a war council on the site where the town was platted (Perkey 198; J. Olson 171-72).

As recently as 1868, Red Cloud's war councils had been aimed at expelling white settlers from the lands north of the Platte River—guaranteed the Sioux in perpetuity as part of the 1851 Laramie Treaty—in western Nebraska, northern Wyoming and Montana. That year a second Laramie Treaty initiated the process that would eventually force Red Cloud to accept semi-reservation status in northwestern Nebraska and that, finally, after the illegal white incursions into the Black Hills in the mid-1870s, would lead to his expulsion from Nebraska altogether.

Nonetheless, in 1870 the Black Hills catastrophe, originally provoked by the discovery there of gold, could not be foreseen: names like Sitting Bull, Crazy Horse and Custer were relatively unknown. In the very months that Red Cloud, Nebraska, was being founded, Chief Red Cloud was completing a treaty in Washington, D.C. In exchange for peace along Nebraska's Platte River Valley— with its just completed trans-continental railroad that the Indians had successfully sabotaged in the 1866-68 war—the Oglalla Sioux were guaranteed possession of the Black Hills and the Powder River country. The 'warring tribes with dirty habits' would be placed in the margins of Nebraska's text; they could continue to 'harass' settlers elsewhere as long as Nebraska prospered. Chief Red Cloud's treaty symbolised this compromise; Red Cloud, Nebraska, opening up what had been Indian territory, profited from its provisions (Brown, chapters 5,6,8,12; Baltensperger 37-52; J. Olson 128-41).

The settlers of Red Cloud under Silas Garber—soon to become governor of the state—may have believed that the name they chose for their town could serve as an emblem for the peace that Chief Red Cloud had made— had been forced to make—possible. That peace, however, was tenuous; provoked by continued white expansion into their territory, the Sioux continued a resistance which James Olson has argued was 'the most serious opposition they [the whites] encountered in the whole of America's westward expansion' (128-29). The events of 1876, and in particular Custer's astonishing defeat—the most serious blow the U.S. Army suffered in all of the Indian Wars—demonstrated anew at what cost such 'peace' had to be won. The hopes generated by Red Cloud's 1870 Washington visit had dissipated amidst a series of bloody wars that, within twenty years, would see the systematic genocide of Red Cloud's people and the deaths of hundreds of white soldiers. Red Cloud became a reminder, for those who chose to remember, that its prosperity and security were predicated upon the removal and elimination of the people for whose chief it was named— people who still occupied most of Nebraska as late as the American Civil War, as Cather herself admitted in a 1923 *Nation* article:

> Before 1860 civilization did no more than nibble at the eastern edge of the State, along the river bluffs. Lincoln, the present capital, was open prairie; and the whole of the great plain to the westward was still a sunny wilderness, where the tall red grass and the buffalo and the Indian hunter were undisturbed (236).

Despite the implications of her *Nation* article, Cather usually chose not to remember the presence of Native Americans in Nebraska, or, perhaps more accurately, she literally seemed to forget their existence. While her short history of Nebraska does acknowledge the Indians' erstwhile presence, it does not try to account for their removal—nor explain how the peoples who roamed the prairies 'undisturbed' were eventually disturbed enough to disappear and make possible the agricultural paradise that she proclaims Nebraska to be.

The name Cather chooses in *My Ántonia* for her fictional Red Cloud, 'Black Hawk,' is suggestive in this context. The Black Hawk War of 1831-32 represented the opening skirmish in the white effort to steal the Plains; Chief Black Hawk's defeat, that is to say, might legitimately stand as the opening moment in Cather's genealogy of the settlement of Nebraska. Cather herself would probably not have known much more of this historical Black Hawk than the residents of Red Cloud would have known of the chief after whom their town was named. Instead, Cather would probably have known only the mythological Black Hawk, a version of the chief popularised through numerous reprintings of his autobiography—an autobiography interpreted and written for an American audience by a U.S. Army officer. As Richard Slotkin has observed in his expose of the mythology of the American frontier, the 'autobiography' of Chief Black Hawk was one of the first texts in the nineteenth-century cult of nostalgia that would increasingly come to surround white perceptions of Native American peoples. As the Indian threat decreased, Slotkin argues, the nostalgic impulse toward the Indians increased (356–60).

Within a year of what was, for the Indians, a disastrous blow, and even as President Jackson was completing the Cherokee removal to Oklahoma, Black Hawk's 'autobiography' was on the market and his heroisation had begun. Cather's account of 'Black Hawk' involved a similar *white*wash on behalf of late-nineteenth-century Nebraska, relegating the Sioux—and Wounded Knee—to a place 'far away,' a 'column of print' on the margins of her celebration of the pioneer instinct. The little girl who had been photographed as Hiawatha had grown up to memorialise the 'highly romanticised legends, some in Hiawatha style,' that, according to Slote, had conditioned Cather's perception of the Nebraska frontier from the start.

Perhaps Cather's most famous evocation of that frontier—not just in *My Ántonia* but in all of her fiction—is the plow which, as Jim enjoys his farewell picnic with the 'hired girls,' is suddenly transformed into a monolithic emblem of the future of the land. The scene occurs at the close of the penultimate chapter of Book II, as Jim prepares to take leave of Black Hawk. As the sun sinks in the west, it magnifies to gigantic proportions a plow that has been left standing in the field: 'it stood out against the sun . . . black against the molten red. There it was, heroic in size, a picture writing on the sun' (245).

Paul Olson, in his reading of the Virgilian influences on *My Ántonia*, draws a parallel and contrast between this passage and that moment in the eighth book of the *Aeneid* (616-43) when Aeneas sees the weapons with which he will be permitted to forge Rome's future. Not only does Aeneas see his sword and his shield inscribed with scenes of the Roman future, but he also envisions his bronze breastplate 'massive and ruddy coloured like to some lowing cloud/When it catches fire from the rays of the sun and glows afar' (qtd. in Olson 282). Olson reasons that the inverse nature of the parallel is intended to suggest Cather's preference for the *Georgics*; as he sees it, when she does not invoke Virgil's pastoral writings directly, as in Jim's study in Lincoln, she obliquely signals her preference by revising the warrior epic to suit her agrarian picture of Nebraska's genealogy: 'Her [Ántonia's] journey ends in a garden, a family garden, as the more perfect world which the *Georgics* propose. Her place is the patria ... [with Cather suggesting that] the ancient epic, celebrating as it had the myth of military might, iron law, and male dominance, had run its course' (284).

Olson's explanation is fine—as far as it goes. But it fails to account for the sudden disappearance of this splendid vision—as the plow is enveloped in the darkness that quickly spreads over the prairie—at chapter's close; indeed, Cather's text seems to suggest that the myth that has 'run its course' is as much the pastoral vision that she has just evoked as the warrior epic which that vision replaces.

Olson likewise neglects to mention the extremely imperial narrative fragment that immediately precedes the magnification of the plow: Jim's relation to the 'hired girls' of the Coronado legend. According to Jim's retelling of the story, a farmer north of Black Hawk, while breaking sod, turned up a Spanish sword engraved with the name of a munitions maker in Cordova. For Jim and his school chum Charlie Harling, this discovery indicates that the Coronado expedition, which reportedly had not advanced further north than central Kansas, must have made it as far north as the southern Nebraska Republican River valley in which the novel is set. The girls ask Jim why Coronado never went back to Spain. 'I couldn't,' he admits, 'tell them. I only knew the schoolbooks said he "died in the wilderness of a broken heart"' (244).

The discrepancy Jim tacitly acknowledges between the textual history through which he has learned about Coronado and 'what actually happened'—the contexts that 'historical' narrative displaces—gestures toward Cather's own uneasy awareness that the Coronado expedition was not quite what the Nebraskan school texts might have claimed it was. *Death Comes for the Archbishop* in particular makes repeated reference to the fact that 'the Spaniards had treated them [the pueblo Indians of the southwest] very badly long ago' (53), specifically referring to cruelties perpetrated by Coronado's soldiers against the Pecos Indians during the march toward the fabled cities of Quivera (125).

The realities were even worse than Cather's references to slavery and concubinage in this 1927 novel might suggest. Beginning with the Arenal pueblo, Spanish troops under Coronado and Cardenas massacred the populations of twelve pueblos of the Tigeux Indians in the winter of 1540; over thirty of the inhabitants of the Arenal pueblo, surrendering after receiving a promise of fair treatment, were burned alive (Day 118-27; Udall 144-46).

Coronado's behavior toward the Indians was too much even for Spain's administrators in Mexico, never known for their overly kind treatment of the Indians. During his *residencia*—an examination of conduct and policy that all Spanish officials were required to undergo upon completion of their duties—in 1544, Coronado was accused by his own men of inhumane treatment of the Indians in both northern Mexico and in the Tigeux country along the Rio Grande river in New Mexico (Hammond 75; Day 165-68). As punishment for his conduct, he was stripped of his post as governor of New Galicia (Day 172). Coronado may or may not have died of a 'broken heart.' What is certain is that, despite a partial rehabilitation in 1549, he died disgraced by his government for his inhumane treatment of New Spain's native population.

Coronado's inhumane treatment might, too, help explain what a Spanish sword is doing in Nebraskan soil—why, that is, it did not accompany its owner back to Mexico. For Cather's inclusion of this apparently inconsequential romantic detail alludes to a Spanish expedition that, unlike Coronado's, really did cross the Republican River and explore south-central Nebraska. In June of 1720, accompanied by forty-five Spanish soliders, over sixty Indians, an interpreter and a priest, Pedro de Villasur set out from Santa Fe to re-establish Spanish control of the Great Plains, a control strongly contested by the French and some eastern Plains native peoples with whom they were allied. Somewhere in central Nebraska—the exact location has never been ascertained—the expedition was ambushed and almost completely annihilated by a contingent of Pawnee Indians. While most of the Indians accompanying the Spanish apparently escaped, only thirteen of the Spanish soldiers made it back to Santa Fe (J. Olson 30-31; Thomas 72-79).

In an ironic way, then, Jim and Charlie were right: Coronado really had made it to Nebraska—at least by reputation. If a Spanish sword is found north of Black Hawk, Coronado's reputation probably had a lot to do with it ending up there. De Villasur's expedition reaped the whirlwind that Coronado's cruelty had sown.

The truth behind the Coronado legend belies the 'georgic' vision that Cather's plow seems designed to evoke. No matter how successfully *My Ántonia* appears to bury the reminders of the wars whose consequence was to 'open' Nebraska for farming, the genealogy of that agricultural triumph refuses to disappear. Plowing, in Nebraska, is inextricably intertwined with the sword. And in a paradigmatic example of the return of the repressed, the sword and everything it stands for 'turn up' in Cather's narrative at the very place where she most powerfully calls forth the symbolic plow; meant to replace the sword, the plow rediscovers it instead. If the sun finally sets on Jim's pastoral vision, it is because the Edenic possibilities which that vision seems to entail have been called into question.

Jim tacitly alludes to the dessication of Eden when he retells the story of his battle with the snake (45-48). Blanche Gelfant sees this scene as an example of the return of the repressed in its classically Freudian sexual sense, claiming that the snake 'forces him [Jim] to confront deeply repressed images, to acknowledge for the only time the effect of "horrible unconscious memories"' (88). I would supplement Gelfant's reading—convincing as it is—by pointing to Jim's actual description of the snake as old enough to have 'been there when white men first came, left on from buffalo and Indian times' (47). Those times, for Jim, are relatively recent; he calculates the snake to be about twenty-four years old. To the extent that we are justified in seeing Jim as an autobiographical persona for Cather, this would place the snake's birth around 1860—immediately preceding the passage of the Homestead Act (1862) which initiated large-scale immigration into and the subsequent domestication of Nebraska's still wide-open spaces. Jim's battle with the snake, then, represents a metonymic displacement of the true genealogy of Nebraska's white settlement: the Indian Wars of the 1860s that were planned in conjunction with the passage of the Homestead Act and that made its implementation possible (Trachtenberg 30).

There can be no Eden in Nebraska, because its origins are not innocent. Much like the unhealed wheel-ruts in the wagon road that 'looked like gashes torn by a grizzly's claws' (371), the 'road of [Manifest] Destiny' (372) in which these ruts are embedded—the road that Cather grandiloquently recalls at the close of her Nebraska history—is slashed by violence. His circular road, though, gashes and all, necessarily awakens memories of the mysterious Indian ceremonial ground—that 'great circle where the Indian used to ride'—which had so powerfully moved Jim when he was a boy (62). However peripheral to Jim's later experience—and the Nebraskan story with which it is intertwined—the historical realities which that circle evokes refuse to disappear.

Jim's infamous road at the close of *My Ántonia* also recalls the road for which he works as a lawyer, that 'great Western railway' that 'runs and branches' through Nebraska, leaving scars far more permanent—and serious—than those Jim can trace to wagon-ruts. When the introduction to *My Ántonia* connects Jim's 'personal passion' for 'the great country through which his railway runs and branches' with 'its development,' it is unclear whether the 'it' refers to the railroad or to the United States. There is no solution to this ambiguity—nor need there be. The U.S. government's expansionist ideology and genocidal policy of Indian 'removal' were intimately and specifically connected to plans for the construction of a transcontinental railroad which were being formulated as early as the 1840s.

Hence it is hardly surprising that Jim Burden works for the railroads; it would be more surprising if he did not. As someone who has engineered a cleaned up version of Nebraska's past, himself controlled by an author who associated 'towering locomotives' charging 'over the great Western land' with 'power, conquest, and triumph' (qtd. in O'Brien 85), Jim quite fittingly works for the industry that epitomised and engineered American progress —while rarely calculating the cost of that progress to America's indigenous people. As Glen Love writes, 'For Cather, as for Jim Burden, the railroad seems to have been accepted as simply a part of the geographical and cultural given of the prairie. The railroad was there when they arrived, and thus it belongs' (144).

It had not always 'belonged,' and Cather herself, in the middle of an article celebrating the comforts of the Burlington Railroad—the road that runs through Black Hawk in *My Ántonia* and which runs through the actual town of Red Cloud—recognised that the 'sudden transition' from the harsh western prairie to the comforts of a railroad dining car had 'something of the black art about it and seemed altogether unnatural' (*World* 838). We can see just how unnatural—and the extent, consequently, to which Cather's narrative 'railroads' its readers—by reviewing the history of how Nebraska was wrested from the Plains Indians.

When Andrew Jackson stole parts of the southeastern United States from the Indians in 1830, he initiated a process that resulted, in 1834, in the Indian Intercourse Act, which guaranteed the Indians possession of most American lands west of the Mississippi, including all of the present state of Nebraska (J. Olson 67). Though subsequent territorial adjustments appropriated substantial portions of this 'Indian land' including most of the spaces between the Mississippi and Missouri Rivers, the Indians were still in possession of all of Nebraska when Stephen Douglas, recently elected congressman from Illinois, arose from the floor of the House in 1844 and proposed his first bill to organise Nebraska as a territory (J. Olson 69-70).

Douglas's initiative was, to say the least, peculiar, since territorial organisation was supposed to follow an accumulation of white settlers in a region. Not surprisingly, however, given the 1834 agreement with the Indians, the only whites in Nebraska in the mid-1840s were a few missionaries, traders and advance squatters, none of whom was very concerned with his/her official position (92). Douglas's real reason for proposing the Bill was less concerned with these few white transients than with the possibility of placing the eastern terminus of the newly proposed transcontinental railroad in Chicago and running it through Nebraska's easily traversable Platte River valley. With this in mind, Douglas had recently invested in Chicago real estate (Limerick 92). Still, as long as he and his constituency were confronted with the lingering fiction of a permanent Indian territory, the proposed routes would begin elsewhere—as indeed all four of the routes proposed during the 1840s did (J. Olson 68-69).

With the introduction of his Bill and his decade-long fight for the creation of a Nebraska territory, Douglas served notice to Secretary of War Jefferson Davis that no more Indians should be allowed into Nebraska. 'The Indian barrier must be removed,' he wrote; otherwise the United States would sacrifice its 'immense interests and possession on the Pacific' to a 'vast wilderness fifteen hundred miles in breadth, filled with hostile savages, and cutting off all direct communication' (qtd. in Limerick 93). Douglas got his wish. The Nebraska Territory was created in 1854, even though a census taken in November of that year showed only twenty-seven hundred whites living in the state—most of them either residing on the eastern fringe of the territory along the Missouri or transients who actually lived in Kansas (J. Olson 88).

Many of the Indian tribes living in eastern Nebraska were either confined to reservations or forced to 'trade' their ancient lands for trinkets and new guarantees of lands further West. The success of this program of removal, combined with the dramatic rise in population as a result of the Homestead Act (intended to consolidate control of these lands) and with the American Civil War, which effectively removed the proposed southern routes from contention, led President Lincoln, in 1863, to choose the Platte River valley as the route that the railroad would follow. The first track was laid that year; by 1867, the rails had reached western Nebraska.

Here, the Sioux, Cheyenne and Arapaho peoples proved more difficult to 'remove' than their eastern neighbors had been. As Chief Spotted Tail of the Brûlé Sioux said to President Grant during the 1870 visit of Red Cloud's delegation, 'The Great Father has made roads stretching east and west. Those roads are the cause of all our troubles.... The country where we live is overrun by whites. All our game is gone.... If you stop your roads we can get our game' (qtd. in Brown 138). Spotted Tail was complaining specifically about white incursions into the Powder River country; by 1870, after all, the transcontinental railroad had been finished for a year. Building it was not easy, however, partly because, from the time of the Sand Creek massacre of 1864, the Indians of western Nebraska systematically tore up tracks and raided supply wagons carrying building materials (J. Olson 114, 137–38).

The outcome of this struggle was inevitable. The whites were too powerful, and there were too many of them. From less than three thousand settlers in 1854, white Nebraskan population rose to thirty thousand by 1860, fifty thousand by 1867, when Nebraska became a state, and one hundred twenty-five thousand by 1870, the year of Red Cloud's eastern visit, the year that Red Cloud, Nebraska was settled. By 1890, just before the economic depression, drought years and emigration that would characterise the nineties, Nebraska had over one million white settlers, almost all of them first generation pioneers (J. Olson 88).

If, as Governor John Thayer of Nebraska claimed in his inaugural address of 1887, the railroads led to Nebraska's settlement a quarter to half century sooner than might otherwise have been expected (Combs 21), one of the reasons was the aggressive propaganda campaign the railroads waged in Europe to lure immigrants to Nebraska. Moreover, the railroads dictated both settlement patterns and the government policy toward the Indians that made settlement feasible.

In 1865, for example, the southern Cheyenne and Arapaho peoples, displaced by the Colorado Gold Rush (1858) and the ensuing Sand Creek massacre (1864), met with representatives of the government to negotiate the site for a reservation. The Indians elected the area between the Smoky Hill River in central Kansas and the Republican River—running through what would become Red Cloud—in southern Nebraska. The government denied their request, knowing as they did that the Burlington planned to open this area for settlement and build a railroad there (Brown 96).

The Cheyenne and Arapaho were forced to move to the Oklahoma territory; Red Cloud was established five years later. Though Indians refusing to accept the 1865 treaty had successfully stymied the first attempt to settle the Republican River valley in 1869, and though they periodically disrupted other attempts at settling the region, such as that at Red Willow in 1871, the prospect of a railroad in the valley—and the railroad's ability to provide the people for settlement—encouraged settlers to believe that if they could hold on for a few years, their ventures into the area would prove successful (J. Olson 170–73). The Burlington dutifully built a spur line through the valley, beginning work in 1878. The line was completed by 1882—a year before Cather traveled it, along with countless immigrant families like the Shimmerdas, to Nebraska.

'The real West to Willa Cather,' writes Slote, 'was the West of settlement, of the immigration of peoples from many parts of the world' (96). It would be misleading to ignore Cather's celebration of these immigrant peoples in novels such as *O Pioneers!* or *My Ántonia*. *My Ántonia* was published in a year of intense xenophobia provoked by the United States government's entry into World War I; on 26 March 1918, Governor Neville of Nebraska successfully engineered the repeal of a law designed to guarantee foreign language instruction in Nebraska's schools as 'vicious, undemocratic, and un-American' (J. Olson 265). In this context, Cather's sensitive portrayal and vigorous defense of immigrant peoples such as the Czechs and the Norwegians can and should be seen as the courageous act that it was.

At the same time, however, one must keep in mind Patricia Nelson Limerick's recent admonition that 'In race relations, the West could make the turn-of-the-century Northeastern urban confrontation between European immigrants and American nativists look like a family reunion' (27). Without taking anything away from Cather's significant achievement, it is nevertheless true that her conception of western history as the story of immigrant settlers blinded her to the effects of such immigration on the

West's native populations. As early as 1852, the Commissioner of Indian Affairs stressed the extent to which Native Americans were suffering 'from the vast number of immigrants who pass through their country, destroying their means of support, and scattering disease and death among them' (qtd. in J. Olson 132). Immigration promoted by the railroads was integral to the accelerated pace at which Nebraskan lands were wrested from the Indians and consolidated as white property.

Moreover, it is important to keep in mind exactly which immigrant groups Cather champions. The Bohemian Czechs she foregrounds in both *O Pioneers!* and *My Ántonia* were used throughout World War I by American propagandists to underscore the United States government's commitment to the right of self-determination. The fact that such propaganda and such a commitment might hasten the dissolution of the Hapsburg Empire of which the Czechs were a subject people might also have had something to do with the Wilson Administration's sudden concern for the Czechs' plight.

It is certainly true that Wilson was fundamentally less concerned with such rights throughout Latin America; as Gabriel Kolko has convincingly demonstrated, one of the reasons that the United States decided to go to war was to protect its own assumed right to intervene militarily, economically and politically in the affairs of any Latin American country without interference from Europe (53–54). Wilson 'celebrated his doctrine of self-determination,' writes Noam Chomsky, 'by invading Mexico, Haiti, and the Dominican Republic' (46).

Furthermore, as Kolko asserts, 'no American leader favored self-determination for Asians and races they felt inferior'; along with his white allies, Wilson later explicitly rejected a statement on racial equality in the covenant of the League of Nations charter (Kolko 55). When one of those 'inferior' Asians approached Wilson's Versailles residence in 1919 begging that the American champion of freedom support the Vietnamese people's right to representation in the French parliament, he was chased away 'like a pest.' The 'pest' was the man who would subsequently be known to history by the name Ho Chi Minh (Chomsky 46).

In this context, Cather's portrait of Ántonia can be read as a text that romanticises the United States's relationship to non Anglo-Saxon peoples. The Czechs, the most Western and consequently least threatening of the Eastern European peoples toward which the government was willing to extend the promise of self-determination, could serve as an ideological figuration of American tolerance, eliding the racism that characterised the United States's relationship to non-Europeans or to its own Black citizen soldiers, vilified, abused and lynched in alarming numbers following their return from France in 1919.

Mention of the 1919 race riots points toward another of Cather's romantic racial portraits in *My Ántonia*, that of the blind Black piano player, Blind D'Arnault (183–92). Gelfant has adequately catalogued the numerous stereotypes of African Americans that enter into Cather's depiction of the man who 'looked like some glistening African god of pleasure, full of strong, savage blood' and the 'buxom young Negro wench' who was his mother (191, 187; Gelfant 80–82).

The racism in this portrait is obvious; less noticeable, perhaps, is the similarity between the function of this romantic text and the function I have attributed to Cather's presentation of the Czechs. During the American Civil War, the people for whom the federal government was supposedly fighting—and to whom it was promising self-determination—were the African Americans. Nebraska ranked second among the territories in the number of volunteers it gave to the Union cause, and it named its capital after the man who had issued the emancipation proclamation (J. Olson 134, 144). Yet even as the Union was reaffirming its commitment to freedom for all peoples, it was implementing its genocidal policy of expansion in the West. The North's victory at Gettysburg in 1863, long seen in American mythology as a landmark in the advance of freedom, allowed the War Department to send eight companies of cavalry West to the Plains (J. Olson 135). They would participate in the campaign that ended in Chivington's programmed massacre of twenty-eight men and one hundred and five Cheyenne and Arapaho women and children at Sand Creek in 1864. In an example of hypocritical double-speak duplicating that employed during World War I, the United States was proclaiming its racial tolerance even as it was conducting a brutal campaign of race hatred.

One might object that such events 'have nothing to do' with *My Ántonia*; they are certainly far removed from Cather's Nebraska world as critics—and Cather—have traditionally described its character and genealogy. As I have attempted to demonstrate, however, that is precisely the point. Recent historians of the West such as Howard Lamar and Limerick have underscored the disparity between 'textual' images of the West and the historical West on a host of issues, ranging from the supposed closing of the frontier to the realities of mining operations, from the exploitative nature of the Plains' agrarian economy to the Western myth of rugged individualism. What I am proposing in this essay is that literary critics look equally hard at some of our canonical texts and conventional shibboleths purporting to explain how the West—as well as any other geographical or ideological territory—was 'won.'

Implicit in any distinction between text and context, story and history, is the assertion that, poststructuralism notwithstanding, some narratives are 'truer' than others are. While admitting, as Jane Tompkins does in her own readings of how the American West was won, that we can never transcend narrative and grasp 'the real' itself, and while admitting that limitations inevitably accompany the interpretive act, we can still argue that some readings are more accurate than others; as Tompkins argues, 'You can show that what someone else asserts to be a fact is false' (76). 'One does not,' writes Jameson, 'have to argue the reality of history: necessity, like Dr Johnson's stone, does that for us' (82).

Such forces of necessity inevitably preserve the historical realities which a text such as *My Ántonia* initially appears to occlude. They are an integral part of Cather's text, imbricated in the very fabric of her narrative, dialogically interacting with her story. If history and text somehow appear distinct, in Cather's novel and in other 'literary' texts, it is less a result of some inherent division between fact and story and more a consequence of our failure to produce readings that elucidate their connection. What such interdisciplinary readings will generate, again and again, is an understanding of the 'material out of which countries are made,' whereby we learn as much about the original materials—and peoples—that narrative employs as we do about how narrative shapes such 'material' for its own ends. Only by way of such approaches can we begin to appreciate the deeper significance of the process of naturalisation that is inherent in the symbolic act, as well as the suppression of history that it entails. Only then can we understand why, if we remember Gettysburg, so many of us seem to have forgotten Sand Creek, and why, if we fondly recall Cather's 'georgic' portrayal of Nebraska, we seem to have amnesia concerning the people who once lived there.

Works Cited

Baltensperger, Bradley H., *Nebraska: A Geography*, London: Westview, 1985.
Bennett, Tony, *Formalism and Marxism*, London: Methuen, 1979.
Brown, Dee, *Bury My Heart at Wounded Knee: An Indian History of the American West*, New York: Washington Square, 1970.
Cather, Willa, *O Pioneers!*, Boston: Houghton, 1913.
—, *My Ántonia*, Boston: Houghton, 1926.
—, *Death Comes for the Archbishop*, New York: Modern Library, 1927.
—, 'Nebraska: The End of the First Cycle.' *The Nation* 117, 1923: pp. 236–38.
—, *The World and the Parish: Willa Cather's Articles and Reviews, 1893-1902*, ed. William M. Curtin, 2 vols., Lincoln: U of Nebraska P, 1970.
Chomsky, Noam, *Turning the Tide: U.S. Intervention in Central America and the Struggle for Peace*, Boston: South End P, 1985.
Combs, Barry B., 'The Union Pacific Railroad and the Early Settlement of Nebraska', *Nebraska History*, 50, 1969: pp. 1–26.
Day, A. Grove, *Coronado and the Discovery of the Southwest*, New York: Meredith, 1967.
Gelfant, Blanche, 'The Forgotten Reaping-Hook: Sex in *My Ántonia*', *American Literature*, 43, 1971: pp. 60–82.
Hammond, George P., *Coronado's Seven Cities*, Albuquerque: United States Coronado Exposition Commission, 1940.

Jameson, Fredric, *The Political Unconscious: Narrative as a Socially Symbolic Act*, Ithaca: Cornell UP, 1981.

Kolko, Gabriel, *Main Currents in Modern American History*, New York: Pantheon, 1984.

Limerick, Patricia Nelson, *The Legacy of Conquest: The Unbroken Past of the American West*, New York: Norton, 1987.

Love, Glen, *New Americans: The Westerner and the Modern Experience in the American Novel*, Lewisburg: Bucknell UP, 1982.

O'Brien, Sharon, *Willa Cather: The Emerging Voice*, New York: Oxford UP, 1987.

Olson, James C., *History of Nebraska*, Lincoln: U of Nebraska P, 1966.

Olson, Paul A., 'The Epic and Great Plains Literature: Rolvaag, Cather, and Neihardt', *Prairie Schooner*, 55, 1981: pp. 263–85.

Perkey, Elton A., *Perkey's Nebraska Place Names*, Lincoln: Nebraska State Historical Society Publications 28, 1982.

Schwind, Jean, 'The Benda Illustrations to *My Ántonia*: Cather's "Silent" Supplement to Jim Burden's Narrative', *PMLA*, 100, 1985: pp. 51–67.

Slote, Bernice, 'Willa Cather and Plains Culture', *Vision and Refuge: Essays on the Literature of the Great Plains*, eds Virginia Faulkner with Frederick C. Luebke, Lincoln: U of Nebraska P., 1982, pp. 93–105.

Slotkin, Richard, *Regeneration Through Violence: The Mythology of the American Frontier: 1600-1860*, Middletown: Wesleyan UP, 1973.

Stouck, David, 'Perspective as Structure and Theme in *My Ántonia*', *Texas Studies in Language and Literature*, 12, 1970: pp. 285–94.

Thomas, A.B., 'The Massacre of the Villasur Expedition', *Nebraska History*, 7, 1924: pp. 68–81.

Tompkins, Jane, 'Indians: Textualism, Morality, and the Problem of History', *'Race,' Writing and Difference*, ed. Henry Louis Gates Jr, Chicago: U of Chicago P, 1986, pp. 59–77.

Trachtenberg, Alan, *The Incorporation of America: Culture and Society in the Gilded Age*, New York: Hill, 1982.

Udall, Stewart L., *To the Inland Empire: Coronado and Our Spanish Legacy*, New York: Doubleday, 1987.

Ideas of History

157
Willa Cather: Idealist Transcendence of Conflict

HARRY B. HENDERSON

After World War I, Willa Cather, like Edith Wharton, turned towards historical subjects, most notably in *Death Comes for the Archbishop* (1927), *My Ántonia* (1918), *Shadows on the Rock* (1931), and *Sapphira and the Slave Girl* (1940). In her work one may see the implications of idealism seized as an antidote to historical scientism, rather than as the key to the science of history as it had been in the old progressive frame of Bancroft, Motley, Twain, and the Whig historians. Willa Cather writes within a basically holist tradition; she is concerned in *Death Comes for the Archbishop* with the clash of races and cultures, the cultural shadings separating Spanish, Indians, and Anglo-Americans. Yet it is a small society as a whole unit that most deeply engages her (this is also true of *Shadows on the Rock*, a novel of seventeenth-century Quebec), and her attention is lavished on all the peculiarities of custom and behavior that mark off an encapsulated time as unlike time-present. She is most deliberate in joining the traditional holistic belief in the absolute barriers between one era and another with the catastrophic note of Henry Adams. 'The world broke in two in 1922 or thereabouts,' she wrote, and her books clearly project a past from which she is separated by an unbridgeable chasm.[1]

Implicitly accepting Adams' polarisation of history into the unified reign of the Virgin and the discontinuous multiplicity of the age of the Dynamo,[2] both *Death Comes for the Archbishop* and *Shadows on the Rock* appropriately have a Catholic orientation. Not only are the principal characters Roman Catholics—in *Death Comes for the Archbishop* they are missionary clerics—but there is an attempt to achieve the sense of stillness and unconcern for historical change that marks the great masterpiece of Catholic historical fiction, Manzoni's *The Betrothed*. While a strong historical sense plays a role in all of Willa Cather's work, *Death Comes for the Archbishop* constitutes her purest attempt to reimagine a past that is not only usable but desirable.

SOURCE   Harry B. Henderson 'Willa Cather: Idealist Transcendence of Conflict', *Versions of the Past: The Historical Imagination in American Fiction*, Oxford: OUP, 1974, pp. 250–53

Death Comes for the Archbishop is the story, conveyed through ten anecdote-like installments, of two Catholic missionaries in the American Southwest in the mid nineteenth century. The aristocratic, intellectual Father Latour and the warm, earthy Father Vaillant come to know their new parishioners in these tales as they carry on busy careers till their deaths — each an archbishop by now — in a West which they have done much to Europeanise, if not to civilise. The characters are most attractive, and the descriptions of New Mexico are superb in a painterly way; yet the tale of men cultivating a civilisation in the semi-wilderness is told too much like *The Swiss Family Robinson* and not enough like *Robinson Crusoe*. The priests fit their roles too well; there are no conflicts between them, and none within, other than those which their roles dictate as commendable; and even these are resolved in too exemplary a manner. Thus, *Death Comes for the Archbishop* gives the unfortunate appearance of marrying the worst features of the Catholic hagiography and the Protestant success story.

This is a severe judgment, but it is important to understand what brought such a finely perceptive writer to such a pass in her most ambitious work. In part, the strength of all Willa Cather's fiction is to be found in her graphic detail, a description of people and things which is not so much holistic as it is the detail of interior decorating, of landscaping, or portraiture; a description of discrete beings, not of relationships. Because the original holist imagination was quintessentially a study of relationships, even at its most conservative it could not ignore the tendency of human relationships to alter according to their own dynamics. In those changing relations and in the threat of change lies the heart of the historical artist's drama.

Perhaps the best critique of the naturalistic form of the historical imagination is that of Georg Lukács in speaking of *Salammbô*, Willa Cather's favorite novel by Flaubert, whom she admired deeply:

> What then can art take from a past conceived in this way? This past appears, more so even than the present, as a gigantic iridescent chaos. Nothing is really objectively and organically connected with the objective character of the present; and for this reason a freely roaming subjectivity can fasten where and how it likes. And since history has been deprived of its real inner greatness — the dialectic of contradictory development, which has been abstracted intellectually — all that remains for the artists of this period is a pictorial and decorative grandeur. History becomes a collection of exotic anecdotes.[3]

And yet *Death Comes for the Archbishop* has a particular quality which is valuable and unique in American literature. The novel is an historical pastoral that attempts to overcome its unreality by an effort of pure idealist imagination. Near the end there are two crucial passages. Willa Cather identifies the conception of time in the novel in the idealist manner of Bradley and Collingwood:

> During those last weeks of the Bishop's life he thought very little about death; it was the past he was leaving. The future would take care of itself. But he had

an intellectual curiosity about dying; about the changes that took place in a man's beliefs and scale of values. More and more life seemed to him an experience of the Ego, in no sense the Ego itself. This conviction, he believed, was something apart from his religious life; it was an enlightenment that came to him as a man, a human creature.... He was soon to have done with calendared time, and it had already ceased to count for him. He sat in the middle of his own consciousness; none of his former states of mind were lost or outgrown. They were all within reach of his hand, and all comprehensible.[4]

The consciousness does not seek the past, but rather frees itself from time. The Ego separates itself from its own past, as well as the communal past. Latour's whole experience is a frontier one, but more than that it is an essentially repeatable one, as old as the Church or as old as mankind. For Willa Cather the past is close to the present in an entirely new way. The old progressive frame had seen all men as identically gifted in rights, reaction to oppression, desire for liberty and truth. The new historical idealism emphasises the repeatable nature of thought and detaches it entirely from the notion of conflict and progress generated by the struggle for natural rights. For Cather, the eternal aspects of consciousness are entirely compatible with historical stasis.

The other passage is an anecdote of the appearance of the Holy Family to the famous missionary of the distant and miraculous past, Father Junipero Serra. The Family had manifested itself in the guise of simple peasants. The worldly Father Latour admires the story aesthetically:

> There is always something charming in the idea of greatness returning to simplicity—the queen making hay among the country girls—but how much more endearing was the belief that They, after so many centuries of history and glory, should return to play Their first parts, in the persons of a humble Mexican family, the lowliest of the lowly, the poorest of the poor,—in a wilderness at the end of the world, where the angels could scarcely find Them![5]

The tale projects in little the impulse of the novel as a whole, in which escape from the present is not so much a defect as a frank goal of art. In this sense *Death Comes for the Archbishop* (though not comparable as an artistic achievement) is as willful an attempt to transcend the present through the past as *The Bridge*.

Notes

1. Willa Cather, *Not Under Forty* (New York: Alfred A. Knopf, 1936), in Prefatory Note.
2. Henry Adams, *The Education of Henry Adams* (New York: Random House, The Modern Library, 1931), Chapter XV, p. 379.
3. Georg Lukács, *The Historical Novel* (Boston: Beacon, 1963), p. 182. First published in Moscow, translated from the German, 1937.
4. Willa Cather, *Death Comes for the Archbishop* (New York: Alfred A. Knopf, 1959), pp. 289-90. Originally published in 1927.
5. *Ibid.*, p. 282.

158
Search & Research: Willa Cather in Quest of History

PATRICIA LEE YONGUE

Godfrey St Peter, in Willa Cather's *The Professor's House* (1925), claims he tried to do something 'quite different' in his eight-volume, prize-winning history, *Spanish Adventurers in North America*, and he indicates that the 'whole plan' of his narrative became clearer in his mind the further he got into the writing of it. He was not attempting 'the usual thing,' which would have been the accumulation of facts from conventional sources, a process leading to ideas likewise conventional and conclusions frequently short-sighted or erroneous. Rather, as an idealistic young scholar beginning his history 'when the desire to do it and the difficulties attending such a project strove together like Macbeth's two spent summers,' St Peter had determined to do 'this dazzling, this beautiful, this utterly impossible thing.'[1] He proceeded to write a history that deliberately eschewed 'all the foolish conventions' about that sort of writing.

According to the few odd pieces of information Willa Cather chose to report about *Spanish Adventurers*—and which information is valuable—the first three volumes were completely misconstrued by reviewers who 'merely thought he was trying to do the usual thing and had not succeeded very well. They recommended to him the more even and genial style of John Fiske' (p. 32), a popular historian of the day whose general popularity increased as his scholarly stature decreased (during the 1890s), when it became too evident that his work lacked inventive and original research. But St Peter had cared little, 'as little as the Spanish Adventurers themselves what Professor So-and-so thought about them.' His reaction, of course, imitates Willa Cather's own active contempt for the narrow-minded reviewers of her personal and

SOURCE   Patricia Lee Yongue, 'Search & Research: Willa Cather in Quest of History', *Southwestern American Literature*, 5, 1975, pp. 27–39

literary behavior and recollects what she noted in her early essay on Thomas Carlyle, who

> went out alone into the solitude and wrestled with great ideas, finding them difficult to express in words, so great, so ungainly were they. He cared little whether his books were popular, whether they were even read. He wrote only that which was in him and which must be written.[2]

Like Carlyle and Willa Cather, St Peter refuses to cater to the vulgar tastes of a pampered public, despite the chiding of publishers and critics.

While *Spanish Adventurers* was never thoroughly appreciated for the singularity of its plan and design, with the fourth volume its effort did generate scattered interest in the United States and England; with the fifth and sixth, that interest began to appear in print and in lectures; and, the seventh and eight volumes brought St Peter international reputation and an Oxford prize in history (p. 33).[3] Precisely what unique view supposedly characterises *Spanish Adventurers*, however, and why Willa Cather, with the exception of a few tempting allusions, left off substantial treatment of the history's nature become problematic features of the novel, since Professor St Peter is recognizably Willa Cather's alter-ego and so his best work must warrant comparison with her own efforts, and especially since history is at the very core of the novel's structural and thematic program.[4]

Spanish Adventurers and its cash award, first of all, triggers the plot activity, for it purchases the new house the Professor is loath to inhabit. His historical research is also exceptional enough to send to his tutelage the young genius, Tom Outland, whose story of his discovery of the Cliff Dweller ruins in Colorado takes up a major portion of the novel (all of Book Two), and whose scientific inventions during his stay with the Professor inadvertently cause St Peter family and professional distress. But after the capsule 'biography' of *Spanish Adventurers,* the ensuing silence is both curious and distracting.

In her essay 'The Novel Démeublé,' in many of her letters, and in view of her general aesthetic methods, Willa Cather pronounced her disdain for extensive use of detail merely for convention's and realism's sake. Such technique, she believed, interfered with the optimum presentation of the 'eternal material of art,' which above all else in her Carlylean view is the business of the artist. So she included in her own fiction only those details directly contributory to its immortal soul. If her claims are accepted unconditionally, then curiosity about the unknown quantities of *Spanish Adventurers* would be inconsequential: all that is essential to the meaning of the novel is reported; what is not essential is omitted, and pursuit of such information is dead-ended guesswork.

On the other hand, *Spanish Adventurers* is a detail important to the integrity of *The Professor's House*. And, again, there is simply too much history in the novel to forego scrutiny of the motivation for the Professor's interest in the Spanish explorers. There is also the fact of Willa Cather's long fascination for the history that developed in the American Southwest, a history that included Spanish participation as well as the culture of the Cliff Dwellers which she studied and incorporated many times into her fiction. While early references to the Spanish explorers occur as the fanciful remarks of little boys, as details with a purpose they are controlled carefully by Willa Cather's imagination (and by her theme of the necessity of the imagination). In the 1909 short story, 'The Enchanted Bluff,' a rather unpolished tale about the imaginative value of the New Mexico Mesa Encantada legend in the lives of six boys from sleepy Sandtown, the importance of the historical seniority of the gold-seeking Spaniards surfaces, a factor de-emphasised by most (like Fiske) in the process of assuming that the country's colonial history is the only 'real' history. 'The Spaniards were all over this country once. . . . Before the Pilgrim Fathers.'[5] A similar bit of information appears in *My Ántonia* (1918), as young Jim Burden — another Willa Cather signature — tells Ántonia that, regardless of what the school textbooks say, Coronado and his men trod the banks of Nebraska's Republican River in their search for Cibola.[6] For Willa Cather, as for the boys from both stories, the Spaniards' effusive spirit, courage, color, and dream — not their gold-greed — are the essential facts in terms of their imaginative value.

Beyond these references, however, there is not much mention of the Spaniards or Spanish explorers until *Death Comes for the Archbishop* (1927) — except, that is, for Professor St Peter's *Spanish Adventurers*. Though her primary interest was always in the ancient Indian civilisations, Willa Cather does include the Spaniards as part of the colorful, vital American history that extended from American Indian to pioneer, that created the American West of fact and feeling, and that served to counteract the overwhelming presence of abstraction, denial, and moral distortion caused by the less happy consequences of the younger Puritan history. She did not scorn the adventurers for their pursuit of gold, as she scorned the Puritans for contributing artless materialism to American civilisation. Investigating why St Peter writes about Spanish adventurers provides some assistance in understanding what critics have often misinterpreted as Willa Cather's 'escape into the past' and what is part of her theory of art and her approach to history, as history is refined by the alembic of art into the Past, Carlyle's idea of the true Past.

Willa Cather was writing journalism in the 1890s and first decade of the twentieth century, a time when interest in the American Southwest was being encouraged on a national level, largely through the enthusiastic and often bombastic efforts of journalist/'explorer' Charles Lummis, who had written an account of the history of the Mesa Encantada which Willa Cather may have read and altered for use in 'The Enchanted Bluff'. There was also some official recognition of Indian ruin sites. Theodore Roosevelt had, in fact, designated Mesa Verde, Tom Outland's Blue Mesa, a national park in

1906, the year of Willa Cather's accession to the prominent staff of *McClure's* magazine in New York. She was writing her best fiction and visiting the Southwest during the time Mabel Dodge Luhan's artists' colony in Taos, New Mexico, was stressing the revival of cultural vigor in post-World War I America 'by drinking deep of the springs of the primitive life of the American Indians of the American Southwest.'[7] Willa Cather did not visit the colony herself until 1925, but she was quite familiar with the Southwest from earlier trips and from extensive reading and discussion.[8] For a long while, the point is, there had been considerable effort to locate real American history in the Southwest and thus to provide the country with a Past that embraced all American history makers who had color, passion, strength, love of the land, and even 'heroic savagery' — spirit-full qualities the Puritans did not transmit to the civilisation they founded.

Although emphasis in this movement was understandably given to the native American Indians, especially considering the Spanish explorers' legendary gold-greed and destruction of Indian civilisations (which destruction, as Professor Larzer Ziff has very recently pointed out by his *Puritanism in America*, is commonly stressed to the exclusion of those massacres of Indian tribes carried out by the Puritan colonists in the name of God), there was also attempt made to give the Spaniards their due as contributors to American spirit, culture, and history. Charles Lummis, whose 1892 book *Some Strange Corners of Our Country* (enlarged in 1925 under the new title *Mesa, Canon and Pueblo*) presents the then little known Southwest as the vital source of America's ethnologic history, also published a very popular book (fifteen editions), *The Spanish Pioneers* (1893), which 'sought to combat the popular conception of cruelty fastened on the conquistadores by Anglo-Saxon writers.'[9] Willa Cather herself, in the novels *The Song of the Lark* (1915), *The Professor's House*, and *Death Comes for the Archbishop*, is careful to intimate that the Indians themselves were partly responsible for their own extinction, because they refused to learn a metal-based technology which would have better equipped them against more warlike tribes, or, in more recent times, because they shunned change completely. The rock of the Acomas had been taken only once — 'by Spaniards in armour.'[10]

The aesthetically advanced Cliff Dwellers, and their descendants, had allowed their beautiful, naturally-endowed culture to deteriorate into a waste land by all avoidance of technological change especially, by a hermetic retreat — like turtles — into their shells, by failure to make any effort to save themselves or actively to expand their customs to the rest of the New World. Rather than standing out against it, the Acomas of *Death Comes for the Archbishop* disappear into the landscape. Willa Cather chides the Indians — and Professor St Peter! — for turning their backs to change, although she herself disliked change intensely; but technological progress and all that it involved was, it seems, one of the many processes she simultaneously supported and renounced.

Be that as it may, the important thing here is that Willa Cather never outrightly attacked the Spanish explorers. She knew of the animosity between them and the Indians, but she pursued a positive, imaginative quantity she saw in the very idea of them as persistent, spirited seekers of Cibola. 'This dazzling, this beautiful, this utterly impossible thing' that St Peter envisioned as *Spanish Adventurers* is metaphoric kin to the sought for Cities of Gold and then, of course, to the joys and disappointments inherent in such a romantic search. Her early short story, 'Eldorado: A Kansas Recessional' (1901), picks up on the ancient South American Indian ritual of the Gilded Man, a tribal chief who would powder his body with precious gold dust and allow himself to be taken to the middle of a lake, where he would wash himself of the gold and let it sink to the bottom of the lake, a sacrifice. As Charles Lummis has explained it somewhat obscurely in *The Spanish Pioneers* (it is not clear whether the chief himself is sacrificed), the Gilded Man, Eldorado, became the American Golden Fleece and part of the Spanish explorers' quest for Cibola, at least in South America.

It is not difficult, or unreasonable, to pursue this image, to proceed from the Cibola of St Peter's imagination to Willa Cather's. *Spanish Adventurers* comes to represent a window offering a view of Willa Cather's creative process and of her definition of the artist's role which includes embracing the golden ideal. Surely one of the major implications of St Peter's rebellion in the writing of his history involves her appraisal of her own literary efforts. Considering her use of the Professor as a vehicle of self-expression, it is first of all significant that she should suggest the analogy between herself and a historian, and secondly, that he should be a historian fighting the trends of his society in general and of his profession in particular. St Peter, on the whole, is a historian in rebellion against his history. *Spanish Adventurers* is a climax in that rebellion.

Willa Cather makes sure that St Peter explicitly calls his *Spanish Adventurers* a narrative, simultaneously endowing it with a more artful personality and removing it from the domain of traditional classification. During the years of the writing of *The Professor's House* and the succeeding novels, especially *Death Comes for the Archbishop*, she herself had insisted on the narrative structure of her works, particularly, as she indicated in letters, because she was made to smart under the criticism of those who found no existing generic slot for her novels. *The Professor's House* is dedicated to Jan Hambourg, 'because he likes narrative.' And *Death Comes for the Archbishop* specifically avoids classification, for, as she wrote to her British friend Stephen Tennant, she finally had done exactly what she pleased with a novel and had felt no obligation whatsoever to employ traditional machinery.[11]

In several respects, Willa Cather was comparing her efforts as a novelist to St Peter's as a historian, and the comparison is neither superficial nor superfluous. She had, for the most part, ensconced herself not only in the 'home pasture' of the West, but in the historical past; her desk, like St Peter's, was, it is true, 'a shelter one could hide behind; it was a hole one could creep into' (p. 161). But even though she and the Professor acknowledged increasing problems with finding delight in the modern world which led to a form of withdrawal, both were finally convinced of the need to continue the creative act (she planning at least *Death Comes for the Archbishop* and he editing the diary of Tom Outland); and, their work had more than escape in mind. At least by making *Spanish Adventurers* a prize-winning history, she seemed to be pointing to an unacclaimed value in her previous work.[12] She, perhaps, also had tried to create something 'quite different,' a narrative with the thrust of Professor Joel Porte's observations about narrative regarding that of Willa Cather's Virginia countryman Edgar Allan Poe (whose work she admired), *The Narrative of A. Gordon Pym*.

> The reader's attention is drawn to the fact that he [Poe] is beginning a *narrative*, not the 'adventures' of A. Gordon Pym. This, in short, is art, not life: the romance is stylized, frequently fantastic, not committed to a *vraisemblable* rendition of experience. And yet the romance can compel belief, in the deepest sense, where the most realistic depiction of life would fail.... But the dedicated reader of romance ... knows that the narrative finally portrays a truth that transcends the veracity of detail.[13]

The probability is that Willa Cather had, at least by 1925, come to regard herself as a historian of sorts and her work as a sort of history. 'A country cares very little about its early history and traditions,' she wrote, 'until it has a great many treats and disappointments, until the first feverish impetus of growth has been checked and it settles down into that quiet, steady course of honest labor and honest gain, which is the only honest way of living. Then it has time to look back on whatever was beautiful or brave in its history, and begins to appreciate the talent and worth that it overlooked or pushed aside in its frequent hurry to be great.'[14] Such 'talent and worth' for Willa Cather resided primarily in the stream of history that gushed forth from the living Rock of the American West, in the irrigating nature-oriented culture of the Indians, the gusto of the Spaniards, the bounty of European tradition, and the idealism of the pioneer—whatever the flaws may have been. The West is her expansive canvas, a narrative.

II

To supplement the assessment of Willa Cather's 'different' fictional intentions, there is further evidence regarding the nature of Professor St Peter's history and its relationship to her work. St Peter not only reiterates the universal symbolic aspect of the historian; he also seems in several particulars to be a profile of the historian/archaeologist Adolph Bandelier (1840–1914), author of fairly revolutionary studies concerning the history of the Southwestern United States. Bandelier, as a matter of fact, put together for the Archaeological Institute of America a series of monographs on the Spanish exploration of North America which were later also included as part of his *The Gilded Man (Eldorado)*, published in 1893, a work with which Willa Cather was familiar.[15]

Bandelier was a name familiar to anyone studying Southwestern history. Exploration of cliff dwellings and renewed concern for Spanish discoveries in North America received widespread coverage at a time, ironically, when American urbanisation issues were also prominent—the metaphoric potential of which situation was obviously apparent to Willa Cather. Bandelier pioneered scientific anthropology in the Southwest, concentrating primarily on the Pueblo Indian civilisation in New Mexico. He became a good friend of Archbishop Lamy, the prototype for Father Latour in *Death Comes for the Archbishop*, and there is a monument bearing his name in Frijoles Canyon, New Mexico, where he worked from 1880 to 1886. Charles Lummis, for whom Bandelier wrote the introduction for *The Spanish Pioneers*, worked hard to generate acclaim for the Swiss-American historian. Bandelier became the 'leading scholar of the aboriginal inhabitants of New Spain and of the Spanish Conquest,' interpreting 'the archaeological past on the basis of the ethnographic present.'[16] While he was in charge of documentary research for the Hemenway Southwestern Archaeological Expedition, Bandelier supplemented what he had learned about American Indians with the discovery of new information about the Spanish conquests. He published four articles and one historical overview as *Contributions to the History of the Southwestern Portion of the United States: Hemenway Southwestern Archaeological Expedition*, Papers of the Archaeological Institute of America, American Series (Cambridge: John Wilson and Son, 1890), V; and the material is also included in *The Gilded Man (Eldorado)*.

Some of the distinguishing features of Bandelier's achievements, curiously enough, match those of Professor St Peter. Willa Cather's Professor is by no means Bandelier in all or even several major respects, but he certainly seems to cut Bandelier's figure insofar as his scholarly aims and approaches to history are concerned. Willa Cather herself may have identified her own intentions as a 'writer' of history with Bandelier's, even though they achieved their goals through different means: he characteristically—and ironically, in terms of Willa Cather's philosophy—by the inclusion of massive chunks of detail, and she by the notable exclusion of detail. Similarities that exist between Bandelier and St Peter, however, are more than coincidental, and they indicate Willa Cather's careful research into America's Southwestern history, despite the altered form in which historical data appears in her fiction.

In his preface to the Papers of the Archaeological Institute of America, Bandelier describes his plan for a projected eight-section study of the Spanish explorers in America.

> It was my plan to treat the history of the Southwest in sections, monographically. The first four papers here published were to have been followed by similar ones on the expedition of Coronado, Chamuscado, Espejo, and Onate, but the material which I accumulated for the purpose is at present beyond my reach.[17]

His study attempted to correct certain misconceptions about Spanish explorations in America and about Spanish-Indian relations by the use of church records he had found and studied.

> To write the history of the Southwest, or any portion thereof, requires the accumulation of a vast amount of material. That material, aside from what Indian traditions afford, is mostly found in Spain. Only a limited number of documents contained in the Archives of the Indies have as yet been published. It had been my wish, after copying whatever the archives at Sante Fe, Santa Clara, El paso del Norde, and Mexico contained, to visit Spain, and secure copies of the large and well preserved mass of documentary material there extant. Sooner or later this work will have to be performed; for there are long periods in the history of New Mexico, for instance, about which Mexican as well as New Mexican archives contain almost nothing.... Without the help of the ecclesiastical archives at Santa Clara I should not have been able to treat of the expedition of Villazur, or to establish the identity of the present New Mexican family of Archibeque with Jean l'Archevegue, the betrayer of LaSalle.[18]

It was not until 1913 that Bandelier got to Spain. In 1911, he had been appointed research assistant by the Carnegie Institute of Washington to collect archival materials in Mexico and Spain, and he ended his work in Mexico in 1912 (when Willa Cather made her first trip to the Southwest). He left for Spain and was working in the ecclesiastical archives in Seville when he died in 1914.

Professor St Peter literally achieves what Bandelier set out to achieve. He completes an eight-volume work called *Spanish Adventurers in North America* which purports to offer originality in research and presentation. Like Bandelier, the Professor seems to concentrate on the Southwest and also to work extensively with unused records. He has worked on *Spanish Adventurers* for fifteen years (almost as many as Bandelier and about as many as Willa Cather had spent studying Southwestern history), spending two Sabbatical years in Spain 'studying records, two summers in the South-west on the trail of his adventurers, another in Old Mexico' (p. 25). Sir Edgar Spilling, the expert on Spanish history from England, comes to the Professor's house to inquire about some of St Peter's sources for the prize-winning history — 'manuscripts shut up in certain mouldering monasteries in Spain' (p. 42).

An additional and quite significant detail relative to St Peter's historical research and his connection with Bandelier is slipped rather quietly into the novel. When Tom Outland tells St Peter the reasons why he has come to him instead of going directly to the university registrar, he explains, 'Your name was the only one here I knew. I read an article by you in a magazine, about Fray Marcos. Father Duchene said it was the only thing with any truth in it he'd read about our country down there' (p. 114). Hearing this, the Professor reflects that 'whenever he wrote for popular periodicals it got him into trouble.' One of Adolph Bandelier's self-declared achievements was the publication of a rather controversial article on Fray Marcos of Nizza, the sixteenth century friar who had accompanied Alvare Nunez Cabeza de Vaca on part of his long journey from Florida to the Pacific. The material appears in the Papers of the Archaeological Institute and in *The Gilded Man*, and the article 'The Discovery of New Mexico by Fray Marcos de Nizza' was published in the *Magazine of Western History* in 1886. In the section on Fray Marcos in the Papers of the Archaeological Institute, Bandelier describes his aim.

> For more than three centuries the character of the man whose name stands at the head of this monograph has been strangely misrepresented. The result of it has been, that almost everything connected with the early history of the discoveries in the North American Southwest has been correspondingly misunderstood. It is my purpose . . . to present the tale of the first trip to Cibola as accurately as possible, with the aid of written and oral evidence, of printed books and manuscripts, as well as of geographical and ethnological facts. I do not wish to be understood as presenting myself as the champion of Fray Marcos. Wherein he has erred, where, and when, I shall be careful to state; but, aside from the fact that it is certainly gratifying to be able to replace a much defamed character in its proper light, it is a duty to science and history to re-establish what is true, and to explain what has for a long time puzzled honest students, as well as intelligent readers.[19]

In 1890, Bandelier published *The Delight Makers*, a novel based on his eight years of ethnological and archaeological research of the Pueblo Indians in New Mexico. 'I was prompted to perform the work by a conviction that however scientific works may tell the truth about the Indian; they exercise always a limited influence upon the general public. . . . By clothing sober facts in the garb of romance I have hoped to make the "Truth about Pueblo Indians" more accessible and perhaps more acceptable to the public in general.'[20] Willa Cather's Professor lectures at length to his class on the failure of science to make men believe 'in the mystery and importance of their own little individual lives' and proclaims that it is art that can *reset* the stage of human history to give value and drama—and Truth—back to life. This is the kind of truth Willa Cather believed in and sought to illustrate in her own retelling of America's history.

While Bandelier's adherence to the Spencerian doctrine of social evolution may not have had Willa Cather's complete acquiescence, there is one important concurrence between Bandelier's idea of history and that of Willa Cather, and even that of historian Henry Adams himself. If the ideas in 'Tom Outland's Story' and in *The Song of the Lark* about the disappearance of the peace-loving Cliff Dwellers who could not defend themselves against more technologically advanced tribes are given credence, Willa Cather expresses some acceptance of a dynamic theory of history much like Adams's. Though her personal preference may have been for the past, her use of the historical past in fiction is not merely a personal response but a thoughtful response to the aesthetic function or potential of the past in society. Bandelier once explained his concern for the past, based on a theory of social evolution, in a way that would have appealed to Willa Cather.

> The value of historical research on the American continent consists not only in the enrichment it affords to the fund of scientific knowledge, which has an indirect influence upon life, but also in the destruction of effects of deeply rooted errors, in which it acts immediately upon practical life. Accordingly as we represent to ourselves a people or a country when they first become known to us, so we shape our expectations of them when we go to establish our home among them. A correct notion of the past furnishes the basis for an intelligent forecasting of the future.[21]

Willa Cather, of course, tried to present 'a correct notion of the past' in aesthetic terms and according to aesthetic as well as strictly personal ideals. Her concern was not so much with including minute historical detail as with extracting and often creating the aesthetic essence of the past, in order to present what she considered eternal truths, aesthetic 'details.' She, too, wanted to reveal the 'true' past in order to illuminate both the present and the future, because she believed that the past as it was completed in the West had more artistic integrity—or could be made to hold more artistic integrity by virtue of an intrinsic vitality and spirit—than either the Puritan past or the puritanic present, and that the present, including Godfrey St Peter, needed to be reminded of its original condition for the sake of its future.

Toward the end of *The Delight Makers*, Bandelier summed up his fictional account of the downfall of the civilisation in the El Rito de los Frijoles with a statement that defines a theme in Willa Cather's fiction. About the ruins of the El Rito civilisation, Bandelier says, 'hovers a charm which binds man to the place where untold centuries ago man lived, loved, suffered, and died as present generations live, suffer, and die in the course of human history.'[22]

Bandelier believed in the indispensable use of the greatest amount of detail to insure historical vividness, accuracy, and impartiality; and Willa Cather remained always shy of extensive detail in order to reinforce aesthetic vividness, truth, and partiality. Even in her probable drawing upon the life and writings of Bandelier, Willa Cather made the characteristic literary decisions concerning what she would and would not use, and what she would modify to suit her nature and that of Professor St Peter. She created, to use St Peter's words, 'splendid effects by excision.' The same is true of Tom Outland's diary, the content of which is based on the actual discovery of the Mesa Verde Cliff Dweller ruins by Richard Wetherill and a friend. Wetherill discovered a pile of ruins from the sale of which he hoped to make a substantial profit; Tom Outland discovers a viable history and an aesthetic code.

Tom's historical discovery of the Cliff Dweller civilisation and St Peter's discovery of his country and its Spanish and Indian history are fundamentally achievements of Willa Cather's imaginative vision and only secondarily the product of research. And the imaginative vision—the symbolic extension of Bandelier's unconventional sources of data—was the only possible means of salvation Willa Cather could see for the individual, for history, and for herself. It is significant, in this respect, that Willa Cather changed the name from Mesa Verde (green mesa) to Blue Mesa, indicating both the imaginative nature of the Cliff Dweller ruins in Tom's and the Professor's life and the structural nature of that portion of the novel. When St Peter remembers his childhood, he does not remember the details. He is not concerned with 'timely' data, historian though he is. He

> remembered blue water . . . the great fact in life, the always possible escape from dullness, was the lake. The sun rose out of it, the day began there; it was like an open door nobody could shut (pp. 29-30).

So, too, the American West and the human imagination.

Notes

1. Willa Cather, *The Professor's House* (New York: Alfred A. Knopf, 1925), p. 25. Further reference to the novel will be documented within the text.
2. Willa Cather, 'Concerning Thomas Carlyle,' *The Kingdom of Art: Willa Cather's First Principles and Critical Statements, 1893-1896*, ed. Bernice Slote (Lincoln: Univ. of Nebraska Press, 1966), p. 424.
3. The pattern of St Peter's professional success corresponds somewhat to Willa Cather's own. She had won a Pulitzer Prize shortly before writing *The Professor's House*.
4. There is agreement among critics that St Peter represents an autobiographical statement. See, for example, James Woodress, *Willa Cather: Her Life and Art* (New York: Pegasus, 1970), pp. 207-208.
5. Willa Cather, 'The Enchanted Bluff,' *Willa Cather's Collected Short Fiction, 1892-1912*, ed. Virginia Faulkner (Lincoln: Univ. of Nebraska Press, 1970), p. 73.
6. Willa Cather, *My Ántonia* (Boston: Houghton Mifflin Company, 1918), p. 243. The continuation of this incident is interesting. Some relics (stirrups and a sword) with Spanish inscriptions had been found by a farmer. Jim records that the hired girls 'began to wonder among themselves. Why had the Spaniards come so far? What must the country have been like, then? Why had Coronado never gone back to Spain, to his riches and his castles and his king? I couldn't tell them. I only knew the schoolbooks said he "died in the wilderness, of a broken heart"' (p. 244).
7. Cf. Nicholas Joost, 'Some Primitives in *The Dial* of the Twenties: Part I,' *Forum*, 10 (Winter, 1972), 34-44. The essay examines the interest of the post-World War I writers in Southwestern Indian history.
8. For an overview of Willa Cather's study of Southwestern history, see Edward A. and Lillian D. Bloom, 'The Genesis of *Death Comes for the Archbishop*,' *American Literature*, 26 (January, 1955), 479-506.
9. See Edwin Bingham, *Charles F. Lummis: Editor of the Southwest* (San Marino, California: The Huntington Library, 1955).
10. See Willa Cather, *The Song of the Lark* (Boston: Houghton Mifflin Company, 1937), pp. 145-148; *The Professor's House*, pp. 220-221 (Outland's peace-loving Indians had immured themselves in their Cliff City, regressed in the arts of war, and were probably destroyed on the plains by a more primitive, barbaric tribe); *Death Comes for the Archbishop* (New York: Alfred A. Knopf, 1927), p. 97, pp. 102-103, 233-235.
11. I wish to thank The Honorable Stephen Wyndham Tennant for sharing his knowledge of and friendship with Willa Cather with me, during my summer visit to Wilsford Manor, 1974. The research opportunity was sponsored by the University of Houston.
12. Although Willa Cather had, as previously mentioned, won a Pulitzer Prize for *One of Ours* (1922), which prize provides a further autobiographical link between her and St Peter, the

Oxford prize she creates for his total, unified effort seems to suggest an unhonored quality of her own work—its unity of spirit and purpose.

13. Joel Porte, *The Romance in America* (Middletown, Connecticut: Wesleyan Univ. Press, 1969), p. 85.

14. Willa Cather, 'Brownville,' *The World and the Parish: Willa Cather's Articles and Reviews, 1893-1902*, ed. William M. Curtin, 2 vols. (Lincoln: Univ. of Nebraska Press, 1970), I, 103-104.

15. Cf. Bloom, *op. cit.*, p. 487. The Blooms mention, through citation of other references to Willa Cather's researches specifically for *Death Comes for the Archbishop*, Bandelier's *The Gilded Man* and some of Lummis's books. It would seem likely, however, that Willa Cather knew of many of these works much earlier. The short stories, 'The Enchanted Bluff' and 'Eldorado: A Kansas Recessional,' draw upon material made available largely by the writings of Lummis and Bandelier, as does *The Professor's House* itself.

16. Bernard L. Fontana, 'A Dedication to the Memory of Adolph F.A. Bandelier,' *Arizona and the West*, 2 (Spring, 1960), 1-5.

17. Adolph Bandelier, *Contributions to the History of the Southwestern Portion of the Southwestern United States: Hemenway Expedition*, Papers of the Archaeological Institute of America, American Series (Cambridge: John Wilson and Son, 1890), V, iii. See also Adolph Bandelier, *The Gilded Man (Eldorado)* (New York: D. Appleton and Company, 1893), p. 199: 'The accomplishment of such enterprise with small means deserves admiration; and we consider that official reports were made . . . we cannot refuse to pay these men, so long decried as "Spanish adventurers," "cruel freebooters," etc., all honor for their achievements. The Spanish government also deserves high praise for the carefulness and farsightedness with which it permitted such enterprises, and preserved written records of them.'

18. Bandelier, *Contributions*, pp. iii-iv.

19. Bandelier, *Contributions*, pp. 106-107.

20. Adolph Bandelier, *The Delight Makers* (New York: Dodd Mead, 1890), p. iii.

21. Bandelier, *The Gilded Man*, pp. 111-112.

22. Bandelier, *The Delight Makers*, p. 436.

159
Willa Cather and History

JAMES WOODRESS

Although Willa Cather is usually associated with Nebraska and the celebration of pioneer life on the prairie, she did not confine her writing to this single area of interest. This fact, of course, is not news to anyone who has dipped more than perfunctorily into Cather's work; and I often have discovered that my friends and students educated in Catholic schools indeed know the other Willa Cather better than the Nebraska one. This other Willa Cather is the novelist who turned to historical fiction in the mid-twenties. This is the author of *Death Comes for the Archbishop*, which re-creates fictionally the life of the first Catholic archbishop of New Mexico, *Shadows on the Rock*, a novel laid in seventeenth-century Quebec, *Sapphira and the Slave Girl*, which takes place in Virginia before the Civil War, and a novel of medieval France, left unfinished at the time she died in 1947.

For the last twenty years of her life, Cather was largely preoccupied with historical fiction. With the exception of *Death Comes for the Archbishop*, most critics have not ranked Cather's late novels as high as the Nebraska stories, but a writer of Cather's stature deserves to be studied in all aspects of her career. She has emerged thirty years after her death as one of the major figures of twentieth century American literature.[1] The purpose of this paper is to inquire into Cather's impulse towards historical fiction. Why did she turn to historical fiction? What was her view of history? How much history did she know? What kind of historical fiction does her historical imagination produce? How good is it as art and as history? The answers to these questions not only illuminate the final two decades of her life, but they also throw light on her early career. Because there was a remarkable unity in Cather's literary life, investigations of one aspect of her career inevitably advance our understanding of other aspects.

Why Cather turned to historical fiction in the mid-twenties can be stated only as a hypothesis. She wrote in the introduction to her volume of essays, *Not Under Forty* (1936), that 'the world broke in two in 1922 or thereabouts' and that she preferred the earlier era. There is no doubt that this statement

SOURCE   James Woodress, 'Willa Cather and History', *Arizona Quarterly*, 34, 1978, pp. 239–54

encapsulates her complex emotional and intellectual dissatisfaction with the twenties; there is biographical and literary evidence to explain it. Thus the turn to historical fiction represents a retreat into the past from a present that Cather found dispiriting and uncongenial. By writing historical fiction she could write about eras and characters that she could empathise with.

One needs to read Cather's fiction of the twenties, from her World War I novel, *One of Ours*, through *My Mortal Enemy*, the last work before *Death Comes for the Archbishop*, in order to assess the malaise that she felt in the period from 1922 to 1926. Death and the defeat of hopes and aspirations strongly mark the novels of this period. A dismayed reaction to the money-grubbing materialism of the twenties runs through them as a recurring theme. *One of Ours* treats the death in France of Claude Wheeler, a Nebraska farm boy who went off to World War I full of idealism and patriotism. Left behind to survive the war and grow increasingly prosperous after Claude's sacrifice are such characters as his brother Bayliss, about whom Claude thinks, 'No battlefield or shattered country he had seen was as ugly as this world would be if men like his brother Bayliss controlled it altogether.'[2]

The next novel was *A Lost Lady*, a small masterpiece in which Cather mourns the passing of the frontier and the pioneer days. Captain Forrester, one of the movers and shakers in the new land, is cut down by a stroke, impoverished by his integrity, and cuckolded by his young wife. At the same time, the new generation of profiteers, represented by the unscrupulous Ivy Peters, who invites comparison with Faulkner's Snopes clan, is left triumphant at the end to exploit the land. The succeeding book was *The Professor's House*, the most autobiographical of Cather's novels. Here the professor is seen at the height of his career, winner of an important literary prize, a man who should have had everything to live for; but he is profoundly depressed by his family and the world around him. He cannot bring himself to leave the old house for the new one his ambitious wife is building with his prize money. One daughter is a crass materialist and her husband is a go-getting entrepreneur. The professor loses his will to live, in fact is eager to die, and at the end of the novel narrowly escapes asphyxiation. The final book of this era was *My Mortal Enemy*, a bitter portrayal of the blighted life of Myra Henshawe. Myra is an unhappy woman who married for love, was disinherited by her father, and lived to discover that money was what she really wanted. Her life ends in poverty, the end of hope, and actual death.

This astringent portrayal of defeat and death in *My Mortal Enemy* marks the end of Cather's own bitter years. It is her final comment on the destructive power of money and a society that worships the golden calf. What began rather mildly in the satire on materialism in *One of Ours*, stepped up in tempo with the portrayal of Ivy Peters in *A Lost Lady* and went on to annihilate psychologically Professor St Peter, finally destroyed Myra Henshawe and her husband. There is much of Cather in the professor and more than a trace of her in Myra Henshawe, though not in Myra's desire for money, which never was a Cather vice. But Myra had an ability to hate, as did Cather, who believed in creative hate, as she has her character Thea Kronborg say in *The Song of the Lark* (1915). She may have glimpsed in Myra the kind of bitter person she might have become, if she had not had her art to sustain her.

Not long after writing this novel Cather astonished her friend Elizabeth Sergeant by asking if she thought psychoanalysis might do her some good. There is no evidence that Cather ever consulted a psychiatrist, but the very fact she raised the question documents the emotional crisis that she passed through in the years following 1922 when the world broke in two. There also are other biographical data that suggest the crisis of this period. One certainly is Cather's very success as a novelist following the publication of *One of Ours*. This novel was a best seller and brought her the Pulitzer Prize and the end of the years of struggle. For a writer who was fond of quoting the French historian Michelet, '*le but n'est rien; le chemin c'est tout,*' financial success was somewhat traumatic, as it was for her character Professor St Peter. In 1922 Cather was forty-nine, perhaps going through change of life, and to a person of her modest tastes the prospect of abundant royalty checks stretching off into the future was disturbing. This situation, coupled with the general cultural climate of the twenties which sent Hemingway and others of the 'lost generation' into exile in Europe, produced the crisis that turned Cather to the past. Finally, there were several illnesses in this period that kept Cather idle, especially a nasty bout with neuritis that prevented her from writing for an entire summer. She always hated herself when she was sick.

If Cather had not been a tough-minded character wholly committed to her art, the crisis might have immobilised her. As it was, she began coping with her spiritual and emotional problems at precisely the time 'the world broke in two.' In 1922 she joined the Episcopal Church and for the rest of her life was a devoted, active member of that faith. Even before *My Mortal Enemy* was published she was spending her summers (1925 and 1926) in New Mexico gathering material for *Death Comes for the Archbishop*. By the time *My Mortal Enemy* reached the bookstores she was already deep in the nineteenth century. It was a good thing that she found this retreat from the present as soon as she did, because even greater personal blows were about to fall. In 1927 she was evicted from the Bank Street apartment in Greenwich Village, where she had lived for fifteen years, when her building was torn down to make way for a new subway. Then 1928 began with the death of her father, to whom she had been very close, and it ended with her mother's paralytic stroke. *Death Comes for the Archbishop* was a refuge and a solace. She hated to finish the book and told her old friend Ida Tarbell that writing the novel had been the most unalloyed pleasure of her life.[3] Cather never lost the sense of alienation that engulfed her in this decade, but she did not lapse into silence and embitterment. *Death Comes for the Archbishop* was literally her salvation.

The seed that grew into this novel, however, had been planted many years before. She had been visiting the Southwest since 1912. Shortly after she resigned her managing editorship of *McClure's Magazine*, she went west to visit her brother who worked for the Santa Fe Railroad. She and her friend Edith Lewis returned in 1916. Then in 1924 after meeting Frieda and D.H. Lawrence in New York, Cather and Lewis planned another trip west in the summer of 1925. When they arrived in Santa Fe, Cather happened onto a book privately printed in Pueblo, Colorado, in 1908, W.J. Howlett's *Life of the Right Reverend Joseph P. Machebeuf*. This was the story of the priest who had been vicar to Archbishop Lamy of New Mexico. Cather was so excited about this book that she stayed up all night reading it. The idea for *Death Comes for the Archbishop* came to her in a flash, and she quickly plotted her story.

As she says in a letter she wrote to the editor of *Commonweal* in 1927, she long had felt that the story of the Catholic Church in the Southwest was one of that area's most interesting tales.[4] Father Howlett's book gave her enough background material to stimulate her imagination. The book, however, is mostly about Father Machebeuf, who was sent to Colorado in 1860, just nine years after arriving in Santa Fe with Bishop Lamy, and only about 100 pages deal with his work in New Mexico. Cather's knowledge of Lamy's career actually was quite limited, though she mined Howlett's book extensively. She also read up on New Mexican history in other sources and made use of her observations during her various trips to the Southwest. But in the end it was her imagination that supplied most of the material, for perhaps ninety percent of the novel is fiction.[5]

Thus we have Willa Cather at the age of fifty-four publishing her first historical novel. The retreat into the past in her fiction, nevertheless, does not represent a complete break with her earlier work. Although her first novel, *Alexander's Bridge*, could be subtitled 'A Tale of Today,' all of her other novels down to 1927, when *Death Comes for the Archbishop* was published, deal in part with the recent past. Her second novel, *O Pioneers!* begins in Nebraska in the pioneer era. Her third, *The Song of the Lark*, creates most evocatively Cather's own childhood in the young life of its heroine. *My Ántonia*, which came next in 1918, is a drama of memory, also utilising Cather's own experiences of childhood and adolescence. *One of Ours* begins twenty years in the past; *A Lost Lady* is laid in Cather's childhood. *The Professor's House* contains a long insert, 'Tom Outland's Story,' that goes back in time to the early part of the century. And *My Mortal Enemy* begins many years before its conclusion. It seems that Cather was always on the verge of becoming a writer of historical fiction, and when she found her subject for *Death Comes for the Archbishop*, she leaped back in time to the middle of the nineteenth century, to the days of the New Mexico Territory just after the War with Mexico. Five years later she jumped back another century and a half for *Shadows on the Rock* and was immersed in medieval France when she died.

Historical fiction was always one of Cather's interests. Although she was an omnivorous reader and devoured all books that came her way, she was especially fond of romance laid in times past. Alexander Dumas's historical novels were great favorites, especially *The Count of Monte Cristo*. *Henry Esmond* was a title in her personal library when she was an adolescent in Red Cloud. John Esten Cooke's historical romances of Virginia were well known to her and probably furnished the inspiration for one of her apprenticeship stories laid in colonial Virginia. During her journalistic career she gave favorable reviews to Hendryk Sienkiewicz's *Quo Vadis?*, S. Weir Mitchell's *Hugh Wynne*, and she bestowed extravagant praise on Mary Johnston's *To Have and To Hold*. In praising Johnston she made clear that she had read a good many contemporary historical novels and found most of them bad. 'Since the days of Hawthorne,' she wrote, 'attempts to utilise American history in fiction have, for the most part, miscarried.' There had been plenty of historical novels, but they were 'histories without accuracy and romances without romance.'[6]

Narrative poetry with a historical setting also captivated her. *Sohrab and Rustum*, Matthew Arnold's narrative poem of medieval Persia, was a work that her father liked to read to the big children, and Cather later read it to her younger brothers and sisters. She also was fond of Keats's uses of the past, especially 'The Eve of St Agnes' with its sensuous evocation of ancient castles and customs. Realism as practiced and promoted by William Dean Howells she cared for not at all. In fact, she was contemptuous of the fictional work that dealt with ordinary people doing commonplace things. She preferred *The Prisoner of Zenda* any day to *The Rise of Silas Lapham*.

It is probably safe to say that Cather never formulated her views about history. So far as I know, the only essay that she ever wrote on any historian was the essay she wrote on Carlyle during her first year at the University of Nebraska in March, 1891. But it was Carlyle the shaggy, untamed romantic iconoclast who appealed to her youthful yearnings, not Carlyle the historian. Yet she had been reading *The French Revolution*, and her essay refers tangentially to Carlyle's ability to bring alive the Revolution because of his great love and sympathy for humanity. This 'gift of sympathy,' as she later termed it, became a key to her critical theory and a necessary ingredient in all great literature. Thus one could infer from this early statement that she viewed the writing of fiction and the writing of history as analagous activities requiring similar emotional commitment.

Nevertheless, during her journalistic apprenticeship, she reviewed only occasional works of history or biography. In these years in Lincoln and later Pittsburgh she was primarily a drama critic and reviewer of belletristic works. She might have reviewed, if she had wanted to, the work of contemporary historians such as Paul Leicester Ford, John Fiske, or Brooks Adams, but she did not. As a child she certainly read the standard works of history that were in the family bookcase, and Edith Lewis reports that in 1928 she 'had long been a reader of Francis Parkman,'[7] but in no sense was she an avid reader of history. The only overt statement I can find that she ever made about history was the opening sentence of her high school graduation speech, which begins: 'All human history is a record of an emigration, an exodus from barbarism to civilisation.'[8] This is no doubt the conventional wisdom of 1890 and is not Cather's view of history a third of a century later when she plunged into the world of Bishop Lamy. This sentiment of the high school speech is the view of the Romantic historians of the mid-nineteenth century, Bancroft, Motley, Prescott, and Parkman, whose works Cather must have known then at least by reputation. These historians subscribed fully to the nineteenth-century faith in the idea of progress. Human society was steadily progressing onward and upward. From the Old World to the New the course of history was moving from tyranny and oppression to ever greater freedom. Monarchies were giving way to democracies; economic exploitation was giving way to freedom of opportunity; class structure was giving way to social mobility. Cather at the age of sixteen would have believed in this philosophy of history. At the same time her reading of Carlyle and Emerson (*Heroes and Hero Worship* and *Representative Men*) would have convinced her of the importance of the great man in the large dramas of history. This too was part of the view of the Romantic historians. She probably knew how Bancroft had treated George Washington, Motley had viewed William of Orange, Parkman had dealt with William Pitt, and Prescott had depicted Hernando Cortes—all as representative men who had come along at the proper time to play leading roles in the drama of their peoples.[9]

By the time Cather was fifty and the world had broken in two, she had discarded the easy optimism of the nineteenth century and the progressive theory of history of the Romantic historians. After World War I she felt that neither the United States nor Europe would ever be the same. Passionate Francophile that she was, Cather grieved over the slaughter and destruction in France. One could no longer believe that either Providence or the natural laws of history were moving the world inexorably from tyranny to liberty or from barbarism to civilisation. She became more convinced of this, inevitably, as the Depression of the thirties blighted the lives of her friends and drought ruined their farms. Tyranny returned in Hitler's Germany and Mussolini's Italy, and World War II, which came in the twilight of her career, plunged her into deep depression.

It was in the context of twentieth-century history that Cather wrote *Death Comes for the Archbishop, Shadows on the Rock, Sapphira and the Slave Girl*, and began a story laid in Avignon in the Middle Ages. If she could no longer believe in the progressive theory of history, she could still believe in Representative Men. Jean Latour / Lamy, her archbishop, was one. He was a man for all seasons during the early days of New Mexico. So too were Count Frontenac and Bishop Laval in the early days of Quebec. We do not know how Cather would have developed her story of fourteenth-century Avignon, but Pope Benedict XII was to have been in it—no doubt as a representative man of his time. *Sapphira and the Slave Girl* has no important historical figure in it and must be discussed separately later.

From sentiments expressed in *Death Comes for the Archbishop* one can see clearly that Cather in the mid-twenties viewed history as a series of disconnected epochs, each to be dealt with separately. The old Archbishop muses at the end of his life that his career has spanned a historic period.

> As the darkness faded into the grey of a winter morning, he listened for the church bells, — and for another sound, that always amused him here; the whistle of a locomotive. Yes, he had come with the buffalo, and he had lived to see railway trains running into Santa Fé. He had accomplished an historic period.[10]

It is also clear that he feels the good old days are passing. Already the air is changing with the taming of the wild land. As a young man before going to New Mexico, he had been in Kansas and Texas, which since had been made into rich farming areas, and 'the air had quite lost that lightness, that dry aromatic odour. . . . one could breathe that only on the bright edges of the world. . . .'[11] New Mexico was going the way of states farther east. Cather might have included Nebraska with Kansas and Texas if she had been speaking as author rather than reflecting through Father Latour. The Golden Age was passing and what was coming next was sure to be greatly diminished. This nostalgic note of loss is quite typical of Cather's fiction, whether it is laid in the near past, as are *O Pioneers!* and *My Ántonia*, or in the remoter past of the historical fiction.

Cather's Archbishop Latour, however, is quite a different person in his attitudes towards progress from his actual prototype Archbishop Lamy. Father Latour expresses Cather's twentieth-century feelings about the past. Archbishop Lamy was one of the prime movers in getting the railroad to come to Santa Fe. He viewed it, as did most of the settlers in the West before the railroad, as a blessing. It would bring New Mexico closer to the East, bring supplies cheaper and more abundantly than the wagon trains that toiled over the Santa Fe Trail, and it would bring new settlers to fill in the empty spaces and help pacify the marauding Navajos and Comanches. It is pure Willa Cather when Father Latour's old Navajo friend Eusabio comes on the cars to visit him before he dies and comments: 'Men travel faster now, but I do not know if they go to better things.'[12]

When Cather found Quebec as the setting for her next historical novel, she was particularly interested in the sense she felt there of arrested time. Quebec seemed timeless. Built on a rock, which she treats metaphorically as well as physically, Quebec had retained its integrity into the twentieth century. While the world elsewhere was in turmoil, the city on the St Lawrence seemed still the city of Frontenac and Laval. Thus in this novel Cather celebrates the durability of this Canadian outpost of French civilisation. For a moment at least in writing this novel she could stop the clock and pretend that the good old days would last forever. Here apparently was an exception to the cyclical nature of history.

After the death of old Bishop Laval towards the end of *Shadows on the Rock*, the new bishop, St-Vallier, recently returned from France, describes conditions at home at the close of the reign of Louis XIV. He speaks to the apothecary Auclair, who is one of the major figures in the novel: 'At home the old age is dying, but the new is still hidden. . . . The changes in the nations are all those of the old growing older. You have done well to remain here where nothing changes.' And in the final paragraph of the novel, Auclair reflects that he was indeed fortunate to spend his old age 'where nothing changed; to watch his grandsons grow up in a country where the death of the King, the probable evils of a long regency, would never touch them.'[13]

What kind of historical fiction then did Cather write with the attitudes towards and the uses of history that the above paragraphs describe? Historical romance, of course. Her work is similar in concept and execution to the greatest of all American historical novels, *The Scarlet Letter*. Cather would have made the same distinction that Hawthorne did in differentiating between the novel and the romance. Just as Hawthorne wanted a larger scope for his invention than the strict adherence to probability required in the novel, so Cather wanted the larger latitude of romance. Both Hawthorne and Cather aimed at a basic reality in their fiction, not the reality of minute fidelity to historic fact. One might call it poetic truth.

Cather actually called it 'a kind of spiritual verity' in the review previously quoted of Johnston's *To Have and To Hold*:

> To how much historical accuracy Miss Johnston may lay claim I cannot say. But certainly she has a kind of spiritual verity, a faculty of making other times and other conditions stand forth in their beautiful perspective, of calling back forgotten tragedies across the years like the strains of distant music.[14]

This is a fair statement of what Cather herself was to attempt in her historical fiction three decades later. She liked Mary Johnston's novel in addition because it did 'not sink history into the slough of sentimentality,' and if the author had worked up her historical sources, she had 'the grace not to show it.' Also she had spared her readers the cross references.

Both Hawthorne and Cather spare the reader the cross references, and there is no doubt that Cather's historical fiction, like *The Scarlet Letter*, has the air of truth. Her historical fiction pulses with life. One may not view history as romantically as she did, however. Father Latour's mission certainly did not proceed as smoothly as Cather describes it, and there is an idealisation of action that contrasts pointedly with the historic facts. Many of the episodes of the novel are pure invention. The tone of the novel comes more from Father Howlett's book and Cather's attitudes than from history, for Howlett was a co-worker with Father Machebeuf. He implicitly viewed the work of Lamy and Machebeuf as the inevitable working out of God's plan for New Mexico. There were hardships, of course, but civilisation and

Catholicism proceeded inexorably. Yet looked back upon from the perspective of a century, this is largely true. Archbishop Lamy and his vicar *were* in large measure the civilisers of New Mexico.[15]

In *Shadows on the Rock* the character of Count Frontenac is taken from Parkman, while the figure of Bishop Laval is drawn from a sympathetic Canadian historian. Thus Cather found sources in history for the characters she *wanted* to portray. Instead of doing her research first and planning her novel later, she approached history with some preconceived ideas. Even so, the novel is a superb historical re-creation. The settings are rendered with a painter's eye, and the work is fashioned with the consummate craftsmanship and style that characterise all of Cather's work. I think, however, that *Death Comes for the Archbishop* is a far greater work, a novel of extraordinary sensitivity and polish. Cather knew the Southwest thoroughly before she began to write, planned her novel carefully, and carried out her plan successfully. She thought it her best novel, and time may prove her right.[16]

Shadows on the Rock is not so good a book, but some of the reasons for this are not particularly relevant to this discussion. Cather's mother was dying in a Pasadena sanatorium while the book was in progress and her creative powers, I think, were beginning to decline. Also she did not know Quebec as well as she knew the Southwest. She discovered the subject quite by chance when she happened to visit Quebec one summer en route to her cottage on Grand Manan Island off New Brunswick. Her friend and companion Edith Lewis got sick in Quebec, and Cather had a chance to roam the city. Later she visited the city three more times while she was writing the novel. She also read or reread a good bit of Parkman in preparation for this novel, and she looked up many other historical sources. A rather large amount of historical research went into the book. In contrast she had to 'work up' the material much more than she did for *Death Comes for the Archbishop*, which she had been preparing unconsciously to write for fifteen years. In sum, I agree with Carl Van Doren, who found *Shadows on the Rock* 'dramatically thin' but 'pictorially rich.'[17]

I have not said much yet about *Sapphira and the Slave Girl*, because it is a different sort of historical novel from the other two. Cather in this book went back to her Virginia origin for her setting. It is a novel that has its inspiration in family history and a childhood memory. The story deals with the escape through the Underground Railroad of a slave Nancy, who has fallen victim to the jealousy of Sapphira, her owner. The person who helps Nancy escape to Canada is a fictional version of Cather's grandmother. The childhood memory that triggered the novel was the recollection of seeing Nancy return home some twenty years later when Cather was a small child.

There are no important historical personages in this novel, though real characters furnished the starting point for the fiction. Cather drew on her own memories of Virginia, visited the area while she was writing the novel, and invited other people's reminiscences. The result is competent fiction, a good re-creation of the Shenandoah Valley before the Civil War. If the novel is not up to Cather's best, one has to remember that she was in her mid-sixties when she wrote it. The strain of finishing the book left her with a severe case of tendonitis of the right thumb, and when the book appeared she was wearing her arm in a sling with her thumb taped to a splint. Cather's nostalgic views of the good old days being better than the present, of course, cannot apply in this novel, which has to deal with slavery. Her chief interests in writing this book were to create some interesting characters, relate a dramatic tale, and set the narrative in the Shenandoah Valley that she remembered from her childhood. The nostalgia came in the evocation of place. It is interesting to note that Cather's last completed novel was the only one she wrote with its setting in her native Virginia. But this story of Virginia before the Civil War is consistent with her retreat into history in the fiction of her last two decades. The novel was published on her sixty-seventh birthday, December seventh, the day Pearl Harbor was attacked. Who could blame a writer for finding the past more attractive than the present?

Notes

1. Jackson Bryer's *Fifteen Modern American Authors* (1969), later expanded into *Sixteen Modern American Authors* (1974), includes Cather among the writers it covers. She is the only woman writer of this group. These authors were selected by a consensus of specialists in American literature, and this volume seems to have established the canon of our major writers of the first half of this century. The others are Anderson, Crane, Dreiser, Eliot, Faulkner, Fitzgerald, Frost, Hemingway, O'Neill, Pound, Robinson, Steinbeck, Stevens, Williams, and Wolfe.

2. *One of Ours*, (New York: Alfred A. Knopf, 1922), p. 419.

3. James Woodress, *Willa Cather: Her Life and Art* (New York: Pegasus, 1970), p. 225.

4. This letter is reprinted in *Willa Cather on Writing: Critical Studies on Writing as an Art* (New York: Alfred A. Knopf, 1949), pp. 3–13.

5. Edward A. and Lillian D. Bloom in an excellent chapter, 'On the Composition of a Novel,' in their *Willa Cather's Gift of Sympathy* (Carbondale: Southern Illinois University Press, 1962), pp. 197–236, have made an extensive analysis of Cather's use of sources. They have examined at least nine works that she drew on besides Howlett, and for the last they have prepared a table of correspondences (pp. 221–22).

6. Published in the Pittsburgh *Leader*, Jan. 11, 1898; reprinted in William M. Curtin, ed., *The World and the Parish: Willa Cather's Articles and Reviews, 1893-1902* (Lincoln: University of Nebraska Press, 1970), II, 740–41.

7. *Willa Cather Living: A Personal Record* (New York: Alfred A. Knopf, 1953), p. 151.

8. Printed in the Red Cloud *Chief* in 1890 and quoted by Bernice Slote in 'The Secret Web,' in *Five Essays on Willa Cather: The Merrimack Symposium* (North Andover, Mass.: Merrimack College, 1974), p. 8.

9. I am indebted to David Levin's *History as Romantic Art* (Stanford: Stanford University Press, 1959) for these generalisations about the Romantic historians.

Harry B. Henderson III in *Versions of the Past: The Historical Imagination in American Fiction* (New York: Oxford University Press, 1974) takes a different view of this group. He would place Bancroft and Motley in the 'progressive' category, that is among those who believed in progress, but he places Prescott and Parkman in a category he calls 'holist,' by which he means that the last two have a more sophisticated concept of history, not as evolving along a continuum but as moving in cycles with each historic epoch requiring separate study. The 'holist' concept he sees as a more modern view of history than the 'progressive' view.

10. *Death Comes for the Archbishop*, (New York: Alfred A. Knopf, 1927), p. 274.

11. *Ibid.*, p. 276.
12. *Ibid.*, p. 294.
13. (New York: Alfred A. Knopf, 1981), pp. 277, 280.
14. *The World and the Parish*, II, 742.
15. Paul Horgan in his excellent biography of the Archbishop, *Lamy of Santa Fe: His Life and Times* (New York: Farrar, Straus and Giroux, 1975), covers exhaustively the career of this exemplary French priest who left his native Auvergne in 1839 to become a missionary priest in the New World. Although there is not space here to list them, there are dozens of differences between the historical figure and Cather's character. Anyone interested in this comparison will find Horgan's book fascinating.
16. Henderson, op cit., p. 251, takes a negative view, which I do not share, of *Death Comes for the Archbishop*: '. . . the tale of men cultivating a civilization in the semi-wilderness is told too much like *The Swiss Family Robinson* and not enough like *Robinson Crusoe*. The priests fit their roles too well; there are no conflicts between them, and none within, other than those which their roles dictate as commendable; and even these are resolved in too exemplary a manner. Thus, *Death Comes for the Archbishop* gives the unfortunate appearance of marrying the worst features of the Catholic hagiography and the Protestant success story.'
17. New York *Herald Tribune*, Aug. 2, 1931. E.K. Brown's *Willa Cather: A Critical Biography* (New York: Alfred A. Knopf, 1953) contains an excellent chapter on *Shadows on the Rock* (pp. 266–86). Brown deals in some detail with Cather's sources and her use of them: the *Jesuit Relations*, Abbé Henri Arthur Scott's life of Laval, La Hontan's *Voyages*, the *Makers of Canada*, which she owned, and others.

160
The Professor's House and the Issues of History

◆

DAVID STOUCK

In most of her novels and stories, Willa Cather gives ancestry to her characters. In *O Pioneers!* there is a portrait of Alexandra's grandfather who lost his fortune to a young wife. In *My Ántonia* the narrator's grandparents are central figures in the first half of the book, and we have there as well a portrait of Ántonia's paternal grandmother, a proud woman, wellborn, class conscious. Lineage is important in *Sapphira and the Slave Girl* to both the black families and the white, encompassing four generations. And if we were to draw up a genealogy for Godfrey St Peter in *The Professor's House*, we could designate seven generations, for we are told something about St Peter's 'remote grandfather' (his grandfather's grandfather) who trekked across Europe into Russia with Napoleon's army.

This contrasts strikingly with most American writers: the protagonists of Dreiser, Hemingway, or Dos Passos very often have no specified ancestry, not even parents being named. The American protagonist is archetypally a new Adam; the idea of ancestry is antithetical to the concept of a Natty Bumppo, an Ishmael, or even a Huckleberry Finn, who is orphaned early in his story. In F. Scott Fitzgerald's famous novel *The Great Gatsby*, shabby and inadequate parents are discarded by Jay Gatsby in favor of heroic and mythic ones—figures like Dan Cody, the Kaiser; finally we are told Gatsby is the child of his own imagination, the son of God. Cather, of course, is not unique in giving her characters ancestry: Hawthorne and Faulkner place their characters in a complex setting of personal and community history. But for the narrator of *The Scarlet Letter* and for characters like the Compsons and McCaslins, history is tragic and memory is a mode in which the sins of the fathers are visited on the succeeding generations.

The evoking of ancestral voices marks Cather's art. Characters typically

SOURCE   David Stouck, '*The Professor's House* and the Issues of History', *Willa Cather: Family, Community and History*, ed. John J. Murphy, Provo, UT: Brigham Young University Press, 1990, pp. 201–11

remember the words and gestures of their forebears, and Cather's narrators frequently quote classic and favorite authors. This intertextual weaving together of voices embodies a dialogue with the past that is both emotionally and intellectually at the center of Cather's art. Cather wrote historical novels — *Death Comes for the Archbishop* and *Shadows on the Rock* are among the finest American fictions in this genre, and we know at the time of her death she was working on another historical novel set in medieval France—but the book in which she most attentively auditions voices from the past and directly confronts the meaning of history is a story of a family. In *The Professor's House*, a 'wasteland' novel of the 1920s, Willa Cather extends the meaning of family and community to a comprehensive vision of human history.

I

Godfrey St Peter in *The Professor's House* is not a historian by accident—this *is* a book about history. The first question we must ask is from what philosophical premise did Cather view history? Her first recorded statement on the subject can be found in her high school graduation speech. There she said: 'All human history is a record of an emigration, an exodus from barbarism to civilisation' (Bohlke 141). James Woodress points out that Cather was voicing the 'conventional wisdom' of her day, that behind her words is the optimistic nineteenth-century view of history with its unlimited faith in the idea of human progress (247). American historians like George Bancroft and John Motley saw humanity advancing on an irreversible path of progress, whereon tyranny inevitably gave way to freedom, monarchies yielded to democracies, and class-structure gave way to equality and material well-being. This was the Romantic view of history, grounded philosophically in Hegel's argument that human history is the progress of reason. It was also a biblical version of history, advancing from Genesis to Revelation, from humankind's fall from Eden to restoration in the New Jerusalem.

Cather may have believed in this philosophy of history when she was sixteen, but as she grew older she would have recognised this view as inimical to her imagination, for as Harry B. Henderson points out, the aim of the progressive view in nineteenth-century America was to organise 'the imaginative and emotional resources of people to accept and advance social change' (37). Cather, to the contrary, was a staunch defender of the status quo. Even as a young woman she felt about Nebraska that the Golden Age had passed and that the age succeeding was a greatly diminished one.

As a classics student at university, reading in the history, philosophy, and literature of the ancient civilisations, Cather adopted a cyclical approach to history. She viewed the rise and fall of Greece and Rome not as a progressive drama of human advancement, but as history repeating itself. The title and the epigraph of *The Troll Garden* refer to the cycles of decaying civilisations and the reconquering of nature. This view of history is voiced by Carl Linstrum in *O Pioneers!* when he looks at the little graveyard on the prairie and says to Alexandra:

> Now the old story has begun to write itself over. . . . Isn't it queer: there are only two or three human stories, and they go on repeating themselves as fiercely as if they had never happened before. (119)

Accordingly, Cather's great plains joins a universal geography that includes the steppes of Russia, the grainfields of Virgil's *patria*. A civilisation may decline, but another will be born in which humankind's energies are renewed: Troy and Athens will be succeeded by Rome, and the garden of the Roman trolls will be taken over by the Teutonic forest children. This view of history allowed Cather to celebrate the beginnings of a new country in Nebraska and to ignore the randomness of history and some of its harsher realities, such as the displacement of the region's native peoples. It also allowed her to accept the inevitable tarnishing of the pioneer ideals: in *A Lost Lady* there is an ironic acceptance of the decline of Marian Forrester and the emergence of Ivy Peters in the drama of Nebraska history. In spite of the downward path, this was a reassuring view of history for Cather.

But in 1922 or thereabouts 'the world broke in two' for Cather, or so it seemed to her by 1936 (Woodress 240). What this statement may have meant in personal terms we cannot know, but in *The Professor's House*, the first novel written after this break, Cather's view of history has altered. She presents us with a despairing view of history after the Renaissance, a rejection of the age of progress dependent on science and technology, with no reassurance any longer that history is cyclical. In this novel we come to recognise that Cather is a conservative in a historically profound sense of the word. In *The Professor's House*, she holds up a classical view (the Greek view) of human experience, one in which philosophical truths derive from natural right, free of all dependence on the events of history. It is an ideal of contemplation as the highest form of civilised activity, expanded after the advent of Christianity to include charity — love for one's fellow human beings.

The great difference after the Renaissance, with the advent of modern science in the age of Newton and Locke, was that humankind no longer saw itself as part of nature, but for the first time as the controller of nature in a way that established radically new priorities and values for human life. Human beings were no longer content to adjust to the rhythms of the natural world; the goal of living was no longer to be in comfortable harmony with nature, but to master and control its energies. The drive to technology became an end in itself — production and consumption became the goal of living, replacing the ideals of contemplation and charity as the highest good. From this 'progressive' course of history Willa Cather withdrew. Significantly, there runs through *The Professor's House* an endorsement of classical and medieval civilisations — their philosophies, literature, and art.

II

A central imaginative preoccupation in *The Professor's House* and in Cather's work as a whole stems from the fact that as North Americans we belong to a civilisation with no history before the age of science and progress. When the European settlers crossed the Atlantic Ocean, they entered an alien land and conquered it with their technology. These were the people who had broken with the Greek and Christian ideals; these were the Calvinist Protestants, northern Europeans who brought with them the new physical and moral science—what we describe as the capitalist work ethic. We have then, as North Americans of European origin, no history that goes back before conscious memory. We have no experience of our land that can be called aboriginal, because in all regions there is some consciousness of our making the land our own. Unless we have native Indian ancestry, there can be nothing immemorial for us because we ourselves have made what is here—the farms, the towns and cities—all the encampments on the road to economic mastery. From the outset, on this continent we have lived divided from the earth.

Cather's own yearning for an aboriginal relation to the land emerges in many passages in her writing. In the conclusion to *O Pioneers!*, Alexandra Bergson, though not born in Nebraska, will be happy at her death to become part of the earth she has cultivated. Thea Kronborg, in *The Song of the Lark*, discovers the meaning of art in an Arizona canyon when she surrenders herself to the elements (the earth, sun, water, sky). In *My Ántonia*, Cather suggests that perhaps non-Protestant Europeans could relate to the land in the old primal way. When Jim Burden first sees the Shimerdas, they are coming out of their cave—out of the earth—and, as Susan Rosowski has noted, they are animal forms (78), a suggestion of human evolution. One of Ántonia's brothers has webbed fingers and makes sounds like a rooster crowing; another is foxlike; the cave itself is 'warm like a badger hole' (75). This vision is repeated at the end of the book when Ántonia and her children emerge out of the fruit cellar in the earth, a veritable explosion of life.

Other figures in Cather's fiction, less certain of purpose or direction, are cut off from this relationship to place but are haunted by a desire to be reconnected, to be grounded, as it were. One thinks of Carl Linstrum in *O Pioneers!*, Niel Herbert in *A Lost Lady*, and, of course, Jim Burden. There broods over these figures an unmistakable feeling of pathos and loss. They respond sensitively to complex human situations, but more urgently they seek to recover, in the very movement of nature's seasons, a sense of humanity's lost relationship to itself. They are characters who travel the country, are lost, deracinated, cannot locate themselves in a landscape or create a home. Their return to the Nebraska country of their family and childhood is an attempt to return to self and the elusive promise of happiness.

Cather's landscapes are colored emotionally by this search for a people and a culture rooted in place. The peasant immigrants of her early fictions seem to enjoy that intimate relation to their land, yet a melancholy attaches to these figures because they have been uprooted from their homelands and some, like Mr Shimerda, do not survive. As Cather grew increasingly disenchanted with American life in the 1920s, with the machines and money-grubbing that beset Claude Wheeler in *One of Ours*, she looked to the oldest cultures of North America, those of the pueblo Indians in the Southwest, to locate that lost world where a people lived in an aboriginal relationship to place. Also, in the cultures of the Navajo and Mexicans described in *Death Comes for the Archbishop* she celebrates a continuous, living tradition of people and place that is immemorial. Cather turned to Quebec in *Shadows on the Rock* because the way of life she found there—language and religion bound to the land—had not changed for three hundred years.

The importance of the land, the emotional value of home and family, the despair over technological destruction and waste, the wholeness of the classical and Catholic visions of life—these become the familiar and repeated themes in Cather's later works, articulated with special urgency in *The Professor's House*. Historically, what Cather envisions in this unhappy novel is technology as a comprehensive fate for the modern world, a fate that tragically cuts people off from their ability to know and love what is intrinsically good.

III

Willa Cather dramatises this vision in terms of a man's home, his family, and the academic community in which he works. The novel opens with Godfrey St Peter having to leave his house, the place in which he has worked and which has given his life meaning. He resists this rupture with the past and holds on to his old study and to his garden, where he has actually lived close to the earth. But St Peter has never known continuity or wholeness to his life; he has always been a man divided against himself, living two lives, a division rooted in his ancestry. Although this is a novel about family and the professor's meditation on his past, there are almost no memories of Godfrey St Peter's parents. We are told simply (but it is significant) that his mother was a practical, 'strong-willed Methodist,' his father a 'gentle, weaned-away Catholic' (30). His mother's family, English-speaking Protestants, represent progressive modern civilisation, while his father's family, French Canadians, come from a Catholic peasant culture with its roots in pre-technological society.

What does family mean for Willa Cather? In its ideal form it represents wholeness, the earthly unity celebrated in the last section of *My Ántonia*, the heavenly ideal imaged in the Holy Family in *Shadows on the Rock*. What is a child? A child is a measure of the gaps, a product of the tensions that exist in the family. Godfrey St Peter has been reared a Methodist but is nostalgic for a Catholic past. His radical inner division symbolises the dilemma of modern humanity. He is a man of the twentieth century, but he yearns for the more meaningful life of the Middle Ages; he is a man adrift between the Dynamo and the Virgin. He carries within himself the natural desire for worldly activity and accomplishments, but also the deep instinct to give first place to imaginative thought and contemplation. This is why he continues to rent his old house—'to have room to think,' he tells his old landlord. The old German appreciates his tenant's sentiments, for he too has 'so many t'ings to t'ink about' (52).

The professor's harsh judgments of the world around him are generated by his rejection of modern science and what he believes is an unthinking technology. 'No . . . I don't myself think much of science as a phase of human development,' he says to Tod Miller, one of the few gifted students in his class. 'It has given us a lot of ingenious toys,' he says, but they simply 'take our attention away from the real problems' (67–68), namely the meaning of human existence. St Peter identifies the Middle Ages and early Renaissance, the high period of Catholicism, as the time in Western civilisation when the individual's life was most meaningful. He says to his students:

> As long as every man and woman who crowded into the cathedrals on Easter Sunday was a principal in a gorgeous drama with God, glittering angels on one side and the shadows of evil coming and going on the other, life was a rich thing. . . . And that's what makes men happy, believing in the mystery and importance of their own little individual lives. (68)

Religion is what gives human lives meaning and purpose and creates community. St Peter cites the medieval cathedral-builders, the sculptors, painters, and glass-workers, whose works of art testify to the strength of vision and purpose in their age.

The professor concludes his lecture by asking Miller to tell him next week what science has done for humankind besides bringing great comfort. Earlier in his talk, St Peter complained that the 'laboratory, not the Lamb of God,' has taken 'away the sins of the world.' By this he means that humankind, in controlling nature, has reduced the mystery in life, become oblivious of God and knowledge of evil and good, and eliminated the need for 'miracles and great temptations and revelations' (68). The professor accordingly still values what we can't control or fully understand. If humankind were to eliminate or ignore this realm, then nothing could happen that we hadn't chosen, and so there would be no standard higher than our wills. Excellence depends on encounters with meaning beyond our control. St Peter (who would be horrified by genetic engineering, artificial intelligence, etc.) reflects that 'the most important things in his life had been determined by chance' (257). The coming of Tom Outland to his door, for instance, was a fantastic stroke of chance, perhaps the most important event in his life.

The professor's yearning for a more deeply meaningful and morally coherent world fixes on the Middle Ages and early Renaissance. He admires not only its art but also the wholeness and the enterprise of the Catholic faith. His histories of the Spanish Adventurers concern the transfer of a Catholic culture to the New World. When the first three volumes are reviewed with little real interest, it is recommended that he adopt the more even and genial style of John Fiske. This is a significant allusion because Fiske was the New England historian and philosopher who popularised scientific evolutionary theory in the United States, adapting it to an optimistic theory of human progress. His vision would have been an anathema to the professor because it scientifically endorsed the course of free enterprise liberalism and the spirit of moral relativism. St Peter's profound conservatism, on the other hand, is indicated in the writers that his son-in-law, Louie Marsellus, envisions entertaining him with in Paris. One of these is Paul Bourget, a novelist who urged a traditional morality against modern scientific theory. (Bourget's 1889 novel, *Le Disciple*, portrays the pernicious influence of a highly regarded Positivist philosopher on an impressionable young man.) Louie also wants the professor to dine with Emile Faguet, a deeply conservative French literary critic. Louie regrets that Gaston Paris, the eminent medievalist, is now dead. When Louie suggests dining with Anatole France, a socialist, the professor replies that he has never made his acquaintance, implying that he has known the others personally.

All these French writers believed that science and the spirit of relativism have brought human society to a moral crisis. This is apparent to the professor in the life of his own family and community, although in their frenetic pursuit of wealth and social status, the people around him seem scarcely aware of the unsatisfactory nature of their lives. The ideal of wholeness, of thoughtful action, which the professor carries within him as a moral measure, is at every turn betrayed in his family. His two daughters, Rosamond and Kathleen, are filled with envy and hatred for each other, as they focus their energies on competitively acquiring material possessions — new houses, furnishings, clothes, jewelry. His sons-in-law are drawn into this rivalry. The professor recognises they are both good men but corrupted by the values of their society. Scott McGregor so envies Louie Marsellus's good fortune, he mean-spiritedly blackballs Marsellus's application to join the Arts and Letters Club.

Marsellus, electrical engineer turned entrepreneur, embodies much of the professor's moral dilemma. Leaving for New York on a business trip, Louie kisses his hand to the family again and again from the platform of the 'Twentieth Century observation car' (152). Louie stands identified with the energy and spirit of the modern era, what Henry Adams meant by the Dynamo, but when the train has pulled away, the professor feels the distinct loss of this man's warm energies and generosity. However, Louie represents everything that troubles the professor — technological expertise, business acumen, pursuit of learning and the arts for status and ornament; his Jewishness is merely the social occasion for deeper strife in this family. Mrs

St Peter is also actively involved in the family's pursuit of wealth and status, and the professor feels sharply estranged from her. As his wife and the Marselluses plan a trip to Europe, for another 'orgy of acquisition,' he recognises that he can no longer be part of this group.

The academic community in which he lives and works also fails to sustain the professor during his crisis. Like his family, it is eroded by the liberal values of a scientific and commercial age. During his career he has fought for the importance of the humanities, for the idea of a university education grounded in cultural studies. But the vulgarising of education has proceeded inexorably, with top appointments going to those who worked with the regents to turn the university into a trade school, those willing 'to give the taxpayers what they wanted' (140). There is no one in Hamilton with whom the professor can share a community of ideas and values. The only unspoiled things left for him at the close of Book One are those that predate the modern world: the lake where he swam as a boy, his garden where he is close to the earth, the curiosity and desire of a gifted student for knowledge and wisdom.

IV

The most curious and gifted of his students was Tom Outland, whose story of youthful adventure and disappointment mirrors the professor's own idealistic quest and defeat. Tom was an orphan and homeless, the quintessential modern man, completely detached from a sense of origins. But in contrast to the stories of Natty Bumppo, Ishmael, or Jake Barnes, the discovery of ancestors is an important part of Tom Outland's experience. Tom's story is of an American boy finding a symbolic home in an aboriginal premodern culture and discovering as well a nurturing relationship with the elements—the rock and sun and water and air that are each so important to life on the Blue Mesa. He finds ancestors—specifically Mother Eve—in what the Belgian priest, Father Duchene, describes as 'a provident and rather *thoughtful* people' (220; emphasis added).

The priest's description of the Indian Cliff City echoes the classical ideal of a civil society that achieves its order and purpose through natural right. From the symmetry and design of the buildings, the shapes and decorations of the pottery, and the evidence of some astronomy, the priest concludes that the Indians lived in this city for something more than food and shelter:

> 'I see them here, isolated, cut off from other tribes, working out their destiny, making their mesa more and more worthy to be a home for man, purifying life by religious ceremonies and observances, caring respectfully for their dead, protecting the children, doubtless entertaining some feelings of affection and sentiment for this stronghold where they were at once so safe and so comfortable.' (220)

There is a vision here of community similar to the Greek idea of the *polis*, the small city-state where individual actions counted, where daily tasks brought people together, where life had an element of ceremony. Suggested here, too, is the idea of autochthony: the strong feeling for a place where one is rooted and has one's being. Father Duchene says there is something sacred about such a place—a place where, over the generations, humanity has lifted itself out of mere brutality to create a civilisation. Most importantly, this happened on the mesa 'without the influence of example or emulation, with no incentive but some natural yearning for order and security' (221).

The Greek ideal of a civilisation that fulfills the natural yearning of humanity for order and security, and the soul's longing for goodness, is a crucial concept here. Looking at it from a mythic frame of reference, John N. Swift writes that the passage 'suggests that human experience is neither fragmentary nor random,' because without any kind of model, the Indians have built a city that expresses a universal human desire for order, security, and love. The prehistoric city, says Swift, is a mythic paradigm by which all 'historical existence can be measured' (303). St Peter sees the modern world as much less noble, preoccupied with food and shelter and comfort, and without a religious feeling for nature or a transcendent ideal. The professor sees the members of his family and community wholly motivated by emulation and greed, by the desire for wealth and social status. The Marselluses are building an expensive country house that will proclaim their superior wealth to all the community. It will not be of the community, nor will it be indigenous in design and materials; instead it will be a Norwegian manor house in the Middle West, a source of pride and an object of envy. It would have no place in a civilisation envisioned by the ancient philosophers nor in that deduced by Father Duchene as having once existed on the Blue Mesa.

For Tom Outland, the tragic fact is that the Indian civilisation has disappeared and modern men and women can value it only in terms of its commercial possibilities (the selling of artifacts) or as a means to acquire promotions and status in a bureaucratic society. After he has been sorely disillusioned in Washington and has found most of the artifacts sold by his friend Roddy Blake, Tom spends a summer on the mesa alone where he comes to understand 'possession,' not in a material sense but in terms of contemplation. He says, 'For me the mesa was no longer an adventure, but a religious emotion. I had read of filial piety in the Latin poets, and I knew that was what I felt for this place' (251). For Tom the mesa is a place of origins, and accordingly what he feels is a religious response to its ancestral and timeless character, something he had intuited almost from the first when he looked up through the falling snow and saw the city looking down into the canyon 'with the calmness of eternity' (201).

When Tom takes his place in the modern world he becomes a scientist; he develops a theory of space that leads to the invention of the Outland engine. Then he is killed in a war that is the product of modern technology and dubious morality, and his memory is defiled in the moral miasma in technology's wake, for his invention brings much misery over inheritance.

In the final section of the novel the professor, living alone, has shed his secondary, social self and returned to the boy, his primitive, original being. We are told, 'He was only interested in earth and woods and water. . . . He was earth and would return to earth' (265). He has become like his father's father, the old French Canadian in his eighties who so often was lost in profound, continuous meditation. He remembers his own personal ancestors (it is in this section we are given a glimpse of his great-great-grandfather and the emigration to Canada), but he also hears the ancestral voices of writers and great men of history. He finds something curiously comforting in the lines Longfellow translated from the Anglo-Saxon poem 'The Grave':

For thee a house was built
Ere thou wast born;
For thee a mould was made
Ere thou of woman camest. (272)

He probably recalls reading with Tom the only surviving piece by the Latin poet Lucretius, the *De Rerum Natura* (*The Nature of Things*), a poetical rendering of the philosophy of Epicurus (176). Although its central argument is an atomic theory of life, it decries earthly ambitions ('what vanity . . . the discovery of gold . . . the craving of power and fame'), speaks in one of the most moving passages against the fear of dying, and extols the private life of withdrawal to the garden, the life of quiet study and companionship. St Peter's desire to escape his family — the squabbling and envy and hatred that surrounds him — makes him think of the legend of Euripides' living in a cave by the sea in old age. (In a similar way perhaps, the looting of the Cliff City for its commercially valuable artifacts made Tom remember most keenly those lines from the *Aeneid* where Aeneas is asked to describe the sack of Troy, his ancestral city [113].)

The professor's death wish is not only suicidal in a personal way, but a wish to return human culture to its simplest elements, to revert to a world before modern science and technology corrupted humanity's finest instincts for contemplation and charity. Saving the professor from extinction is surely the meaning of the dressmaker's role in the novel. Augusta represents a vestige of that Catholic world of his paternal forebears whose values predate the age of progress, a world where faith and love still provide guideposts to the search for life's meaning, the world of the Virgin as opposed to the Dynamo. It is through Augusta, another instance of chance in his life, that Godfrey St Peter feels he can resume living, be outward bound, and once again feel 'the ground under his feet' (283).

Willa Cather believed with her professor in truths freed from historical contingency. She believed with classical man in trying to rise above one's earthly passions, to enthrone virtue and reason, with medieval man in the preeminent Christian value of charity. She was not a modern; she thought outside of modern assumptions, and from that vantage she saw twentieth-century life sapped by moral relativism and epistemological skepticism. The family, that primal experience of wholeness, was one of the moral absolutes to which she clung. She has been labelled nostalgic and antiquarian, but Cather never reviews the past for purely antiquarian reasons or ancestor worship; instead she looks to see if in its thought and art there are things lost that we need here today, to see if it is possible to glimpse the moving image of eternity.

Modernism and Modernity

161
Modernism: The Case of Willa Cather

◆

PHYLLIS ROSE

In the 1950s David Daiches cannily predicted that literary historians would have difficulty placing Willa Cather.[1] He did not foresee that Cather's work would be underrated because it was hard to place, but such may have been the case. It could be said that Cather has been ignored because she was a woman, but that would not explain why her rediscovery has taken ten years longer than Virginia Woolf's. Generally perceived as a traditionalist, Cather has been patronised. Many people read her for pleasure, but for the past twenty years few have taught her works or written about them. The novels seem curiously self-evident. They are defiantly smooth and elegant, lacking the rough edges that so often provide convenient starting points for literary analysis. To a critical tradition that has valued complexity, ambiguity, even obscurity, the hard-won simplicities of Cather's art seem merely simple. Her lucidity can be read as shallowness; her massive, abstract forms can be—and have been—viewed as naively traditional, the appropriate vehicle for an art essentially nostalgic and elegaic.

Although I am deeply distrustful of the way in which, for twentieth-century writers, the term 'modernist' is not merely an honorific but the precondition of attention from literary critics and scholars, I will nonetheless try to show ways in which Willa Cather's work is allied to modernism. I do this by way of redressing a balance. Her public stance was so belligerently reactionary (perhaps in order to mask the radically unacceptable nature of her private life) that she herself encouraged the flattening of her work into a glorification of the past, a lament for the shabbiness of the present, which has persisted for decades. The writer who titled a collection of essays *Not Under Forty* would have been the last person to feel congratulated at being called a modernist. But it is time to risk her wrath. In part because of her defensive self-presentation, in part because her fiction so perfectly embodies certain

SOURCE Phyllis Rose, 'Modernism: The Case of Willa Cather', *Modernism Reconsidered*, ed. Robert Kieley, Cambridge, Mass: Harvard University Press, 1983, pp. 123–45

aesthetic ideals of modernism—monumentality, functionalism, anonymity—we have overlooked its innovative nature. To see its modernist elements is to readjust and enrich our response to her work—and also to widen our notions of modernism. If Cather is a modernist, she is a tempered, transitional modernist closer to Hardy than to Pound. Nonetheless, her work is moved in important ways by a modernist urge to simplify and to suggest the eternal through the particular. Because we have paid more attention to other aspects of literary modernism—the overtly experimental, the representation of subjectivity, the literary analogues of cubist collage—we react to Cather's novels as though we have stumbled across some giant work of nature, a boulder, something so massive that it seems inhuman, uncrafted. But I would suggest that what we have stumbled upon in fact is something like the literary equivalent of an Arp, a Brancusi, a Moore.

I would point first of all to her scale. I do not mean, of course, the size of her books, for they are conspicuously slender, little masterpieces of economy; I mean the size of the subjects to which her imagination responds. In her strongest work, the land is as much a presence as the human characters, and the landscapes that move her imagination are large and unbroken ones, the plains and fields of the American Midwest, the canyonlands and deserts of the South-west. Reading *O Pioneers!*, *My Ántonia,* or *Death Comes for the Archbishop,* we experience the exhilarating potential of clear blank spaces.[2] Few novels I can think of are less cluttered than these; they offer the breathing space of all outdoors, and one feels that Cather may be describing herself when she says of Alexandra Bergson, the Swedish immigrant farmer who is her first great female protagonist, that she was uncertain in her indoor tastes and expressed herself best in her fields, that properly speaking her house was the out-of-doors.[3]

The vast Nebraska prairie, which Cather saw for the first time when she was ten, transplanted from the hill-enclosed perspectives of Virginia, determined—or answered to—her sense of scale. Whether it happened when she was ten, or, as seems more likely to me, when as a grown woman, a harried and successful magazine editor in New York, she turned her inner eye back to the landscape of her childhood, the landscape of her dreams, the impact of the prairie on her sense of self was probably such as her narrative stand-in, Jim Burden, describes in *My Ántonia*:

> There seemed to be nothing to see; no fences, creeks, or trees, no hills or fields. If there was a road, I could not make it out in the faint starlight. There was nothing but land: not a country at all, but the material out of which countries are made . . . I had the feeling that the world was left behind, that we had got over the edge of it, and were outside men's jurisdiction. I had never before looked up at the sky when there was not a familiar mountain ridge against it. But this was the complete dome of heaven, all there was of it . . . I don't think I was homesick. If we never arrived anywhere, it did not matter. Between that earth and that sky I felt erased, blotted out.[4]

To feel 'erased, blotted out' is not, from Cather's perspective, such a bad thing. The scale of the landscape erases trivialities of personality, and in one of the most beautiful passages in American literature Cather presents Jim at his happiest, most fully alive, when he has become a mere creature on the earth, sitting in his grandmother's garden, resting his back against a sun-warmed pumpkin, his individuality transcended.

> I kept as still as I could. Nothing happened. I did not expect anything to happen. I was something that lay under the sun and felt it, like the pumpkins, and I did not want to be anything more. I was entirely happy. Perhaps we feel like that when we die and become part of something entire, whether it is sun and air, or goodness and knowledge. At any rate, that is happiness; to be dissolved into something complete and great (p. 18).

Against the background of the plains, only the biggest stories stand out, only stories based on the largest, strongest, most elemental emotions. 'There are only two or three human stories,' Cather wrote in *O Pioneers!*, 'and they go on repeating themselves as fiercely as if they had never happened before; like the larks in this country, that have been singing the same five notes over for thousands of years' (p. 119). If you approach *O Pioneers!* as a naturalistic account of the conquest of new land, four-fifths of the book is anticlimactic, even irrelevant, and you must wonder why the story of the adulterous love of Emil Bergson and Marie Shabata and their murder by her jealous husband is taking up so much space in a book about pioneers. In fact, the love of Emil and Marie, growing as inevitably as Frank's murderous jealousy, is the focus of the story, along with the autumnal attachment of Alexandra Bergson and Carl Lindstrum, Alexandra's ambition, and her fatigue. The rhythms of the seasons are matched by the natural growth of human emotions. Typically, Cather uses a metaphor of seed-corn to compare Emil's guilty passion for Marie with the happy love of his friend, Amédée:

> From two ears that had grown up side by side, the grains of one shot joyfully into the light, projecting themselves into the future, and the grains from the other lay still in the earth and rotted; and nobody knew why (p. 164).

As in ballads, motivation is played down; motives in such oft-enacted human stories are assumed to speak for themselves. Amédée dies in the prime of life of a ruptured appendix; Emil dies from the gunshot blast of a man who is so enraged he hardly knows what he is doing and who is presented as acting with no conscious volition. In a curious way, both deaths seem equally natural in this novel which presents the life of man and the life of earth as concurrent, equivalent.

In the American Southwest, which Cather visited for the first time in 1912, she found not only another monumental landscape but the temporal equivalent for the vast spaces of the Midwest. For these were not, like the plains, uninhabited spaces whose history was just beginning. Here and there, tucked in the great half-dome caverns on the cliff-sides of canyons, were the remains of an ancient, civilised people. The cliff-dwelling Indians had lived, cultivated the land, and, in their weavings and pottery, produced art, long before Europeans had landed on American soil. The effect of Anasazi art and architecture on Cather's aesthetic was profound, but for the moment I want to concentrate merely on the imaginative impact of a long-inhabited, long-abandoned monumental landscape. It lengthened the past. If you included the Indians, American history, which had seemed so small and cramped a thing, suddenly became vast. When Thea Kronborg in *The Song of the Lark* and Tom Outland of *The Professor's House* encounter the canyonlands, the effect on their senses of themselves is like the effect of the prairie on Jim Burden: it obliterates the trivial and raises them, spiritually, to its own scale, uniting them to something larger than themselves.

Cather's imagination craved and fed on large scale, both in time and space, and her books repeatedly struggle to break outside the confines of town or city life and make their way, quite against the grain of the narrative, back to the wilderness. *The Song of the Lark* gets to Panther Canyon by way of the unlikely premise that Thea Kronborg, studying music in Chicago, needs the experience of exactly that locale to change her from a good artist into a great one. The relationship between Tom Outland's story of the discovery of the cliff-dweller ruins on the Blue Mesa (a version of the true story of the discovery of Mesa Verde by Richard Wetherill) bears an even more tenuous plot connection to the rest of *The Professor's House*, which concerns a transitional crisis in the life of a midwestern university professor. Thematic justification for the interpolated story may of course be found, but I find it more interesting to note how it does *not* fit into the rest of the novel. In the sudden, eccentric switch to the southwestern locale, we witness a Catherian compulsion. Explaining it, however, as an experiment in form (a tactic that would have been more persuasive had she not done something so similar in *The Song of the Lark*), Cather said she wanted to reproduce the effect of a square window opening onto a distant prospect set into a Dutch genre painting of a warmly furnished interior. She said she wanted the reader first to stifle amidst the trappings of American bourgeois domesticity, then to feel the clean air blowing in from the mesa.[5] This suggests that the contrast between inside and outside worlds is essential to the power of both. But the effect of the massive dislocation within *The Professor's House* is less like the effect of Dutch genre painting, which carefully subordinates one scale to the other, than it is like the effect of surrealism, with its willful changes of scale and its reminders, within a canvas, of the artificiality of the canvas—Magritte's painting of a view out the window blocked by a painting of a view out the window, or Charles Sheeler's ironic *The Artist Looks at Nature* which depicts Sheeler out-of-doors, painting a kitchen interior. It is Cather herself who stifles in the house-bound, small-town scenes, craves open air, and inserts the outdoors into the indoors as willfully as Sheeler's self-portrait does the reverse, justifying the change however she can. (The novel's epigraph, a quotation from itself, also seems a justification of the form: 'A turquoise set in silver, wasn't it? . . . Yes, a turquoise set in dull silver.') The first part of the novel seems to me strained—overly didactic, underlining all points, the dialogue forced—but when we move to the mesa, the writing achieves that effortless symbolic quality which is Cather's distinctive note and best achievement, in which everything seems radiant and significant, but in a way no one could precisely explain.

The pattern in *The Song of the Lark* and *The Professor's House* is repeated in her work as a whole. She alternates between two modes—a more conventional realism, which is evoked when she sets herself the task of describing people in groups, living in houses, and a more abstract and lyrical mode, evoked by people against a landscape. Writing about indoor people—Thea Kronborg, Bartley Alexander, Godfrey St Peter—she writes in small strokes, with more circumstantial detail, with more accounts of what people think and say. Her first novel, *Alexander's Bridge*, was in this mode and has always reminded readers of the work of Henry James and Edith Wharton. Later, Cather preferred to think of *O Pioneers!* as her first novel, because it was the one in which she discovered the lyrical mode that she considered her authentic style. It is the mode in which her best books—*My Ántonia*, and *Death Comes for the Archbishop* as well as *O Pioneers!*—are written.[6] Deeply associated with it, perhaps necessary to generate it, is the quality I have been calling scale.

I have already touched on the way in which scale determines an approach to character, but I would like to go into it more fully. The illusion of grandeur in her protagonists is another feature of Cather's most exhilarating work, and this illusion, I suggest, depends on simplification.

We are first introduced to Alexandra Bergson, for example, through the eyes of a traveling salesman who is never named, whose role is never developed, whose sole function is to provide a perspective on the heroine. And what does he think of her? That she is 'a fine human creature' who makes him wish he was more of a man. That is, she makes an impact without individuation. Although Alexandra has a good deal of character—she is placid, firm, in some ways a visionary (about the future of the Divide), yet wholly unimaginative about other people's emotions—Cather's presentation of her consists of broad strokes. Alexandra is not clever in the manner of city-bred and well-educated people, such as the characters Cather had written about in *Alexander's Bridge*; and that absence of cleverness allowed—perhaps forced—Cather to treat character in a new way in *O Pioneers!*. Alexandra cannot be an interesting 'center of consciousness' in a Jamesian sense, because her consciousness is insufficiently complex. Nor is it the most important part of her.

> Her personal life, her own realisation of herself, was almost a subconscious existence; like an underground river that came to the surface only here and there, at intervals months apart, and then sank again to flow under her fields. (p. 203)

Her conscious mind is a 'white book, with clear writing about weather and beasts and growing things. Not many people would have cared to read it' (p. 205). So we do not explore her consciousness. We see her resolutely from the outside, and this, along with Cather's persistent contrast of her in terms of size to those around her ('"What a hopeless position you are in, Alexandra!" [Carl] exclaimed feverishly. "It is your fate to be always surrounded by little men,"' p. 181), creates the illusion of grandeur which is a distinguishing trait of Cather's heroines, although they may be as different in background and personality as Ántonia Shimerda and Marian Forrester.

For Jamesian centers of consciousness, Cather substitutes objects of admiration. Her favorite narrator is the adoring young person, usually a man, creating out of some woman a creature with mythic resonance: Jim Burden and Ántonia, Niel Herbert and Marian Forrester in *A Lost Lady*, also Nellie Birdseye and Myra Henshawe in *My Mortal Enemy*. Ántonia provides the best example, for she is not so much characterised as mythicised from the opening – 'This girl seemed to mean to us the country, the conditions, the whole adventure of our childhood' – to the conclusion:

> She lent herself to immemorial attitudes which we recognise by instinct as universal and true . . . She had only to stand in the orchard, to put her hand on a little crab tree and look up at the apples, to make you feel the goodness of planting and tending and harvesting at last . . . She was a rich mine of life, like the founders of early races. (p. 353)

Ántonia lingers in the mind more as a goddess of fertility than as an individuated woman; to Jim, certainly, she is archetypal woman, her face 'the closest, realest face, under all the shadows of women's faces' (p. 322).

Cather shared the impatience with individuated character that she saw reflected in the way southwestern Indians spoke English or Spanish, dropping the definite articles: not 'the mountain' but 'mountain'; not 'the woman' but 'woman.'[7] She often presents her characters as conduits for a divine spirit, raised above human powers by some force above or below consciousness, approaching the condition of gods, goddesses, or saints. In her portrait of Archbishop Latour, who could so easily have been made to seem a cathedral-building, executive, and managerial paragon, Cather goes out of her way to deemphasise willed activity. We see him first when he is lost in the desert, able to forget his own thirst through meditation on and identification with Christ's agony on the cross, and from then on, his 'story' is largely a record of his finding or losing the spirit of God. Cather repeatedly chooses artists as subjects because she has an archaic sense of the way, in performing or creating, they are possessed by divine inspiration, a sacred breath that blows away consciousness of the petty circumstances of their lives, so that Thea Kronborg, for example, can look harried and fatigued in the afternoon, but that night, performing at the Met, she is the essence of youthful idealism.

Cather's art is peculiarly keen at registering surges of energy and at noting the presence or absence of spirit—in an innocent girl like Lucy Gayheart or in an amoral woman like Marian Forrester, who resembles Lucy only in that she puts her whole heart into everything she does. Indeed, most of Cather's heroines—Lucy, Marian, Ántonia, and Alexandra—have the capacity, sometimes harmful to themselves, to live so intensely that they seem like powers more than people, and one sometimes feels that Cather has set herself the task of portraying pure spirit divorced from circumstance, that background and circumstance are merely accidents, and that in the earth-mother Ántonia as in the bitchy, bitter Myra Henshawe, what is essential is the vital breath. Although she would have been appalled by the terms 'blood knowledge' and 'head knowledge,' Cather resembles Lawrence in her desire to bypass the conscious and intellectual elements in her characters in quest of the instinctual and unconscious. These elements she found most accessible in simple people like the farmers of the Divide, in the devout, like the Old World Catholics of her later books, or, in their ideal imagined form, Indians. (When Mabel Dodge married Tony Luhan, a Taos Indian, and many of her friends asked how she could do it, Willa Cather reportedly said, 'How could she not?')

But if Cather and Lawrence were in some sense after the same thing in their characters, they went about it in very different ways, and she attacks him as a mere cataloguer of physical sensations and emotions in her most important critical statement, 'The Novel Démeublé.' Most of this essay is a rather predictable attack on the novel of physical realism which she calls 'over-furnished,' overly devoted to description and observation. Balzac serves as her example of misguided labor, as Bennett, Wells, and Galsworthy served in Virginia Woolf's comparable manifestos, 'Modern Fiction' and 'Mr Bennett and Mrs Brown.' Balzac, says Cather, wanted to put the city of Paris on paper, with all its houses, upholstery, games of chance and pleasure, even its foods. This was a mistake, she believes.

> The things by which he still lives, the types of greed and avarice and ambition and vanity and lost innocence of heart which he created—are as vital today as they were then. But their material surroundings, upon which he expended such labor and pains ... the eye glides over them.[8]

At this point Cather moves away from Woolf, who rejected physical realism in favor of psychological realism, outer for inner, including Lawrence in her camp, and moves instead toward an aesthetic of the archetypal, toward Jung rather than Freud. In a brilliant maneuver, she asserts that it is possible to be a materialistic enumerator about the inner life as well as the outer and offers Lawrence as her example. Cataloguing sensations, he robs the great stories of their intrinsic grandeur. 'Can one imagine anything more terrible than the story of *Romeo and Juliet* rewritten in prose by D.H. Lawrence?'[9] The minds of one's characters can be overfurnished, too, and in detailing the crockery and footstools of their interior life we can lose track of the distinctive forms of their humanity.

In her insistence on presenting her characters from the outside, in her refusal to explore their subjectivity, Cather seems to fly most conspicuously in the face of modernism, but that is because we have overidentified modernism in the novel with the techniques of interior monologue and stream of consciousness. Interior monologue and Cather's resolutely external treatment are equally reactions against traditional characterisation. If we posit a traditional method of characterisation in which the inner expresses itself in the outer—both action and physical surroundings—in which character is compassable, knowable, and if we think of this as a middle-distance shot, then interior monologue may be thought of as a close-up, emphasising uniqueness and individuality to the point of unknowability, and Cather's method of characterisation as a kind of long shot, emphasising the archetypal and eternally human, acknowledging individuality, perhaps, but not exploring it. Joyce tried to incorporate both the close-up and the long shot in his presentation of Leopold Bloom by suggesting that this highly individuated man was an avatar of Odysseus; Virginia Woolf seems to want to present eternal types in *The Waves* and to some extent in *Between the Acts*; and Lawrence likes to show his characters in the grip of cosmic forces, wrenched away from the personal. By abandoning the attempt to represent interior consciousness, by her resolute externality, Cather in her own way participated in the attempt to render the generally human as opposed to the individual. This is what I mean by the urge to abstraction in her handling of character (although 'abstraction' is inevitably an imprecise and somewhat irritating word as applied to literature): her downplaying of individuality, her lack of interest in 'personality' as opposed to essential force.

Heroic simplification is the essence of Cather's approach to character, and I will offer a visual analogy of this which Cather herself provides. In *My Ántonia*, Jim Burden and the Bohemian girls picnic on the banks of the river, and, as the sun begins to set, they notice a curious and striking phenomenon:

> Just as the lower edge of the red disk rested on the high fields against the horizon, a great black figure suddenly appeared on the face of the sun. We sprang to our feet, straining our eyes toward it. In a moment we realised what it was. On some upland farm, a plough had been left standing in the field. The sun was sinking just behind it. Magnified across the distance by the horizontal light, it stood out against the sun, was exactly contained within the circle of the disk; the handles, the tongue, the share—black against the molten red. There it was, heroic in size, a picture writing against the sun. (p. 245)

When the sun goes down further, the plough sinks back into its own littleness somewhere on the prairie, but it is the moment of heroic magnification that intrigues Willa Cather.

Naive readers responding to *O Pioneers!* or *My Ántonia* or *Death Comes for the Archbishop* have trouble seeing these works as novels. They appear to be collections of vignettes or sketches, and the connection between the parts is not always evident. This response is useful, reminding us how unconventional Cather's approach to form really is. Except in *The Song of the Lark*, her most traditional novel, Cather pays no more attention to plot than Woolf does in *To the Lighthouse* and looks for unity to mood. 'It is hard now to realise how revolutionary in form *My Ántonia* was at that time in America,' wrote Edith Lewis, Cather's companion. 'It seemed to many people to have no form.'[10]

In the first part of *My Ántonia*, for example, one comes suddenly upon a story so powerful that it threatens to throw the novel off track: the story of Pavel and Peter, who, back in Russia, had been carrying a bride and groom home from their wedding in a sled over snow by moonlight, when the entire party was set upon by wolves. To lighten their load and make it to safety, Pavel and Peter throw the bride out of the sled to be devoured by the wolves. At first this violent, horrific story seems separate from the novel as a whole, but with time one's mind weaves it into the fabric. It serves as a prologue to the grim winter in which Mr Shimerda, unable to endure longer the hostility of nature, shoots himself. And in the sacrifice of the bride so that Pavel and Peter may reach the safety of town, the story states, with the starkness of folktale, the theme of sexuality sacrificed to advancement which is the heart of the book. But the real power of the story, it seems to me, comes from our awareness that Pavel and Peter are ordinary men whose lives had once been suddenly shifted into the realm of elemental forces, then dropped back down again into the ordinary, men metaphorically struck by lightning who go back the next day—or the next month—to milking cows. Their detachment from their horrendous experience is what is so moving, precisely their failure to incorporate it into the texture of their lives. The narrative exemplifies the way in which Cather's fiction moves between the quotidian and the elemental, not forcing the former to render up its potential for transcendence, nor demanding that the latter be everywhere manifest, but acknowledging the abrupt transformations of the ordinary into the ghastly or elemental or transcendent.

Other writers, hardly modernists, have used inset stories—Cervantes and Dickens, for example. But in Cather the folktale material is not framed by the rest of the narrative; it penetrates it, bringing what might be read merely as naturalistic narrative into the realm of the mythic, so that, later in the novel, we are aesthetically prepared, though still surprised and shocked, when a tramp wanders in from the prairie, climbs onto a threshing machine, waves his hand gaily, and jumps head first into the blades. Why should a tramp be immune to despair? Heroic emotions are not just for heroes.

Cather routinely works with mythic incident (Jim's killing of the giant rattlesnake, a dragon-slaying episode that proves his manhood, although the rattlesnake is definitely a rattlesnake at the same time as it is, psychically, a dragon), with folk material, and with dreams. Naturalism coexists with symbolism. Lena Lingard may be an upwardly mobile, sexy, independent dressmaker in Lincoln, Nebraska, when Jim is a student there, but she is at the same time what she appears to him in a dream: a woman in a wheat field with a scythe, both a symbol of harvest and a figure threatening death, the pleasant death of his will and ambition by surrender to her compelling sensuality. Lena, the Danish laundry girls, and the three Bohemian Marys are to Jim—and Cather—joyous, evocative figures out of Virgilian rural life ('If there were no girls like them in the world, there would be no poetry'), and Jim, the student, is simultaneously Virgil ('For I shall be the first if I live to bring the Muse into my country,' p. 264).

With such an emphasis on the timeless, with the way in which human beings embody recurrent impulses and attitudes, with Swedish immigrant girls in Nebraska as avatars of Virgilian rustics, no wonder *My Ántonia* defies the traditional temporal organisation of plot. Dorothy Van Ghent has noted how, out of homely American detail, Cather composes in *My Ántonia* 'certain frieze-like entablatures that have the character of ancient ritual and sculpture.'[11] 'The suffering of change, the sense of irreparable loss in time, is one polarity of the work; the other polarity is the timelessness of those images associated with Ántonia, with the grave of the suicide at the crossroads, with the mute fortitude of the hired men and the pastoral poetry of the hired girls, and most of all with the earth itself.'[12] In appreciating Cather's instinct for the timeless, Van Ghent begins to see the implications in formal terms of that instinct, the 'frieze-like entablatures,' the sculptural and abstract forms throughout Cather's work. 'The boldest and most beautiful of Willa Cather's fictions are characterised by a sense of the past not as an irrecoverable quality of events, wasted in history, but as persistent human truths—salvaged, redeemed—by virtue of memory and art.'[13]

Most critics have noticed only the nostalgia, the 'sense of irreparable loss in time' in Cather's work, a thematic emphasis that leads them to misperceive her art as traditional. This is like confounding Georgia O'Keeffe's skulls, crosses, and flowers with Landseer's dogs. Leon Edel, for example, demanding a representational three-dimensionality foreign to Cather's art, can only be dissatisfied with *The Professor's House* for offering, as he says repeatedly in his 'psychoanalytic' reading of that novel, no explanation for the professor's depression.[14] Forced to invent a narrative wholly outside the text, Edel offers an explanation, essentially that Cather herself was regressive, infantile, and so depressed when she was deprived of Isabelle McClung's maternal attention by her marriage to Jan Hambourg that she wrote her depression into Godfrey St Peter without enough distinction between herself and her character to provide him with motivation. But Cather has her own notion of personal development, which is very well articulated in *The Professor's House*: she imagines childhood as a stage of pure being, divorced from accomplishment; in the middle years, from adolescence on, fueled by sexual energy, one asserts one's identity both through one's work and family life; old age is a return to a stage of pure being, a sadder or a richer childhood. The professor is at the end of the second stage of his life, his identity played out, his daughters grown and his work accomplished; his depression marks his transition to the third stage. In *Death Comes for the Archbishop* Cather would present her protagonist as having successfully performed the transition that was so difficult and painful for Professor St Peter. The Archbishop

> was soon to have done with calendared time, and it had already ceased to count for him. He sat in the middle of his own consciousness; none of his former states of mind were lost or outgrown. They were all within reach of his hand, and all comprehensible. (p. 290)

Van Ghent, with her interest in primitive religion and myth, can understand what Cather is trying to do in her representation of old age. Edel, with his interest in Freudian analysis of a crude sort, insisting on the individual etiology of every 'symptom,' cannot even begin to understand. For him, *Death Comes for the Archbishop*, one of Cather's masterpieces, is an exercise in nostalgia, signaling Cather's final retreat into the past. That, indeed, is the way most critics of the forties and fifties — all dominated by a moralistic response to Cather, all disposed to condemn her for retreating into the past, all viewing her as a traditionalist — saw that book.[15]

In fact, from a formal point of view, *Death Comes for the Archbishop*, that extraordinary compilation of vivid scenes and great stories which ignores chronological time, is the most daring and innovative of Cather's works. It perfectly embodies the anti-illusionist aesthetic which many of her early books strove for. I will quote Cather's own excellent description of what she was trying to accomplish and, I believe, did accomplish:

> I had all my life wanted to do something in the style of legend, which is absolutely the reverse of dramatic treatment. Since I first saw the Puvis de Chavannes frescoes of the life of St Genevieve in my student days, I have wished that I could try something a little like that in prose; something without accent, with none of the artificial elements of composition. In the Golden Legend the martyrdoms of the saints are no more dwelt upon than are the trivial incidents of their lives; it is as though all human experiences, measured against one supreme spiritual experience, were of about the same importance. The essence of such writing is not to hold the note, not to use an incident for all there is in it — but to touch and pass on. I felt that such writing would be a discipline in these days when the 'situation' is made to count for so much in writing, when the general tendency is to force things up. In this kind of writing the mood is the thing — all the little figures and stories are mere improvisations that come out of it.[16]

Cather had begun her writing career imitating the 'dramatic treatment' of Henry James. But what she had always been moving toward was what she calls here 'legend.' The distinctive note of modernism appears in her aspiration to do 'something without accent,' in her impatience with 'artificial elements of composition,' with traditional climaxes and resolutions ('not a single button sewn on as the Bond Street tailors would have it,' said Virginia Woolf).[17] Musically speaking, this lifelong lover of opera repudiates the operatic ('holding the note') as a model for fiction and turns instead—rather astonishingly—to jazz, with its emphasis on mood-generating 'improvisations.'

The attempt to write 'something in the style of legend' involved the pursuit of another aesthetic quality: anonymity. This was hard for Cather to achieve. She had been a high school teacher; more important, she had suffered in her youth from the disapproval of her community, who regarded her nonconformity with distaste. She could never quite stop telling them off for it, and the theme of opposition between philistine materialism and artistic dedication too often evokes a marring didacticism in her work. The way she overcame the urge to preach was by complete submission to her material, which she said she learned from the example of Sarah Orne Jewett. And when she suppressed herself, she did it more completely than any writer I can think of.

The clarity and simplicity—the sheer absence of eccentricity—of Cather's prose style contributes to the effect of anonymity. She adheres to the traditional structure of the English sentence—subject, verb, object—as the surest way of suppressing individuality. Rarely does one find any complicated syntax. There are passages in Cather's writing that stop the heart with their beauty, but they are never purple passages in the usual sense. They tend, as in this passage, to depict moments of quiet, and they are signaled, if at all, by a toning down of the prose rather than a keying up:

> In stopping to take a breath, I happened to glance up at the canyon wall. I wish I could tell you what I saw there, just *as* I saw it, on that first morning, through a veil of lightly falling snow. Far up above me, a thousand feet or so, set in a great cavern in the face of the cliff, I saw a little city of stone, asleep. It was as still as sculpture—and something like that. It all hung together, seemed to have a kind of composition: pale little houses of stone nestling close to one another, perched on top of each other, with flat roofs, narrow windows, straight walls, and in the middle of the group, a round tower . . . It was red in colour, even on that grey day. In sunlight it was the colour of winter oak-leaves. A fringe of cedars grew along the edge of the cavern, like a garden. They were the only living things. Such silence and stillness and respose—immortal repose. That village sat looking down into the canyon with the calmness of eternity.[18]

Although the moment Cather describes here is characteristic—the small and particular raised to the monumental, the once-busy seen in eternal repose—the force of this passage resides as much in its style, in the calm, methodical notation of colors and shapes, the note of awe suggested with no overtones of hysteria, as in its content. It insists on the sculptural qualities of its subject, as Cather tends to in her descriptions of prairie and sky as well.

The prose is by no means flowery, but neither is it as stark as it might be, as Hemingway's is, for example, There is a softness about it which comes from Cather's willingness to offer neutral elaboration. 'In the sunlight it was the colour of winter oak-leaves'—this is a nice detail but not hypercharged, as it might appear in Hemingway, where the excessively stripped-down quality of the prose makes everything seem almost too significant. Cather's range is more comfortable, and the effect is to reduce, symbolically, the glare. Georgia O'Keeffe comes to mind again, as opposed to Dali or Magritte.

O'Keeffe, Sheeler, and other visual artists allied, however loosely, with Precisionism in America offer a good example of aesthetic urges similar to Cather's, generated from analogous but different sources and worked out quite independently. The aim of the Precisionists was simplification of form, and this joined an impulse toward monumentalising ordinary objects —Sheeler's 'Totems in Steel,' for example, a rendering of steel girders on a building project, or his eerie stairwells or imperious ladder-back chairs, or O'Keeffe's resonant adobe houses. Cather particularly recalls O'Keeffe in her response to the Southwest, in her homage to the scale of the American landscape, in her ability to monumentalise the ordinary, and in her gift for generating a sense of mystery out of simplified forms.[19] Cather's sources of inspiration invite comparison with Sheeler's. Sheeler's formalism fed on a deeply native tradition which was not in itself modernist: he was a student of Shaker furniture and Shaker barns. Similarly, Cather took strength from what she saw as a native example of functionalism, the stories of Sarah Orne Jewett. In describing Jewett's work, Cather distinguished between two kinds of beauty: the beauty of the Chinese junk, which comes from ornamentation and embellishment, and the beauty of the racing yacht, in which every line is subsumed to purpose.[20] The beauty of Jewett's prose, to Cather, was the sleek, functional, pared-down beauty of the yacht, and although it is possible to imagine a stripping down and functionalism that goes well beyond Cather's—Hemingway, again—that is certainly the beauty she aspired to herself.

Every great writer is an innovator, forging his or her own style in the face of the seductive force of the conventional. We must mean more than that when we use the term 'modernist.' Critics of the sixties tended to identify modernism in the novel with subjectivity, but newer accounts of modernism tend to emphasise art's awareness of its own artificial status.[21] The modernists themselves, however, did not unanimously recognise that what they were producing was semiotically precocious fiction; nor were all of them effective theorists of their own positions. Joyce talked about the artist refined out of existence. Eliot talked about art as an escape from personality. Flaubert aspired to write a novel about nothing. Woolf talked about capturing the luminous halo of life. In this company, Cather, with her talk of the 'novel *démeublé*,' seems the least critically sophisticated, yet it is certainly in this company that she belongs. In modernist critical writings, including Cather's, certain themes recur: an urge to shake loose of clutter, a refusal to accept the mimetic function of art as previously defined, a feeling that a certain 'spirit' was escaping the older forms, an urge toward anonymity. The vessel is emphasised rather than the content; art is imagined as a fragile container for the ineffable substance of life. Thea Kronborg speaks for Cather:

> What was any art but an attempt to make a sheath, a mould in which to imprison for a moment the shining, elusive element which is life itself, — life hurrying past us and running away, too strong to stop, too sweet to lose? The Indian women had held it in their jars.[22]

The modernists were aware of art as created artifact, not as a mirror reflecting reality or a camera eye absorbing and imprinting it. Nothing could be further from the modernist temper than Dreiser's boast about *Sister Carrie* that it was not intended as a piece of literary craftsmanship but as a picture of conditions. The modernists often, like Cather, looked to Flaubert as their Ur-aesthetician, with his emphasis on style, surface, disciplined craft; but the wittiest theorist of modernism was Oscar Wilde, whose assertion that life imitates art may be seen as the key to the modernist spirit.

If we describe the modernists as self-conscious artificers who rejected mimesis as their chief business, we risk overemphasising the intellectual, game-playing, Nabokovian element in modernism. Not all experiment took place for the sake of experiment, but out of a conviction that the old forms did not capture something important in life, a 'spirit,' a force, a religious or spiritual dimension existing somewhere below or above consciousness but beyond the purviews of traditional fiction. Hence modernism's impatience with describing the here-and-now and its persistent urge to see the here-and-now in the light of, united to, all of human history: Eliot in *The Waste Land*, Pound in the *Cantos*, Joyce in *Ulysses*, and, I would suggest, Cather, in her continuing effort to tie contemporary life to a past that stretched back, in America, to the cliff dwellers and to see all human life in relation to the enduring earth.

An interest in the past and particularly in primitive cultures characterised the early twentieth century and was not just a piece of isolated nostalgia or conservatism on the part of Willa Cather. Gauguin had been impressed by Aztec sculpture at the Paris Exposition as early as 1889. Vlaminck began collecting African sculpture around 1903 and was followed in his enthusiasm for primitive art by Derain, Matisse, Modigliani, Brancusi, Moore, and Picasso, who, in 1907, incorporated renderings of African sculptures into *Les Demoiselles d'Avignon*.[23] Picasso had visited Altamira in 1902 to see the neolithic cave paintings. Lawrence left the Old World for the New in search of civilisations more ancient than the former could offer. The same impulse drove Cather to Walnut Canyon, Arizona, and later to Mesa Verde, where she found in the buildings and pottery of the Anasazi an objective correlative for aesthetic impulses she had felt in herself. Form in these cliff-dwellings followed function; the buildings blended with the landscape; towns were set inside natural caverns with the cliffs themselves providing protection from the elements. The pottery was elegantly functional, embellished only with abstract designs. No more in these designs than in Indian pictographs, no more than in the cave paintings of Altamira or in certain Greek vase painting, was there an attempt to imitate three-dimensionality on a flat surface. It is no surprise that a woman so moved by this art should also have responded strongly to the frescoes of Puvis de Chavannes, whose flat, almost friezelike figures emphasise the picture plane and refuse to create the illusion of receding space. Although Puvis de Chavannes was not himself a modernist figure, he influenced Seurat, Gauguin, Matisse, and Picasso. Most modern painting has stemmed from a refusal like his to create the illusion of three-dimensional space, often encouraged by the example of primitive, non-Western, or pre-Renaissance art. Cather's antinaturalistic *Death Comes for the Archbishop*, a series of stories so arranged as to blur the distinction between the past and the present, the miraculous and the mundane, is, I would argue, a true even if somewhat surprising example in literature of the modernist aesthetic in art, and much of her early work should be seen as moving in that direction.[24]

Visual analogues for Cather's modernism are many. The determining factor, as in so much modernist painting which exploded out of the confines of easel-sized canvases, is scale. One thinks of the wall-sized works of Picasso and Matisse, such as *Guernica* and *The Dance of Life*; one thinks of the giant canvases of Jackson Pollock and the vast areas, made to seem even vaster by their minimalist treatment, of works by Rothko, Frankenthaler, Barnett Newman; one thinks of the murals of Orozsco and Thomas Hart Benton. To work on that scale involves simplification. The reduction to essential forms, which began in the visual arts with Cézanne, finds a literary analogue in Cather's insistence on there being only a few human stories which are told over and over. Her refusal to follow the twists and turns of her characters' individual thoughts, her insistence on seeing them as 'human creatures,' subject to an endlessly recurring cycle of emotions, recalls Cézanne's insistence that the cone, the circle, and the square are at the basis of everything we see. If her novels seem consequently simple, their simplicity has the same aim as Klee's figures, Matisse's late abstract cutouts, or Picasso's consciously childlike drawings. It is a simplicity that aims to capture the elemental and enduring and that requires the greatest art to produce.

However fragmented their initial impact, both *The Waste Land* in its relation to *The Golden Bough* and *Ulysses* in its relation to the *Odyssey* attempt to transcend the complexity of modern life by annexing the structural simplicities of myth. Embracing multiplicity but animated by an urge to abstraction, they attempt to search through the historical and accidental to the fundamental. The appropriate stance for the artist in the face of such mythic and archetypal material is anonymity. The appropriate style is no style. Joyce in *Ulysses* sought to approximate 'no style' by parodying all styles. Gertrude Stein and Hemingway sought to produce an anonymous surface by means of prose styles of the utmost plainness, stripped of all ornament and connotation. But the lucid prose of Willa Cather makes even Hemingway's sentences look mannered. And as for Gertrude Stein, it is one of the many ironies of modernism that the pursuit of simplicity and anonymity produced works of such futile complexity and obtrusive personality. Like many other modernist artists, Cather sought to bypass consciousness and the circumstantial details with which it concerns itself and to produce an art that appealed to the most elemental layers of our minds. Her enduring popularity with readers shows that she succeeded, and critics ought now to take account of her success.[25]

Notes

1. David Daiches, *Willa Cather: A Critical Introduction* (Ithaca, New York: Cornell University Press, 1951), p. 189.
2. I borrow the phrase from Robert Pinsky, whose tribute to Cather forms an important part of his epic poem, *An Explanation of America* (Princeton, N.J.: Princeton University Press, 1979).
3. Willa Cather, *O Pioneers!* (Boston: Houghton Mifflin, n.d.), p. 84. Further citations of this work, identified by page numbers in the text, refer to this edition.
4. Willa Cather, *My Ántonia* (Boston: Houghton Mifflin, n.d.), pp. 15–16. Further citations of this work, identified by page numbers in the text, refer to this edition.
5. Willa Cather, 'On *The Professor's House*,' in *Willa Cather on Writing* (New York: Knopf, 1949), p. 31.
6. See Cather, 'My First Novels [There Were Two],' in *Willa Cather on Writing*, pp. 91–97.
7. See Cather, *Death Comes for the Archbishop* (New York: Vintage Books, 1971), p. 91. Further citations of this work, identified by page numbers in the text, refer to this edition.
8. *Willa Cather on Writing*, pp. 38–39.
9. Ibid., p. 42.
10. Edith Lewis, *Willa Cather Living* (New York: Knopf, 1953), p. 107.
11. Dorothy Van Ghent, *Willa Cather*, University of Minnesota Pamphlets on American Writers, no. 36 (Minneapolis: University of Minnesota Press, 1964), p. 23. Like just about everything Van Ghent wrote, this is an inspired piece of literary criticism and the best short appreciation of Cather that exists. The closest thing to a standard biography of Cather is E.K. Brown, *Willa Cather: A Critical Biography* (New York: Knopf, 1953), completed by Leon Edel after Brown's death. Also useful is James Woodress, *Willa Cather: Her Life and Art* (New York: Pegasus, 1970), and Dorothy Tuck McFarland's brief treatment of all the novels, *Willa Cather* (New York: Frederick Ungar, 1972).
12. Van Ghent, *Willa Cather*, pp. 24–25.
13. Ibid., p. 5.
14. In Leon Edel, *Literary Biography* (New York: Doubleday, 1959), pp. 99–122. Edel's brief overview of Cather's career, a lecture printed as a pamphlet and called 'The Paradox of Success,' is equally punitive, arguing that Cather projects her personal experience onto American history—life is good and interesting to her when she is struggling for success, but once she achieves it everything goes flat, and she becomes nostalgic for the past and its struggles. Consequently, Edel sees Cather's career in three stages: the great early period (*O Pioneers!*, *The Song of the Lark*, *My Ántonia*), the middle years of disillusionment (*One of Ours*, *A Lost Lady*, *The Professor's House*, *My Mortal Enemy*), and the final period of nostalgia (*Death Comes for the Archbishop*, *Shadows on the Rock*, *Lucy Gayheart*). This means that her 'early period' lasted about five years (1913–1918), her middle period seven (1919–1926), while her late period extended

over the last twenty years of her life. I prefer to see the period of Cather's greatest creativity as running from 1913, with the publication of *O Pioneers!*, right through to 1927, the year in which *Death Comes for the Archbishop* was published. That was also the year Cather had to leave the Bank Street apartment in which she and Edith Lewis had lived very comfortably from 1912. Lewis says their enforced departure from Bank Street marked an epoch in Cather's life, and without meaning to imply that her creativity was tied to that apartment, I will say that to regard the years from 1912 to 1927 as a single 'period' makes more sense than Edel's three-stage paradigm.

15. Maxwell Geismar is typical, reproving Cather for 'this movement *back* in terms of time and place, this movement *away* from the real areas of human feeling,' in *The Last of the Provincials: The American Novel, 1915-1925* (Boston: Houghton Mifflin, 1947), p. 196, but Kazin, Trilling, and Daiches are equally agreed that Cather is concerned only with the past and are equally censorious. See Alfred Kazin, 'Elegy and Satire: Willa Cather and Ellen Glasgow,' in *On Native Grounds* (New York: Harcourt Brace, 1942), pp. 247-264; Lionel Trilling, 'Willa Cather,' in *After the Genteel Tradition*, ed. Malcolm Cowley (New York: Norton, 1937), pp. 52-63; and David Daiches, *Willa Cather: A Critical Introduction*, cited above. James Schroeter, in *Willa Cather and Her Critics* (Ithaca: Cornell University Press, 1967), suggests it was Cather's status in the thirties as a literary darling of right-wing critics that generated the attack from the left, of which he offers as an example Granville Hicks's 'The Case against Willa Cather' (1933). Left and right, however, differed little in what they saw in Cather's work; they differed only in whether or not they approved of it.

Nina Baym has argued that critics of American literature have always been more interested in defining the American 'character' and American cultural essence than in literary questions, and she shows how this preoccupation has led to the exclusion of women writers from the canon of American literature. See 'Melodramas of Beset Manhood: How Theories of American Fiction Exclude Women Authors,' *American Quarterly*, 33, no. 2 (Summer 1981), 123-139. In Cather's case, the persistent approach to her work in terms of content (the search for 'cultural essence') has led to a misunderstanding of the novels' form, which further distorts readers' perceptions of their content.

16. *Willa Cather on Writing*, pp. 9-10.

17. Virginia Woolf, 'Modern Fiction,' in *Collected Essays*, 4 vols. (New York: Harcourt, Brace and World, 1967), II, 106. 'The accent falls differently from of old; the moment of importance came not here but there; so that, if a writer were a free man and not a slave, if he could write what he chose, not what he must, if he could base his work on his own feeling and not upon convention, there would be no plot, no comedy, no tragedy, no love interest or catastrophe in the accepted style, and perhaps not a single button sewn on as the Bond Street tailors would have it.'

18. Willa Cather, *The Professor's House* (New York: Vintage Books, 1973), p. 201.

19. See Jules David Prown and Barbara Rose, *American Painting* (New York: Rizzoli, 1977), p. 144. On Sheeler, see Martin Friedman, *Charles Sheeler* (New York: Watson-Guptill Publications, 1975). The thrill of the native discovery of abstraction is recorded—so ecstatically as to verge on the comic—in the Daybooks of Edward Weston, particularly in those sections dealing with his 1930 photographs of peppers: 'Twenty years of effort ... have gone into the making of this pepper, which I consider a peak of achievement. It is classic, completely satisfying—a pepper—but more than a pepper: abstract, in that it is completely outside subject matter. It has no psychological attributes, no human emotions are aroused: this new pepper takes one beyond the world we know in the conscious mind. To be sure much of my work has this quality,—many of my last year's peppers, but this one, and in fact all the new ones, take one into an inner reality—the absolute—with a clear understanding, a mystic revealment.' *Edward Weston: The Flame of Recognition*, ed. Nancy Newhall (Millerton, N.Y.: Aperture Monograph. 1975), p. 34.

20. See Willa Cather, 'Preface to *The Best Short Stories of Sarah Orne Jewett*,' in *Willa Cather on Writing*, pp. 57-58. She takes the image from Gilbert Murray, who used it to define the beauty of ancient Greek literature.

21. See David Lodge, *Modernism, Antimodernism, and Postmodernism* (Birmingham, England: University of Birmingham Press, 1977).

22. Willa Cather, *The Song of the Lark* (Lincoln: University of Nebraska Press, 1978), p. 304.

23. Stieglitz channeled the European interest in primitivism into America, organising a show of African sculpture at his gallery in New York in 1914. For an excellent summary of modern artists' interest in primitive art (a term the author would dislike), see Douglas Newton, 'The Art

of Africa, the Pacific Islands, and the Americas,' *The Metropolitan Museum of Art Bulletin*, 39, no. 2 (Fall 1981), especially pp. 7–10.

24. For Puvis de Chavannes' influence on modernist painting, see Robert Hughes, *The Shock of the New* (New York: Knopf, 1981), p. 116. For my sense of how the modernist novel is engaged in 'transmuting the time world of history into the timeless world of myth' and of how the reaction against temporal sequence is the key to its form, and for much else, including analogies between modernist literature and the visual arts and an account of how naturalistic and non-naturalistic styles have tended to alternate through history, I am indebted to Joseph Frank's 'Spatial Form in Modern Literature,' in *The Widening Gyre: Crisis and Mastery in Modern Literature* (Bloomington, Ind. and London: Indiana University Press, 1963), pp. 3–62.

25. I would like to express my gratitude to Paul Alpers and to Alex Zwerdling for discussions of the material in this essay and critiques of the manuscript and to the students in my course on Willa Cather in the spring quarter of 1982 at the University of California, Berkeley, for specific insights and general enthusiasm.

162
From *Shifting Gears: Technology, Literature, Culture in Modernist America*

CECELIA TICHI

[. . .] This was the world of *Alexander's Bridge* (1912), the title of Willa Cather's first major novel, which concerns a master bridge engineer of worldwide renown. Cather's form is at least as important as her subject. *Alexander's Bridge* is committed to the values of the waning Romantic era. If Wright speaks for artists exploiting the machine age, Cather typifies those others who felt threatened by the engineering power from which they felt excluded. In the novel, Alexander's bridge is not a structure but an organic symbol. It is not an artifact of component parts but an evocation of the spiritual-psychological state of the man whose life it represents. Its significance does not lie in its statement on design, but only in what the symbol reveals about the spiritual state of the person it represents. Its importance lies in what it means, and its meaning lies beyond itself. As a structure with its own design integrity, it is negligible, unimportant.

Cather only flirts once with the idea of a component-part aesthetics of engineering. The bridges of her engineer-character do have, she concedes, artistic value. 'Have you ever seen his first suspension bridge in Canada?' asks her engineer's wife, showing a photograph of the bridge to Alexander's former professor. The impeccably tasteful Mrs Alexander describes the 'bridal' bridge as spanning the 'wildest river, with mists and clouds always battling about it . . . as delicate as a cobweb hanging in the sky' (17–18).

The figure of the cobweb has great potential for perception of the gear-and-girder world. It could have given Cather easy access to an appreciation

SOURCE   Cecelia Tichi, from *Shifting Gears: Technology, Literature, Culture in Modernist America*, Chapel Hill: University of North Carolina Press, 1987, pp. 173–80

of component-part design in nature and culture. As one journalist wrote, 'A suspension bridge represents the highest mechanical, mathematical, and engineering skill, and yet is only the adaptation of a spider's web to man's requirements' ('Natural Form and Mechanical Design' 463). Cather could have looked into the aesthetic values of the structure, exploited them, and welcomed the engineer as a fellow in the arts. In turn, she could have gained an invaluable sense of the potential that the novelist could have as a designer in the contemporary world.

Yet Cather felt threat, not fellowship. In fiction she held fast to the traditional romantic worldview. In that world fiction was synonymous with story, its form presumed to be organically whole. It was formally natural, not constructed. It hearkened always to a preindustrial world of spiritual values thought to be inherent in nature. Cather's identity and fictional realm belonged to the world Thoreau described when he called poetry a 'natural fruit' and said that 'man bears a poem . . . as naturally as the oak bears an acorn and the vine a gourd.' That fidelity to a unified, spiritually whole, organic world set Cather in opposition to the world of gear-and-girder technology in which trees, animals, and engines were all perceived as constructions. The romantic Cather could only see the encroachment of engineers and their worldview as a threat. She used fiction to try to expose the danger of the engineers and to plead for the restoration of a waning world.

Cather typifies those writers and artists who were frightened and angry, and motivated principally by their sense of immediate danger. They, too, lived in urban areas replete with machines and steel-framed structures. But they saw no imaginative opportunities in the component parts of structural or mechanical engineering. Feeling threatened by technology, they reacted with attacks on the engineer, his bridges, his buildings, his machines. They disparaged the technological mind as narrow, dangerous, and unimaginative, and invited readers to rededicate themselves to the traditional source of spiritual vitality, the written word kept pure and uncontaminated by technological influences. Willa Cather, Sherwood Anderson, and the young Lewis Mumford belong in this group.

Early in the twentieth century, then, Alexander's bridge was directly opposed to Frank Lloyd Wright's blocks. They represented two separate and distinct worlds. In 1912, in fact, Cather declared war on modern technology in two works of fiction, a short story and a novel.

Cather's story, 'Behind the Singer Tower,' is set in the aftermath of a catastrophic hotel fire in which over three hundred people have died, among them many corporation presidents and dignitaries. The luxury hotel 'was the complete expression of the New York idea in architecture.' In price and proportion it 'outscaled everything in the known world.' Yet its interior burned with 'incredible speed.' Its fire escapes melted as some guests plunged hundreds of feet toward 'cobwebby life nets.' As the aura of invincibility vanishes, the charnel house exposes the myth of so-called fireproof tall buildings and discredits the skyscraper per se. 'The New York idea [will] be called to account by every state in the Union, by all the capitals of the world.'

From a motor launch offshore in the Hudson River the narrator, a newspaperman, recounts the events of the fire and observes the city skyline. The 'incredible towers of stone and steel' seem a lonely, confused grouping, and he imagines the city to be protesting, asserting its helplessness and its outrage at those responsible for this new vertical profile. He ponders American values gone awry.

> Our whole scheme of life and progress and profit [is] perpendicular. There [is] nothing for us but height . . . [W]e depend upon the ever-growing possibilities of girders and rivets as Holland depends upon her dikes (44, 46).

The conversation in the launch turns toward other buildings and the engineers who plan them. Here Cather's tone turns vitriolic in its anti-Semitism. One of the passengers remarks on 'what a Jewy thing the Singer Tower is when it's lit up' (46). The group blames the ideals of open immigration for the enormity of the commercial skyscraper. Then the story recounts the life of the engineer who built the burned hotel. He is half Jewish and thereby genetically corrupt. All his motives are commercial. Readers are left to surmise that the catastrophe has been caused by criminal negligence fostered by his Semitic greed.

In its own structure 'Behind the Singer Tower' is uncertain. Its narrative parts seem cobbled together. But the story makes a clear, strong statement against the power Cather discerns in the engineer. A greedy heathen, he builds the structures to which human life is sacrificed, from the foundation workers to the window washers who plunge to their deaths at the rate of one a day, to the guests and employees seduced and destroyed by the engineers' hubris masquerading as expertise. But the story also suggests the extent to which Cather felt threatened by the engineers' new world. Even as a charred ruin it is 'massive and brutally unconcerned,' the very material embodiment of its designers. The author's bigotry is a measure of her anxiety.

The source of that anxiety was amply revealed in *Alexander's Bridge* (1912), the novel focused on another engineering failure. We meet Bartley Alexander, the great engineer, in mid-life and discover that Cather's protagonist conforms biographically to the engineers of the popular novels. By birth a poor westerner, Alexander worked his way to Paris to study, thereafter becoming the protégé of an eminent bridge engineer who, facing death, designates Alexander his heir apparent. The young engineer succeeds and has since married a wealthy and elegant Bostonian who represents fine taste and eastern tradition. We see their Beacon Hill life together as one of formal ritual, of elegant dinners, of tea in the drawing room. Cather makes it clear that the couple deeply love and admire each other. As for Alexander's career, at forty-three he is a man rich in honors, moving with professional ease between Britain and America, and lecturing in Japan at the emperor's request. He has several bridges under construction throughout the United States but is primarily involved in 'the most important piece of bridge-building going on in the world,' a Canadian bridge over the St Lawrence River 'designed to be the longest cantilever in existence' (36-37).

Alexander, however, is a man in crisis. 'His existence was becoming a network of great and little details' (38). The success he thought would bring freedom and power has proven to be confining. Vowing in youth to preserve his personal liberty, he finds himself instead 'a public man . . . a cautious board member, a Nestor *de pontibus*.' He yearns to recapture the vitality of his youth, the 'wild light-heartedness' and vibrant consciousness he calls 'Life itself.' Instead, facing the 'dead calm' of middle age (and in a foreshadowing of his death by drowning) Alexander begins to feel 'buried alive.' The novel recounts the story of his life-and-death struggle between his youthful and mature selves.

Cather exploits the engineer's youth-and-mid-life crisis through the traditional literary opposition between fair and dark women. She sets the brunette Bostonian, Winifred Alexander, against the blond Irish actress, Hilda Burgoyne, the engineer's former lover now celebrated for her work on the London stage. Their reacquaintance during his stay in London turns into a resumption of the old love affair of his youth, which in turn intensifies his personal battle. Alexander's wife appeals to that civilised part of him which has learned to value 'the harmony of beautiful things that have lived together without obtrusion of ugliness or change . . . those warm consonances of color . . . blending and mellowing before he was born' (9-10). The free-spirited Hilda, on the other hand, speaks to his pagan energies, which Cather accents by imbuing her life—from her dress to the food she serves—with the tones of golden yellow that signify sexuality. The engineer's divided self is enacted in his attraction to both women and dramatised in his transatlantic crossings on a 'bridge' of steamships as he tries in vain to stabilise the conflict within.

That conflict, meanwhile, takes another symbolic form in Alexander's professional life. The niggardly commission for the Canadian bridge forces him to specify construction materials about which he feels uncertain and to design the structure close to its maximal stress limit. 'They've crowded me too much on the cost,' he says to the house guest who is Alexander's former college professor. 'It's all very well if everything goes well, but these estimates have never been used for anything of such length before' (63-64).

Here Cather makes the Canadian bridge the symbol of the engineer's tortured psyche. The professor's intuition of Alexander's 'weak spot where some day strain would tell . . . a big crack zigzagging from top to bottom' proves to be accurate, as Alexander himself acknowledges (12, 114). No sooner does he envision the terrifying personal cataclysm of 'the crack in the wall, the crash, the cloud of dust' than he is brought face to face with the moment of his death at the collapse of his great bridge, the symbol of himself. Responding to an emergency call to its construction site, Alexander has found the bridge members ready to buckle from stress. Moments too late he orders work stopped and the workmen off, then dies as the uncompleted bridge on which he stands tears 'itself to pieces with roaring and grinding and noises that were like the shrieks of a steam whistle' (125). He drowns in the clutches of panicked workmen, but we are meant to understand that the collapse of the bridge symbolises the destruction of a man unable to reconcile two antagonistic parts of his psyche.

In Alexander's torment Cather's readers can recognise at once her recurrent preoccupation with themes of the divided self, which can also be found in such novels as *My Ántonia* (1918) and *A Lost Lady* (1923). *Alexander's Bridge*, however, engages us here because it makes a trenchant statement about the antagonism Cather felt between the literary artist and the engineer. For one thing, she saw the master engineer as a figure whose distinction she thought dubious. In London her protagonist need be introduced only as 'Bartley Alexander, the American engineer,' and he is recognised on sight while traveling upcountry in New England on a railroad day coach (27, 112). As a journalist Cather had interviewed many artists and literary lions, and she appreciated celebrity status as an index of power. To cast Alexander accordingly in her novel was to acknowledge the contemporary prominence of the engineer.

By basing her novel on an actual engineering disaster, however, Cather implies that such prominence is unwarranted. In 1912 she would have expected her readers to grasp a dreadful historical connection between her story and recent events. In August 1907, the Quebec bridge on which Alexander's own is based had collapsed when a main compression member buckled, turning 19,000 tons of structural steel into twisted wreckage and killing eighty-two workmen. In the government inquiry that followed the disaster, the board charged that the bridge was designed for economy and not strength and that the dead load estimate was too low—both problems Cather attributes to the failure of Alexander's bridge. Just as in the story, 'Behind the Singer Tower,' Cather exploits a major engineering failure in fiction. This time she relies on public memory to support her suggestion that the engineer is fallible and that his personal flaws can kill and maim those who rely on his expertise.

Cather goes further, in fact, to characterise the master engineer as a machine-age barbarian. Bartley Alexander's very physique is the grotesque embodiment of technological power. His head is a catapult, his shoulders a bridge pier (9). 'The machinery was always pounding away in this man . . . [who] was only a powerful machine' (13, 39). (Cather, like most writers, fails to make a distinction between machines and structures, and so intermixes images from both.)

She also shows the engineer's barbarity of mind. The antithesis of the artist, her engineer is neither reflective nor introspective. 'Away with perspective! No past, no future for Bartley; just the fiery moment' (7, 8, 13). His former professor remembers him as 'the most tremendous response to stimuli [he has] ever known' (8). It is significant that an elderly aunt of Alexander's wife greatly admired the young engineer, for the aunt 'liked men of action . . . and had a great contempt for music and philosophy' (18-19). The contempt extends to literature. In the course of the novel Alexander writes two lengthy and important letters, one to his wife and the other to his lover; yet Cather, overlooking this, has him claim that mere 'marks on paper' mean nothing to him (108).

Cather's portrait of Bartley Alexander could be dismissive were she not fearful that the future belonged to him and his kind. He is the modern American successor to the great Victorian activists, Benjamin Disraeli, 'Pasha' Gordon, and the explorer David Livingstone (11). He is a 'natural force . . . always on the edge of danger and change.' He is a 'bridge into the future' because he is one of the people 'who make the play,' while most others 'are only onlookers at the best' (15, 17, 101, 138).

As one of the 'onlookers,' the novelist can only seek consolation in the qualities thought to be lacking in the engineer, reflection and perspective. These too, Cather argues, are powers. They enable her to see and to understand the fault line in Alexander's nature. They endow the writer with the power of insight lacking in those whose minds can only formulate 'definite' things. For those of technological minds are baffled by the collapse of the bridge and shocked at the accidental death of its designer. 'According to all human calculations, it simply couldn't happen,' says a young engineer, incredulous amid the twisted steel and the bodies of the drowned workmen (129). Of course the novelist knows better. The artist working routinely in the world which surpasses that of mere mathematical calculation understands the naiveté of the young engineer, even if he represents modern America.

If the public continues to believe that the American mind at its truest is the mind of an engineer or mechanic, as one character suggests, then America, says Cather, is a nation in jeopardy. Her eulogy for the drowned engineer contains a warning of the kind only the writer can provide. The novelist's voice, introspective and reflective, teaches that 'the mind that society had come to regard as a powerful and reliable machine, dedicated to its service, may for a long time have been sick within itself and bent upon its own destruction' (131). By showing the disastrous personal and social consequences of that sickness, Cather suggests that the literary voices are those best heeded by a people otherwise condemned to be the victims of their own misplaced faith in technology and its proponents. Her Alexander is an emperor of havoc, and one feels she takes a certain resentful satisfaction in the failure of his bridge.

The novel also shows a degree of authorial anxiety not allayed by the catastrophic fictional climax. For now, Cather must acknowledge the power of the engineer. Her best hope is that in the long run the the writer will prevail, not the engineer. Surrounded by the industrial technology of Pittsburgh, Cather spoke of herself and of all artists when she said that the music of her Pittsburgh friend, the composer Ethelbert Nevin, 'will live when the armour plate made at Homestead [steel works] is eaten away with rust,' since 'it is possible for a lyric to outlive a battle-ship and a nation's songs to outlive its navy' (Byrne and Snyder 34). This, in essence, is the argument she tries to write large in *Alexander's Bridge*, even though readers suspect the sentiment must come from massive denial of the industrial-age realities confronting her daily in Pittsburgh and New York, the cities where she lived in maturity. [. . .]

163
From Fiction's Vacuoles: Tracing What Willa Cather Left Out

JO ANN MIDDLETON

[. . .] Willa Cather's technique involves the effects of juxtaposition and the gaps that it produces. Because Cather sees a work of art as a whole, we are well advised to regard the details and the gaps of juxtaposition also as part of the whole. In a comment about Willa Cather's method of writing, Edith Lewis provides a clue to an understanding of the importance of this artistic technique:

> In writing the story, it was the flooding force of a great wealth of impressions that she had to control. She could have written two or three *Sapphiras* out of her material; and in fact she did write, in her first draft, twice as much as she used. She always said it was what she left out that counted.[1]

In the juxtaposition of two seemingly unrelated episodes, scenes, events, or details, the reader will experience an intense moment of realisation, drawing on or based in both elements, but occurring in neither. Perhaps the most intriguing and perplexing aspect of Willa Cather's work is the effect on the reader of what he or she cannot find on the written page. 'What was left out' is significant in a special way for Cather; in fact, Miss Lewis also writes that 'occasionally she outlined beforehand her plan for a novel; but she always left out its real theme, the secret treasure at its heart, the thing that gave it its reason for being.'[2] What was left out must therefore be significant for the reader, because it is in that void that we find the real meaning of her work. We also begin to suspect that we are being manipulated by the artist's use of this technique in such a way that we cooperate in the story that appears in print and the story that exists in the blank spaces. Indeed, we have no choice but to participate in what Emerson calls 'creative reading.'

SOURCE   Jo Ann Middleton, from 'Fiction's Vacuoles: Tracing What Willa Cather Left Out', *Willa Cather's Modernism: A Study of Style and Technique*, Rutherford, N.J., Fairleigh Dickenson University Press, 1990, pp. 51–65, 144–46

Dealing with a writer who places so much importance on what she leaves out—and who tells us so—can be exasperating because it is difficult to explicate the ephemeral. Cather herself tries to identify what, for her, is the essence of creation:

> Whatever is felt upon the page without being specifically there—that, one might say, is created. It is the inexplicable presence of the thing not named, of the overtone divined by the ear but not heard by it, the verbal mood, the emotional aura of the fact or the thing or the deed, that gives high quality to the novel or the drama, as well as to poetry itself.[3]

Here she uses metaphor, a poet's tool, in an attempt to explain the 'inexplicable,' but the metaphors she uses still leave us unsatisfied, with no appreciation of the concrete effect she actually has on the consciousness of her reader. In his preface to *On Writing*, Stephen Tennant calls Cather's vision 'a poet's vision, simplified by an extraordinary natural honesty and warmth';[4] however, when he discusses 'Willa Cather's preoccupation as an artist—the bringing into being of something beyond the situation or character of a story, something beyond the story itself, the unseen vision, the unheard echo, which attend all experience,'[5] his only extension of Cather's own metaphor is the image of 'the room beyond,' which minimally enlarges our understanding.

In any discussion of Willa Cather's style, we must try to describe in the available vague language real gaps in both the content and form of her fiction. Given her own statements about the importance of these gaps, we are compelled to keep looking for a point of entry. Some critics note her increasing use of this technique in her later books, in which it does become pronounced, unfavorably. For instance, Granville Hicks uses the phrase 'highly episodic' in his discussion of *Death Comes for the Archbishop*,[6] and Lionel Trilling refers to her essay, 'The Novel Démeublé,' as 'the rationale of a method which Miss Cather had partly anticipated in her earlier works and which she fully developed a decade later in *Shadows on the Rock*.' He continues with a comment that illustrates not only the inadequacy of language to pinpoint the technique but also his own inadequacy to understand it: 'And it is no less obvious that this technical method is not merely a literary manner but the expression of a point of view toward which Miss Cather had always been moving—with results that, to many of her readers, can only indicate the subtle failure of her admirable talent.'[7]

Others feel the power and simplicity that Cather attains through this puzzling technique and try various ways of defining it. Rebecca West calls it 'that feat of making a composition out of the different states of being';[8] E.K. Brown says, 'Her vision is of essences . . . [S]he could disengage her essential subject and make it tell upon the reader with a greater directness and power, help it to remain uncluttered in his mind.'[9] In *Willa Cather's Imagination*, David Stouck discusses *Death Comes for the Archbishop* as a book that moves, then, not in familiar chronological sequence but through the juxtaposition of episodes and narratives which are loosely associated with the ideal of saintliness, and which offer an edifying or emotional contrast to each other. . . . Any action in the novel is almost always described 'after the event'; what is important is not the event, but the effect.[10]

The effect, as we have seen, is all-important, and these critics are perceptive enough to appreciate any technique that can achieve that effect. They all deal with the events of the story as given, however; they do not address themselves to the gaps between the events and to the functions those gaps perform, because they do not have the critical vocabulary to do so.

Edward and Lillian Bloom do address this problem of critical vocabulary directly in their book, *Willa Cather's Gift of Sympathy*. They point out Cather's own inability to define clearly her technique, and they suggest that it was necessary for her 'to fall back upon a language of subjective response.' They continue:

> This haziness—if such it may be called—was unavoidable, for she was reflecting rather than asserting, and her subject matter was of such private intensity that it simply did not lend itself to a critical rationale. . . . Terms such as 'desire,' 'yearning,' and 'spirit' may seem elusive when attempts are made to compress them into these definitions. They are abundantly clear in narrative context, however, generally eliciting the response of feeling when incisive statement is inadequate.[11]

Incisive statement is inadequate because, thus far, we have been unable to address the problem of 'what was left out.' Our discussions have considered what was included; now we must begin to confront the voids that shape these modern texts and give us the space in which to experience an astonishing, emotional 'reader response.' Once we can name the unnamed, we can begin to see how Cather uses it.

I would like to propose that we borrow a term used in science, a biologic or botanical metaphor, to name this elusive technique. We can call the unwritten but essential part of Willa Cather's fiction, the *vacuole*. I suggest this term because it functions in the same way for science that we need it to function in our understanding of Willa Cather, and because it fills our need for an identifying critical term with which to address the artistic technique Cather employs. It is far more manageable than the unwieldy terminology of current reader-response analysis: *lacunae of indeterminacy, blanks, negations,* or *indeterminate areas in imagination*; it recognises the structural significance of the technique as well as its referentiality better than the term *allusion*; and it is more precise than *gap*, because it carries with it the weight of its scientific meaning as well.

There occur in nature, specifically in cells themselves, empty spaces which scientists have named *vacuoles*. Although they are now discovering that some vacuoles are not actually empty—just as the gaps between the details in juxtaposition are not really empty once the reader has perceived their significance—biologists and botanists as well as physicians and physiologists still use the term for both animal and plant cell definition. In both kinds of cell, the vacuole helps to maintain the structure of the cell. In animal cells, the vacuole often performs functions such as storage, ingestion, digestion, excretion, and expulsion of excess water; plant cell vacuoles also 'serve to expand the plant cell without diluting its cytoplasm,'[12] thus enabling the plants themselves to attain a large size without accumulating the bulk that would make metabolism difficult. In 'Problems in Water Relations of Plants and Cells,' Paul J. Kramer explains that

> we are concerned with vacuoles as osmotic systems that develop the turgor pressure essential for mechanical support of unlilgnified tissues, for certain movements of plant structures such as the leaves of sensitive plants, for opening of stomata and for cell expansion. Loss of turgor pressure as a result of dehydration causes cessation of growth and wilting.[13]

In other words, both plant and animal vacuoles appear empty, though neither actually is empty; both are supported by, and in turn support, the structure of the cell; plant vacuoles, in fact, allow the plant to develop a structure that is greater in size than would logically, or scientifically, be expected.

In addition to these specific meanings of vacuole, scientists are apt to use the word in a more general sense to refer to any unusual empty space in the natural order. For instance, to a geologist, a fluid inclusion in a mineral is a vacuole. In his definition of vacuole, which refers only to cytology, Joseph G. Hoffman notes the wide variety of those phenomena called vacuoles, pointing out that 'they come and go and vary widely in size.'[14] Thus, the term is vested with a wide range of applications for its use in understanding Willa Cather's literary technique, referring to gaps in plot sequence, which any reader may notice, and also to those absences resulting from Cather's selection of detail, which only a reader familiar with the history of her composition would know with equal significance. Its usefulness derives from its potential to identify structural absences that, in fact, allow for a fuller story than should be technically possible; the excisions themselves vary widely in size. The beauty of the term is its adaptability to the text at hand.

In science, as in art, language reverberates with many layers of meaning and association. I.A. Richards points out that 'a metaphor may be illustrative or diagrammatical, providing a concrete instance of a relation which would otherwise have to be stated in abstract terms. This is the most common scientific or prose use of metaphor.'[15] It is interesting to note that the scientist is as particular as the poet about the connotative power of the word. In the interest of clarification and specificity, S.M. McGee-Russell proposes a further refinement of vacuole: 'it is now desirable to have some special terminology to describe them and set them apart from other organelles. For an empty-seeming vacuole I suggest the term colamphora.'[16] The term McGee-Russell suggests is the name of an ancient Greek, two-handled water vessel. We are reminded of Owen Barfield's conclusion: 'How essentially parochial is the fashionable distinction between Poetry and Science as modes of expression.'[17] We must agree, therefore, that the vacuole serves as a metaphor in the scientific or prose sense: it represents an abstract relation in a concrete term.

Richards reminds us, however, that 'metaphor had yet further uses. It is the supreme agent by which disparate and hitherto unconnected things are brought together in poetry for the sake of their effects upon attitude and impulse which spring from their collocation and from the combination which the mind then establishes between them.'[18] For vacuole to work poetically, it must be the catalytic agent for the imagination. Willa Cather once told Elizabeth Sergeant that

> she could only describe this coming together of the two elements of the book [*O Pioneers!*] as a sudden inner explosion and enlightenment. She had experienced it before only in the conception of a poem. Now she would hope always for similar experience in creating a novel, for the explosion seemed to bring with it the inevitable shape that is not plotted but designs itself. She now believed that the least possible tinkering with the form — revealed from within — the better.[19]

Emily Dickinson said that this same explosion took the top of her head off;[20] Barfield more sedately describes this experience as a 'felt change of consciousness,' the goal of the 'aesthetic imagination,' and he explains, '"consciousness" embraces all my awareness of my surroundings at any given moment, and "surroundings" includes my own feelings. By "felt" I mean to signify that the change itself is noticed, or attended to.'[21] The explosion of understanding that Cather experienced in the coming together of the two elements of *O Pioneers!* is reflected in its form; the gap between the first two parts of the novel sets us up for an aesthetic explosion of our own. Barfield calls this '*Living* poetry . . . the present stir of aesthetic imagination lights up only when the normal continuum of this process is interrupted in such a manner that a gap is created, and an earlier impinges directly upon a later — a more living upon a more conscious.'[22] This gap can be a thirteen-year space between parts of a work, or a minute space between disparate details, or an unexpected space between scenes; however, it is in this space, or vacuole, that we experience the insight arising from the juxtaposition of Cather's often disjointed elements. It is the vacuole that gives the novel its form, arising from the carefully selected material itself; it is the vacuole that sustains the structure of the work without overloading it. Among the scant details of *My Mortal Enemy* lie the unseen but swollen vacuoles of meaning in which the reader experiences the poetic change of consciousness that is the result of art.

With *O Pioneers!* Willa Cather recognised the power and rhythm she could create by the selective placement of vacuoles, and the books that follow all result from her increasing mastery of this technique, which allows her to leave out what counts. If we look closely at *Alexander's Bridge*, however, we can see the seeds of the novel *démeublé* even in this early work. As Cather becomes more and more the consummate artisan, she learns with increasing skill how to handle the elements of metaphor, the vacuole itself, and the aesthetic consciousness of her readers. It is possible to trace Cather's use of the vacuole as a technical tool throughout her work; in this study we will consider only the novels, because ample material exists for study and illustration here of both this specific technique, and her increasing experimentation with the novel's artistic form and its aesthetic effect.

In an essay called 'My First Novels [There Were Two],' Cather discusses her early novels, mentioning, in fact, not only the first two books, but the first four. Her famous comparison of *Alexander's Bridge* to a studio picture is followed by an even more interesting statement:

> The impressions I tried to communicate on paper were genuine, but they were very shallow. I still find people who like that book because it follows the most conventional pattern, . . . Soon after the book was published I went for six months to Arizona and New Mexico. The longer I stayed in a country I really did care about, and among people who were a part of the country, the more unnecessary and superficial a book like *Alexander's Bridge* seemed to me. I did no writing down there, but I recovered from the conventional editorial point of view.[23]

Her use of the words *shallow, superficial,* and *conventional* is the clue to her lack of satisfaction with the book. Cather finds the vacuoles that add depth to the actual story missing here. In this work, all information is given to the reader; because appreciation of the work is a direct result of involvement in it, the reader responds in a pleasant, perhaps moving, but superficial way. It seems that Cather's problem with *Alexander's Bridge* is twofold: she is uncomfortable with its affinity to James and Wharton as well as its debt to Poe and Adams,[24] and she knows that it does not create a world beyond its pages. At one point, however, we are invited to bridge a gap. Chapter 9 ends in Bartley's apartment with our attention closely focused on Hilda and Bartley; chapter 10 begins with the long, distancing viewpoint of 'a Boston lawyer who had been trying a case in Vermont.'[25] By the time we have our bearings, we are back in Bartley's consciousness. This gap, though minute, triggers a subconscious reaction that all is not right. The reader's uneasiness arises from the effect of the vacuole. In her introduction to *Alexander's Bridge*, Bernice Slote notes that the work does contain many of the themes and techniques of the later novels; she also adds that 'its crisply balanced form is the body carefully chosen to support the theme.'[26] Even in the clearly balanced form, we can find the unsettling gap that will become the form-determining vacuole of *O Pioneers!*

We have already noted Cather's description of the writing of *O Pioneers!* as an explosion similar to the conception of a poem. She says in 'My First Novels':

> Here was no arranging or 'inventing'; everything was spontaneous and took its own place, right or wrong. . . . Since I wrote this book for myself, I ignored all the situations and accents that were then generally thought to be necessary.[27]

By ignoring the expected situations and accents, she challenges the reader to a greater involvement in the story. Here, the superficial reading is possible, but the real—and very carefully contrived—story is not on the page. As James Woodress reminds us:

> The structure of *O Pioneers!* has troubled a good many readers. Its loose organization, gaps, and digressions have made it seem a flawed work of art. Despite Cather's insistence that the material dictated the form, and the story told itself, art is not nature, and any artist must select and arrange incident and character. Like any other novelist, Cather brings order out of chaos in creating a literary work. She gets away with loose organization, however, because plot is probably the least important part of a novel. Readers want a book to stir their emotions, stimulate their imagination; they want characters who live and breathe; images that linger in the memory after the book is closed. All of these things Cather does well.[28]

Cather is able to do all of these things well because she controls her reader's response to the events she does record. We have already mentioned earlier the thirteen-year hiatus between parts 1 and 2, which is the most obvious change in form. Here the distancing that we saw in *Alexander's Bridge* is further emphasised by a tense change from the traditional story-telling past tense to the attention-demanding present tense.

> It is sixteen years since John Bergson died. His wife now lies beside him, and the white shaft that marks their grave gleams across the wheat fields. Could he rise from beneath it, he would not know the country under which he has been asleep. The shaggy coat of the prairie, which they had lifted to make him a bed, has vanished forever.[29]

Consider the jump that the reader must make from the last sentences of part 1:

> She had never known before how much the country meant to her. The chirping of the insects in the long grass had been like the sweetest music. She had felt as if her heart were hiding down there, somewhere with the quail and the plover and all the little wild things that crooned or buzzed in the sun. Under the long shaggy ridge, she felt the future stirring. (71)

The reader is jolted here by the juxtaposition of the two images: the future sleeping under the shaggy prairie and the Bergsons sleeping there as well. Both point ahead to the final image of the book, which is also foreshadowed by Alexandra's feeling that her own heart was 'hiding down there': 'Fortunate country, that is one day to receive hearts like Alexandra's into its bosom, to give them out again in the yellow wheat, in the rustling corn, in the shining eyes of youth!' (309). At this last point in the book, however, Cather uses the vacuole for timing and distancing; we are put off guard, and when the insight comes, it has the effect of an explosion because it is unexpected. By placing the accents in the 'wrong' places throughout the book, she keeps us aware of not only the actual situations we are given, but the ones we normally anticipate in fiction.

The Song of the Lark is Willa Cather's experiment with 'the full-blooded method which told everything about everybody' and which, she tells us, 'was not natural to me.'[30] In her preface to the book, Cather observes:

> The story set out to tell of an artist's awakening and struggle; her floundering escape from a smug, domestic, self-satisfied provincial world of utter ignorance. It should have been content to do that. I should have disregarded conventional design and stopped where my first conception stopped, telling the latter part of the story by suggestion merely.[31]

Again we notice that disapproving word *conventional*. Both this book and *Alexander's Bridge* follow someone else's rules too closely. We should also notice, however, that Cather has enough confidence in her own method to assert that she *could* tell the latter part of the story by mere suggestion. There are gaps in Thea's story—for instance, she never actually marries Ottenburg; however, when Cather turns to *My Ántonia*, she remembers the lesson she has learned in writing *The Song of the Lark*:

> Too much detail is apt, like any other form of extravagance, to become slightly vulgar; and it quite destroys in a book a very satisfying element analogous to what painters call 'composition.'

By this time, composition has come to include both the suggestive detail and the significant vacuole that attends it.

With *My Ántonia*, Cather reaches a balance between vacuole and detail that can best be considered as poetry. The image of the plough against the sun is supported by and resonates with our consciousness of all that it took to tame the prairie; the vanishing road, 'like gashes torn by a grizzly's claws,'[33] recalls other roads, both those described in the book and those that we know have existed for Jim in the world beyond the novel. We can create for ourselves from the scant details the New York life Jim lives, and we can comprehend the entire relationship between Ántonia and Cuzak by reading: 'Clearly, she was the impulse, and he the corrective' (358).

Jim says, 'It must have been the scarcity of detail in that tawny landscape that made detail so precious' (29). In *My Ántonia* the detail is precious both because it is scarce and because it is loaded with implication. Discovering the implication, filling the vacuole, readers are drawn into the poetic creation, just as Cather intends them to be.

In a 1921 interview with Eva Mahoney for the *Omaha World-Herald*, Cather discussed her technique in writing *One of Ours* (which she originally called *Claude*):

> The hero is just a red-headed prairie boy.... I have cut out all descriptive work in this book—the thing I do best. I have cut out all picture making because that boy does not see pictures. It was hard to cease to do the thing that I do best, but

we all have to pay the price for everything we accomplish, and because I was willing to pay so much to write about this boy I felt that I had a right to do so.[34]

Here, the vacuoles, the descriptions that are missing, are a clue to her method of characterising Claude; what he does not see is essential to our understanding of him.

Although he does not refer to it by name, James Woodress points out one of the vacuoles in *One of Ours* that underlines the lack of 'picture making' in the book. Discussing Claude's disastrous marriage to Enid, he not only locates a gap for us, he locates the source for the actual incident as well:

> On their wedding night, as the Denver Express carries them off for their honeymoon, Enid locks Claude out of their stateroom. This incident, Cather told a friend, actually happened to a young man she knew in Pittsburgh; otherwise she never would have had the courage to use it.[35]

Here, Cather transforms memory into art, employing the vacuole that real life suggests, and invites her readers to bring to the scene their own comprehension of frustration—not only the sexual frustration of the thwarted bridegroom but all the frustration of life itself.

We might consider Willa Cather's next novel, *A Lost Lady*, as entirely a characterisation. Certainly it can be read as a simple story of a young man's disillusionment with an older, beautiful, and charming woman; indeed, we should note that Hollywood twice exploited the cinematic qualities of the book. Beginning with the title itself and the numerous meanings of the word *lost*, the reader brings so many conscious and unconscious associations to its details that we have several different novels arising from the same seemingly simple story. In this work, Cather uses the vacuole to swell the story beyond the limits of its structure. For instance, the spaces give us a place to reflect on the provocative names of the characters: Ivy Peters, Niel Herbert, Captain Forrester.[36] The book can be read as Mrs Forrester's story, as Niel's story, as Captain Forrester's story; it can be read as social allegory; it can be read as a book about art itself. The number of readings one can have is determined by the number of ways in which the reader can fill the vacuoles.

Willa Cather herself called *The Professor's House* 'two experiments in form.' She explains:

> The first is the device often used by the early French and Spanish novelists: that of inserting the *Nouvelle* into the *Roman*. . . . But the experiment which interested me was something a little more vague, and was very much akin to the arrangement followed in sonatas in which the academic sonata form was handled somewhat freely.[37]

Her metaphor explains the three-part structure of the book and also clarifies her return in the third part to the characters and situation of the first. Her image of the turquoise set in dull silver might apply as well to our metaphor, the vacuole. In this book, it is necessary to fill the void for the reader, because most readers cannot bring Cather's experience of the Southwest to parts 1 and 3. *The Professor's House* probably demands more effort on the reader's part than any of the other works; it certainly requires several readings for the experience of the vacuole, that is, 'Tom Outland's Story,' to impinge on our appreciation of Godfrey St Peter's story.

In a review of *My Mortal Enemy* entitled 'Willa Cather Fumbles for Another Lost Lady,' Louis Kronenberger comments unfavorably on the book's brevity:

> Compression and selection grow naturally stronger in most good writers as they master their medium. But in *My Mortal Enemy* they have been carried too far. All bones and no flesh is never a wise method. In this instance Miss Cather has done ever worse—though she has used very little, she has not always used the bones. Significant things are left out, and the reader is left not only unsatisfied, but also puzzled.[38]

Certainly this short work makes every detail count: both placement and timing of the vacuoles draw the reader into the story in such a way that reading it can be an exhausting experience. Vacuoles are used here as gaps in the plot, as signals to both emotional changes and to narrative voice changes, and as the keys to an entire structure of relevance beyond the page. For instance, Nellie says at one point:

> For many years I associated Mrs Henshawe with that music, thought of that aria as being mysteriously related to something in her nature that one rarely saw, but nearly always felt; a compelling, passionate, overmastering something for which I had no name, but which was audible, visible in the air that night, as she sat crouching in the shadow. When I wanted to recall powerfully that hidden richness in her, I had only to close my eyes and sing to myself: '*Casta diva, casta diva!*'[39]

In *Music in Willa Cather's Fiction*, Richard Giannone discusses the aria, which, as Cather tells us in the novel, comes from the opera *Norma*.[40] He elucidates this reference fully, explaining the resemblances between Myra and Norma. It is also fascinating to discover that the next line after the aria is 'mira, Norma, mira.' What makes this a vacuole and not merely a literary allusion is the very real amplification of Myra's character that the whole of the opera *Norma* provides. Every detail and reference in the book can in some fashion be expanded in just this way. If this is the case, then we can experience in *My Mortal Enemy* a novel with the breadth and density of *The Song of the Lark*.

We have mentioned the critical dismay at the episodic nature of *Death Comes for the Archbishop*; even those who praise its mood have some difficulty classifying this work as a novel. Because Cather intends to arouse the aesthetic imagination of her reader, she supplies both fact and vacuole; the emotional and psychological impact of this beautifully written novel comes in part from the reader's own consciousness of the process of creation. The scene with the Bishop of Durango, in which Father Latour secures the letters containing his credentials and establishing his authority, takes place only in our imagination, but it is as real as if Cather had described it and is perhaps more significant than if it had actually appeared on the page. We have such a vivid impression of Father Vaillant that we understand without any explanation the characteristics of his own bishopric in Colorado. This book is extraordinary because we are not particularly aware that the conventional main events are missing; it is only when we search for some specific bit of information that we should be able to locate that we realise we have absorbed it in the gaps, we have been manipulated through the vacuoles. We are less aware of our own efforts in this book than in any other; we are only cognisant of that 'felt change' in our consciousness and understanding of human relations.

Marion Marsh Brown and Ruth Crone call *Shadows on the Rock* 'a long lyric prose poem, sincere, genuine and charming,'[41] and John Randall agrees with their assessment of the book:

> All of Willa Cather's novels can be considered to be extended lyrics in prose; on this basis *Shadows on the Rock* is better constructed than the previous novel because in it the unity of lyric tone is consistently maintained.[42]

Cather creates this tone through the small, homey, familiar details she uses in presenting this fairly circumscribed world of seventeenth-century Quebec. By juxtaposing the serenity of the town with glimpses of the wilderness that surrounds it, however, Cather creates a vacuole in which we instinctively know how much this serenity costs. When we read the novel, the vacuoles give us space for reflection; the gap between Cécile's understanding of Mother Catherine de Saint-Augustin and Mother Juschereau's view of her allows us to reflect on the gap between civilised France and civilised Quebec more efficiently than any description could. This example demonstrates Catherian compression at its best. The vacuoles in *Shadows on the Rock* account for the intentionally nostalgic air about the book; the leisurely movement of the story is controlled by their placement. David Stouck says:

> The painterly quality for which Willa Cather's style is distinguished is strongly developed here; each chapter in the novel constitutes a self-controlled, essentially plastic scene and almost every sequence of the book is set in a descriptive tableau which superbly evokes the colors and textures of the Quebec landscape.[43]

When we first approach *Lucy Gayheart*, it appears to be, as Maxwell Geismar says, 'a standard and almost stereotyped story in our literature; the love affair of the young provincial girl who seeks an artistic career and the sophisticated city-man who represents all the glamour of artistic success.' He continues in admiration of the technique that can persuade readers to forget what they see:

> what Cather had managed to create in the reader of her story is hardly so much that 'willing suspension of disbelief' which the literary critic delights in, but a

sort of inevitable and unwitting acceptance of the artist's intention—an intention that is hardly limited to a picture of love's delights.[44]

We have seen that Cather intentionally enlists the reader's participation in the creation of her work; 'unwitting' or aware, we are forced by the inevitable effect of the work's structure to accept her premises. In this particular novel, vacuoles are left between each of the books, but they follow scenes of such emotional intensity that we rush into the void propelled by our own momentum. We feel Lucy's anguish at Sebastian's death more deeply because we do not see it. We respond to Harry Gordon's remorse and guilt with his own helplessness because we bridge the twenty-five years he has endured it in the time it takes to turn the page; the horror is fresh to us—we have just perceived it—in the same way that it remains fresh to Harry after all those intervening years.

In this work, Cather also uses the vacuole as a void that invites the reader to enrich the story through association. References to specific works of music are significant in this novel, as they are in both *The Song of the Lark*, and *My Mortal Enemy*; in *Lucy Gayheart*, we find references to some of Cather's other novels. The Chicago Art Institute appears here with its promise of the immortality of art for Lucy as well as for Thea in *The Song of the Lark*; drowning is the cause of death for Bartley Alexander, Sebastian, and, finally, Lucy.[45] Both of the earlier works elucidate and amplify the events and themes of *Lucy Gayheart*.

Edith Lewis calls *Sapphira and the Slave Girl* 'uncharacteristic,'

> in the sense that one does not find in it the qualities one most looks to find; the qualities that most predominate in the writer's other work. But this, perhaps, comes not so much from a lack, as from an emergence, a substitution of other latent traits in the writer's development. It is written austerely, with very little of that warmth and generous expansion so many of her readers delight in.... Nothing is stressed—incidents, scenes are touched on so lightly, one is hardly aware of their having more than a surface significance. Yet one finds—I find, at least—that they have a curiously imperishable quality.[46]

The quality that Lewis calls curious can be attributed to Cather's childlike world view, which Pers described. In this novel Cather tests the imaginative ability of the child's vision and her reader's ability to participate in that vision. Lewis's point that one is scarcely aware of what is significant is a tribute to Cather's crafted contrivance of the vacuoles supporting the work. The various digressions within the book are such a part of the apparently seamless whole that the reader's response to them is almost unconscious. As Susan Rosowski points out, however, 'the overall effect of these disruptions is that this novel, which seems to offer a retreat into the past, contains the distinctly modern search for meaning in an estranged world.'[47]

Sapphira and the Slave Girl gives us ambiguities and the space in which to experience them; by the end of the novel, we are as ambiguous about Sapphira as her husband, daughter, and Nancy's mother Till. The final chapter, which takes place twenty-five years after the rest of the book and includes the child Willa as a character, threatens to become a Cather 'convention,' an epilogue following a vacuole of compressed time. Here, though, the central action of this last part is related by Till and sends us back in time; we are forced to cross the gap both coming and going. Even in this late book, Cather remains in charge of her material, her technique, and her reader.

Willa Cather manipulates the few details of her work to produce the greatest emotional impact on her reader in a deliberate way. We have also noted the many ways in which she uses the void, or the vacuole, to achieve many of her artistic goals. Implicit in this theory of reader manipulation is a theory of reader response. . . . Willa Cather not only anticipates the modern attitude toward juxtaposition and experimentation in technique, but she also anticipates the integral role of the reader in the creative process of modern literature.

Notes

1. Lewis, *Cather Living*, 183.
2. Ibid., 155.
3. Cather, 'Novel Démeublé,' in *Forty*, 50.
4. Stephen Tennant, 'The Room Beyond' in *Writing*, xiv.
5. Lewis, *Cather Living*, 138.
6. Hicks, 'Case against Cather,' in *Cather and Critics*, 145.
7. Trilling, 'Willa Cather,' in *After the Genteel Tradition*, ed. Malcolm Cowley (Carbondale: Southern Illinois University Press, 1964), 48.
8. West, 'Classic Artist,' in *Cather and Critics*, 63.
9. Brown, 'Willa Cather,' in ibid., 85.
10. Stouck, *Imagination*, 133.
11. Bloom and Bloom, *Gift of Sympathy*, 197-98.
12. Phillip Sheeler and Donald Bianchi, *Cell Biology: Structure, Biochemistry, and Function* (New York: John Wiley & Sons, 1983), 41.
13. Paul J. Kramer, 'Problems in Water Relations of Plants and Cells,' in *International Review of Cytology*, ed. G.H. Bourne and J.F. Danielli, assist. ed. K.W. Jean (New York: Academic Press, 1983), 263.
14. Joseph G. Hoffman, *The Life and Death of Cells* (Garden City, N.Y.: Hanover House Books, 1957), 27.
15. I.A. Richards, *Principles of Literary Criticism* (New York: Harcourt, Brace & World, 1925), 239.
16. S.M. McGee-Russell, 'The Method of Combined Observations with Light and Electron Microscopes Applied to the Study of Histochemical Colourations in Nerve Cells and Oocytes,' in *Cell Structure and its Interpretations: Essays Presented to John Randel Baker F.R.S.*, ed. S.M. McGee-Russell and K.F.A. Ross (London: Edward Arnold, 1968), 200.
17. Owen Barfield, *Poetic Diction* (Middletown, Conn.: Wesleyan University Press, 1973), 138.
18. Richards, *Literary Criticism*, 239-40.
19. Sergeant, *Memoir*, 116.
20. Philip Gerber agrees with this assessment: 'Had she heard Emily Dickinson say that one knew poetry by the effect it produced—something akin to knowing that the top of one's head had been taken off—she would have been bound to approve, since her own theories rest upon similar recognition' (*Cather*, 13).
21. Barfield, *Poetic Diction*, 48-49.
22. Ibid., 179.
23. Cather, 'My First Novels,' in *Writing*, 92.

24. Skaggs 'Poe's Shadow,' 365–74.
25. Willa Cather, *Alexander's Bridge* (Lincoln: University of Nebraska Press, 1977), 112.
26. Slote, 'Introduction,' in ibid., xxvi.
27. Cather, 'My First Novels,' in *Writing*, 92–93.
28. Woodress, *Literary Life*, 245.
29. Willa Cather, *O Pioneers!* (Boston: Houghton Mifflin Company, 1941), 75. Subsequent citations from this work are noted parenthetically in the text.
30. Cather, 'My First Novels,' in *Writing*, 96.
31. Willa Cather, *The Song of the Lark* (Boston: Houghton Mifflin, 1965), iii–iv.
32. Cather, 'My First Novels,' in *Writing*, 97. Susan Rosowski makes an interesting point: 'In many respects it was not until *The Song of the Lark* that Cather came to terms with her heritage. For the first time she used a midwestern point of view and spoke with a midwestern narrative voice. This highly particularized, personal point of view combined with the detailed narrative is the aspect of the novel most criticized; Cather herself believed she had "taken the wrong road" with her "full blooded method." Yet perhaps that fullness was what Cather needed to make her materials her own' (*Voyage Perilous*, 74). We should also recall Cather's own statements regarding the value of her overwritten journalism in developing her later, simpler style.
33. Willa Cather, *My Ántonia* (Boston: Houghton Mifflin Company, 1954), 371. Subsequent citations from this work are noted parenthetically in the text.
34. Willa Cather, interview with Eva Mahoney, 'How Willa Cather Found Herself,' *Omaha World-Herald*, 27 November 1921, in Bohlke, *Cather in Person*, 39.
35. Woodress, *Literary Life*, 324.
36. This reading of the names in *A Lost Lady* was first presented to me in a seminar discussion by Merrill Maguire Skaggs, Spring 1984.
37. Cather, 'On *The Professor's House*,' in *Writing*, 31.
38. Louis Kronenberger, 'Willa Cather Fumbles for Another Lost Lady,' *New York Times Book Review*, 24 October 1926, 2.
39. Willa Cather, *My Mortal Enemy* (New York: Vintage Books, 1954), 48. Subsequent citations from this work are noted parenthetically in the text.
40. Richard Giannone, *Music in Willa Cather's Fiction* (Lincoln: University of Nebraska Press, 1968), 179–83.
41. Brown and Crone, *Cather*, 130.
42. Randall, *Landscape*, 341.
43. Stouck, *Imagination*, 151.
44. Maxwell Geismar, 'Willa Cather: Lady in the Wilderness,' in *Cather and Critics*, 194.
45. Having established that Cather uses those intensely remembered scenes from her past to create intensely moving scenes in her writing, we can indicate the source of these drownings. Woodress points out the correspondence between *Alexander's Bridge* and events surrounding the disaster of 1907, which occurred when a bridge under construction near Quebec collapsed, killing eighty men, including the chief engineer, Theodore Cooper (*Literary Life*, 217). We can find ties between the real episode and the fictional account. The emotional intensity with which these drownings are recorded also lies in Cather's own personal experience and her own emotional response to that experience, which she translates into deeply felt art. Willa Cather worked as a columnist in Lincoln with a young man who left for another job in New York. Bernice Slote tells us that 'on June 13, 1897, Lincoln learned that Morton Smith had drowned in the Hudson River—his catboat had been hit by a sudden squall and capsized' (*Kingdom of Art*, 25). The effect of this news on Willa Cather is recorded in *Alexander's Bridge* and *Lucy Gayheart*.
46. Lewis, *Cather Living*, 185.
47. Rosowski, *Voyage Perilous*, 239.

164
Excavating Artistry in Willa Cather's Novels

KATHLEEN WHEELER

Brought up on a farm in Red Cloud, Nebraska, Cather embarked on a successful career as editor and arts critic in Pittsburgh and New York, and while on an assignment in Boston in 1908, met Sarah Orne Jewett, the great New England stylist who influenced Cather from the start. Travels to Europe and throughout America probably affected her less than her journeys to the magical American Southwest, which she discovered in the Spring of 1912, on a visit to Arizona. Subsequent explorations of these sublimely inspiring ruins of the cliff-dwellers in Walnut Canyon and elsewhere were to haunt her for the rest of her life. Excavation of Cliff City becomes in *The Professor's House* a metaphor both for writing and for reading, and for the archaeological strata and layerings of the human mind and of language itself, as Michel Foucault was later to elaborate. Excavation functions not, however, to suggest the discovery of meanings hidden under a surface text. Rather, the labour of excavating is shown by Tom Outland to be intrinsically rewarding as a process of imaginative discovery, suggestive of the actual lives of the people who, mysteriously, carved out these towns of art and then disappeared as silently as they came. No hidden meanings then, but the joy of work as play, is the sense which this metaphor conveys in that novel within a novel.

    Cather's interest in the novel as novel (as a work of art), and not simply as a repository of ideas and opinions of the author, led to an emphasis upon the intricacies and techniques that constitute her art. Moreover, oppositions that had been thematic aspects of most of her novels provided the material for the fundamental conflict between mediocrity and excellence, between the pretentious and the genuinely cultivated mind, between the imprisonment of the human spirit in small, mean, petty concerns of ambition and success, and provided thematic material for the fulfilment of the human

SOURCE   Kathleen Wheeler, 'Excavating Artistry in Willa Cather's Novels', commissioned for this volume spirit by releasing the elemental, creative forces within it, whether through art, nature, religion, or loving human relationship. Mediocrity and fear of the unconventional or new was, then, the true enemy of art and fulfilment. Among the many 'literary' aspects of her novels, the use of landscape as a principle of artistic unity, her use of complex narrative techniques and personas, her sophisticated emblematic imagery, her foregrounding of storytelling, and her original style stand out as major devices of central importance in appreciating her art. It is well known that, deeply impressed as Cather was by the realism and, later, naturalism, of Flaubert, Balzac, Maupassant, Zola, and others, she, like Chopin and Wharton, eventually reacted against these as a model for her own writing. Widely read in the literature of many languages, familiar with Greek, Latin, German, French, and English classics as well as with American literature (such as Jewett, Emerson, Freeman, Poe, Hawthorne, Crane, Wharton, James, Gilman), Cather came early in her career to reject realism as restricting the imagination to the ordinary and social superficialities of life. Cather, like Hawthorne, embraced what she termed the romance 'as the highest form of fiction', and emphasised the great value she placed upon the elemental force of the creative imagination. By 'romance' Cather anticipated Flannery O'Connor with the idea that at the basis of all spiritual achievement is a thoroughgoing commitment to the physical, 'the sensuous, and to nature and the natural within humanity itself.'[1] For Cather, as for Blake and Coleridge, the forces of life and artistic creation are one. Both are natural forces of a powerful and mysterious nature, which Cather explored in order to find ways of opening out, to herself and to others, its energy and restorative vitality for constructive purposes. For she knew that, undirected and unshaped, such powerful natural energy could destroy everything.

Cather, then, rejected what she saw as the contrived artifices of much writing, the 'over-furnishing' of the novel that realism and naturalism had turned into a cult.[2] She sought rather to simplify, to sweep away old props which had lost the power of novelty, and to reveal nature's fundamental life forces operating in humans through the creation of living characters in ordinary situations. She wished, moreover, to free the novel into the open spaces she had experienced in the stupendous and overwhelming landscape of the Great Plains and the magical southwestern United States. Consequently, she emphasised the idea that art 'should simplify. That, indeed, is very nearly the whole of the higher artistic process; finding what conventions of form and what detail one can do without and yet preserve the spirit of the whole'.[3] Cather explained that art must simplify by compression, not simply by excision. The artist simplifies by compressing many subordinate elements into a few main elements, yet the subordinate elements remain hovering in the background or atmosphere by means of suggestion. Coleridge had argued for 'compression' in similar terms, shortly after writing 'Kubla Khan' in 1797.[4] For Cather, the many good conceptions which are finally sacrificed to the better conception still hover in the life of that conception by means of suggestion: 'All that one has suppressed and cut away is there to the reader's consciousness as much as if it were in type on the page'.[5] The reader then must excavate the novel, to find its details. Contrary to the realist and naturalist technique of detailed, explicit enumeration and cataloguing of gritty facts, Cather argued in Keatsian language that

> whatever is felt upon the page without being specifically named there—that, one might say is created. It is the inexplicable presence of the thing not named, of the overtone divined by the ear but not heard by it, the verbal mood, the emotional aura of the fact or the thing or the deed, that gives high quality to the novel or the drama, as well as to poetry itself.[6]

The cram-jammed detail and enumeration of realism destroys such suggestion and compression, at the same time that it cramps and restricts imaginative forces to attention to the familiar and social. Cather's emphasis upon the 'spirit of the whole' and on compression in art are founded in Coleridgean and Romantic theories, and are related to Cather's preoccupation, of an almost classical kind, with what she saw in the landscape of the Southwest, with the exquisite, timeless, but human-made cliff dwellings so harmoniously set in the natural scenery. What she saw there was harmony, proportion, and the perfect integration of the human with nature. A novel, she thought, could, through the imaginative techniques of simplification and unity, achieve such proportion and harmony, by which she meant that the end is always kept in view, through understatement, restraint, and the control over the elements that make up the unity. Harmony further suggests the familiar technique of using contrasts and oppositions (one major mode of simplification and compression) to contribute to the clarity of the conception as a whole. Cather structured her novels with certain fundamental contrasts and oppositions that contain within themselves a whole array of specific issues. She then achieved continuity by raising these principal contrasts to the level of unifying structures, of stratifications of meanings, of emblems and symbols, or by using recurring imagery suggestive of elemental oppositions.

Finally, memory, and the excavation of the individual's past, plays the vital role in Cather's art of keeping her in touch with powerful early life experience, providing continuity with her present adult self.[5] The opposite, but not contrary force of imagination selects and shapes that material of life experience which memory provides but cannot shape without the power of a highly sophisticated and carefully developed imaginative genius. Through memory as intermediary medium and imagination as agent, adult and elemental childhood experiences are excavated and then shaped into a continuity and unity, which is the pre-condition of genius for Cather, as for Rhys and Porter.

Cather's idea of a 'magical memory', which she, like Porter and Rhys, so often extolled, is contrasted with the merely mechanical realist faculty of recall. Such a magical memory was, for Cather, a faculty integrated into imagination, and not something contrary to it. Indeed, such memory and remembrance are seen as powerful means of arousing their close relation, the imagination, into creativity. Moreover, both genuine memory as well as imagination, opposites though they may be in some sense, are the true contraries of all that is mechanical, artificial, and contrived. In her reflections on the relation between instinct, or intuition, and conscious craft, Cather concluded that the craft and techniques must be learned thoroughly, and then 'forgotten' or unlearned. Technique for Cather was always subordinate and indirect in its relation to the intuitive, unlike realist practices. Craft and technique become 'natural' to the thoroughly accomplished artist; they become a second nature always guided by that mysterious faculty, intuitive imaginativeness, that 'spirit of the whole'. Craft and technique are as essential as intuition, but, Cather argued, should never dominate it. This was one of the failures of realism for Cather. Cather portrayed the artistic process as something mysterious which cannot be fathomed or measured by the reasoning, conscious intellect. But she also made it clear that art is never merely a matter of spontaneous overflow, or untutored intuition. Thus, there is no simple dichotomy or opposition between those mysterious faculties, memory and imagination. Magical memory is for Cather a kind of imaginativeness. Yet without the greater creative and shaping power of imagination, memory can never produce works of art.

Personified in Cather's narrative techniques, memory could be seen as a kind of astute observer and recoverer as well as preserver of one's past experience, and its importance for the imaginative shaping of its material is reflected in Cather's designing of complex narrative points of view expressive of these different faculties. In clearing away the furnishings of realism and even of the conventional romance novel, Cather sought, then, to express the complexity of the artistic process, and of human life. Cather sought to escape what she and so many other artists saw as the imprisoning, confining effects of artistic forms that had become conventional stereotypes, such as the realist novel and even the form of conventional romance. New experiences, she argued, call for new forms of expressions, for new techniques, new crafts. She claimed to seek to avoid both the usual fictional patterns, of plots, of love, courtship, adventure, family conflicts, and so on, while she sought to use the 'details of everyday life', instead of these larger, more public issues to provide the material for her fiction. Yet she used those details sparsely, emblematically, even sometimes allegorically. Above all, she used them to re-create a 'powerful sense of place', as Eudora Welty has described this central element of fictional narrative. Locality and natural landscape become a Blakean metaphor in Cather's novels for imagination itself. Or rather, nature is the metaphor for imagination, hardly a surprising reversal of relations since, for Cather, as for Blake, imagination is the human form of nature's elemental forces.[7]

Cather used framework techniques, stories within stories, personas, and a 'nouvelle' within a 'roman', in the best Spanish and French manner, to express the metaphor of memory and imagination as observers and transformers of experience, both past and present. Cather also used metaphors of excavation and discovery in 'Tom Outland's Story' to represent the importance of memory (she also gently mocks the futility of realist cataloguing in Tom's rejection of his own catalogue of Cliff City). Excavation becomes, indeed, a multiple symbol for writing, reading, and experience of the past, as will be discussed below. While these strategies may complicate her tales at the surface level, they make possible both simplification and compression at deeper levels. They also make possible a level of critical self-consciousness within the text, which is the very essence of art, namely a self-watching, a self-awareness of the text's own artistry. Cather achieved her goal without the realist's enumerating or cataloging, through the mysterious power of suggestion, that strange sense of things present, hovering above, without being specifically named. An atmosphere of openness, of spaciousness, of great vistas and distances, the very opposite of realism, is the essence for her of imaginativeness. She found in the vast, open landscape of New Mexico and Colorado an evocation of powerful forces and happenings by means of the barest, most meager traces in its geological history. Moreover, Cather's use of landscape and artistic strategies, of personas and frameworks, also provided the distance and spaciousness needed for the level of self-conscious criticism found in any work of art, and which makes possible an artistic response more self-conscious than the merely sentimental and naïve subjugation of the artefact to the reader's unexamined, unconscious values, desires, and prejudices.

The complex methods and narrative strategies of Willa Cather indicate that experience is of several different kinds. Experience can be merely 'had', in which case it goes unnoticed by the conscious mind, though it may be stored in the unconscious. Experience can also be noticed and observed, and in that case it is raised to a second-order level of experience. It becomes known, conscious, and can be material for a third level of experience, namely, reflection upon conscious experience. At this third level, experience is now reflected upon, analysed, and, as such, yields further experience of a knowledge kind. Finally, one may reflect on the processes of seeing, observation, and even reflection or analysis itself. By this means, brute, 'had' experience is refined, by stages, into experience which eventually can lead to the production of works of art and science, or to imaginative living. Cather, through her narrative complexities, managed to convey these levels of experience, and to show that ignorance, passivity, and mediocrity, those primitive enemies of art, love, and life itself, result from a failure to go through these stages of rarefying experience into its highest degree of imaginative awareness, involving ultimately a detached self-consciousness.

The literature on *My Ántonia* suggests that this novel has been poorly understood, though for easily understandable reasons. Its strategies of narrative personas, framework devices, and innumerable stories within stories have at times been accused of being artificial and unconvincing. Further, Cather has been repeatedly criticised for her portrayal of Ántonia as a kind of ideal woman, an earth-mother. The novel has been accused of having no integrity of structure; it is said to be merely a set of stories strung together. The sections on the hired girls and Lena are described as crippling and explicable diversions from the main issue of Jim's and Ántonia's relationship. These criticisms have had little effect upon the popularity of one of Cather's finest novels, demonstrably one of her finest, if the errors leading to these misreadings are uncovered.

One of the great, unrecognised artistic achievements of *My Ántonia* is a distancing of the author from the text in order that Cather should portray not the ideal woman, but a male notion of the ideal woman. This is a shift that demands artistic detachment; Cather's text is designed such that one of its primary subject matters is an analysis of the male psyche and its fantasies about women, sexuality, and male–female relationships. Once the reader makes this artistically crucial shift, she can never read the novel again allowing Jim Burden's sentimental and nostalgic longings for the past and for a mother to dominate her reading. Otherwise, an uncritical reading blinds the reader to the realisation of the crushing indictment the text utters about destructive fantasies.[8] Hence the novel begins with a blatant and parodic framework, and a thoroughly fanciful narrative persona, all too often dismissed by critics as not to be taken seriously.[9] These satirical strategies are designed precisely, however, to be seen through by the reader, but in an artistically significant way. That is, they should alert her to the fact that the point of view is a male's fond but warped point of view on women. By shifting brazenly and artificially the authority of the contents of the novel on to Jim Burden, Cather makes *My Ántonia* into a 'masterpiece' of exposure of male idealisation of women, of male nostalgia, as well as exposing male attitudes toward sex, female independence, and toward other types of independent women. Such women as Lena and the young Ántonia are shown in the novel to threaten men and to thwart the realisation of their hopelessly unrealistic, immature fantasies of wife as mother. As such, these sections on Lena and the hired girls are crucial to the text, not the digressions they are usually said to be.

By her prefatorial disclaimers, Cather was being overtly ironic, in the sense that she meant something other than what she said. She was trying to write a new kind of novel, without the conventional forms, arrangements, furnishings, patterns, structures, themes, or styles, of realist novels. She was both anticipating an incomprehending readership and gently mocking it for its narrow, unimaginative, and stubborn concept of what the novel might be and what it might become (and, analogously, of what women might be and what they might become). By creating this frame, which in crucial ways enriches the book, she jokingly, ironically distanced herself from the content of the text, by making Burden a fictional counterpart to herself. She also made polemical aesthetic statements in her preface, as she called attention to central aesthetic issues of form, arrangement, memory, and how writing and reading take place. Basically, she called attention to the communicative situation involved in all story-telling: first, she referred ironically to Jim's making Ántonia 'come alive' for (the fictional) Cather on the train through Iowa by his 'relating stories' about her. Second, Cather emphasised the fact that she would now read his 'thing', his 'account', and presumably, edit it for us to read later. The import of these ironic, self-referential, framing strategies, though simple and easy to follow, has been neglected by readers. Yet they are crucial in leading to a realisation of a level of self-criticism embedded in the text, a criticism of reading, and a representation of the self-conscious nature of life, and art, as well as of the complex, mysterious relation between craft, imagination, and memory. These three latter elements become explicit parts of the subject matter of the novel, as are their interrelations. Memory, along with criticism embedded in art, is overtly an issue and is personified to some degree by Burden himself; additionally, artistic energy becomes a metaphorical subject as characterised by Ántonia. Her natural energy and vitality, and their relation to her womanliness and her idealness are an issue for the reader. Her energy and creativity are the source and the material for Jim's subsequent work of art. No single allegories are possible here, though the issues of relationship are clearly present. They are present, perhaps, but in the only sense acceptable to Cather, namely, hovering over the work, as overtones, as metaphors, 'on the page without being specifically named there'.[10] That 'inexplicable presence of the thing not named' is what provides much of the unity, the end which is always kept in view if a harmony of the elements and proportion of part to whole are to be achieved: 'that, one might say, is created.'

In the above sections discussing narrative strategies, ironic frameworks, and the artistic significance of personas, Cather's profound and continuous response to the sublimity and mystery of nature, with its twin life and death forces, has only been touched upon. Her response to the country of the cliff dwellers, like that of such great artists as Georgia O'Keeffe, permeates her work, even where it is 'absent', or rather, where it is only one of those overtones or suggestions more 'inexplicably present' in the text than if landscape had been overtly invoked. Cather's fascination and respect for what one might call a naked, Blakean energy of nature, whether used for positive or destructive ends, has brought criticism from a number of critics.[11] Like Blake, however, Cather saw clearly that the most deadly enemy of fulfillment and creativity was not misuse of vital, powerful energy, destructive as it can be at times, so much as the passivity and mediocrity which stifles imagination hourly and daily. *The Song of the Lark* is a constant meditation upon the deadliness and suffocation of genius by convention and narrow-mindedness, which sees in all excellence danger and threat to entrenched ways of living. Like William Blake, Cather believed that the only 'truths' for human beings were this vital energy and its diminution, death. Yet, paradoxically, she saw death as a natural part of energy, so that the real death to be feared most is death-in-life, namely, the mediocrity of ordinary everyday life: it alone kills the spirit and leads to a death-in-life existence.

In the exquisite cliff dwellings, Cather was inordinately inspired to see nature inset with human life in the most harmonious, perfect proportion she had ever found:

> But the really splendid thing about our city, the thing that made it delightful to work there, and must have made it delightful to live there, was the setting. The town hung like a bird's nest in the cliff, looking off into the box canyon below, and beyond into the wide valley we called Cow Canyon, facing an ocean of clear air. A people who had the hardihood to build there, and who lived day after day looking down upon such grandeur, who came and went by those hazardous trails, must have been, as we often told each other, a fine people. But what had become of them? What catastrophe had overwhelmed them? (p. 213)

Life and death were at one in those canyons, while any duality between nature and art or nature and human life was overcome. There, she saw humanity and art as themselves natural, as in nature, continuous with and one with nature, not above it or outside it or alienated from it, as in modern city life. The abysses and the endless dualities that modern life created between art and nature, and between the spiritual and the physical, were overcome in those tiny, perfectly wrought cities set into the natural arches of the high cliffs in the canyons.

Nature, that most fully developed 'character' in Cather's novels (and personified explicity in Ántonia), not only provides a sense of the sheer immensity of space and energy surrounding life. Nature seems itself all alive, whether organic or inorganic, and death is portrayed as a natural part of a living nature. Absolute dualities between life and death are overcome for Cather through imaginative, relational apprehension. Nature also acts as one of the unifying principles of her novels, as Cather explores, time and again, as one of her central thematic preoccupations, woman's relation to nature and how nature's stupendous energies can be released by the human imagination for fulfillment and art. Moreover, the unfathomable mystery and wonder of how nature could have come into being, of how it is that there is anything at all, informs most of her writings with a pagan, religious dimension, just as it permeated Dorothy Richardson's *Pilgrimage*.

Cather wrote in her preface to *The Song of the Lark* that style is the artist's very self. Some of her most exquisite prose occurs in the passages describing the canyons of the Southwest, where the cliff dwellings seemed more like outcroppings and outgrowths of nature itself, not intrusions into it, as are the towns and cities of civilisation usually are. The naturalness, harmony, and proportion of those cliff cities became a kind of model, ideal, and inspiration for Cather, as she sought to develop a style of writing and a formal structure that were 'like' the cliff dwellings. Her rejection of realism, with its overcrowded furnishings, her rejection of the traditional romance with all its props of plot, drama, and thematics, and her craving for a spaciousness, austerity, and harmony in her style arose from her powerful response to the wild natural beauty she saw in the perfect congruence of humanity, art, and nature. Her forms and style, then, can be understood as an imaginative expression or representation of the cliff canyons, that is, as emblematic of them and as metaphors for them. Her style is a constant striving to re-enact in language the harmony, proportion, and integration of the congruence of nature, the human, and art which she experienced there. Moreover, her novels, as artefacts, also seek to emulate in their shape and form the exquisite, austere beauty and natural order of the cliff cities.

Cather's use of nature occurs in quite strikingly different ways, from its permeating utterly the atmosphere of *Death Comes for the Archbishop* (1927), to being an incredibly effective inset ("Tom Outland's Story') in *The Professor's House* (1925). Earlier, nature was used as a pivotal and recurrent force in Thea Kronberg's life (in *The Song of the Lark*, 1915), and it provided the entire background and much of the vitality of *My Ántonia* (1918) and *O Pioneers!* (1913). While in Cather's other novels nature impinges in less obviously powerful ways, it is rarely absent, whether the setting is the Great Plains and prairies, the Southwest, or Virginia. Even where events may take one of the characters to a large East Coast city like New York, or Washington, the deadly absence of the nurturing qualities of nature are a powerful, unnamed 'presence'. Those nurturing qualities still permeate the style of the novel, reminding the reader by suggestion and overtone that life-forces cut off from nature wither.

In terms of artistic craft, Cather's most strikingly successful, overt uses of nature may be the 'Tom Outland's Story' inset of *The Professor's House*, and in *Death Comes for the Archbishop*. Yet there are powerful sections in *The Song of the Lark*: Thea returns to the Southwest to revitalise her seriously life-endangering, failing energy. Powerful as nature is as an atmosphere, background, and even stage upon which the events of *My Ántonia* and *O Pioneers!* are enacted, the plains and prairies fail to provide the imaginative richness of the Southwest, where the integrated nature–art–humanity strides in as central unifying force. Hence, in *My Ántonia*, the force of nature is embodied in the central character. If we examine Cather's design in *The Professor's House* (and *Death Comes for the Archbishop*), the emblematic quality of her structure and style as an attempt to re-create the canyon-city perfection will become more evident, both in the novel and in the reading experience of the novel, where the reader is drawn into an excavation, like Tom Outland, of a work of art which turns out to be nothing other than a process of the construction of one's very individuality. Excavation, then, is a central, unifying emblem for both art and for reading or aesthetic response; it constitutes indeed a 'recipe' for reading imaginatively.

In *The Professor's House*, the 'Tom Outland's Story' turns the whole novel inside out by a stroke of magic, shifting the artistic emphasis to an apparently a-central, or, at least, supplementary element (to use one of Derrida's favourite techniques). Structurally, the novel is divided into three sections, vastly varying in length. 'The Family', book one, is some 165 pages; book three, 'The Professor', is only 26 pages, while the inset, book two ('Tom Outland's Story') is 74 pages. Outland's story is a stunning piece of prose, a priceless work of art, inset into a larger framework. What seems to be the novel turns out, in a sense, only to be the frame for (arguably) the most successful piece of prose writing Cather ever produced. This 'inversion' of novel into framework, and an apparent interruption or intrusion transformed into the centre-piece, suggests the role of disruption in imaginative creation. A kind of reversal of values is announced, whereby the novel becomes a mere setting for the story within the novel, the novel almost an annoying distraction from the real substance at hand, namely, the elemental forces of nature that nurture women and men and reproduce themselves in imaginative human artefacts.

There are many complications in *The Professor's House*, which one can only mention in passing here. Issues regarding the relation of author to reader, creation to interpretation, and the problem of the nature of language and communication arise as a result of the story within the novel. Tom is the teller, allegedly, of the inner tale, while the professor is the chosen listener. Since Cather selects this 'tale within a tale' form of art, instead of giving us Tom's experiences 'directly', she is clearly, as in so many of her novels, making story-telling and listening overt subject-matter. To complicate matters, the professor is overtly the subject of the outer tale, the novel, but he is also made the transmitter to the reader of Outland's story. In *My Ántonia* Jim Burden allegedly 'tells' Ántonia's story (Cather transmitted it to us) and Ántonia is overtly the subject of '*My Ántonia*' (the Burden MS, not the novel). The doubling of characters in both novels suggests, however, not only fantasies of wholeness through love and affection, but also a more sophisticated suggestion of the collapse of absolutely distinct identities, so that teller is the listener's double. Jim and Ántonia, and the professor and Tom, lose their separate identities and merge into each other. The notion of an autonomous, discrete 'self', is parodied, while the identities and activities of the two corresponding processes (interpretation versus the creation of 'fictions'—themselves being interpretations) overlap and merge. The dualities of speaker-listener and story-interpretation show these opposite roles to be more alike than different; or at least their alleged difference (activity versus passivity) is shown to have been misrepresented as more absolute than it is.

As in Coleridge's 'Ancient Mariner', the listener is carefully chosen. These tales of the Mariner's, and Outland's, and Burden's can only be told to certain chosen people, perhaps even because the teller could not even tell the story without the stimulation or inspiration of having 'the right listener'. It is suggested here that landscape and persona devices, along with style, can select readers to whom Cather herself also tells various tales, the meaning of each tale being determined by the point of view from which the reader assumes Cather to be speaking. That is, the interpretations of readers vary decidedly depending on the point of view they themselves take, and the view they mistakenly ascribe to Cather. This in turn depends in part upon whether it is repressed by the reader. One may deny the textual gestures of self-consciousness in these novels only by a determined blindness to the artistic facts. Note, for example, the humorous way Cather engaged in self-referential tactics shortly before and during the initial part of the Outland story. Tom is said to have 'always kept back' (p. 176) the story that he 'at last told' to St Peter. This is also the story that Cather kept back from her readers for 165 pages! Moreover, Outland begins his story by saying 'the thing that sidetracked me and made me so late coming to college was a somewhat unusual accident, a string of accidents. It began with a poker game' (179). Cather delighted in raising the issue of the role of blind chance and accidents in life, but what really makes one smile here is the ironic, indirect reference to the fact that the reader is now being 'sidetracked' from St Peter's story to Outland's, which also began with a poker game! Poker-faced Cather could also be said to have begun with a poker game with her readers: the novel began with St Peter's story masquerading as the mainline. It turns out to be itself a side-tracking from the Outland story.

Further gestures toward self-consciousness and irony occur if we consider the names of Cather's characters. Jim 'Burden' unburdens his soul and his MS to a fictional Willa Cather. He becomes an awful burden to the reader, as well, who sees his male fantasies embarrassingly revealed. Tom Outland's name, on the other hand, suggests something beyond convention, unusual and exotic, though not without a touch of parody. The professor's name is the most parodic of all, Napoleon Godfrey St Peter, and to be forced to refer to him all the time as St Peter has a remarkably satiric effect. Named after warriors, crusaders, and adventurers, his life-work devoted to an account of *Spanish Adventurers in North America*, he seems an appropriate person to 'receive' Tom Outland's gift of the incredible story of the discovery and excavation of the cliff dwellings. But we must not take him too nostalgically, too seriously, or we fail to see Cather's gentle fun-poking criticism, on the one hand of the 'burdens', and on the other hand, of the males who fantasise that a life of adventure would have been the key to happiness. Integration, balance, and the need to connect up our differing human needs, is emphasised: 'only connect' as Forster said. 'Thea' 'Kronberg' in *The Song of the Lark*, has a doubly funny name, the use of the Greek word for goddess suggesting paganism, since the Christian myth, invoked in 'St Peter', always involves a male God. This use of names in fiction overtly to allegorise is a very conventional, but nevertheless effective technique of self-consciousness, much akin to Bowles', Chopin's, Stevie Smith's, Mansfield's, and others' puns on naming.

Related, however, to the above-mentioned issue of author–reader, mainline–sideline interactions is the question of Cather's portrayal of the relation of imagination to perception. Coleridge described this as the relation of secondary to primary imagination, meaning that basic perception itself is imaginative, artistic creation being a secondary 'echo' of that primary form of human mental activity. Shelley followed Coleridge's insistence that the poet's mental activity is not a special kind of behavior, but the paradigmatic form of all human mental activity, namely perception itself. The latter, as Derrida has recently suggested, is not to be conceived of as a passive receptivity, but as active creativity (though the latter degenerates through time and custom into 'dead metaphors'). Cather's style, her use of landscape description, and her narrative techniques suggest the awareness that perception is imagination, and that the reader's perception must become, like the author's, imaginative and creative if the text is to be anything but a 'dead metaphor'. Cather's style, that is, reveals the primacy of imagination in all perception, and the fact that interpretation, emblemised as excavation, is involved in what often passes for 'mere' description. Cather's meta-narrative devices show that fact and history are imbued with fiction, to use a familiar phrase; by taking fact and history literally, we forget, first, that any point of view is always only one possible perspective, and second, that truth is 'an army of metaphors', to use Nietzsche's phrase.

In 'Tom Outland's Story', other remarkable passages testify to similar preoccupations of Cather with the way language works preeminently figuratively to reveal that basic perception is essentially imaginative. The following passage demonstrates the perceptual creation of order out of chaos through metaphor, simile, personification, symbol, and allegory, as a process of excavating layers of meaning both in life experience, in language, and in art:

> I happened to glance up at the canyon wall. I wish I could tell you what I saw there, just as I saw it, on the first morning, through a veil of lightly falling snow. Far up above me, a thousand feet or so, set in a great cavern in the face of the cliff, I saw a little city of stone, asleep. It was as still as sculpture—and something like that. It all hung together, seemed to have a kind of composition: pale little houses of stone nestling close to one another, perched on top of each other, with flat roofs, narrow windows, straight walls, and in the middle of the group, a round tower.
>
> It was beautifully proportioned, that tower, swelling out to a larger girth a little above the base, then growing slender again. There was something symmetrical and powerful about the swell of the masonry. The tower was the fine thing that held all the jumble of houses together and made them mean something. It was red in colour, even on that grey day. In sunlight it was the colour of winter oak-leaves. A fringe of cedars grew along the edge of the cavern, like a garden. They were the only living things. Such silence and stillness and repose

—immortal repose. That village sat looking down into the canyon with the calmness of eternity. The falling snow-flakes, sprinkling the pinions, gave it a special kind of solemnity. I can't describe it. It was more like sculpture than anything else. I knew at once that I had come upon the city of some extinct civilization, hidden away in this inaccessible mesa for centuries, preserved in the dry air and almost perpetual sunlight like a fly in amber, guarded by the cliffs and the river and the desert. (pp. 201-2)

Phrases such as 'the face of the cliff', the 'little city of stone asleep', 'still as a sculpture', 'it was more like a sculpture than anything else', the 'solemnity', 'that village sat looking down into the canyon with the calmness of eternity', all these are gestures of personification, metaphor, and simile. Special to this passage is the way Cather both speaks of the scene as a still-life composition in painting, and then paints for her readers that very still-life composition in words. This is a technique she often used in the other novels. It is characteristic of her style, a characteristic that writers like Katherine Mansfield developed to a high degree of art. Yet all the while, hovering as an unspoken presence, is the metaphor that just such linguistic events of personification and figuration as occur in basic writing and reading also occur in perception itself: brute experience is raised to a high, imaginative quality by precisely these compositional, linguistic processes of perception which use metaphor, figures of speech, personification, imagery and symbol to layer, structure, and order the various elements of an experience so as to create a whole, unified effect. This passage is also a metaphor for Cather's ideal of the structure of her novels. Novels are compositions which for Cather are beautifully proportioned, with some one element or number of elements working, as does the tower in the cliff city, to hold all the separate elements of the novel together and make them meaningful. Later passages reinforce the metaphor of the cliff-dwelling canyons as a metaphor for language and art, and particularly, to Cather, for her kind of art. The cliff cities combined artistic craft with domestic life in perfect integration, just as Cather sought to integrate her artistic structures with the thematics, namely the lives of her characters. Nature's relation to humankind is clarified in Father Duchene's insight that the cliff dwellers 'built themselves into this mesa and humanised it':[12]

> Like you, I feel a reverence for this place. Wherever humanity has made that hardest of all starts and lifted itself out of mere brutality, is a sacred spot. Your people were cut off here without the influence of example or emulation, with no incentive but some natural yearning for order and security. They built themselves into this mesa and humanised it. (p. 221)

'Tom Outland's Story' has a further significance in *The Professor's House*, which markedly enriches its aesthetic function for the reader as a story within a novel. The discovery of Cliff City, along with Blake's and Outland's patient excavation of it, are described by Cather in such a way as to create a fascinating, complex analogy with reading. The tremendous efforts the two men have to make to get into the heart of the mesa at all become, for them, for the reader, and for the author, a rite of passage, an initiation into the mysteries of nature and imagination. The discovery of the completely unexpected magical hidden cliff dwellings add further layers of meaning to the journey metaphor. The men manage, moreover, only with great difficulty, to climb the canyon wall up to one of the cliff dwellings, Cliff City. There, the excavation of the incredible city in the sky and all its ancient, extraordinary furnishing turns Outland's story into an intricate, symbolic elaboration of processes of imaginative perception, writing, and reading. The details of Cather's own struggle to create her construction of this elaborate metaphor of imaginative activity in its three major modes of perception, artistic creation, and aesthetic response bear examination. For such details of the various phases of the journey reveal the methods of imaginative activity and, hence, are instructive as intimations to the reader of how to lift herself from a passive, 'lazy-onlooker' attitude into a more active, participatory response.

Cather begins her emblematic account of the men's sojourn near the fascinating mesa with a description of the mesa as monumental and impassable. In a characteristic gesture of irony, she has the foreman in charge of Blake and Outland issue a prohibition to Outland against trying to enter or climb the dangerous mesa:

> Nobody has ever got into it yet. The cliffs are like the base of a monument, all the way round. The only way into it is through that deep canyon . . . you can't get in by that, because the river's too deep to ford and too swift to swim . . . if you boys try any nonsense of that sort, I'll fire you quick. You'd break your neck and lose the land for us. (p. 191)

Outland, however, cannot resist the power of the great mesa:

> The mesa was our only neighbour, and the closer we got to it, the more tantalizing it was. It was no longer a blue, featureless lump, as it had been from a distance, the sky-line was like the profile of a big beast lying down . . . When I got up at daybreak and went down to the river to get water, our camp would be cold and grey, but the mesa would be red with sunshine, and all the slim cedars along the rocks would be gold-metallic, like tarnished gold-foil . . . early in the afternoon . . . the sunset colour would begin to stream up from behind it. Then the mesa was like one great ink-black rock against a sky on fire.
>
> No wonder the thing bothered us and tempted us; it was always before us and was always changing. (pp. 191-3)

In this description, distinctions between the alive and the inert are completely abolished; nature is all alive, whether organic or inorganic, as it was for Coleridge. Moreover description and interpretation are indistinguishable; seeing is imagining, perception is itself visionary, as the light of imagination is projected into the verbal description of fiery nature. Personification, metaphor, metonymy, simile, powerful imagery, paradox, ambiguity, symbol, and allegory are all used by Cather in this passage to awaken the reader to imaginative participation, to 'seeing' imagination itself in action and thereby becoming imaginative.

Further personifications, similes, metaphors, and other rhetorical devices follow, as Cather metaphorically depicts her own and Outland's increasingly imaginative perception, their 'humanising of nature'. His eventual transgression of the prohibition expresses Cather's understanding of the role of disruption and disobedience in imaginative creation, while the apparent impassability of the giant mesa is an acknowledgement of the tremendous labour and courage demanded for imaginative undertaking, whether creation or reading. It is also a signal to the reader of the energy demanded of her, and Cather's step by step account of Outland's laborious undertaking becomes a symbolic recipe for the reader's struggle to penetrate into the text and discover its hidden beauties and its 'architecture'; to excavate its layers and strata of embodied artistry, not, however, to discover, hermeneutically, a hidden meaning. Rather, excavation is itself the goal — as activity of an imaginative, creative kind becomes not only the means of engaging with art, but the end itself. As Outland came to see, the value of the excavation of Cliff City was completely intrinsic to the process, as a metaphor for imaginative living.

Outland began by reconnoitering the mesa, first riding all the way around it, to get a sense of it, concluding that the only way into the mesa is via the dangerous river passing out of it. (Likewise, Cather showed the reader that she must climb back up the 'stream of narration' to get into the deeper layers of the text's existence.) Once Outland succeeded in fording the river, he made his way up the canyon, which, it turns out, has a well-marked trail! A sense of other-worldliness gradually entered into this multi-layered narrative, when Tom spoke of the air as the purest he had ever known: 'It made my mouth and nostril smart like charged water, seemed to go to my head a little and produce a kind of exaltation' (p. 200). For the water, he had a similar reverence:

> I've never anywhere tasted water like it; as cold as ice, and so pure . . . the water looked like liquid crystal, absolutely colorless . . . it threw off the sunlight like a diamond. (p. 209)

After much 'rough scrambling' through the floor of the canyon which had become 'a mass of huge boulders, great pieces of rock . . . as big as haystacks' (p. 200), Outland stopped to catch his breath, and for the first time glanced up at the canyon wall: there he saw 'a little city of stone, asleep' (see quotation of full passage above, pages 159–60), and was so overcome with its magical presence that he hesitated to tell his comrade. Cather's breathtaking description of Outland's initial aesthetic response to Cliff City is a remarkable linguistic description of aesthetic experience itself, and as such is emblematic of imaginative reading, acting as a model for readerly participation. Yet she spared no detail in the narrative to emphasise the labour and determination Outland needed before he caught even a glimpse of the hidden city from the canyon below. And Cather indicated clearly, moreover, that Outland had not had the slightest knowledge of what he might find, if anything, once he penetrated the canyon.

Later Outland communicated his unexpected discovery to Blake, and they decided to devote themselves to climbing up the canyon wall to the cliff dwelling to explore it. After an arduous week, they made their way via a broken trail to the threshold, and 'stepped upon the ledge that was the floor of the Cliff City' (p. 207). Outland gave St Peter a detailed description of the architectural layout of the little cliff city and the innumerable household objects—the pots, jars, bowls, mats, baskets, clay ovens, implements—which they found lying about undisturbed. They spent weeks building a passable road before they started 'what we called excavating' (p. 211), another metaphor for excavating 'meaning' from the novel. Outland bought a book and wrote into it an exact description of each object found, and in another ledger he wrote an 'account of the day's work'. Later, he was to abandon this latter book which he came to call a diary, as antithetical to his eventual response and relation to Cliff City (p. 252 and see p. 223), a metaphor for Cather's rejection of realism.

It would be reductive and unimaginative to seek explicit allegories for Cather's careful construction of Outland's story, but the intricate artistry of his tale invites reading analogies and metaphors of imaginative activity which greatly enrich the text. Outland's arduous journey entails several more stages in addition to the one described above, each of which is instructive for the reader in Cather's marvellous allegory of the reading imagination: Outland journeyed to Washington to announce his discovery, but no one took any interest in it. He was devastated by the stupidity of the bureaucrats, and horrified at the regimented life of the hundreds of 'little black-coated men pouring out of white buildings. Queer how much more depressing they are than workmen coming out of a factory' (p. 236). Suffering from a 'low-spiritedness I had never known before' (p. 233), he 'wanted nothing but to get back to the mesa and live a free life and breathe free air again' (p. 236). He returned to New Mexico only to learn to his horror that Blake had sold the entire furnishings of the City to a German collector who had already shipped them to Europe while Outland was in Washington. He quarrelled with his friend Blake, who departed deeply hurt and feeling gravely misunderstood, and Outland decided to stay alone in the mesa all summer. The writing and reading analogy now becomes explicit and pronounced:

> that was the first night I was ever really on the mesa at all—the first night that all of me was there. This was the first time I ever saw it *as a whole*. It all came together in my understanding, as a series of experiments do when you begin to see where they are leading. Something had happened in me that made it possible for me to co-ordinate and simplify, and that process, going on in my mind,

brought with it great happiness. It was possession. The excitement of my first discovery was a very pale feeling compared to this one. For me the mesa was no longer an adventure, but a religious emotion. I had read of filial piety in the Latin poets, and I knew that was what I felt for this place. It had formerly been mixed up with other motives; but now that they were gone, I had my happiness unalloyed. (pp. 250-1)

'To co-ordinate and simplify', these are the words Cather used to describe the essence of creative activity, whether in writing or in reading. Up to this point in the narrative, analogies of different responses in reading and varied interpretations have been multi-fold: Father Duchene gave a long, detailed verbal interpretation of the furnishings of Cliff City (pp. 218-21), Blake and Outland's responses are contrasted — and lead to a terrible clash, the Washington bureaucrats don't care, but a German collector grabs up the valuable artefacts. After all these different responses to that work of art, 'Cliff City', are narrated, and after the multiple stages of Outland's imaginative activity are portrayed, Cather suddenly transmuted Outland's own aesthetic responses into another realm, as a mere 'adventure' has become a 'religious emotion':

> I can scarcely hope that life will give me another summer like that one. It was my high tide. Every morning, when the sun's rays first hit the mesa top, while the rest of the world was in shadow, I wakened with the feeling that I had found everything, instead of having lost everything. Nothing tired me. Up there alone, a close neighbour to the sun, I seemed to get the solar energy in some direct way. (p. 251)

Outland's rejection of his day-book and cataloguing follow this aesthetic experience of wholeness and of the primal energising effects of nature and the sun on the solitary mesa:

> All that summer, I never went up to the Eagle's Nest to get my diary — indeed, it's probably there yet. I didn't feel the need of that record. It would have been going backward. I didn't want to go back and unravel things step by step. Perhaps I was afraid that I would lose the whole in the parts. At any rate, I didn't go for my record. (p. 252)

Emblematically, this passage represents Cather's rejection of realism, its cataloguing and recording of detail, its 'props' and 'furnishings', and her commitment to something she saw as greater than such rational description, namely the aesthetic experience of unity and the imaginative creation of it. Nevertheless, there is a definite suggestion that this stage of detailed enumeration and intense familiarity with concrete particulars is a stage of experience that must be gone through, not skipped out. Had Tom not become intimate with the Cliff City's furnishings, he would never have been able to achieve the sense of wholeness and vision that he later gained. Similarly, author and reader must attend to detail, to concretes, in order to gain an experience of the whole aesthetic unit of an artefact. Later, Outland acknowledged the tragedy of the broken friendship with Blake over a disagreement about possession, over material objects, no matter how beautiful or valuable aesthetically and no matter how selfless his moral position. Cather thereby implied that imagination in art (or love in friendships) has, ultimately, little to do with possessions, as she forcefully argued in 'The Novel Démeublé', and as Outland came to believe by the end of his story. The interweaving of several distinct levels of thematics into Outland's story —developing friendship and its destruction, the relation of humans to nature, the nature of imaginative activity, and the essential quality of art as unifying—gives the text a powerful, multilayered complexity which is completed by Cather's inversion of history and fiction. St Peter's life-work was a 'historical' account of the exploration of America by the Spanish, while Outland's story was a living narrative of his own experience as a discoverer and explorer of the New Mexico cliff dwellings. Outland was making history while St Peter was writing about it; St Peter saw Outland as a personification of imagination, while Outland's narrative became for him a complex metaphor for the various stages of imaginative experience. As such, St Peter imaginatively identified with Outland, inspired as he was by Outland's story, and saw Outland as his ideal youthful self, as his own imagination in action. St Peter's ability to enter into Outland's story is a model for the reader, as is Outland's ability to enter into the beauty of the cliff dwellings and both excavate and appreciate them in a way such that aesthetic appreciation, through excavation, leads to almost religious fulfillment.

As in *My Ántonia*, the narrative of this novel is elaborately structured; indeed, it is Cather's most complex novel. Its Chinese-box structure is aesthetically unobtrusive (unlike *My Ántonia*), but irresolvably complex, as the central 'origin' of the story is a mystery, namely, the irrecoverable life of the cliff dwellers—why they built such cities, and why they deserted them: 'What had become of them?' (p. 213). To sum up, Cather's complex narrative involves the Professor, a writer of 'history' (fiction?), engaged in a powerful emotional conflict with life and death, as he struggled with *tedium vitae*. Within this 'framework novel' is set Outland's story, narrated to St Peter in the midst of the latter's struggle with the forces of death and suicide impulses. This framework about the failure of imaginative energies (one of Cather's central preoccupations throughout her writings) contrasts by opposition with Outland's story of adventure and imaginative living. But this centrepiece, the Outland story, is itself a story which gains its inspiration from another imaginative life—the past life of the cliff dwellers, who built their marvellous, awe-inspiring cities, and then mysteriously disappeared, leaving their work of art, the city, behind them, as a testimony and embodiment of their own imaginativeness. The city inspired Outland as an embodiment of his imagination, just as Outland himself, and his story, inspired St Peter. Cather was at pains to emphasise, moreover, that the city is a perfect integration of the natural and the human, this congruence constituting for her the definition of art. The city is a work of art, not a mere historical relic; it is an embodiment of the artistic power, the 'humaneness', of the people who built it and lived there. The collapse of the distinction between history and art is completed as Outland's account of his own history is the fiction at the heart of the novel. *The Professor's House* stands as Cather's most eloquent statement of the inadequacy of any notion which makes literature or art secondary to history and reality, such as 'new historicism' does. And her novels reject any hermeneutic interpretation of excavation as the relevation of hidden meaning. Excavation is valuable in itself. It is the intrinsically valuable activity of imaginative creation, both in artefact and in aesthetic response, but most especially in perception and life experience. The workplay is the écriture of Derrida, not the search for hidden, discoverable meanings of Ricoeur or Gadamer.

It is not exaggeration to suggest, then, again, that nature, understood as imagination, is the central character of Cather's novel, present even where it is not literally named in the pages of some of her novels. Nature, Cather suggested, is the most elemental need of humankind; cut off from nature our spirit is lost. Deeper than family, Freudian, or Oedipal conflicts in the unconscious is the terrible deprivation and conflict that occurs in the spirit of humans when deprived of a close, nurturing, harmonious, and constant interaction with nature. For Cather, nature is our nature as humans, our living, vital, creative being. Without keeping in touch with nature (and our own nature, namely, imagination) we become dehumanised, denaturalised 'cogs in a machine'. Our speech becomes a series of dead metaphors, a string of parroted clichés; our feelings and thoughts borrowed, hackneyed, stereotyped, predictable reactions rather than individual, imaginative responses. Cather's novels show that our individuality never develops if we lose touch with nature and therefore with imagination. No amount of art, cultivation, or religion can stifle that need for creation, and without the constant restorative effects of nature, humans become unimaginative and dehumanised. Genuine humanity is in need of the sustenance that a relation with nature (that most fully drawn and living character of her novels) brings. This 'serious', almost religious attitude to nature (as imagination) which Cather's novels suggest should not, however, blind us to the playfulness throughout Cather's artistry. Nor should it make us insensitive to her irony and wit.

Cather, like Tom Outland and Jim Burden, seeks a reader sympathetic and imaginatively responsive to her unnamed 'presences' hovering over the page. The reader may realise that both she and her mode of reading are implicated in the tales. The experience, struggles, and conflicts of the protagonists are a depiction of each reader's psychological life-experience, not merely the struggle of someone else which readers passively watch. These struggles, when artistically portrayed in Cather's novels, always involve at some crucial level the effort to make meaning, to interpret, and to read actively. They involve universal conflicts, which unconsciously or consciously we all are undergoing. Thus, Tom Outland, the Professor, Jim

Burden, Ántonia, Thea, and other characters are engaged in the struggle to make meaning of their lives. They must cope with the conflicting demands of the need for solitude and for relationship, the need for nature and for art. Those conflicts portrayed in the novels mirror our own, if only we are imaginative enough to experience that 'recognition' scene (so central a literary technique of Greek tragedy). Moreover, Cather's style reveals the primacy of imagination in basic perception itself, as well as in the interpretation involved in apparently mere description.

Death Comes for the Archbishop (1927) is one of Cather's most exquisite and mature novels. Yet, judging from the literature on Cather and the American novel, this fine achievement is a little unrecognised. In an utterly different genre of fiction from the experiments of *The Song of the Lark* (1915) or *The Professor's House* (1925), on the one hand, and *My Mortal Enemy* (1926) or *A Lost Lady* (1923) on the other, the narrative techniques and stylistic devices of *Death Comes* seem at first to be most like the story-telling techniques and structures of *My Ántonia* (1918). Plot is subordinated to the demands of some of those 'dozens of stories' which lie behind any good novel, many of which are themselves sacrificed to the demands of the explicit stories which do remain in these two fictions, and which constitute this late, remarkable artefact of 1927. Perhaps, surprisingly, there is no lack of integrity or unity, however, in this apparently anecdotal novel, virtually plotless, overall at least, but with endless plots within the stories. These stories are told sometimes by the 'author', sometimes by the characters as recent events, sometimes as very distant memories, or even as stories within stories—all contained within that timeless, inexhaustibly powerful, and all-pervasive, world-wide literary convention of the journey. Journeys pervade the text from start to finish; only a very few significant stories do not involve journeys crucially. Events occur during journeys, or as a result of departures or arrivals; detours are frequent due to storm, human threats or error, or illness. The use of the journey convention functions more, however, as an artistically enriching metaphorical element to create stimulating analogies both with life and also with reading, perception, and artistic creation—as in *The Professor's House*—than as, pre-eminently, a unifying technique, though of course this metaphorical complexity does unify the novel as well. Storytellers, audiences, methods of narration, the magical relation of memory to imagination, all are fascinating thematic elements which, while they never obtrude on the reader to the detriment of the overt thematic interests so deeply engaged with by Cather, still are there on the page as suggested, metafictional elements, at least for those readers interested as much in the art of fiction as in its wonderful, rich content.

The primary method, however, of unifying the various stories of the novel—so that Cather achieved a Coleridgean integrity of part to whole she openly admired—is precisely in this rarefied novel's artistic congruence of 'art', or formal, structural narrative dimension, and that vivid content. This may seem like a tautology until one realises that the implied, though often overt thematic content of nearly every story in the text is human spirituality in all its diverse manifestations, which makes art and religion—in their genuine realities—one. Indeed, the entire novel could be described as one long, steady, but marvellously diverse meditation on the human imagination in its explicit manifestation in religion and the religious life, whether through charity to strangers, religious love of God, or deep companionship and friendship—at the level of overt content, in any case. Imagination is shown to be, as Shelley argued, the very source of all love itself, whether of God, of men and women to each other, or of friendship: 'the great secret of morals is love . . . the great instrument of moral good is the imagination . . . poetry strengthens the faculty which is the organ of the moral nature . . . as exercise strengthens a limb' ('A Defence of Poetry'). Cather's novel takes as its unifying structural/thematic principle this integral relation between religion, art, and life—focusing on characters and on occasions of intense imaginativeness, and arousing in the receptive reader the realisation that the overtly religious theme conveys a universally accepted truth: between the genuinely religious and the genuinely aesthetic, there is no gap, because of an essential, shared spirituality or imaginativeness which is the inspiration of both. Cather's art was her religion, but Father Vaillant and Bishop Latour's religion is truly their art. And in all three cases, life lived imaginatively becomes an occasion for the construction of a work of art, as each character builds herself or himself out of elemental materials into a beautiful creation. Not only for this reason, though, for each character becomes a whole, but a whole which is also an enriching part of the entire network of human community in which they are embedded, and this 'partness', this belonging, is achieved only through intense, imaginative sympathy and humanity. In this way, each of Cather's characters, nearly all of whom become narrators at one point or another, functions as embodiments of the imagination in its various stages of development or, tragically, of decay.

If Cather's subject matter is the imagination, and if this novel traces it in its religious manifestations as though religion were art itself, then content becomes fused with form in one of the finest examples of artistic congruence in the Twentieth Century novel, along with Ellen Glasgow's *The Sheltered Life* (1932), Faulkner's *The Sound and the Fury* (1929), and Kate O'Brien's *Mary Lavelle* (1936), to give only a few more well-known examples. Congruence occurs, that is, because the structure of *Death Comes for the Archbishop* is also that of the faculty of imagination. Cather, for example, dispenses with logical, 'calendared time' (Bishop Latour, also, 'was soon to have done with calendared time . . . he sat in the middle of his own consciousness . . . all [his former states of mind] were within reach of his hand, and all comprehensible', 288-9), in an anti-realist gesture. Taking the Romantic metaphors of the structure of imagination as radial, or as also a field, 'whose centre is everywhere and whose circumference is nowhere', or as 'the snake with the tail in its mouth', or as the 'self-circling energies', or the 'upwardly spiralling force', Cather rejected the linear plot and developmental structure of conventional fiction, and instead created an astonishingly emblematic artefact whose structure designedly and overtly, self-consciously reflects the radial, networking metaphorical working of the human imagination. Every story, every event, every character, every image, every journey is designed to circle back on the others and shed a new, related light on the element in question, or add an increment of meaning or transform the field of relationships into multiple dimensionality. The significance of each element is thereby heightened to the point of an inexhaustible nexus of meaning. Take the example of Bishop Latour's extraordinary experience in 'Hidden Water' (Book I, ii). Only 254 pages later does the reader learn that this is also legible as a miraculous event, and that the characters he met are readable as legendary figures from Biblical times. Indeed, we only learn this if we circle back in our memories, take up pages 22–29, and relate them to 276–81. This example is only one of the most memorable of dozens of such reflected lights, which create radiation effects and networks of relations or meanings that supercharge the text with endless imaginative possibilities.

The other central, systematically occurring artistic technique of this novel, which is a hallmark of much (though not all) of Cather's finest fiction, is the use of nature and landscape. The sheer elemental, primitive force of nature in the American Southwest is, as usual, conveyed—oxymoronically— by the analogy with the human: nature humanised, and indeed, humanity 'naturised'. Coleridge had given Cather her terminology when he argued in the *Shakespearean Criticism* that the most intense form of imaginativeness is the humanising of nature. Take this fine example of Cather's self-conscious artistry, with all its thematic overtones:

> The landscape one longed for when one was far away, the thing all about one, the world one actually lived in, was the sky—the sky! . . . Travelling with Eusabio was like travelling with the landscape made human . . . It was the Indian manner to vanish into the landscape, not to stand out against it . . . they seemed to have none of the European's desire to 'master' nature, to arrange and re-create . . . It was as if the great country were asleep, and they wished to carry on their lives without awakening it . . . winding among the sand waves as if it were [their] business to pass unseen and unheard through a country awakening with spring . . . They coursed over the sand . . . like the shadows that eagles cast in their strong, unhurried flight. (229–32)

While this analogy between nature and the human is evident throughout *Death Comes*, Cather also made use of typical Edith Wharton-like effects of natural light as a metaphor of imaginative seeing, too. Here is a typical instantiation of light as a metaphor for perception, reading, and art:

> They took the old road to the northeast, through the sharp red sand-hills spotted with juniper, and the Bishop accompanied them as far as the loop where

> the road wound out on the top of one of those conical hills, giving the departing traveller his last glimpse of Santa Fé. There Father Joseph drew rein and looked back at the town lying rosy in the morning light, the mountain behind it, and the hills close about it like two encircling arms. '*Auspice, Maria!*' he murmured as he turned his back on these familiar things. (250-1)

Here light, perspective, foreground, background, and central focus all play on painting metaphors to install the reader in yet another of dozens of opportunities for aesthetic experience.

Cather had, one might argue, an aversion for the overt self-consciousness of modernism and post-modernism, but—like Cervantes, Shakespeare, Goethe, and others—she was too much of an artist to miss any opportunity to enrich her elements with emblematic significances of the whole. That is, wherever possible, every discrete element of the text functions as a metaphor, an emblem of the novel's long meditation on the Passion, whether religious, artistic, or human life in its daily ordinariness. The apparently inconsequential matter of a wooden parrot is a good example of the infusion of passion into simple incidents in the Bishop's life in New Mexico:

> ... the sole ornament in the padre's poor, bare little *sala* was a wooden parrot ... It was cut from a single stick of wood, exactly the size of a living bird ... the wings and tail and neck feathers were just indicated by the tool, and thinly painted ... though scarcely carved at all, merely smoothed into shape, it was strangely lifelike; a wooden pattern of parrots, as it were. (82-3)

There follows a story of the mystical meaning of the bird for the pueblo Indians, a 'bird of wonder and desire'.

This image is clearly another emblem of Cather's idea of the artefact, and, as such, another metaphor for her novel; this novel itself can seem to the uninitiated reader as 'light', thinly painted, and merely smoothed into shape: just a collection of anecdotes, really, hardly a Tolstoyan epic. But what exquisite artistry and lifelikeness all at once! And such lifelikeness, by which Cather set much store, so different from the copying mentality of realist representation. Perhaps this is, ultimately, what sets Cather apart from many other novelists or poets, namely, the passionate commitment to art as life itself, lived intensely—not art set apart from life in a museum or library or concert hall. Life—that is the art which Cather everywhere describes; it is the thrust of *My Ántonia*, who forges a self and a family, and wrenches a rich existence out of that treacherous Great Plain. It is the heart of *The Professor's House*, and the very meaning of *The Song of the Lark*. For Thea, life and art are utterly fused, and of course A.S. Byatt is quite mistaken if she really believes that Part VI, etc., should not have been deleted. Cather and William Heinemann were quite right about it. All of part six could have been in the novel by suggestion, not by such crass enumeration, for 'success is never so interesting as struggle'. Never so interesting, and never so artistic; only struggle is artistic. There is nothing, then, at the end of *The Song of the Lark* which could not have been much better achieved by means of hints and prognostications in I–V.

Rarely, however, did Cather's tact fail her, and even in *The Song of the Lark* it is not disfiguring, just odd and superfluous, like an over-long tail on a horse! Usually, her genial irony was fully awake, constantly guiding her intuition, and providing readers with innumerable opportunities for reminding ourselves that what we call artistic perception is in fact the basis of all perception, before it degenerates into unperceptive habit and custom and cliché. References are made, for example, by the narrator to James Fenimore Cooper — through whom the Cardinal 'sees' the Native Americans — or to the lost El Greco — which hovers over the whole diverse narrative like the metaphor of a human soul. Or take the passage described below, and see it as an example of how our perception of nature is constructed out of cultural expectations, conventions, and preconceptions — and not 'natural' at all!

The following long passage from *Death Comes for the Archbishop* shows Willa Cather at work in the effort to free the reader from notions of perception and reading as passive receptivity of already constituted external objects, on the one hand, and already fixed ideas, beliefs, and values of the author on the other. If we look closely at the following passage from *Death Comes for the Archbishop*, we can see how interpretation, perception, figuration, and communication, which are all issues at the heart of reading and writing, become metaphorical subject matter of Cather's novels. These texts are designed for the reader to use as mirrors in which to view one's own wakening into a greater imaginativeness about perception in general and reading in particular. They create the possibility for a greater self-awareness about the pitfalls that surround efforts to read and interpret, pitfalls such as the tendency to make reductive gestures aimed at increasing certainty and determinacy about textual meanings, and the tendency to read for fixed content, instead of for the awakening to active participation in the making of metaphors:

> One afternoon in the autumn of 1851 a solitary horseman, followed by a pack-mule, was pushing through an arid stretch of country somewhere in central New Mexico. He had lost his way and was trying to get back to the trail, with only his compass and his sense of direction for guides. The difficulty was that the country in which he found himself was so featureless — or rather that it was crowded with features all exactly alike. As far as he could see, on every side, the landscape was heaped up into monotonous red sand-hills, not much larger than haycocks, and very much the shape of haycocks. One could not have believed that in the number of square miles a man is able to sweep with the eye there could be so many uniform red hills. He had been riding among them since early morning, and the look of the country had no more changed than if he had stood still. He must have travelled through thirty miles of these conical red hills, winding his way in the narrow cracks between them, and he had begun to think that he would never see anything else. They were so exactly like one another that he seemed to be wandering in some geometrical nightmare; flattened cones, they were, more the shape of Mexican ovens than haycocks — yes, exactly

the shape of Mexican ovens, red as brick-dust, and naked of vegetation except for small juniper trees. And the junipers, too were the shape of Mexican ovens. Every conical hill was spotted with smaller cones of juniper, a uniform yellowish green, as the hills were a uniform red. The hills thrust out of the ground so thickly that they seemed to be pushing each other, elbowing each other aside, tipping each other over.

The blunted pyramid, repeated so many hundred times upon his retina and crowding down upon him in the heat, had confused the traveller, who was sensitive to the shape of things.

'Mais c'est fantastique!' he muttered, closing his eyes to rest them from the intrusive omnipresence of the triangle.

When he opened his eyes again, his glance immediately fell upon one juniper which differed in shape from the others. It was not a thick-growing cone, but a naked, twisted trunk, perhaps ten feet high, and at the top it parted into two lateral, flat-lying branches, with a little crest of green in the centre, just above the cleavage. Living vegetation could not present more faithfully the form of the Cross.

There is much wit and irony in this passage, a quite mocking irony, and also sympathy, of the tendency, when one has lost one's way, whether in nature or in reading, to make the strange and uncertain into something familiar and meaningful. An attentive reading of this passage, however, turns up some delightful metaphors of the processes of perception, of interpretation, and of making meaning of surrounding elements. (It is also a gentle parody of the enumerating and cataloging of detail of the realist.)

The solitary horseman has 'lost his way and was trying to get back to the trail', very much the feeling readers often have toward texts; the featurelessness of the landscape, which makes difficulties for the horseman, is suddenly changed to its opposite, and the landscape is now 'crowded with features all exactly alike'. Monotonous red sand-hills then become, under the solitary horseman's continuing gaze, likened to haycocks, this change being a clear move toward metaphor. The whole landscape is then described by means of another metaphor, namely, a 'geometrical nightmare', and the haycocks become mathematical cones. Next the observer decides they are not, after all, haycocks or geometrical cones so much as Mexican ovens, 'yes, exactly the shape of Mexican ovens'. His efforts to make sense of and interpret the landscape take him to another extreme. He identifies the red sand-hills with the contrasting yellowish-green juniper trees: 'And the junipers, too, were the shape of Mexican ovens.' Cather wittily confronts her reader with this quite incredible resolution of yellowish green, living juniper trees and red sand-hills into the identical interpretation of not haycocks, not cones, but Mexican ovens. Now everything in the landscape, whether green junipers or red hills, is like a Mexican oven. The narrative persona seems openly to intrude, in the next line, as simile, pushed to metaphor, gives way further to personification: 'The hills thrust out of the ground so quickly that they seemed to be pushing each other, elbowing each other aside, tipping them over.' This example of 'humanising nature' (as Coleridge liked to describe one of the primary activities of imagination) is yet another example of imaginative perception seeking to establish order in the midst of chaos and unfamiliarity, by means of similes and metaphors.[13] The hills, after this personification of the landscape, now become blunted pyramids, another geometrical metaphor, and in a gesture of gentle wit, the narrator humorously remarks, in justification of all the previous metaphors, that 'the traveler was sensitive to the shape of things.' Pyramids unobtrusively give way to triangles, and, finally, to crown the passage, one juniper stands out from all the 'featureless' hills and trees, in the form of the Cross!

This passage is a humorous and remarkable exemplification of the various processes of 'meaning-making' involved in perception and interpretation in general, and is characteristic of Cather's novels. Cather's metaphors, similes, and personifications show that perception is not merely a 'passive beholding of already constituted entities'. Rather, it involves imaginative activity at its most basic levels. The 'description' of this landscape, like Cather's other landscape descriptions, is shot through with self-referential depictions of the imaginative perception, or figuration, involved in both writing and in efforts to read meaning into the text. Metaphors, similes, personifications, and, finally, gross allegory are shown to be a part of all such 'description'; realist notions of the possibility of objective description collapse, as Cather exposed all description to be interpretations of a highly subjective kind. The final, delightfully parodic religious allegory gently satirises and exposes the superstitious tendency to reduce nature to religious iconography and artistic, imaginative play to familiar, recuperable, or univocal meanings. The passage, while overtly serious, sets imaginative art and genuine spirituality against allegorisation, and proceeding in a dead-pan, poker-faced tone, eventually releases humour and irony about the priest's final allegory. For that final allegory is an 'emblem', a type, a metaphor for unimaginative reading and allegories unconsciously imposed by readers on to texts, as, for example, the systematic idealisation of Ántonia, and others. Cather ironically exposed idealisation for what it is, namely, a crucifixion of imaginative response, and the surest means to dehumanisation and death-in-life through reducing the human spirit to mediocrity. All her novels, without exception, depict, through sophisticated techniques, the struggle between mediocrity (the life of passive fantasy) and imagination, by confronting the reader directly with parodies of reductive readings and with models of imaginative perception.

Cather's final irony, her gentle final gesture in *Death Comes...*, is an Emily Dickinson-like metaphor of the arrival of death as a carriage:

> He continued to murmur, to move his hands a little, and Magdalena thought he was trying to ask for something... but in reality the Bishop was not there at all: he was standing in a tip-tilted green field among his native mountains, and he was trying to give consolation to a young man who was being torn in two before his eyes by the desire to go and the necessity to stay. He was trying to forge

a new Will in that devout and exhausted priest; and the time was short, for the diligence for Paris was already rumbling down the mountain gorge.

Not only does the realisation that this past 'memory' is a metaphor of Bishop Latour's own present state (desire to die, necessity to live—or *vice versa*) release the novel from 'calendared time'. Not only does it remind the reader that the principal narrative strategy is one of stories of self-circling energies; not only does it foreground how meaning is enriched by relationships with other meanings and events. Not only does it suggest that the very nature of imagination is a journeying or shuttling from one metaphor or point of view or element to another, to yet another, then circling back again to relate them all together in various kinds of temporary unity. The passage also reminds the reader that Bishop Latour and Father Vaillant—the two character-strands which weave in and out throughout the novel in unity and yet in distinction—are also head and heart, thought and feeling, and like Contento and Angelica, while distinguishable, should never be wholly divided. As the Bishop said to Father Vaillant before his next and final departure:

> If you take Contento, I will ask you to take Angelica as well. They have a great affection for each other; why separate them indefinitely? Once could not explain to them. They have worked long together. (250)

Compare these two distinguished fathers of the Church of Rome to a couple of white mules? Oh, ironic Willa!

Notes

1. See Flannery O'Connor, *Mystery and Manners: Occasional Prose* (London: 1972), especially the essay, 'Some Aspects of the Grotesque in Southern Fiction', pp. 36–50, and 'The Nature and Aims of Fiction', pp. 63–86.
2. 'The novel démeublé', in *On Writing*, foreword by S. Tennant (New York: 1968), pp. 33–44.
3. 'On the Art of Fiction', in *On Writing, op. cit.*
4. See Coleridge: 'A little compression would make it a beautiful poem. *Study Compression!*–'. *Collected Letters*, ed. E.L. Griggs (Oxford: 1956), I, 351.
5. 'On the Art of Fiction', in *On Writing, op. cit.*, 102.
6. 'The novel démeublé', in *On Writing, op. cit.*, 41–2.
7. William Blake, letter to Dr Trusler, 23 August 1799: 'To the Eyes of the Man of Imagination, Nature is Imagination itself'.
8. Kate Fulbrook, in *Free Women* (Brighton: 1990), discussed this issue, and it is taken up by Chopin and Rhys.
9. A.S. Byatt, preface to *A Lost Lady* (London: 198). And see James Schroeter, ed., *Willa Cather and her Critics* (Ithaca and London: 1967), 20–4, on narrative personas.
10. 'The novel démeublé', 41.
11. See Kate Fulbrook, *Free Women, op. cit.*, 33–56, who seems disturbed by Cather's emphasis on naked energies of a Dionysiac, Nietzschean kind.
12. Coleridge practically defined imagination as the faculty of 'humanising nature' in his *Shakespearean Criticism*, which a close reading reveals to be Cather's artistic hornbook. See Thomas Raysor's edition (London and New York: 1960), especially vol. I, pages 199 ff., on 'The Characteristics of Shakespeare'.
13. See Schroeter, *op. cit.*, 22–4, and 62–71, for Rebecca West on *Death Comes* as 'the feat of making a composition out of the juxtaposition of different states of being'.

The Literature of Place

165
The Two or More Worlds of Willa Cather

◆

MARCUS CUNLIFFE

In 1923 Frederick Jackson Turner, the famous historian of the frontier, remarked that 'American history and American literature cannot be understood apart from each other.' Most of us would accept Turner's comment as a truism. Yet the problem of the relation between historical and literary approaches is more complicated than that. Thus, so far as I can determine, Willa Cather did not read Turner's enormously influential essays, though they set the pattern for an entire generation of American historians, from about 1900 to 1930; and Turner for his part, though in 1924 he told a correspondent that 'a valuable study might be made of the pioneer woman and her place in history,'[1] seems never to have read Willa Cather.

We shall come back later to the parallels and divergences in these two figures. For the moment, my point is that, for the purposes of historians, some imaginative writers lend themselves more readily than others to classroom citation. The historian appears to feel most at home with novelists who discuss public issues in their work, or who take stands on issues in their capacity as citizens. In covering the years from 1880 to 1930 or thereabouts, the historian of the United States fastens upon such authors as Edward Bellamy, William Dean Howells, Mark Twain, Frank Norris, Winston Churchill, Sinclair Lewis, and Scott Fitzgerald. He instances Bellamy's *Looking Backward* (1888) as a novel directly concerned with social abuses and social reform. He is fascinated by the development of a social conscience in Howells's novels. He is interested in the more oblique social satire of Twain's *Connecticut Yankee* (1889), in which Twain's illustrator Dan Beard supplied caricatures for a rogues' gallery of contemporary Europeans and Americans. The historian refers students to Norris's *The Octopus* (1901) for a view of the struggle between farmers and capitalists in California, and to

SOURCE Marcus Cunliffe, 'The Two or More Worlds of Willa Cather', *The Art of Willa Cather*, eds Bernice Slote and Virginia Faulkner, Lincoln: University of Nebraska Press, 1974, pp. 21-42, 259-60.

The Pit (1903) for an account of the frenzied operations of the stock market in Chicago. Churchill's novels supply material for an understanding of political corruption in the so-called called Progressive Era. Sinclair Lewis and Scott Fitzgerald are treated as chroniclers of the America of the 1920s. Or the historian brings in those writers who associated themselves with the causes and controversies of their day: Howells for his courageous stand on behalf of Chicago's Haymarket anarchists in 1886, Twain as an anti-imperialist, in the wake of the Spanish-American War, Upton Sinclair and Jack London as socialists, and so on.

Willa Cather, being much less easy to handle, has been comparatively neglected by historians. She is of course less preoccupied with purely local affairs than Sarah Orne Jewett, or with abstractions of behavior than Henry James—two fellow writers whom she much admired, and whose work has likewise not supplied much leverage for historians. Willa Cather is a precise observer. With James we usually have only the vaguest explanation of what his characters do for a living, or how much money they make. In Cather's case the material circumstances are often recorded with some exactness. The dollars and cents are set forth. Financial disasters and successes are fairly prominent in her plots. Some of her characters, we learn, are much affected by the dramas of the time. We are told for example that Rodney Blake in *The Professor's House* (1925) feels strongly about the Chicago anarchists and about the Dreyfus trial in France. But such allusions remain peripheral; they are never at the center of the story.

As for her personal response to public issues, this too seems unemphatic—at least when set beside those of the other contemporary writers I have mentioned. In his lively book *The Landscape and the Looking Glass* (1960), John H. Randall suggests that Willa Cather was considerably influenced by the Populist ferment of Nebraska in the 1890s. This may well be true. But taking her work as a whole, I do not feel that the Populist outlook was crucial and enduring for her. The esthetic modes of the decade, which Mr Randall also stresses, strike me as having fixed her attitudes in profounder ways. None of Willa Cather's formidable pioneer women emulates the Populist leader Mary Leese, who urged farmers to 'raise less corn and more hell.' In the next decade, after 1900, America became highly politicised (to use a jargon word of a later period). Political reform, temperance, women's rights, housing and working conditions, pacifism, conservation: these activities aroused a multitude of energetic and articulate Americans—women as well as men. One thinks for example of Jane Addams, the founder of the Chicago slum settlement known as Hull House, who flung herself into a variety of causes, including that of Theodore Roosevelt's 'Bull Moose' Progressivism in 1912. There was abundant opportunity for the writer, through the spread of what Roosevelt called muckraking journalism. Willa Cather, with her editorial job on *McClure's Magazine*, the most lively of all the muckraking periodicals, was set in the midst of Progressivism. Yet for whatever temperamental reasons, she seems to have stood apart from the indignations and aspirations of the Progressive Era. Nor did she seek to attune herself closely to the *Zeitgeist* in later years. Her war novel *One of Ours* (1922) is to my mind a somewhat better book than most critics have been prepared to acknowledge. But it does not reveal a comprehensive grasp of the moods of wartime America or of the immediate postwar atmosphere. Her subsequent treatment of the American scene, for instance in *The Professor's House*, is intelligent but diffuse, as if the author is unsure whether valediction or malediction is the fitter response.

Historians in their classes might have been able to draw upon Cather's writings to illustrate theories of art and literature. Here too she has failed to oblige them. Her ideas on writing are well stated and in my view perfectly sound. But she seems to have declined to jump through the right hoops at the right moment. She did not in the 1890s become identified with the new advocates of naturalism in literature, though self-professedly 'Western' writers such as Frank Norris and Hamlin Garland asserted that truth in literature was something that the authors of their region were peculiarly qualified to produce. Willa Cather did not stake out a claim for herself as a woman writer. Though some of her principal characters are women, they display an almost mannish shrewdness and vigor; and in some of her novels the viewpoint is in more ways than one that of a man. Not for Cather, then, the combination of feminine perception and technical experiment evident in the stream-of-consciousness fiction of her English contemporaries Dorothy Richardson and Virginia Woolf. She may in *One of Ours* have expressed an innocent idealism that actually existed. But the historian prefers to conclude that the American experience in World War I was best rendered in the youthful avant-garde prose of John Dos Passos's *Three Soldiers* (1921) and E.E. Cummings's *The Enormous Room* (1922). Her much-quoted observation that the world broke in two in the year 1922 could be taken as her own recognition that she could not imaginatively make the transition from the old universe to the new, in part because she had never sought to keep abreast of literary fashion. So, according to this interpretation, she was able to enjoy talking with D.H. Lawrence when she met him in New York and then through Mabel Dodge Luhan in New Mexico,[2] but would never have been able to stomach most of Lawrence's fiction—any more than she could appreciate James Joyce's *Ulysses* or the plays of Eugene O'Neill. I suppose historians ought not to be blamed too much for their indifference to Willa Cather, seen as spokesman for her time, when some literary critics have also displayed a good deal of uneasiness, and have tended to categorise her as a 'traditional' novelist. That may amount to a confession that they are unable to devise any suitable definition or 'placing' for Willa Cather.

So much for the superficial problems that have—at least so far as historians are concerned—kept some of us from including her within the familiar range of cultural references. My main argument however is of a different order. It is that each of us is, after all, a prisoner of the *Zeitgeist*; that Willa Cather does, for the historian and possibly for the student of literature, help to shed light on her own age; and that by approaching her from this external position one may gain an additional appreciation of her individual quality. In particular, I wish to examine her as both a product and an exponent of a whole set of tensions between West and East. To some extent these are universal tensions, affecting all 'advanced' civilisations at the end of the nineteenth century, and indeed all societies aware of a difference between the provincial life and that of the metropolis.

Within the American framework, it is clear—to begin with—that some Easterners treated the West with a casualness amounting on occasion to contempt. At various times the New Englander Henry Adams observed that the whole country west of the Alleghenies might as well be scrapped. 'I do not like the western type of man,' was the similar verdict of the New York journalist E.L. Godkin, editor of the *Nation*. The young literary scholar George Edward Woodberry, bemoaning the fate that had exiled him as a teacher at the University of Nebraska, told a Boston friend that the Nebraska faculty was split between Eastern and Western members. Nebraska society was 'characterised by blank Philistinism intellectually and barren selfishness morally.' The undergraduates were unkempt and wore 'shirt fronts of outrageous uncleanness.' 'This life,' he lamented, 'requires a hardihood of the senses and susceptibilities of which you have little conception, I fear. . . . I doubt very much whether the hardihood I gain will not be a deterioration into barbarism, not sinew for civilization.' In about 1890 the Johns Hopkins historian Herbert Baxter Adams, reared in New England and trained in Germany, was offered a temptingly well-paid professorship at the University of Chicago, which for him was in the West. Pondering the advantages and disadvantages of his present post as against the new future one, Adams drew up a balance sheet. He headed one column 'Chicago,' the other 'Baltimore':

CHICAGO	BALTIMORE
Rush	Quiet
Broken	Continuity
Experiment	Experience
New People	Society
Boom	Conservatism
Advantage	Duty
All new	Assured position
Moving	Settled
Lost	Identification

It is not difficult to guess from this choice of vocabulary that Adams decided to stay put.[3] For a convinced Easterner, the West was raw, rude, and remote. It was worse than the provinces, in a European scheme, in being not just relatively but almost absolutely uncultivated.

However, as in the case of the European metropolis-provinces polarity, the disdain of the Easterner was often matched by the self-abasement of the sensitive Westerner. A special feature of the American Westerner was that he was often not a native provincial but someone who had come out to the West from the East, and felt he was regressing into barbarism. This was for instance the initial reaction of the young California writer Bret Harte, who had grown up in New York City. In his contributions to San Francisco magazines, during the middle 1860s, Harte sighed at the ugliness of such American place-names as Poker Flat, Red Dog, and One Horse Flat. In another piece he wrote: 'The less said about the motives of some of our pioneers the better; very many were more concerned in getting away from where they were, than in going to any particular place.' A few years later, as editor of the *Overland Monthly*, Harte poured scorn on the Society of California Pioneers, and claimed that what the West needed instead was a Society for the Suppression of Local Pride.[4]

It was not necessary to be a settler from the East to denigrate the West. Edgar W. Howe, a thirty-year-old newspaper editor in Kansas, poured out his accumulated bitterness in a novel entitled *The Story of a Country Town* (1883). One of the characters in the novel says:

> Haven't you noticed that when a Western man gets a considerable sum of money together, he goes East to live? Well, what does it mean except that the good sense which enabled him to make money teaches him that the society there is preferable to ours? . . . Men who are prosperous . . . do not come West, but it is the unfortunate, the poor, the indigent, the sick . . . who came here to grow up with the country, having failed to grow up with the country where they came from.

Nor was it necessary for a Westerner to apologise for coming East. The classic Dick Whittington-ish story of the ambitious and talented person in all eras and countries is that he demonstrates his ability by leaving the country for the city, the provinces for the metropolis. Ambition itself dictates the move; and the consolation for the provinces is that such-and-such a famous individual is 'from' their area. They gain or hope to gain a minor glory from what is in fact an abandonment. There is a pathos in this recurrent drama. Sometimes the native sophisticate almost entirely loses his original feeling for the home place, as seems to have happened with William Dean Howells in relation to his Ohio childhood. Sometimes the escaper makes his living out of his store of recollections, as in large part Bret Harte did with California. Sometimes, as with Mark Twain, his best writing deals with the scenes of his early life. Usually, however, he does not go back again except on visits. Missouri-born Twain, comfortably installed in Connecticut, wrote to an old friend in 1876 about Southern politics:

> I think I comprehend their position there—perfect freedom to vote just as you choose, provided you choose to vote as *other people* think, social ostracism otherwise. . . . Fortunately a good deal of experience of men enabled me to choose my residence wisely. I live in the freest part of the country.

But the provinces-metropolis analogy is inexact as applied to the American polarity of West and East, and this not merely because the American 'West' was an area whose geographical boundaries and whose other characteristics were continually shifting. There was the further complicating factor that in the American myth, as it has been delineated by Henry Nash Smith and others, the West was never simply the back-of-beyond. It was also, and to a growing degree as the nineteenth century wore on, the land of America's destiny, the locus of the westering impulse evoked in Walt Whitman's poem 'Passage to India' (a poem that Bret Harte, incidentally, rejected when it was submitted to his *Overland Monthly*). After his death in 1865 Abraham Lincoln began to be deified as a great Western symbolic hero—the 'first American' in the words of J.R. Lowell's Harvard Commemoration Ode. *The American Commonwealth* (1889), a widely read assessment by the Scottish observer James Bryce, insisted that the West was the most American part of the United States. In the traditional legend, the provinces are fatally and irretrievably backward, vis-à-vis the metropolis. In part of the American formulation, the West is not backward but forward: the place of the future.[5] According to this reversal, in important respects the 'latest' is not to be found in the East but in the West; and even the 'latest' in the limited sense of the latest fashions in books and clothes was swiftly becoming available in Western metropolises—including the Chicago that Herbert Baxter Adams had so summarily dismissed. This other mood was expressed in Carl Sandburg's *Chicago Poems* (1914):

> *I speak of new cities and new people.*
> *I tell you the past is a bucket of ashes. . . .*
> *I tell you there is nothing in the world*
>   *only an ocean of to-morrows,*
>   *a sky of to-morrows.*

As the nineteenth century drew to a close, Westerners were inclined to argue the strengths of their region as measured by both kinds of up-to-dateness. The historian Charles A. Beard, who had grown up in Indiana, later remembered his annoyance in the 1890s at the prevailing Eastern assumption 'that all of us beyond the Alleghenies, if not the Hudson, were almost, if not quite, uncouth savages.'[6] Frederick Jackson Turner, then a young teacher at the University of Wisconsin, was exasperated by an 1891 article in the *Century Magazine* by that proper Bostonian, Henry Cabot Lodge. Lodge analysed over fourteen thousand entries in *Appleton's Encyclopedia of American Biography* to prove to his own satisfaction that practically all the talent in the United States had derived from New England, New York, and adjacent states. A generation later, in 1926, Turner offered a rebuttal on behalf of the West in the shape of an article (*Yale Review*, July 1926) entitled 'Children of the Pioneers.' Turner had been working on it for years. His biographer Ray Billington tells us: 'It was crammed with the names of westerners who had succeeded in business, government, and the arts . . .; his westerners, he believed, gained Lincolnesque stature by their dedication to the interests of the ordinary people, inventing or writing or worshipping or painting to glorify and instruct the common man.'[7]

When therefore Turner delivered his paper 'The Significance of the Frontier in American History' at a conference in Chicago in 1893, the moment was exactly right. Instead of bowing to the Lodgeish assurance that the West was, so to speak, on probation and perhaps unlikely to pass the test, Turner declared that everything vitally democratic in American life had developed from the frontier experience. Within a few years every historian of note was beginning to incorporate the Turner frontier thesis in his interpretation of the national past. In Turner's lifetime, to his gratified amusement, references to the frontier spirit even became common in the utterances of politicians. There was the additional gratification that the children of the pioneers were moving into more and more prominence, in their own areas and among the strongholds of the East. He himself exemplified the process by accepting a chair at Harvard with effect from 1910; Harvard had already given him an honorary degree in the previous year.

One reason for the rapid spread of a new congratulatory attitude to the West, already touched upon, was that certain Easterners were not eager to claim kinship with the West out of a troubled sense that the East was no longer the repository of clear-cut, wholesome American values. 'Their' America was altering rapidly, and for the worse as they saw it, under the impact of urbanisation, industrialisation, and immigration. In the West, patrician, Harvard-educated young men like Theodore Roosevelt and his classmate Owen Wister found adventure, simplicity, manliness—indeed gentlemanliness, for they discerned chivalric qualities in the inhabitants of the great outdoors, especially those of the cattle and mountain territories. Their West, in the words of what is said to have been Roosevelt's favorite song, was the place 'Where seldom is heard a discouraging word, / And the skies are not cloudy all day.' Their celebration of the natural gentleman, the pioneer, the rugged individualist, is nicely analysed by G. Edward White in *The Eastern Establishment and the Frontier Experience* (1968). Roosevelt, Wister, and the artist-writer Frederic Remington, extended the romanticising of the West that was beginning to be essayed in works such as Mark Twain's *Roughing It* (1872) and the stories of Bret Harte. Roosevelt, who had praised the printed version of Turner's 1893 lecture, saw eye to eye with him too as to the future importance of the West. 'I think it will be a good thing for this country,' he told Turner in an 1896 letter, 'when the West, as it used to be called, the Centre, as it really is, grows so big that it can no more be jealous of the East.'[8]

Yet we can see that there was much ambiguity in these hymns to the West, whoever sang them. If a Westerner came East, or an Easterner went out West, what did they represent, and to whom? If the West evolved into the Center, in what ways could it remain distinctive? George Santayana, speaking of Whitman, has said that there is a sad contradiction in the very activity of pioneering. Once the pioneer arrives wherever he is going, he begins to 'improve'—that is, spoil—the wilderness environment that temporarily ennobled him. The uncertainties are indicated in the device chosen by Bret Harte for the title page of the *Overland Monthly* (which started publication in 1868), as well as in the actual name of the magazine. The founders of the magazine had decided upon a picture of a grizzly bear: an appropriate emblem since California was the Bear Flag state. But the bear on his own did not seem sufficient. Harte's solution was to add a railroad track beneath the bear's paws. Before the change, said Mark Twain, the bear 'simply stood there snarling over his shoulder at nothing.' With the change, 'behold he was a magnificent success!—the ancient symbol of California savagery snarling at the approaching type of high and progressive Civilization, the first Overland locomotive!' The transcontinental railroad was then within a year of completion. But what was being symbolised? In a contest with a locomotive, the bear would clearly lose. The completion of the railroad would inevitably link California with the East, and diminish whatever spirit of wilderness the bear typified.[9] In fact the railroad soon took Harte off to the East, all the way to Boston and an agreement to produce Western tales and poems for the *Atlantic Monthly*. And in any case, it had been the Eastern appetite for stories of the Wild West that had made the dandified Bret Harte realise that he had stumbled upon a literary bonanza. Was the West then truly America's future, in any but the materialistic sense of a region awaiting exploitation? As a spiritual heritage, was it not disappearing almost overnight?

This ambiguity is fully apparent in the career of Frederick Jackson Turner. Did the value of the West for America lie in the formative, bygone stages of pioneering, as his frontier thesis appeared to say? He took as starting point in his 1893 paper the United States census announcement that the frontier as a continuous line of open country had ceased to exist. Yet he was offended when a critic charged him with having said that the frontier was ended, and labored to prove that, through the 'children of the pioneers,' the West was culturally and materially displaying a favorable balance of trade in relation to the country as a whole. Having moved to the East from his native Wisconsin, Turner continued to think of himself as a Westerner. He retained a lifelong affection, indeed a personal need, for regular re-immersion in wild landscape. But he was never able to admit to himself imaginatively that his old West might have had serious shortcomings, in narrowness and crudeness of spirit, or that the new West might soon become indistinguishable from the East. In *Historians Against History* (1965) David Noble portrays Turner as one of several American historians who have woven scholarly legends of some splendid past era but who have been psychologically unable to come to grips with American evolution up to recent times.

One curious aspect of Turner's view of the frontier West, which he shared with various Easterners, was that he liked to think of the pioneers as being pre-eminently of old, that is 'Anglo-Saxon,' stock. He knew perfectly well with one part of his mind that this was historically not so. As a boy in Portage, Wisconsin, he had grown up in a polyglot community.[10] As a scholar he compiled material on immigrant settlement, and recommended graduate students to turn their attention to immigration history. Marcus Hansen, the author of excellent studies on American immigration, was a Turner student. But in some other part of his mind Turner revealed a distaste not only for the city immigrants but also for those on the frontier. This is clearly brought out in the few references to Willa Cather in Turner's printed correspondence. These occur in exchanges with Mrs Alice Forbes Perkins Hooper, an exuberant and affluent lady who had spent her childhood in Burlington, Iowa, where her father was president of the Burlington railroad. He had extended the Burlington track through Nebraska. Mrs Hooper had already met Willa Cather by 1913, when she wrote to her friend Turner to say in passing that she had just read *O Pioneers!* and thought it 'disappointing.' Apparently she expected Willa Cather to 'help us sometime'— presumably in lauding the pioneering enterprise of President Perkins. She implied that Willa Cather had failed to capture the atmosphere of Nebraska because she had come to Red Cloud late in the day and really knew little about it. Turner replied facetiously, also picking up a notion of Mrs Perkins that it would be pleasant to make a return pilgrimage to Nebraska in a private railroad car:

> But is a young thing who doesn't know her own birthplace [?] qualified to write historical fiction anyway? I haven't read *O Pioneers* and I'll *not* until I can make that historical pilgrimage with a real pioneer, possessed of the memory, the maps and the imagination which belong only to oldest inhabitants. . . . As for me, give me Red Cloud *wie es eigentlich gewesen*, or give me nothing![11]

A decade afterward, in *A Lost Lady*, Cather did speak glowingly of the aristocratic boldness and integrity of the railroad builders, as personified by Captain Forrester. But Mrs Hooper, as she informed Turner, resented the book:

> She drew upon her imagination and our family in Burlington and gave an absolutely false and arrogant impression of my mother and of me tho' she would probably say she had never heard of us. I didn't care for her a bit when I met her . . ., tho' I must admit some of her stories are excellent.[12]

I leave it to Cather scholars to determine whether there is any foundation for this supposed source of *A Lost Lady*. More relevant to my own account is the agreement of Turner and Mrs Hooper, as he told her in a letter of March 1925, that Willa Cather and some other novelists had overstressed the non-British side of frontier settlement. He added: 'The constructive work of the men of means, bankers, railway builders, etc. will also be recognised again after the present criticism of all things American has died down.'[13] Turner's outlook is clarified in a letter he sent in the same year to his fellow historian Arthur M. Schlesinger (another Middle Westerner):

> I imagine that some of the attempts to minimize the frontier theme, in the broad sense in which I used it, are part of the pessimistic reaction against the old America that have followed the World War—the reaction against pioneer ideals, against distinctively American things historically . . . to write in terms of European experience, and of the class struggle incident to industrialism. But we cannot altogether get away from the facts of American history, however far we go in the way of adopting the Old World![14]

It is time to recapitulate the discussion, and to bring it back closer to Willa Cather. In setting her beside Frederick Jackson Turner, the first point to stress is an oddity: the oddity that two writers so distinguished in their respective ways as interpreters of the American Western experience should have had so little to say to one another, directly or indirectly.

The second point is that, in my view, this mutual neglect reveals more of a deficiency in Turner than in Willa Cather. As an imaginative writer she was entitled to be idiosyncratic—to read whatever suited her own needs and to ignore whatever did not speak to her. Turner, as his many admiring colleagues and students have testified, was a compulsively inquisitive and accumulative scholar. He had a feeling for the poetry of his subject. He sought eloquence as well as clarity in his own writing. 'I always wanted to be an artist,' he told a former student, 'tho' a truthful one.' He cherished Emerson's phrase 'the nervous, rocky West'; and these lines from Tennyson's 'Ulysses':

> *for my purpose holds*
> *To sail beyond the sunset, and the baths*
> *Of all the western stars, until I die.*

He was moved by Rudyard Kipling's 'Explorer' poem, and also Kipling's 'The Foreloper':

> *He shall desire loneliness, and his desire shall bring*
> *Hard on his heels a thousand wheels, a people and a king . . .*
> *For he must blaze a nation's way, with hatchet and with brand,*
> *Till on his last-won wilderness an empire's bulwarks stand.*

Turner often, too, recited some lines from Robinson Jeffers's 'Californians' in his history lectures. But this appears to me a limited and rather commonplace record.[15] Turner's biographer does not indicate that he ever read Whitman, from whom Willa Cather borrowed her title *O Pioneers!* He showed some knowledge of Vachel Lindsay's poetry in a letter of 1914, but only a cautious enthusiasm: 'I can't say I think he is the authentic voice of the Middle West, as his friends assert.' Turner appears to have remained unaware of or unaffected by Lindsay's lovely poem 'Bryan, Bryan, Bryan, Bryan' from which Willa Cather took the epigraph—'Bidding the Eagles of the West fly on'—and the title of the final section of *One of Ours*.

A third point is that comparison with Turner strengthens her reputation at the expense of his. In other words, both have been accused of various deficiencies; there is a kind of parallelism in these supposed deficiencies; and Turner's seem to betray a greater deficiency of imaginative scope. Thus, critics have suggested that Willa Cather's mindset was formed quite early, and restricted her. But by this test Turner, too, a dozen years her senior, had a restricted range. After the 1890s he wrote little, and tended to repeat the essential themes he had hit upon by the time he was thirty-five. On the specific matter of immigrant frontier settlement, he appears to have been surprisingly reluctant to admit its significance. The reason, one supposes, is that like Theodore Roosevelt, Woodrow Wilson, and other historical writers of the day, he had formed an emotional image of the frontier West as the embodiment of 'pure' Americanism, by which he and they meant old-stock Americanism. Willa Cather, for whatever personal reasons, showed a more original appreciation of the valuable un-Americanness of some aspects of the immigrant contribution, though possibly she may have overemphasised what Turner underemphasised.

This line of inquiry comes dangerously close, one might think, to a negative assertion that if Willa Cather is a defective writer, we will not put her at the bottom of the class because her celebrated historian-contemporary proves to be even worse. That is not my intention. In both cases, something of the quality that made them so excitingly fresh to readers of their day has evaporated, or is now so much part of our imaginative heritage that we take it for granted. Nevertheless, I would like to pursue a fourth point, also expressible negatively—though it leads toward a more positive conclusion. This point, illustrated not only by Turner but by a number of 'Western' authors, is that the West in fact offers an extraordinarily elusive and frustrating theme—splendid for manifestoes and brief bursts of oratory but very difficult to handle with subtlety and compassion. The literary shortcomings of, say, Hamlin Garland, Frank Norris, Jack London, and Owen Wister show a tendency to substitute geography for humanity, to be programmatic and declamatory, and to slide into either rancor and self-pity or grandiose sentimentality. Garland shifted in his literary career from bitter little pictures to roseate reminiscence. Norris in his short life could not decide whether the bigness of the West was monstrous or glorious. A comparable stridency and unevenness marred the abundantly gifted Jack London—and can for that matter be detected in the British explorer of other far-off frontiers, Rudyard Kipling. Owen Wister, in company with Roosevelt and Remington, tended to stage heroic but stereotyped melodrama against a spectacular backdrop—making the scenery somehow more interesting than the performers.

The explanation, I believe, lies in the nature of their subject rather than in their own lack of literary ability. No doubt it was a *big* subject, but what precisely *was* it? The West was an embodiment of tender and powerful yearnings in mankind, of the kind hinted at in Wordsworth's phrase 'something evermore about to be,' or Emerson's haunting juxtaposition of 'the grey past, the white future,' or Kipling's 'Foreloper,' or James Elroy Flecker's *Hassan*: 'We are the pilgrims, master, and we shall go / Always a little further.' The West was the land of possibility, 'a fairer land than prose' as Emily Dickinson put it. Vachel Lindsay caught this quality of make-believe in his evocation of what the Nebraska politician William Jennings Bryan stood for in his campaign of 1896:

> *And these children and their sons*
> *At last rode through the cactus,*
> *A cliff of mighty cowboys*
> *On the lope,*
> *With gun and rope.*
> *And all the way to frightened Maine the old East heard them call,*
> *And saw our Bryan by a mile lead the wall*
> *Of men and whirling flowers and beasts,*
> *The bard and the prophet of them all.*
> *Prairie avenger, mountain lion,*
> *Bryan, Bryan, Bryan, Bryan. . . .*[16]

That was the poetic essence of the West, a dream toward which to travel, an area of *becoming* rather than *being*. It has proved an enduring poetic myth, as a host of novels, films, and TV episodes testify. Understandably they concentrate upon the sharpest and most poignant part of the story—the first ranches, the first breaking of the sod, and even more compulsively the journey into the West, the movement of the wagons, the encampments, the Indian raids, and so on. But such sagas are fixated upon a transitory moment, and upon two-dimensional displays of masculinity, of lone-wolf heroism on the part of men who, like Peter Pan in J.M. Barrie's Never-Never Land, resist involvement in the subsequent chapters of the tale.

These subsequent chapters constitute the prose rather than the poetry of the Western story. Historians and novelists have the obligation to put things in sequence, to tell us what happens next. But if what happens next is in some ways a letdown, an anticlimax, as with the later career of William Jennings Bryan, they run into serious difficulties. They can try to confine themselves to chapter one, but that may seem an evasion. They can pretend there was no spiritual deterioration, as I think Turner preferred to do; but that is another evasion, not far removed from the superficialities of mere boosterism. They can turn sour, as Edgar Howe did in his novel of Kansas small-town claustrophobia, or insist that if 'Go West, young man' was a stirring injunction, then 'Go East, young man (or woman)' was an equally imperative need for talented Westerners. But to portray the West as a psychic wasteland is to miss the poetry, both of exhilaration and of the elegiac, that infuses the prosaic aspects of the theme.

When all these difficulties are considered, it is no wonder that the literature of the West has been so uneven, and so dominated by John-Wayneish, Marlboro-Country clichés of rugged maleness. What is a wonder is that

Willa Cather, a woman reared in what might look like the tired fag-end of Late Victorian parlor-culture, was able to turn so much of her situation to advantage. Perhaps she was not able entirely to transcend her difficulties. Now and then I feel she is perilously near to cliché, that she is asserting a truth somewhat editorially, instead of conveying it, and even occasionally against the grain of the narrative; and that she is in such instances rescued in part by the sheer excellence of her prose—a kind of perfection of plainsong.

Nevertheless the achievement is remarkable; and my argument, to reiterate, is not that Willa Cather merely stands out in a field of second-raters, but that she made fine fiction out of alluring yet extremely intransigent material. Thus, to deal for the moment only with her handling of Nebraska, she covers all the basic stages of settlement as enumerated by Frederick Jackson Turner and other historians. There is the unmitigatedly bare landscape as young Jim Burden sees it at the beginning of *My Ántonia*: 'I had the feeling that the world was left behind, that we had got over the edge of it, and were outside man's jurisdiction' (p. 7). There are the daunting early struggles of the newly-arrived farmers, recounted for example in *My Ántonia* and in *O Pioneers!*. There is the satisfaction that comes to good farmers from seeing their patch of prairie gradually turn into something fruitful, handsome, and orderly: a prosperity worked for, and fitting. There is the accretion of memories, of vast significance to particular individuals though not related to public events. 'Whatever we had missed,' as Jim concludes of his lifelong friendship with Ántonia, 'we possessed together the precious, the incommunicable past' (p. 372).

Nor does Willa Cather avoid the grubbier sides of Western life. She stresses the drabness and narrowness of the little towns, and the glum resentfulness of some of the farmers. Like William Faulkner, she contrasts the generosity of the older order with the mean rapacity of would-be local tycoons such as Wick Cutter in *My Ántonia* and Ivy Peters in *A Lost Lady*. She reaches up to the present day—her present day—in *The Professor's House*. The gallery of characters is less linked and extensive than with Faulkner's Yoknapatawpha Country, but it is surprisingly comprehensive. Moreover, she appreciates the magic of 'Eastern' culture, whether represented by college education or by music and the theatre, and freely concedes that those who have the opportunity and wish to take it are likely to head away from the home place, and may become estranged from it. Certain settlers are, so to speak, likely to become unsettled. Kipling says of the pioneer: 'He shall desire loneliness, and loneliness shall bring / Hard on his heels a thousand wheels, a people and a king.' There is, I think, a tinge of irony but only a tinge, in that précis of the pioneer experience. Willa Cather makes room for it with more honesty than any writer familiar to me.

The reason, I believe, is that with an instinctive wisdom she declined to identify herself as either a professional Westerner, or as one of that band of esthetes in Greenwich Village or the Left Bank who, especially in the 1920s, announced that they were escapees from the prison of the central states of America. With the dispassionate egotism of the genuine artist, Willa Cather abstracted and universalised her own situation. This idea is very well put by Dorothy Van Ghent, who calls Cather's creative spirit 'primitive' and 'psychologically archaic,' and observes that 'out of homely American detail'—for instance in *My Ántonia*—'are composed certain friezelike entablatures that have the character of ancient ritual and sculpture.'[17] Instead of dwelling upon the uniqueness of the American frontier, as Turner did, she sensed the recurrence of immemorial predicaments and hopes. *Tempora mutantur, nos et mutamur in illis*: both the sadness of frontier failure and the subtler regrets that came from frontier success, had for her a larger dimension, stretching back to the poetry of Virgil and Horace.

It is obvious that she was not a person of a completely equable temperament. In younger life she was a rebel, in middle age increasingly dismayed by what she took to be the progressive vulgarisation of the world. Nevertheless there was an assurance in what she wrote. Her likes and dislikes and her convictions were established early. In some respects they appear conventional. But they gave her a frame and a tone, and suggested a literary method. The result is a curiously measured, wise style—that of a tribal elder who can explain the underlying order in even the most disorderly events.

Thus for Willa Cather there simply was no dramatic opposition between West and East, between 'frontier' and 'civilisation.' She knew well that there were differences of circumstances, which might be considerable. But she was not committed, as Turner and some of her contemporaries were, to the attractive yet oversimplified East-West polarity. Certainly she knew the strengths and weaknesses of each theoretical mode. Within the sophisticated world, refinement could become preciosity, and art artifice. On the frontier, hardihood could degenerate into callousness, boldness into brutality. She realised that the two extremes existed; she had after all a firsthand acquaintance with both.

Yet to her, frontier and civilisation were not so much opposites as coordinates. The true human being in Willa Cather's realm is innately civilised, though books and travel may heighten one's sensibility. The true human being is at home in all environments, and is a respecter both of persons and of places. The false human being, to be found in all environments, is a hater and a spoiler, both of persons and of places. Those are Willa Cather's opposites. They are not complicated. But they work better for literary purposes than the artificial *versuses*, the false male-female, tough-effete antitheses of a good deal of popular frontier fiction—in which for example the reader or viewer is triggered to identify the villain as the man who arrives wearing gloves and a fancy hat, unless this man almost immediately gets into a victorious fight with some local tough and so proves he is not really a corrupt dude, despite appearances. In Cather's fiction, indeed, the pioneer may well be cultivated and—in the best sense of the word—worldly, as with one or two of the priests in *Death Comes for the Archbishop*, or Captain Forrester and some of his visitors in *A Lost Lady*. Nor is he necessarily an innovator, at least not in any reckless fashion. '"Change is not always progress,"' according to Euclide Auclair in *Shadows on the Rock* (p. 119). As in *Shadows on the Rock*, Willa Cather is fond of comparing good pioneers with bad pioneers. Auclair's patron, Bishop Laval, has respected the needs of the Quebec citizens. His system is overturned by a seemingly more sophisticated cleric in the name of progress. Tom Outland in *The Professor's House* likewise respects the remnants of the Indian mesa culture he has discovered, whereas his companion Blake—though he may believe in justice for the Haymarket anarchists and for Captain Dreyfus—is unable to keep faith with Tom or with the mesa Indians. In other words, Willa Cather refuses to be saddled with the orthodox polarities of supposed East-West behavior. Her proper pioneer is not the spoiler Santayana described, but a conserver and a bringer of beauty. Unlike Theodore Roosevelt, he does not worship the wilderness by killing its animals. In his supreme form, he is as attuned to the ecology as an Indian.

Willa Cather's other main coordinates are time and space. Clearly one of the problems of writing about the West, especially in her time, is that while the space-dimension is extremely large the time-dimension is extremely small. Some writers, as we have seen, shrink the time-dimension to an almost infinitesimally brief period—a sort of imaginary moment suspended between past and future. This could be said, not too unfairly, of the essential idea in Turner's frontier thesis, which is that the initial contact between settler and wilderness brings about a psychic rebirth. In Cather's case, awareness of the time-dimension is among the essential attributes of a true human being. She, and some of her principal characters extend their consciousness of time-past through exposure to the culture of Europe. Her novel *One of Ours* makes an interesting attempt to convey the impact of such an exposure upon an open-minded young man from Nebraska when he goes to France with the American army. In *One of Ours* the theme becomes entangled with other aims. But in her most successful explorations of the time-dimension—Tom Outland's story in *The Professor's House*, *Death Comes for the Archbishop*, and rather less powerfully in *Shadows on the Rock*—she establishes with beautiful economy and authority various previous layers of North American pioneering. If this was her way of reacting against the disagreeable realities of postwar America, she managed to universalise her private concerns, and to transform them into extraordinarily distanced and consoling images. She probably could not have accomplished this had she not been in search of American pasts appropriate to her. Other Americans were involved in similar quests; so for that matter was D.H. Lawrence. Henry Adams, her senior by a generation, had more or less concluded that medieval France was his spiritual home, and that ever since the thirteenth century the world had been going downhill. Van Wyck Brooks, her junior by thirteen years, argued in his first batch of books that while America badly needed a 'usable past,' it did not truly possess one. The heritage, he thought, was warped and stunted.

It would be too much to claim that Willa Cather single-handedly supplied the usable past for her country. She did however furnish some authentic and most valuable fragments. They could be no more than fragments or vestiges, like the Coronado sword in *My Ántonia*, because the record itself within the United States was fragmentary and discontinuous. Imaginatively, though, she brought them into a continuum. Figuratively, it could be said that she was the discoverer of the cliff dwellings at Mesa Verde and the pueblo on the plateau at Ácoma. She restored them to the American historical consciousness, and thereby enriched it. I myself, as a wandering student of American history, went to see them a quarter of a century ago, having read about them in Willa Cather, and know that they enlarged the meaning of that history for me.

We come back finally to the question I started with. Why is Willa Cather not given her due in the average history class? In a way the question is misleading. I presume that courses on the history of the frontier do include her. My point was that during her lifetime she did not conspicuously say the right things at the obvious moments. Like all important artists she was essentially a private person, not a platform performer. Yet looking back, we can see that she did after all mirror her own time, in her own ways, and speak for it. She helped her country to understand itself and its momentous, momentary heritage, and she brought dignity instead of rhetoric to such understanding. Perhaps she is too good for the historians, in their everyday teaching. For generally, in spite of what Turner said about the mutuality of history and literature, the historians are ill at ease with first-rate imaginative material. They can get more out of literature that lies nearer the surface, unmistakably signalling its intentions and its provenance.

Her 'Americanness' is not in question. But perhaps she is best compared with two other novelist-contemporaries who were not American: Thomas Hardy and Joseph Conrad. None of them lived snugly. All three were deeply aware of the pain, the dislocation, the loss, and the element of heroism, in ordinary lives. All three ranged widely through time and space. They were secret, sympathetic sharers in the hurts and hopes of people who are not full belongers. Hardy, not born into assured status, sensed the anguish of semi-outcasts like Tess and Jude. Conrad, the Polish-born sea-captain, knew that the surfaces of life were merely surfaces. Willa Cather was finely sensitive to the problems of women who refused to accept their conventional sexual-domestic roles, and by extension to the problems of 'ethnic' immigrants stranded on the American prairie. Each recognised that, on both a geographical and a psychological plane, the profoundest possibilities of self-knowledge, for people of spirit, are raised not in the well-defined centers of established society but on the equivocal peripheries. What each perceived, we may conclude, was that every worthwhile pioneer is in part an exile — and that such doubleness of insight is both mournful and miraculous.

Notes

1. Ray Allen Billington, *Frederick Jackson Turner: Historian, Scholar, Teacher* (New York: Oxford University Press, 1973), pp. 491-92.

2. Lewis, *Willa Cather Living*, pp. 138-39, 143.

3. Examples cited in Richard Hofstadter, *The Progressive Historians: Turner, Beard, Parrington* (New York: Vintage Books, 1970), pp. 54-55, 67.

4. George R. Stewart, *Bret Harte: Argonaut and Exile* (1935; repr. Port Washington, N.Y.: Kennikat Press, 1964), pp. 150-51, 175.

5. Turner too voiced this sentiment. He wrote in 1887: 'I am placed in a *new* society, which is just beginning to realize that it has made a place for itself by mastering the wilderness and peopling the prairie, and is now ready to take its great course in universal history. It is something of a compensation to be among the advance guard of new social ideas and among a people whose destiny is all unknown. *The west looks to the future, the east toward the past.*' Quoted in Hofstadter, *The Progressive Historians*, p. 63.

6. Hofstadter, *The Progressive Historians*, p. 54.

7. Billington, *Frederick Jackson Turner*, pp. 399-400. The article, 'Children of the Pioneers,' was reprinted in Turner's *The Significance of Sections in American History* (New York: Henry Holt, 1932), pp. 193-206. In a letter of 23 December 1925 to his friend Mrs Alice Hooper, Turner says that in the article 'I examine whether the prediction of "barbarism" made for them when their parents were going west — middle nineteenth century — proved true. It's really wonderful what places the children have filled, not only in the world of constructive business where vision was demanded, but also in the realms of art and literature, science, religion etc. etc.' Ray Allen Billington, ed., *'Dear Lady:' The Letters of Frederick Jackson Turner and Alice Forbes Perkins Hooper, 1910-1932* (San Marino, Cal.: Huntington Library, 1970), p. 373.

8. G. Edward White, *The Eastern Establishment and the Western Experience: The West of Frederic Remington, Theodore Roosevelt, and Owen Wister* (New Haven: Yale University Press, 1968), pp 191-92.

9. Stewart, *Bret Harte*, p. 159.

10. Wilbur R. Jacobs, ed., *The Historical World of Frederick Jackson Turner* (New Haven: Yale University Press, 1968), pp. 55-62.

11. Billington, ed., *'Dear Lady,'* pp. 147-49. The full citation is on p. 29 n, above.

12. Ibid., p. 448.

13. Ibid., p. 365.

14. Jacobs, ed., *Historical World of Turner*, p. 164.

15. Billington, *Frederick Jackson Turner*, pp. 426-27. The Emerson allusion is from Emerson's 1844 lecture, 'The Young American'; see Hofstadter, *The Progressive Historians*, pp. 56-57.

16. Vachel Lindsay, *Collected Poems* (New York: Macmillan, 1925), p. 99. He notes having written this poem at the Guanella Ranch, Empire, Colorado, in August 1919.

17. Van Ghent, *Willa Cather*, pp. 5, 22-23.

166
Willa Cather and the Fatality of Place: *O Pioneers!*, *My Ántonia* and *A Lost Lady*

SUSAN J. ROSOWSKI

'Geography is a terribly fatal thing sometimes,' Willa Cather wrote in 1895, announcing an idea that runs through her writings and is especially important to her Nebraska fiction (*Courier* 8). For the first thirty years of her career (1893–1923), Cather explored the relationship between an artist and her region; her fiction during this period provides a superb example of the ways in which one writer worked out an essential relationship between geography and literature.

In her early stories Cather treated her Nebraska settings much as early cartographers treated those embarrassing blanks on their maps: as voids to be filled in by something familiar. And, like decorative bestiaries, Cather's conventional plots may have been a welcome distraction for an artist contemplating unknown territory, but ultimately they were unsatisfactory: fanciful plots, like fanciful creatures, leave the most interesting matters unexplored. To release the land from that void, Cather wrote her first major novel, *O Pioneers!*, in the manner of a fairy tale, a mode of magic transformations by which she could make the land her hero. In two subsequent books, Cather returned the land to a circumstantial world and completed a brilliant trilogy of place: in *My Ántonia* she told of her country's incarnation, and in *A Lost Lady* of its tragic fall.

Willa Cather's confrontation with the land began when she was nine years old and moved with her family from Virginia to Nebraska, where she

SOURCE   Susan J. Rosowski, 'Willa Cather and the Fatality of Place: *O Pioneers!*, *My Ántonia*, and *A Lost Lady*', *Geography and Literature: A Meeting of the Disciplines*, eds William Mallory and Paul Simpson-Housley, Syracuse: Syracuse University Press, 1987, pp. 81–94

felt she had been 'thrown out into a country as bare as a piece of sheet iron' (*Special Correspondence*). The land stretched out before her, empty of the familiar mountains and trees, and she felt an overwhelming loneliness. Years later, when Cather began to write, this same land again stretched before her, although this time figuratively rather than literally. Nebraska was an inescapable fact of her creative experience, yet it was alien to the 'kingdom of art' she desperately wanted to enter—a wilderness untreated by any serious writer. Indeed, until Willa Cather wrote about it, nobody ever thought Nebraska was beautiful (Lewis 17).

Not surprisingly, Cather began by thinking of geography as an implacable and malevolent fate. In her early stories—'Peter' (1892), 'Lou the Prophet' (1892), 'On the Divide' (1896), 'El Dorado: a Kansas Recessional' (1901)—the land appears an evil genius that determines the lives of the people struggling upon it. 'On the Divide,' for example, is a story of human futility in the face of the impossible odds imposed by place. Canute Canuteson is a Norwegian immigrant who has settled in Nebraska, along Rattlesnake Creek, the only human being within twenty miles, and his shanty seems lost amidst the plains that stretch away on every side. Inside the shanty, Canute—'the wreck of ten winters on the Divide'—stares out the window into endless space and upon an eternally treacherous country (495). Each spring, the plains

> stretch green and rustle with the promise of Eden, showing long grassy lagoons full of clear water and cattle whose hoofs are stained with wild roses. Before autumn the lagoons are dried up, and the ground is burnt dry and hard until it blisters and cracks open.

By the onset of winter, decay has begun, and when Canute looks upon his land he sees 'white leprous patches of frozen earth where the hogs had gnawed even the sod away.' Though Canute cannot impose order upon the land, he can interpret his relationship to it. In a series of pictures along his window sills, he carves a hieroglyphic of human struggle against the fatality of place. Men are plowing, praying, fighting with serpents, dancing with skeletons, and through it all 'evil geniuses' hang over them: 'little horned imps sitting on their shoulders and on their horses' heads,' skulls hanging over their heads, serpents coiling among the vines and foliage.

By presenting a call for human beings to come to terms with their environment, the setting posed the right dilemma for Cather: she as an artist was confronting untreated materials much as her characters were confronting empty space. Yet in 1896 Cather seemed not ready to follow through with that dilemma, for in her plot she turned her attention elsewhere—to a melodramatic love story imposed upon that setting. Canute abducts the fetching but rather silly Lena, brings her (and then a minister) to his shanty, forces a marriage, and then returns the minister to his home. Lena, left alone, first weeps, then feels sympathy for the man who has lived in such wretched loneliness; the story ends as she calls him from the plains into the shanty.

Through love, Canute Canuteson apparently takes a measure of solace from the land.

In other early stories Cather's other characters also escape the fatality of place: they flee, they go mad, they commit suicide. At best, they endure. No character finds happiness *through* the land, though; none works out a resolution in terms of it.

That was all to change with *O Pioneers!*, the book in which as the dedication to Carrie Miner Sherwood's copy says, Cather 'hit the home pasture' (Bennett 222). Cather firmly placed the central conflict of her creative life at the heart of her first Nebraska novel. Immigrants, leaving behind civilisation and entering a wilderness, move out of time and into an elemental confrontation with space. 'The great fact was the land itself, which seemed to overwhelm the little beginnings of human society that struggled in its sombre wastes' (15), Cather wrote in her opening description, and until her characters came to terms with that fact, nothing else would be possible. This is literature wedded to geography, a creative artist considering how to establish a spatial context within which human society might operate and using her art to make dramatic the terms of that struggle.

The opening scene of *O Pioneers!* is one of the most powerful expressions in American literature of the need for spatial order. The little town of Hanover consists of buildings 'set about haphazard on the tough prairie sod. . . . None of them had any appearance of permanence.' Houses stray off by themselves, heading straight for the open plain; a little country boy feels overwhelmed by a strange, perplexing village; a kitten is lost atop a telegraph pole; a girl stares blindly into the distance. Outside town the new country is even more starkly bewildering, for it is an uncharted region of unending grass and featureless land. 'Of all the bewildering things about a new country,' Willa Cather wrote, 'the absence of human landmarks is one of the most depressing and disheartening' (19).

Initial attempts to impose order only demonstrate how immense the task is. Most of the houses 'were built of the sod itself, and were only the unescapable ground in another form. The roads were but faint tracks in the grass, and the fields were scarcely noticeable' (19). As if mocking the puny efforts of men and women to establish boundaries, the grass grows back over everything, hiding not only the graves in the Norwegian cemetery but even the wire fence that encloses it. Most important in a new country, where the plow is the vital imprint of human existence, '[t]he record of the plow was insignificant, like the feeble scratches on stone left by prehistoric races, so indeterminate that they may, after all, be only the markings of glaciers, and not a record of human strivings' (19-20).

These are the conditions that Cather's homesteaders, the Bergsons, confront. John Bergson had come with his wife, daughter, and two sons to tame the land, but after eleven long years he has worn himself out, having made 'but little impression' upon it. As he lies dying in his shanty surrounded by unending fields, he realises that

> it was still a wild thing that had its ugly moods; and no one knew when they were likely to come, or why. Mischance hung over it. Its Genius was unfriendly to man.

The words sound familiar: Cather had long been writing about the fatality of place as an evil genius. Yet with *O Pioneers!* there is a profound difference. Until now, she had written about geography *as* fate; in *O Pioneers!* she wrote of her Nebraska as suffering *from* fate. It was as though Cather realised that, for her, the true struggle was not a physical one, of human strength pitted against an unbroken land; rather, the essential challenge was to recognise the order inherent in the land, and to love the land for it. It was a challenge, in short, to see beauty.

To show her characters achieving a relationship with the land, Cather turned to a mode far removed from that usually associated with geography. She used a fairy tale, 'the best model we have of the way in which the psyche integrates the experiential world with its own needs and desires and explicates its being in the world to itself' (Metzger 8). In fairy tales chaos can be transformed into order, evil into good, ugliness into beauty; in a fairy tale a Nebraska wasteland could be transformed into a fertile farm, and an artist's native materials could be released into art. Cather could write metaphorically of the Nebraska prairie as a heroic youth destined to languish in darkness until, awakened by love (that miracle that has broken countless spells in countless fairy tales), it stretched with energy so powerful that it transformed itself into a New World Eden.

Cather adopted more than just the general characteristics of the fairy tale, however. As a simple plot synopsis reveals, her story of human love and the land seems like an Americanised version of 'Beauty and the Beast.' In the latter tale as in Cather's novel, the action is set against a background of fallen status and misplaced persons. A father descended from a family of power and fortune has lost everything and moved to a little house in the country, far from the city and culture in which he flourished. There, isolated from all they had once known, his children have to work like peasants just to survive. The one gem among their fallen fortunes is a beautiful daughter. She is, of course, the key to salvation, which is offered if the father will sacrifice her, a condition he reluctantly accepts. As her father gives Beauty to the Beast, so John Bergson pledges Alexandra to the land; and as Beauty vows to remain, so Alexandra promises she will never leave.

A period of testing follows, during which Alexandra—as isolated on the land as is Beauty in the Beast's castle—proves herself faithful. Through three long years of drought and failure, she remains true until, much as Beauty visits the human world, Alexandra visits the farms in the valley.

There false love is tested against true when Beauty's sisters ask her to desert the Beast (as Alexandra's brothers ask her to leave the Divide). But separation has enabled Beauty to discover her true feelings for the Beast and Alexandra to realise hers for the Divide, and both women return, newly conscious of their love.

The return triggers the transformation at the heart of the fairy tale — the kind of transformation by means of which human beings participate in something close to magic. When she returns to the Divide, Alexandra sees it for the first time as 'beautiful . . . rich and strong, and glorious.' (The words could as easily be those of Beauty for her newly seen Beast.) But it is not enough that Beauty love the Beast; to break the spell she must agree to marry him. And here too, Cather's story resembles the fairy tale, for Alexandra returns to the Divide as a bride to her groom. The scene is one of the most dramatic in all of Cather's fiction, for in it a human imagination joins with the land in an epiphany of place:

> When the road began to climb the first long swells of the Divide, Alexandra hummed an old Swedish hymn, and [her brother] wondered why his sister looked so happy. Her face was so radiant that he felt shy about asking her. For the first time, perhaps, since that land emerged from the waters of geologic ages, a human face was set toward it with love and yearning. It seemed beautiful to her, rich and strong and glorious. Her eyes drank in the breadth of it, until her tears blinded her. Then the Genius of the Divide, the great, free spirit which breathes across it, must have bent lower than it ever bent to a human will before. The history of every country begins in the heart of a man or a woman. (65)

The spell is broken and transformation follows. As the Beast becomes a handsome prince, so the Divide becomes a new kingdom in which Alexandra will reign. Contrast makes the transformation dramatic. Cather's first section, 'The Wild Land,' had opened with an approach to the Bergson homestead, lost in a bewildering wasteland; the second section, 'Neighboring Fields,' opens with a second approach to the same homestead, which is now well-ordered space:

> They drove westward toward Norway Creek, and toward a big white house that stood on a hill, several miles across the fields. There were so many sheds and outbuildings grouped about it that the place looked not unlike a tiny village. A stranger, approaching it, could not help noticing the beauty and fruitfulness of the outlying fields. There was something individual about the great farm, a most unusual trimness and care for detail. On either side of the road, for a mile before you reached the foot of the hill, stood tall osage orange hedges, their glossy green marking off the yellow fields. South of the hill, in a low, sheltered swale, surrounded by a mulberry hedge, was the orchard, its fruit trees knee-deep in timothy grass. Any one thereabouts would have told you that this was one of the richest farms on the Divide, and that the farmer was a woman, Alexandra Bergson. (83)

Here are the directions and measurements of a map, but all infused with magic: from chaos has come order, from a wasteland a great, rich farm. And to this magic (common to all fairy tales) Cather has added the magic of human individuality. This is *Alexandra's* farm, and her hand is everywhere apparent—in its 'most unusual trimness' and care for detail. In Alexandra's farm, as great and rich as any fairy tale kingdom, the most prized treasure is domestic security. Her landscape is comforting and protective: tall osage orange hedges protect the road leading to it; then another hedge surrounds a 'low, sheltered swale,' within which is an orchard whose fruit trees protect the timothy grass. Finally, lest there be any question about the individuality she is writing of, Cather specifies in the climactic detail of her description, 'and the farmer was a woman.'

The scene illustrates one of the most interesting aspects of Cather's treatment of geography: the extent to which she acknowledges gender as a factor influencing the relationship between a group or individual and the environment. Cather reinforces the point in subsequent descriptions: as a domesticated wilderness, Alexandra's farm is engendered space:

> When you go out of the house into the flower garden, there you feel again the order and fine arrangement manifest all over the great farm; in the fencing and hedging, the windbreaks and sheds, in the symmetrical pasture ponds, planted with scrub willows to give shade to the cattle in fly-time. There is even a white row of beehives in the orchard, under the walnut tree. You feel that, properly, Alexandra's house is the big out-of-doors, and that it is in the soil that she expresses herself best. (83–84)

Through it all, Alexandra is united to the land—no longer as a betrothed to her lover, but as a wife to her husband. As has been apparent from the beginning, she is different from the people about her; not unexpectedly, her house is 'curiously unfurnished and uneven in comfort,' as if she has conformed to human ways only indifferently. Alexandra's sojourn among human beings is a lonely one, for she is as unlike them as any fairy princess residing among mortals. In the end Alexandra will marry Carl Linstrum, her friend from childhood, and their companionship will provide solace from her loneliness. But their marriage will be distinct from the union Alexandra has with the land, and Carl is a fit human spouse because he recognises that difference: 'You belong to the land,' he murmurs to Alexandra before they marry, 'as you have always said. Now more than ever.'

Cather concludes her book by distinguishing Alexandra's relationship with the land from artificial, documentary kinds of possession. Just as the grass once grew over the fences placed upon it, so the names on 'official' records will change. It is as futile to try to will the land to others as it is to try to will the sunset: 'We come and go, but the land is always here. And the people who love it and understand it are the people who own it—for a little while' (308). When she dies Alexandra will join the immortality of nature, its unending cycles of birth and death, day and night, summer and winter. Her final embrace will be with that land: 'Fortunate country, that is one day to receive hearts like Alexandra's into its bosom, to give them out again in the yellow wheat, in the rustling corn, in the shining eyes of youth,' says the narrator in the Whitmanesque last line of the book.

In the end that book is far more than a celebration of taming the land: *O Pioneers!* is Willa Cather's celebration of an artist's ability to release a geographical region into beauty. Cather gave her own dilemma to Alexandra Bergson: a country that stretched before her 'as unknown to art as it was to the pioneer' (Lewis 17) — then she gave herself to that land as surely as did her heroine. Cather recalled that 'the country insisted on being the Hero and she did not interfere, for the story came out of the long grasses' (Sergeant 92). As if following the dictates of that hero, she gave her book the loose structure of newly broken sod, organised it by the seasons, and created for it a spouse: the pioneer Alexandra Bergson.

After *O Pioneers!* Willa Cather was never again to confront so centrally the problem of establishing spatial order. However, she wrote further about the fatality of place — first in *My Ántonia* (1918), telling of its incarnation; then, in *A Lost Lady* (1923), of its tragic fall.

After writing of the union of Alexandra and the Divide (Human Love and the Land), in her next novel of the land Willa Cather created Ántonia Shimerda, and it is as if we are seeing the child of that union. Like Alexandra Bergson, Ántonia belongs to the land, but there is an immense difference between the characters' relationship to it. Alexandra is an otherworldly figure, often described by details of gold and light: she 'looked as if she had walked straight out of the morning itself' (126). But whereas Alexandra is ethereal and is identified with light, Ántonia is physical and identified with the earth. As a matter of fact, we meet the young Ántonia as she emerges from a hole in the bank of the prairie, and though we know that she has come from her family's dugout, the effect is almost as if the earth itself has given birth to her. When a middle-aged Ántonia again emerges from the earth, we know that she comes from her fruit cellar; yet when her children follow her it is 'a veritable explosion of life out of the dark cave into the sunlight' (*My Ántonia* 339). As the narrator comments, Ántonia is 'a rich mine of life' (353); she is a child of nature who has followed her destiny to be an earth mother, and through her new race springs.

In *My Ántonia* space is again transformed, though not by the land itself (as in *O Pioneers!*) but by Ántonia. When Ántonia is a child sleeping in a hole in her family's cave, the earth seems nature's womb for her, its human child. And when she is a mother, Ántonia again fuses the human and natural worlds. She draws Jim into her house, where she introduces her children to him; then, as if taking him to another room of her home, she leads him into the apple orchard. She had earlier told Jim about her human children; she now tells him about one tree after another, stopping before each as if to introduce it, telling how she cared for them when they were young and on her mind 'like children.' 'I love them as if they were people,' she said, rubbing her hand over the bark.

As they will that evening sit in the Cuzak parlor with the children playing nearby, Jim and Ántonia in the afternoon sit in the orchard, a natural parlor with hedges for walls, the sky for a ceiling, and grape leaves for curtains. With the children playing nearby, the scene is a domestic idyll:

> Ántonia leaned her elbows on the table. There was the deepest peace in that orchard. It was surrounded by a triple enclosure; the wire fence, then a hedge of thorny locusts, then the mulberry hedge which kept out the hot winds of summer and held fast to the protecting snows of winter. The hedges were so tall that we could see nothing but the blue sky above them, neither the barn nor the windmill. The afternoon sun poured down on us through the drying grape leaves. The orchard seemed full of sun, like a cup, and we could smell the ripe apples on the trees. (341)

A second domesticated wilderness established by a female pioneer, the scene again suggests how Cather included gender as a critical factor in the process by which individuals or groups establish a relationship to environment. Cather's male pioneers characteristically attempt to impose order upon the land, to dominate and to conquer it—and they characteristically fail. In *O Pioneers!* Alexandra's father dies worn out by the struggle, and her brothers are buffoons, one thoughtlessly rash, the other unimaginatively physical. Both would have returned to the city were it not for Alexandra. In *My Ántonia* Cather again associates with her male characters an impulse to conquer space, to chart it and move inside it. Jim Burden is a legal counsel for the great Western railways. He is identified with roads—those by which he enters and leaves Ántonia's farms, and those of the railroad, by which he has helped to develop the West. He travels *through* space, while Ántonia, on the other hand, lives *within* space. She is identified with a kitchen within a house, a grape arbor within an orchard, a fruit cellar within the ground, all within a farm. She has organised space by multiple enclosures, within which 'there is the deepest peace.' Cather's female pioneers order space not in terms of progress or power, but in terms of mutuality. Both Alexandra's and Ántonia's farms have the beauty of productive land interacting with its human inhabitants: the earth loved by Alexandra yielded to the plow, while the orchard tended by Ántonia filled the air with the perfume of its fruit.

Cather closed *My Ántonia* as she closed *O Pioneers!*—with a final scene of contrasting geographies. After he leaves Ántonia's farm, Jim Burden spends a disappointing day in Black Hawk, then takes a satisfying walk outside of town, where he stumbles upon 'a bit of the first road that went from Black Hawk out to the north country. . . .' This was all that was left of that original road on which he and Ántonia first entered Nebraska, and it provides a dramatic contrast to subsequent thoroughfares cut through it. Highways were surveyed across the country, following the dictates of instruments rather than of the land. As if describing a brief time in which human lives conformed to nature, their harmony threatened by progress, Cather writes that

> this half-mile or so within the pasture fence was all that was left of that old road which used to run like a wild thing across the open prairie, clinging to the high places and circling and doubling like a rabbit before the hounds. (371)

In *O Pioneers!* and *My Ántonia*, imagination and gender primarily determine the relationship of a people to their environment; in *A Lost Lady*, status, class, and power also influence that relationship. Cather opens *A Lost Lady* by establishing that in approximately 1883 there were

> two distinct social strata in the prairie States; the homesteaders and handworkers who were there to make a living, and the bankers and gentlemen ranchers who came from the Atlantic seaboard to invest money and to 'develop our great West,' as they used to tell us. (9–10)

Alexandra Bergson and Ántonia Shimerda Cuzak, homesteaders who made a living with the land, were both members of the first stratum; Daniel and Marian Forrester are of the second. Captain Forrester is a railroad man, 'a contractor, who had built hundreds of miles of road for the Burlington — over the sage brush and cattle country, and on up into the Black Hills' (10). He, like the bankers and gentlemen ranchers from the East, came first to invest money and (as if an afterthought — the irony is subtle but present) to develop the West.

A Lost Lady tells about land that is 'Captain Forrester's property' — not a farm but a site he had selected for its beauty, then kept as a fancy he could afford to humor. With this as her setting, Cather suggests an aesthetics detached from utility and, as such, a beauty that is vulnerable against a rising tide of materialism. Incongruities emphasise that tension. The Forresters seem out of place in the country, these city people of elegant manners, the likes of whom Niel Herbert, the Sweetwater boy who recalls them, had never met before. And their house is similarly incongruous, an ugly building with narrow porches and 'fussy, fragile pillars,' by which 'every honest stick of timber was tortured by the turning-lathe into something hideous.' Yet even such a house is made beautiful by the land, with its 'fine cottonwood grove that threw sheltering arms to left and right and grew all down the hillside behind it,' and, especially, by the marsh beyond it. The marsh is a major symbol of the novel: its delicate ecology suggests a fragile beauty that is all the more precious because it is so easily destroyed by change. Here, Captain Forrester built his house and brought his beautiful young wife, and their lives too have the beauty — and tension — of something fleeting: the friendships of people stopping briefly on their way elsewhere; the loveliness of a young woman growing older; even the presence of the Forresters themselves, for in the beginning they lived in Sweetwater only a few months of each year.

In *A Lost Lady* — the third member of what I am interpreting as a trilogy of place — Cather writes of ironic reversals brought with time. Where the human inhabitants in Cather's early stories suffered from a fatality of place, their descendents in *A Lost Lady* have become the evil geniuses beneath which the land suffers. Captain Forrester loses his fortune, ages, and dies, and a shyster lawyer, Ivy Peters, gains control of the Forrester properties — both the delicate marsh and the beautiful wife. Ivy Peters is the extreme perversion of tendencies evident throughout the second social stratum, whose members come west not to live with the land but to make money from it. Peters practices law but farms 'a little on the side,' as one of his many 'iron[s] in the fire.' He first rents, then purchases the Forrester place, and he drains the marsh. Having done so he

> had obliterated a few acres of something he hated, though he could not name it, and had asserted his power over the people who had loved those unproductive meadows for their idleness and silvery beauty. (106)

Men like Ivy Peters, oblivious to the identity of the land, see it only as another commodity, to be cut up and sold as goods are processed in a factory:

> The Old West had been settled by dreamers, great-hearted adventurers who were unpractical to the point of magnificence; a courteous brotherhood, strong in attack but weak in defense, who could conquer but could not hold. Now all the vast territory they had won was to be at the mercy of men like Ivy Peters, . . . The space, the colour, the princely carelessness of the pioneer they would destroy and cut up into profitable bits, as the match factory splinters the primeval forest. All the way from the Missouri to the mountains this generation of shrewd young men, trained to petty economies by hard times, would do exactly what Ivy Peters had done when he drained the Forrester marsh. (106–107)

Reduced to profitable parcels, the land contains little to hold its human inhabitants, and *A Lost Lady* ends with its major characters dislocated. Marian Forrester has gone west and remarried, her second husband an Englishman she had met in California and with whom she now lives on a ranch in South America. (Again, incongruities abound.) The characters who once lived in Sweetwater have become part of a modern environment, in which people meet by chance in hotels, able to speak only briefly before passing on to somewhere else, or leaving behind messages received too late to answer. The Nebraska land appears only as a grave upon which flowers are placed each year.

A Lost Lady was to be Cather's last novel about the land that had figured so importantly in her creative life. She used Nebraska as a setting of only one other novel, and in *Lucy Gayheart* (1935) it exists more as a symbolic extension of character than in its own right. It was as though Cather had completed her region's story with *A Lost Lady*. The land was a magical hero of *O Pioneers!*, transforming the material world into a rich kingdom; by *My Ántonia* it had taken on human form, but with its vulnerability. Finally, in *A Lost Lady*, that land had suffered beneath the very race it had given rise to.

Tragedy often concludes with a summation of tragic experience, a return to the commonplace with a reflection upon what has passed (Greene 100).

The description could be of 'Nebraska—The End of the First Cycle,' an essay first published in September, 1923, the same month as *A Lost Lady*. Cather began the essay with a description of the country (now organised as a state):

> The state of Nebraska is part of the great plain which stretches west of the Missouri River, gradually rising until it reaches the Rocky Mountains. The character of all this country between the river and the mountain is essentially the same throughout its extent: a rolling, alluvial plain, growing gradually more sandy toward the west, until it breaks into the white sand-hills of western Nebraska and Kansas and eastern Colorado. From east to west this plain measures something over five hundred miles. (236–38)

This is textbook geography, of course—so familiar we unthinkingly accept it as true. But after presenting it as such, Cather questions its implications by tracing the 'social history' of Nebraska. From one point of view it is a history of progress, and Cather provides the dates and figures of growth and prosperity. But there is another way of seeing the land, Cather suggests: not as an object to be charted, but as a living part of nature, to be understood and respected. When passing through the state, one should look about him: 'the country has no secrets; it is as open as an honest human face.' As she had in her novels, Cather treats the land as a character, with its own identity and integrity; for such a subject documentary geography is inadequate. The land has yielded farms that, like neighbors in a natural community, 'rub shoulders'; to write of it Cather uses the metaphors of literature.

By doing so Cather wrote once again of living *with* the land. She had ended *O Pioneers!* with a paean to sympathetic interaction: '[f]ortunate country, that is one day to receive hearts like Alexandra's into its bosom, to give them out again in the yellow wheat, in the rustling corn, in the shining eyes of youth' (309). A decade later, in 'Nebraska: The End of the First Cycle,' she echoed these words:

> I have always the hope that something went into the ground with those pioneers that will one day come out again, something that will come out not only in sturdy traits of character, but in elasticity of mind, in an honest attitude toward the realities of life, in certain qualities of feeling and imagination.

Though her early certainty was by now no more than a plaintive hope, Cather's belief in an essential relationship with place remained firm, as did her linking to the land traits of character, attitudes, qualities of feelings, and imagination.

Cather ended her 1923 essay with a warning about the geography we are creating, the result of 'the ugly crest of materialism' created by a marketplace mentality. Like a coating of dust, a new surface of things 'has settled down over our prairies,' gaudy, artificial, tawdry. The danger is that, should we allow this social environment to harden 'into molds and crusts', a saving relationship to nature will be lost. Like Alexandra Bergson, Willa Cather believed that we belong to the land. We shape our environments, of course: we order them in the fields we plow, the houses we build, the highways we survey. But just as surely, our environments shape us, and geography remains 'a terribly fatal thing, sometimes.'

Works Cited

Bennett, Mildred R., *The World of Willa Cather*, Lincoln: University of Nebraska Press, 1961.
Cather, Willa, *A Lost Lady*, (1923), New York: Random House, 1972.
—, *My Ántonia*, (1918), Boston: Houghton Mifflin, 1961.
—, 'Nebraska—The End of the First Cycle', *The Nation*, 5, September 1923: pp. 236–38.
—, *O Pioneers!*, (1913), Boston: Houghton Mifflin, 1962.
—, 'On the Divide', *Willa Cather's Collected Short Fiction*, ed. Virginia Faulkner, Lincoln: University of Nebraska Press, 1970.
Courier, 28 September 1895, p. 8; rptd Slote, pp. 281–82.
Greene, William Chase, *Moira: Fate, Good, and Evil in Greek Thought*, Cambridge: Harvard University Press, 1944.
Lewis, Edith, *Willa Cather Living: A Personal Record*, (1953), Lincoln: University of Nebraska Press, 1976.
Metzger, Michael M., Preface, *Fairy Tales as Ways of Knowing: Essays on Marchen in Psychology, Society and Literature*, eds Metzger and Katharina Mommsen. Las Vegas: Peter Lang, 1981.
Sergeant, Elizabeth Shepley, *Willa Cather: A Memoir*, (1953), Lincoln: University of Nebraska Press, 1963.
Slote, Bernice, ed., *The Kingdom of Art: Willa Cather's First Principles and Critical Statements 1893-1896*, Lincoln: University of Nebraska Press, 1966.
Special Correspondence of the [Philadelphia] Record, 9 August 1913; rptd Slote, pp. 446–49.

167
The Cliff Dweller Thrill

DAVID HARRELL

Even as a child, Willa Cather was fascinated by the cliff dwellers. In a seldom noted interview from 1925, Cather says, 'When I was a little girl nothing in the world gave me such a moment as the idea of the cliff dwellers, of whole civilizations before ours linking me to the soil.'[1]

Edith Lewis recalls this childhood fascination when she comments upon Cather's trip to Walnut Canyon in 1912:

> she had never seen any cliff-dwellings before; but she and her brothers had thought and speculated about them since they were children. The cliff-dwellers were one of the native myths of the American West; children knew about them before they were conscious of knowing about them.[2]

In the absence of other, more specific, information, one is hard pressed to account for the particular sources of this knowledge. Even if the Cather children did know about cliff dwellings 'before they were conscious of knowing about them'—responding, perhaps, to the mystique of the Santa Fe and Oregon trails or other westward attractions—their knowledge had to come from somewhere. It seems unlikely that during the 1870s at Willow Shade, in Frederick County, Virginia, there would have been anything said about cliff dwellings in the far Southwest, virtually a world away. There were frequent visitors 'from all over,' including Washington, D.C.,[3] and in 1913 Cather told an interviewer that she had met 'traveled people' in Virginia;[4] but at that time Mesa Verde and its Anasazi neighbors were known to few people outside the Southwest. This would not be the case for long, however.

When her family moved to Nebraska in 1883, young Willa Cather was in a better location to learn about the cliff dwellers. With rapt attention, probably, she listened to the stories told by the drivers of wagon trains between Nebraska and the mines in Colorado. Already the landscape was making an impression on her as these drivers told of losing count of the days of the week and month as their wagons passed over a long stretch of trackless

SOURCE   David Harrell, 'The Cliff Dweller Thrill', *From Mesa Verde to The Professor's House*, Albuquerque: University of New Mexico Press, 1992, pp. 8–33, pp. 226–233

grass.⁵ Perhaps from these same drivers Cather heard stories of mysterious ancient villages built into inaccessible places in nearly inaccessible canyons.

Passengers on the railroad are another possible source. During the last third of the nineteenth century, there was a great deal of road building in the Rocky Mountain region to gain access to the mines that were extracting coal and precious metals; and in 1882 Red Cloud became a division point on the Burlington and Missouri Railroad connecting Chicago, Kansas City, and Denver.⁶ Like other children in town, Cather gravitated toward the depot to watch passengers deboard to take their meals.⁷ Perhaps some of them, fresh from Denver, had picked up rumors of cliff dwellings and were still chatting about them as they piled into the diner. Stories overheard there were probably repeated throughout the town so that Cather could have picked up news from farther west almost anywhere in or around Red Cloud.

Another, and more likely, means of early exposure was Cather's reading, an activity whose far-ranging importance Cather scholars have always recognised. Bernice Slote speaks for many others when she calls Cather's reading 'the stream of experience most central to her own creativity.'⁸ This point notwithstanding, Slote also cautions that

> every account of backgrounds and books read—in general, the literary influences and sources of a writer's work—has its own seeds of disaster, for the bare alignment of book, time, and person says little of the interplay and transformation when the particular ingredients are combined.⁹

There is little danger of such disaster here, however: with rare exceptions, the most one can do in the case of Mesa Verde is to make broad suggestions about possible exposure to printed materials. In fact, one longs for more instances of 'the bare alignment of book, time, and person' because when they can be examined they show that Cather's use of such material is almost always an expansion, at the very least a rearrangement, not a simple reproduction or a 'rigid, unimaginative paraphrase.'¹⁰ Moreover, these alterations provide valuable insights into Cather's creative designs.

One who read 'constantly and indiscriminately,' Cather had the run of two libraries in Red Cloud, that of her family and that of her neighbors, Mr and Mrs Charles Wiener. She augmented these eclectic collections by starting one of her own, which consisted partly of paperbacks that Cather chose as the means of payment for her work in the local drugstore. The earliest accession date recorded in any of the volumes in this personal library is 1888,¹¹ the same year that Richard Wetherill and Charlie Mason discovered Cliff Palace at Mesa Verde.

In 1888 Cather also reached the age of fifteen, the year by which she said a writer had absorbed most of his basic materials. If she had wanted to read anything about the cliff dwellers during this formative period, she would have had a limited number of titles to choose from because by that time Mesa Verde, as well as other southwestern cliff dwellings, had appeared in print infrequently. There were a few articles in popular magazines such as *Scribner's Monthly* and *Popular Science Monthly*, but the most notable publications of this period were the reports of the Hayden expeditions.

Under the leadership of Ferdinand Vandiveer Hayden, these surveys were the best publicised and the most widely known of those performed by the four major survey teams that, during the 1860s and 1870s, explored and mapped the territories west of the 100th meridian, which runs almost equidistant between Kearney and North Platte, Nebraska. Between 1874 and 1877, Hayden survey crews led by pioneer photographer William H. Jackson made excursions into the Four Corners region to find reputed cliff dwellings around Mesa Verde. Their first discovery was the ruin that became known as Two Story House, which was called to their attention by their guide, miner and Mancos resident John Moss. Although Jackson and his crew missed the major ruins later discovered by the Wetherills, their efforts produced the best early documentation of cliff dwellings, and, in the words of one commentator, made Hayden himself 'world-famous.'[12] Because the Wetherills obtained copies of these reports (and read them with great interest), one could assume that copies were available to other people as well—perhaps even to Willa Cather. In fact, there are some interesting similarities between 'Tom Outland's Story' and parts of a Hayden article by William Henry Holmes, but without something more substantial to connect Cather with this report, there is little to be made of the parallels.[13]

Beyond the things that Cather might have read or heard during her childhood or adolescence, numerous possibilities emerge. By 1890, when Cather enrolled at the University of Nebraska in Lincoln, the number of Mesa Verde publications had begun to increase; and by 1895, the year she graduated, several major studies had been published, including articles by W.R. Birdsall and S.D. Peet and books by Frederick H. Chapin and Gustaf Nordenskiold. Then late in 1896 Cather's boss at *The Home Monthly*, James W. Axtell, left Cather to tend to the magazine while he toured the West.[14] Perhaps he returned with stories of the cliff dwellers.

Also during the 1890s the Denver & Rio Grande (D&RG) Railroad heavily and widely promoted its scenic tours through the Rocky Mountain region.[15] In fact, one of the railroad's turn-of-the-century brochures even highlights the family that would play a crucial role in the composition of 'Tom Outland's Story':

> At Mancos headquarters should be made at the Alamo Ranch, owned and conducted by Wetherill & Sons, which is located in beautiful grounds about two miles from the railroad station in a lovely valley, fertile and well watered and in an advanced stage of cultivation. Conveyance to the ranch may be procured at Mancos, or the Messrs. Wetherill will meet parties who have corresponded with them.[16]

Even though Cather's brother Douglass worked for another line, the Southern Pacific, there is a good chance that he was familiar with the advertising matter of the D&RG. In those days of heavy railroad activity, competing and complementary lines alike often engaged in mutually beneficial arrangements; and one company bought stock in another with considerable frequency. Moreover, the D&RG sent its circulars all over the world.[17] Such publicity, together with the work of her own organisation, allowed one early champion of Mesa Verde to boast in 1904, 'To-day who does not know of the Cliff Dwellings?'[18]

By 1915, the year Cather and Edith Lewis visited Mesa Verde, the park bibliography comprised more than forty titles, many of them by Jesse Walter Fewkes, the Smithsonian archaeologist whom they met there. Evidently, Cather was reading something during this period because Sergeant says that by 1920 or so Cather had read 'some archaeology,' although she 'had done very little reading in anthropology.' That subject, Sergeant said, was one that she 'had to work at' to stimulate Cather's interest.[19] Moreover, because Cather read several books in researching material for *Death Comes for the Archbishop*, it is reasonable to assume that by the early 1920s she was doing similar research for *The Professor's House*.

By 1924, the year that Cather was completing *The Professor's House*, the number of publications about Mesa Verde had increased so dramatically that one could spend years trying to locate and read all the works that Cather might have seen. Happily, however, the field can be narrowed, both logically and conveniently, to include at this point only the works of two authors, one of whom Cather mentions by name and the other whom she actually met.[20]

Popular belief to the contrary, Gustaf Nordenskiold was not a baron, but he was a descendant of a prominent family of Swedish Finns. He was also a scientist and an adventurer who, by the age of twenty-one, had already been on an expedition to Spitsbergen to collect fossils, to study the flora and fauna, and to measure and photograph glaciers. It was on this expedition that Nordenskiold developed tuberculosis, which he sought to relieve by traveling in warmer climates throughout the world. On 27 May 1891, he arrived in New York City, and a month later he was in Denver. There he visited museums and libraries and sought out local scientists. One of them was Alice Eastwood, a botanist who had recently come from southern Colorado and who told him about the work of the Wetherill family among some extraordinary cliff dwellings at Mesa Verde. With a letter of introduction from Miss Eastwood, Nordenskiold arrived at the Alamo Ranch in late June or early July.[21] He quickly became friends with the Wetherills and hired them to assist him in excavating a number of ruins and in making a collection of artifacts, which he took back to Sweden.[22] There he wrote and published *The Cliff Dwellers of the Mesa Verde*, the first extensive scientific study of those ruins and a book that remains useful even today.

That Cather knew something about Nordenskiold—and also about his book—is evident from the opening paragraph of her 1916 newspaper essay about Mesa Verde:

> Twenty-five years ago an adventurous young Swede, the Baron Nordenskjold [sic], started on a trip around the world, sailing westward. When he got to Denver he heard rumors about certain cliff dweller remains that had been found in the extreme southwest corner of Colorado. He went down to the Mesa Verde and got no farther on his trip around the world. He stayed on the mesa for some months and then went back to Stockholm and wrote and published the book which first made the Mesa Verde known to the world. Later the book was translated but the English edition also was published in Stockholm. There is no American edition.[23]

Cather probably read Nordenskiold's book before her trip to Mesa Verde. The newspaper story proves that she knew of it before January 1916, and there seems not to have been a copy of it at the park in 1915. Although the records of the park library do not include the dates, the accession numbers assigned to both the Swedish and English editions of Nordenskiold's book are high enough to suggest that they were acquired later.[24] Even as late as 1923 Superintendent Jesse Nusbaum had to borrow a copy from somewhere else.[25] As one of the Wetherills' friends observed, Nordenskiold's book 'was not widely distributed.'[26] One reason, surely, is that the twenty-dollar price was quite high for that time. Richard Wetherill was one of many who commented on the cost, but he hastened to add in a letter to his friend Gustaf that he and his family would do all they could to promote the sale of it among libraries and archaeological and historical societies.[27] The libraries in Pittsburgh, Washington, and New York would have been likely repositories where Cather might have found a copy.

It is with good reason, then, that Susan Rosowski and Bernice Slote suggest that Cather knew the book 'at the time of her visit and that it is more important to *The Professor's House* than has been recognised':

> The volume would have been well suited to ideas Cather associated with the Mesa Verde. By combining scientific objectivity with personal recollection, Nordenskiold provided a transition between an ancient and a modern world, his story a heroic adventure that has been brought into the twentieth century by being made scientifically credible.[28]

After noting some of the archaeological details found both in Nordenskiold and in 'Tom Outland's Story,' Rosowski and Slote further suggest that *The Cliff Dwellers* 'is a source she [Cather] may have drawn upon . . .,' one that 'anticipates the strongly personal mood Cather was to associate with the Mesa Verde.'[29] Indeed, these scholars draw an interesting parallel between the feeling Tom Outland has for Cliff City and the poetic sentiments expressed in this passage from Nordenskiold, a description of Spring House:

> What a striking view these ruins present at a distance! The explorer pictures to himself a whole town in miniature under the lofty vault of rock in the cliff

before him. But the town is a deserted one; not a sound breaks the silence, and not a movement meets the eye, among those gloomy, half-ruined walls whose contours stand off sharply from the darkness of the inner cave.[30]

With these similarities in mind, one would expect a more extensive comparison of the two texts to reveal even more parallels. And so it does. In almost all instances, Cather's treatment is more concise, more metaphorical, more imaginative—in a word, more artistic—but it was probably Nordenskiold who was responsible for the fact or the scientific concept, which Cather adapted into her art.

One of the first signs of ancient inhabitation noted by Tom Outland and Roddy Blake is 'a number of straight mounds, like plough furrows, running from the river, inland.' This they identify as 'an old irrigation main.'[31] Perhaps Cather saw for herself the prototype of this irrigation system near the mesa-top ruin of Far View House; or perhaps she read about it in Nordenskiold, who identifies certain low walls that cross shallow depressions as 'the ruins of reservoirs' and who notes an apparent irrigation system of ditches and reservoirs on Chapin Mesa 'above the great ruins,'[32] evidently referring to the location of Far View House.

Tom Outland's discovery of a second cliff dwelling may be a reflection of what Cather read in Nordenskiold.

> Not far from this place [Cliff Palace], but in a different cañon, they [Richard Wetherill and Charlie Mason] discovered on the same day another very large cliff-dwelling; to this they gave the name of Sprucetree House, from a great spruce that jutted forth from the ruins.[33]

Though in a better state of preservation, Spruce Tree House never received the attention lavished upon the larger and more spectacular Cliff Palace. For his part, Outland makes only a brief reference to his second discovery and then, after using it to draw a conclusion, never mentions it again:

> When I at last turned away [from viewing Cliff City], I saw still another canyon branching out of this one, and in its wall still another arch, with another group of buildings. The notion struck me like a rifle ball that this mesa had once been like a bee-hive; it was full of little cliff-hung villages, it had been the home of a powerful tribe, a particular civilization.[34] (*PH* 202)

To gain access to Cliff City, Outland and Blake use as a ladder 'an old dried cedar trunk, with toe-notches cut in it,' which they find lying beside one of the gaps in the ledge (*PH* 207). Interestingly, Nordenskiold mentions at least twice his surprise at finding no signs of ladders whatsoever; but he also notes that he and the Wetherills used a 'long notched tree-trunk to serve as a ladder.'[35]

Once they begin exploring Cliff City, Outland and Blake find a number of conditions and artifacts whose antecedents are probably in Nordenskiold's book, considering the similarities in both diction and detail. In addition to the similarities noted by Rosowski and Slote, Cather's two characters echo Nordenskiold's terms exactly when they mention cedar joists that had been 'felled with stone axes' (*PH* 212); Outland and Blake find 'what seemed like cotton cloth' (*PH* 213), and Nordenskiold notes 'pieces of cotton cloth'; Outland and Blake discover 'sheepskins tanned with the fleece on them' (*PH* 213), and Nordenskiold determines that the hides he found were 'probably chiefly of deer and mountain-sheep'; when Outland and Blake discover Mother Eve, they notice that she still has 'a great deal of coarse black hair' (*PH* 214), and Nordenskiold describes a mummy whose hair 'was black and rather coarse, [and which] still hung to the head,'[36] As for Mother Eve herself, 'she had dried into a mummy in that water-drinking air' (*PH* 214), a circumstance also noted by Nordenskiold, though in somewhat less picturesque diction: 'The entire absence of moisture had presumably been enough without further preparation to transform the corpse to a mummy.'[37]

Still other similarities require a little more comment. Marveling at the construction skills displayed by the ancient home builders, Tom Outland says that the 'little poles that lay across them [the cedar joists] and held up the clay floor of the chamber above, were smoothly polished' (*PH* 212). This description is probably a condensation and paraphrase of a similar passage from Nordenskiold:

> Thick beams of cedar or piñon and across them thin poles, laid close together, form the floors between the stories. In some cases long sticks were laid in pairs across the cedar beams at a distance of some decimetres between the pairs, a layer of twigs and cedar bast was placed over these sticks, and the whole was covered with clay, which was smoothed and dried.[38]

Another example of close borrowing is Outland's description of the doors in Cliff City: 'The door lintels were carefully fitted (the doors were stone slabs held in place by wooden bars fitted into hasps)' (*PH* 213). Nordenskiold says almost the same thing although at greater length, and he includes additional detail:

> the door [is] a thin, flat, rectangular stone slab of suitable size. Through two loops on the outside of the wall, made of osiers inserted in the chinks between the stones, and placed one on each side of the doorway, a thin stick was passed, thus forming a kind of bolt.[39]

In one room of Cliff City, Outland observes 'a painted border, little tents, like Indian tepees, in brilliant red' (*PH* 213). Minus the analogy to tepees, which southwestern cliff dwellers would probably not have seen, Nordenskiold finds the same thing in one of the rooms in a small ruin in Cliff Canyon and in a room in Spruce Tree House (the latter Cather may have seen for herself, of course). Describing a dark red border around the lower part of a wall, Nordenskiold says 'this red paint projects upwards in triangular points [tent-like shapes, one might say], arranged in threes, and above them is a row of small round dots of red.'[40] 'It is difficult to conceive the idea which suggested this singular design,' he adds later.[41]

Another detail perhaps taken from Nordenskiold is Tom Outland's camera. When he goes to Washington, Outland takes with him 'some good pieces of pottery . . . and all the photographs Blake and I had taken. We had only a small kodak,' he says, whose pictures 'didn't make much show' (*PH* 226). Both Nordenskiold and the Wetherills used a Kodak too, at a time, incidentally, when cameras of this sort were new to the market.[42] For Nordenskiold, however, the Kodak was only a temporary substitute for his own more versatile view camera, which finally arrived, it seems, in late August.[43] But it was the more humble Kodak that inspired the name of one of the ruins, Kodak House, because 'we kept one of these apparatuses hidden for some time in one of the rooms.'[44]

'Probably these people burned their dead' (*PH* 215), Tom Outland surmises, echoing what Cather had already said in her 1916 essay in spite of extensive evidence to the contrary in just about anything she may have seen or heard. Yet, after three pages summarising the various methods of burial that he and the Wetherills found, Nordenskiold does provide Cather with a scientific basis for Outland's hypothesis:

> That cremation, however, was sometimes practiced by the cliff-dwellers, seems probable from the fact that Richard Wetherill observed in the same ruin where the above-mentioned burial chamber was found [a small ruin in Pool Canyon, a branch of Navajo Canyon] bodies which had apparently been burnt together with the pottery belonging to the dead.[45]

Cather also seems to have derived some of Father Duchene's actions and theories from Nordenskiold. Like Nordenskiold, Father Duchene cuts down a tree to count the annual growth rings as a way of estimating the age of the dwelling. The underlying assumption in both cases is that the tree could not have grown where it did until after the inhabitants had abandoned the village. The tree Nordenskiold cut down was

> a huge spruce . . . projecting from the wall of an estufa. We counted the rings, which were very distinct, twice over, the results being respectively 167 and 169. I had supposed from the thickness of the tree that the number of the rings was much greater.[46]

In the case of Father Duchene's cedar tree, which had been growing 'in the middle of the deep trail worn in the stone,' the number of rings *is* much greater, 336 to be exact, some of them 'so scant that [they] . . . were invisible except with a glass' (*PH* 218).

When Father Duchene 'measured the heads of the mummies and declared they had good skulls' (*PH* 217), he did so probably on the authority of Professor G. Retzius, a colleague of Gustaf Nordenskiold's whose illustrated thirty-page appendix to *The Cliff Dwellers* recounts in exacting detail the results of his measurements of the skulls brought back by Nordenskiold. Whatever was left of Wm. Cather, M.D., probably found this appendix, technical in the extreme, to be fascinating reading.

Finally, Cather may also owe to Gustaf Nordenskiold some of the amazement that Tom Outland feels when he first sees Cliff City, even beyond what Rosowski and Slote have already noted. With its point of view, its evocative language, and its imaginative use of detail, the following passage anticipates Tom Outland's awestruck effort to describe just what he saw there, *as* he saw it, when he happened upon that 'little city of stone, asleep,' 'set in a great cavern in the face of the cliff' (*PH* 201):

> Strange and indescribable is the impression on the traveller, when, after a long and tiring ride through the boundless, monotonous piñon forest, he suddenly halts on the brink of the precipice, and in the opposite cliff beholds the ruins of the Cliff Palace, framed in the massive vault of rock above and in a bed of sunlit cedar and piñon trees below. This ruin well deserves its name, for with its round towers and high walls rising out of the heaps of stones deep in the mysterious twilight of the cavern, and defying in their sheltered site the ravages of time, it resembles at a distance an enchanted castle.[47]

Although Nordenskiold's book was probably unavailable at Mesa Verde in 1915, another helpful source was there: the park brochure for that season, titled *The Prehistoric Cliff Dwellings/Mesa Verde National Park*. In fact, copies of this succinct and informative publication must have been available in abundance because in February of that year park superintendent Thomas Rickner ordered twice as many copies as he had the season before,[48] and the increase in visitors fell far short of that projection.[49] The author of the brochure is not credited, but certain internal evidence points to Smithsonian archaeologist Jesse Walter Fewkes.[50] Cather does not acknowledge this document as a source—after all, it was neither as significant nor as picturesque as Nordenskiold's *Cliff Dwellers* or as the Howlett biography of Bishop Machebeuf that inspired *Death Comes for the Archbishop*—but it is unlikely that she could have missed it and quite improbable that, having seen it, she failed to use it.

The style of the brochure is not especially inviting, but the document contains a wealth of archaeological and anthropological detail. In addition, there are frequent quotations from Nordenskiold's book, including his account of the discovery of Cliff Palace by Richard Wetherill and Charlie Mason, which Cather must have found handy. Her use of this source in addition to Nordenskiold is suggested not just by the reappearance of some of the details in 'Tom Outland's Story' but also by the reuse of similar terms to describe them.[51]

Nordenskiold's surprise at the absence of ladders notwithstanding, the brochure affirms that the cliff dwellers placed 'notched logs . . . along the street to be used by visitors.'[52] Cather turns such a ladder into an effective symbol by having her visitors use it to bridge not only a short gap in space but also an extensive gap in time.

Once they begin exploring the interior of Cliff City, Outland and Blake find 'a row of grinding stones' arranged in the 'back court' (*PH* 209); in one room of Cliff Palace, the brochure says, there was a row of four grinding stones, or *metates*.[53] The brochure also contains a detailed account of the doors used in the ruins. Although this description differs a little from Nordenskiold's, it might have further encouraged Cather to include this feature in her own description of Cliff City, especially since the brochure directed readers to a reconstruction of this type of door in Spruce Tree House.[54]

Some of Father Duchene's observations may have come from the park brochure, too. For instance, the priest concludes that the two 'square towers on the mesa top . . . were unquestionably granaries' (*PH* 218), while the brochure notes that each clan in a village had 'inclosures, for granaries or storage of corn.'[55] Likewise, Father Duchene's characterisation of Cliff City as a 'stronghold' (*PH* 218 and 221) might have been suggested by the numerous references throughout the brochure to the defensive advantages of a cliff dwelling, references somewhat more emphatic than those in Nordenskiold: the inhabitants were 'protected from human enemies below'; '[i]n each of these villages is an elaborate system of fortification'; and 'this room [in Spruce Tree House] was believed to be a bastion for defense. . . .'[56]

Finally, the comments about towers in each composition most strongly suggest a connection between the park brochure and Cather's story. Cather probably saw Nordenskiold's acknowledgment of the round tower in Cliff Palace, but she would have found nothing there to suggest that it was anything of particular significance, as Nordenskiold simply mentions it in passing.[57] In the brochure, however, references to towers run like a motif from beginning to end. In 1875 William Henry Holmes 'drew attention to the remarkable stone towers so characteristic of the region'; four of the villages at Mesa Verde have 'watch towers 30 feet high'; and one of the most striking features of Cliff Palace is its 'tapering loopholed tower,' a conspicuous landmark known as the 'Round Tower':[58]

> The most prominent and picturesque building in Cliff Palace is the Round Tower, situated about midway in its length on a high angular rock, which raises it in full view above all the terraces. . . .
> The Round Tower, formerly two stories high . . . was little damaged during the centuries elapsing since Cliff Palace was abandoned and needed little repair. The walls show most beautiful examples of aboriginal masonry, perhaps the finest north of Mexico. Almost perfectly symmetrical in form, the stones that compose the walls are skillfully dressed, fitted to one another, and carefully laid. This tower was evidently ceremonial in function, or it may have served as an observatory, for which purpose it is well situated. The presence of small peepholes through which one can look far down the canyon supports the theory that the tower was a lookout. . . .[59]

This is the tower that Cather distills into its poetic essence and transforms into a chief symbol, as Outland tries to describe the 'round tower' that so struck him when he saw it 'in the middle of the group' of 'pale little houses of stone':

> It was beautifully proportioned, that tower, swelling out to a larger girth a little above the base, then growing slender again. There was something symmetrical and powerful about the swell of the masonry. The tower was the fine thing that held all the jumble of houses together and made them mean something. (*PH* 210)

To Tom Outland's hypothesis that the structure was used as a watch tower, Father Duchene adds his theory that, 'from the curious placing of those narrow slits, like windows, I believe it was used for astronomical observations' (*PH* 219). If Cather had wanted scientific authority for this theory, she could have found it not only in the passage quoted above, but also in the brochure's description of the openings in a circular room of Spruce Tree House, 'through which the sun priest watched the setting sun to determine the times for ceremonies.'[60]

The park brochure may not have been the only one of Jesse Walter Fewkes's publications that Cather read. She could have come across his work in any number of popular and accessible periodicals, or she could have been led to him by the bibliography in the park brochure, by Fewkes himself when she met him, or by Nordenskiold, who cites Fewkes as one of his sources and even suggests that he was personally acquainted with him.[61] If Nordenskiold's spruce tree was not old enough, a stump that Fewkes found 'on top of the highest wall of Sun Temple' would have been. In an article for *Scientific American*, Fewkes counted '360 annual rings of growth which germinated after the top of the walls that form the mound had fallen.'[62] (Interestingly, Fewkes was working at Sun Temple in the summer of 1915.) In another article, cited by the *Literary Digest*, Fewkes reports finding 'an astronomical observatory used by the cliff-dwellers in calculating time for their farming operations.'[63] Even more directly than the park brochure, this piece could have suggested Father Duchene's assumption. Both of these articles appeared in time for Cather to have seen them and used them. Finally, an even earlier publication (1910) would have been especially helpful in bolstering Tom Outland's theory that the cliff dwellers practiced cremation. According to Fewkes's excavation of Cliff Palace, there is 'no doubt that the inhabitants . . . cremated perhaps the greater number of their dead in special walled enclosures for that purpose,' a practice that Fewkes claims to have verified in other cliff houses as well.[64] Of course, none of this establishes the alignment of book, time, and person; but considering Fewkes's fame, Cather's habit of omnivorous reading, her interest in cliff dwellings, and the textual similarities, one would be surprised if Cather did not use these sources.

In addition to what she read by Nordenskiold and Fewkes, Cather had several other kinds of opportunities to learn about the cliff dwellings at Mesa Verde. One such opportunity was news of a woman whose energy and devotion to her cause Cather would probably have admired, Virginia

Donaghe McClurg. There is no record that Cather ever met McClurg,[65] but this irrepressible champion of Colorado's cliff dwellings was so much in the news that Cather could hardly have missed hearing about her. John March believes that Cather was familiar with McClurg's writings because some of Tom Outland's experiences 'parallel those of Miss McClurg.'[66] If nothing else, the name McClurg must have aroused Cather's interest because of its similarity to the names of two people dear to her, S.S. McClure and Isabel McClung.

McClurg (then Virginia Donaghe) was one of the earliest tourists to visit Mesa Verde, first in 1882 and then in 1886.[67] During these early visits she was a guest of the Wetherills.[68] Al Wetherill remembered her as an 'enthusiastic and tireless worker . . . [whose] persistence overcame all indifference . . . [and who] was able, through long and tireless effort, to interest the government, where we had failed in our attempts.'[69]

McClurg was so enthralled by what she saw at Mesa Verde that during the 1890s

> she turned into a one-woman crusade, passionately devoted to saving the ruins and creating a park. She launched an emotional campaign in Colorado to awaken the public, and her message was soon transmitted to the rest of the American public.[70]

Quite tireless in her efforts, McClurg attended meetings, gave speeches, wrote articles, and lobbied congressmen and presidents. She also instigated the founding of the Colorado Cliff Dwellings Association, an off-shoot of the Colorado Federation of Women's Clubs, perhaps the organisation most responsible for the preservation of the ruins at Mesa Verde. McClurg was assisted by many people, of course, among them Lucy Peabody, who eventually succeeded in having Mesa Verde established as a national park rather than a state one, as McClurg had wanted, but only after a nasty public airing of factionalism within the association that occupied the press for most of February and March 1906.[71] As one who kept up with current events, Cather probably read some of the coverage of this dispute and may, therefore, have learned of both women.

Evidently, McClurg took advantage of every opportunity to spread the word about Mesa Verde. In 1893 she lectured at the International Folk Lore Congress of the Chicago World's Fair and presented a series of lectures in the Anthropological Building at the fair, 'being the only woman so honored.' The next year she gave a similar lecture series in Denver.[72] In 1900 she served as a delegate from the United States to the ethnological congresses at the Paris exposition, where she was decorated by the French government. Then in 1904 Virginia McClurg and her husband embarked upon another lecture tour, which took them to Chicago, the University of Michigan, the University of Wisconsin, the Board of Public Instruction of New York City, and finally to St Louis for the World's Fair.[73]

If Cather heard of McClurg nowhere else, she must have read about her when she was in Washington in 1900-01 helping her cousin Howard Gore with the hasty preparation of the report of the United States Commission to the Paris Exposition. Acting in two capacities, as Juror in Chief and as Director of the Organisation of International Congresses, Gore was responsible for two of the six volumes of the report. McClurg's name appears three times in Volume Six, the Report of the Director of the Organisation of International Congresses. She is listed in the official register of persons attending the twelfth session of the International Congress of Americanists and is included as one of the presenters under the heading 'Archaeology': 'Mme. McClurg, of Colorado, U.S.A., "Prehistoric Pueblo Country" (with lantern [that is, slides]).' Finally, she is included among twenty-one other people as one of the 'Officiers de L'Instruction Publique,'[74] apparently not the most prestigious of the titles bestowed by the French officials but one of which she was nonetheless proud.

Incidentally, Volume Six also lists the papers presented at previous sessions of the International Congress of Americanists. At the seventh session in Berlin in 1888 there were two presentations about the Hemenway expeditions in other parts of the Southwest, both by men well known for their work in the American Southwest: Frank Hamilton Cushing (though his paper was read by someone else) and a Mr Bandelier, certainly Adolph. At the eighth session in Paris in 1890, a paper called 'The cliff dwellers of the Sierra Madre' notes 'the discoveries of the subject of this paper by Messrs. Jackson and Holmes. . . .' Then at the tenth session in Stockholm in 1894 there were three papers that would surely have interested Cather: 'A la memoire de Mme. Mary Hemenway,' by one Madam Nuttal; 'Sur la disparition des Cliff-dwellers,' by a Mr Charnay; and 'Recherches nouvelles dans les ruines et les tombeaux de Mesa Verde,' by M. Gustave Nordenskiold.[75] Once again Cather's path to Mesa Verde crossed those of others who had been there before.

Although Virginia McClurg did attend the World's Columbian Exposition of 1893, Willa Cather, according to James Woodress, did not. 'So far as any documentary evidence goes, Cather's first visit to Chicago was in the spring of 1895 when she went there to attend the opera.'[76] There is no question, however, that Cather knew about the fair. She could have learned of it from Howard Gore, who served as a juror in the Department of Liberal Arts, or she could have read about it in the newspapers. This 'grandest exhibition of modern times'[77] was good copy in the press nationwide, with writers by the dozen exuding hyperbolic praise; therefore, it could scarcely have escaped the notice of an insatiable reader heading toward her own career in journalism. In fact, Cather mentions the fair in one of her 1895 reviews when she writes disparagingly of Eddie Foy, the 'highest salaried man on the American stage,' for making an exhibition of himself one night 'during the

World's Fair.'[78] And in three of her early stories Cather shows not only her own awareness of the fair but depends upon the reader's knowledge as well when she uses the event as a reliable means of establishing time or place.[79]

More than just a handy literary device, however, the World's Fair could have afforded Cather a preview of the major cliff dwellings at Mesa Verde. Near the Anthropological Building (where Virginia McClurg was lecturing), in the southeast corner of the grounds, workmen had constructed out of 'timbers, iron and staff' an enormous replica of Battle Rock in Colorado's McElmo Canyon. Upon entering the structure,

> through a cavern made to produce the effect of a canyon, it was difficult for the visitor to comprehend that he was not in the country of the people who, ages ago, peopled the mesas and tablelands of the Southwest. The houses, perched far up the cliffs in places apparently inaccessible, were reproduced on a scale of one-sixth their real size. . . .[80]

The cliff houses themselves were replicas of Square Tower House, Balcony House, and Cliff Palace.[81] Had Cather toured this amazing structure and examined the display of artifacts, she would have come face to face with the prototype of Mother Eve, the mummy of a woman found by the Wetherills and named 'She.'[82]

Another attraction at the fair was the exhibit of cliff dweller artifacts by the state of Colorado. Because most of the items on display had been collected by Richard Wetherill and his brothers, Richard was sent there in September to answer questions from visitors. He was exhilarated and encouraged by the interest expressed, which contrasted sharply with the indifference he had encountered from people in Colorado the first few times he and his brothers showed a collection of artifacts.[83]

After the fair closed, Cather had other chances to see the artifacts that had been displayed in the man-made canyon because the collection was transferred to the museum of the University of Pennsylvania in Philadelphia, where it was first exhibited in 1895. This time, apparently, there was greater attention to scientific presentation. Critics received the exhibit quite favorably while condemning 'the meaningless display . . . at the Exposition.' Even if she did not see the museum exhibit, Cather probably read about it in the Pittsburgh papers because there was considerable publicity surrounding the arrival of the collection in Philadelphia.[84] In February 1896 the museum bought the collection for $14,500, with money provided by Phebe A. Hearst.[85]

Because Cather seems only to have heard of it and not to have visited it, the Chicago World's Fair and the cliff dweller exhibits it housed can be presented only as part of the collective culture from which Cather was already extracting facts and impressions, even if, as Lewis suggests, she was doing it unknowingly. Be that as it may, Cather knew precisely what she was doing in 1912 when she boarded a train for Winslow, Arizona, to visit her brother Douglass.

This trip to Arizona has long been recognised for its importance to Willa Cather's discovery of herself as an artist and to the composition of another of her novels, *The Song of the Lark* (1915). With her brother as guide, Cather spent several unforgettable hours touring Walnut Canyon, about ten miles east of Flagstaff, where she got her first look at ancient cliff dwellings. The result, of course, is Thea Kronborg's sojourn of self-discovery among 'The Ancient People' in Panther Canyon. This literary benefit aside, simply because it afforded Cather her first impression of ancient cliff dwellings, the Walnut Canyon experience helped shape 'Tom Outland's Story,' too: crystallizing images, defining themes, and suggesting symbols. In addition, the trip to Arizona seems to have introduced Cather to an important source for this later story.

In a brief remark often overlooked, Elizabeth Sergeant says that Cather once told her that the 'cliff-dweller part [of "Tom Outland's Story"] was based . . . on a true story that Willa had heard on the Navajo Reservation from a famous family of Indian traders, the Wetherills.'[86] Quite explicitly, this statement points to a Wetherill source other than the one in Mancos in 1915: Mesa Verde, after all, is in Ute country, whereas Walnut Canyon is in Navajo country. Furthermore, the rest of the details in Sergeant's statement coincide with the history of one branch of the Wetherill family. In 1911, after learning the ways and gaining the trust of the Navajo in several other parts of Arizona, John and Louisa Wetherill moved their trading post and their family to Kayenta, about 160 miles north of Flagstaff. Therefore, they must be the 'famous family of Indian traders' to whom Sergeant refers.

This connection raises the possibility that it might have been John Wetherill in Arizona whom Cather had in mind in 1938 when she wrote the letter explaining the Wetherill origin of 'Tom Outland's Story.' Cather mentions neither the name of the man nor of the place; and it is only from Lewis, thirteen years after the first publication of Cather's letter, that readers have learned of a Wetherill source in Mancos in 1915 and therefore assumed that he was Cather's only one.

Because the Kayenta guest register from this period disappeared many years ago,[87] it is impossible to say whether Cather met this famous family at their trading post; but she need not have gone to Kayenta to hear about John and Louisa or even to meet them. Never one to stay put for long, John Wetherill was often traveling about the country, frequently as a guide for one expedition or another, although he seems to have been close to home in 1912.[88] The list of people whom he helped to 'discover' and to excavate various ruins is a Who's Who of southwestern archaeology. Also, he traveled frequently to Flagstaff for supplies,[89] over a road that he and his partner Clyde Colville had helped build.[90] Like John, Louisa too was often away from the post, usually to offer some form of aid to the Navajo—as interpreter, as peacemaker, as healer. In fact, she was so immersed in the Navajo culture that a widely believed legend made her a descendant of a particular Navajo family.[91]

It is little wonder, then, that the Wetherill trading post at Kayenta soon became one of the most famous in the Southwest.[92] Not only were the proprietors friendly and honest, their trading post 'was the only patch of lawn in seventy miles of desert, and with the cottonwoods which grew near-by, and the trees which they themselves [John and Louisa] set out, it soon was an oasis of shade and coolness.'[93] Surely Cather's brother Douglass was familiar with it and with the people who ran it, if for no other reason than that the parties that John Wetherill guided would have passed through Winslow on their way to Flagstaff.[94] And just as surely, Cather heard of the Wetherill name and reputation at this time, even if she had somehow managed to miss it in one of her earlier opportunities.

The other Wetherill brother in Mancos should still be regarded as Cather's principal family source, largely because Cather's contact with him is more extensively documented. But here is additional evidence of Cather's early knowledge of Mesa Verde history and the part played by the Wetherills, and yet another inducement, as if one were needed, for her to visit the place herself.

In 1914 Cather came a little closer to Mesa Verde by visiting a museum in the East, anticipating Claude Wheeler's visit to the Capitol in Denver to see 'the collection of Cliff Dweller remains.'[95] Accompanied by Sergeant 'on a fine afternoon in May,' Cather attended an exhibit of cliff dweller artifacts at the American Museum of Natural History in New York. There she saw 'tan pots with ridged designs in relief, and great black and red pots with complex geometrical patterns,' prototypes, no doubt, of the pots that Tom Outland would find.[96]

Evidently, Cather went to the museum for the same reason that 'she had been going to singing lessons, hearing voices tested, [and] getting into a behind-the-scenes opera row': to replenish her energy for the book she was working on at the time, *The Song of the Lark*. 'When a book did not write itself, she knew enough to leave her manuscript and do something that was germane to the story, in another way . . . ,' Sergeant says.[97] At this museum, Cather found even more than she had hoped for. Although there is no extant catalog of the exhibit she saw, it is 'safe to say . . . that the Hall [that housed the exhibit] included some or all of two collections acquired from the Wetherills. . . .'[98]

Three months later, Cather was back in the Southwest again, having escaped the heat in Red Cloud. Little is known about this trip, other than Cather's gloomy observation that not even among the Sangre de Cristo Mountains, east of Santa Fe, could one escape the looming menace of the war in Europe, which endangered 'everything one most cared about. . . .'[99] It was not until 1922, or thereabouts, that Cather's world broke in two, but already the crack was forming.

Perhaps it was such discouraging signs in the modern world to the East that sent Cather on a personal quest to an ancient one in the West, toward a time when people followed their 'natural yearning for order and security' and 'built themselves into . . . [a] mesa and humanized it' (*PH* 221). According to Sergeant, Cather was never very interested in or even sympathetic toward living Indians,[100] so she probably would not have been flattered to have any of them claim her as a descendant. But these ancient ones appealed to her across the centuries, grabbed her imagination (and perhaps also her hope), and never let go. In 1925 Cather described this feeling as 'the cliff dweller thrill,' one of the sensations she had wanted to get into the book she had just finished, *The Professor's House*.[101]

As many readers have observed, the ancient cliff dwellers represented for Cather an ideal society more stable and harmonious than her own. *The Song of the Lark* (1915) introduces this dichotomy, and *The Professor's House* (1925) formalises it and emphasises it. In between came *One of Ours* (1922) and *A Lost Lady* (1923), each in its own way an examination of how the present often abandons the ideals of the past. To the extent that the past reminds people of these ideals it can beneficially affect the course of present events. Writing in 1926, Stuart Sherman was perhaps the first in a long line of commentators to affirm that Cather 'has been clarifying for us our sense of what we have in common with the generation[s] before 1900, and our sense of the points at which we have departed from the old paths.'[102] With each reminder that Cather encountered—from the stories heard in childhood to the visit to a museum as an adult—the grip of the ancient ones tightened until finally all the disparate times, places, and events coalesced in Cather's own discovery of Mesa Verde in the summer of 1915. The same fingers whose imprints could still be seen on potsherds hundreds of years old had already left their mark on Willa Cather's soul.

Notes

1. Fanny Butcher, 'Willa Cather Tells Purpose of New Novel,' *Chicago Daily Tribune* 12 Sept. 1925: 9. Early in 1988 my wife, Yolanda, happened upon an excerpt from this interview in *El Palacio*, the magazine of the Museum of New Mexico. Then late in 1989 I finally located the interview itself. It should also be noted, though, that Mary Miritello made her own discovery of the interview after seeing a reference to it in a dissertation. See 'The "design of life" in Willa Cather's *The Professor's House*,' Fourth National Seminar on Willa Cather, Santa Fe, New Mexico, 21 June 1990.

2. Edith Lewis, *Willa Cather Living: A Personal Record*, New York: Knopf, 1953, p. 81.

3. James Woodress, *Willa Cather: A Literary Life*, Lincoln: U of Nebraska Press, 1987, p. 25.

4. Willa Cather, *Willa Cather in Person: Interviews, Speeches and Letters*, ed. L. Brent Bohlke (Lincoln: U of Nebraska P, 1986) 10. Subsequent citations will appear in the text, with the abbreviation *WCP* substituting for the full title.

5. Woodress, *Literary Life*, 5. It was this very terrain that, more than three hundred years before, had prompted Coronado to assign a man to count the number of steps that the army took on its eastward march to Quivira. Things had not changed much in three hundred years. When he approached that unending expanse of plain from the east, Willa's uncle George

Cather 'measured the circumference of one of the back [wagon] wheels, tied a rag on the rim so they could more easily count the revolutions and started across the prairie. George had a compass to keep him going in the right direction. His wife sat in the back of the wagon, counted revolutions and computed mileage' (Mildred Bennett, *The World of Willa Cather*, new ed. [Lincoln: Bison-U of Nebraska P, 1961] 12).

6. Richard C. Overton, *Burlington Route: A History of the Burlington Lines* (New York: Alfred A. Knopf, 1965) 186-87.

7. Bennett, *World*, 43-44.

8. Bernice Slote, *The Kingdom of Art: Willa Cather's First Principles and Critical Statements 1893-1896*, ed. Bernice Slote, Lincoln: U of Nebraska Press, 1966, p. 35.

9. Slote, *Kingdom of Art*, 42.

10. Edward and Lillian Bloom, 'The Genesis of *Death Comes for the Archbishop*,' *American Literature* 26 (Jan. 1955): 488.

11. Woodress, *Literary Life*, 49-51.

12. Jack L. Benham, 'Publishers Preface and Introduction,' *Mesa Verde and the Four Corners* (Ouray, Colorado: Bear Creek Publishing, 1981) N. pag.

13. Even so, it might be interesting to mention a few of the similarities between Cather's story and Holmes's essay: 'Report on the Ancient Ruins of Southwestern Colorado, Examined During the Summers of 1875 and 1876,' 1878, reprinted in *Hayden Survey, 1874-1876: Mesa Verde and the Four Corners* (Ouray, Colorado: Bear Creek Publishing, 1981): 383-408. Like Cather in 'Tom Outland's Story,' Holmes discusses the secure positions of the cliff dwellings (384), the possibility that the towers were used for religious ceremonies or as watch towers (384-85), the skill displayed in the masonry (385), the presence of springs in some of the cliffs themselves (396), and the ample evidence of the cliff dwellers' 'art of ornamentation' in the bowls and other pottery, some perhaps of 'foreign origin' (403).

14. Kathleen D. Byrne and Richard C. Snyder, *Chrysalis: Willa Cather in Pittsburgh, 1896-1906* (Pittsburgh: The Historical Society of Western Pennsylvania, 1982) 4-5.

15. Lucius Beebe and Charles Clegg, *Rio Grande: Mainline of the Rockies* (Berkeley: Howell-North, 1962) 198.

16. *The Cliff Dwellers of Southwestern Colorado*, promotional brochure, the Denver and Rio Grande Railroad [1897], State Historical Society of Colorado, Denver, N. pag.

17. Jackson Thode, foreword, in *Health, Wealth and Pleasure in Colorado and New Mexico* (1881; Santa Fe: Museum of New Mexico Press, 1980) ii.

18. Virginia Donaghe McClurg, *Two Annual Addresses: Pueblo, 1903; Denver, 1904*, Mesa Verde Research Center, Mesa Verde National Park, Colorado, N. pag.

19. Elizabeth Shepley Sergeant, *Willa Cather: A Memoir* (1953; Lincoln: U of Nebraska P, 1967) 165.

20. Another book about the Southwest that Cather seems to have read is *Rocky Mountain Flowers*, by Frederic E. and Edith S. Clements (1914). At least, she said she wished she had written it (see *WCP* 47; Bennett, *World*, 246; and Sergeant, 165). A highly technical catalog of scientific data about regional plants, this book seems an unlikely object for the authorship desires of a romanticist. It does contain some beautiful illustrations, but it seems less concerned with beauty and more with science. Some of the plants growing in Cather's Blue Mesa are listed here, but others are not. Thus, the influence of this book upon 'Tom Outland's Story' seems negligible. This is not to say that Cather was unconcerned about the botanical authenticity of her story, however. Every plant she mentions has been found either in New Mexico or Colorado. For more on Cather's concern with botanical accuracy, see Bennett, *World*, 141.

21. Irv Diamond, letter to the author, 8 and 9 Mar. 1991.

22. Olof W. Arrhenius, *Stones Speak and Waters Sing: The Life and Works of Gustaf Nordenskiold*, ed. Robert H. Lister and Florence C. Lister (Colorado: Mesa Verde National Park and Mesa Verde Museum Association, [1984]) 4-5 ff.

23. Willa Cather, 'Mesa Verde Wonderland Is Easy to Reach,' *Denver Times* 31 Jan. 1916: 7. Subsequent citations will appear in the text, with the abbreviation 'MV' substituting for the full title. Incidentally, now there are three American editions of Nordenskiold's book. Two of them are listed by Rosowski and Slote (92): Antiquities of the New World Series, Vol. 12, AMS Press; and the Beautiful Rio Grande Classic edition, which is the one used here. Finally, the Mesa Verde Museum Association recently published a paperback edition of the original 1893 English version.

24. Beverly Cunningham, letter to the author, 15 Feb. 1989.
25. Duane A. Smith, letter to the author, 14 May 1987.
26. Herbert L. Cowing, letter to Frank McNitt, 13 Mar. 1953, Frank McNitt Collection, New Mexico State Records Center and Archives, Santa Fe.
27. Richard Wetherill, letter to Gustaf Nordenskiold, 21 Dec. 1893, Mesa Verde Research Center, Mesa Verde National Park.
28. Susan J. Rosowski and Bernice Slote, 'Willa Cather's 1916 Mesa-Verde Essay: The Genesis of *The Professor's House*,' *Prairie Schooner*, 58, 1984, p. 87.
29. Rosowski and Slote, 87.
30. Quoted in Rosowski and Slote, 87.
31. Willa Cather, *The Professor's House* (New York: Alfred A. Knopf, 1925) 198. Subsequent citations will appear in the text, with the abbreviation *PH* substituting for the full title.
32. Gustaf Nordenskiold, *The Cliff Dwellers of the Mesa Verde*, trans. D. Lloyd Morgan (1893; Glorieta, New Mexico: The Rio Grande Press, 1979) 73-74.
33. Nordenskiold, 12. Actually, it was Wetherill alone who discovered Spruce Tree House after he and Mason separated to look for other ruins. Then the next day he and Mason together happened upon Square Tower House (see Frank McNitt, *Richard Wetherill: Anasazi*, rev. ed. [Albuquerque: U of New Mexico P, 1966] 25).
34. Later in the story, Roddy Blake finds 'four other villages, smaller than the first' (*PH* 204).
35. Nordenskiold, 30. In an article for a scholarly journal, Nordenskiold describes the access to the upper floor of a dwelling in Spruce Tree House: 'no ladder seems to have been used, several stones projecting from the wall providing instead the necessary foothold' (*Letters of Gustaf Nordenskiold*, ed. Irving L. Diamond and Daniel M. Olson, trans. Daniel M. Olson, (Mesa Verde National Park: The Mesa Verde Museum Association, 1991) 71.
36. Nordenskiold, *The Cliff Dwellers*, 96, 20, 19, and 39.
37. Nordenskiold, *The Cliff Dwellers*, 39.
38. Nordenskiold, *The Cliff Dwellers*, 54.
39. Nordenskiold, *The Cliff Dwellers*, 52.
40. Nordenskiold, *The Cliff Dwellers*, 16.
41. Nordenskiold, *The Cliff Dwellers*, 108.
42. Edward Oxford, 'George Eastman: The Man Who Wrought the Kodak,' *American History Illustrated* (Sept. 1988): 16 ff.
43. Arrhenius, 25-26.
44. Nordenskiold, *The Cliff Dwellers*, 21, n. 1. See also Benjamin Alfred Wetherill, *The Wetherills of the Mesa Verde: Autobiography of Benjamin Alfred Wetherill*, ed. Maurine S. Fletcher (1977; Lincoln: U of Nebraska P, 1987) 119.
45. Nordenskiold, *The Cliff Dwellers*, 49.
46. Nordenskiold, *The Cliff Dwellers*, 56.
47. Nordenskiold, *The Cliff Dwellers*, 59.
48. Thomas Rickner, letter to the Secretary of the Interior, 13 Feb. 1915, Mesa Verde National Park Library, Vault.
49. Duane A. Smith, *Mesa Verde National Park: Shadows of the Centuries* (Lawrence: U of Kansas P, 1988) 211.
50. Twice 'the author' of the brochure alludes to other publications of his: 'the descriptions of the Hopi Kiva rites elsewhere published by the author' (12) and 'my report on Spruce Tree House' (22). Fewkes published several studies of Hopi rituals, and his 1909 report on Spruce Tree House is listed in the brochure's bibliography. The anonymous author also mentions in passing that he has 'exhumed the skeleton of an adult' from a particular room. Fewkes was the first professional archaeologist to do extensive work at Mesa Verde, and he was still at work when Cather and Lewis were there.
51. One other indication that Cather had read this brochure is that in her 1916 essay she calls Nordenskiold 'Baron,' as the brochure does, although mistakenly. Of course, it is possible that she picked up the title in conversation with someone (her Wetherill contacts would have called him Gustaf), but seeing it in print in an official publication would more likely incline her to use it herself.
52. *The Prehistoric Cliff Dwellings: Mesa Verde National Park, Southwestern Colorado* (Washington: GPO, 1915) 8.
53. *Prehistoric Cliff Dwellings*, 23.

54. *Prehistoric Cliff Dwellings*, 9.
55. *Prehistoric Cliff Dwellings*, 3.
56. *Prehistoric Cliff Dwellings*, 2, 5,10.
57. Nordenskiold, *The Cliff Dwellers*, 61-62.
58. *Prehistoric Cliff Dwellings*, 1-2, 5, 18.
59. *Prehistoric Cliff Dwellings*, 24.
60. *Prehistoric Cliff Dwellings*, 10. This astronomical theory is still current among modern scientists. See 'Anasazis May Have Had Stars in Their Eyes,' *Albuquerque Journal* 10 Jul. 1990: E1.
61. Nordenskiold, *The Cliff Dwellers*, 56. According to Irv Diamond, Nordenskiold and Fewkes probably never met. Nordenskiold did write to Fewkes after the publication of *Cliff Dwellers of the Mesa Verde*, saying he hoped to see him at the Americanists Conference in Stockholm in 1894; but Fewkes's name does not appear in the published proceedings (letter to the author, 8 and 9 Mar. 1991).
62. Jesse W. Fewkes, 'Ancient Remains in Colorado: The Mesa Verde National Park, Landmark of a Lost Race,' *Scientific American* 122 (29 May 1920): 609.
63. Jesse W. Fewkes, 'A Prehistoric Observatory,' *Literary Digest* 75 (11 Nov. 1922): 27.
64. Jesse W. Fewkes, 'Cremation in Cliff-Dwellings,' *Records of the Past* 9 (May-June 1910): 155.
65. Janet Robertson, letter to the author, 26 Sept. 1987.
66. John March, *A Reader's Companion to the Fiction of Willa Cather*, ed. Marilyn Arnold, Westport: Greenwood Press, 1995, p. 598.
67. D. Smith, *Mesa Verde*, 41.
68. Janet Robertson, letter to the author, 4 Mar. 1989.
69. Wetherill, 192.
70. D. Smith, *Mesa Verde*, 41.
71. D. Smith, *Mesa Verde*, 42 ff.
72. Arthur Chapman, 'Mesa Verde Relics Are Preserved by Women,' *The Denver Times* 29 June 1915: 1.
73. McClurg, N. pag.
74. J.H. Gore, *Report of the Director of the Organization of International Congresses*, in *Report of the Commissioner-General for the United States to the International Universal Exposition, Paris, 1900*, 6 vols. (Washington: GPO, 1901) 6: 41, 42, 354.
75. Gore, 31, 33, 37. Another connection between Cather and McClurg is little more than a curiosity, but it bears noting. One of the pieces written about McClurg appeared in the July [1902] issue of *Woman's Home Companion*, a magazine that during the twenties and thirties published several of Cather's short stories and whose editor, Frederick Collins, was one of the reorganisers of *McClure's* in 1910.
76. James Woodress, letter to the author, 16 Jan. 1989.
77. Robert Grant, 'People Who Did Not Go to the Fair,' *The Cosmopolitan* 16 (Dec. 1893): 161.
78. Willa Cather, *The Kingdom of Art: Willa Cather's First Principles and Critical Statements, 1893-1896*, ed. Bernice Slote (Lincoln: U of Nebraska P, 1966): 196. Subsequent citations of Willa Cather's words from this book will appear in the text, with the abbreviation *KA* substituting for the full title.
79. For these World's Fair allusions I am indebted to John March (letter to the author, 27 Jan. 1989). The three stories are 'The Count of Crow's Nest' (1896), 'A Death in the Desert' (1905), and 'The Bohemian Girl' (1912); for the precise references see pp. 449, 199, and 5 respectively in *Willa Cather's Collected Short Fiction, 1892-1912*, rev. ed., ed. Virginia Faulkner (Lincoln: U of Nebraska P, 1970). Subsequent citations will appear in the text, with the abbreviation *CSF* substituting for the full title.
80. *The Wonders of the World's Fair*, souvenir ed. (Buffalo: Barnes, Hengerer & Co., [1894]) 111.
81. Smith, *Mesa Verde*, 36.
82. Ricardo Torres-Reyes, *An Administrative History of Mesa Verde National Park* (Washington: United States Department of the Interior, National Park Service, 1970) 379.
83. McNitt, *Richard Wetherill*, 56-57. Eleven years later Richard and his youngest brother Win took a better organised presentation to St Louis for that World's Fair (McNitt, *Richard Wetherill*, 214-15). For Cather, this was another missed opportunity to meet the man who would inspire her story.

84. Alessandro Pezzati, letter to the author, 28 June 1989.

85. Floyd W. Sharrock, 'The Hazzard Collection,' ts., 1962, the University Museum Archives, University of Pennsylvania, Philadelphia, 15.

86. Sergeant, 204.

87. Harvey Leake, letter to the author, 3 Apr. 1989.

88. Frances Gillmor and Louisa Wade Wetherill, *Traders to the Navajos: The Story of the Wetherills of Kayenta* (Boston: Houghton Mifflin Company, 1934) 103.

89. Leake.

90. Gillmor and Wetherill, 191.

91. Gillmor and Wetherill, 107.

92. McNitt, *Richard Wetherill*, 210.

93. Gillmor and Wetherill, 192.

94. Often the parties themselves included famous people. Perhaps the most notable was Theodore Roosevelt, who came there in the summer of 1913, a year after Cather's trip to Arizona, and hired John Wetherill to take him and his party to Rainbow Bridge (Gillmor and Wetherill 193-94), a recently discovered phenomenon about forty miles northwest of Kayenta, just across the Utah border. Not long afterward, Roosevelt wrote for *Outlook* magazine a characteristically exuberant account of his adventure, heaping praise upon John and Louisa Wetherill.

95. Willa Cather, *One of Ours* (1922; New York: Vintage Books, 1971) 103. Subsequent citations will appear in the text, with the abbreviation *OO* substituting for the full title.

96. Sergeant, 122-23.

97. Sergeant, 124.

98. Belinda Kaye, letter to the author, 21 Jan. 1988.

99. Woodress, *A Literary Life*, 259. See also David Stouck, 'Cather's *Archbishop* and Travel Writing,' *Western American Literature* 17.1 (Spring 1982): 4.

100. Sergeant, 164-65, 207-08. One obvious exception is Tony Luhan.

101. Butcher, 'Purpose,' 9.

102. Stuart Sherman, *Critical Woodcuts* (New York: Charles Scribner's Sons, 1926) 32.

168
Willa Cather's Ecology of Place

◆

SUSAN J. ROSOWSKI

I propose to write of a Willa Cather we've scarcely met, the Cather who while growing up in Red Cloud went on rounds with Dr McKeeby, observing him as he diagnosed and treated his patients; and the Cather who in her high school graduation speech described success as becoming 'a great anatomist or a brilliant naturalist.' This Cather entered the University of Nebraska in 1890 intending to study science, and she arrived at precisely the time that the pioneering work being done there in botany and ecology placed the University at the forefront of those fields. Having joined its faculty in 1884, Charles E. Bessey was transforming 'raw youths from the new farmlands of booming Nebraska into missionaries for science' (Tobey 9). The intellectual climate created by Bessey and his circle was nothing short of extraordinary, formed by a common appreciation of being at the frontier of knowledge offered by the unbroken prairies and plains spreading around them.

Out of his work in the Midwest Bessey wrote *Botany for High Schools and Colleges* (1880), the textbook that revolutionised botany by directing attention away from other people's taxonomies and toward the field, where one might study nature.[1] Among his students and among Cather's friends was F.E. Clements (class of '94), an intense young man with the soul of a poet who formulated principles of both plant and animal ecology, now best known for the facilitation hypothesis of ecological succession. Among the University's students also was Edith Schwartz, who would marry Fred Clements and coauthor with him scientific papers (she received her own Ph.D. degree in botany in 1904), as well as write with him popular guides to plants of the plains and Rocky Mountains. Yet another student was Roscoe Pound (brother of Cather's friend Louise Pound), whose genius inspired those around him to explore the philosophical issues most relevant to biology. Pound was to receive his Ph.D. in botany and to head the state's

SOURCE Susan J. Rosowski, 'Willa Cather's Ecology of Place', *Western American Literature*, 30, 1995, pp. 37–51

survey of Nebraska flora before moving on to Harvard, where he became Dean of the Law College.

Developed in response to practical problems facing the state's farmers, ecology at the University of Nebraska was articulated in language that invited participation by the nonprofessional. Along with their more academic writing, these scientists wrote books for the schools, prepared reports for the state's citizens, and published popular guides to plants of a region. Courses of study (the scientific and the phiolosphical) and subjects of inquiry (nature and human) come together in a field that describes itself in terms common to both,[2] and ecology had a human face—sometimes literally. In *Flower Families and Ancestors*, for example, the Clementses wrote that 'The faces of flowers are much like those of people in bearing the impress of experience more or less plainly stamped upon them' (1). Plants 'bear' flowers and provide 'parental care'; they co-operate and compete; they establish a 'community,' and so on. Making the activity of science as accessible as its subject, the founding ecologists described what they did in the familiar terms of reading a story. As Edith Clements was to reflect in her memoir, 'The ecologist adds his pages to the book of knowledge by reading in the vegetation of the world, not only the story of its past and of the present, but he can foretell its future as well' (*Adventures in Ecology* 11).

Being at the University of Nebraska in the early 1890s meant that one 'could not have avoided the Bessey influence' (Knoll, 'Interview'; see also *Prairie University*). With a student population of 500 when Cather arrived and 1500 when she left, the University was akin to a small town where everybody knew everybody—and where everybody looked to Bessey as their 'model of excellence,' the one 'who set the pace.' His 'influence was everywhere, in all the departments—in the English and the language departments (where A.H. Edgren called himself a linguistic scientist) and in the history department (where F.M. Fling advocated conducting historical research by scientific principles) and, of course, in the sciences.'[3] As a 'second prep' student intending to pursue the scientific course of study, in 1890 Cather was allowed to take freshman chemistry, where she was directly in the science (and therefore Bessey) program. When in 1891 Cather changed her field of study to literature, her friendships (with Louise Pound, Edith Schwartz and Fred Clements) and her animosities (with Roscoe Pound) made personal her ongoing sensitivity to Bessey's presence.[4]

Most important, Cather gave witness to Bessey's influence in her fiction, as seen in the contrast of stories she wrote while a freshman to those four years later. In 1892 Cather described nature in sweeping generalisations and conventional asides: the plains was a place where 'there was nothing but sun, and grass, and sky' ('Peter') and where a settler realised that 'unless rain fell, ... his entire crop would be ruined' ('Lou, the Prophet' 1892). By the time she was graduated, Cather was writing with the authenticity of direct observation. In 'On the Divide' (1896), for example, she described the effect of weather on crops in precise scientific detail: when 'scorching dusty winds ... blow up over the bluffs from Kansas,' they dry up the sap in the corn leaves, and 'the yellow scorch creeps down over the tender inside leaves about the ear.' Far from dismissing nature as a conventional backdrop, Cather was reading drama in the vegetation about her: winds blow *over bluffs*, and as if in stealthy attack, yellow scorch *creeps* down tender *inside* leaves *about* the ear of corn.

Displacement followed, as if nature's drama was competing with and finally pushing aside that of its human inhabitants in Cather's writing. The real story of 'The Treasure of Far Island' (1902) concerns not the world-famous playwright who returns to his hometown for the woman he had loved from childhood, but instead the ongoing life of an oval sand bar, with all the changes that come with alterations in the weather:

> In the middle of the island, which is always above water except in flood time, grow thousands of yellow-green creek willows and cottonwood seedlings, brilliantly green, even when the hottest winds blow, by reason of the surrounding moisture.

In 'El Dorado: A Kansas Recessional' (1906), a human plot of thwarted speculation in land and love pales beside the more memorable story of a valley in western Kansas where a 'turbid, muddy little stream . . . crawls along between naked bluffs, choked and split by sand bars.' Cather's setting tells nature's story of community and competition:

> Beyond the river with its belt of amber woodland rose the bluffs, ragged, broken, covered with shaggy red grass and bare of trees, save for the few stunted oaks that grew upon their steep sides. They were pathetic little trees, that sent their roots down through thirty feet of hard clay bluff to the river level. . . . They seldom, if ever, bore acorns; it took all the nourishment that soil could give just to exist.

In the same vein 'The Enchanted Bluff' (1909) opens with the narrator's reading the story that nature is telling:

> Every spring the swollen stream undermined a bluff to the east, or bit out a few acres of corn field to the west and whirled the soil away to deposit it in spumy mud banks somewhere else. When the water fell low in midsummer, new sand bars were thus exposed to dry and whiten in the August sun. Sometimes these were banked so firmly that the fury of the next freshet failed to unseat them; the little willow seedlings emerged triumphantly from the yellow froth, broke into spring leaves, shot up into summer growth, and with their mesh of roots bound together the moist sand beneath them against the batterings of another April.

Interaction of species with the soil influenced by wind, water and humidity, and culminating in a triumphant emergence or climax—this is a narrative structured by the ecological model evolving at Nebraska during the years that Cather was a student there. And as the Bessey model directed attention to the field and responded to practical problems identified by the state's farmers, Cather wrote her plains stories with reference to a real world[5] where blight and chinch bugs threaten crops, and settlers seeking farming methods appropriate to their land plant sod corn, introduce winter wheat, and debate whether to plant red clover or alfalfa.

Not surprisingly, perhaps, the one area in which Cather was a social reformer concerned advocating a culture that is native to a place. She lectured to community groups, sounding like a stump speaker in campaigning for an 'appreciation of . . . native prairies,' counseling women to 'study trees, flowers and other beauties of the state instead of turning back to Botticelli and early art,' and urging Nebraskans to take action 'to protect the native trees, especially the giant cottonwoods' (Bohlke 40). She championed Nebraska wild flowers with special fervor:

> There is no place in the world that has more beautiful ones. But they have no common names. In England, in any European country, they would all have beautiful names like eglantine, primrose, and celandine. As a child I gave them all names of my own. I used to gather great armfuls of them and sit and cry over them. They were so lovely, and no one seemed to care for them at all! (Bohlke 47)

What has long been charged to nostalgia for the past is strikingly similar to the principles that ecologists today argue as a model for our future: Cather argued against standardisation and for diversity; she argued against Middle Westerners aping the East and for them to have 'their own particular kind of life'; she urged cities to develop individuality (Bohlke 150–51).

Devoting her attention to her place led Cather to redefine her region. Again, antecedents exist in those early botanists, for as Bessey had turned from other people's taxonomies to the field, so Cather turned from other's maps and toward imagining her own. 'I wonder where this river really does begin!' her character muses while sitting on a sandbar in 'The Enchanted Bluff' (1909); in response Cather reflects '[t]hat was an old and a favorite mystery which the map did not clearly explain,' then speculates about what lay beyond that map, where 'the little black line stopped somewhere in western Kansas; but since rivers generally rose in mountains, it was only reasonable to suppose that ours came from the Rockies.' She cast her version of history in terms of a regional character:

> The state of Nebraska is part of the great plain which stretches west of the Missouri River, gradually rising until it reaches the Rocky Mountains. The character of all this country between the river and the mountains is essentially the same throughout its extent: a rolling, alluvial plain, growing gradually more sandy toward the west, until it breaks into the white sandhills of western Nebraska and Kansas and eastern Colorado. From east to west this plain measures something over five hundred miles; in appearance it resembles the wheat lands of Russia, which fed the continent of Europe for so many years. Like Little Russia it is watered by slow-flowing, muddy rivers, which run full in the spring, often cutting into the farm lands along their banks; but by midsummer they lie low and shrunken, their current split by glistening white sand-bars half overgrown with scrub willows.

> The climate, with its extremes of temperature, gives to this plateau the variety which, to the casual eye at least, it lacks. There we have short, bitter winters; windy, flower-laden springs; long, hot summers; triumphant autumns that last until Christmas—a season of perpetual sunlight, blazing blue skies, and frosty nights. In this newest part of the New World autumn is the season of beauty and sentiment, as spring is in the Old World. ('Nebraska: The End of the First Cycle' 1)[6]

As for her own aspirations—after writing *O Pioneers!*, *The Song of the Lark* and *My Ántonia*, Cather said 'There is one book that I would rather have produced than all my novels. That is the Clements botany dealing with the wild flowers of the west' (Bohlke 47).[7] Hyperbole? Perhaps, but an indicative one. She never made such claims about other fields, and in making this one, she gave voice to the appreciation of botany and ecology that informed her fiction.

It is not only that Cather observed nature closely, however, nor is it solely that she wrote of place by principles of ecology; botanical and ecological principles helped shape Cather's very idea of art. To illustrate I propose jumping generations to read Cather alongside *Becoming Native To This Place*, in which Wes Jackson issues a call to

> Imagine our continent with thousands of plant and animal breeders practicing their art (and their science) to meet the *regional* necessities of farmers across a less homogenized agricultural landscape. Imagine these men and women breeding crops and livestock for their neighbors, 'developing elegant solutions predicated on the uniqueness of place'. (49)

By her example, Cather issued her own call (and here I paraphrase Jackson) to imagine our continent with thousands of writers practicing their art to meet the *regional* necessities across a less homogenised literary landscape and to imagine these men and women writing for their neighbors, 'developing elegant solutions predicated on the uniqueness of place.' Imagining solutions predicated on the uniqueness of place is the principle Cather followed in *O Pioneers!* when she dismissed preconceptions of what a novel should be and wrote a story that 'came out of the long grasses.' The country insisted on being the Hero of her story, she said simply, and she did not interfere (Sergeant 92). Positioning herself in conversation with nature (the phrase is Wendell Berry's), Cather responded with not only the plot but the form of *O Pioneers!*. The book had no skeleton, she wrote of it, and then explained that the country she was writing about had no skeleton either. That was a country without rocks or ridges, where the black soil ran through one's fingers. Its softness somehow influenced the mood and structure of her novel (WC to ES; 22 April 1913; see Sergeant 97).

In the opening pages of her story Cather announces her premise that 'the great fact was the land itself, which seemed to overwhelm the little beginnings of human society that struggled in its sombre wastes' (21). She then writes about becoming native to a place, a process her characters undertake with humility. John Bergson is the homesteader who 'knew every ridge and draw and gully between him and the horizon,' and who 'had an idea that no one understood how to farm it properly' (26–7); Alexandra Bergson is the daughter with whom he discusses this often, and who must learn to read this land for the lessons it teaches, then to map it by the ecological principles she has learned. That is the challenge facing Alexandra—the land, unmapped and spreading out before them: 'Of all the bewildering things about a new country, the absence of human landmarks is one of the most depressing and disheartening' (25).

Beginning with the Bergson homestead, Cather describes what it is to acquire the 'feel' of a place in all its particularity, realised by its contrast to the rough country across the country line where the hermit Crazy Ivar has his homestead. Setting out to visit him there,

> the Bergson wagon lurched along over the rough hummocks and grass banks, followed the bottom of winding draws, or skirted the margin of wide lagoons, where the golden coreopsis grew up out of the clear water and the wild ducks rose with a whirr of wings. (38)

When Alexandra and her brothers leave 'the lagoons and the red grass behind them,' their journey traces an ecological map in describing the contours of the land.

> In Crazy Ivar's country the grass was short and gray, the draws deeper than they were in the Bergsons' neighborhood, and the land was all broken up into hillocks and clay ridges. The wild flowers disappeared, and only in the bottom of the draws and gullies grew a few of the very toughest and hardiest: shoestring, and ironweed, and snow-on-the-mountain. (39)

'To consult nature, we turn to . . . one hundred acres of never-plowed native prairie' (43), writes Wes Jackson: on never plowed acres of native prairie, Alexandra finds Ivar, quoting from his Norwegian Bible about adaptation of species to place: the trees are nesting sites for birds, 'The high hills are a refuge for the wild goats; and the rocks for the conies' (38). Thus Cather, like Jackson, turns to tradition for

> time-honored arrangements [to] inform us of what has worked without our running the empirical experiment. . . . This is another way of saying that we must turn to nature to inform us, to serve as a reference, must turn our thoughts to building a science of ecology that reflects a consultation of nature. Ecology is the most likely discipline to engage in a courtship with agriculture as we anticipate a marriage. (25)

In just such a courtship, Alexandra visits farms in the river country, talks with farmers, observes—and only then returns to the Divide.

> For the first time, perhaps, since that land emerged from the waters of geologic ages, a human face was set toward it with love and yearning. It seemed beautiful to her, rich and strong and glorious. Her eyes drank in the breadth of it, until her tears blinded her. Then the Genius of the Divide, the great, free spirit which breathes across it, must have bent lower than it ever bent to a human will before. (64)

It is the moment from which all else springs: Alexandra's relationship to place and Cather's orientation of herself. For Cather, its effect was to fix the points of the compass.

By invoking the Genius of the Divide and paying tribute to it as 'the great, free spirit which breathes across it,' Cather established a lineage going back before the Bible that Ivar was reading, to the classical, pagan belief in which genius is the tutelary and controlling spirit connected with a place. This is the idea of genius to which Virgil refers when at the outset of the Georgics he advises that

> *Care must be taken to observe the winds*
> *And changing skies, what modes and habits be*
> *The region's heritage, what gift each place*
> *Bears or denies. These acres favor corn,*
> *In yonder, vines grow better; elsewhere spring*
> *Fruit-orchards and a wealth of unsown green.*
> . . .
> *Such are the laws, the lasting covenants,*
> *Which Nature's power ordains for place and time,*
> . . .
>
> (*Georgics* I: 57–62)

In the tradition of the *Georgics*, Alexandra's education consists of learning 'the laws, the lasting covenants,' which Nature's power ordains for her place —that is, the Divide.

That 'new consciousness of the country,' that 'new relation to it' is the gravitational center of *O Pioneers!*: from it evolves the mosaic of a neighborhood and region. Without human landmarks, mapping occurs neither by rectangular surveys nor by grid or property lines, but by ecological realities. Norway Creek is the point of reference for the Bergson homestead, 'a shallow, muddy stream that sometimes flowed, and sometimes stood still, at the bottom of a winding ravine with steep, shelving sides overgrown with brush and cottonwoods and dwarf ash. This creek gave a sort of identity to the farms that bordered upon it' (25). From it extends the neighborhood, within which points on the map signal the individual's participation in community: the wheatfield corner between the Shabatas' and Alexandra's places, with the path that led from one to the other and the stile over the fences that separated them.

The map extends further still by journeys taken by members of a community. To the east is Lincoln, where Emil Bergson went to the University and Frank Shabata was imprisoned in the penitentiary; beyond that was Omaha, where Marie Tovesky grew up, where Frank gave himself up to the police, and where Emil was planning to read law; farther still was Iowa, where Carrie Jensen, the sister of one of Alexandra's hired men, visited relatives. Chicago is where John Bergson's younger brother went after giving up his homestead 'to work in a fancy bakery and distinguish himself in a

Swedish athletic club' (27), and then Ann Arbor, Michigan (where Alexandra planned to visit Emil in law school), and New York, where Carl Linstrum lived, and where the Wall Street that Lou Bergson wishes to blow up is. To the north there is the Norwegian graveyard, then Hanover, and then Hastings, whose baseball team played the Saint-Agnes boys, and the French country, where Emil kissed Marie at the Catholic fair. To the west is San Francisco, and to the South is the river twenty miles away, where Mrs Bergson sent the boys to fish for channel cat twice every summer; and then Mexico, where Emil went to try to escape his love for Marie. Behind it all lies Stockholm and the Old Country, and back of that geologic time, when glaciers left faint markings upon rocks. Metaphoric ripples extend outward: 'Like the plains of Lombardy,' the Divide 'seems to rise a little to meet the sun' (74). And beyond it are the stars upon which Alexandra gazed as she leaned against her windmill.

It is a map drawn by principles of community: when seen by a point of view rooted in place, France is kin and the stars are neighbors. Place and region—the terms are different in kind, and that difference is critical to an understanding of Cather. Place is not a nation or a region or even a province, but 'the little rural neighborhood ... where the poet was born,' as Cather was to quote Virgil's *Georgics* in *My Ántonia*—Virgil's 'father's fields, "sloping down to the river and to the old beech trees with broken tops"' (256). Place—as Cather writes of it—is a matter of consciousness, a point of view rooted in nature that is individual and particular. Place is known, whereas a region is mapped; the relationship to place determines the terms of one's map. And for the writer, *place is to region as voice is to language*: it is 'the thing that is [the writer's] very own' that 'cannot be defined or explained any more than the quality of a beautiful speaking voice can be' ('Katherine Mansfield' 134-35). In the words of Eudora Welty, 'place is where [the writer] has roots, place is where he stands; in his experience out of which he writes, it provides the base of reference; in his work, the point of view' (117).

By a point of view rooted in place, the part and the whole interpenetrate—this is the lesson that Cather makes dramatic in the scene immediately following Alexandra's invocation of the Genius of the Divide. That night, leaning against her windmill, Alexandra stands 'looking at the stars which glittered so keenly through the frosty autumn air.' 'She always loved to watch them,' Cather explains,

> to think of their vastness and distance, and of their ordered march. It fortified her to reflect upon the great operations of nature, and when she thought of the law that lay behind them, she felt a sense of personal security. That night she had a new consciousness of the country, felt almost a new relation to it. (68-69)

With Alexandra gazing at the stars, reflecting upon the laws that govern them all, the scene demonstrates the ecological or dialectical approach asserting, according to Jackson, that

> creating the world is involved in our every act.... What we desire arranges the genetic code in all of our major crops and livestock. We cannot avoid participating in the creation, and it is in agriculture, far and away our largest and most basic artifact, that human culture and the creation totally interpenetrate. (22)

The dialectical approach of ecology is seen in the structure of *O Pioneers!* more generally. Desire affects the genetic code, Jackson writes, as if in explanation of the apparently miraculous transformation of the Wild Land into Neighboring Fields; by seeing her place with love and yearning, Alexandra participates in creation. Thus Cather jumps ahead sixteen years to describe the Divide 'now thickly populated,' where 'the rich soil yields heavy harvests; the dry, bracing climate and the smoothness of the land make labor easy for men and beasts,' and 'the furrows of a single field often lie a mile in length' (74). Similarly, for her novel's conclusion Cather describes the dialectic of Alexandra's eventual return to the land itself:

> Fortunate country, that is one day to receive hearts like Alexandra's into its bosom, to give them out again in the yellow wheat, in the rustling corn, in the shining eyes of youth! (274)

Interpenetration of part and whole is the principle also behind Cather's narration, with its movement between the inclusive and the particular. Scenes begin with a point of view similar to that of a camera lens opening very wide to take in the expanse of the Divide; they then narrow upon the particular, to focus upon a moment in Alexandra's garden or in Marie's orchard. The story's voice similarly alternates between that of creation itself (as if the Genius of the Divide is speaking) to that of its inhabitants—Alexandra and Carl and the rest of the human voices, of course, but also a windmill vibrating in the wind and coyotes howling for food.

Beyond the workings of a single novel, and ecological dialectic provides the principle of a sustainable culture underlying the remarkable longevity of Cather's career. Nearly three decades separate her first novel (*Alexander's Bridge*) from her last (*Sapphira and the Slave Girl*), years notable for the consistency and quality of Cather's output. After a decade of writing about Nebraska (*O Pioneers!* appeared in 1913, *A Lost Lady* in 1923), Cather turned elsewhere—to Michigan, the American Southwest, France, Quebec, and Virginia. As the farmer insures the continuing yield of biological resources by controlled periodic harvesting, Cather was to return again and again to the Divide and Red Cloud for her material, rested by alternating crops. As so often was the case, Cather drew upon botany and ecology to describe her relation to her region:

> 'Next to writing I love best to prowl around the Western country, seeing little towns and how the people live in them. To me, the real West begins with the Missouri. Colorado, Nebraska, Arizona, New Mexico, and Nevada do not seem like separate states to me, but are linked together in my mind like one big country.
>
> 'In my writing, however, I do not want to become too identified with that

region. There is little of the West in *The Professor's House*, the book I am working on now. Using one setting all the time is very like planting a field with corn season after season. I believe in rotation of crops.' (Bohlke 76)

By such a view, fiction is a sustainable culture. From her first published story, 'Peter' (1892) to *My Ántonia* (1918) and then again in 'Neighbor Rosicky' (1932), for example, forty years pass in which four generations of a fictional family appear, drawn from four generations of the actual family Cather had known as a child, and with whom she visited and corresponded throughout her life. The Sadilek-Pavelka family has an ongoing, self perpetuating life in Cather's writing, appearing as the Sadelacks, the Shimerdas, the Cuzaks, and the Rosickys; and they continue today with the descendants of Annie Sadilek and John Pavelka: one granddaughter (Antonette Turner) now tells visitors to Webster County about the time her grandmother was photographed for *Life*, and a grandson (Kent Pavelka) is the sports announcer known in these parts as 'the voice of Nebraska football.'

Beneath these human stories is the place that Cather claimed as her own. With the Divide at the center, a neighborhood and a region extend, for convenience labeled Red Cloud and Webster County on the map but flashing into the fiction with the particularity of a little neighborhood: the enchanted bluff upon which boys sit about a watchfire, the fruit cave from which Ántonia's children burst forth, the farm fields into which Claude Wheeler throws himself, the marsh to which Marian Forrester brings cookies to boys playing, the Republican River upon which Lucy Gayheart skates in winter, the farm for which Anton Rosicky feels blessed, and beyond the fiction, still spreading out before one. 'We come and go, but the land is always there,' Cather wrote in *O Pioneers!*.

In *Writing in Place: The New American Regionalism* Michael Kowalewski calls for 'a new attention to place in literary studies' that 'might help alter the model itself, perhaps by way of a few new metaphors, like photosynthesis or an ecology of the self, in place of omnipresent notions of "constructed" identity.' Kowalewski cautions, however, that 'the force of such a new emphasis will only be successful if the "ecology" turns out to be something challengingly new. . . . The new regional studies must be capable of exploring regional identity without reverting to mere localism.' For a new way of exploring regional identity in literary studies, I suggest that we return to the wellsprings from which those metaphors have taken on meaning—to the likes of Bessey, Clements, and Pound. There in the creative ferment of ecology's beginnings, the founding generation assumed that regional identity yielded knowledge, and 'mere localism' wasn't even an issue. By such a revisiting, we might find 'something challengingly new' in placing familiar texts in new contexts—Willa Cather as the heir to Charles Bessey, for example, and as the forerunner to Wes Jackson.

Notes

1. For example, Bessey began Chapter I by directing his reader toward observation: 'If we examine a thin slice of any growing part of a plant (Fig. 1) under the microscope of a moderately highpower (400 to 500 diameters), there may be seen large numbers of cavities which are more or less filled with an almost transparent semi-fluid substance.'
2. After directing his reader to look at a plant through a microscope in the opening sentence of his botany textbook, Bessey explains,

> This substance is the *living portion of the plant*, the active, vital thing which gives to it its sensibility to heat, cold, and other agents, and the power of moving, of appropriating food, and of increasing its size; it is, in fact, *that which is sensitive, which moves, appropriates food, and increases in size*. This sensitive, moving, assimilating, and growing substance is named PROTOPLASM. (1)

3. Robert E. Knoll, personal interviews September 1994 and 12 March 1995.
4. Indeed, the genealogy of Bessey's influence upon Cather is a subject unto itself. As Kari Ronning has noted in 'Willa Cather's University Days,' Fling's required research with primary sources (which reflected Bessey's stress upon field work) resembles the assignment that gives Claude his happiest moments in *One of Ours*, and 'Many years later Cather would use similar research methods in historical novels like *Death Comes for the Archbishop* and *Shadows on the Rock*' (15).

Cather's sensitivity to things botanical at the University is dramatically apparent in the vitriolic quality of her 1894 attack upon Roscoe Pound:

> He was, by the lengthy words he used, a member of the botanical seminar. He called everything by its longest and most Latin name, and the less his victim knows about botany the more confidential he becomes and the more copiously he empties forth Latin words upon him. . . . He loves to take rather weak minded persons and . . . botany them into a shapeless mass. ('Pastels in Prose,' 4–5)

While Cather was a student, the botanical seminar, or 'Bot Sem' as it was known, was both the most prestigious intellectual assembly at the University, and it was also closed to women. The happier side of Cather's sensitivity to botany at the University appears in her ongoing interest in the research of the Clementses, as I note later in this essay.

5. In this, too, Cather was in the tradition of the Nebraska ecologists, and of the University of Nebraska as a land-grant institution. Whereas the University of Chicago, Nebraska's major competitor in grassland ecology, provided a model of pure research and 'epitomized . . . the ethic of the ivory tower' in its 'dedication . . . to pure research, unsullied by immediate problem solving,' the University of Nebraska as a land-grant university, responded to the needs of ordinary citizens. Bessey was hired at University of Nebraska as dean of the Industrial College, professor of botany and horticulture, and Nebraska state botanist (Tobey 10, 123 et passim). Similarly, the dynamic ecology the Clements formulated 'grew out of and returned for nourishment to the practical soil of agriculture' (126 Tobey). Moreover, the concept of community was as basic to the Nebraska scientists' working relationships as to their theory of ecology; whereas scientists at Chicago worked as individuals, those at Nebraska formed a research group of collaboration and cooperation.
6. Compare Pound's description of physiography and climatology in *Phytogeography of Nebraska* (1900), pp. 31 ff.
7. The interview misspelling of 'Clemens' is presumably that of the interviewer or a typesetter.

Works Cited

Bessey, Charles E., *Botany for High Schools and Colleges*, 4th ed., New York: Henry Holt and Company, 1885.

Bohlke, L. Brent, ed., *Willa Cather in Person; Interviews, Speeches, and Letters*, Lincoln: University of Nebraska Press, 1986.

Cather, Willa, *Collected Short Fiction, 1892-1912*, ed. Virginia Faulkner; Intro. Mildred R. Bennett. Lincoln: University of Nebraska Press, 1970.

—, 'Katherine Mansfield', *Not Under Forty*, New York: Knopf, 1936, pp. 123-47.

—, *My Ántonia*, eds Charles Mignon with Kari Ronning, Lincoln: University of Nebraska Press, 1994.

—, 'Nebraska: The End of the First Cycle', *The Nation*, September 5, 1923, rptd *Roundup: A Nebraska Reader*, ed. Virginia Faulkner, Lincoln: University of Nebraska Press, 1957, pp. 1-8.

—, *O Pioneers!*, eds Susan J. Rosowski and Charles W. Mignon with Kathleen Danker, Lincoln: University of Nebraska Press, 1992.

—, 'Pastels in Prose', *The Hesperian*, March 10, 1894; pp. 4-5.

Clements, Edith Gertrude Schwartz. *Adventures in Ecology: Half a Million Miles: From Mud to Macadam*, New York: Pageant Press, 1960.

Clements, Frederic E. and Edith S. Clements, *Flower Families and Ancestors*, New York: The H.W. Wilson Company, 1928.

Jackson, Wes, *Becoming Native To This Place*, Lexington: University Press of Kentucky, 1994.

Kowalewski, Michael, 'Writing in Place: The New American Regionalism', *American Literary History*, 6.1, 1994: pp. 171-83.

Knoll, Robert E., Personal Interview, Lincoln, Nebraska. September 1994; 13 March 1995.

Pound, Roscoe and Frederic R. Clements, *The Phytogeography of Nebraska: I General Survey*, 2nd ed., Lincoln: The Botanical Seminar, 1900.

Ronning, Kari, 'Cather the Student', *Willa Cather's University Days*, Lincoln, Nebraska: Center for Great Plains Studies, 1985, pp. 14-17.

Sergeant, Elizabeth Shepley, *Willa Cather: A Memoir*, Philadelphia: J.B. Lippincott Company. 1953.

Tobey, Ronald C., *Saving the Prairies: The Life Cycle of the Founding School of American Plant Ecology, 1895-1955*, Berkeley: University of California Press, 1981.

Virgil. *The Georgics and Eclogues of Virgil*, trans. Theodore Chickering Williams, Cambridge: Harvard University Press, 1915.

Welty, Eudora, 'Place in Fiction', *The Eye of the Story: Selected Essays and Reviews*, New York: Random House, 1978, pp. 116-33.

Canon Studies

169
No Stone Unturned: Popular versus Professional Evaluations of Willa Cather

◆

DAVID STINEBACK

In *The Song of the Lark* (Willa Cather's third novel, published in 1915), Thea Kronberg goes to one of her father's regular prayer meetings in Moonstone, Colorado, and hears an old woman who 'never missed a Wednesday night [and] came all the way up from the depot settlement.' Cather describes the woman this way:

> She always wore a black crocheted 'fascinator' over her thin white hair, and she made long, tremulous prayers, full of railroad terminology. She had six sons in the service of different railroads, and she always prayed 'for the boys on the road, who know not at what moment they may be cut off. When, in Thy divine wisdom, their hour is upon them, may they, O our Heavenly Father, see only white lights along the road to Eternity.' She used to speak, too, of 'the engines that race with death'; and though she looked so old and little when she was on her knees, and her voice was so shaky, her prayers had a thrill of speed and danger in them; they made one think of the deep black cañons, the slender trestles, the pounding trains. Thea liked to look at her sunken eyes that seemed full of wisdom, at her black thread gloves, much too long in the fingers and so meekly folded one over the other. Her face was brown, and worn away as rocks are worn by water. There are many ways of describing that colour of age, but in reality it is not like parchment, or like any of the things it is said to be like. That brownness and that texture of skin are found only in the faces of old human creatures, who have worked hard and who have always been poor.

When Thea reaches home, she buries herself in Tolstoy's *Anna Karenina*, hoping for release from the 'mournfulness' of her evening's experience. We

SOURCE David Stineback, 'No Stone Unturned: Popular versus Professional Evaluations of Willa Cather', *Prospects*, 7, 1982, pp. 167–76

are told, however, that she will eventually find the old faces at her father's prayer meeting 'as full of meaning, as mysteriously marked by Destiny, as the people who danced the mazurka under the elegant Korsunsky.'[1]

Reading Willa Cather's novels is like going to the Reverend Mr Kronberg's prayer meetings: they too work on one's emotions in a less than voluntary way and finally leave a residue of deep, often painful meaning that lasts. But if they reveal, as Cather says elsewhere in *The Song of the Lark*, that no one keeps the warm feeling of the friendliness of the world for very long, they also show us that everyone's being in the same decrepit vehicle is far from the worst of fates, especially if we look one another in the eye with pity and forgiveness. Our reality can become as meaningful as the reality in Cather's works if we permit the human connections between her characters and ourselves, as Thea did between Tolstoy and her own experience with the railroad woman. 'A novel,' Cather once asserted, 'is merely a work of imagination in which a writer tries to present the experience and emotions of a group of people by the light of his own.'[2] That group of people, in Cather's case at least, always includes us—her readers—as well as her characters.

This has not, however, been the judgment of Cather scholars over the years. Academic critics—those who write scholarly books and articles—not only have measured Cather's achievement by inappropriate standards but have frequently patronised her in the process. Perhaps this is no surprise when it comes from Cather's detractors, particularly if one considers the subtle and experimental nature of her fiction; but misrepresentation and condescension have also characterised the scholarship of her professed admirers, who have made 'damning with faint praise' an unconscious art.

The most striking example of scholarly mistreatment concerns the distinctive form of Cather's fiction. Cather was so committed to characterisation—its breadth, depth, and varying modes—that she perversely and repeatedly reduced her plots to a series of seemingly innocuous events and generally refused even to highlight the dramatic potential of those events when she had the chance. Indeed, her weakest novels— *One of Ours* (1922), *Shadows on the Rock* (1931), and *Lucy Gayheart* (1935) — suffer from her inability or unwillingness to replace a lapsed interest in characterisation with an interest in the details of setting and plot. Yet no critic since the 1920s has emphasised, much less analysed, the extremity of Cather's commitment to characterisation as a conscious artistic principle. On the contrary, critics have consistently argued that Cather complacently exploited her fictional characters as expressions of her own troubled character and that in the process, she repeatedly passed moral judgments on those characters and the values they seem to embody.

Three major critical approaches to Cather's work reflect these assumptions. First and most familiar to Cather readers is the *political* criticism of the 1930s and after. Offended by the historical nature of Cather's later novels and some of her nonfictional judgments on American society, Granville

Hicks, Lionel Trilling, Maxwell Geismar, and others concentrated on what they felt was Cather's excessive gentility and charged her with artistic cowardice in the face of pressing moral issues in American society. A glaring example of this critical approach is Hicks's famous assertion that 'Miss Cather has never once tried to see contemporary life as it is; she sees only that it lacks what the past, at least in her idealisation of it, had. Thus she has been barred from the task that has occupied most of the world's great artists, the expression of what is central and fundamental in her own age.' Much more recently and with less animus, Morton Dauwen Zabel elaborated on this characterisation of Cather:

> Her devotion to the past and its perished beauty was sincere but inevitably limited by a didactic principle and threatened by the inflexibility of an idealistic convention.... But it must also be granted that she lived through a cleavage and a crisis in something more than American life; that she saw 'the end of an era, the sunset of the pioneer'; that it 'was already gone, that age; nothing could ever bring it back'; and she defined the pathos, if not the challenge and moral imperative, its passing imposed on every survivor and writer concerned with it. She did not succeed in surmounting the confines of her special transition and the resentment it induced in her, and she did not write the kind of books that assure the future or the energy of a literature. That opportunity she consciously rejected.[3]

Yet, for all its passion, the political critics' rhetoric about 'contemporary life as it is' and 'rejected opportunities' amounts to little more than an insistent preference for urban settings, which Cather used only occasionally in her novels.

Second, and somewhat at odds with the political criticism of Cather's novels, is the *sociological* criticism that began after the appearance of *O Pioneers!* in 1913. From H.L. Mencken and Carl Van Doren to the major critical works on Cather by E.K. Brown, John Randall, and Edward and Lillian Bloom, the sociological critics have responded to the ostensible 'themes' of Cather's novels rather than their settings. Thus early in her career Cather seemed to be another 'revolt from the village' novelist, particularly in *The Song of the Lark*. Then, with *One of Ours, A Lost Lady*, and *The Professor's House* in the early 1920s, she appeared to be deeply offended by the materialism and corruption of twentieth-century American society. Other themes took shape in the hands of succeeding critics: the pioneer spirit, frontier pastoralism, traditional values of all kinds. Alfred Kazin best summarised the essence of this sociological approach and suggested its difference from the political rejection of Cather:

> The very intensity of her nostalgia had from the first led her beyond nostalgia; it had given her the conviction that the values of the world she had lost were the primary values, and everything else merely their degradation.... It was this conflict, a conflict that went *beyond classes* and could be represented only as a struggle between grandeur and meanness, the two poles of her world, that became the great theme of her novels.[4]

Third and, though least visible, growing in appeal among scholars is the *psychological* criticism initiated by Leon Edel in the 1950s and used implicitly by some of Cather's recent commentators and explicitly by Blanche Gelfant, the most provocative of the newer Cather critics. The psychological critics are not interested in setting or theme. Instead, although they accept the general characterisation of Cather as nostalgic and moralistic, they place the source of her creativity in her unconscious and use the boldest imagery in her novels to generate hidden meaning. Thus James Woodress described *The Professor's House* as a compulsive spiritual autobiography and offhandedly called the character of Tom Outland Cather's 'dream self,' and Gelfant found countless images of sexual inhibition in *My Ántonia* (1918) of which Cather, nevertheless, was supposed to be completely unaware. Gelfant's conclusion is typical of this mode of criticism:

> Like most novelists, Cather writes out of an obsessive concern to which her art gives various and varied expression. . . . *My Ántonia* is a magnificent and warped testimony to the mind's image making power, an implicit commentary on how that creative power serves the mind's need to ignore and deny whatever is reprehensible in whatever one loves.[5]

To repeat, all three groups of critics—political, sociological, and psychological—assume that Cather, to a distinctive degree, subordinates her characters to autobiographical and moral impulses. My own reading of Cather's twelve novels, however, leads me to the *opposite conclusion*: not merely that characterisation is her primary strength as a novelist (as opposed to setting, theme, or suggestive imagery) but even that her characters are strikingly autonomous, biographically and morally. Time and again Cather seems to create people for their own sake, that is, for the human variety they suggest. Moreover, Cather's persistent sense of natural fatality in life gives her character portrayals a distinctly *amoral*, unsentimental quality, something like the characterisation in Thomas Hardy's novels.

Certainly Hardy would have sympathised with Cather's assertion that 'conditions and circumstances, not their own wishes, dictate the actions of men.'[6] But Cather constantly refuses to make the clash of personalities in her novels more dramatic by resorting to some of the melodramatic coincidences of plot for which Hardy is notorious. She leaves us with an array of characters whose lives are grim and not very exciting, and whose virtues and vices are seldom pure. Yet, in their very familiarity and ordinariness, her characters have personalities that are remarkably complex and lives that are remarkably meaningful. To the common charge that Cather is too provincial to be a great novelist, one can offer this reply: Thanks to her ability to draw readers deep into the emotions of a variety of characters, on an almost subliminal level, she may be the least provincial of all twentieth-century American novelists.

Fortunately for Willa Cather, academic criticism is not the only form of literary evaluation. When one turns to the popular reviews of her books (those appearing in daily or weekly publications),[7] one discovers (1) that popular reviewers had a better understanding than Cather scholars of her strengths and weaknesses as a writer and (2) that the reviewers seldom felt the need to pass moral judgments on Cather herself. Some of the reviewers, such as Joseph Wood Krutch, Newton Arvin, and Howard Mumford Jones, were established scholars; few of these, however, had written or went on to write about Cather at greater length in their scholarship. Most of the reviewers were less well known but no less perceptive than the established scholars.

One obvious reason for paying attention to any group of reviews is that an author's individual works are, by and large, not neglected by reviewers. The number of times a book is reviewed has little to do with its quality, of course, but the opposite tendency of academic critics to shy away from works in an author's canon that seem qualitatively weaker or less relevant to their theses is even more misleading. Unlike popular reviewers, professional scholars repeatedly debate the nature and worth of certain works that have been deemed the 'classics' of a particular writer. But what if the supposedly weaker works aren't weaker? And what if there are no 'classics'? In Cather's case, for example, critics have analysed *My Ántonia* and *Death Comes for the Archbishop* (1927) over and over again; yet her first novel, *Alexander's Bridge* (1912), and her eighth novel, *My Mortal Enemy* (1926), though treated with aversion by scholars, are fine novels that need not automatically take a backseat to any of her other works.

But, again, the reviews of Cather's novels are particularly perceptive, comprehensive in number and scope. First, the reviews contain passing observations about individual Cather novels that are unequaled in any scholarly studies. Second, they contain general approaches to individual novels that are preferable to any proposed by Cather scholars. And third, they contain descriptions of Cather's technique and vision throughout her career that are more insightful than those found in formal Cather scholarship.

Passing observations on particular works that nonetheless seem perfect in their perception include Mary Ross's statement that in *Sapphira and the Slave Girl* (1940) Cather reveals 'without moralism . . . the mixed values of a crumbling society,' and Frances Robbins's description of Cather in *Death Comes for the Archbishop* as a 'hagiographer' who 'has produced something sounding out from a thousand years ago'; like Bishop Latour's tolling Angelus, the novel 'rings': 'While its note lasts,' Robbins said, 'life is broken up and held in suspension.' Ross's comments appeared in the *New York Herald Tribune* (December 8, 1940, p. 1) and Robbins's in *The Outlook* (October 26, 1927, p. 25); nothing, however, could be more fitting than Dorothy Van Doren's statement in *The Nation* (August 12, 1931, p. 161) that the characters in *Shadows on the Rock* seem to have 'completed their earthly existence before the tale began and are engaged in shadowy and painless struggles with their past.'

More significant are the general critical approaches to individual works that are superior to those suggested by academic critics. Randolph Bourne's description of Cather's goal in *My Ántonia* is a good example of an original and fertile approach: 'Her purpose is neither to illustrate eternal truths nor to set before us the crowded gallery of a whole society. . . . In [*My Ántonia*] the stiff moral molds are broken and she writes what we can wholly understand' (*The Dial*, December 14, 1918, p. 557). Or consider Henry Seidel Canby's statement (in *The Saturday Review of Literature*, September 26, 1925, p. 151) that Cather, in *The Professor's House*,

> . . . believes, as no Englishman or Frenchman can be convinced of, and no native novelist since Hawthorne has practiced, that there is a profundity in American life. A profundity not merely instinctive as Sherwood Anderson is revealing, but a conscious spiritual profundity which poets like Robert Frost and Edwin Arlington Robinson have long seen. [*The Professor's House*], more than *O Pioneers!*, is a pioneering book.

The following year, writing for the same journal (October 23, 1926, p. 234), Lee Wilson Dodd sensed perfectly the connection between technique and emotion in *My Mortal Enemy*:

> Willa Cather is a cool, scrupulous mistress of her medium, her material, and all its human, social, and philosophical overtones. She has no desire merely to stir our mere facile emotions. It is not our nerves she would trouble, but our minds — or whatever it is that we most deeply and personally are!

Finally and most significantly, the reviews of Cather's novels contain general evaluations of her art that are on target. Moses Harper wrote in *The New Republic* (September 16, 1925, p. 106), 'In all her work [there is] a slow solid sanity. She is one of the sanest of our writers.' Ludwig Lewisohn, in *The Nation* (October 11, 1922, p. 338): Willa Cather has 'a brooding earnestness of mind, with reverence tempering her rebellion, and with patience softening her protest.' Harry Lorin Binsse, in *Commonweal* (January 10, 1941, p. 307): Her writing 'can, on occasion, seem mannered and even a little thin. Sometimes her people are very close to being lay-figures, and seem to lack any particularising touch.' And Wilbur Cross, in *The Saturday Review of Literature* (August 22, 1931, p. 67) on the way Cather's philosophy of life seems to revolve around two questions: 'Are we but shadows projected upon a scene? . . . Or are [others] but shadows to us after all?'

From particular to general, such observations in the reviews of Cather's novels are very valuable; but the most important point to make in favor of popular reviews transcends incidental descriptions of Cather's works and career, as impressive as those descriptions may be. If it is easy to find such passages in the reviews, it is not hard to find occasional impressive observations in scholarly studies. In this respect, therefore, the qualitative difference between the two modes of criticism is not terribly dramatic.

Rather, the conclusive superiority of reviews to formal scholarship on

Cather lies in the *overall impression* of perception one gets from many reviews taken together. The general thrust of the reviews—their standards and even their brief argumentation—is preferable to the general thrust of formal Cather scholarship.

For one thing, the reviews are less belligerent. Few (except in the case of *Death Comes for the Archbishop*) express categorical admiration or deprecation; instead, most contain a sensible mixture of praise and criticism that seems to increase their authoritativeness. An anonymous reviewer in *The Nation* (November 2, 1918, p. 523), for example, commented that Cather's style in *My Ántonia* 'has distinction, not manner, . . . the style of an artist whose imagination is at home in her own land,' yet concluded that Cather's portrait of that land is 'rendered too quietly . . . to catch the eye of the seeker for color and movement of the picturesque or dramatic order.' Similarly, the reviewer of *Sapphira and the Slave Girl* in *The Saturday Review of Literature* (December 14, 1940, p. 5) was perfectly willing to complain about the complacent autobiographical ending of the novel because he so much admired the earlier 'quiet narrative which [built] up characters and situations with such easy brushstrokes that the reader is not aware of the intensity of the situations developing until they take over the story.' Even those reviewers who *are* categorical in either their general estimates of Cather or their specific comments on individual novels are less disputatious throughout the rest of the reviews.

Second, the popular reviewers are for the most part *more* sensitive to style and structure than are Cather scholars. Take, for example, Sidnie Greenbie's assertion in the *Springfield Republican* (November 13, 1927, p. 7F) that Cather has 'such control over her technique' in *Death Comes for the Archbishop* 'that she can take out all the expected elements of fiction,' or the *New Republic* reviewer's shrewd comment (November 24, 1926, p. 23) that *My Mortal Enemy* has a 'mineral quality' that may seem 'merely smoothly polished' and his conclusion that Cather at times 'invades' her own narrators, as in *The Professor's House* when Tom Outland's masculinity seems to have been 'extinguished' by Cather and replaced by a 'certain spacious, but for him rather feminine sensitiveness.' All in all, the popular reviewers constantly grappled with the relationship between the unusual forms of Cather's novels and their sense of her vision of reality. Margaret Cheney Dawson, in a *New York Herald Tribune* review (July 31, 1932, p. 3), summarised this struggle well:

> For all the analysis that has been expended to discover and describe the essence of her books there seems to be something so elusive about their character that not only do we fail to name it, we sometimes fail to know whether or not it is present.

Such sensitivity to style and structure, repeated over and over again in the reviews, leaves the clear impression that Cather was a very conscious artist—

not one governed by fears and obsessions, as most scholars have patronisingly argued.

Finally, the reviewers—in contrast to scholars—seldom stressed the presence or absence of moral issues in Cather's works and, therefore, seldom gave themselves an easy opportunity to indulge in moral judgments on Cather herself. Typical terms used by popular reviewers to describe Cather's art were 'sober,' 'subtle,' 'severe,' 'unobtrusive,' 'realistic'—none of which need carry any moral connotation. Moses Harper's description of the main character in *The Professor's House* (*The New Republic*, September 16, 1925) suggests this emphasis on aesthetic effects over moral ideas:

> Like most of Miss Cather's characters, he is drawn in the round, with calm, warm, generous strokes, a figure never in the same place, ever turning slowly a new side to us, changing, growing, even when the growth points a little sadly to a kind of death before death, a premonitory halt before the last stop.

Why should reviews of Cather's works have been more perceptive in these many ways than formal Cather scholarship? It does not seem to be a matter of the reviewer's vocation; many were scholars in their own right. Nor does it seem to be the result of not having a personal point of view; strong feelings are just as apparent in the reviews as in scholarly articles and books on Cather, even if they aren't presented as vehemently. I think the best answer may be the most obvious one: The difference is a matter of format; some writers are better served by reviews than by scholarship because of the way those authors write and think. For instance, Cather was such a subtle writer that the intensified analysis characteristic of academic studies may have become too frustrating for scholars and, therefore, found its outlet in the kind of petulance that was directed at Cather the person, even by critics as illustrious as Lionel Trilling, Alfred Kazin, and Leon Edel. It may be, too, that Cather's 'vision,' in the words of an anonymous reviewer (*The Nation*, September 25, 1920, p. 352), had 'come to be of an intense and naked clearness'—so much so that her clarity has become an emotional rather than intellectual challenge to, as Dodd put it, 'whatever it is that we most deeply and personally are.'

Finally, the paradoxical combination of the two qualities I just mentioned—clarity and subtlety—seems to me to be particularly rare in American fiction, and thus difficult for scholars to appreciate. Among American novelists, Cather had, for example, by far the most acute sense of social change as a fact of life in American society, yet she also had the ability to understand and display the effects of social change—in its most private forms—on the minds of her characters. Perhaps this sense of time passing and its psychological consequences has frightened Cather's academic critics, whose job—far more than a reviewer's—is to freeze time with theories and categories. If there is one thing I am sure of, Willa Cather doesn't lend herself to the freezing of time: Her fictional world is in a constant state of flux, and her reviewers at least have had to move in and through that world with their own sense of tenuousness intact. Joseph Wood Krutch, in his review of *The Professor's House* in *The Nation* (September 23, 1925, p. 336), described the academic critics' predicament well: 'There is nothing that indicates more clearly the nature of Miss Cather's peculiar excellence than the fact that the intention of her works generally defies any [abstract intellectual] attempt at restatement.' Only through a critical format that is as unpresumptuous as her vision of human struggle has Willa Cather received a measure of critical justice.

Notes

1. *The Song of the Lark* (Boston: Houghton Mifflin, 1937), pp. 162, 165.
2. 'On *Death Comes for the Archbishop*,' in Stephen Tennant, ed., *Willa Cather on Writing* (New York: Alfred A. Knopf, 1949), pp. 12–13.
3. Hicks's comment appears in 'The Case Against Willa Cather,' *English Journal*, November 1933, p. 708, and Zabel's in *Craft and Character in Modern Fiction* (New York: Viking Press, 1959), pp. 273, 274. See also Lionel Trilling, 'Willa Cather,' in Malcolm Cowley, ed., *After the Genteel Tradition: American Writers Since 1910* (New York: W.W. Norton, 1937), pp. 52–63; Philip Rahv, 'The Slump in American Writing,' *American Mercury*, February 1940, pp. 185–91; and Maxwell Geismar, *The Last of the Provincials* (Boston: Houghton Mifflin, 1947). Robert Footman, 'The Genius of Willa Cather,' *American Literature*, May 1938, pp. 123–41, is an early embodiment of all three 'critical approaches' I'm describing and a good example of 'damning with faint praise.' The two essays by Willa Cather that most infuriated the political critics were 'The Novel Démeublé,' *The New Republic*, April 12, 1922, Part II, pp. 5–6, and 'Escapism,' *Commonweal*, April 17, 1936, pp. 674–79, both of which are in *Willa Cather on Writing*.
4. Italics added. Kazin's statement is in *On Native Grounds* (New York: Reynal & Hitchcock, 1942), p. 251. A good introduction to the heavy critical emphasis on sociological themes in Cather's work is provided by James Schroeter, ed., *Willa Cather and Her Critics* (Ithaca, N.Y.: Cornell University Press, 1967), which contains healthy selections from, among others: H.L. Mencken's *Smart Set* reviews; Carl Van Doren's *Contemporary American Novelists: 1900-1920* (New York: Macmillan, 1922); E.K. Brown's *Yale Review* article, 'Homage to Willa Cather,' Autumn, 1946, pp. 77–92, the ideas of which were expanded in *Willa Cather: A Critical Biography* (New York: Alfred A. Knopf, 1953); John Randall's *The Landscape and the Looking Glass: Willa Cather's Search for Value* (Boston: Houghton Mifflin, 1960), and Edward and Lillian Bloom's *Willa Cather's Gift of Sympathy* (Carbondale: Southern Illinois University Press, 1962). Schroeter himself contributes one of the more vicious scholarly analyses of Cather: 'Willa Cather and *The Professor's House*,' an investigation of Cather's supposed anti-Semitism reprinted from the *Yale Review*, Summer 1965, pp. 494–512.
5. Edel's work on Cather includes a chapter on *The Professor's House* in *Literary Biography* (Toronto: University of Toronto Press, 1957) and *Willa Cather: The Paradox of Success* (Washington, D.C.: Library of Congress, 1960), an especially patronising pamphlet that is reprinted in Schroeter. See James Woodress, *Willa Cather: Her Life and Art* (New York: Pegasus, 1970) for evidence, even in a 'safe' treatment of Cather, of the aggressive influence of Edel; Gelfant's statement is from 'The Forgotten Reaping-Hook: Sex in *My Ántonia*,' *American Literature*, March 1971, pp. 60–82, a fascinating but improbable application of Freud to Cather. Another recent psychological study of *My Ántonia* is William J. Stuckey, '*My Ántonia*: A Rose for Miss Cather,' *Studies in the Novel*, Fall 1972, pp. 473–83.

Here, by way of contrast, let me mention a few academic studies of Cather from a general point of view that could serve as reliable introductions to the characteristics of her imagination. T.K. Whipple's 'Willa Cather,' in *Spokesmen: Modern Writers and American Life* (New York: Appleton, 1928), pp. 139–60, provides the best intuitive understanding of Cather's art, though of course it has nothing to say about her last three novels, published after 1928. Dorothy Van Ghent's *Willa Cather* (Minneapolis: University of Minnesota Press, 1964) is a brief, sensitive treatment of all of Cather's fiction. And David Stouck's *Willa Cather's Imagination* (Lincoln:

University of Nebraska Press, 1975), despite its fondness for rigid categorisation, has the virtue of being the first book to take Cather on her own terms, as a very conscientious craftsman.

6. 'A Chance Meeting,' in *Not Under Forty* (New York: Alfred A. Knopf, 1936), p. 40.

7. I limited my research to daily or weekly publications that had reviewed more than two of Cather's sixteen works of fiction: *Commonweal* (7 reviews), *The Dial* (3), *The Independent* (7), *The Nation* (13), *The New Republic* (11), *The Outlook* (7), *The Saturday Review of Literature* (9), and the *Boston Transcript* (10), *Christian Science Monitor* (4), *New York Herald Tribune* (11), *New York Times* (20), and *Springfield Republican* (5). Only the *New York Evening Post* (7 reviews) was not consulted. Two extensive bibliographies were of great help: Phyllis Martin Hutchinson, 'The Writings of Willa Cather: A List of Works by and About Her,' *Bulletin of the New York Public Library*, June–August 1956, pp. 267-88, 338-56, 378-400, and Bernice Slote, 'Willa Cather,' in Jackson Bryer, ed., *Sixteen Modern American Authors* (rev. ed.; Durham, N.C.: Duke University Press, 1974), pp. 29-73.

170
Becoming Noncanonical: The Case Against Willa Cather

SHARON O'BRIEN

In the 1920s Willa Cather achieved both critical acclaim and popular success. So confident was she of her ability to attract contemporary and future readers that in 1927 she asked her publisher Alfred Knopf for a one percent increase in her royalties for *Death Comes for the Archbishop*. Believing that this novel's reputation—and sales—would outlast her lifetime, she prophesied that someday Knopf's son would be paying royalties to her niece.[1]

Cather's literary and economic faith in *Death Comes for the Archbishop* has been vindicated; considered one of her finest novels, the book continues to sell in paperback. But her literary reputation has not been maintained at the height it attained in the 1920s, when critics and reviewers deemed her a major American novelist. During the 1930s and 1940s, she was increasingly subjected to attacks by reviewers who not only disliked novels like *Shadows on the Rock* (1931) and *Lucy Gayheart* (1935) but who also questioned her literary stature, arguing that she was a minor, not a major, writer. As Clifton Fadiman phrased it in a typical commentary that appeared in *The Nation* in 1932, Cather's intensifying preoccupation with the historical past might 'permanently transport her to regions where minor works of art may be created, but major ones never,' an unfortunate fate since the author of *The Song of the Lark* (1915) and *My Ántonia* (1918) had not been a 'minor writer, but a major one.'[2] Fadiman's assessment was prophetic. Although Cather has won a place in the American literary canon, it is not a high one; she has been considered an important writer and yet somehow not a 'major' one, somehow not an equal colleague of Hawthorne, James, or Faulkner, and perhaps not even in the same realm as Fitzgerald, Hemingway, or Dreiser.

SOURCE Sharon O'Brien, 'Becoming Noncanonical: The Case Against Willa Cather', *American Quarterly*, 40, 1988, pp. 110-26

Fadiman assumed that he and his fellow reviewers were merely recording, not constructing, Cather's decline. Yet recent developments in literary theory have questioned traditional assumptions of literary value and evaluation, requiring that we cease to regard the American literary canon as an objective, impartial list of those classic writers whose works have simply withstood the test of time. Several critics and writers have challenged the view that literary value arises from timeless, universal qualities inherent in the work, qualities most effectively seen and described by trained literary scholars. Reader-response criticism has called our attention to the ways in which meaning and value, as well as the aesthetic criteria used to determine these, are the products of the social, political, and ideological assumptions that readers bring to texts, which are thus not stable or fixed entities. Other studies of canon formation have pointed out that the assessment of literary value and the selection of certain texts and writers as 'classic' or 'major' are not based solely on aesthetic criteria; rather, the construction of a literary canon results from a complex process of cultural production and transmission in which publishers, reviewers, editors, literary critics, and teachers structure the interaction between the text and the reader.[3]

Understanding the ways in which the literary canon is shaped and perpetuated—a process requiring the inclusion of some writers and the exclusion or marginalisation of others—thus can help us to see the role of professional readers in determining literary value, and so give us insight into the 'interests, institutional practices, and social arrangements that sustain the canon of classic works.'[4] Examining Willa Cather's varying reputation offers particularly fruitful insights into the complex dynamics of literary evaluation and preservation. Unlike Hawthorne, whose reputation grew steadily (although for historically changing reasons) from the publication of his first stories, and unlike Kate Chopin, Sarah Orne Jewett, or Harriet Beecher Stowe, women writers who have never been considered 'major,' Willa Cather possessed canonical status during the 1920s only to lose it in the 1930s. If we attribute a writer's literary reputation not to the inherent value and stable meaning of his or her work but to the historical circumstances in which that work is published, read, interpreted, and evaluated, then Willa Cather's ascent and decline is a case study in the politics of canon formation.

Cather's unmaking did not result merely from the political and social climate of the 1930s, even though the nation's economic plight led some left-wing reviewers and critics to attack what they considered her conservatism and escapism. Cather's literary decline coincided with, and was in part a product of, the self-conscious attempt of reviewers, critics, and academics to create an American literary canon. Although this endeavor began in the 1920s, it flowered during the 1930s and 1940s—the years when college professors and men of letters were struggling to establish American literature as a respectable field of professional inquiry within English departments. In doing so, they felt the need, as Perry Miller later phrased it, to 'make clear which are the few peaks and which the many low-lying hills.'[5] For the most part, the literary men who defined the canon during this period placed Willa Cather in the foothills of American literature—the appropriate landscape, many critics assumed, for a woman writer.

To situate Cather's decanonisation historically, I will first review the social and literary circumstances that led to her establishment as a major writer in the 1920s. Then I will turn to the historical, ideological, and institutional forces that contributed to her demotion from 'major' to 'minor' writer in the 1930s and 1940s; finally I will explore Cather's creative (and human) response to her literary decline—an increasing reliance upon nonprofessional readers as her professional readers became more hostile. By examining the making and the unmaking of a major writer, I hope to illuminate the social, political, and ideological dynamics of canon formation in twentieth-century America.

Cather's first novel—*Alexander's Bridge* (1912)—was politely praised by reviewers impressed by the beginning writer's command of style and characterisation even as they noted her apprenticeship to Henry James and Edith Wharton. In his review in *Smart Set*, H.L. Mencken observed that most novice writers in America chose to model themselves either after E. Phillips Oppenheim or Marie Corelli, allying themselves either to the 'School of Plot' or the 'School of Piffle.' Cather had aimed higher, however, and despite a 'certain triteness,' she was, Mencken thought, a 'promising' writer.[6] Although not proclaiming Cather a major novelist, Mencken thus made an important distinction: here was a serious, not a popular, writer.

After Cather left the drawing room for the prairies and turned to her Nebraska past in *O Pioneers!* and *The Song of the Lark*, she began to draw increased attention from reviewers who saw emerging an authentic American voice, a challenge both to a meritricious popular taste and a decaying genteel tradition. With the publication of *My Ántonia* in 1918, critics who took it as their mission to define and to encourage an indigenous and vigorous American literature promoted Cather from a promising to a major American novelist. Eager to displace the waning influence of New England literary culture, to challenge middle-class pieties, to establish an American literary tradition separate from (and perhaps equal to) that of England, and to solidify their own roles as cultural arbiters, critics like H.L. Mencken, Randolph Bourne, Heywood Broun and Carl Van Doren linked Willa Cather with Theodore Dreiser and Sherwood Anderson as writers bringing a new realism to American letters. Bourne praised Cather's breaking of 'stiff moral molds' and leaving the ranks of 'provincial' writers with *My Ántonia*; meanwhile, delighted with the 'extraordinary reality' he found in the novel, Mencken became Cather's particular champion.[7] Hoping to wean American teachers and readers from their servile worship of England's literature, such critics found Cather's progress from the London of *Alexander's Bridge* to the Nebraska of *My Ántonia* a paradigmatic, and exemplary, journey.

Cather's first supporters were, by and large, journalists and men of letters who waged their campaign for a national literature with a 'distinctively American spirit' outside the academy.[8] Indeed, professors of English who preferred philological dissections of Chaucer to the living vitality of American authors were anathema to these literary radicals; Bourne, for example, characterised his English courses at Columbia as 'dead rituals in which academic priests mumbled their trite commentary.'[9] Among Cather's first advocates, only Carl Van Doren was an academic; during the 'teens he was teaching American literature at Columbia. But he, like Mencken and Bourne, was a literary maverick whose devotion to the study and promotion of American literature led to his editorship of the *Cambridge History of American Literature* (1917–1921). Although continuing to teach at Columbia, Van Doren soon moved into the literary world outside the academy, becoming literary editor of *The Nation* in 1919 and of the *Century* in 1922.

In the first major assessment of Cather in a literary history, *Contemporary American Novelists: 1900-1920* (1922), Van Doren compared her favorably to her mentor Sarah Orne Jewett (to whom *O Pioneers!* was dedicated), claiming that the 'thin, fine gentility' of Jewett's world faded beside the 'rich vigor' of Cather's pioneer fiction whose 'spaciousness' and epic sweep owed more to Whitman than to Jewett. Noting that Cather's epics featured female heroes, Van Doren nevertheless found them able to represent what he considered a universal American story: 'the struggle of some elected individual to outgrow the restrictions . . . of numbing circumstances.'[10] Dedicated to challenging 'numbing' social and literary conventions themselves, the critics and reviewers who defined Cather as a major writer in the late 'teens and early twenties saw in her work an analog to their own critical enterprise, the struggle of elected individuals to challenge and regenerate a native American culture.

Endorsed by these important cultural arbiters, Cather enjoyed a remarkably prolific and creative period in the 1920s. Six books appeared in seven years: *Youth and the Bright Medusa* (1921), *One of Ours* (1922), *A Lost Lady* (1923), *The Professor's House* (1925), *My Mortal Enemy* (1926), and *Death Comes for the Archbishop* (1927). Although some of these novels received mixed reviews, Cather's literary reputation continued to ascend throughout the decade as she gained the external signs of literary esteem; she won the Pulitzer Prize for *One of Ours*; she was granted honorary degrees from Yale, Columbia and the University of Michigan; she was invited to Breadloaf and the McDowell colony; she was elected to the National Institute of Arts and Letters; and she was awarded the American Academy of Arts and Letters Howells Medal for *Death Comes for the Archbishop*. Further evidence of

Cather's firm position as a major contemporary writer was the selection of *Death Comes for the Archbishop* by the College Entrance Board as a text for high school students to prepare: this was sound cause for congratulation, Houghton Mifflin editor Ferris Greenslet informed Cather, because selection meant that a book had been definitely established as an American classic.[11]

During the same years Cather enjoyed the American writer's dream of uniting critical approval with popular success as her aesthetic and financial worth increased: she was given high rankings in several literary polls; she hired an agent; she moved from Houghton Mifflin to Knopf largely because she thought that her Boston publisher did not sufficiently appreciate—and promote—her novels; her sales increased along with her reputation; her novels began to interest Hollywood producers, and *A Lost Lady* was made into a movie.[12]

By the end of the 1920s, then, Cather seemed to be firmly established as a major writer whose works had attracted both critical and popular acclaim. Yet premonitions of the attacks to come can be seen in the negative, even hostile reviews gained by *One of Ours*, Cather's novel of World War I. The book was generally dismissed by male reviewers as a woman writer's romanticised, outmoded view of modern combat. It was, Mencken charged—evidently using the worst epithet he could imagine—very like the work of a 'lady novelist.'[13] For the first time, Cather was explicitly judged as limited because of her gender. Trespassing on the preserve of masculine fiction in the last section of the novel, in which her hero Claude Wheeler enters the war in France, Cather had trod on forbidden ground and so, many reviewers agreed, exposed the limitations of the female imagination.[14]

That Cather had feared and anticipated such criticism is evident in an important letter she sent to H.L. Mencken shortly before he reviewed the novel. Cather began by reminding Mencken of their common ground: they were both enemies of a debased, popular American literature, she wrote, both committed to overturning Booth Tarkington platitudes and raising American literature to a higher plane. She went on to reveal many anxieties: that her gender might have prevented her from making a soldier's story seem authentic and powerful; that male critics might assess her novel more accurately than she could, simply because their gender gave them privileged access to a war story, whether or not they had ever seen combat; and that she might deserve punishment for having attempted such an unfeminine design. Please read the novel soon, Cather asked Mencken, because she might be hit by a taxicab if he delayed. The novel might be a complete mistake, she confided, but he would be a good man to smell out falsity. If, despite her best efforts, she had told her soldier's story in a sentimental, old-maid way, she called on Mencken to tell her so loudly, like a man: he should rub it in, because she would deserve it.[15] Cather's fear that she might be guilty of being a woman writer attempting a masculine subject and hence deserve punishment was realised when Mencken gave her the pounding she anticipated. The last half of *One of Ours*, he charged, degenerated to the 'level of a serial in the *Ladies' Home Journal*.'[16]

Mencken's and other attacks on *One of Ours* suggest that Cather—the supposed realist—might not be able to deal adequately with contemporary social and political issues; at the same time, they equate such issues with masculine experience and claim that a woman writer's imagination could not encompass this expansive territory. During the 1930s and 1940s, the politics of gender evident in the negative reviews of *One of Ours* became more prominent as a small but influential group of reviewers and academic critics decided to take on Willa Cather.

In some ways Cather's reputation continued to rise during the 1930s. She was reviewed well in journals like *The Saturday Review* and *Commonweal*, she gained more prizes and honorary degrees, and *Shadows on the Rock* was an immediate best-seller.[17] But with this novel—set in seventeenth-century Quebec—she began to anger a new generation of critics and reviewers who, influenced by the economic and social collapse of the Depression as well as by Marxist political thought, believed that art should grapple with the stern social, political, and economic realities of its time. Although their reviews and articles did not dominate in numbers, this rising generation of Marxist and liberal critics and reviewers—including Granville Hicks, Newton Arvin, Louis Kronenberg, Edmund Wilson, Lionel Trilling, Maxwell Geismar, and Alfred Kazin—were highly influential, taking over from Mencken and Van Doren as cultural arbiters and shapers of the canon. As Cather seemed to retreat further and further into the past in search of an orderly and harmonious world, travelling first to the nineteenth-century Southwest and then to seventeenth-century Quebec, the pages of left-wing journals like the *New Republic* and *The Nation* as well as those of the *New York Times Book Review* began to fill with criticism of Cather as a romantic, nostalgic writer who could not cope with the present. Cather wrote, contended Newton Arvin in a typical commentary in *The New Republic*, as if 'mass production and technological unemployment and cyclical depressions and the struggle between the classes did not exist,' and so she failed to 'come to grips with the real life of her time.'[18]

By 1933 the attack had infiltrated even the staid pages of the *English Journal*, the publication of the National Council of Teachers of English, which hosted Granville Hicks' now-famous essay 'The Case Against Willa Cather.' Hicks equated Cather's literary decline with her growing political conservatism. Cather had 'never once tried to see contemporary life as it is,' he charged. Fleeing to an idealised conception of a heroic past, she had been 'barred from the task that has occupied most of the world's great artists, the expression of what is central and fundamental in her own age.' Having surrendered to a 'supine romanticism,' Hicks argued, Cather could no longer examine 'life as it is.'[19] What had seemed like the individual's rebellion against mediocrity to Carl Van Doren struck reviewers in the 1930s as bourgeois humanism and disdain for the masses: Cather and her literary reputation were caught in the midst of a generational and ideological shift in American literary culture as a new cohort of critics began to apply different standards to determine literary merit. As the writer whose reputation rested on the estimation of the previous generation of reviewers as well as one who invited rebuttal by openly declaring in 1936 that 'economics and art are strangers,' Willa Cather was an easy target for socially conscious critics.[20]

At first glance, the charges against Cather in the 1930s and later arose from the politics of class rather than of gender. Indeed the left-wing attacks against Thornton Wilder—viewed, like Cather, as an old-fashioned humanist—were, if anything, more vicious than the dismissals of Cather.[21] Hence this was not simply or exclusively an attempt to exclude a woman writer from the company of great writers. Yet a subtext in the attacks on Cather suggests that gender may have been the dominant, if unacknowledged, variable in shaping the case against Willa Cather. In his influential literary history, *The Last of the Provincials* (1947), Maxwell Geismar introduced his discussion of Willa Cather by saying: 'In approaching our first feminine writer among the dozen or so contemporary American novelists who deserve a full literary consideration, it is essential, of course, not to consider her as a "feminine" writer.'[22] Yet Geismar and his colleagues throughout the 1930s and 1940s invariably did consider Cather as a 'feminine' writer as they set up a set of metaphoric equivalences: 'feminine,' 'romantic,' 'sentimental,' 'soft,' and 'small,' a circle of associations that led them, seemingly inevitably, from 'woman' to 'minor writer.'

Granville Hicks concluded his review of *Shadows on the Rock* by stating that 'today, perhaps even more than in the past, it takes stern stuff to make a novelist. Miss Cather, one is forced to conclude, has always been soft; and now she has abandoned herself to softness.'[23] Hicks' implicit assumption that the world of contemporary social and economic issues realistically described is 'masculine' and that a failure to demonstrate 'stern stuff' in writing of this world is 'feminine'—and therefore inferior—becomes explicit in Lionel Trilling's seemingly more judicious (and certainly more influential) essay in Malcolm Cowley's important literary history, *After the Genteel Tradition* (1937). Trilling linked Cather's decision to write historical fiction with a 'defiant' rejection of her own time, which he in turn associated with her fondness for limited female interests. Commenting on *Shadows on the Rock* (in which Cather uses food preparation and preservation to explore women's contributions to the establishment and preservation of culture and society), Trilling found that her 'mystical concern with pots and pans' did not seem more than an 'oblique defense of gentility or very far from the gaudy domesticity of bourgeois accumulation glorified in the Woman's Home Companion.'[24] Seemingly kinder, in *On Native Grounds* (1942), Alfred

Kazin continued this association of 'female' and 'minor' when he concluded that if Cather's 'world became increasingly elegiac and soft, it was riches in a little room.'[25]

And so Cather's demotion from major to minor writer in the reviews of the 1930s and the literary histories which followed was connected not only with the left-wing critics' explicit application of aesthetic criteria which demanded social relevance from all writers, male as well as female, but also with their implicit application of aesthetic criteria which equated social and literary relevance with masculinity. The question remains, however, why it was that the male critics and reviewers of the 1930s sought to unmake a major writer who had been made by the male critics and reviewers of the teens and twenties. Why was gender any more a factor in the reviewing process in 1930 than in 1920?

That gender became the underlying, and arguably the most important, source of the attacks on Cather has to do not simply with individual male-biased readings of texts by women writers but with the social, political, and institutional situation of Cather's 1930s reviewers. The 1920s critics who established Cather's reputation could play a paternal role in relationship to a young woman writer, but the young critics seeking to establish themselves in the 1930s were sons seeking to displace their fathers professionally and ideologically — Mencken, for example, came under fire from the new liberal establishment for his reactionary political stance. At the same time they were sons confronting a maternal presence their fathers had left as a literary legacy, a woman writer of the first rank. In attacking Willa Cather, the leftist critics who came of age in the 1930s were thus engaged in a complex oedipal drama, seeking both to replace the older generation of male critics and to repudiate a powerful maternal literary figure by defining her as limited.

The fact that many of the 1930s reviews refer not only to Cather's softness and smallness but also to the size and power of her matriarchal heroines — and to the size and power of her previous reputation — suggests that the critics' overt stress on the weakness and smallness of her imagination arose, at least in part, from a covert acknowledgment of the strength and expanse of Cather's heroines, of her literary imagination, and of her literary reputation. Cather's 'dominant and increasingly inaccessible women' seem to be 'always surrounded by little men,' complained Maxwell Geismar, and this observation characterises the relationship between Cather and the new generation of critics at the beginning of the decade: a dominant and increasingly inaccessible woman surrounded by men concerned with the issue of size.[26]

Several members of this new generation of critics and reviewers were playing a new professional and institutional role that also contributed to Cather's displacement as a major writer. Whereas most of Cather's early critics were journalists, professional reviewers, and editors who combatted gentility and Philistinism from outside the academy, the majority of

Cather's critics in later decades were, for all or part of their professional careers, teachers of literature within English departments as well as book reviewers and authors of literary histories: Newton Arvin (Smith), Alfred Kazin (CCNY), Granville Hicks (Rensselaer), Maxwell Geismar (Sarah Lawrence), Henry Seidel Canby (Yale), and Lionel Trilling (Columbia).

Those who attended college or graduate school in the 1960s and 1970s — when American literature and American studies held firm, if not always highly respectable, positions within the academy — may need to be reminded of the ideological and institutional pressures faced by scholars and teachers of American literature in the decades before World War II. 'To those of us who had a special interest in American literature,' remembers Jay B. Hubbell, 'it seemed that, as Vernon L. Parrington once phrased it in a letter to me, "There are too many Anglo-Saxon hounds guarding the sacred degree." . . . It seems clear to me now that some of us who were interested in American literature were suffering from feelings of inferiority.'[27] Such feelings are easy to understand. Not only were pioneers of American literary study like Hubbell surrounded by critics and colleagues who doubted that their native literature was worthy of serious study, but there was almost no institutional recognition of American literature in the teens and twenties: very few courses in colleges and universities, little encouragement of graduate studies, no journals, and no sessions devoted to American literature at the Modern Language Association.[28]

By the end of the 1920s and throughout the 1930s and 1940s, however, important changes took place as the study of American literature became increasingly professionalised. These decades were marked by the increasing presence of American literature in curricula and the development of graduate programs in American civilisation; the founding of professional journals (*New England Quarterly* [1928] and *American Literature* [1929]); convention sessions on American literature at the MLA (beginning in 1928); and the publication of literary histories and studies of individual American writers.[29] Seeking to stake out the new territory of American literature as an important field of scholarly inquiry, surrounded by Shakespearians and Miltonists who questioned whether Americans had produced a worthy national literature, after 1930 scholars, critics, and reviewers were increasingly concerned with defining and codifying an American literary canon, the establishment of which would both reflect and justify their own professional enterprise.

In so doing, they systematically overlooked or excluded women writers from the highest reaches of the newly emerging canon, defining their work as either 'minor' or as 'major' but second rank: if Americans were to have a first-rate canon to compete with that already possessed by the British, it would have to be male.[30] Hence from the late 1920s through the 1940s we have the phenomenon of academic critics simultaneously defining American women writers as minor and promoting American male writers as major, as if these were yoked, interdependent aspects of the same project: F.O. Matthiesson praising Sarah Orne Jewett in his 1929 biography, even as he defined her art as regional and limited and went on to exclude her and other women writers from his *American Renaissance* (1941); Newton Arvin dismissing Cather at the same time that he was elevating Hawthorne and Whitman; Granville Hicks demoting Cather and Wharton while he promoted Dreiser and Anderson in *The Great Tradition* (1933); Henry Seidel Canby comparing Cather unfavorably to Lewis in Robert Spiller's *The Literary History of the United States* (1948). Canby's assessment of Cather in *LHUS* summarises and preserves her literary decline, at the same time revealing the important role the ideology of gender had played in her diminishment:

> Her art was not a big art. It does not respond to the troubled sense of American might and magnitude realized but not directed, and felt so strongly by such men as Sinclair Lewis in the same decades. It is national in significance, but not in scope. Her colleagues among the men 'sweated sore' over that job, whereas her books rise free and are far more creative than critical. She is preservative, almost antiquarian, content with much space in little room—feminine in this, and in her passionate revelation of the values which conserve the life of the emotions.[31]

The equation Canby makes between gender and literary size ('feminine' = 'little') raises an important issue. It is possible that the same pattern that social historians see characterising the establishment of the medical profession in America also informs the professionalisation of American literature in the 1930s and 1940s: during the informal, uncodified beginnings of a profession women may play powerful roles, but the process of professionalisation is also one of masculinisation. Hence—just as midwives were exiled as the American Medical Association became established—women writers were required to leave the highest reaches of the canon, as if their presence there would somehow make it questionable that the American literary canon and the work of those who sought to establish it were serious enterprises.[32]

Willa Cather was aware that a male-dominated publishing and critical establishment was attempting to reduce her stature, an awareness that informs her changing literary relationship with Sarah Orne Jewett during the 1920s and 1930s. Jewett had been an important influence in Cather's personal and professional life, and when Cather dedicated *O Pioneers!* to Jewett she was acknowledging her mentor's role in her literary emergence. By the mid-1920s Cather was the established writer and Jewett the diminished one, however, and when she edited her collection of Jewett's fiction in 1925 for Houghton Mifflin Cather was determined literally and figuratively to increase Jewett's size. She told editor Ferris Greenslet that the existing editions of Jewett's fiction were simply too small—people would refuse to take them out of libraries, she explained, because they assumed they were children's books.³³ Greenslet promised her a larger edition, and in her introduction Cather addressed her real aim—increasing Jewett's literary stature—by grouping *The Country of the Pointed Firs* with *Huckleberry Finn* and *The Scarlet Letter* as three American texts which would, in her view, withstand time and change.

By the mid-1930s, however, Cather had less confidence in her ability to guarantee Jewett—and herself—a place in the American literary canon. Just as her literary value was beginning to be questioned, so was Jewett being relegated to a footnote in American literary history by the shapers of the canon. Granville Hicks' assessment of Jewett is typical of the more generous evaluations: although declaring her 'only a minor writer,' he acknowledged that she was 'master' of delicate insights, and so a 'master of a tiny realm,' a 'little world.' But Hicks undercut even this faint praise (which echoes the metaphors of size used to limit Cather's significance), indulging in an *ad feminam* attack: after granting Jewett 'powers of perception,' he went on to say that 'in other respects she was merely a New England old maid, who had a private income, traveled abroad, read the *Atlantic Monthly*, and believed in piety, progress, and propriety.'³⁴

Distressed by such dismissals of Jewett as a minor writer whose spinsterish eccentricity and genteel prudishness prevented her from addressing important subjects, Cather revised her 1925 preface to *The Country of the Pointed Firs* in her essay 'Miss Jewett,' published in *Not Under Forty* (1936). She removed her prediction of Jewett's longevity and classic status, attributing the fact that Jewett possessed a 'limited audience' to the development of a new class of unsympathetic readers: young urbanites, born in New York City and educated at New York universities, 'violently inoculated with Freud,' and most likely of foreign descent, perhaps Jewish or German.³⁵ In 'Miss Jewett' Cather describes these unpleasant people as readers, not as critics, but a letter she wrote to Zoë Akins shortly after *Not Under Forty* was published reveals that she had in mind professional readers: those reviewers and critics whom she termed her 'haters,' among them Trilling and Geismar. In a 1945 letter to Ferris Greenslet, she added a reference to Hicks as one of her tormentors.³⁶ Nowhere does Cather suggest that she was changing her own estimation of Jewett's work or that her own fiction was declining in quality; rather, her essays and letters throughout the 1930s suggest her recognition that the social, political, and institutional structures defining the production and the reception of literary texts were changing, relegating both Jewett's and her fiction to marginality. She sensed that the politics of gender might have something to do with this decline: the critics cursed her, she wrote to Sinclair Lewis, because she did not write like a man.³⁷

The essays Cather included in *Not Under Forty* reflect her one attempt to fight the power of professional readers and critics on their own terms, by seizing power herself and publishing her own book of literary and cultural criticism. Her essays on the 'novel démeublé,' on Mrs Fields, on Sarah Orne

Jewett, and on Katherine Mansfield show her distaste for a contemporary society that dishonors the past; they also show a woman writer's attempt to claim and to preserve a female literary heritage. *Not Under Forty* itself received negative reviews from critics who saw here only more evidence of Cather's escapism and marginality, and she was so distressed by the attacks that she resolved never to express her critical opinions in print again. She realised that she had revealed herself particularly in her essay on Jewett, she told Zoë Akins, and although the criticism made her angry she had learned her lesson: she would be silent.[38]

Unable to silence reviewers and critics or to affect the cultural climate, Cather sought to control the way her books would be read and interpreted by refusing to let them be shaped and defined by literary and academic institutions. She limited the excerpts from her fiction that could appear in anthologies and refused permission to include any of her work in anthologies intended for use in high schools or colleges; she also successfully prevented the publication of cheaper editions of her books. As Alfred A. Knopf recalls, Cather did not want her books to be read in the classroom, because if readers were exposed to her in a coercive environment they might 'grow up hating her.'[39]

Cather refused such dissemination of her fiction because her view of the relationship between writer and reader was based on the private model of friendship. 'When we find ourselves on shipboard, among hundreds of strangers,' she wrote in 'Miss Jewett,' 'we very soon recognise those who are sympathetic to us. We like a writer much as we like individuals for what he is, simply, underneath his accomplishment.'[40] Since the act of reading, ideally, was like striking up a friendship—with the same qualities of freedom, choice, and sympathy—Cather did not want readers to be forced to read her. So strongly did she wish readers to discover her novels independently that she even refused to allow her books to be adopted by book clubs throughout the 1920s. She relented only with *Shadows on the Rock*, in part responding to the private claims of friendship: her good friend Dorothy Canfield Fisher, then one of the judges of the Book-of-the-Month Club, wrote her a long letter defending the club's policies.

Paradoxically, Cather's attempts to ensure that readers would approach her work freely and sympathetically were cutting off institutional means for ensuring the accessibility of her novels and for solidifying her literary reputation. So to us it may seem that Cather was limiting her readership by restricting the ways in which people could encounter her books (and so revealing literary and social elitism), but from her perspective she was trying to preserve her novels from the cultural and literary institutions that were seeking to define, interpret, and limit her work. In a sense, she was trying to preserve the independence and autonomy she valued in the writer/reader bond from the social and institutional forces that were increasingly structuring it in the 1930s and 1940s—reviews, scholarly articles, anthologies, book clubs, high school and college curricula. Cather could have faith in the endurance of this bond, separated from the power of professional readers and critics, because during the period of her literary decline she was receiving hundreds of letters from readers who reaffirmed her faith in herself and in her work. Some of these she included in her own letters to old friends and supporters, thus creating an informal, supportive network of readers through her correspondence.

The links Cather maintained with readers through letter-writing became particularly important during World War II, years of pain, isolation, and depression that were occasionally lightened by the hundreds of letters she received (and answered) from soldiers who were reading her books in Armed Services Editions—a form of cultural transmission that she did not find offensive. During the last years of her life, Edith Lewis tells us, Cather took increasing pleasure in her correspondence with readers from all over the world:

> ... letters that were truly from 'the people,' not from any particular class of people, bringing to her their gratitude, their homage, their affection, in the kind of language she most appreciated—the language art cannot invent—were a sort of giving back to her, a return in kind, of the qualities of feeling she had herself expended in her writing career.

Although, sadly, we do not have these letters, Lewis selects some quotations to suggest their range and quality: '"I would love to count myself your friend."—"Your books have somehow helped me, a boy from Wisconsin, to take heart again in my effort to rebuild my health and life." . . . "I am glad you are alive, and have written so many splendid books."' Finding a 'great anonymous affirmation of her art' in these private voices, Cather tried to answer each one personally.[41]

So Cather found in these letters evidence that the writer/reader relationship could resemble the private bonds of affection and friendship; her letters from readers doubtless helped her to keep writing by offsetting the criticisms of her professional readers. Perhaps she found some assurance in them that her work would continue to be read and appreciated, even if not considered 'major' by scholars and critics. In a sense she has been right; although not placed among the 'peaks' of the American literary canon, Cather has continued to have a wide popular readership, a readership which preceded (and may be independent from) the recent revival of interest in her work in the academy.

Although Cather would have wanted to attribute this continuing readership to the same private, intuitive sympathies that create friendship, literary and cultural institutions have played a central role in keeping Cather's work alive—paradoxically by modifying the restrictions she sought to place on them. After her death Cather's executors negotiated an agreement with Houghton Mifflin, publisher of Cather's first four novels, that allowed the publication of *My Ántonia* and *O Pioneers!* in educational editions for high schools and the inclusion of *My Ántonia* in college anthologies. Twenty years later, seeing that Cather's sales were declining (in part because hardback editions were becoming too expensive for classroom use), Alfred Knopf persuaded Edith Lewis to agree that Cather's novels should be brought out in paperback.[42] Currently all of Cather's novels and most of her short stories are available in this form. Thus, even though individual readers may regard discovering a Cather novel as comparable to beginning a friendship, her continuing readership must be connected with the social, economic, and institutional structures that have kept her work in print and available to readers.

Over the last fifteen years Cather's stock in the academy and the canon has also been slowly rising, judging from the increasing appearance of her fiction in college curricula, the number of sessions at the Modern Language Association devoted to her work, and the publication of numerous articles in professional journals, biographies, and book-length studies of her fiction. A new consensus about her literary values has still not emerged, however, in part because past evaluations like 'Her art was not a big art' still have shaping power, and in part because many of the feminist scholars and critics who are focusing new attention on her work are simultaneously questioning the politics of canon formation.[43] What is clear is that a new generation of professional readers—looking at Willa Cather through different interpretive frameworks from those of her 1930s reviewers—is seeing a more significant, complex, and interesting writer than the conservative, 'antiquarian' novelist described by Trilling, Hicks, and Canby.

Since Cather valued the nonacademic over the professional reader (no matter how sympathetic), she might not be entirely pleased by this development. For a student to encounter *O Pioneers!* in a course on American women writers rather than in a high school anthology might not strike her as an improvement, since she valued only acts of reading arising from choice and affinity. Yet Cather herself did not fully recognise that the seemingly private act of reading is itself structured by public forces and power relationships: we simply do not read writers whose work has not been published, evaluated, preserved, and transmitted by social, economic, and literary institutions of some sort. In fact, Cather could imagine the act of reading as private and intuitive only because she had attained at least a minimal place in the canon and a secure place in the structure of publishing as one of Alfred Knopf's most important authors.

Her relatively privileged position allowed Cather to ignore the social and institutional forces that had granted her a certain amount of literary power. Had she been even more disenfranchised during the 1930s and 1940s, as was a writer like Zora Neale Hurston, she might not have been able to compare reading with friendship because she would have seen more clearly the powerful forces that limited her ability to attract friendly readers. In fact, Cather's metaphor of the shipboard friendship—based on her experience as a passenger on the luxurious ocean liners of the 1920s—reveals this paradox, suggesting she could envision the writer/reader bond as private precisely because of public institutions that placed her at least in the lower levels of the American literary canon. To develop such a shipboard friendship, one must be already a member of an elite, privileged group of travelers that includes a few people while excluding many more, much the way a literary canon exalts some writers and eliminates others.

Notes

1. Alfred A. Knopf, 'Miss Cather,' *The Art of Willa Cather*, ed. Bernice Slote and Virginia Faulkner (Lincoln, Neb., 1974), 210.
2. Clifton Fadiman, 'Willa Cather: The Past Recaptured,' *The Nation* (Dec. 7, 1932): 563.
3. Important book-length studies of the politics of canon formation in the United States are Jane Tompkins, *Sensational Designs: The Cultural Work of American Fiction, 1790-1860* (New York, 1985), esp. 186-201 and Cathy N. Davidson, *Revolution and the Word: The Rise of the Novel in America* (New York, 1986), esp. 254-62. See also Nina Baym, 'Melodramas of Beset Manhood: How Theories of American Fiction Exclude Women Authors,' *American Quarterly* 33 (Summer 1981): 123-39; Annette Kolodny, 'The Integrity of Memory: Creating a New Literary History in the United States,' *American Literature* 57 (May 1985): 291-307; Paul Lauter, 'Race and Gender in the Shaping of the American Literary Canon: A Case Study from the Twenties,' *Feminist Studies* 9 (Fall 1983): 435-464. For a study of the links among literary theory, pedagogy, and canonisation see William E. Cain, *The Crisis in Criticism: Theory, Literature, and Reform in English Studies* (Baltimore, 1984). I have been helped in my understanding of canon formation by Barbara Herrnstein Smith's theoretical essay, 'Contingencies of Value' in *Canons*, ed. Robert von Hallberg (Chicago, 1984), 5-40.
4. Tompkins, *Sensational Designs*, 37.
5. *Major Writers of America*, ed. Perry Miller (New York, 1962), xvii (quoted in Kolodny, 'The Integrity of Memory,' 295). See David Stineback, 'No Stone Unturned: Popular Versus Professional Evaluations of Willa Cather,' *Prospects* 7 (1982): 167-76 for a different view of Cather's reviewers and critics.
6. H.L. Mencken, review of *Alexander's Bridge*, in *Critical Essays on Willa Cather* ed. John J. Murphy (Boston, 1984), 96.
7. Randolph Bourne, review of *My Ántonia* in *Critical Essays on Willa Cather*, ed. John J. Murphy (Boston, 1984), 96; H.L. Mencken, review of *My Ántonia*, *Willa Cather and Her Critics*, ed. James Schroeter (Ithaca, 1967), 8. See ' "America's Coming-of-Age" Criticism: Early Views' in ibid., 1-5. For a discussion of Bourne's and Mencken's roles in promoting American literature and shaping literary taste, see Kermit Vanderbilt, *American Literature and the Academy: The Roots, Growth, and Maturity of a Profession* (Philadelphia, 1986), 205-13.
8. Bourne, quoted Vanderbilt, *American Literature*, 207.
9. Quoted in ibid., 206.
10. Carl Van Doren, 'Willa Cather,' in Schroeter, *Willa Cather*, 13-19.
11. Ferris Greenslet to Willa Cather, 21 Oct. 1932, Houghton Library, Harvard University, Cambridge, Mass.
12. For a survey of the polls, see Jay B. Hubbell, *Who Are the Major American Writers?* (Durham, 1972), 201-35.
13. Review of *One of Ours* in Schroeter, *Willa Cather*, 10-12.
14. For a discussion of the reviews of *One of Ours*, see Barry Gross, 'Willa Cather and the "American Metaphysic,"' *Midamerica* 8, ed. David D. Anderson (East Lansing, 1981), 68-78.
15. Willa Cather to H.L. Mencken, 6 Feb. 1922, Enoch Pratt Library, Baltimore, Md.
16. Schroeter, *Willa Cather*, 10.
17. For a selection of the positive reviews and assessments, see Schroeter, *Willa Cather* and Murphy, *Critical Essays*.
18. Newton Arvin, 'Quebec, Nebraska, and Pittsburgh,' *New Republic* (Aug 19, 1931): 345.

19. Schroeter, *Willa Cather*, 139-47.
20. Willa Cather, 'Escapism,' in *Willa Cather on Writing* (New York, 1949), 27.
21. See Daniel Aaron, *Writers on the Left: Episodes in American Literary Communism* (New York, 1961), 241-43.
22. Schroeter, *Willa Cather*, 171.
23. Granville Hicks, *Forum* (Sept. 1931).
24. Schroeter, *Willa Cather*, 148-55. The critical attacks by Trilling and others on *Shadows on the Rock* support Nina Baym's argument that theories of American literature exclude women authors because the myth of America—the story of the untrammeled individual confronting an untamed wilderness—is in fact gender-coded (see Baym, 'Melodramas of Beset Manhood'). Interestingly, *Shadows*—the novel that signified Cather's peripheral status to many reviewers— is a version of the mythic American story, the establishment of a society in the wilderness. Cather, however, was challenging the gender-coded myth of America: her protagonist is not the individual male but the collective culture, and the culture manages to inscribe itself upon the wilderness without the acts of violence and domination which, in Cather's view were not as central to the story of settlement as the acts of peace and accommodation. 'And really,' she wrote in a letter published in *The Saturday Review* in 1931, 'a new society begins with the salad dressing more than with the destruction of Indian villages' (*Willa Cather on Writing*, 16). Critics could view the novel as peripheral because, although it addresses the central American story of immigration, transplanting, and resettlement, it does not tell the male version of that story.
25. Schroeter, *Willa Cather*, 170. The same imagery of size was used by Fred Lewis Pattee who praised Cather's novels, which he nonetheless described as 'cameo cuttings' (*The New American Literature, 1890-1930* [New York, 1930], 265).
26. Schroeter, *Willa Cather*, 187.
27. Jay B. Hubbell, *South and Southwest: Literary Essays and Reminiscences* (Durham, 1965), 22-23.
28. For a discussion of this period in the history of American literary study, see Vanderbilt, *American Literature*, 243-70, and Hubbell, *South and Southwest*, 3-48.
29. For an institutional history of the development of American Studies that traces some of these developments, see Gene Wise, ' "Paradigm Dramas" in American Studies: A Cultural and Institutional History of the Movement,' *American Quarterly* 31: 293-337. See also Gene Wise, 'An American Studies Calendar' in ibid., 407-47.
30. See Lauter, 'Race and Gender,' for a fuller analysis of role played by the politics of gender in the shaping of the canon.
31. *Literary History of the United States*, Vol. 2, eds. Robert E. Spiller, Willand Thorp, Thomas H. Johnson, and Henry Seidel Canby (New York, 1918), 1216.
32. See Barbara Ehrenreich and Deirdre English, *For Her Own Good: One Hundred and Fifty Years of the Experts' Advice to Women* (New York, 1979) and Margaret W. Rossiter, *Women Scientists in America: Struggles and Strategies in 1940* (Baltimore, 1982). Lauter also correlates the establishment of the canon with professionalisation and the consequent marginalisation of women writers ('Race and Gender,' 446-48).
33. Willa Cather to Ferris Greenslet, 17 Feb. 1924, Houghton Library, Harvard University, Cambridge, Mass.
34. Granville Hicks, *The Great Tradition: An Interpretation of American Literature since the Civil War* (New York, 1933), 104-05. Waldo Frank was even more contemptuous in a 1925 review of Cather's edition of Jewett's stories: 'We must all snatch from our coming days the nodding wish to turn from the rot of our world into a sweet-scented realm of senile wishes, in order to enjoy Miss Jewett' (*New Republic* 44 [Oct. 14, 1925]: 204. Van Wyck Brooks' assessment makes clear the role played by gender in Jewett's decline: 'Her vision was certainly limited. It scarcely embraced the world of men, and vigorous, masculine life of towns like Gloucester, astir with Yankee enterprise and bustle, lay quite outside her province' *New England: Indian Summer* (New York, 1940), 347-48.
35. Willa Cather, 'Miss Jewett,' in *Not Under Forty* (New York, 1936), 92-93.
36. Willa Cather to Zoë Akins, 28 Oct. 1937, Huntington Library, San Marino, Calif. and Willa Cather to Ferris Greenslet, 31 Jan. 1945, Houghton Library, Harvard Univ., Cambridge, Mass.
37. Willa Cather to Sinclair Lewis, n.d., Beineke Library, Yale University, New Haven, Conn.
38. Willa Cather to Zoë Akins, 28 Oct. 1937, Huntington Library, San Marino, Calif.

39. Knopf, 'Miss Cather,' 211.
40. 'Miss Jewett,' 94.
41. Edith Lewis, *Willa Cather Living: A Personal Record* (New York, 1953), 186-88.
42. For an account of these negotiations, see Knopf, 'Miss Cather,' 222-24.
43. I include myself among such critics. My biography of Willa Cather (*Willa Cather: The Emerging Voice* [New York, 1987]), which draws on feminist and psychoanalytic theory, describes Cather's attainment of literary identity and authority but does not argue that her fiction deserves a higher rank in the literary canon.

171
Categorical Cather: Reading the Canon(s)

◆

DEBORAH CARLIN

When Betty Jean Steinshouer began touring her one-woman Willa Cather performance, she tried 'to duplicate Cather's evening dress. I got a lot of brocade, shawls, and brightly colored things because I knew she liked to dress up and wear hats and all that.'[1] But her audiences, Steinshouer soon realised, were upset. They had a different vision of Cather in their minds' eye. So she began to wear the costume made famous by a photograph Edward Steichen took of Cather in the 1920s, in which the author sports a sailor's middy blouse, red tie, and dark skirt. 'The middy blouse and the tie is sort of the Cather symbol,' Steinshouer admitted. 'I decided, at least in that way, to give people what they wanted and what makes them feel comfortable — that they're really seeing Willa Cather.'

And according to Steinshouer, people *do* want to see and experience Cather. 'Everybody loves Willa Cather. People just come out of the woodwork. I am always astonished at the level at which she moves people, and it pretty much extends across all boundaries — economic, class, race, everything.' Steinshouer does not work from a script, and each of her performances includes a period during which she takes questions from the audience in character. When asked what essential attributes of Cather she tries to re-create in her performance, Steinshouer replied, 'I use a lot of her humor. She's very, very funny and people don't expect that because they think of her as having this somber tone of hardship and sternness. There's no sag in her. She's very opinionated. She loved to debate. I tried to bring out that part of her that would find the winners of the debates at the University of Nebraska and then debate them in public where she could humiliate them. She has some sharp edges.'

Steinshouer believes that one reason that Cather appeals to the public at large is because 'she is so fully balanced. To use Maswell's term, she's

SOURCE   Deborah Carlin, 'Categorical Cather: Reading the Canon(s)', *Cather, Canon and the Politics of Reading*, Amherst: University of Massachusetts Press, 1992, pp. 3–26, 177–82

"self-actualized." She writes about everyday people who struggle. Only a well-adjusted person could take all of the pain and failure and problems of everyday life and exalt it to the level she does. So that a young person reading her books might think, "Oh, this is terribly boring: there's no sex, there's no real violence" (the violence that's in there is so real it's almost unbearable). But she makes the everyday lives of Americans significant.' With Cather, Steinshouer has realised over the years, 'people see an inner glimpse of themselves.'

While Steinshouer quite literally takes Cather to the people, the Willa Cather Pioneer Memorial Society and Education Foundation is busy preserving and promoting the life and art of Willa Cather within Nebraska and throughout the world.[2] Both academic and popular, the Willa Cather industry that operates out of Red Cloud, Nebraska, is akin to a small business run by a family utterly passionate about and deeply devoted to its product. The Cather Historical Center houses not only a significant collection of Cather's letters and papers, but also displays scenes from her novels in dioramas.[3] Officials of the Memorial have retitled the Red Cloud environs 'Catherland,' offering guided and self-guided tours through many of the places that appear in Cather's fiction. An advertisement of 'Extraordinary Christmas Ideas' touts Cather Country Confections (six different jellies) and Willa Cather Limited Edition Brass Bookends. Girl Scout National Headquarters even created a Willa Cather Merit Badge in 1963.[4] One 1988 letter, written by Nancy Picchi from South Orange, New Jersey, and published in the *Willa Cather Pioneer Memorial Newsletter*, typifies what constitutes Cather's popular appeal for these devotees.

> It's been difficult getting back to the mundane details of work after the excitement of the Amtrak Sisters' Western Tour. Again, I would like to express my appreciation to you for your hospitality and attention. When I should be writing a grant proposal, I find myself day-dreaming about Red Cloud. I am very impressed by the work that you and your dedicated band of Catherites have accomplished in Red Cloud. The restoration of the Cather Homestead is a gift to all of us; it preserves an important place in American literature and a special time in American history....
>
> I have begun my Willa Cather Society proselytizing and have a core of believers ready to sign on the dotted line. I am always surprised by how many well-educated Americans have never read a novel by Willa Cather. I have now taken to carrying copies of *O Pioneers!* and *My Ántonia* with me and distributing them to these poor souls. I feel as if I am distributing manna in the wilderness....
>
> Yesterday my husband, Bern, and I received a letter from the Statue of Liberty-Ellis Island Foundation describing the work that has been done to restore Ellis Island as a monument to the immigrants that helped to build this country. As I read this letter, I kept thinking of Red Cloud and Catherland; while Ellis Island symbolises the beginning of the American dream for these immigrants, Red Cloud and Nebraska represent the actual realization of that dream.[5]

For Nancy Picchi, the Cather Homestead, like Ellis Island and the Statue of Liberty, is a historical monument because of its place within a particular national and even mythic grid of American history. The historical narrative within which Picchi locates and is able to read both *O Pioneers!* and *My Ántonia* is one of immigration and 'realization.' The relevance of Cather's America is its continuation of and progression within a narrative that posits the 'American experience' as one of late-nineteenth-century immigration to the United States and early twentieth-century accommodation to an expansive landscape and culture in which the self could be defined anew. The yawning Nebraska prairie then is not so far removed, at least imaginatively and ideologically, from the Lower East Side tenements, and both mark particularly 'American' spaces of experience. Picchi's reading of the American dream as a drama of rebirth parallels her own conversion to Cather, and prompts her, with the conviction of the newly enlightened, to disseminate the gospel of Cather in an urban, northeastern wilderness that has not read and does not appreciate her work. Picchi, in other words, has been awakened to the historical and American significance of Willa Cather, and like all acolytes ('Catherites'), she resolves to share her newfound knowledge with an ignorant world.

Such passionate devotion constitutes simply one of the reading communities in which the person and the prose of Willa Cather are appropriated, claimed, and somehow signified.[6] Such reading communities organise themselves unconsciously around what Barbara Herrnstein Smith has termed 'contingencies of value,' an evaluative frame of reference in which an object, a text, or an author 'is likely to perform certain particular (though taken-for-granted) functions for some particular (though only implicitly defined) set of subjects under some particular (unspecified but assumed) set or range of conditions.'[7] Though such significations of value characterise virtually all critical treatments of 'major' writers, Cather, because she 'belongs to no school,'[8] is especially subject to the revision, reification, and renunciation of widely disparate readerly contingents. Whether viewed as an American icon, a woman writer, a lesbian, a cosmopolitan Midwesterner, a conservative Republican, a scathing journalist, an antimodernist, or an embittered elegist, Cather remains an anomaly in American literature and her fiction is peculiarly hard to place. Despite her popular appeal, Cather lingers in the margins of the American literary canon. As Sharon O'Brien has noted, Cather's literary rank 'is not a high one; she has been considered an important writer and yet somehow not a major one, somehow not an equal colleague of Hawthorne, James, or Faulkner, and perhaps not even in the same realm as Fitzgerald, Hemingway, or Dreiser.'[9] The current and frequently rancorous debate about canons and the curriculum seems to bear this out. In a 1988 letter to the *New York Times Magazine*, responding to a previous piece on the controversies surrounding the literary canon, C. Webster Wheelock closed his jeremiad with the following peroration: 'Any professor who lets [Charles Brockden] Brown or [Zora Neale] Hurston shoulder aside works by James, Melville, *or even Cather*, ought to be required personally to give a tuition refund to *her* students' (emphasis added).¹⁰ Though one might wonder why Wheelock imagines the offending professor to be female, it is nonetheless interesting that removing Cather from the canon constitutes a criminal offense in his scheme, if, albeit, a lesser one.

Wheelock's qualified inclusion does suggest, however, that Cather has made it into some versions of an American literary canon. But what soon becomes apparent about canonical inclusions of Cather is that they are limited to the first half of her oeuvre, those early pioneer novels — *O Pioneers!* (1913), *The Song of the Lark* (1915), and *My Ántonia* (1918) — that celebrate American manifest destiny and the settling of the West. Spanning both popular and critical assessments, Cather's canonical value resides in the heroic myth of national destiny that a vast array of readers recognise in these early novels. In the 1978 'Films for the Humanities' series, 'Exploring American Literature' and 'Women in American Literature,' for example, 'Willa Cather's America' is composed of 'the wild American land and the people on it, and the heroism required to transplant the Old World culture to the harsh, vast New World.' What is unique about this version of Cather's literary relevance is its staying power; nearly fifty years earlier, Alfred Kazin praised Cather's early novels for their ability to inspire 'the individual discovery of power, the joy of fulfilling oneself in the satisfaction of an appointed destiny.'¹¹ What designates these early novels as canonical then is their appeal to reading publics as stories already inscribed within the national imagination. They are recognizable versions of what Sharon O'Brien characterises as 'America's story,' yet startlingly original in their evocation of the pioneer experience as, essentially, 'epics of women.'

> Unlike many of her female literary predecessors and contemporaries . . . Cather did not limit herself to telling a conventional female narrative. Alexandra Bergson's taming of the wild land embodies the history of her culture as Cather makes a female character representative of the American experiment without seeming to be self-conscious about doing so. Having experienced dislocation, loss, and resettlement herself, unlike her contemporaries Edith Wharton and Ellen Glasgow, Cather could claim this dominant subject in American culture and literature as her own and envision the heroic leader of the pioneer venture as female.¹²

Because of this mythic and historical resonance, Cather's early novels are the ones regularly taught in high schools and colleges. Of the seventeen Cather texts appearing on the progressive college and university syllabi collected by Paul Lauter in *Reconstructing American Literature*, only one, *Death Comes for the Archbishop* (1927), is drawn from the eight novels Cather wrote after 1925. *My Ántonia*, conversely, appears six times, *O Pioneers!* four, and *A Lost Lady* (1922) and *The Song of the Lark* each turn up once. Early short stories account for the final four inclusions.¹³ What is identifiably canonical within Cather's nearly fifty years of fiction writing then is, paradoxically, a small number of texts that embody the expansive West of the American imagination.

To say that Cather's fiction is noncanonical then is not entirely accurate, for obviously the early novels have attained a kind of thematic, canonical inclusion.[14] But certain, persistent questions remain about Cather and the canon generally, and this study will attempt to articulate at least some of them. Why, for instance, are the majority of Cather's late fictions rigorously unread?[15] Why are they either ignored in or excluded from canons? What is it exactly that renders them, if not absolutely noncanonical, then conventionally unclassifiable in the prevailing critical assessments of Cather's work? Why, in other words, are they difficult to read?

Such questions necessitate an examination of the way differing contingents of academic readers have addressed the late novels—those written after 1925 and until Cather's death in 1947—because public and popular acceptance of the late fiction kept Cather on best-seller lists throughout her career. These *academic* reading communities fall, broadly, into four categories: those concerned with art, style, and form in Cather's fiction; those who attempt to place Cather historically and thematically in the 'main currents' of twentieth-century American literature; feminist critics; and lesbian feminist scholars. Each of these contingents have a vested interest in the politics of its own reading(s), and each represents the *idea* of Willa Cather in a radically different way.

Looking at Willa Cather as the consummate artist whose works are best understood as being fundamentally about art itself is the most prevalent approach in Cather studies, and for good reason. Begun by the pioneering work of Mildred Bennett, whose 1951 *The World of Willa Cather* introduced readers to the midwestern and biographical concerns informing Cather's fiction, this method is most closely associated with scholars at the University of Nebraska and with that university's press, which has published virtually all Cather's writing on art.[16] Composed predominantly of New Critical textual readings, investigations of Cather's artistry locate recurring biographical and thematic issues that center around what Cather firmly believed was the exceptional and necessary role of the artist in society: to preserve that which is true and good by a careful attention to human nature and a command of one's artistic medium. The Willa Cather enshrined within the Nebraska community is the embodiment of American individualism; her diligence and talent enabled her to achieve her dream of becoming the (dis)embodiment of artistic distance, intensity, and integrity. The more personal and private aspects of her life are carefully veiled and ultimately subordinated to a biographical history determined solely by artistic growth and achievement.[17] What such an approach ignores, however, are the ramifications of Cather's gender and presumed sexual preference upon her choice of subjects and strategies of representation. In this reading, art becomes the ultimate 'meaning' of her considerably diverse novels.

More recently some critics have attempted to redefine Cather's work within the boundaries of canonical modernism or as arising out of and consequently affiliated, in style and technique, with a modernist impulse. Susan J. Rosowski, for instance, in her important study of Cather's novels entitled *The Voyage Perilous: Willa Cather's Romanticism* (1986), contends that 'the essential characteristic of romanticism concerns a mode of perception by which the imagination is used in its synthesising or creative powers to transform and give meaning to an alien or meaningless material world. In this sense, the Romantics inaugurated modern literature.' Tracing thematic manifestations of both romanticism and gothicism throughout Cather's fiction, Rosowski charts Cather's sensitivity 'to feelings we term modern: a sense of alienation and historical discontinuity.'[18] What is liberating about this approach is that by arguing that experimentation with content and/or form is what characterises both Cather's fiction and standard texts of high modernism, Rosowski's proposition allows for the incorporation of the later novels into the critical debate on canon. Phyllis Rose, who, along with Rosowski, argues pointedly for an essentially modernist interpretation of Cather's work, has suggested that impulse and design are relevant categories to examine in evaluating Cather as a canonical modernist.

> In modernist critical writings, including Cather's, certain themes recur: an urge to shake loose of clutter, a refusal to accept the mimetic function of art as previously defined, a feeling that a certain 'spirit' was escaping the older forms, an urge toward anonymity. The vessel is emphasised rather than the content; art is imagined as a fragile container for the ineffable substance of life. The modernists were aware of art as a created artifact, not as a mirror reflecting reality or a camera eye absorbing and imprinting it.[19]

The critical writing to which Rose alludes is Cather's best-known essay, 'The Novel Démeublé,' in which she seems to move away from certain aspects of literary 'realism' toward some allusive and purposefully indefinite articulation of her own method. Cather begins the essay by redefining what realism is *not*; it is, she suggests cryptically, 'an attitude of the mind,' not 'the cataloguing of a great number of material objects, in explaining mechanical processes, the methods of operating manufactories and trade.'[20] Though she purposefully reduces realism to an aesthetic she can then discard, what Cather does advocate in the title of her essay is a housecleaning of sorts, a stripping down of narrative to its essential minimum, unencumbered by too many 'realistic' details and by authorial intervention. She praises the artistic innovation of those

> younger writers [who] are trying to break away from mere verisimilitude, and, following the development of modern painting, to interpret imaginatively the material and social investiture of their characters; to present their scene by suggestion rather than by enumeration (48).[21]

'The higher processes of art,' she concludes, 'are all processes of simplification' (48–49), of 'unfurnishing' the too cluttered house of fiction. What Cather arrives at finally in the essay is an aesthetic method determined by absence and allusion:

> Whatever is felt upon the page without being specifically named there—that, one might say, is created. It is the inexplicable presence of the thing not named, of the overtone divined by the ear but not heard by it, the verbal mood, the emotional aura of the fact or the thing or the deed, that gives high quality to the novel or the drama, as well as to poetry itself. (50)

What leads critics like Rose and others to identify this elusive definition as somehow modernist is its seeming repudiation of definite and explicable form, its emphasis on 'presence,' 'mood,' and 'aura,' and its implication that audience response is dictated more by divination than by apprehension.

Janis P. Stout, in her recent *Strategies of Reticence* (1990), suggests that this textual 'reticence' in Cather's fictions is intimately linked to the loud silence surrounding issues of sexual preference in her life: 'The aesthetic principle that Cather consciously and capably defended and that she followed in so craftly a fashion was chosen, at least in part, because it accorded so well with her need to find a strategy of avoidance and suppression. The need fueled the theoretical affiliation that gave it aesthetic respectability.'[22] Hermione Lee, Cather's most recent biographer, also examines Cather's life and fictional language through the lens of a modernist sensibility. Lee, in her *Willa Cather: Double Lives* (1989), suggests that Cather's conscious aesthetic of elimination and excision in language 'isn't just a matter of making a sophisticated narrative read like the story-tellings of an oral culture. It is a communication (more "modernist," ambiguous and strange than it looks at first sight) which can find a way into the incommunicable; the silent; the obscure.'[23] Avoiding the interrelation between biography and aesthetics that Stout and, to a lesser extent, Lee persuasively suggest, other critics have turned to language alone as the arena in which to locate Cather's modernism. Robert J. Nelson, for example, in his *Willa Cather and France: In Search of the Lost Language* (1988), argues that Cather's refusal to conform to knowable and signifiable language practices creates a radical modernism, resulting in 'a countertext if not an antitext . . . by the author's own desire.'[24] And Jo Ann Middleton, in *Willa Cather's Modernism: A Study of Style and Technique* (1990), appropriates the biological term 'vacuole,' using it as a way to better 'understand Catherian absences.' Despite such silences, gaps, and absences, Cather's novels, as Middleton points out, remain 'deceptively simple to read' and, on several levels, to comprehend, which is what accounts for her particularly broad and popular appeal.[25] Wallace Stevens, one of Cather's many admirers, cautioned a friend in a letter that 'she takes so much pains to conceal her sophistication that it is easy to miss her quality.'[26] Indeed, I would suggest that it is the lucidity and seeming readability of Cather's concise prose that make her novels difficult to place squarely within canonical modernism as we know it, despite the efforts of critics to redefine the parameters of what 'modernism' as a term signifies and, more important, to extend what is excluded a priori within that signification.[27]

Hugh Kenner's intriguing essay, for example, 'The Making of the

Modernist Canon' (1984), illustrates the numerous ways in which the conventional definition of modernism would necessarily not concern itself with Willa Cather.[28] In Kenner's historical narration of modernism, it is an engagement with international influences and movements that makes the modern artistic sensibility.

> As the capital [London] ingathered, the provinces stirred. Poems were mailed to *The Egoist* by William Carlos Williams from New Jersey and by Marianne Moore from New York. Williams had known Pound at college; Miss Moore revered the example of James. Though they stayed settled in America all their lives they were never tempted to make easy rhymes for the natives. Their generation, aware of emissaries in London—Pound, Eliot, H.D.—could look toward London for contact with more than mere Englishness. The next American generation, that of Hemingway, Fitzgerald and Faulkner, also drew profit from the transatlantic example. By the time of its apprenticeship there were modern masterworks to study, notably *Ulysses* and *The Wasteland*. However rootedly local, American writing, thanks to twenty years of looking abroad, has enjoyed ever since an inwardness with the international, the technological century. (370)

Kenner's ostensible purpose in this essay is to pose the questions: 'The canon of literary modernism: how did that get made? Is it made yet?' (365). But in his own history of modernism, Kenner is himself making the canon in the narration of its making. He establishes two conditions: first, that Americans who claim title to modernism transcend their own provincial literature by never making 'easy rhymes for the natives.' In other words, to write either for or within the literal confines of an American sensibility is to remain stuck in the mire of popular, not high (modernist) art. Kenner implicitly links Williams to Pound, Moore to James, thereby providing proof that each moved beyond his and her own national borders toward modernist pioneers who had already made the literal move to Europe. This requisite club membership in the modernist canon is especially problematic for Cather whose first novel, *Alexander's Bridge* (1912), is a 'failed' imitation of James, and whose artistic mentor was the extremely marginalised and conceptually provincial regionalist Sarah Orne Jewett.[29] 'Easy rhymes for the natives' also condemns economic success as a sign of the fatal popular embrace, excluding from consideration such 'best-selling' authors as Cather herself.

Kenner's second condition is an artistic incorporation of continental models, what he refers to as 'an inwardness with the international.' The models he singles out, significantly, are *Ulysses* and *The Waste Land*, both of which originate from writers in exile from their own, limiting national conditions. The way one locates 'an inwardness with the international,' however, must necessarily be within a text, an *external* manifestation which then Kenner, or any critic, reads, interprets, and signifies as the product of this 'inwardness with the international.' In other words, the proof again lies in what any critic valorises in a text as 'modernist,' which then is read as the causal effect of a writer's internalisation of 'modern masterworks.' By this logic, *Ulysses* and *The Waste Land* become the ur-texts through which all subsequent *American* modernism is defined.

It seems also worth noting that within this passage Kenner has, in effect, created his own modernist canon, one that includes Williams, Moore, Pound, Joyce, James, Eliot, Hemingway, Faulkner, and Fitzgerald. This is less an examination of how the modernist canon was made and more a reiteration of what we already know it to be. And within the definition Kenner provides, Cather could not possibly be identified as or even remotely considered to be a modernist. Despite her own cosmopolitan travels, interests, and affinities, Cather remains somehow too American, too nationally oriented. The answer to Kenner's second question then, 'Is [the canon] made yet?' is an unequivocal 'yes,' because the question itself, as the essay articulates, is a purely rhetorical one.

Cather, however, has not simply been ignored within critical studies of the modernist canon such as Kenner's. Rather, from the 1930s onward, she has been labeled as and harangued for being, quintessentially, an antimodernist. And certainly her own critical writing during this period did nothing to repudiate this image. On the contrary, Cather seemed to delight in fanning the flames of critical indignation, an act that had particular consequences on her literary reputation for approximately forty years.

The contemporary critical attack on Cather began in 1933 with the publication of Granville Hicks's essay, 'The Case against Willa Cather.'[30] In it Hicks critiqued what appeared to him to be 'the political conservatism' evident in all Cather's work, embodied most clearly in her nostalgic evocation 'of the frontier, and . . . the heroism of earlier days' (140). Though Hicks conceded that both *O Pioneers!* and *My Ántonia* 'have their importance in American literature' because they contain 'a basis in reality' (141), he was less charitable toward Cather's subsequent fiction. Essentially, Hicks was the first critic to align Cather's personal sensibility with the work she produced, arguing that Cather could not sustain her vision of America's heroic idealism in the midst of the modern world: 'as she looked at the life about her, her despair grew' (143). Hicks's final assessment of Cather is harsh. Concluding that 'her romantic dreams involve the distortion of life' (146), he dismisses Cather as a writer who has nothing relevant to say about the twentieth century: 'Miss Cather has never once tried to see contemporary life as it is; she sees only that it lacks what the past, at least in her idealisation of it, had. Thus she has been barred from the task that has occupied most of the world's great artists, the expression of what is central and fundamental in her own age' (144).

Cather, not surprisingly, perceived these to be fighting words. And the critical essays she wrote during the thirties respond to Hicks's attack with a rhetoric of hyperbolic posturing and defensive rationalisation. The Preface to *Not Under Forty* (1936), for instance, announces dramatically that 'the world broke in two in 1922 or thereabouts, and the persons and prejudices recalled in these sketches slid back into yesterday's seven thousand years.' Rather than counter Hicks's characterisation of her as antimodern, Cather embraced it. 'It is for the backward,' she declared unapologetically, 'and by one of their number, that these sketches were written.... the book will have little interest for people under forty years of age.' In that same year she published her specific response to Hicks in a letter to the *Commonweal* entitled, 'Escapism.' In it Cather begins with the rhetorical question, 'What has art ever been but escape?' and justifies her position by arguing that art is devoted to universal, human experiences, not simply contemporary, economic ones.[31] The difference between Cather and Hicks lies in their separate notions of what, literally, escapism means. Cather adopts one sense of the word—the diversion of the mind to purely imaginative activity—to insist that 'true' artists must be allowed to exist in their own separate sphere, 'left out of the social and industrial routine' (21). Art, she implies, is by necessity apolitical, because only then does it transcend social propaganda and the petty details of daily life that weigh down and ultimately destroy the human and experiential 'truth' to which all 'great' fiction aspires. Hicks, conversely, conceives of literature as essentially and necessarily political. Escapism in his terms constitutes a betrayal of one's social and human responsibility, an evasion of unpleasant reality through what he characterises as Cather's compensatory nostalgia. Both believe that art should aspire to 'truth,' but each defines it legitimately and oppositionally, within the operative meanings of the word 'escapist' itself.

Confirming rather than contradicting Hicks's reading of her fiction, Cather's theoretical writing inadvertently contributed to the critical devaluation of her work throughout the thirties and forties.[32] Sharon O'Brien has commented on how certain critics during these decades—Hicks, Kazin, and Trilling especially—engaged in an *ad feminam* attack of Cather that was in part motivated by their desire to define themselves in opposition to the paternal power and influence of the literary critics who had immediately preceded them: 'At the same time they were sons confronting a maternal presence their fathers had left as a literary legacy, a woman writer of the first rank. In attacking Willa Cather, the leftist critics who came of age in the 1930s were thus engaged in a complex oedipal drama, seeking both to replace the older generation of male critics and to repudiate a powerful maternal literary figure by defining her as limited.' O'Brien accounts for the virulent antifeminism of these attacks by historicising the role that gender played in the formation of the canon. Noting that increased professionalisation of American literary studies occurred during these decades, she surmises that critics regularly delegated women writers to lesser and 'minor' ranks so as to ensure that a vigorous, virile, and national American literature existed to rival that of an English tradition in which the male masters—Chaucer, Shakespeare, and Milton—had already been enshrined.[33]

O'Brien's work is important in determining why Cather was the brunt of such vicious attacks during these decades, but it does not discuss fully the canonical consequences of this critical invective, especially upon Cather's late fiction that was being both written and published at the time.[34] For what distinguishes the critical rhetoric of this decade is not only a none too subtle misogyny about what is 'feminine,' and therefore, nostalgic and regressive, in Cather's fiction, but also an interpretation that links explicitly Cather's personal life to her fictional texts. Alfred Kazin, for example, simply reiterates Hicks's claims that Cather's early fiction was her only important contribution to American literature, and that as her career progressed, her novels deteriorated. Kazin himself charts a teleology of personal and artistic decline that exactly parallels what he reads as the 'meaning' of Cather's later fictions: 'The climax in Willa Cather's career came with two short novels she published between 1923 and 1925, *A Lost Lady* and *The Professor's House*. They were parables of the decline and fall of the great tradition, her own tradition. . . . Later, as it seemed, she became merely sentimental, and her direct criticism of contemporary types and manners was often petulant and intolerant.'[35] Equating Cather personally with her texts ('They were parables of the decline and fall. . . . she became merely sentimental'), Kazin identifies the 'climax' of her career in the years between 1923 and 1925, when Cather was nearing fifty. What is telling in his diction, however, is his characterisation of both her and her work as 'petulant,' 'intolerant,' and 'sentimental,' words frequently associated with the elderly, especially women.

Other attacks are more relentlessly personal. Leon Edel argues in his ironically titled 'Homage to Willa Cather' that after 1922 Cather 'was a creature of old and fixed habits and she could not swim with the stream. This made for deep loyalties and abiding affections. It also tended to dry up the fount of her inspiration; there was no sustenance in the present.'[36] In this extraordinary passage, Edel equates Cather's inability to produce what he deems 'great' fiction with an encoded asexual signification: she is a 'creature' in his diction, 'old and fixed,' whose 'fount' has dried up, offering 'no sustenance' in the present. In one sense, Edel is describing what he sees as Cather's refusal to accomodate herself to the modern American world of the twenties, thirties, and forties. Yet the associations conveyed by his imagery suggest as well that Cather had herself become an aged crone, whose withered body (fount/breasts) betrays her inability to offer 'sustenance in the present' (both for herself and for the reader), during precisely that period in which she wrote her final seven major works of fiction. Edel's critique is, essentially, a postmenopausal condemnation of Cather and her late fiction as being past their prime; they are outdated, they are uninteresting, they are old-womanish.

The canonical consequence of such psychologising has been the creation of an entire school of criticism that reads Willa Cather the author as virtually indistinguishable from her works, especially the later ones.[37] Moreover, these later assessments accept unquestioningly the early critical formula that

Cather's novels climax in the twenties, then spiral downward in a trajectory of despair, decline, and artistic degeneration. Such assumptions allow both John H. Randall and David Daiches, for example, to conflate Cather with her late novels in the following critical evaluations.

> Another sign of artistic weakening makes its appearance about this time: the main characters, when the stress becomes too acute, beat a mental retreat to an earlier and less frustrating phase of their existence; in other words, they regress.... the actions of her later protagonists seem to be projections of some unfortunate personal traits of her own.... The kindest thing which can be said of the later crisis novels is that they present a world-view at once idiosyncratic and bizarre. I am inclined to make the severer judgment that they embody an outlook on life so distorted and falsified as to be practically worthless as an interpretation of human experience.[38]
>
> A strong inventive imagination was not one of Willa Cather's gifts. Her memory had to be stirred, her emotions involved, some autobiographical impulse had to be touched, however indirectly, before she could produce her best and strongest work. And her best work *is* strong: she possessed the kind of masculine sensibility which drew nourishment from simple, elemental situations to subtilize them and make them persuasive symbols of aspects of experience.... In retreating from the earthy situations of her earlier Midwestern novels she had finally lost altogether the epic touch, and, though she had gained other qualities, none of them were so convincingly her own.[39]

The biographical basis of these readings is self-evident; Cather's art weakens as her life progresses. Yet these passages impart an interpretation about Cather and her fiction that prevails even today. This reading centers upon the idea that Willa Cather's life and art embody a traditionalism that is vigorous when it evokes the pioneer West, but rigid and genteel from the 1920s onward. Accordingly, Cather lost herself and her artistic strength within the wasteland of an urban, postwar world. She could not regain the 'masculine sensibility' that invigorated her early, manifest destiny fiction. Instead, she became feminised; she weakened artistically, she retreated, she regressed, she began to see the world in 'idiosyncratic and bizarre' ways. As the scope of society Cather explores in the late fiction narrows, so does her art devolve. This logic is exacerbated by the fact that most of the later novels and stories are concerned primarily with female protagonists who struggle with and even sometimes resist the social constraints imposed upon them because of gender. The late novels are devalued not specifically because they are less masculine, but because they are about telling women's stories. Thus do critical judgments reveal themselves to be a thinly disguised misogyny. Lionel Trilling's pronouncement then, that 'so self-conscious and defiant a rejection of her own time must make her talent increasingly irrelevant and tangential—for any time,'[40] stands as only one of many such interpretations that have contributed to the now canonical acceptance of the 'fact' that Cather's late works are artistically inept, tired failures not worth reading.[41]

One might suppose that the surge of feminist criticism in the early seventies would have addressed this devaluation of the later works, especially since they are, for the most part, stories about women. Yet in certain instances just the opposite was true. Carolyn Heilbrun, in a curiously reductive reading of the late novels, bemoans what she sees as the loss of 'strong heroines' in Cather's late fictions: 'Equally indicative of the female urge toward the destruction and denial of female destiny is the woman novelist who manages to achieve an autonomous woman character in perhaps one or two novels, and then relinquishes the central role to men. Willa Cather is such an author. . . . After *My Ántonia*, the struggle is over, the imagination has failed in its creation of women, and has shifted to male heroes.'[42] This is essentially the same attitude toward the late works as that entertained by male critics from the thirties through the sixties, only it offers an opposing explanation for failure. Heilbrun reads Cather's work as becoming more, rather than less, masculine. One wonders how she manages to ignore the female heroines in *My Mortal Enemy* (1926), *Shadows on the Rock* (1931), 'Old Mrs Harris' (1931), *Lucy Gayheart* (1935), and *Sapphira and the Slave Girl* (1940), except for the possibility that she may not find them all likable or admirable and thus refuses to designate them as 'heroic.' A similar, though thematically unrelated, elision of the later novels occurs in Gilbert and Gubar's analysis of Cather in *Sexchanges*, volume two of their *No Man's Land*. Though Gilbert and Gubar's premise, in keeping with the larger intent of their investigation, is that 'Cather quarreled with contemporary America in general and with the "laws" that govern heterosexual relations in particular,' they spend the majority of their chapter examining the ways in which the women construct autonomy in the early novels and mention the later ones only in passing.[43] Within feminist studies on Cather, Judith Fryer's *Felicitous Space* devotes sustained analysis to two of the later novels as they represent imagined and real spaces inhabited by women characters.[44] Susan Rosowski, Janis Stout, and Hermione Lee, however, have pioneered feminist approaches to Cather's fiction which encompass issues either expressed in or related to the later novels. Rosowski (1986) and Lee (1989) address Cather's entire oeuvre (including the later novels) from a feminist perspective in their thematic and biographical studies, respectively. Stout, similarly, argues that, in general, Cather's works could be termed feminist in that they alternate between 'sometimes proclaiming a feminist vision, sometimes depicting the perniciousness or merely the invalidity of the varying forces arrayed against a feminist vision, or, more simply, arrayed against women.'[45] Important as these works are, they do not address what I will argue are not so much differences as readerly difficulties that arise in the later texts but are not in the earlier ones. The focus of these feminist critics is more sweeping and synthetic in approach; my methodology will tend toward the more disjunctive and particular.

Lesbian feminist criticism has not, curiously, expressed an interest in Cather's late fiction, despite the numerous critiques of heterosexuality throughout the late novels and the presence of subtle, homoerotic, and homosocial allusions within them. Though Cather was explicitly introduced as a lesbian writer by Jane Rule as early as 1975,[46] it was not until the publication of Sharon O'Brien's ground-breaking essay, '"The Thing Not Named": Willa Cather as a Lesbian Writer' (1984), which was followed by her 1987 psychoanalytic biography charting Cather's emergence as a female-identified writer, that Cather's lesbianism became common parlance in academic conferences and critical essays. And while the term 'lesbian' undoubtedly makes some readers and critics of Cather uncomfortable, and perhaps even raises the hackles of others, it also raises the political stakes of Cather criticism generally. For the impressive array of scholarship O'Brien has marshaled—especially her discovery of Cather's love letters to Louise Pound which hint at Cather's own awareness that her feelings for Pound would be viewed as 'unnatural'[47]—makes it difficult, if not impossible, to ignore Cather's sexual and emotional preferences in critical works linking the life with the works that still predominate in Cather scholarship.[48] O'Brien's work, in other words, constitutes a watershed in Cather criticism and raises the following inevitable questions: What does it mean to read Cather as a lesbian writer? If, indeed, we acknowledge that Cather was a self-identified lesbian, as O'Brien claims, then does it necessarily follow that she was, because of this erotic preference, a *lesbian* writer? How can we, and do we, read lesbian traces in Cather's fiction?

In her 1984 essay, O'Brien suggests that Cather's use of the phrase 'the thing not named' in 'The Novel Démeublé' marks a particularly significant instance of absence in Cather's work and raises the problem of unnameability in general: 'Whereas phrases like *overtone, verbal mood* and *emotional aura* suggest ineffable realms of experience and feeling—complex or barely sensed signifieds for which there is no precise verbal signifier—Cather's startling phrase *the thing not named* has another connotation: an aspect of experience possessing a name that the writer does not, or cannot, employ.' O'Brien herself suggests the connection between what she calls 'Cather's startling phrase' and Oscar Wilde's coining of 'the Love that dared not speak its name,' and concludes that though Cather appears in the passage as 'the modernist writer endorsing allusive, suggestive art and inviting the reader's participation in the creation of literary meaning,' she must also be read as 'the lesbian writer forced to disguise or to conceal the emotional aura of her fiction, reassuring herself that the reader fills the absence in the text by intuiting the subterranean, unwritten text.'[49] O'Brien's essay has been formative in the subsequent lesbian-centered criticism of Cather. By naming the unnameable thing 'lesbian,' O'Brien transforms a reader's interaction with the multiple significations of Cather's texts—'presence,' 'overtone,' 'mood,' and 'aura'—and instead *seems* to suggest that one can 'fill the absence in the text' with the 'unwritten text' that is lesbian experience. Though O'Brien will later in her essay complicate the reading of lesbianism as the 'unwritten text' of Cather's novels, most critics who have appropriated Cather as a lesbian writer read quite literally the existence of a 'subterranean, unwritten text' that is, essentially, lesbian.[50] In these readings, considering Cather as a lesbian writer not only illuminates unexamined or contradictory aspects of the texts, but it also constitutes the repressed *meaning* of the texts as well.

In order to arrive at a lesbian-centered interpretation of a text that inscribes lesbianism as an unnameable absence, critics have begun to read the fictions as either coded or engaged in an elaborate masquerade that displaces their lesbian nature. Early in the critical formulation of lesbian criticism, Catherine Stimpson argued that because 'the violent yoking of homosexuality and deviancy has been so pervasive in the modern period,' the lesbian writer who 'wished to name her experience but . . . feared plain speech' would of necessity 'encrypt her text in another sense and use codes.'[51] Reading Cather's fiction as sexually coded is prevalent among current scholarship; at the 1989 Santa Fe Conference on Willa Cather, for example, a number of papers directed their interpretations toward the 'unwritten' text. Focusing primarily on the early fiction, the papers had titles ranging from 'Unnatural Excitement and Narrative Masquerade: The Lesbian Aesthetic in *Alexander's Bridge*,' and 'The Sub/Versions and Silences in Alexandra's "White Book": A Lesbian Feminist Reading of *O Pioneers!*' to 'The Unescapable Ground in Another Form: Lesbian Identity in Willa Cather's *O Pioneers!*' Masquerade, subversion, silence, *another form*: what distinguishes these readings is the implicit assumption that the fiction masks, submerges, and even distorts the lesbianism that resides, albeit coded, in the texts. The critical task then becomes one of decoding, uncovering, and recovering what has been unwritten, unmentionable, and unnamed. Yet it also involves a mode of interpretation that reads between and beyond what is literally inscribed on the page, basing its interpretive burden of proof on the life rather than the text. It is because Cather is a lesbian that Judith Fetterley can claim, for instance, that 'the central situation in many of her novels and stories is an indirect expression of a lesbian sensibility,'[52] *not* because that sensibility is necessarily readable in the text.

Another method of coding to which critics point in Cather's fiction is her use of male narrators in love with, usually, women unavailable to them. Read as a persona of the author, these male narrators allow Cather, as Bonnie Zimmerman suggests, 'to express safely her emotional and erotic feelings for other women.'[53] Joanna Russ also reads the novels in this way: focusing primarily on *O Pioneers!* (1913) and *One of Ours* (1922), Russ contends that the sexually ambiguous heterosexual relationships in these novels (between Emil and Marie, and Claude and Enid respectively) embody masquerades of Cather's own relations with unattainable women, emphasising 'emotional deprivation' and 'the impossibility and hopelessness of the situation.' Like many Cather critics before her, Russ is trying to account for the markedly nonsexual nature of heterosexual relationships in Cather's fiction. Her conclusion is that 'if one goes back and translates the situations in Cather's novels into lesbian situations, the fictions often make clearer sense.'[54]

Yet 'clearer sense' is ultimately *not* what Sharon O'Brien advocates in the essay that informs many of these readings. Though O'Brien frequently employs the terms 'masquerade,' 'disguise,' and 'displacement,' she cautions against what is at once a too literal and, paradoxically, nonliteral reading of the fiction, which would claim 'that the overt, written text conceals a subtext that is the "real" story Cather would have written had she been able.' O'Brien instead offers a dialectic of reading, suggesting that 'we need to examine . . . what is named and what is not,' keeping in mind that 'authorial intention and meaning may oscillate between the two and thus be indeterminate.' We misread Cather's work altogether, she insists, if we assume 'that what is not named is the "real" text, the one Cather would have written in a different social environment.'[55]

Despite O'Brien's well-reasoned cautions, an emphasis on the 'real' lesbian text is precisely what characterises the majority of lesbian-centered readings of Cather.[56] Even more problematic is the way such readings continue to valorise the early fiction at the expense of Cather's later work. Deborah Lambert, for example, seems to reiterate Heilbrun's argument when she asserts that 'after certain early work, in which she created strong and achieving women, like herself, she abandoned her female characters to the most conventional and traditional roles; analogously, she began to deny or distort the sexuality of her principal characters.'[57] Equating Cather the woman with her female characters—a move extraordinarily similar to the one made by the early male critics of the thirties—Lambert identifies a 'lesbian' text as one that features 'strong and achieving women' who in some way parallel the personal attributes of their author. In this reading, only those novels that conform to a standard of politically correct representation both valorised by the critic and read as part of the author's lesbian character ('strong and achieving') are themselves lesbian texts. Bonnie Zimmerman warns that 'there is a danger in this attempt to establish a characteristic lesbian vision or literary value system. . . . In an attempt to say *this* is what defines lesbian literature, we are easily tempted to read selectively, omitting what is foreign to our theories.'[58] Despite this caution, what is excluded from lesbian feminist explorations of Cather's novels is the way in which the later fiction examines and self-consciously addresses not only the social and gendered conventions within which women try to create space for the self, but also the kinds of narrative conventions that shape how one tells a woman's story. In viewing the novels solely as a reflection or a masquerade of Cather's life, lesbian feminist readings necessarily ignore the ways in which Cather's lesbianism might affect textual representation, complicating and even contradicting the representation of heterosexual romance that Lambert identifies as too 'conventional and traditional.'

It is necessary to return then to the question of why these late novels seem so difficult to place in any critical category. Part of the reason, at least, seems to be that no critical vocabulary exists with which to discuss them, other than one that affixes derogatory labels—petulant traditionalism, too conventional, a failure of the imagination—in order to dismiss them entirely from critical discourse. The later novels then, do not conform to any of the paradigms through which we have been conditioned to read Cather's fiction. Yet another reason why Cather's late fiction eludes easy classification is that she was self-consciously experimenting with both narrative structure and technique after 1922. Her 'Four Letters'—'On *Death Comes for the Archbishop*,' 'On *Shadows on the Rock*,' 'Escapism,' and 'On *The Professor's House*'—address the new techniques she was attempting to incorporate into her novels, which she alluded to as 'experiments in form.' These experiments were primarily worked out through 'different kinds of method' in narrative, which Cather signified as perhaps a more appropriate term than 'novel' for some of her work. One of these 'experiments' was 'that of inserting the *Nouvelle* into the *Roman*,'[59] the self-conscious placement of separate and distinct short stories within the novel as a whole. One effect of such experimentation is the decentering of her narratives, which are marked by a shifting and mercurial focalisation rather than a single determining and easily apprehensible vision. Multiple perspective and narration figure prominently in these novels and often occur in deliberate opposition to the attempt of a particular text to sustain thematic coherence. A certain textual self-reflexiveness operates in all Cather's late works consequently; her fictions recognise and frequently comment upon their own status as fiction. Art and artifice become permeable, and thus confusing categories.

In a 1933 NBC radio broadcast, Cather commented on what she saw as the limitations in form of the contemporary American novel, which she believed was confined 'to two themes; how the young man got his girl, whether by matrimony or otherwise, and how he succeeded in business.'[60] As a woman novelist interested in telling stories about women in American society, Cather concluded that only

> when we learn to give our purpose the form that exactly clothes it and no more; when we make a form for every story instead of trying to crowd it into one of the stock moulds on the shelf, then we shall be on the right road, at least. . . . We won't face the fact that it's the formula itself which is pernicious, the frame-up. (170)

In her late fiction especially, Cather experiments with these 'pernicious formulas' and the ways in which women have been (re)presented within them. As Susan J. Rosowski has noted in her trenchant analysis of women in Cather's fiction, 'Cather devotes works long recognised as among her most powerful to gradually narrowing the question of what it is to be a woman. She places her female characters within increasingly complex and restrictive contexts.'[61] Thus the seemingly more 'conventional' and 'traditional' kinds of novels Cather writes late in her career—the novel of romance, the historical novel, the bildungsroman, and novels that return to her familial and midwestern origins—self-consciously address the difficulties and tensions of writing women's stories within conventional narrative frames. The late texts experiment with genres generally, exploring how written history is created from an oral tradition of tale-telling, for example, and specifically, in their self-reflexive revision of inherited notions of what exactly constitutes a woman's tale, or a tale about a woman.

One would think then that feminist critics would have immediately embraced Cather's analysis of gender and of gendered plots in the late fiction, had it not been for the problematic 'heroines' whose stories she tells. The late novels offer two types of female protagonists: powerful and embittered middle-aged women whom it is difficult to like, much less sympathise with, and more conventional, young, pliable, and almost too good ingenues. Neither of these categories of characters makes possible a feminist interpretation interested in praising 'strong and admirable' heroines like Ántonia Shimerda, Alexandra Bergson, or Thea Kronborg. Moreover, as Gilbert and Gubar have noted, Cather's work in general and the late novels in particular 'expressed skepticism not only about conventional sex roles but also about the possibility of changing them.'[62] In other words, Cather's late fictions incorporate what are commonly understood as feminist issues—power, autonomy, career aspirations, financial independence—but are not necessarily feminist. Transgressive gestures of sexual expression, of power, of role reversals appear early in the novels, but are contained, managed, and sometimes even contradicted within each text by its end.[63] Thus the problems and disruptions that the stories of these female characters engender—such as the way in which 'the figure of the crippled or ill matriarch represents the limitations of women's power in patriarchy'[64]—are resolutely rewritten into some kind of narrative, if not textual, containment. The feminist critic Adrienne Munich has suggested why such interior narrative contradictions inevitably arise in women's novels. Such a female-centered tale exhibits, she argues, 'profound disjunctions and throws barriers around its "feminist consciousness" that betray profound discomfort about what is being expressed. I would argue that all western literature will exhibit some defensiveness about this subject. Female authored work cannot escape varieties of sexual malaise; identification with dominance has colonised most imaginations.'[65] The narrative disjunctions in Cather's texts cut two ways. It is just as impossible to read those novels unambivalently as feminist as it is to accept the frequently conventional way they will attempt to negotiate their own closure, believable only if one represses or ignores meanings that the texts have raised earlier in their narratives. One way then to reclaim the later novels as 'women's texts' is to acknowledge just how frustratingly feminist and potentially antifeminist they are simultaneously. Cather, one is forced to accept, will always demand to have her texts read both ways, and at once.

Cather's late novels, in fact, all attempt to inscribe what Ross Chambers defines as 'readability,' a concept I will use throughout this study as the focus of my own reading. 'Readerly texts,' according to Chambers,

> claim the power to produce new meanings in ever new circumstances (they lay claim to status as artistic discourse), but at the same time they are concerned, if not to claim a single univocal sense as central to their meaning, then at least to define the range of possible meanings that they can admit, to the exclusion of other possible meanings and relevances. This is what is meant as their 'readability.' It is as if for them the deferring of meaning from which they benefit as art requires careful control so as not to get out of hand—and it would be possible to show in many texts of the nineteenth century, for instance, that their sense of writing as a phenomenon of entropy, of slippage, or of drift is carefully balanced by a negentropic appeal to the act of reading as an ordering, fixing, or channeling phenomenon.[66]

Chambers's characterisation of a nineteenth-century authorial sensibility that appears in certain texts sums up the feelings of many critics about how Cather herself escapes into art in these late novels and about how her art constitutes a reaction against the entropy, slippage, and drift of the modern world. Yet each of the late works examined in this study—*My Mortal Enemy, Shadows on the Rock,* 'Old Mrs Harris,' *Lucy Gayheart,* and *Sapphira and the Slave Girl*—questions the very possibility of arriving at any ordered or fixed meaning through the process of reading and interpretation. At the same time that the texts elicit certain readings, by trying to enclose the story within a conventional ending, they inevitably confound the reader's ability to affix an order or a meaning by incorporating within the narrative a multiplicity of contradictory perspectives and interpretations. Cather's late texts then are essentially at odds with the limits of interpretability posed throughout their narratives. They desire comprehension and readability, while they simultaneously encode a sense of narrative deferral and artistic self-referentiality. They both are and are not readable, and they incorporate this difference within their own complex and complicating narratives.

My desire in this book is to challenge previous canonical assumptions about the late novels, though I do not wish to argue that they are necessarily 'better' or more complex than the earlier fiction. I wish primarily to bring these texts back into the critical discourse about Cather's work in general, now reread with increasing interest and theoretical sophistication.[67] I have, consequently, tried to be rigorously honest in these readings by framing them as exactly that, readings in the plural rather than the singular sense. For I am certain that these texts have the capacity to elicit and inspire other readings, which I hope will contribute to the critical dialogue and debate about Cather, whose narratives are some of the most complex and subtle in all twentieth-century American literature. I must also acknowledge the important study on Cather's late novels that precedes mine. Merrill Maguire Skaggs's *After the World Broke in Two: The Later Novels of Willa Cather,* addresses the same texts and time frame as my own study. Skaggs, however, conceives of and interprets these late novels within the perspective of an intellectual biography, assuming 'that this most autobiographical of writers leaves traces of her intellectual struggles and passions in the texts of her novels.'[68] As will become apparent, my own critical approach differs dramatically from Skaggs's, yet our respective analyses might best be read as complementary rather than as contradictory.

During the long process of reading and writing about these texts, I have been consistently challenged, frequently frustrated, always intrigued, but never bored. Their ability to sustain my interest and curiosity over a period of years testifies, I think, to their complexity and their readability. And though I resolutely believe that Cather's texts are not reducible to a simple moral or unified meaning, I have learned one significant lesson: reading Willa Cather is never as simple as it seems.

Notes

1. All quotations are drawn from a phone interview (April 21, 1991), which Ms Steinshouer was kind enough to allow me to conduct.

2. The Willa Cather Pioneer Memorial (WCPM) was founded in 1955, and in May 1962 it opened the Willa Cather Museum in Red Cloud. In April 1963, the society began to offer tours of the museum and of the surrounding Red Cloud environs, and in the fall of that same year 'Catherland' was adopted as the name for the historical and fictional sites the memorial encompassed.

3. The centerpiece for the diorama, 'The Sculptor's Funeral,' for example, is an old-fashioned casket donated to the WCPM by the Brown Mortuary in Superior, Nebraska.

4. *Willa Cather Pioneer Memorial Newsletter* 7, no. 1 (Spring 1963).

5. *Willa Cather Pioneer Memorial Newsletter* 32, no. 4 (Winter 1988): 39–41.

6. I am indebted to Sharon O'Brien for introducing the idea of 'reading communities' into my thinking about Cather and the canon.

7. Barbara Herrnstein Smith, 'Contingencies of Value,' in *Canons*, ed. Robert von Hallberg (Chicago: University of Chicago Press, 1984), 24. Cf. Herrnstein Smith's expansion of this essay into *Contingencies of Value: Alternative Perspectives for Critical Theory* (Cambridge: Harvard University Press, 1988).

8. Vernon L. Parrington, *Main Currents in American Thought*, vol. 3, *The Beginnings of Critical Realism in America* (New York: Harcourt, Brace and Company, 1927), 383.

9. Sharon O'Brien, 'Becoming Non-Canonical: The Case against Willa Cather,' *American Quarterly* 40 (March 1988): 110. See also David Stineback's two essays, 'No Stone Unturned: Popular Versus Professional Evaluations of Willa Cather,' *Prospects* 7 (1982): 167–76, and 'The Case against Willa Cather,' *Canadian Review of American Studies* 15 (Winter 1984): 385–95, in which he declares that 'no major American novelist in the twentieth century has been as misunderstood and mistreated by literary critics as Willa Cather' (385).

10. *New York Times Magazine*, July 10, 1988, p. 24.

11. Alfred Kazin, *On Native Grounds* (1942; New York: Harcourt, Brace Jovanovich, 1970), 251.

12. Sharon O'Brien, *Willa Cather: The Emerging Voice* (New York: Oxford University Press, 1987), 74. The phrase 'Epics of Women' is the title of Parrington's chapter on Cather in *The Beginnings of Critical Realism*, 382. Cf. Cecelia Tichi's conclusion in 'Women Writers and the New Woman,' from *The Columbia Literary History of the United States*, ed. Emery Elliott (New York: Columbia University Press, 1988): 'The American land, then, is the center of woman's power in Cather's fiction. Her heroines—the "Amazonian" Alexandra Bergson of *O, Pioneers!*, Ántonia Shimerda of *My Ántonia*, Thea Kronborg of *Song of the Lark*—all embody its characteristics. They enact its generative values, its natural cycles, the moods of its changing weather, its very spatial expensiveness [*sic*]' (605).

13. Paul Lauter, *Reconstructing American Literature: Courses, Syllabi, Issues* (Old Waterbury, N.Y.: Feminist Press, 1983).

14. Though Cather appears in some introductory and advanced historical courses in the Lauter compilation [Introduction to American Literature (5); American Literature: Early Modern Period (121); Introduction to Later American Literature (56); American Literature 1865-1914 (99); American Literature 1914-present (124)], her novels are also included in a number of thematic courses, including Regionalism (196), Black and Ethnic Literature (176), The American Dream (210), Her-Land: American Literature of Women and the Land (194), and Twentieth-Century Novels by Women (160). The most recent thematic study that encompasses all Cather's novels without disparaging or dismissing any of them is Susan Rosowski's *The Voyage Perilous: Willa Cather's Romanticism* (Lincoln: University of Nebraska Press, 1986). Conversely, John H. Randall's *The Landscape and the Looking Glass: Willa Cather's Search for Meaning* (Boston: Houghton Mifflin Company, 1960) and even Jamie Ambrosie's recent *Willa Cather: Writing at the Frontier* (Oxford: Berg, 1988) read the later novels as failures within the parameters of their own critical and thematic concerns.

15. The two late novels that do sustain more critical attention and approbation are *The Professor's House* (1925) and *Death Comes for the Archbishop* (1927). Significantly, they are also the only late novels whose protagonists are male.

16. See, for example, William Curtin, ed., *The World and the Parish*, 2 vols. (Lincoln: University of Nebraska Press, 1970); Bernice Slote, ed., *The Kingdom of Art: Willa Cather's First Principles and Critical Statements, 1893-1896* (Lincoln: University of Nebraska Press, 1966); Bernice Slote and Virginia Faulkner, eds., *The Art of Willa Cather* (Lincoln: University of Nebraska Press, 1973); Brent L. Bohlke, ed., *Willa Cather in Person: Interviews, Speeches, and Letters* (Lincoln: University of Nebraska Press, 1986); Willa Cather, *Not Under Forty* (1936; Lincoln: University of Nebraska Press, 1988); and Willa Cather, *Willa Cather on Writing* (1949; Lincoln: University of Nebraska Press, 1988).

17. See, for example, E.K. Brown and Leon Edel, *Willa Cather: A Critical Biography* (1953; New York: Avon Books, 1980), and James Woodress, *Willa Cather: Her Life and Art* (New York: Western, 1975) and *Willa Cather: A Literary Life* (Lincoln: University of Nebraska Press, 1987).

18. Rosowski, *The Voyage Perilous*, x, xiii.

19. Phyllis Rose, *Writing of Women: Essays in a Renaissance* (Middletown, Conn.: Wesleyan University Press, 1986), 150. See also Lillian D. Bloom and Edward A. Bloom, 'The Poetics of Willa Cather,' in *Five Essays on Willa Cather: The Merrimack Symposium*, ed. John J. Murphy (North Andover, Mass.: Merrimack College, 1974), 97-119.

20. Cather, *Not Under Forty*, 45. All further references to this work will appear in the text.

21. See both Elizabeth Sergeant, *Willa Cather, A Memoir* (Philadelphia: Lippincott, 1953), 34-39, 43, and Sharon O'Brien, *Willa Cather: The Emerging Voice*, 151-52, on Cather's equation of realism with social reportage and muckraking.

22. Janis P. Stout, *Strategies of Reticence: Silence and Meaning in the Works of Jane Austen, Willa Cather, Katherine Anne Porter, and Joan Didion* (Charlottesville: University Press of Virginia, 1990), 67.

23. Hermione Lee, *Willa Cather: Double Lives* (New York: Pantheon, 1989), 17.

24. Robert J. Nelson, *Willa Cather and France: In Search of the Lost Language* (Urbana: University of Illinois Press, 1988), 2. Though Nelson relies extensively on an almost incomprehensible Lacanian analysis for much of his study, his final chapter raises pertinent and unresolved questions in Cather studies with regard to theoretical approaches (127-52).

25. Jo Ann Middleton, *Willa Cather's Modernism: A Study of Style and Technique* (Rutherford, N.J.: Fairleigh Dickinson University Press, 1990), 21. Cf. Lee, *Willa Cather: Double Lifes*, 4.

26. Stevens, quoted in Woodress, *Willa Cather: A Literary Life*, 487.

27. See Ann Ardis's recent study, *New Women, New Novels: Feminism and Early Modernism* (New Brunswick: Rutgers University Press, 1990), and Rachel Blau DuPlessis's *Writing Beyond the Ending: Narrative Strategies of Twentieth-Century Women Writers* (Bloomington: Indiana University Press, 1985). DuPlessis, however, does not include Cather in her assessment of twentieth-century women modernists because she believes Cather's work adheres more to a nineteenth-century sensibility.

28. Hugh Kenner, 'The Making of the Modernist Canon,' in Von Hallberg, *Canons*, 363-75. All further references to Kenner's essay will appear in the text.

29. See Cather's essays, 'My First Novels [There Were Two],' in *Willa Cather on Writing*, 89–97, and 'Miss Jewett,' in *Not Under Forty*, 76–95.

30. Granville Hicks, 'The Case against Willa Cather,' was originally published in the *English Journal* and was reprinted in *Willa Cather and Her Critics*, ed. James Schroeter (1947; Ithaca: Cornell University Press, 1967), 139–47. All further references to this essay will appear in the text.

31. 'Escapism,' in *Willa Cather on Writing*, 18. All further references to this essay will appear in the text.

32. See Slote and Faulkner, *The Art of Willa Cather*, 150–51, for a panel discussion about whether Cather actually possessed and articulated a theory of fiction.

33. O'Brien, 'Becoming Non-Canonical,' 117, 118–19.

34. O'Brien notes only that 'a new consensus about her literary values has still not emerged, however, in part because evaluations like "Her art was not a big art" still have shaping power' (ibid., 123).

35. Kazin, *On Native Ground*, 251, 253.

36. Leon Edel, 'Homage to Willa Cather,' in Slote and Faulkner, *The Art of Willa Cather*, 203.

37. The lone dissenting voice in early Cather criticism is that of Arthur Hobson Quinn, who argues that 'it is the usual critical mistake to speak of Willa Cather as though her main significance lay as a representative of the Far West. While she has represented life in that region with unusual insight and sympathy, she has not been limited to that locality, nor indeed is locality an element of supreme importance in her fiction. She is quite unprovincial, and her significance lies much more in the artistry of her method than in her material. . . . her greatest books came after 1922, and . . . none of them owe their power to the description of the farming life of Nebraska' (*American Fiction: An Historical and Critical Survey* ([New York: D. Appleton-Century, 1936], 683, 696).

38. Randall, *The Landscape and the Looking Glass*, 159–60.

39. David Daiches, *Willa Cather: A Critical Introduction* (Ithaca: Cornell University Press, 1951), 132.

40. Lionel Trilling, 'Willa Cather,' in Schroeter, *Willa Cather and Her Critics*, 153.

41. If this seems hyperbolic, consider my experience during a job interview at MLA with a large and respected state university in 1986. I was asked just what was 'an ostensibly bright young woman, as my letters of recommendation claimed, *doing* writing on the lesser novels of Willa Cather?' The implicit suggestion seemed to be that I was not so bright as I thought, especially for choosing an 'inferior' group of texts as both a dissertation topic and a marketing strategy. My polite rejoinder that 'later was not necessarily synonymous with lesser' met with bemused condescension, if little else. Needless to say, I did not get the job.

42. Carolyn Heilbrun, *Reinventing Womanhood* (New York: W.W. Norton, 1978), 79, 81.

43. Sandra M. Gilbert and Susan Gubar, 'Lighting Out for the Territories: Willa Cather's Lost Horizons,' *No Man's Land: The Place of the Woman Writer in the Twentieth Century*, vol. 2, *Sexchanges* (New Haven: Yale University Press, 1989), 169–212 (quotation is from p. 173). Gilbert and Gubar devote one paragraph to *My Mortal Enemy* (206), and mention *Shadows on the Rock* briefly (210).

44. In *Felicitous Space* (Chapel Hill: University of North Carolina Press, 1986), Judith Fryer discusses at length only *Shadows on the Rock* (319–41) and *Sapphira and the Slave Girl* (262–73).

45. Stout, *Strategies of Reticence*, 68.

46. In her chapter on Cather in *Lesbian Images* (New York: Pocket Books, 1976), Rule argues, paradoxically, against engaging in lesbian readings of Cather's work. Addressing what she sees as the predominantly homophobic origins of the negative assessments of Cather by Lionel Trilling and others, she suggests that 'these grossly inaccurate critical generalisations can only be explained by a desire of each of these men to imply that Willa Cather's "basic psychology," "personal failure," or "temperament" negatively influenced her vision. What they want out in the light of day is her emotional and erotic preference for women, and, if they cannot have irrefutable biographical facts or cannot use them in print, they will distort their reading of her fiction to make their discrediting point' (78–79).

47. O'Brien, *Willa Cather: The Emerging Voice*, 133–37. See also O'Brien's useful and lucid definition of the term 'lesbian,' which she argues depends upon a lesbian 'sense of self' within a historical and cultural milieu (127–28).

48. The most recent of these is Hermione Lee's *Willa Cather: Double Lives*.

49. Sharon O'Brien, '"The Thing Not Named": Willa Cather as a Lesbian Writer,' *Signs* 9 (1984): 576, 577.

50. Perhaps the most literal of such readings is Timothy Dow Adams's 'My Gay Ántonia: The Politics of Willa Cather's Lesbianism,' in *Historical, Literary, and Erotic Aspects of Lesbianism*, ed. Monika Kehoe (New York: Harrington Park Press, 1986), 89–98, in which he argues that 'both Jim and Ántonia were imagined by Willa Cather as homosexuals' (91).

51. Catherine Stimpson, 'Zero Degree Deviancy: The Lesbian Novel in English,' in *Writing and Sexual Difference*, ed. Elizabeth Abel (Chicago: University of Chicago Press, 1982), 244, 246.

52. Judith Fetterley, '*My Ántonia,* Jim Burden, and the Dilemma of the Lesbian Writer,' in *Gender Studies*, ed. Judith Spector (Bowling Green: Bowling Green State University Popular Press, 1986), 43.

53. Bonnie Zimmerman, 'What has never been: an overview of lesbian feminist criticism,' in *The New Feminist Criticism*, ed. Elaine Showalter (New York: Pantheon Books, 1985), 207.

54. Joanna Russ, 'To Write "Like a Woman": Transformations of Identity in the Work of Willa Cather,' in Kehoe, *Historical, Literary and Erotic Aspects of Lesbianism*, 81, 83.

55. O'Brien, 'The Thing Not Named,' 597, 598.

56. At least a part of this interpretive emphasis can be attributed to the ambivalence in O'Brien's essay vis-à-vis its own stance toward a lesbian reading. For though O'Brien turns her argument toward ambiguity and openendedness halfway through the essay ['In deciding whether to define Willa Cather as a lesbian writer and then in determining her individual experience of lesbianism, we cannot use silence—her failure to weave the emotional threads central to her life directly into her fiction—as a clear basis for deduction' (ibid., 580)], her wariness at using silence as the basis for interpretation contradicts her suggestive, but nonetheless unambiguous, reading that 'the thing not named' signifies lesbianism in the essay's opening pages.

57. Deborah Lambert, 'The Defeat of a Hero: Autonomy and Sexuality in *My Ántonia*,' *American Literature* 53 (1982): 677.

58. Zimmerman, 'What has never been,' 214.

59. These quotations from *Willa Cather on Writing* can be found in 'On *The Professor's House*' (30), 'On *Shadows on the Rock*' (14), and 'On *Death Comes for the Archbishop*' (12).

60. Bohlke, *Willa Cather in Person*, 169. All further references to this work will appear in the text.

61. Susan J. Rosowski, 'Willa Cather's Women,' *Studies in American Fiction* 9, no. 2 (1981): 274.

62. Gilbert and Gubar, *Sexchanges*, 173. Compare Rosowski's argument that 'Cather focuses squarely on the implications for women of cultural myths concerning them' ('Willa Cather's Women,' 265).

63. See Susan J. Rosowski's important essay, 'Willa Cather's Subverted Endings and Gendered Time,' in *Cather Studies*, vol. 1, ed. Susan J. Rosowski (Lincoln: University of Nebraska Press, 1990), 68–88. My own study expands and builds upon much of Rosowski's earlier work.

64. O'Brien, *Willa Cather: The Emerging Voice*, 41.

65. Adrienne Munich, 'Notorious signs, feminist criticism and literary tradition,' *Making a Difference: Feminist Literary Criticism*, ed. Gayle Green and Coppélia Kahn (London: Methuen, 1985), 250–51.

66. Ross Chambers, *Story and Situation: Narrative Seduction and the Power of Fiction* (Minneapolis: University of Minnesota Press, 1984), 26.

67. See, for instance, the New Historicist approach to Cather illustrated by Walter Benn Michaels's, 'The Vanishing American,' *American Literary History* 2 (Summer 1990): 220–41.

68. Merrill Maguire Skaggs, *After the World Broke in Two: The Later Novels of Willa Cather* (Charlottesville: University Press of Virginia, 1990), 10.

Gender Studies

172
From Performing Heroinism: The Myth of Corinne

◆

ELLEN MOERS

[. . .] From George Sand's *Consuelo* (1842) to Willa Cather's *Song of the Lark* (1915), the prima donna justified the myth of Corinne; the miracle of operatic performance served as could no other to show off a woman's genius. For a great voice does indeed transport an audience to an ideal existence, as Mme de Staël wrote of Corinne's tarantella; and it excuses any degree of hyperbole. There is only one voice like it in a century, as Flora Tristan could write of her opera singer heroine in *Méphis;* and readers cannot quibble with Willa Cather's elitism (though we may be troubled by its vehemence) when she says of Thea Kronborg that 'she is uncommon, in a common, common world.'

For the feminist, such as Flora Tristan, the opera singer makes a heroine who is strong, willful, and grand; an international traveler; a solitary, but with a subservient entourage in attendance. Men adore her, but there is no other kind of heroine, not even the saint, who can so plausibly be made a chaste as well as a mature and desirable woman. George Sand keeps Consuelo a virgin, even a married virgin, for more than a thousand pages. And George Eliot has her prima donna, in *Armgart*, reject a nobleman's proposal of marriage in coldly elitist terms:

> Armgart. . . . *Seek the woman you deserve,*
> *All grace, all goodness, who has not yet found*
> *A meaning in her life, nor any end*
> *Beyond fulfilling yours. The type abounds.*
> Graf. *And happily, for the world.*
> Armgart. *Yes, happily.*
> *Let it excuse me that my kind is rare:*
> *Commonness is its own security.*

SOURCE   Ellen Moers, from 'Performing Heroinism: The Myth of Corinne', *Literary Women*, London: Women's Press, 1978, pp. 189–92, 255–9

Mme de Staël put the matter even more drily in relation to literary women. 'Many men prefer,' she wrote in the 1814 preface to her *Letters on Rousseau*, 'wives who are solely involved with household cares . . . and incapable of understanding anything else. It's a matter of taste; and anyway, as the number of distinguished women is very small, those who don't want one have a wide choice.'

Both George Sand and Willa Cather loved the opera and both knew opera singers well; neither novelist had any musical talent. Intimacy without rivalry explains their success with the woman of opera as heroic stand-in for the woman of letters. In the Venetian scenes of *Consuelo*, the Chicago scenes of *The Song of the Lark* (and several Cather short stories), both showed the brutal physical labor, the rigorous technique, and the first-rate training of the singer to be almost as important to her art as the qualities of mind and feeling upon which, as literary artists, they primarily insisted. (Just as did Mrs Gaskell in her portrait of Margaret, the Manchester folk singer, in *Mary Barton*: though blind and working-class, she is a thorough professional.)

George Sand met Pauline Garcia, the model for Consuelo, in 1839; she became a prima donna almost as important in the history of opera as her older sister Maria Malibran. Pauline Garcia married Louis Viardot, the distinguished journalist with whom George Sand collaborated on the *Revue Indépendante*—where *Consuelo* first appeared in 1842: a literary, political, and musical manifesto, as well as a version of the myth of Corinne.

It was the most famous treatment of the opera singer in nineteenth-century fiction, and every woman of more than ordinary distinction read *Consuelo* or at least knew that it was there. Charlotte Brontë read it; her feminist friend Mary Taylor wrote her from New Zealand that it was worth learning French just to read it. George Eliot read it; her friend Sara Hennell wrote her that '*Consuelo* is the only thing to compare with' *The Mill on the Floss*. Elizabeth Barrett cited it to Robert Browning; Queen Victoria found it '*dreadfully* interesting'; and if there was one reason why Willa Cather kept George Sand's portrait over her mantelpiece as late as the 1930s, it was surely *Consuelo*.

Sand's and Cather's opera singers have education without genteel refinement, distinction without birth, and the manners of a queen, an artist, and a woman of the people, all in one. Like real singers too, and in this way significantly different from real actresses, their heroines did not need to be and were not beauties. Consuelo, illegitimate daughter of a gypsy, studies in Venice under Porpora (a real figure: George Sand was writing a historical novel, including personages from early eighteenth-century musical history); she triumphs at the court of Frederick the Great, and along the way acquires the title which she never uses of Countess of Rudolstadt. Thea Kronborg is a girl from the prairies who studies in Chicago; her teacher is a disciple of Theodore Thomas (the real conductor); she triumphs in New York at the Metropolitan and becomes the great Wagnerian soprano of international reputation that Olive Fremstad was in fact. Fremstad was, as much as Willa Cather herself, the model for the heroine of *The Song of the Lark*, Cather's most realistically documented as well as most autobiographical novel. Cather met the Swedish-American singer as a journalist, worshiped her as a friend, and dreaded her reaction to her portrait as heroine. But the soprano reassured her, when they met in Nebraska after *The Song of the Lark* appeared. It was the only such book, Fremstad said, where she felt 'there was something doing' in the artist.

What is Thea Kronborg's secret, someone asks Harsanyi, the piano teacher who first discovers that her musicality is of an operatic nature. '"Her secret? It is every artist's secret"—he waved his hand—"passion. That is all. It is an open secret, and perfectly safe. Like heroism, it is inimitable in cheap materials."' That Cather credo, often quoted, says much about her attitude as a writer; but there is more than passion to the heroine of *The Song of the Lark*. Here is the way Cather handles the beginning of Thea's professional career: the discovery by Harsanyi that she has the makings of a great voice.

Thea has been paying her way in Chicago, including her piano lessons, by singing in a church choir. One night in the Harsanyis' shabby parlor, after their lesson, and after the family dinner to which Thea is invited, the teacher on impulse asks her to sing.

> When she finished, Harsanyi sprang from his chair and dropped lightly upon his toes, a kind of *entre-chat* that he sometimes executed when he formed a sudden resolution, or when he was about to follow a pure intuition, against reason. His wife knew from his manner that he was intensely interested. He went quickly to the piano....
>
> 'Sing *ah–ah* for me, as I indicate.' He kept his right hand on the keyboard and put his left to her throat, placing the tips of his delicate fingers over her larynx. 'Again—until your breath is gone.—Trill between the two tones, always; good! Again; excellent!—Now up—stay there. E and F. Not so good, is it? F is always a hard one.—Now, try the half-tone....'
>
> 'Now, once more; carry it up and then down, *ah—ah.*' He put his hand back to her throat and sat with his head bent, his one eye closed. He loved to hear a big voice throb in a relaxed, natural throat, and he was thinking that no one had ever felt this voice vibrate before. It was like a wild bird that had flown into his studio on Middleton Street from goodness knew how far! No one knew that it had come, or even that it existed; least of all the strange, crude girl in whose throat it beat its passionate wings. What a simple thing it was, he reflected; why had he never guessed it before? Everything about her indicated it—the big mouth, the wide jaw and chin, the strong white teeth, the deep laugh. The machine was so simple and strong, seemed to be so easily operated. She sang from the bottom of herself. Her breath came from down where her laugh came from, the deep laugh which Mrs Harsanyi had once called 'the laugh of the people.' A relaxed throat, a voice that lay on the breath, that had never been forced off the breath; it rose and fell in the air-column like the little balls which are put to shine in the jet of a fountain.

The rough physicality of the scene (the teacher's hand on Thea's throat) —the inelegant surroundings—the absence of sexual overtones—the twangy Americanisms—all set off the image of the bird and of the fountain, so exquisitely phrased, which Cather uses to make her point about the otherwordly quality of genius, that uncommon thing, which is to take possession of her heroine and command of her public. But just as much as Corinne's, Thea's genius is the kind that demands, that cannot exist without public response, vibrating here for the first time in the fingers of the piano teacher.

[. . .]

The female landscape knows no nationality or century. George Sand's *Vallée-Noire*, as described for example at the beginning of *Le Meunier d'Angibault*, with its rough and dusky terrain, its *traînes* or twisting lanes leading to stagnant pools, is something more than a real place in Le Berry; it is, as Sand writes, 'a continual enchantment for the imagination, with very real dangers for those who, adventurously, . . . attempt these seductive, capricious, and prefidious detours.' And Isak Dinesen's Africa, which she said was 'a landscape that had not its like in all the world,' is remarkably like the landscapes Willa Cather saw on the mesa and on the Divide.

The very names that women writers have given to their personal landscapes—indeed, have imposed on their homeland through sheer force of language—are sexually suggestive: the Black Valley, the Divide, the Red Deeps; the first and the third of these names were entirely George Sand's and George Eliot's inventions. Before raising the serious question of the relationship of these places to external reality and to the literature they inspired, I should perhaps deal with the more trivial problem of embarrassment itself—the awkwardness of discussing female sexual imagery in women's literature.

Embarrassment was certainly my own reaction when accidentally, because of Gertrude Stein, I began to find a proliferation of this material in women's literature; and as I tried to lecture or write about it, felt concerned that even to raise the subject would tend to insult the memory and downgrade the writing of the greatest among women writers. The austere dignity of Willa Cather gave me pause, for in her work the female landscape is either a central issue or it is not there at all; Cather's greatness, finally, resides not in her womanliness as a writer but in the bardic role she played in the history of the prairie land. 'The history of every country begins in the heart of a man or a woman': no line she wrote can more justly be quoted in tribute to her work.

Reflection, however, brought an end to embarrassment and produced this chapter; for why should female eroticism be less important or more demeaning to literary criticism than male eroticism? Common observation and common sense, well before the age of American sexual sociology, have long informed us that women like men have sexual desires; and sexual parts conducive through sight and touch to female sexual pleasure. Surely it would be more insulting to assume that those women writers who worked on the deepest level of the imagination toward the creation of literature should have entirely ignored their own bodies and sensations as sources for metaphor. Common sense also taught us, long ago, that Portnoy's complaint is hardly of an exclusively masculine nature; and that virgin girls are no more shut out from sexual experience than their male counterparts. In women's literature of the nineteenth century especially, the Child is here as elsewhere Mother to the Woman.

Let us therefore call a spade a spade—and there I am brought to a full stop, because the first metaphor that comes to mind is entirely inappropriate to this subject; what am I to call it? Language itself, the material which women writers have for centuries been refashioning to their needs, is at fault. For the female landscape there should be a term equivalent to 'phallic symbol,' to employ in civil discourse without raising a snigger of embarrassment. No one, surely, thought of Carlyle as a foul-mouthed old man when, in the *Latter-Day Pamphlets*, he fulminated against the '*new* astonishing Phallus-Worship' of the age, 'with universal Balzac-Sand melodies and litanies.' No one, surely, reflected at the time that 'Phallus-Worship' might apply to Balzac, but would never do for George Sand.

Phallus is an *un*embarrassing word because it is Greek, meaning *penis*, which is Latin and somewhat less easy to use; the only English equivalents are unacceptable. Furthermore, in English usage *phallus* refers to an *image* of the male organ which in various lands and eras has been an object of veneration (as equivalent female images have been as well). By extension, therefore, *phallus* serves as an iconographical term, with little anatomical reference remaining, for a symbol in literature as well as art and ritual. What the criticism of women's literature requires is an equivalent female term, which does not, I believe, exist. If there is anything the recent wide availability of printed pornography has taught us, it is the meagerness in layman's English of sexual terms.

The terms of female sex that do exist were clearly fabricated by a male mind, back before the days of widespread female literacy. For example, the term for the canal leading to and from the womb is *vagina*, Latin for sheath or scabbard: thus only a single function of the canal, and biologically its less important, is evoked—that of a tight receptacle for the male organ, visualised as a sword. (As passageway to life for the newborn infant, the canal walls miraculously stretch and expand as no scabbard or sheath can do.) Even were the word *vagina* less biased toward masculine interest, the canal it refers to has almost no place, so far as I have discovered, in the female literary imagination (just as, all recent medical studies indicate, it has no nerve endings, no sensual outlet to consciousness). Instead, the female landscape is that 'complicated topography' to which Freud referred: external, accessible, a prominent, uneven terrain, not a hidden passageway or chamber.

The womb, as we all know, is the most important female organ, but where it is and what it is like is information available only to the medical specialist, not to writers of either sex. (Neither of the ancient words for womb would therefore serve our present purpose: the Latin, *uterus*; or the Greek, *hystera*, with its old-fashioned psychoanalytical associations, quite unscientifically based.) *Pubes* is the Latin word and our for the pubic hair of both sexes; *vulva*, from the Latin, refers principally to an opening, not to a complex totality; and *pudenda*, which used to be genteelly translated as the private parts, derives from the Latin word for shame, which is what we are trying to dispense with.

Mons Veneris at least offers geographical suggestions, but they are the wrong ones: mountain (*mons*), as we don't need Freud to tell us, is descriptive of the male organ but not the female, which is hilly, high-lying, and hard in the female landscapes of literature, but never Alpine. And *Veneris* shows once again that a man, not a woman, invented the term: for the mountain of Venus is a place sacred to heterosexual love and masculine worship, not a Temple of Solitude consecrated to Diana, the goddess of virgins.

It would be easy enough to invent a female equivalent for 'phallic symbol' by combining the Greek for place (*topos*) as in topography; and some form of the Greek for woman which gives us words like gynecology. But the air of literary debate is already so littered with Greek words used by critics who share my own ignorance of Greek and access to a dictionary that I don't have the heart for perpetrating further damage to literary ecology. I do suggest, however, that nothing be done with the female term. Ivy Compton-Burnett heard as a child from her doctor father (who was of the homeopathic persuasion): 'pelvic power.'

Willa Cather's dissatisfaction with *The Song of the Lark*, which she severely cut and virtually repudiated in 1932 on the occasion of its republication, extended to more than its title, for it is a cluttered, disorganised work with too much detail drawn from her own and Olive Fremstad's biography, and too little evidence of the Cather fire which, especially in the short novels of the 1920s, burned away all impurities. Still, far down as *The Song of the Lark* must be placed in the Cather scale, there are wonderful things in the novel, as well as the most thoroughly elaborated female landscape in literature. The whole Panther Cañon section of the novel (Part IV: 'The Ancient People') is concerned with female self-assertion in terms of landscape; and the dedication to female landscape carries with it here the fullest possible tally of spiritual, historical, national, and artistic associations. Whether Cather's later dissatisfaction with the novel included a realisation of the unguarded sexuality of her cañon topography there is no way to know.

'Panther Cañon was like a thousand others,' it begins,

> —one of those abrupt fissures with which the earth in the Southwest is riddled. ... It was accessible only at its head. The cañon walls, for the first two hundred feet below the surface, were perpendicular cliffs, striped with even-running strata of rock. From there on to the bottom the sides were less abrupt, were

shelving, and lightly fringed with piñons and dwarf cedars. The effect was that of a gentler cañon within a wilder one. The dead city lay at the point where the perpendicular outer wall ceased and the V-shaped inner gorge began. There a stratum of rock, softer than those above, had been hollowed out by the action of time until it was like a deep groove. . . .

The associations come tumbling out. Thea explores 'the long horizontal groove' of the cañon. She inspects the deserted, prehistoric ruins of the Ancient People—'clean with the cleanness of sun-baked, wind-swept places.' She moves in alone, with nothing but a blanket, to take up residence in one of the ruined rooms. There she discovers the pottery made by the Indian women, 'their most direct appeal to water, the envelope and sheath of the precious element itself.' She bathes in a pool hidden at the bottom of the cañon and, as the sun and water strike her body, ponders the relationship between the stream, the pottery—and her own art: 'what was any art but an effort to make a sheath, a mould in which to imprison for a moment the shinning, elusive element which is life itself?' Her own artistic commitment makes her one with the Indian women, who with their pottery began the creation of beauty

> even here, in this crack in the world, so far back in the night of the past! Down here at the beginning, that painful thing was already stirring; the seed of sorrow, and of so much delight.

Thea relishes her aloneness: it is a physical sensation—'keenly alive, lying on that insensible shelf of stone, when her body bounded like a rubber ball away from its hardness.' She perceives that this physical vitality—'a lightness in the body and a driving power in the blood'—is the source of her art; of her voice as a singer. She makes then a decision that is a major turning point: toward study in Germany, away from family life. She will risk everything on 'older and higher obligations' rather 'than meekly draw the plough under the rod of parental guidance.' Then her lover arrives; he discovers that Thea is 'not a nesting-bird'; and the great golden eagle comes sailing across the sky over the cañon. 'From a cleft in the heart of the world she saluted it. . . .'

The first point to be made about this section of *The Song of the Lark* is that it rests on an actual episode in the life of Willa Cather the writer, not of Olive Fremstad the opera singer. In the spring of 1912 Cather left New York and her work on *McClure's* to vist her brother in the Southwest, where she explored cañons and Indian ruins. For various reasons the experience was crucial, providing for Cather the means of self-discovery as woman and artist; from it we date her serious beginnings as a novelist.

But the second thing that must be said is that this plainly sexual landscape closely parallels other places evoked by women writers for the same purpose of solitary, feminine assertion. (All are outdoor places, with one interesting partial exception, the hard, uneven terrain of the courtyard of the German school where Miriam, the heroine of Dorothy Richardson's *Pilgrimage*, affirms her female solitude.) The height, the sky, the horizontal vistas, the aboriginal openness, the dry hard ground, the pottery colors, even the 'light delicate foliage . . . in horizontal layers . . . a strange appearance as if the whole wood were faintly vibrating' are in Isak Dinesen's Africa as well as in Cather country; and exultation is sounded by both writers. Dinesen writes: 'In the highlands you woke up in the morning and thought: Here I am, where I ought to be.'

The whole opening chapter of *Out of Africa* is so exquisitely phrased, so deserving of its place as a classic of modern English prose (by a writer whose native language was Danish!) that Dinesen leads at once to the third point: whatever component of sexuality enters into these literary landscapes, its inspirational residue is of the highest, not the lowest order.

Cather's greatest prose as a landscapist is not in *The Song of the Lark*, but in other works where she returns, more in control, to the mesaland: 'Tom Outland's Story' in *The Professor's House*, and in *Death Comes for the Archbishop*. The greatest of her landscapes are those inspired by the land she knew best, the Nebraska prairies, in *O Pioneers!* and *My Ántonia*, and some of her stories. The same sense of earthbound ecstasy fills them all, of physical dissolution on a limitless, undulating, high-lying plain under a limitless sky; of a solitary, primordial land antecedent to, perhaps hostile to human life. 'There seemed to be nothing to see,' she writes through the eyes of Jim Burden, the narrator of *My Ántonia*, who is transported at the age of ten from the lush mountain valleys of Virginia to the barren open land of frontier Nebraska, much as Willa Cather was herself. 'There was nothing but land; not a country at all, but the material out of which countries are made. . . . Between that earth and that sky I felt erased, blotted out.'

173
Willa Cather: 1876–1947

JANE RULE

For Willa Cather, an almost exact contemporary of Gertrude Stein, the question of being publicly identified as a lesbian never surfaced. She called those biographers who try to reduce great artists to psychological cripples, explaining away their gifts and visions in neuroses and childhood traumas, 'tomb breakers.' In her will she ordered that none of her letters be quoted. Elizabeth Shepley Sergeant, her friend and one of her biographers, explains, 'The prose she used in friendly correspondence was colloquial, vivid, frank, at times emotional, more like her casual talk than the subtle, equable prose she developed in her finest novels and stories. She feared the betrayal, in print, of that heat and abundance that surged up in her. In her art she transformed heat to a plasticity. . . .'[1] Perhaps the most intimate and important letters Willa Cather wrote were those to Isabelle McClung, with whom she had lived sporadically from 1901 to 1915, when Isabelle McClung married. At her death in 1938 those letters were returned to Willa Cather, who week by week burned bundles of them until they were all destroyed. Edith Lewis, Willa Cather's most intimate friend, in her modest and perceptive biography, originally undertaken only as notes for an official biographer, says, 'I have written about Willa Cather as I knew her; but with the feeling it is not in any form of biographical writing, but in art alone, that the deepest truth about human beings is to be found.'[2] In this account, Willa Cather's relationships with other people are mentioned only when they fire her imagination for a book, as her friendship with the singer Olive Fremstad provided material for *The Song of the Lark*; or when they take her away from her writing, as happened in both her mother's and Isabelle McClung Hambourg's long dying.

Later critics and biographers are restive about a lack of frankness in these dealings with Willa Cather's life. James Schroeter, in a discussion of Willa Cather's supposed anti-Semitism, suggests that, since Isabelle McClung's

SOURCE Jane Rule, 'Willa Cather: 1876–1947', *Lesbian Images*, Trumansburg, NY: Crossing Press, 1982, pp. 74–87

husband was Jewish, 'the hatred, I believe, has two separate roots. The deepest was a psychological root, which so far has resisted efforts people have made to drag it into light—although some day, if the picture of Willa Cather as a frank, hearty westerner with a taste for French cooking is ever going to be replaced by a picture of more complex reality, it will have to be.'[3] Lionel Trilling diagnoses what he sees as her failing creative power in her last novels with a similar suggestiveness. 'It has always been a personal failure of her talent that prevented her from involving her people in truly dramatic relations with each other. (Her women, for example, always stand in the mother or daughter relation to men; they are never truly lovers.) But at least once upon a time her people were involved in a dramatic relationship with themselves or with their environments.'[4] John H. Randall III warns, 'But I believe she is dangerously idiosyncratic in seeing spontaneous relations between the sexes as being uniformly dangerous and unrewarding as she makes them out to be. This view reflects her own particular upbringing and temperament—particularly the latter—and it severely limits her art.'[5]

None of these critical observations is true. Willa Cather hated neither the Jewish character, Louie Marsellus, in *The Professor's House*, as any careful reading of the book would make clear, nor Isabelle McClung's husband, to whom the book is dedicated. The women in her novels are often essentially lovers, and in *My Ántonia*, the book Willa Cather herself liked most, Ántonia's marriage is as fine and unsentimental a portrait of domestic happiness as there is in fiction. These grossly inaccurate critical generalisations can only be explained by a desire of each of these men to imply that Willa Cather's 'basic psychology,' 'personal failure,' or 'temperament' negatively influenced her vision. What they want out in the light of day is her emotional and erotic preference for women, and, if they cannot have irrefutable biographical facts or cannot use them in print, they will distort their reading of her fiction to make their discrediting point. No lesbian can write about heterosexual experience without 'dangerous idiosyncrasy' which must therefore be found in Willa Cather's work whether it is there or not.

There is enough evidence, even in the most circumspect of the earliest biographical material, to indicate that for Willa Cather men were great friends and companions but of no interest to her erotically. She excused herself from marriage on the grounds that she was married to her art, but that did not prevent her from living with the McClung family in Pittsburgh for nine years, sharing a bedroom with Isabelle, using an attic room as a study. When she moved to New York finally to take a better job, she lived with Edith Lewis, a relationship which lasted until Willa Cather's death in 1947. James Woodress, her most recent biographer, describes Isabelle McClung as 'the one great romance of her life'[6] and Edith Lewis as 'a rival for Willa Cather's affection'[7] because Willa Cather was dividing her time between her houshold with Edith Lewis in New York and the McClung household in Pittsburgh long before Judge McClung died and Isabelle married.

Whatever the erotic content of these relationships, they were practically very different. Isabelle was a beautiful young woman from a wealthy Pittsburgh family with a connoisseur's interest in the arts. She and Willa Cather met in the dressing room of an actress they both admired. Willa Cather's position in the McClung household was obviously a compromise, for Isabelle put it to her father that either Willa Cather stayed there or Isabelle left home. Willa Cather was not making enough money during those years in journalism and schoolteaching to support herself very comfortably, and she and Isabelle could not have taken holidays in New England and Europe without Judge McClung's approval and subsidy.

In 1915, when Willa Cather was living in New York, she was offered an opportunity to go to Germany to write articles there, and she wanted Isabelle to go with her. Judge McClung vetoed the trip, and Willa Cather finally went instead to the South-west with Edith Lewis. That fall, when Judge McClung died, leaving Isabelle rich and independent, she chose to marry Jan Hambourg, a violinist. Elizabeth Sergeant suggests that the loss of both the sanctuary of the McClung household, where Willa Cather had been able to write, and of Isabelle were emotionally devastating. Still it was not long after these events that Willa Cather was writing *My Ántonia*, her most serene and loving book. She visited with the Hambourgs, and, though she never went to stay for months at a time as they suggested she might, even setting up special rooms in their house for her, she was with Isabelle, tending her for some time during her final illness. Isabelle's death was a great grief, for it seemed to Willa Cather that Isabelle was the one person for whom all her books were written.

Friends and biographers have much less to say about Edith Lewis. Her own book makes it clear that she shared not only a domestic life with Willa Cather for nearly forty years but also was her companion in many of her travels and was often with her in late years at the island retreat they built. She worked with Willa Cather, proofreading manuscripts, a task she describes as one of their greatest pleasures. But Edith Lewis doesn't intrude on the scene she describes. She had work of her own to do. When Willa Cather was making an excellent living from her writing and would have much preferred to live away from New York, she did not move because Edith Lewis enjoyed her job in the city. The only direct comment Elizabeth Sergeant makes about their relationship is: 'Though they had gone their own ways and lived their own lives, their companionship was deeply founded and delightful.'[8] If Edith Lewis did not cut the romantic figure in Willa Cather's life assigned to Isabelle McClung, neither did she become a secretary-companion like Amy Lowell's actress or a colorful wife like Alice B. Toklas. She has no public image at all.

Willa Cather's burning of her letters to Isabelle and her refusal to have any of her letters quoted were minor gestures in a whole pattern of protecting her personal life so that she and those she loved could live without the invasions and distortions of fame.

The choice of privacy does not seem surprising under the circumstances until one looks at Willa Cather as an adolescent and very young woman. The oldest child of a large family, growing up in a small town in Nebraska, she was not averse to being different and making that difference obvious. At fifteen, she cut her hair like a boy's, wore masculine clothes, took male parts in plays, and signed her name 'William Cather, M.D.' In a friend's album she answered stock questions with good-humored lack of self-protection.

> The trait I admire most in a woman: Flirting
> The trait I admire most in a man: an original mind
> The fault for which I have the most toleration in another person: passion
> The fault for which I have the least toleration in another person: lack of nerve
> The qualification or accomplishments I most desire in a matrimonial partner: lamblike meekness
> As a traveling companion, I would most highly appreciate: a cultured gentleman
> The greatest wonder according to my estimation is: a good looking woman.[9]

Her college classmates and some of her early students remember her as masculine in dress, voice, and manner.

After her second year in college, she was persuaded to let her hair grow and modify her dress. She did not modify her aggressive manner of mind, her hard judgments of anything second rate in the arts. Edith Lewis describes her when she first met her in Lincoln as 'a young, rebellious mind, impatient of all camouflage.'[10] 'She was naturally a very fearless person, fearless in matters of thought, of social convention.'[11] Even as late as in her thirties, when Elizabeth Sergeant first met her, Willa Cather gave the impression of 'a powerful, almost masculine personality.'[12] 'This Miss Cather filled the whole space between door and window to brimming, as a man might do.'[13] Yet those who had expected her to become what was then called 'bohemain' did not reckon with her economically conservative needs or her desire to be admired and respected by those she cared about. Her habitual attachments to women of accomplishment and refinement transformed her from a brash, self-advertising adolescent from a raw Nebraska town into a cultured woman who commanded great respect for her integrity of mind and literary gifts. She not only no longer needed to attract attention to herself, she needed to protect her privacy for her work and those close to her.

Most interpreters of Willa Cather's work sooner or later remark on her 'masculine sensibility' either in noting her preference for male narrators or her realistic and therefore not flattering explorations of heterosexual relationships. For some it is a virtue which places her above the more delicate and limited talents of other women writers. Others, like John H. Randall III, make personal accusations: 'she could accept fertility in crops more easily than in human beings, the reason being her fear of physical passion and the dependence on others which it entails.'[14] In an introduction to *My Mortal Enemy*, Marcus Klein quotes from an essay on Katherine Mansfield by Willa Cather: 'Human relationships are the tragic necessity of human life; that they can never be wholly satisfactory, that every ego is half the time greedily seeking them, and half the time pulling away from them.'[15] He goes on to suggest a thesis for examining all Willa Cather's fiction: 'it is the struggle to get beyond the necessity of human relationships that is the secret history of all Willa Cather's novels, only as time went on, as the struggle turned, one supposes, more desperate, its nature becomes more apparent.'[16] Elizabeth Sergeant sees this theme in Willa Cather as sourced in 'the passion which takes a woman of exceptional gifts away from the usual instinctive woman's lot of marriage and children to fulfill a directive that is altogether impersonal.'[17]

What actually characterises Willa Cather's mind is not a masculine sensibility at all but a capacity to transcend the conventions of what is masculine and what is feminine to see the more complex humanity of her characters. Ántonia, the character who so richly fulfills 'the usual instinctive woman's lot' in a remarkably happy marriage and fine, loving sons, has physical strength and vitality as well as warmth, tenderness, and compassion. 'Oh, better I like to work out of doors than in the house . . . I not care that your grandmother says it makes me like a man. I like to be like a man.'[18] In the frontier of Nebraska only those with such strength and pleasure in it can survive. Ántonia's father, a frail, gentle artist, commits suicide in despair at crop failures and harsh winters. Willa Cather does not judge him. And she understands, too, Lena Lingard, who chooses to go to Lincoln and run a dress shop rather than marry. 'She remembered home as a place where there were always too many children, a cross man, and work piling up around a sick woman.'[19]

Willa Cather's method of creating character is to submerge herself in that character, to achieve a total sympathy which will render the character authentically, inevitably, past judgment. Even the morally most objectionable of her characters, by this method, commands compassion and even at times admiration. Myra, the main character in *My Mortal Enemy*, has married against her rich uncle's wishes, been disowned, and created a myth about herself because she has lived 'for love.' The destruction of that myth is the intention of the novel in which Myra's cynicism and misery become more and more apparent. Early in the story, she is making remarks like 'Love itself draws a woman nearly all the bad luck in the world; why, for mercy's sake, add opals?'[20] She speculates about a developing love affair: 'very likely hell will come of it.'[21] Much later she diagnoses her own failure. 'We were never really happy. I am a greedy, selfish, worldly woman; I wanted success and a place in the world.'[22] Her husband is gallant and gentle with her through illness, preserving the illusion of their relationship through all her denials of it. He even survives her final question: 'Why must I die like this, alone with my mortal enemy?'[23] Though her own evaluation of herself is accurate, the ruthless honesty of her judgment and the pure energy of her anger are somehow admirable. The book is not a condemnation of marriage any more than *My Ántonia* is propaganda for marriage. It is an accurate portrait of a woman who exchanged self-knowledge for illusion and consciously suffered the consequences.

Willa Cather can be just as sympathetic with a woman who is frailly feminine, like Mrs Forrester in *A Lost Lady*, a woman who is entirely dependent on her husband's strength, integrity, and social position to give her a protective atmosphere in which to charm everyone. When he loses his money and becomes ill, she turns where she can for support and approval, even to Ivy Peters, a crude young lawyer who despises and envies all she stands for. Though Niel Herbert, the narrator, is shocked and disillusioned by her affairs, he stays protective and half in love with Mrs Forrester through her decline. Instead of judging her harshly, he comes instead to admire her husband more, to see in him not only the traditional masculine virtues of strength and integrity but also the insight and compassion reflected in his attitude toward his wife.

Though many male writers have been concerned with the role and nature of the artist, Willa Cather is nearly alone among female writers in her preoccupation with this theme. Most of the stories in *Youth and the Bright Medusa* deal with artists, and two of her novels, *Lucy Gayheart* and *The Song of the Lark*, are studies of women artists, a pianist and a singer.

Lucy Gayheart, though set apart by her talent and vitality from childhood, 'the parlor cat'[24] as compared to her older sister's 'kitchen cat,' is constitutionally dependent, afraid to acknowledge her gift even to herself, and lacking in ambition. Her relationship with Harry Gordon, the most eligible young man in the small town where she grows up, is a real alternative to a musical career. 'Lucy shut her eyes and leaned on Harry's shoulder to escape from what she had gone so far to snatch. It was too bright and too sharp. It hurt, and made one feel small and lost.'[25] When she goes to Chicago to study, she is not driven by her own needs but by her infatuation with a singer, Clement Sebastian, for whom she is to play.

> She had never been nervous when Auerbach [her teacher] asked her to play for his friends; he had told her this was because she was not ambitious—and that was her greatest fault. But this time it was different. If she didn't please Sebastian, she would probably never meet him again. If she did please him— But that possibility frightened her more than the other.[26]

The relationship that develops between them is not sexual. 'He sometimes thought of her as rather boyish, because she was so square. It was more like a chivalrous loyalty than a young passion.'[27] Sebastian is probably a decorous portrait of a homosexual since, except for Lucy, his most important relationships have been with an adopted boy who had to be sent away because Sebastian's wife became jealous, a male friend of his youth, and his male accompanist. When Harry comes to Chicago to press Lucy to marry him, she untruthfully confesses that Sebastian is her lover as the only way to explain her real passion, which is the music she shares with him. When Sebastian and his accompanist are killed in a boating accident, Lucy has a breakdown and returns home, needing to make some contact with Harry, even though she knows that he has married. 'If he should put his hand on her, or look directly into her eyes and flash the old signal, she believed it would waken something and start the machinery going to carry her along.'[28] There is no one, now that Sebastian is dead, to encourage her. Her Chicago teacher has said to her,

> 'In the musical profession there are many disappointments. A nice house and a garden in a little town with money enough not to worry, a family — that's the best life.... Even for women of great talent and great ambition — I don't know. Some have good success, but I don't envy them.'[29]

Mrs Ramsey, the town's wise woman who is concerned about Lucy, gives her these clichés: 'I don't like to see young people with talent take it too seriously. Life is short; gather roses while you may.' 'Nothing really matters but living — accomplishments are the ornaments of life, they come second.'[30] Against these views is set one frail evening, during which Lucy hears a soprano in a traveling show. 'She felt she must run away tonight, by any train, back to a world that strove after excellence.'[31] Lucy is killed before her resolve can be tested, but it seems clear that she did not have the toughness and independence of spirit necessary for any artist, particularly a woman, to survive and perfect her gift.

Thea Kronburg, in *The Song of the Lark*, is a different breed of woman, one who recognises her gift and holds it to herself against any damage. She is not only not frightened of it but knows that it is both center and goal. In the small community where she lives, she associates with those few people who will help nurture her as an artist: Dr Archie, who recognises early that she is an unusual child, lends her books, takes her on his rounds, talks seriously with her; Mr Wunsch, her alcoholic music teacher who is considered too disreputable by most people in the town to be suitable as a music teacher for their children; Spanish Johnny, a Mexican with fine natural musicianship and a passion for his art. Thea's mother does what she can to give her gifted daughter space to grow, and Ray Kennedy, a sentimental railway man, who dreams of marrying her when she is old enough, is more usefully killed in an accident, his life insurance money left to Thea so that she can go to Chicago to continue her studies. She works her teachers as hard as she works herself, studying first piano and then voice. Without social grace, with only the strength and vitality of her gift, she is in a pure way ruthless.

Exhausted from study and trying to earn a living, she goes home for a rest, but, as she later reflects on a better kind of holiday in Arizona,

> There was certainly no kindly Providence that directed one's life; and one's parents did not in the least care what became of one, so long as one did not misbehave and endanger their comfort. One's life was at the mercy of blind chance. She had better take it in her own hands and lose everything than meekly draw

the plough under the rod of parental guidance. She had seen it when she was at home last summer—the hostility of comfortable, self-satisfied people toward serious effort. Even to her father it seemed indecorous. Whenever she spoke seriously, he looked apologetic. Yet she had clung fast to whatever was left of Moonstone in her mind. No more of that! The Cliff-Dwellers had lengthened her past. She had older and higher obligations.[32]

Willa Cather is as willful with the plot as Thea is with her life. She provides Thea with Fred Ottenburg, a rich young businessman and music lover who has the intelligence and sensitivity to understand her, who wants nothing more of his own life than to serve her and help her in her career. But Willa Cather also provides him with a wife so that he can't clutter up Thea's emotional life as she begins her rigorous training for opera. Dr Archie provides the money for her to go to Germany, from which she does not return even for her mother's illness and death because her career is at a crucial point. In a triumphant return to New York, she appears to the people who have loved and helped her to be totally absorbed in her singing without anything left for them. 'I have no private life,'[33] she explains. In an epilogue, she finally marries Fred Ottenburg, but her life has been one in which both she and other people have had to make great personal sacrifices. The triumph of her art exacts a price higher than most are willing to pay. When one of her teachers is asked for the secret of her success, he answers simply, 'Passion,' the fault Willa Cather from girlhood is most willing to forgive.

Willa Cather knew she had put much of herself as well as her friend, Olive Fremstad, into the portrait of Thea Kronburg. Olive Fremstad said, when she had read the book, she could not tell where she left off and Willa Cather began. Though Willa Cather gave a great deal of personal time to her family and attended her mother's last illness, she understood how much of herself must be reserved for her work. There is no condemnation of Thea Kronburg by those who care for her. They come to understand her position, and the loss of a personal life is not presented as a great grief against the fierce joy of a fulfilled and fulfilling voice. The book is dedicated to Isabelle McClung.

The character in which critics most identify Willa Cather is not Thea Kronburg but St Peter, the main character in *The Professor's House*. 'He is what Willa Cather herself has always been or hoped to be—a pioneer in mind, a Catholic by instinct, French by inclination, a Spiritual aristocrat with democratic manners.'[34] Not only are his tastes and accomplishments similar to those of Willa Cather, but the crisis he is going through seems one which might parallel Willa Cather's loss of her old writing room at the McClung's and of Isabelle.

No novel by a writer of real gifts should be read as veiled autobiography. All successful fiction is transformed and transcended biography. Willa Cather often acknowledged one or several models, as well as identification with aspects of many of her characters, and she knew that the best material for fiction is what is in the writer's natural domain.

A creative writer can do his best only with what lies within range and character of his deepest sympathies[35] . . . It is a common fallacy that a writer, if he is talented enough can achieve this poignant quality by improving upon his subject matter, by using his 'imagination' upon it and twisting it to suit his purpose. The truth is by such a process (which is not imaginative at all!) he can at best produce only a brilliant sham which, like a badly built house, looks poor and shabby after a few years.[36]

The Professor's House is an authentic building, obviously drawing on the deep sources of Willa Cather's experience and perception. It is not, however, an inexact translation of her personal life.

St Peter is a successful, middle-aged scholar with a wife and two married daughters. Prize money from publications has made it possible for him to build a new house, and one of his sons-in-law has made a lot of money commercialising another man's discovery. When St Peter refuses to move his study out of the old house and excuses himself from a trip to France his son-in-law has planned for the family, St Peter gives himself the opportunity to examine the effect material success has had on all of them. His daughters, who have been very close, are now envious and suspicious of each other. His wife is entirely enamored of her successful son-in-law, and St Peter finds himself indifferent to them all. His chief attachment is to young Tom Outland, killed in the war, whose story is told in a separate section of the book. In Tom are all the values of youth with its passion and integrity, the very things everyone has now lost. St Peter's brooding and his increasing dread of his family's return make him careless of his own safety, and he is nearly killed by a faulty stove in his old study. Augusta, the stolid Catholic seamstress, finds him in time. He seems resigned to being alive. 'Theoretically he knew that life is possible, maybe even pleasant, without joy, without passionate griefs. But it had never occurred to him that he might have to live like that.'[37] For a man who really loved his wife, his children, his work, 'surely the saddest thing in the world is falling out of love.'[38] One of the most telling observations in the book is 'the complexion of a man's life was largely determined by how well or ill his original self and his nature as modified by sex rubbed on together,'[39] those two perhaps very different, intimately connected parts of the human personality. St Peter's obviously were wearing mortally thin.

Willa Cather suffered crises of her own, some of them perhaps related to the conflict between her original self and the self modified by her own sexual nature. She certainly knew the profound discomforts as well as the pleasures of success. And she shared with St Peter the horror of what is lost in the worship of material progress. But it was Willa Cather's vitality and passion which created *The Professor's House*, and she was to go on from there to write her greatest book, *Death Comes for the Archbishop*.

Willa Cather wrote two books about French Catholics in the new world, *Death Comes for the Archbishop* and *Shadows on the Rock*, and Catholicism is Myra's refuge in *My Mortal Enemy*, hinted at also for St Peter when he is rescued by

Augusta. Willa Cather was not a Catholic. When she finally was confirmed, she joined the Episcopal Church with her parents, the closest alternative which still allowed the Protestant privacy of individual conscience. Her sympathy with the Catholic Church and her knowledge of it made many of her Catholic readers assume she was one of them, an error which gave her great pleasure.

Though Willa Cather did not write a book about love between women, *Death Comes for the Archbishop* is, among many other things, the study of a relationship between two men, Bishop Latour and Father Valliant, vowed to celibacy as French Catholic missionaries in the Southwest. Their attachment to each other from the time they are boys together studying for the priesthood in France to Father Valliant's death after years of hard service is quietly developed throughout the book. Father Valliant, a remarkably homely and frail-bodied man, is overtly emotional, friendly, enduring, a man of action. Bishop Latour is an intellectual, handsome and refined in his tastes, naturally an introvert. The two men, during their years as missionaries in the same territory, rarely have the opportunity to be together. If Father Valliant lies ill somewhere in an Indian encampment, Bishop Latour rides out with medicine, grateful to bring his friend home for some period of rest. Occasionally Latour sends for Valliant on no more than a slight pretext simply to have his company, but Valliant is always restless to be at work; at the same time he is sympathetic, for he understands that, while he makes friends easily everywhere, Latour does not. Here is a relationship in which the erotic plays no part, in which work always takes precedence over affectionate need. Though it is neither sentimentalised nor idealised, it is offered as another of the ways human beings relate to each other and to their work.

Willa Cather was a contemporary of D.H. Lawrence, knew him and enjoyed his company. They shared an enthusiasm for the Southwest. Her only critical comment about his work indicates that she resented his literalness about mental reactions and physical sensations as dehumanising, as reducing to 'animal pulp.'[40] She read Gertrude Stein and could not take her seriously. Willa Cather's literary mentor was Henry James, and, though she learned early not to imitate him, to find her own subject matter, her own style, her own creed of art as simplification, she shared his ability to create an enormous range of characters in accurate, limiting, and illuminating environments. Her sexual tastes, like his, extended rather than limited her sensibilities, whatever social and private burden they may sometimes have been to her. Her only 'dangerous idiosyncrasy' is her great gift of perception and craft, which has always made those who are fearful of the truth uncomfortable before it.

Notes

1. Elizabeth Shepley Sergeant, *Willa Cather, a Memoir* (Philadelphia and New York: J.B. Lippincott Co., 1953), p. 9.
2. Edith Lewis, *Willa Cather Living* (New York: Alfred A. Knopf, Inc., 1953), p. vi.

3. James Schroeter (ed.), 'Willa Cather and *The Professor's House,' Willa Cather and Her Critics* (Ithaca: Cornell University Press, 1967), p. 376.
4. Lionel Trilling, 'Willa Cather,' *Willa Cather and Her Critics*, p. 155.
5. John H. Randall III, 'Interpretation of My Ántonia,' *Willa Cather and Her Critics*, p. 320.
6. James Woodress, *Willa Cather, Her Life & Art* (New York: Pegasus, 1970), p. 86.
7. Ibid., p. 92.
8. Sergeant, op. cit., p. 279.
9. Mildred R. Bennett, *The World of Willa Cather* (Lincoln: University of Nebraska Press, 1961), p. 112.
10. Lewis, op. cit., p. 41.
11. Ibid., p. xiv.
12. Sergeant, op. cit., p. 34.
13. Ibid., p. 34.
14. Randall, op. cit., p. 321.
15. Willa Cather, *Not Under Forty* (New York: Alfred A. Knopf, Inc., 1936), p. 136.
16. Marcus Klein, 'Introduction,' *My Mortal Enemy* by Willa Cather (New York: Vantage Book, 1961), p. xv.
17. Sergeant, op. cit., p. 134.
18. Willa Cather, *My Ántonia* (New York: Houghton Mifflin, 1918), p. 157.
19. Ibid., p. 330.
20. Cather, *My Mortal Enemy*, p. 28.
21. Ibid., p. 31.
22. Ibid., p. 75.
23. Ibid., p. 105.
24. Willa Cather, *Lucy Gayheart* (New York: Alfred A. Knopf, Inc., 1935), p. 170.
25. Ibid., p. 12.
26. Ibid., p. 34.
27. Ibid., p. 81.
28. Ibid., p. 175.
29. Ibid., p. 134.
30. Ibid., p. 165.
31. Ibid., p. 181.
32. Willa Cather, *The Song of the Lark* (Cambridge: Houghton Mifflin, Inc., 1915), pp. 307-8.
33. Ibid., p. 455.
34. Alfred Kazin, 'Willa Cather,' *Willa Cather and Her Critics*, p. 168.
35. Cather, *Not Under Forty*, p. 81.
36. Ibid., p. 79.
37. Willa Cather, *The Professor's House* (New York: Alfred A. Knopf, Inc., 1925), p. 282.
38. Ibid., p. 275.
39. Ibid., p. 282.
40. Cather, *Not Under Forty*, p. 51.

174
The Dangers of Femininity in Willa Cather's Fiction

JENNIFER BAILEY

When she was twenty-one, Willa Cather wrote, 'The mind that can follow a "mission" is not an artistic one. An artist can know no other purpose than his art.... The feminine mind has a hankering for hobbies and missions.'[1] From the outset of her writing career as a journalist, Cather was intensely conscious of what to her seemed a difficult anomaly: being a serious writer and being a woman. She believed that women were conditioned to think and write in a literal and 'horribly subjective' fashion, so that their literary productions were 'an infernal mess.'[2] When she embarked on a full-time writing career at the age of thirty-nine, she insisted that to avoid a feminine mind, one must avoid a feminine way of life:

> One must have the power to refuse most of the rest of life ... to be free, to work at [my] table—that *is* all in all.... There are fates and fates but one cannot live them all. Some would call mine servitude but I call it liberation. Miss Jewett too, turned away from marriage.[3]

Cather's single-minded determination to succeed and her uncompromising way of life that would ensure success as a writer rather than a woman writer prompted her to reject her background in her first pieces of fiction. She lived in rural southern Nebraska for seven years, from the ages of ten to seventeen, and in some early short stories she portrayed small-town life on the Plains as narrow, spiritually crushing and dominated by terrible physical hardship.[4] When she first moved East to work as a teacher in Pittsburgh in 1896, her stories dramatised a terrible conflict between the artistic and cultural life of the East and the philistine life of the Mid-West.[5] Yet she learned how to express her artistic ideas through this particular Midwestern setting.

SOURCE Jennifer Bailey, 'The Dangers of Femininity in Willa Cather's Fiction', *Journal of American Studies*, 16, 1982, pp. 391–406.

In 1912, with advice from Jewett to concentrate positively on the land she knew best germinating in her mind, Cather revisited Red Cloud, Nebraska, where she was brought up, then gave up her job as a reporter for S.S. McClure and wrote *O Pioneers!* On the fly-leaf of a copy she gave to a friend, she wrote:

> This is the first time I walked off on my own feet—everything before was half real and half an imitation of writers whom I admired. In this one I hit the home pasture and found that I was Yance Sorgeson and not Henry James.[6]

Beginning with *O Pioneers!*, Cather wrote her own version of frontier settlement in the latter part of the nineteenth century and showed how the courageous and radical vision of the early settlers was displaced in time by an escapist and febrile idealism. This process in Cather's fiction can be analysed by means of her development of the image of the garden, as land enclosed and/or conserved. It is a concept which she terms not only a garden, but also an orchard and, in *The Professor's House*, the Mesa.

In *Virgin Land* (1950), Henry Nash Smith's account of the penetration of the West, the metaphor of the 'Garden of the World' is used to designate the cultivation of land and the development of settlements by male pioneers. If the land before cultivation was virgin, then the settlement that came after was feminine. G.J. Barker Benfield argues that 'American history is in several ways the interplay between male activity construed as free with the heterosexual obligations of settlement.'[7] In this context then, the woman presides over the house and its immediate surroundings. Her function is to personify and perpetuate social and moral values; qualities which are maintained by her very exclusion from the larger, more spacious environment of the farm or ranch. Because the masculine cultural and literary traditions establish the woman in this stronghold, she is of course perceived as both an ideal and a serious threat.

Women's role in the migration westwards was thus often secondary and reactive. Many were forced against their will to follow their husbands or look for jobs as housekeepers in the West and leave their family and friends behind. Faced with the vast and recalcitrant Plains, a pioneer woman could either be terrified by their intimidating space or exalted by a sense of infinite possibility. Some *were* overcome by the strangeness and hardship of the Western environment and the moral and domestic responsibility that attended this way of life. In 1851, a Nebraskan woman wrote, 'These unbounded prairies have such an air of desolation—and the stillness is very oppressive.'[8] Such women succumbed to the scale and uncertainty of cultivation undertaken by their men and barricaded themselves within houses made claustrophobic by the surrounding space—and some went mad. Dorothy Scarborough's novel *The Wind*, published in 1925, and O.E. Rölvaag's *Giants in the Earth*, published in 1927, record the progressive insanity of such women.

Just as frequently, however, pioneering farmers' wives responded positively to the spacious and strange landscape. In the process of fulfilling their feminine roles as moral and cultural conservers, women could and frequently did discover a real harmony with the larger landscape, the wide open spaces. In 1855, Julia Louisa Lovejoy, a New England wife of a Methodist episcopal minister, wrote,

> It seems . . . impossible that any spot on earth uncultivated by art can be more inviting in appearance than this country. Beautiful rolling prairie, undulating like the waves of the sea, high limestone cliffs with immense bottom-lands stretching into thousands of acres as rich as it is possible for it to be.[9]

This harmony was achieved in conjunction with the establishment of a woman's own particular domain which was the garden, defined in this context, in a literal and prosaic sense. In the case of Elinore Pruitt Stewart, there is evidence that the more positively reponsive and resourceful a woman was as land was settled and cultivated, the more attention she gave to her garden. In *Letters of a Woman Homesteader*, Stewart describes her life after leaving Denver as a widowed mother of one daughter, to be Clyde Stewart's housekeeper in Wyoming in 1909. She marries Clyde Stewart, homesteads her own ranch, begins a second family and insists that frontier life offers the perfect opportunity for a woman to be financially self-sufficient. She concludes her account with a list of her achievements: 'I planted the garden. I had almost an acre of vegetables. I irrigated it and I cultivated it myself. . . . I raised a great many flowers.'[10] The female garden then is land enclosed, protected from the open prairie and large fields of crops which are a male domain. If sexual roles blur as women help their men to run the farm, sexual identity remains separate and intact as women cultivate their garden. It is functional in its supply of vegetables and comforting in its display of flowers.

In female literary versions of land settlement, it is apparent that this kind of experience develops into a serious and significant questioning of a familiar literary tradition based on a masculine ethos. Like all literary versions, these are retrospective and the best, written during the 1920s by Ellen Glasgow, Elizabeth Madox Roberts and Cather, undermine the metaphor of the garden as the apotheosis of moral and social order in the civilised settlement. There is, in other words, a real questioning in the work of these writers of the idealisation of the female domain by male writers. To the female imagination, this domain is seen to deny individual potential. Glasgow, Roberts and Cather reject the notion that the garden of the civilised settlement, with its moral and social order, is personified by the ideal feminine woman. Marriage, when it takes place, is often a source of anguish. In Roberts' novel *The Time of Man*, Ellen Chesser is a poor farmer's wife who finds her salvation in the grandeur of uncultivated land.[11] In contrast, her husband and their many children are a physical outrage. In her remarkable short story, 'Scarecrow,' Roberts suggests an analogy between the cultivation of land and violation of the female. Joan looks after her father's cornfield and can no more prevent the crows from tearing their way into the 'tender sheaves'[12] than she can avoid her rape by the boy who will be her husband. In Glasgow's novel *Barren Ground*, Dorinda Oakley becomes a successful farmer but only after she has dispensed with the illusion of romantic entanglement and anything other than a marriage of convenience. At the end of the novel when it is suggested that she might remarry, Dorinda 'smiled, and her smile was pensive, ironic and infinitely wise. "Oh, I've finished with all that," she rejoined. "I am thankful to have finished with all that."'[13]

The female literary response to land settlement thus tends to move away from the idealised version of the feminine role rather than confirm it. Conventional relationships between women and men, rather than the protagonists' intense desire for solitude, are what is felt to be undesirable or abnormal. In Cather's major novels, this conviction is to be found in the virtual absence of such conventional relationships. Cather herself did feel a deep anxiety about all strong emotional attachment. In her essay on Katherine Mansfield, she argued that all human relationships 'are the tragic necessity of human life . . . they can never be wholly satisfactory . . . every ego is half the time greedily seeking them, and half the time pulling away from them.'[14] This anxiety is expressed even in the successful marriage in *My Ántonia*, which is unique in Cather's fiction. It is presented as a tableau at the novel's conclusion, with no attempt to deal dramatically with the developing emotional bond between Ántonia Shimerda and Anton Cuzak. Despite the mood of fulfillment and images of fecundity that the domestic scene evokes, Cather's narrator Jim Burden observes of Cuzak:

> He was still, as Ántonia said, a city man. . . . Yet his wife had managed to hold him here on a farm, in one of the loneliest countries in the world. . . . This was a fine life, certainly, but it wasn't the kind of life he had wanted to live. I wondered whether the life that was right for one was ever right for two![15]

This kind of reservation expresses what so many of Cather's critics judge to be a flaw in her fiction. Lionel Trilling for example wrote, 'It has always been a personal failure of her talent that prevented her from involving her people in truly dramatic relations with each other.' By this he means that her men and women 'are never truly lovers.'[16] Maxwell Geismar concurs with Trilling's judgment and suggests that Cather could not accept 'the real [that is, imperfect] dynamics of ordinary affairs' because she measured such reality against a mistaken ideal of perfection.[17] But to insist that this absence 'of ordinary affairs' is an artistic limitation is to ignore the function of Cather's conviction as it is transmuted into her writing as a whole.

In her major novels, the strong, free and creative individual is always dramatized by Cather as a woman who is successful because she is unattached and therefore unencumbered by a largely oppressive social role. Alexandra Bergson and Thea Kronberg remain single until their token marriages at the end of *O Pioneers!* and *The Song of the Lark* because, as Carl Linstrum points out to Alexandra, '"It is your fate to be always surrounded by little men. And I am no better than the rest."'[18] The creative imagination of both Alexandra and Thea receives its inspiration from an unsettled wild landscape. There are, however, female characters in Cather's fiction who elicit male adoration that defines their identity. Marie Shabata in *O Pioneers!* and Marian Forrester in *A Lost Lady* are adored and idealised by Emil Bergson and Niel Herbert. This male adoration creates a purposeless, confused, fluttering femininity that threatens or actually effects the destruction of the individual female. In her fiction, Cather equates this fluttering femininity with unproductive land that is enclosed and therefore subject to decay. It is bequeathed as a specious legacy to subsequent generations of males who mourn the loss of a glorious and idealised past.

It has been assumed by most of Cather's critics that she backed to the hilt her insular young observer Niel Herbert and the old railroad man Captain Forrester in *A Lost Lady* and her isolated aesthete and scholar Godfrey St Peter in *The Professor's House*. They are men who remember with deep nostalgia, 'The Old West . . . settled by dreamers, . . . a courteous brotherhood, strong in attack but weak in defence, who could conquer but could not hold.'[19] In fact, it is these sincere but fastidiously conservative men who facilitate the social and moral decline that horrifies them so profoundly. They flounder, confused and weak in a time of change, retreating further and further into a self-contained world of abstract beauty, strenuously creating a past that never existed. To both Niel Herbert and Godfrey St Peter, the failure of the modern era is personified in the corruption of femininity; it is the sexual promiscuity of Marian Forrester or the 'snake's hate'[20] of Rosamund St Peter's greedy materialism that rots the feminine ideal. In *A Lost Lady*, that feminine ideal is validated and enhanced by the conventional pioneer legend. The aging Captain is married to the beautiful, elegant and sensual Marian Forrester. The 'courteous brotherhood' of old Westerners is lovingly conserved and idealised like the artificial artlessness of Marian's femininity and the Captain's unproductive meadows. These meadows are the Captain's garden; his monument to the wilderness of his youth.

Cather wrote about the pioneer farmers she had grown up with. They were European immigrants who could not forget Europe, who struggled to make a living on the Nebraskan prairie in the face of drought, harsh winters, soil erosion and debt. In *O Pioneers!* Mr Bergson never overcomes the shock of the transplantation to an empty, wild country and dies a despairing man. Mrs Bergson is a stoic who will not give up:

> Habit was very strong with Mrs Bergson, and her unremitting efforts to repeat the routine of her old life among new surroundings had done a great deal to

keep the family from disintegrating morally and getting careless in their ways . . . Alexandra often said that if her mother were cast upon a desert island, she would thank God for her deliverance, make a garden, and find something to preserve. (*O Pioneers!*, pp. 28–29)

In *My Ántonia*, Mr and Mrs Burden are successfully established on their land. He runs a profitable but modest farm, she presides over a productive garden and secure, comfortable kitchen. Mr and Mrs Shimerda, newly arrived from Bohemia, cannot adapt. He commits suicide and she relies selfishly and incompetently on the material help of others.

Cather however, was principally interested in the second generation. Like an artist, a successful pioneer 'should have imagination, should be able to enjoy the idea of things more than the things themselves' (*O Pioneers!*, p. 48). A pioneer should, in other words, be capable of ignoring a traditional social order in favour of a not yet realised re-vision and a re-ordered way of life. Like an achieved work of art, a pioneer's farm can be beautiful as well as productive if it is conceived as a complex and functioning whole, rather than discrete entities of crops and animal herds as one realm and garden and orchard as another. Alexandra Bergson is Cather's greatest and most successful pioneer farmer because she is unmarried and female. She looks with love and yearning not at a man but at the land that she will eventually transform into a fertile and ordered farm. Cather demonstrates that Alexandra is justified in the object of her passion in that the land, unlike any man she knows, offers her 'personal security' (*O Pioneers!*, p. 71) and an almost sexual ecstasy of union as the plough cuts the rich earth. Ultimately, Alexandra's farm is like 'a tiny village' because there are both acres of fields *and* an orchard, shed and pasture-ponds *and* a flower garden. By contrast, the house is 'unfinished and uneven in comfort' (p. 83) because Alexandra is not domestic; the house is not an insular environment sharply distinct from the out-of-doors.[21] Cather breaks down the extreme separation of masculine and feminine in all senses of the terms because in the single figure of Alexandra, she demonstrates that a successful pioneer farmer is a radical individual of imaginative foresight and the self-sufficiency to act upon that foresight.

Convention mocks and attacks Alexandra in the shape of her plodding and incompetent brothers Lou and Oscar, who deem her lack of conventional femininity a matter for ridicule and a symptom of moral weakness. Cather shows, however, that femininity without purpose or function is not only undesirable but dangerous. While Lou and Oscar's wives are merely ridiculous in their fussy hats and imported city manners, Marie Shabata, a pretty but married Bohemian girl, is captivating. Emil, Alexandra's favourite and youngest brother, makes Marie the object of his adoration. We are made to see Emil's self-pity as he wonders why he is so cursed, since the more his passion and excitement grow, the more unattainable and capricious Marie becomes. We see Marie's confusion as she insists she once loved her husband Frank because he was so romantic and carried her off against her father's wishes. She combines feminine helplessness with adult suggestiveness and her milieu is not, like Alexandra's, the great out-of-doors, but her orchard to which she retreats frequently. Decades ago, a German pioneer carefully watered the trees; they were part of his livelihood and means of survival. Now it is a neglected and artificial wilderness, dominated by a white mulberry tree whose 'sweet insipid' fruit falls to the ground 'unheeded all summer through' (p. 153). Cather's images of Marie in her orchard stress her insubstantiality, her childishness, her pleading wistfulness. When Emil joins her there for the last time, she is lying beneath the mulberry tree with the fingers of light around her like a net. Caged within her vapid femininity, she is the sacrificial victim to the possessive passions of two young men. When the lovers are discovered in Marie's orchard by Frank, he shoots them both in a fit of crazed jealousy. Alexandra realises too late the truth 'that Marie was after all, Marie; not merely a "married woman"' (p. 285). Marie's selfhood has been all but destroyed by her adult childishness in fulfilling her role as Frank Shabata's wife. Immune in her own female self-sufficiency, Alexandra never perceives that a wife could reach out to another man, least of all to her own brother Emil.

Marie's orchard in *O Pioneers!*, with its rich, sickly, tangled beauty, is an image of the garden, the sequestered land that no male writer would have created. There is corruption in that very arena where conventional versions find ennobling fulfillment. Cather's fiction demonstrates that when the garden, the insular wilderness, has outlived its original function, it becomes the setting for homicide, sadistic violence (as when Ivy Peters slits the eyes of the woodpecker in Captain Forrester's meadows) and sterility. In each case, this realm is personified by male versions of feminity. This can be compared with Faulkner's vision of the sequestered land in *Go Down, Moses*, where the anachronistic wilderness is symbolised by the bear. Here, violence is ceremonial and ritualistic; the participants are male and defiantly alone. The apotheosis is to be found in the awful moral dilemma of Isaac McCaslin, who must either commit himself to the free spirit of the wilderness or to heterosexual responsibilities. He chooses to remain faithful to a disembodied ideal rather than allowing that ideal to be modified by future generations and the mutability of a modern era.

In *My Ántonia*, Cather again wrote about the settlement of the Nebraskan prairie, but as a retrospective account told by an unhappily married man, Jim Burden. The strength of the novel lies in the tension between Jim's possessive nostalgia towards the farm girls of his youth, especially Ántonia Shimerda, and the girls themselves. They are second generation immigrants who come to town to hire out their labour; whose strength, independence, vitality and beauty make them far superior to the respectable girls brought up in Black Hawk, whose 'bodies never moved inside their clothes; their muscles seemed to ask but one thing—not to be disturbed' (*My Ántonia*, p. 199). The hired girls personify the qualities that Jim first perceives as a child on his grandmother's farm and which he associates with the land. Those qualities are an air of freedom, an expansive nature, a willingness to take risks, a heroism that is caught in a vision shared by Jim Burden and the girls on a summer outing. They watch the setting sun and see a plough silhouetted against it, magnified by the horizontal light: 'There it was, heroic in size, a picture writing on the sun' (p. 245). When Burden is at university in Lincoln, a brilliant teacher unfolds the wisdom of Virgil's *Georgics* to him. Burden realises the true significance of the term 'patria'—one's own land. Just 'as the pen was fitted to the matter as the plough is to the furrow,' Burden knows that for him 'if there were no girls like them in the world, there would be no poetry' (pp. 264, 270). It is a true insight to make the connection between people, a place, human passion and artistic and moral ideals. Yet Burden wants the girls, especially Ántonia, to remain forever girls and feminine ones at that. He hates it when Ántonia loses her feminine manners while working on her brother's farm. He is alarmed when she tells him '"Oh, better I like to work out-of-doors than in a house! . . . I not care that your grandmother say it makes me like a man. I like to be like a man." She would toss her head and ask me to feel the muscles swell in her brown arm' (p. 138). He is disgusted when she conceives an illegitimate child by a wastrel. He is emotionally unmoved when he mentions the middle-aged fate of two of the girls, Tiny Soderball and Lena Lingard, who live in unmarried prosperity in California. Burden's emotional commitment ends when the hired girls stop being girls.

It is significant that one of Burden's happiest and earliest memories is of contemplating the sky from the shelter of his grandmother's garden, passive, immovable, not wishing for anything to happen or change. The closing stages of his account are also dominated by a garden which serves the same function. Burden preserves the memory of the young girl in the image of Ántonia in her orchard. Although the triple enclosure of wire fence and hedges of thorny locusts and mulberry holds the 'deepest peace' within, the 'hedges were so tall that we could see nothing but the blue sky above them, neither the barn roof nor the windmill' (p. 341). For Burden, dreams and real experiences, memories and present realities blur and merge as he lives entirely faithful to a succession of nostalgic images sheltered from the harsh mutable world where women grow old and are not always gentle, kind or perfectly happy. While the epitaph for his account is Virgil's mournful line, 'Optima dies . . . prima fugit,' Ántonia herself is busily engaged in the job of bringing up eleven children and helping to run a farm.

My Ántonia is finally an optimistic novel because Burden's feminine idea is flexible enough to incorporate the flirtatious sensuality of the young Lena

Lingard and the wild impulsiveness of Ántonia Shimerda. *A Lost Lady* is a bitter novel because Niel Herbert's notion of femininity is a rigid aesthetic grounded on vague notions of gentility and a pioneer civilisation in the most conventional sense. Herbert is too young to remember the early settlement of the Mid-West, but is impelled to idealise that era in the person of Captain Forrester, the aging pioneer, and his young beautiful wife Marian. Yet 'the great brooding spirit of freedom . . . The space, the colour, the princely carelessness of the pioneer' (p. 104) is confused in Herbert's mind with the Sweet Water society that he remembers as a young man. He values the vitality of the parties, dances and formal midnight dinners given by the Forresters and their glittering winter seasons at Colorado Springs. This strange equation of old pioneer aristocracy with modern social vitality and gaiety is personified by Marian Forrester, who mocks at the 'proprieties she observed' and thus inherits 'the magic of contradictions.' It is Herbert who defines 'the subtlest thrill of her fascination' (p. 75) when he acknowledges to himself that its source lies in her role as the Captain's wife.

As a respected land tycoon, the Captain can afford to humour his fancies. On his property, he has chosen to conserve an area of beautiful pasture and marshland alongside the creek, rather than convert it into highly productive wheatfields. Analogously, Marian is adorned with jewels bought for her by the Captain 'in acknowledgement of things he could not gracefully utter. They must be costly; they must show that he was able to buy them, and that she was worthy to wear them' (p. 48). The creek, which separates the Captain's property from the town of Sweet Water, is allowed to trace its 'artless loops and curves through the broad meadows' (p. 5) for the aesthetic effect produced. Marian, enmeshed in her hammock, welcomes Herbert back from college, 'laughing up at him with the gleam of something elegantly wild, something fantastic and tantalizing,—seemingly so artless, really the most finished artifice!' (p. 109). When the wildness sheds its elegance and the wilderness loses its 'idleness and silvery beauty' (p. 104), it signals the end of an era. Marian has always been a woman of powerful sexuality to which Herbert responds even as a boy. When Marian tends his broken leg, she sheds her rings as a token of her earnestness, and her physical proximity thrills the uncomprehending boy. Marian sheds her rings as she disappears into the woods with the foxy and potent Frank Ellinger. After the Captain's death, she has an affair with the sadistic shyster lawyer Ivy Peters, who drains Marian as he drains the marsh. Herbert rejects her finally in disgust, taking away with him the image of Peters' hands on Marian's breasts as she stands working in the kitchen.

Critics of the novel have argued persistently that Cather created Marian Forrester as a stereotype of nineteenth century genteel femininity in order that she should stand for a civilised ideal. John Randall echoes J.W. Krutch, Alfred Kazin and Henry Steele Commager, when he argues that 'promiscuity becomes a symbol of social degeneration. This equating of the chastity of woman with the moral integrity of a civilization provides the fundamental metaphor upon which the book is based.'[22] But these critics tell only half the story. They fail to note that Herbert, who makes this equation, is a prudish young aesthete who harbours a sexual desire for Marian; a desire of which he is unaware. He reads Byron and Ovid's *Heroides*, revelling with guilty enjoyment in a past world 'that had plunged and glittered and sumptuously sinned long before little Western towns were dreamed of' (p. 79). Early one Spring morning, he wanders ecstatically through the Captain's wild meadows, cutting wild roses, whose colour is 'so intense that it cannot possibly last . . . must fade, like ecstasy,' in order to make a bouquet and lay it outside the French windows of Marian's bedroom. As he does so, he hears Frank Ellinger's laugh and feels a blight settle on his life. 'It was not a moral scruple she had outraged, but an aesthetic ideal' (pp. 82, 84).

Cather's point is clearly that idealistic and limpid young men like Herbert facilitate the rise to economic and social power of Ivy Peters and men like him. After the proof of Marian's promiscuity, after the Captain's plunge into poverty, Herbert will do nothing to help her materially. She relies on Ivy Peters for money and eventually for sex. Herbert clings all the more tenaciously to ideals that have an only incidental connection with real human beings and actual places. The only method by which Marian can assert her identity and refuse to decline as a symbol of a passing age is to use her powerful sexuality. Life on her terms can only be obtained through corrupt means, and she perseveres after the Captain's death, entertaining Sweet Water's young men. There is a coda to the story in which Herbert hears that Marian left Sweet Water and re-married an Englishman in California. Ed Eliot, one of the young men, has seen her in Buenos Aires and tells Herbert that although older, Marian has not changed, especially in her laugh. She still pursues life on her own terms, able to accept change, to accept the future, to take risks in a manner not dissimilar to Alexandra Bergson. Both women are characters who have no patience with men who cling to the past, to convention.

The Professor's House is a bleak novel in which no-one and no belief or value survives intact. Cather's definition of the garden and its symbolic freight becomes more flexible yet just as crucial in this novel. The story of Godfrey St Peter, the scholar, teacher and family man, frames that of Tom Outland who discovered the ancient Indian civilisation on the Blue Mesa in New Mexico. Outland subsequently comes to live with the St Peter family and becomes a brilliant scientific inventor. After his death in the war, his story is recalled by his mentor St Peter. The account of Outland however reaches imaginatively into a further past when a civilisation thrived, perched on rocks high in the mesa. Cather once compared the form of her novel to a Dutch painting, as the overcrowded stuffy foreground of St Peter's house is perceived against the background of 'the fresh air that blew off the Blue

Mesa.'[23] It is a suggestive comparison, although in fact the novel's symbolic structure more accurately describes a series of reducing images endlessly repeating themselves with terrible finality.

The scholarship of St Peter, which has resulted in a magisterial study of Spanish adventurers in North America, has been achieved at the expense of his relationships with his wife and daughters. Outland's reverence for the artefacts of the ancient Indian village costs him the friendship of his loyal partner Roddy Blake, who has sold the artefacts to a German dealer in order to finance Outland through college. Outland stresses his horror significantly: '"I'd as soon have sold my own grandmother as [the mummy] Mother Eve—I'd have sold any living woman first"' (p. 244). This damaging insularity is reiterated in the suggestion of the amateur archeologist Father Duchene that the extreme isolation of the Indian village was a contributory factor to its destruction by a roving tribe.

The rigidity of memories that supplant the reality of the present, the abstraction of ideas that displace the claims of individuals, the distaste for any kind of change, is imaged in St Peter's 'walled-in garden [which] had been the comfort of his life . . . it was a tidy half-acre of glistening gravel and glistening shrubs and bright flowers.' St Peter's landlord Fred Appelhoff remarks with sly humour, '"I don't like dem trees what don't bear not'ing," . . . remembering the Professor's glistening, barren shrubs and the good ground wasted behind his stucco wall' (pp. 14, 51-2). St Peter's garden describes vividly his impotent intellectual sterility. As inventor of the Outland engine, Tom Outland has left a great deal of money, which has occasioned jealousies and squabbles among the St Peter family and Outland's co-worker Doctor Crane. St Peter refuses to become entangled in such materialistic conflict and passes no judgement on his daughter Rosamund and her husband Louie, who built 'Outland' as a vulgarised monument to his achievements. Kathleen, St Peter's younger daughter, considers '"Tom's mesa entirely my own"' and claims to her father '"Our Tom is much nicer than theirs."' To Kathleen's husband Scott, Tom isn't very real anymore. '"Sometimes I think he was just a—a glittering idea"' (pp. 111, 131-2). To Lillian St Peter, Outland was an intruder who paid court to her husband rather than herself. Tom Outland is divided up and parcelled out by the petty jealousies of the family, and St Peter, who has always held himself apart and above his family turmoil, is himself the cause of their destructive jealousies. He has reserved his life for a scholarly reconstruction of Spanish explorers in America, for a vicarious discovery of an ancient Indian civilisation. Everything to be valued is contained in an idea, a memory. His attitude towards his family is similarly contained in an idea—that of chivalry—which dictates '"reserve about one's deepest feelings."' But, as Lillian retorts accurately, '"this reserve—it becomes in itself ostentatious, a vain-glorious vanity"' (pp. 48-9). The more St Peter seeks to contain his wife and daughters within aesthetic and moral ideas, the more they spill out into individuals he finds morally repugnant. '"I was thinking,"' he tells his wife,

> 'about Euripides; how, when he was an old man, he went and lived in a cave by the sea, and it was thought queer, at the time. It seems that houses had become insupportable to him. I wonder whether it was because he had observed women so closely all his life.' (p. 56)

St Peter comes to believe that his jealous and materialistic wife and daughters represent the present, while Tom Outland and his mesa and the study of Spanish adventurers represent a fading and noble past. But the symbolic structure of Cather's novel demonstrates that everything, even the noble past, is flawed. The mesa that is discovered by Outland, preserved in his journal and celebrated in St Peter's reconstruction, conforms to that realm that Cather terms the garden. It is empty, decaying and markedly insular, a monument to the past and, in the manner in which it is valued by Outland and St Peter, as sterile as St Peter's garden. Like the gardens of Cather's earlier novels, there lurks within this mesa the echo of evil. It is not to be found in the snake that kills Henry, the old man working with Outland and Blake. Like Marie Shabata's orchard, like the Captain's meadows, the evil is generated by male versions of ideal femininity and masculine reactions to the corruption of that ideal.

Outland and Blake find the mummified corpse of a young woman who clearly did not die a natural death. The men label her 'Mother Eve' and note that she has kept 'a look of terrible agony.' Father Duchene speculates that she was killed as a result of her sexual infidelity. '"In primitive society the husband is allowed to punish an unfaithful wife with death"' (pp. 214, 223). In the contemporary society of the novel, the husband is able to punish a wife unfaithful to his idealisation of her with contempt. Cather carefully develops symbolic parallels between St Peter's attic study and Outland's mesa. The former shares his study with Augusta the sewing woman, who keeps her two dress-making forms there. One is a 'headless, armless female torso' which, when touched, has a 'dead, opaque, lumpy solidity.' The other is a 'full-length female figure' (p. 18) with no legs and made of wire. When Augusta finally moves out of St Peter's study, he refuses to let her remove the forms. The parallel is obvious. St Peter's attic study high in the air is peopled by the dress forms, just as the mesa is peopled by corpses—'Mother Eve' and three old people that Outland and Blake find preserved in an inner room. While the fate of 'Mother Eve' is to fall into Black Canyon when being transported by the German dealer, St Peter guards his rigid unpleasant female forms, insisting to his protesting daughter Rosamund, '"I don't want to come upon them lying in some dump-heap on the road to the lake"' (p. 60). By the end of the novel, with his intellectual endeavours complete, St Peter is so devoid of feeling that he prefers death to the company of his family. In the event he reconciles himself to a bitter and joyless existence. He recognises that his life as a scholar is over and awaits the return of his wife and pregnant daughter from Europe with apathetic despair.

The exploration and the settlement of North America has of course provided one of the principal challenges to the literary imagination. As this analysis of some of Cather's best fiction demonstrates, familiar motifs in this literary tradition can acquire a different valuation from the point of view of a woman writer. Instead of insisting on the polarisation of a virgin land with a feminine settlement, Cather's female imagination shows how an early pioneering way of life at its best was able to combine and balance in a harmonious whole the primeval land and the civilised settlement. The kind of critique that this imagination conducts against the conventional literary tradition demonstrates that to equate civilised settlement with idealised femininity is to facilitate the revolt of those individuals who are burdened with this symbolic freight. The ideal is therefore made corrupt. It is wrong to fit Cather into a prevailing masculine literary tradition and then fault her for her failure to conform. Whether we are considering critics reading texts or writers 'reading' the world, we are, in the words of Annette Kolodny, 'calling attention to interpretive strategies that are learned, historically determined, and thereby necessarily gender-inflected.'[24] Kolodny's thesis is clearly vindicated in Cather's fiction where femininity, which is a source of stability or moral responsibility in the masculine tradition, is transformed into a dangerous and sometimes destructive force.

Cather was much more fiery and a lot less genteel than her mentor Sarah Orne Jewett. Cather's contemporaries Ellen Glasgow and Elizabeth Madox Roberts were temperamentally different and wrote about the Southern states rather than the Mid-West. But there may be a counter literary tradition waiting to be mapped out that might even extend into our contemporary period. It would certainly help to put some excellent writers into academic and possibly commercial circulation and to do more justice to such dedicated artists as Willa Cather.

Notes

1. Bernice Slote, ed., *The Kingdom of Art: Willa Cather's First Principles and Critical Statements 1893-1896* (Lincoln: University of Nebraska Press, 1966), p. 406.
2. *The Kingdom of Art*, pp. 408, 409.
3. Elizabeth Shepley Sergeant, *Willa Cather A Memoir* (Lincoln: University of Nebraska Press, 1953), pp. 115-16. Cather became a great friend of Sarah Orne Jewett, shortly before Jewett's death in 1909.
4. For example, 'Lou, the Prophet,' first published in *The Hesperian*, 22 (14 October 1892), and 'Peter,' first published in *The Mahogany Tree* (31 May 1892).
5. For example, 'A Death in the Desert,' first published in *Scribners Magazine*, 33 (January 1903), 'A Wagner Matinée,' first published in *Everybody's Magazine*, 10 (February 1904), and 'The Sculptor's Funeral' first published in *McClure's*, 24 (January 1905). All the stories listed

above are included in Willa Cather, *Collected Short Fiction 1892-1912* (Lincoln: University of Nebraska Press, 1965).

6. Mildred Bennett, *The World of Willa Cather* (New York: Dodd, Mead, 1951), caption of the photograph facing p. 196.

7. G.J. Barker Benfield, *The Horrors of the Half-Known Life: Male Attitudes Toward Women and Sexuality in Nineteenth Century America* (New York: Harper and Row, 1977), p. 8.

8. Quoted in J.R. Jeffrey, *Frontier Women: the Trans-Mississippi West, 1840-1880* (New York: Hill and Wang, 1980), p. 151.

9. Quoted in Michael Fellman, 'Julia Louisa Lovejoy Goes West,' *Western Humanities Review*, 31 (Summer 1977), 230.

10. Elinore Pruitt Stewart, *Letters of a Woman Homesteader* (Lincoln: University of Nebraska Press, 1961), pp. 280, 281.

11. Elizabeth Madox Roberts, *The Time of Man* (New York: Viking Press, 1926). This ecstatic release, occasioned by an open, uncultivated or vast landscape, is also found not only in the fiction of Roberts and Cather, but also in Sarah Orne Jewett's *The Country of the Pointed Firs* (New York: New American Library, 1979): 'there above the circle of pointed firs we could look down over all the island, and could see the ocean that circled this and a hundred other bits of island-ground, the mainland shore and all the far horizons. It gave a sudden sense of space, for nothing stopped the eye or hedged one in—that sense of liberty in space and time which great prospects always give' (p. 81). There is a similar affirmation in Agnes Smedley, *Daughter of Earth* (London: Virago, 1977), when Marie Rogers describes her affinity with the Arizona Desert.

12. Elizabeth Madox Roberts, *The Haunted Mirror* (New York: Viking Press, 1932), p. 103.

13. Ellen Glasgow, *Barren Ground* (New York: Sagamore Press Inc., 1957), p. 409. The novel was first published in 1925.

14. Willa Cather, *Not Under Forty* (New York: Alfred A. Knopf, 1936), p. 136.

15. Willa Cather, *My Ántonia* (London: Virago, 1980), pp. 366, 367. Subsequent references will be to this edition and will appear in the text.

16. Lionel Trilling, 'Willa Cather,' repr. in James Schroeter, ed., *Willa Cather and Her Critics* (New York: Cornell University Press, 1967), p. 155.

17. Maxwell Geismar, 'Willa Cather: Lady in the Wilderness,' repr. in *Willa Cather and Her Critics*, p. 193.

18. Willa Cather, *O Pioneers!* (Boston: Houghton Mifflin Company, 1941), p. 181. Subsequent references will be to this edition and will appear in the text.

19. Willa Cather, *A Lost Lady* (London: Virago, 1980), p. 104. Subsequent references will be to this edition and will appear in the text.

20. Willa Cather, *The Professor's House* (London: Virago, 1981), p. 85. Subsequent references will be to this edition and will appear in the text.

21. The notion of a home as a house that merges with its surroundings, so that the distinction between inner and outer space is minimised, is to be found in Jewett's novel *The Country of the Pointed Firs* and in *The Great Meadow* (New York: Viking Press, 1930) by Elizabeth Madox Roberts. Diony Hall, the protagonist of Roberts' novel, is among the first pioneer settlers into Kentucky and learns to accept the wisdom of Daniel Boone: '"You always felt at home in the world," Diony said. "You felt at home with what way the sun rises and how it stands overhead at noon, at home with the ways rivers run and the ways hills are. It's a gift you have, to be natured that way"' (p. 186). The exclusively male prerogative to have '"Elbow room"' (loc. cit.) is finally transferred to Diony. This is the definition of home, rather than the log cabin, whose domestic insularity is made all the more vulnerable by its defensive exclusion of the wilderness.

22. John H. Randall III, *The Landscape and the Looking Glass: Willa Cather's Search for Value* (Boston: Houghton Mifflin Company, 1960), p. 180. See also J.W. Krutch, 'The Lady as Artist,' Alfred Kazin, 'Willa Cather,' and Henry Steele Commager, 'Willa Cather', all repr. in Schroeter, ed.

23. Willa Cather, *On Writing: Critical Studies on Writing as an Art* (New York: Alfred A. Knopf, 1949), pp. 31–32.

24. Annette Kolodny, 'A Map for Rereading: Or, Gender and the Interpretation of Literary Texts,' *New Literary History*, II (1980), p. 452.

175
Mothers, Daughters and the 'Art Necessity': Willa Cather and the Creative Process

SHARON O'BRIEN

Since its inception, as Judith Fetterley observes, feminist literary criticism has been a 'growing, changing, constantly self-transforming phenomenon characterized by a resistance to codification and a refusal to be rigidly defined or to have its parameters prematurely set.'[1] But despite its eclectic, rapidly shifting nature, certain trends in feminist criticism can be discerned. In its early stages, most critics, trained in the techniques of formalist literary analysis, naturally focused on the texts themselves despite their awareness that literature could not be separated from culture or biography. Much early work was thus of the 'images of women in fiction' variety. Such analyses provided scholars with a useful taxonomy of recurrent female stereotypes, most often those employed by male writers who consciously or unconsciously revealed the male vision of woman as Other; whether a female character was Goddess, Mother, or Temptress, she reflected male desires or fears rather than autonomous selfhood.[2] Since this beginning, feminist critics have deepened and varied their approaches to literature as more acquire the interdisciplinary skills that work in women's studies requires, going beyond issues of imagery and characterisation to explore the complex links among writer, culture, and text. Two of the most promising and potentially fruitful approaches are summarised in Cheri Register's recent review essay on feminist criticism in *Signs*.[3] Since I employ both methods in my work on Cather, I will briefly detail them here.

SOURCE   Sharon O'Brien, 'Mothers, Daughters and the "Art Necessity": Willa Cather and the Creative Process', *American Novelists Revisited: Essays in Feminist Criticism*. ed. Fritz Fleischmann, Boston: G.K. Hall, 1982, pp. 265–98

The first approach, centering on the question, Is there a female aesthetic? combines formalist analysis with cultural contexting to determine whether the woman writer and her work reflect distinctly female experience or perceptions. In *The Madwoman in the Attic*, Sandra Gilbert and Susan Gubar argue persuasively that the woman writer in patriarchal culture experiences self, authorship, and creativity differently. Facing a male literary tradition that excludes her, unlike her male counterpart she suffers a feminine 'anxiety of authorship' rather than Harold Bloom's Oedipal 'anxiety of influence.'[4] Gilbert and Gubar find a 'distinctively female literary tradition' connecting Austen, the Brontës, Eliot, Rossetti, and Dickinson. Forced to invert or subvert the images of women inherited from a patriarchal tradition as well as forge a new definition of the artist, these authors create fiction embodying the 'woman writer's own discomfort, her sense of powerlessness, her fear that she inhabits alien and incomprehensible places.'[5]

Growing up in Victorian America when the dominant culture assigned women to the home and men to the world and social conventions and literary traditions conspired to relegate women writers to subordinate status, Willa Cather suffered the same anxiety of authorship Gilbert and Gubar see afflicting her British predecessors. How could one be a woman and a great writer at the same time? This dilemma plagued Cather during her twenties and thirties; until she resolved it she could not commit herself fully to her craft. Her first solution was to repudiate her gender and identify with men, which she did flamboyantly and overtly during her adolescent masquerade as 'William Cather, Jr,' later more discreetly and covertly. Obviously male identification was not a satisfactory answer to her search for identity and vocation. Despite her yearnings she was not male, and as long as she devalued her gender she devalued herself; as long as she devalued herself she did not have the self-confidence to embark seriously on the writing of fiction. Reconciliation of the conflict between feminine identity and artistic vocation was an arduous process. Although she wrote her first short stories in her early twenties, Cather did not complete her first major novel until she was forty. To understand her long apprenticeship and to evaluate patterns in the major fiction concerning woman's search for autonomy and creativity, it is necessary to consider the forces that caused and prolonged Willa Cather's anxiety of authorship—as well as those that allowed her to overcome it.

Patriarchal culture and male literary tradition are not the only forces affecting the woman writer. The other important recent development in feminist literary criticism is psychoanalytic rather than cultural in orientation, concerned with the woman writer's sources of support and strength as well as oppression. Inspired by recent studies combining feminist with psychoanalytic perspectives such as Dorothy Dinnerstein's *The Mermaid and the Minotaur* and Nancy Chodorow's *The Reproduction of Mothering*, feminist critics are displaying new interest in the mother/daughter relationship and in the impact of mothering—and being mothered—on women's lives, identities, and creative expression. As Register points out, viewing 'the mother-daughter relationship as a creative source for women can enhance our work in a number of ways.'[6]

Such an approach is central to understanding the connection between Willa Cather's life and work. Just as her mother dominated her early years, so themes deriving from the mother/child configuration dominate her fiction. As one of her recent critics astutely noted, Cather's bond with her mother provided her with a 'source of conflict' central to her creativity.[7] Her mother provided Cather with a source of support as well as conflict, for this mother/daughter bond—like most—was marked by intense ambivalences and contradictions.[8] The daughter's wish to separate was countered by the desire to remain fused; the drive for an autonomous self was countered by the fear of abandonment and loss. Unlike most women, Cather did not escape the psychodynamics of the mother/daughter bond in her intimate relationships. As a woman whose primary intimacies were with other women, Cather never relinquished the support and nurturance the daughter gains from the mother which, as Chodorow argues, many heterosexual women must forgo since men are culturally and psychologically induced to seek rather than offer nurturance. She also never escaped the accompanying fear that in same-sex intimacies she was losing adult separateness, since she did not have the barrier of gender to differentiate herself from the women she loved. Although the extent to which Cather's bonds with women were overtly sexual is not clear given the scant evidence available, her fiction reveals that she found sexuality and passion troublesome forces. Cather's heroic, creative characters channel their passions into transcendent objects —land, the family, religion, art—whereas her doomed or limited characters indulge in sexual or romantic passion. This essay will explore some of the critical problems that Cather's emotional orientation toward women presents to the feminist critic. Simultaneously identifying with women as subjects and viewing them as objects, Cather created both complex, autonomous heroines struggling toward self-definition and creative expression like Alexandra Bergson and Thea Kronborg, and archetypal female figures that reflect the (usually male) viewer's needs and preoccupations, like the maternal Ántonia Shimerda or the seductive Lena Lingard. Hence any feminist reading of Cather's fiction confronts a paradox: a novel like *The Song of the Lark* (1915) with its triumphant, independent artist-heroine seems feminist before its time, whereas *My Ántonia* (1918)—appearing only three years later—may at first seem as sexist as *Light in August*, with Ántonia the idealised Earth Mother the precursor of Faulkner's bovine Lena Grove. Understanding Cather's psychological and emotional conflicts can help us resolve such paradoxes without having to view her as the unwitting captive of male views of women.

In the first half of this essay, I will be intertwining these two approaches in examining Cather's struggle to combine the seemingly contradictory identities of 'woman' and 'artist,' uniting cultural and psychological analysis in assessing her response to a patriarchal culture and literary tradition as well as analysing her relationship with her mother and the other women whom she loved. In the second half of the essay, I will consider the major fiction in the light of the issues I have raised, concentrating on those major texts that are most pertinent to the questions I am asking. Of course in this brief space I can only suggest approaches to Willa Cather's life and work, not offer a comprehensive overview. I hope to demonstrate one way for a feminist critic to assess the complex interplay among culture, life, and text.

I

As a young woman, Willa Cather associated creative achievement with maleness because she looked for it in culturally sanctioned and prestigious forms: the novel, the poem, the concerto. In later years, however, she recognised the underground stream of female creative expression. Long before the current feminist movement helped us discover the artistry concealed in the sampler or the quilt, Willa Cather understood that female creativity had been forced to flow in acceptable and unobtrusive domestic channels. 'The German housewife who sits before her family on Thanksgiving Day a perfectly roasted goose, is an artist,' she declared in 1927.[9] Although Cather realised it only in retrospect, during her rural childhood in the Shenandoah Valley farming village of Back Creek, Virginia, where she was born in 1873, she had been surrounded by such un-self-conscious women artists. The old women who helped out at the Cather farmhouse during busy seasons—sewing, quilting, preserving—were not only accomplished craftswomen, they were the first storytellers the child encountered. Indigenous artists, in their conversation they were the preservers and transmitters of culture, myth, and folklore. Entranced by their vivid talk, Willa Cather would creep under their quilting frames and listen for hours. Her maternal grandmother Rachel Boak taught her to read and write, thereby providing another unconscious resource for Cather's eventual reconciliation of feminine identity and artistic vocation, since the child's mastery of language and expression was connected with a female presence. When the Cathers moved to the Nebraska Divide in 1884, the nine-year-old Willa encountered more women she would later recognise as artists—the immigrant farm wives who combined storytelling craft with creative skill at women's life-sustaining tasks of cooking, gardening, preserving. Although this exposure to strong, creative women could not counter the culture's association of professional artistry with maleness, it was a resource on which Willa Cather could draw, a tradition of female creativity to which she could look with pride—when she knew how to look.

Willa Cather's own mother, Virginia Boak Cather, was more the spoiled southern lady than the hard-working, self-denying rural farm wife. Beautiful, charming, and imperious, she was the dominant presence in the family, overshadowing her milder husband Charles Cather. A paradoxical woman, she whipped her children to maintain household order while allowing them great freedom in their personal lives.[10] Although she must have found Willa's fondness for male dress trying, she nevertheless saw to it that her eldest daughter had a room of her own, an attic bedroom which reappears in Cather's fiction as the space for autonomy, creativity, and nurturance. She also supported her daughter's wish to attend the University of Nebraska. Evidently Virginia Cather inspired the same devotion in her children the southern belle traditionally evoked in her doting admirers. According to Edith Lewis, the woman who shared Cather's life for forty years, all the children worshipped their mother and dreaded her displeasure.[11] Like the others, Willa bought her gifts to win her favor—delicate clothing, perfume, flowers, all tributes to her mother's beauty.

Willa Cather's relationship with her mother was intense and conflicted. For her as for all children, growing up required a process of separation and individuation, defining the self against the mother with whom the infant was once merged. The process was fraught with ambivalence. Increasing autonomy meant increasing loss, independence was accompanied by fears of abandonment and yearnings to return. Throughout childhood as well as the rest of her life, Cather sought to reconcile the competing needs that separation from the mother brought, trying to balance autonomy—her need for a separate, creative self—with nurturance—her need for close, sustaining human bonds. As Nancy Chodorow and Jane Flax have pointed out, the process of separation and identity formation and the balancing of needs for autonomy and nurturance are far more complex for girls than for boys.[12] Unlike her brother, the girl does not have the barrier of gender to sever identification with the mother; hence forming her own identity is more difficult, there being less clearly demarcated ego boundaries between daughter and mother than between son and mother. And whereas men can combine the joys of autonomy and nurturance by having both a professional career and a domestic life where they are nurtured, most women must sacrifice autonomy for nurturing relationships—or sacrifice nurturance for independence. Willa Cather's early memories and her crude, heavily psychological first short stories reflect these conflicts, centering on the mother/daughter bond and the accompanying issues of separation and individuation, independence and loss, autonomy and nurturance. But before turning to the fiction, we must consider a dramatic episode in Willa Cather's life which will illuminate these conflicts: her adolescent male impersonation period. Her four-year masquerade as William Cather reveals how cultural and psychological pressures conspired to delay her attainment of identity and vocation, preventing her temporarily from realising the alliance between femininity and creativity the Back Creek storytellers embodied.[13]

One of Cather's earliest childhood memories concerned her adopting an identity that 'horrified' her genteel southern mother. The five-year-old Willa, expected to please a visiting judge who was paying her chivalrous compliments, announced defiantly that she was not a little girl but a 'dang'ous nigger,' simultaneously rejecting her mother's standards of lady-like behavior and declaring her separate identity.[14] When Cather was fourteen, newly arrived in the small prairie town of Red Cloud, Nebraska, she adopted another persona that must also have horrified Virginia Cather. Announcing her disdain for the female sex and her membership in the male, Willa cropped her hair to crew-cut length, donned shirts and trousers, and baptised herself anew as 'William Cather, Jr' or, reflecting her career interests, 'William Cather, M.D.'[15] She continued this male role playing for the next four years. Her sustained performance had multiple sources, cultural as well as psychological. The cultural ones are most evident. In Red Cloud, she encountered expectations for female behavior she found confining and unacceptable. As a gifted, independent, spirited girl who intended to be a doctor, Cather rejected a female identity requiring passivity, deference, and submissiveness as well as a role requiring domesticity. Possessing personal traits such as ambition and assertiveness which her society deemed male and desiring a role in the male territory outside woman's domestic sphere, she chose to repudiate her gender rather than her personality or aspirations. Her male masquerade reflected identity conflict, not confusion. Cather pretended to be male because she knew she was female—and in Victorian America, being female meant being confined and regulated.

An angry rejection of a confining sex role was only one source for Cather's rebellion. She was also acting in a psychological drama, propelled by the inner needs for self-definition all girls face in adolescence—some contradictory, most doubtless unconscious. The masquerade, connected with the adolescent's need to define identity, reflects her complex and ambivalent relationship with her mother. As Nancy Chodorow points out, during adolescence the girl engages in a psychological 'replay' of the issues that characterise the Oedipal phase—merging, separation, sameness, identity.[16] The girl wants to separate from mother and form her own identity, yet she dreads the loss of the mother's love; moreover, the mutual identifications characterising the mother/daughter bond complicate the process. In addition, the daughter must confront her emerging sexuality, continue to identify with her mother's sex role while transferring her erotic interest to men. Willa's metamorphosis into William was a creative, daring way of mastering the psychological and emotional difficulties adolescence posed. As William Cather she could reject the mother she perceived as indifferent (the phase began when Virginia Cather, ill after the birth of a male child, could not care for her daughter's hair and Willa had it chopped off). She could also flout her mother's standards of ladylike dress and appearance while at the same time separating from her by adopting an opposed identity; clearly as William Cather she was not the same as her mother. Of course, the extremity of her action suggests the underlying fear that she *was* the same. Her transformation satisfied other conflicting needs. She wanted to strike out at her mother, just as she had 'horrified' her by declaring herself a 'dang'ous nigger,' but she also wanted to continue to seek her love. As William Cather she could do this, competing with the men her mother preferred — her father, her brothers, perhaps the newborn male sibling. Her male identification thus reflects her failure to transfer her emotional/erotic needs from women to men, the process that in heterosexual women occurs during the Oedipal stage and is 'replayed' during adolescence.

Her William Cather solution to identity problems was obviously temporary, and Willa Cather abandoned male dress and coiffure after two years at the University of Nebraska. But a more feminine external appearance did not signify the end of identity conflict. She was still not happy about being a woman; during her college years, she abandoned thoughts of medicine and began to aspire to the artist's lofty role — which was, she realised, a male preserve. America's 'scribbling women' who invaded the literary marketplace during the nineteenth century did not offer her an acceptable tradition. Their fiction she considered trashy, commercial, and woefully limited to women's subjects like romance and domesticity. Such writers could not be literary forebears for a young woman now entranced by the Emersonian notion of the artist as godlike Creator.[17] The artists she worshipped in this category — Carlyle, Shakespeare, James — were male. 'Artist' and 'woman' seemed contradictory identities also because Cather doubted that women could subordinate their need for human affection to the austere demands of art. 'Art of every kind is an exacting master,' she wrote, accepting only 'human sacrifices'; if an artist were to do anything worthwhile, he must make human relationships a 'secondary consideration.'[18] Male artists could make this sacrifice, but had any woman 'ever really had the art instinct, the art necessity?' she wondered. Liberty and solitude were the two 'wings of art,' but what woman could deny her need for human bonds, even if they kept her earthbound?[19]

Cather did meet several actresses and opera singers during her years in Lincoln and Pittsburgh who had committed themselves to artistic careers, but they could not compensate for an insufficient female literary tradition. Operas needed sopranos, plays demanded actresses, but American letters did not require participation by female writers. Moreover, the actresses and opera singers she knew were performers, not original creators of texts; her situation was different. There were a few literary women she admired, although none were American: Austen, the Brontës, in particular the 'great Georges' — Eliot and Sand. But these last, whom she respected the most, she considered 'anything but women' — anomalies, deviants, perhaps male impersonators like William Cather. Given the choices, being 'anything but' a woman was preferable to being female. Willa Cather's youthful advice to women writers who wished to escape the limitations of their traditional sentimental and domestic subject matter reveals how strongly she had internalised the male aesthetic. When a woman writer leaves behind romantic subject matter and attempts a 'stout sea tale' or a 'manly battle yarn'—then, the young woman concluded, she might expect 'something great' from a female author.[20] Abandoning her male persona had solved nothing, since in aspiring to the writer's role she once again encountered forbidden territory and sexual polarisation. Women writers were limited, male writers were universal; to escape female limitations, a woman had to write like a man. But advocating men's subjects for women writers—or attempting them herself—was in effect resuming her William Cather disguise. Manly battle yarns were not the answer.

Cather's view that human relationships were draining forces threatening to autonomy and creativity was not merely a theoretical argument. Although Cather's Nebraska classmates later described her as a loner who had no friends and wanted none, in fact she had several close friends in college as well as an intense and sometimes turbulent intimacy with Louise Pound, a classmate who later became a well-known philologist and folklorist as well as the first woman president of the Modern Language Association.[21] The few existent letters reveal the formerly rebellious William Cather in the role of the moody, beseeching lover—at times jealous, insecure, passionate, depressed, self-pitying.[22] Eventually Louise Pound terminated the relationship, and Cather was devastated for a while. As Carroll Smith-Rosenberg has shown, such intense and romantic friendships between women were common in Victorian America.[23] Close, caring, and compassionate, these intimacies were often the primary emotional bonds in women's lives. In most cases not genitally sexual, these relationships were socially acceptable and considered compatible with woman's role as wife and mother.

But Cather's attachment to Pound had a different quality from the close, secure intimacies Smith-Rosenberg found prevalent in the 1840s and 1850s. Her letters, which were written in the early 1890s, bear out Lillian Faderman's contention that by the late nineteenth century, as women increasingly left the home for college and the professions and Havelock Ellis's and Krafft-Ebbing's work on human sexuality appeared, women's romantic friendships seemed increasingly suspect, ultimately deviant: Americans had discovered lesbianism.[24] Although Cather's letters reveal emotional rather than physical passion, they do reflect an uneasiness that a woman would not have felt in the 1840s. It was unjust, she wrote Pound, that feminine friendships should be unnatural.[25] Her protest suggests an underlying anxiety. Forty years earlier, it would not have occurred to a woman that her intense feelings for a female friend might be 'unnatural.'

It is possible to debate whether Cather's attachment to Louise Pound and later her primary relationships with Isabelle McClung and Edith Lewis were lesbian if we insist that the term imply genital sexuality. There is no evidence in the remaining letters or in Edith Lewis's discreet memoir, *Willa Cather*

Living, that these bonds were sexual as well as emotional, although the fiction reveals Cather's familiarity with the allure and the danger of sexual passion. But such a distinction does not concern me here. Two points are central: Willa Cather invested herself emotionally in other women, and in keeping with the comment to Pound that such intimacies were unnatural, she did not portray them in her fiction. Hence we find her disguising and camouflaging her deepest attractions, which are always translated into heterosexual attachments. Such fictional disguise, which as we will see raises complex interpretive problems, reveals her awareness that female intimacies are not appropriate subject matter for fiction. (By contrast, her mentor Sarah Orne Jewett who had a 'Boston marriage' or stable ménage with Annie Fields during a more innocent era made women's friendships the primary subject of her fiction; she could not understand why Cather chose male personas to express romantic yearning for female characters.)

Willa Cather's first short stories, written between 1892 and 1902, embody both the cultural and the psychological stresses we have been discussing. Aesthetically crude but psychologically revealing, they are worth considering both for the insights they provide into the young writer's inner life and for their anticipation of the major fiction, where she would explore similar themes with far greater control, detachment, and artistry. Cather chose Nebraska settings and immigrant protagonists in several of these stories which expose the harshness of prairie life as well as the social and economic injustices crushing the immigrant farmers. But despite her subject matter she was no Hamlin Garland. Like many young writers, her deepest concern is herself rather than her characters or the social issues she attempts to raise. The prominent motifs in this fiction—the child searching for a maternal figure, the association of erotic and maternal love, the dangers of passion—are her own enduring preoccupations, although here as in her novels she portrays all intense erotic or emotional bonds as heterosexual.

Cather's choice of male protagonists in several of these early stories—among them 'Peter,' 'Lou the Prophet,' 'The Clemency of the Court,' 'The Elopement of Alan Poole,' 'The Burglar's Christmas'—suggests that she was still captive of a culture relegating women to subordinate status. If she could not be a male writer, she could at least create male characters whose universal dilemmas would lift her fiction above that of the scribbling women. The one story featuring a strong, admirable heroine—'Tommy, the Unsentimental'—reveals Cather's continued association of positive human qualities with the male sex. The boyish heroine receives Cather's approval; blunt, intelligent, resourceful, Tommy is, Cather assures us, 'unfeminine.'[26] Her foil, the shrinking, delicate, childlike Miss Jessica who 'wore violet perfume and carried a sunshade,' is useless and ridiculous, Cather's caricature of Victorian America's ideal woman. The author had not progressed too far beyond her William Cather phase. The human qualities she admired she still considered male.

While 'Tommy' reveals the cultural pressures contributing to Cather's identity conflict, paradoxically the stories featuring male protagonists reflect the psychological and emotional dynamics of the mother/daughter bond. In drawing on intensely personal and unconscious material, Cather opted for disguise, projecting herself into male characters—another reason for their prevalence in this fiction. What was she concealing? Let us briefly consider one early story that reveals her inner conflicts with almost embarrassing directness: 'The Burglar's Christmas.' The surface plot is appallingly sentimental. A starving, destitute young man named William (Cather's adolescent pseudonym) is driven by hunger and desperation to rob a fashionable Chicago mansion on Christmas Eve. Obsessed with obtaining food, he slips upstairs and surreptitiously enters a richly furnished bedroom, opens a dressing-case and begins pocketing the rings, watches, and bracelets he finds. Suddenly the thief discovers a disturbingly familiar object: the silver drinking mug he used as a little child! Before he or the reader has time to puzzle this out, his mother enters the room. It is her bedroom, this is his parents' house. (The reason for the unlikely coincidence and the son's ignorance of his parents' whereabouts is later awkwardly and unconvincingly explained.) An angelic presence, his mother embraces her prodigal son, forgives all and assures him of her undying, unconditional love while she gets him dinner.

Despite its glaring aesthetic deficiencies, 'The Burglar's Christmas' is a crucial story in the Cather canon because its psychological themes connect both to her life and to her later fiction. They center on issues of nurturance, separation, and identity. Having failed at an autonomous adult existence, William returns home to posses and be possessed by his mother who offers endless nurturance. But he must pay the price of regression for regaining this bliss; the twenty-four-year-old man becomes a small child finding 'refuge and protection' in his mother's arms. At the story's end, he seems to have traveled even farther back into the past, for the 'rich content' he experiences sitting by a warm fire with hunger satisfied and sleep descending suggests the infant's satiated pleasure more than the little boy's happiness. He has returned to the oral stage, the period in human development symbolised by the baby's silver drinking mug.

The story's imagery of the theft suggests that this is an Oedipal as well as a pre-Oedipal fantasy, for the mother is an erotic as well as a nurturing figure: the son guiltily steals along passageways and corridors, finds his way to the 'darkened chamber' where the 'jewels and trinkets were kept,' forces open his mother's dressing case, and begins stealing her jewels. Such imagery hardly needs commentary. But one does not need the resources of Freudian theory to see the eroticism in this mother/child reunion. Not only does the mother seem beautiful and seductive to the son, with her 'superb white throat and shoulders' and her 'impetuous and wayward mouth,' but their embraces are also marked by intense sensuality (his mother's kiss 'burnt him like fire'). Cather seems to be describing the reunion of long-separated lovers, not mother and son.

In following her protagonist back to childhood and infancy, Cather reveals both the identity problems Chodorow finds in the mother/daughter relationship and the conflict between autonomy and nurturance that Jane Flax analyses. In regaining his mother, William loses a separate identity. '"We are of one blood,"' his mother tells him. '"Even as a child, I felt your likeness to me . . . I have lived all your life before you. You have never had an impulse that I have not known, you have never touched a brink that my feet have not trod."' The mother's terrifying declaration of their sameness becomes psychologically more understandable when we take William as a mask for Willa; the fusion then suggests the mutual identifications existing between mother and daughter. The protagonist's inability to balance autonomy and nurturance also suggests the mother/daughter configuration. On his own, he is starving and destitute; independence means emotional abandonment. But in returning to his mother's love, he must abandon adult separateness and independence. This seemingly clichéd piece of magazine fiction, a sentimental reworking of the prodigal son motif, thus in fact reflects the author's unconscious desires and fears. The text's artlessness is connected with her lack of control of her material as well as her technical inexperience. There is no controlling authorial presence in the story, no separation between the author's and the character's viewpoint, no criticism of his urge to regress—in fact the rapturous ending implies that we are to read William's sinking into passive gratification as positive. Of course, the biographical parallels are suggestive but not complete, for in writing the story and expressing the fantasy, Cather resisted the regressive impulses to which her protagonist succumbed. But the fact that the fantasy is presented uncritically with the young author unaware of what she is concealing and revealing demonstrates that Cather did not yet have mastery over her material, either psychologically or technically.

Other early stories reveal similar psychological themes. In 'The Clemency of the Court,' the orphaned Russian immigrant Serge finds that he can return to his idealised mother only in death and dies assuming the fetal position; in 'The Elopement of Alan Poole,' the hero unites with his sweetheart only as he is dying and she, a 'little Madonna of the Hills,' assumes the mother's role ('"Oh my boy! my boy!" Nell cried as she rocked herself over him as a mother does over a little baby.')[27] Regaining the mother/lover is thus literally equated with death in these stories, in contrast to the metaphoric death William achieved as he slid into passive nonbeing. The mother figure in all the stories is alluring because she offers love and nurturance, but terrifying because she threatens loss of self; to regain the infant's preconscious oneness with the mother is to be obliterated, to die. Since Cather connects maternal and erotic love, the sexual drive has a threatening regressive component, similarly leading to self-annihilation and ultimately the obliteration of death. Although drawing on childhood drives and conflicts, doubtless these early stories owed something to Cather's contemporary relationship with Louise Pound.

This immature early work raises critical problems that will persist in the major fiction. In 'Elopement,' for example, is Cather revealing her hostility to adult heterosexual passion and to her male rivals by killing off the male lover? Or, if Alan is a mask for herself, is she revealing her own discomfort with the erotic/emotional drives? Or both? (The same questions can later be asked of the lovers' murder in *O Pioneers!*) Clearly the interpretation shifts if we consider the male protagonist a mask for a female author who must disguise homosexual themes to her audience and perhaps to herself. Another problematic pattern that will persist is Cather's occasional portrayal of women characters in traditional stereotypic guises, women as Other. For example, Nell, the 'Madonna of the Hills,' is the idealised virgin/mother one might expect to find in fiction by a male writer. Like other aspects of her early work, this figure will reappear in novels like *My Ántonia* and *A Lost Lady* where Cather consciously explores the ways in which men (or women?) invest women with meaning.

The fear expressed in Cather's early journalism and fiction that human relationships must be sacrificed for art must have lessened in 1899. In that year she met Isabelle McClung, the beautiful daughter of a Pittsburgh judge who was to be her great love. With Isabelle Cather found a sustaining affection that promoted rather than impeded creativity, since Isabelle was devoted to nurturing her friend's talent; she also discovered a loving maternal presence whom she did not have to share with father or siblings. Isabelle continued to support Cather's creative life until her marriage to violinist Jan Hambourg in 1916. Even after Cather moved to New York and was sharing an apartment with Edith Lewis, she would return to Pittsburgh and Isabelle to write. Shortly after their meeting, Isabelle invited Cather to move into the McClung household; the two women shared a bedroom but Isabelle provided her friend with an attic study where she could be alone to write, so Cather had spaces for both intimacy and solitary work. Achieving the delicate balance between nurturance and autonomy with a motherly friend who wanted her to write, Cather experienced a creative explosion. She published six stories the year after meeting Isabelle and two books shortly after — *April Twilights* (1903), a pallid collection of poems, and *The Troll Garden* (1905), a collection of short stories containing her first work of real literary merit.

Whereas the early stories were either stilted imitations of other writers or barely disguised personal fantasies, in *The Troll Garden* stories, Cather created fully realised characters who are not merely projections of the author's inner conflicts. Unlike the regressive William, for example, the rebellious Paul in her well-known short story 'Paul's Case' who greedily seeks beauty amid Pittsburgh's grimy commercialism exists in a thickly textured, realistic world. Cather was drawing on her own rebellious adolescence in creating this character, but she was not limited by her own experience; hence Paul exists outside of herself and thus can exist for the reader. This successful, well-crafted story reveals the connection between her technical and personal advances. Paul is driven by the same regressive urges that sent William home to mother; his lust for music, fine wine, and delicate clothes masks an urge for passive gratification, not active creation, in a world of 'basking ease.' But in this story, Cather manages point of view beautifully, maintaining a consistent ironic detachment from her character, a critique of his capitulation to the regressive pull that seemed so enticing in 'The Burglar's Christmas.' The story reveals her in control of her material, both psychic and literary.

Most of the stories in the collection concern art and artists, exploring in particular the external and internal forces that cause artists to succeed or fail. As in her college journalism, the great artists are men—Harvey Merrick in 'The Sculptor's Funeral,' Hugh Treffinger in 'The Marriage of Phaedra,' Raymond d'Esquerré in 'A Garden Lodge,' Adriance Hilgarde in 'A Death in the Desert.' But the stories also demonstrate progress in Cather's resolution of feminine identity with artistic vocation. Revealingly, the male artists are all absent or dead, and the author is more interested in the failed artists who are her protagonists—all female. Katherine Gaylord, Aunt Georgianna, and Caroline Noble are her first significant female protagonists who are neither mannish Tommys nor silly Miss Jessicas; nor are they stereotyped figures seen only through men's eyes. Although they do not equal the men's artistic achievements, it is important that Cather is now writing about women who posses creativity—albeit creativity that is denied, distorted, or repressed by cultural pressures and psychological necessities. The female characters' defeat reflects Cather's understanding of the difficulties facing the woman artist, including that of confronting a patriarchal artistic tradition (suggested by the absent or dead male artists in the stories), but the fact that they possess creative gifts at all reveals her new awareness that women are not innately limited as artists, an insight that can be connected with her development of her own creative powers and growing artistic self-confidence. Moreover, Cather's choice of female protagonists in four of the seven stories shows a new interest in exploring female identity and experience. The decision reflects her increasing identification with her own sex.

A crucial turning point in Cather's resolution of feminine identity and art came a few years after *The Troll Garden* was published when she met Sarah Orne Jewett, then celebrated for *The Country of the Pointed Firs* as well as her other stories of Maine life. Their brief friendship was central in Cather's decision to commit herself to the artist's vocation. On assignment in Boston for *McClure's* magazine (she had moved to New York to work for S.S. McClure in 1905), Cather met Jewett at the gracious Charles Street home of Annie Fields in 1909. As a gifted American woman writer whom Cather revered, Jewett embodied the female literary tradition the younger woman had been seeking. She was, to use Gilbert and Gubar's term, the literary 'foremother' who provides the daughter/artist with a tradition and a lineage. In addition, as a well-bred New England lady, Jewett was not 'anything but' a woman; she was, Cather later commented approvingly, 'a lady, in the old high sense,' perhaps a northern version of Virginia Cather's southern lady.[28] In any case, for a brief time Jewett was model, mentor, and mother for her young protégée, offering support and encouragement for her work, proffering literary advice, and delicately suggesting that Cather leave her draining magazine job to devote herself solely to her writing. Jewett also predicted Cather's ultimate literary direction. One day, she thought, Cather would write about her 'own country' and embody Nebraska's land and people in fiction just as Jewett had honored her beloved Maine.[29] Jewett's influence continued after her death a year later. Her memory inspired Cather finally to embark on her first novel in 1912. After paying a pilgrimage to Jewett's house in South Berwick, she 'felt goaded,' she told a friend. 'It was as if Miss Jewett's spirit, which filled the place, had warned her that time was flying.'[30]

Cather knew she had to take the final step, quit her job and commit herself to writng, and yet she was understandably fearful. Even if it now seemed possible that a woman could be a great writer, as a single woman who had to make her own living she was reluctant to give up a secure income. In 1912 she managed a compromise and took a leave from *McClure's* to write *Alexander's Bridge*. She was not yet ready to trust herself and turn to her 'own country,' though, for the novel with its international settings and drawing room conversations shows her still in the grip of Henry James. Cather later disparaged the novel, viewing it as the apprentice writer's awkward, imitative venture and comparing it unfavorably to *O Pioneers!*[31] It seemed a bastard child to the mature writer, and in the Library Edition of her fiction, she denied *Alexander's Bridge* its rightful place, offering *O Pioneers!* as her 'First' novel. The plot was largely conventional, a mid-life crisis superimposed on a romantic triangle. Bartley Alexander, a successful middle-aged bridge builder, is torn between his American wife and everything she stands for (self-discipline, professional success, adult responsibility) and his English mistress and everything she stands for (self-gratification, romance, youth). His yearning to recapture his own youth through Hilda proves Bartley's moral/psychological flaw. In the novel's melodramatic and symbolically incvitable conclusion, the similarly flawed bridge he has been building collapses, and he is drowned in the St Lawrence River.

Although the novel's settings are artificial and the dialogue stilted, its themes connect with some of Cather's enduring preoccupations; it is not as atypical as she would have us think. Alexander is the heroic, creative individual of pioneer force and energy, anticipating Alexandra Bergson, Thea Kronborg, and Godfrey St Peter, but unlike them, he is driven by the urge for romantic love that Cather finds so disastrous. Bartley displays the urge to recapture his lost youth that links him with other Cather protagonists like Jim Burden and Godfrey St Peter as well as the regressive William. But although the author sympathises with Bartley's wish to retrace time, she surrounds him with imagery of flux and change—oceans, rivers, clocks— that remind the reader that time and adulthood cannot be denied. As in 'Paul's Case,' the distance between author's and character's point of view reveals Cather's technical and psychological growth; she projects some of her deepest desires into Bartley, but is detached from them at the same time.

Like much of Cather's fiction, the novel poses some perplexing interpretive problems when regarded from a feminist perspective. Cather again chooses a male protagonist to explore erotic and regressive drives, and the women in his life are flat, stereotypic figures: the patient wife, the enticing mistress. Does this mean that Cather was still captive of a patriarchal culture and literary tradition and thus was choosing a male protagonist and women characters as conceived by men in order to seem 'universal' rather than limited and feminine? Or was Bartley another mask for the female writer who had to camouflage her own 'unnatural' intimacies in fiction? Do the female stereotypes reveal the author's psychological and emotional realities rather than her slavish adherence to patriarchal images of women, since for her women did embody her desires and fears and were thus objects as well as subjects? Perhaps all these possibilities are true, with cultural and psychological forces intersecting to produce a novel that seems to have sexist patterns linking it with works by male writers for whom woman is Other. In her later novels like *My Ántonia* and *A Lost Lady*, Cather is more aware of the way men project meaning onto women and interpret them in terms of their own needs and fears. That process in fact becomes the subject of both novels.

II

In 1913 Cather took Jewett's advice and decided to write about her 'own country,' the Nebraska farmland and its immigrant settlers. In combining memory with imagination, she created the first novel she later felt was her own. *O Pioneers!* celebrates the pioneer-immigrants who tamed the stubborn land and founded a civilisation; it is Willa Cather's epic. The heroic protagonist is a woman who makes the land flourish when the men around her have failed, broken in spirit by the soil's resistance to cultivation. Alexandra Bergson is a new heroine both in American literature and in Cather's fiction: strong, autonomous, creative, she is neither the female figure of male fantasy nor a doomed heroine like Chopin's Edna Pontellier or Wharton's Lily Bart who cannot achieve self-definition in an oppressive society. Alexandra's triumph reflects the author's. Although the novel is not directly autobiographical, since Alexandra is artist as well as pioneer, her achievement reflects Cather's now successful welding of the formerly mutually exclusive identities, artist and woman. Accepting her gender, newly confident of her creative powers, freed from subservience to the male literary tradition (there is no trace of James's influence in the novel, which fittingly is dedicated to Sarah Orne Jewett), Cather could at last create a heroine who redeems the failed female artists in *The Troll Garden*.

Alexandra is the novel's supreme artist. Her selfless passion for the land, which she regards with 'love and yearning,' rather than the men's antagonism, parallels the unselfish love Cather thought the artist must have for subject matter.[32] As a farmer/artist, Alexandra creates order and beauty in the natural world, shaping and forming what was chaotic and barren: 'it is in the soil that she expresses herself best' (p. 84). Later her childhood friend and suitor Carl Linstrum makes the artist/pioneer equation explicit. "'I've been away engraving other men's pictures,'" he tells her, '"while you've stayed here and made your own"' (p. 116). Cather reverses the pattern of *The Troll Garden*: the woman is now the authentic creator, the man the mere copyist. In her bond with the fertile soil—the dominant maternal presence in the novel—Alexandra the artist/daughter combines autonomy and merging with something beyond the self. With the soil she can both assert the self and give it up, imposing order in cultivation and fusing physically and spiritually with the soil, feeling its 'joyous germination' in her own body (p. 204). Alexandra both nurtures the land and receives sustenance from it, playing the roles of both mother and daughter. But in losing the self in joyous identification with the land, she does not suffer William's regressiveness or Alan Poole's obliteration; this merging with a maternal force, which allows her to be separate and connected at the same time, leads to flourishing life rather than self-annihilation—just as giving up the self in the act of writing did for Willa Cather. (The artist should be 'so in love with his subject matter,' she commented, that 'he forgets "self" in his passion.'[33]) In creating a female hero who is artist as well as pioneer, Cather reveals a new awareness that her creative 'foremothers' extended back beyond Sarah Orne Jewett to the strong rural women she had known in childhood and youth, the immigrant farm wives who introduced her to narrative. A lineage of creativity links mother and daughter in the novel as well. Mrs Bergson, the immigrant farm wife, makes a garden in the desert as soon as she arrives, just as her daughter Alexandra would do on an epic scale.

Alexandra ultimately discovers a nurturing relationship in addition to her tie with the land. At the novel's end, depressed by the murder of her brother Emil and Marie Shabata, she acknowledges her need for human companionship and turns to her ever-faithful friend and suitor Carl for support and affection. But their union will not contain the destructive force of sexual passion. '"When friends marry, they are safe,"' Alexandra reassures herself, envisioning a future protected from the dangerous forces that destroyed Marie and Emil (p. 309).

Cather wrote *O Pioneers!* when she realised that two previously written short stories should be combined: 'Alexandra,' a 1911 version of the heroine's taming of the soil, and 'The White Mulberry Tree,' a tragic tale written a year later in which a crazed Bohemian farmer kills his wife, Marie, and her young Swedish lover—the source for the lovers' subplot. She felt a 'sudden inner explosion and enlightenment' when she realised the two stories belonged together; obeying a command that seemed to issue from the tales themselves, she combined them to create her 'two-part pastoral.'[34] Many critics feel that the fusion of the two fictional elements is imperfect, with the lovers' subplot an unnecessary diversion. But as I have argued elsewhere, the stories are linked thematically.[35] Both are parables about passion. Alexandra Bergson's taming of the soil chronicles the heroic results of passion regulated and channeled into the land rather than into human relationships, while the lovers' doom records the destructive outcome of sexual passion indulged and unleashed. Like 'The Elopement of Alan Poole,' the subplot reflects Cather's uneasiness with romantic/erotic love, which she portrays here as narcissistic, solipsistic, and regressive. Marie and Emil fall in love with the images they create of each other and are most intense when they are separated. Thus they do not really connect with anything or anyone beyond their own egos, in contrast to the self-transcendent Alexandra.

Alexandra should please any feminist critic or reader looking for full-bodied, complex, autonomous female characters who transcend stereotypes traditionally defining and limiting women. Her portrayal suggests that Willa Cather, although politically never aligned with feminist causes, imaginatively had broken the cultural molds circumscribing female identity. But a perplexing inconsistency emerges for the feminist critic in considering Marie Shabata, the impetuous heroine whose self-indulgent romanticism leads to destruction. At first she seems to be more complex than the stereotypic temptress; warm, generous, and vibrant, she was, as Carl tells Alexandra, ' "the best you had here"' (p. 305), and throughout the novel Cather portrays her sympathetically. And yet at the novel's end, we learn that the tragedy was caused by Marie; Carl, who is the voice of reason and psychological insight in the novel, tells Alexandra that ' "There are women who spread ruin around them through no fault of theirs, just by being too beautiful, too full of life and love. They can't help it"' (p. 304). The generalising rhetoric ('There are women who . . .') reveals that Marie is being categorised as the seductive Eve who spread ruin among men. Evidently Emil and Frank do not share moral responsibility for the tragedy. Why does a women writer both challenge the traditional stereotypes confining women and reinforce them in the same novel? It is possible that at the time Cather was only partially free of cultural views of women, and her inconsistency determined the characterisation of the contrasted women. On the other hand, it is likely that her portrayal of Marie reveals her own unacknowledged conflicts, since here as elsewhere in her fiction she portrays all attraction as heterosexual. Since in life she both identified with women and viewed them as objects of desire, in fiction she could portray women both as autonomous, three-dimensional female subjects and as stereotyped or idealised objects of fear or longing.

In writing *O Pioneers!* Cather experienced the creative process in a new way. Instead of consciously controlling and shaping her material, she felt that the book wrote itself. Powerful forces seemed to be using her as their agent, and she yielded to a nonrational force she called the 'wisdom of intuition.'[36] This self-abandonment to a powerful force and joyous loss of self in the creative process Cather connected with the novel's composition suggests that she was letting down psychic barriers. With her internal conflicts surrounding identity and vocation resolved, the writing of fiction could be an expansive process of 'letting go with the heart.'[37] From now on she found writing blissful. The joy Cather experienced in the creative process is connected with her achievement of harmony between conflicting psychic opposites. In writing she could be both connected to a larger force and separate, balancing needs for nurturance and autonomy. In *My Ántonia* she defined happiness as being 'dissolved into something complete and great' (p. 18), and all her comments on the creative process suggest that she found such self-annihilation in merging with loved subject matter or characters, just as Alexandra thrilled in fusing with the land. But like Alexandra, Cather could also maintain separateness; such loss of self was neither regressive nor final. Hence in writing, Cather resolved the conflict we have seen as particularly intense in mother/daughter relationships.

The creative process provided nurturance as well as self-dissolution; like Edith Wharton, Cather characteristically used the language of starving and feeding to describe the act of writing. The writer without a subject is starving or half-nourished, the writer who finds her material is nourished and sustained.[38] But if the writer is the nourished child (the relationship of writer to subject matter is like that of baby to the 'mother's breast,' Cather once commented), she is also the mother, creating the book as child and nourishing its characters.[39] Cather thus also used metaphors of gestation, birth, and separation to describe her relationship to her novels, referring to the way she 'fed' characters in creating them.[40] Once Cather could give herself up to the creative process in this way, having resolved the conflicts that had kept 'woman' and 'artist' apart, her novels followed in a steady stream. After the long apprenticeship period ended with *O Pioneers!* there would be no creative dry spells. Her next novel, *The Song of the Lark* (1915), appeared two years later. In it Cather introduced another strong, creative heroine to American literature; Thea Kronborg might have been Alexandra Bergson's sister.

At last sure of her creative powers after discovering both her 'own country' and the creative process in *O Pioneers!* Cather wrote her most autobiographical novel in celebrating the woman as artist. Although ostensibly based on the career of opera singer Olive Fremstad, *The Song of the Lark* owes more to Cather's discovery of the 'art necessity' within herself. Thea's slow, stumbling growth as an artist parallels Cather's own laborious discovery of identity and vocation; in addition, Thea's mystic turning point—her sojourn at Panther Canyon where she undergoes a conversion experience to art— directly reflects Cather's trip to the Southwest where she saw the ruins of the Cliff-Dwellers in Walnut Canyon, an experience that deeply stirred her and later 'took root and grew and flowered in her mind into artistic creation' when she returned to the East and wrote *O Pioneers!*[41] In choosing to make her alter ego Thea a singer, Cather revealed her now firm wedding of femininity and creativity. As a gifted soprano, Thea can not separate her art from her body. Anatomy does not relegate woman to a restricted destiny; gender is the basis of artistic expression. The pattern of Cather's journalism and early fiction is reversed here: the novel's male characters are worshippers at Thea's shrine.

Thea's artistic triumph involves personal costs, for her personal life wanes as her artistic life flourishes. Art is not incompatible with feminine identity here but it is with the feminine role as culturally defined, for the artist cannot be answerable to the demands of human relationships requiring female self-abnegation. But the options Cather gives her heroine—the artist's solitary devotion to her craft and a possibly confining marriage— were not the only ones available to the author. Cather was constrained from giving Thea the possibility she had chosen for herself, an intimate relationship with a nurturing woman friend. Whereas Thea triumphs alone, Cather wrote *The Song of the Lark* while tended by Isabelle McClung and Edith Lewis, who filled Isabelle's role in New York.

But Cather does grant Thea her mother and the land. Bearing some resemblance to Virginia Cather, Mrs Kronborg recognises Thea's specialness and promotes her talent, providing her a private space for creativity within the house—Thea's beloved attic room, a duplicate of Willa Cather's. Thea also has the land to which she escapes for freedom and self-expression. The sand hills that she loves anticipate the topography of Panther Canyon, as Thea seeks out a feminine landscape with a 'great amphitheater' called 'Pedro's Cup,' 'cut out in the hills' along with 'winding ravines . . . full of soft sand.'[42] Like Alexandra she draws physical and spiritual strength from this affinity.

Nowhere is Thea's life-sustaining union with the land's maternal power more dramatic than in her journey to the Southwest, where she spends days in Panther Canyon, home of the ancient Cliff-Dwellers; it is, as Ellen Moers observes, 'the most thoroughly elaborated female landscape in literature.'[43]

> The canyon walls, for the first two hundred feet below the surface, were perpendicular cliffs, striped with even-running strata of rocks. From there on to the bottom the sides were less abrupt, were shelving, and lightly fringed with *piñons* and dwarf cedars. The effect was that of a gentler canyon within a wilder one. The dead city lay at the point where the perpendicular outer wall ceased and the V-shaped inner gorge began. There a stratum of rock, softer than those

> above, had been hollowed out by the action of time until it was like a deep groove running along the sides of the canyon. In this hollow (like a great fold in the rock) the Ancient People had built their houses of yellowish stone and mortar. [p. 297]

Thea explores the 'long horizontal grove' and finds among the ruins of the Cliff-Dwellers' houses a safe, protected retreat where she lingers for days: a 'cave,' a 'rock-room' where she can touch the stone roof with her finger tips (p. 298). The feminine imagery surrounding this 'nest in the high cliff' suggests both Thea's attic room and her 'Cup' in the sand hills. Cather does not associate Thea's withdrawal into her womb/cave with regressiveness; she is not William who seeks only passive, infantile merging with the mother. Her journey is a mythic return to the primitive, maternal sources of life and energy to gain strength for her return to the world, the cave a place for rebirth rather than death. Her retreat into the rock-room is the heroine's equivalent of the epic hero's journey to the underworld, and Thea emerges from her interlude with maternal powers whole, integrated, and ready to commit herself to art.[44]

Willa Cather makes the linkage between this landscape and feminine creative power even more explicit when Thea discovers shards of pottery crafted by the Indian women. She uncovers a connection between herself and her long-dead artistic foremothers, for in crafting pots to hold the precious water, the Indian women were both sustaining life and expressing artistry; their vessels were beautiful as well as functional. Bathing in a nearby stream, Thea feels 'a continuity of life that reached back into the old time,' back to the Indian women who held life in their jars just as they created it in their bodies (p. 304). This continuity provides her with a connection to feminine creativity outside the patriarchal artistic tradition.[45] Thea recognises her resemblance to her foremothers: 'In singing one made a vessel of one's throat and nostrils and held it on one's breath, caught the stream in a scale of natural intervals' just as the Indian women caught the stream of water and life in their jars (p. 304).

In writing *My Ántonia* (1918), considered by many critics her finest novel, Cather drew once more on the past for inspiration, this time transforming her childhood memories of the Bohemian farm girl Annie Sadilek into artistic expression. In Ántonia Shimerda, Cather offers a different version of the creative woman. Like Alexandra and Thea, she is linked with the land and its generative power, but Ántonia does not self-consciously shape or transform its energies into art. Like Cather's farm wife whose Thanksgiving meals rivaled novels and operas, Ántonia is linked with the un-self-conscious, ongoing creative processes of life. Connected with fertility and nurturance, she tends her children and her garden with equal care. When Jim Burden returns to her farmhouse after a twenty-year absence, he sees the miracle of birth she suggests re-enacted before his eyes. After leaving the fruit cave with Ántonia, he looks back to see her children 'running up the steps together, big and little, tow heads and gold heads and brown, and flashing little naked legs; a veritable explosion of life out of the dark cave into the sunlight.'[46] The use of the womb/cave image implies her difference from Thea. In *The Song of the Lark*, the cave was the retreat from which the daughter was reborn as autonomous artist; here it reflects the mother's powerful fertility. Jim's meditation on Ántonia's transcendent meaning further suggests her alliance with the life force: 'she had only to stand in the orchard, to put her hand on a little crab tree and look up at the apples, to make you feel the goodness of planting and tending and harvesting at last' (p. 353). By the end of the novel, Ántonia is an archetypal figure, the Earth Mother who nourishes all life. 'She was a rich mine of life,' Jim reflects, 'like the founders of early races' (p. 353).

Jim's romantic vision of Ántonia as the mother of sons who stood 'tall and straight' makes any simplistic feminist reading of the novel suspect. Ántonia is strong and admirable and she endures (despite missing teeth and weathered skin), but like Faulkner's Dilsey or Lena Grove, she is not a complex human being but a mythic figure viewed through male eyes. Jim's construct (the book is *My Ántonia*), she is not an autonomous subject but another version of woman as Other. But Cather, unlike Faulkner, is not promoting a romanticised male myth about women; whereas Faulkner creates Lena, Jim creates the mythic Ántonia. The reader has seen her realistically described in the early chapters and so is aware of how Jim transforms her in the final pages of the novel. In the unusual Introduction where Cather introduces Jim Burden to the reader as the actual author of the novel, she stresses that *My Ántonia* is *his* version of Ántonia when she has him change the title from *Ántonia* to *My Ántonia*, the addition suggesting both possession and subjectivity.

Critical debate has centered on whether Jim's deification of Ántonia is positive or not, and hence on whether he is a reliable narrator. Although most critics trust Jim's perceptions and see the novel as a celebration of Ántonia and the American frontier, in a provocative, ground-breaking article Blanche Gelfant argued that Jim's perceptions are untrustworthy. Beset by sexual fears, she contends, he eulogises the asexual mother Ántonia and shuns the sensual Lena, celebrating childhood and the past because he is afraid to grow up. Thus his romanticising of Ántonia stems from his own inadequacies. 'He can love only that which time had made safe and irrefragable—his memories,' and thus Jim 'succumbs to immobilizing regressive needs.'[47] Gelfant's article illuminates patterns in the novel unnoticed by other critics that reveal the fear of sex and passion we have seen in 'The Elopement of Alan Poole' and *O Pioneers!*: Pavel and Peter's terrible story of the bride fed to the wolves; Jim's fight with the phallic snake whose 'loathsome, fluid motion' makes him sick (p. 45); Jim's disturbing dream of the seductive Lena with a threatening reaping hook in her hand; Wick Cutter's attempted rape of Jim in Ántonia's bed. In contrast to 'Elopement' and 'The Burglar's Christmas,' here Cather splits the erotic and the maternal sides of the mother between Lena and Ántonia, and Jim is drawn irresistibly toward Ántonia and the safety of a passionless relationship mediated by distance and memory.

The question of whether he 'succumbs to immobilizing regressive needs' is complex, and the answer to it depends on an analysis of the relationship between author and narrator, which unfortunately is also extremely complex. Does Jim speak for Cather? Or is there ironic distance between author and narrator? The answer to both questions is yes. At times Jim is Cather's mask and spokesman, whereas at others she is ironically detached from him. This wavering distance between author and narrator makes settled interpretation difficult and probably accounts for the novel's conflicting readings; it's hard to locate Cather's point of view in this text. In the introduction Cather seems to make her separation from Jim Burden definitive by insisting that he, not she, wrote the narrative the reader is going to encounter. This unusual device, which Cather employs nowhere else, suggests that she wished to stress their separation. Her choice of a male narrator might at first seem further evidence of her wish to create a distinction between author and character, but this differentiation lessens when we note that many of the incidents of Jim's early years parallel hers. In addition, as we have seen, Cather frequently chooses male characters as masks, and since the Black Hawk years of Jim's acquaintance with Ántonia cover his adolescence, the period when Cather masqueraded as William, the sex difference between author and narrator does not seem that significant. Cather's paradoxical detachment from Jim and fusion with him continues throughout the text. At times she undercuts his perceptions; for example, the reader sees the irony when Jim first declares his superiority to the cowardly Black Hawk boys who fear the sensuous hired girls, and then flees from Lena Lingard to the celibate scholarly world ruled by the aptly named Gaston Cleric. But in the novel's conclusion Cather does not seem to question Jim's transformation of Ántonia into a 'rich mine of life' nor challenge his view that in returning to Ántonia and childhood he is 'coming home to [him] self' (p. 371). Does this mean that Cather is being both sexist and regressive here, viewing her heroine through the filter of a limiting female stereotype and celebrating the joys of returning to childhood? It does not seem to me that she is unthinkingly perpetuating and sanctioning limiting male views of women. First of all, Jim Burden is more the author's mask than a fully imagined male character, so in the novel's conclusion we are presented with a *woman's* construction of another woman's meaning, with Cather again resorting to camouflage when revealing her deepest preoccupations.[48] In addition, although the Earth Mother can be a limiting stereotype, the image of woman as possessing mythic powers of fertility and nurturance could be interpreted as Cather's re-claiming and reworking of a male-perpetuated stereotype which she uses to enhance rather than limit woman's dignity and stature.

The question of whether we should call this a regressive fantasy remains. Gelfant argues that 'retrospection, a superbly creative act for Cather, becomes for Jim a negative gesture.'[49] In this view, Cather is driven by the same urges as her narrator—to return to the past and retrieve the child's relationship with the mother—but she writes a novel from these urges, whereas the narrator is passive and empty, a 'wasteland' figure.[50] Certainly Cather's satisfying of regressive urges in the creative process was a positive way of dealing with such impulses, but I would argue that Jim does the same. Finally he is not regressive in the sense that William was in 'The Burglar's Christmas'; Jim, as Cather's fiction has it, does not merely narrate a story. He *writes the novel*. He thus is Cather's alter ego, the author compelled to create by the conflicts he cannot fully resolve in life, moved like Willa Cather to write by his yearning for a lost maternal figure, Ántonia Shimerda/Annie Sadilek.

After attempting a war novel in *One of Ours* (1921), inspired by the death of a nephew in World War I rather than a return of her youthful urge to write a 'manly battle yarn,' Cather returned to another version of *My Ántonia*'s compelling story in *A Lost Lady* (1923) where once again a male adolescent worships an idealised mother figure whom he views in terms of his own subjective needs.[51] But here Cather's control of authorial distance is consistent and unerring, as suggested by her decision to make Niel Herbert a limited center of consciousness within a third-person narration rather than a first-person narrator. The origin of this novel was also the loss of a maternal woman Cather had known in childhood. When she heard of the death of Mrs Silas Garber, 'a woman I loved very much in my childhood,' she created the lovely, alluring, and finally desperate Marian Forrester whose decline parallels the decay of pioneer values in America.[52] The book embodies cultural as well as personal loss, reflecting the disaffection with modern American society that pervades Cather's fiction in the 1920s. Her famous statement that 'The world broke in two in 1922 or thereabouts' embodies her repudiation of a present she saw as materialistic, spiritually bankrupt, and ignoble.[53] But although both *A Lost Lady* and *The Professor's House* (1925) reflect Cather's disaffection with the present, both novels make commitments to continuing and to accepting change, process, and life's inevitable disappointments. In dealing with the theme of loss in *A Lost Lady*, she turns once again to her most compelling preoccupation and deals with the child's search for the mother. But this novel both expresses these yearnings and examines them at the same time, with the omniscient author ironically undercutting the regressive impulses of the point-of-view character.

The union of the cultural and personal loss is embodied in the title. The 'lost lady' is America's virgin land, raped and pillaged by men like Ivy Peters, the novel's Snopes-like villain who corrupts the spiritual and imaginative vision of the West's pioneers, draining the Forresters' marsh to make it commercially profitable. The 'lost lady' is also the heroine and by extension the mother of earliest childhood whom we all must lose. In contrast to Ántonia, Marian Forrester is more erotic than maternal. Cather, aware of the sexual drive in the child's passion for the mother, adopts a male persona in order to explore this dynamic. Niel Herbert allows her to present the Oedipal drama in the conventional son/mother terms, and since the novel concerns the adolescent's unacknowledged desires for the mother figure, the male persona is consistent with her own posturing as William Cather during the same years. Niel Herbert is the youthful perceiver who first idealises and romanticises the lost lady, then viciously repudiates her. Unable to acknowledge his own unconscious sexual drives which would sully his idealised courtly lady, he reacts with excessive disgust and revulsion when he discovers that she satisfies her sexual needs with other men—first the animalistic Frank Ellinger, then the repulsive Ivy Peters to whom she turns after her husband dies. Furious that his idealised mother prefers life on any terms— as well as another man to himself—Niel is filled with 'weary contempt' when Marian refuses to 'immolate herself' after her husband's death and 'die with the pioneer period to which she belonged' so that his memory of her can remain pure and unsullied (p. 169). Like Hawthorne's Young Goodman Brown or Aylmer, Niel cannot accept either woman's sexuality or her human limitations. To him Marian is either goddess or whore, Virgin Mary or sullied Eve. But as Cather shows us, such images are Niel's constructions built from his own desires and fears, not accurate interpretations of Marian Forrester. Although some readers have assumed that Cather repudiates Marian Forrester along with Niel, this is not the case. She delicately and consistently separates her point of view from his, ironically undercutting his perceptions by suggesting the unconscious motivations for his judgments.

The contrast between Niel's and Cather's perspectives can best be seen in the central scene where Niel, the courtly lover, pays what seems to be a religious pilgrimage to Marian Forrester, rising in the 'unsullied' dawn to pick a bouquet of roses as his offering (p. 85). When he hears Frank Ellinger's laughter from her bedroom, his excessive response suggests the child's feelings of loss, anger, and betrayal when he realises that the mother's sexual attentions are given elsewhere. He hurls the flowers in the mud, murmuring '"lilies that fester smell far worse than weeds"' (p. 87). Although Niel thinks that his motives are pure and intends that the flowers will give Marian a 'sudden distaste for coarse wordlings like Frank Ellinger,' Cather makes it clear that he is propelled by sexual desire and jealousy (p. 85). The pilgrim's destination, ironically, is the lady's bedroom which he hopes to reach 'before Frank Ellinger could intrude his unwelcome presence,' and the landscape through which he moves is erotically charged, reflecting his unacknowledged sexual design (p. 84). Although Cather is drawing on the same drives that spilled over in 'The Burglar's Christmas,' here she is in control—distanced, judging, separate from her adolescent viewer. She demonstrates both Niel's self-deception and his life-denying unwillingness to accept time, change, and sexuality, in the process providing the reader with a fuller portrait of Marian Forrester than Niel will ever see.[54]

In her next novel, *The Professor's House* (1925), Cather indulged in veiled autobiography, expressing her inner conflicts once more through a male protagonist, Godfrey St Peter, the middle-aged professor who unaccountably does not want to leave his familiar old house for the gleaming new one he has bought and which his wife loves. Unlike Niel or Jim, he does not worship an idealised mother figure, but he is obsessively attached to the attic room in his old house where he has written all his books, a room he shares only with the seamstress Augusta and her sewing dummies. As Leon Edel has noted, the professor's unreasoning, stubborn attachment to his womblike retreat suggests the child's wish to remain attached to the mother. Hence the novel's ending, where the professor accidentally almost suffocates in the room by overturning an oil lamp, is psychologically sound: 'Appropriately enough, Willa Cather ends her story with the professor nearly suffocating in his room. To remain in the womb beyond one's time is indeed to suffocate.'[55] Edel links the professor's excessive depression and infantile attachment to the room he must leave with the author's extratextual conflicts. The book reflects, he argues, Cather's depression and grief at the loss of Isabelle McClung, who after marrying Jan Hambourg could offer her friend neither her exclusive attention nor the protective attic room where Cather used to write. But as we have seen, the drives Cather was drawing on here antedate the relationship with Isabelle, although doubtless that loss was the immediate source for the novel.

The professor, Edel points out, 'wants his mother to be both a mother and an erotic stimulus and above all he wants to possess her exclusively.'[56] Hence he is another version of the regressive William. But from the beginning of the novel, Cather makes it clear that he can never attain these desires. *The Professor's House* is no unmediated authorial fantasy but a carefully crafted novel in which Cather both expresses regressive yearnings through her protagonist and analyses them as the omniscient author. Fulfilling childish dreams for blissful union with a mother figure is impossible, she implies, for throughout the novel women are connected with disappointment, rejection, and loss. Even the two symbolic figures that could be idealised—the sewing dummies in the attic room which the professor could clothe or complete to suit the requirements of his imagination—are disturbingly indifferent. The first, called 'the bust' because it is 'richly developed in the part for which it was named,' should represent maternal nurturance, but it is repeatedly disappointing: 'Though this figure looked so ample and billowy (as if you might lay your head upon its deep-breathing softness and rest safe forever), if you touched it you suffered a severe shock, no matter how many times you had touched it before. It presented the most unsympathetic surface imaginable.'[57] The second form, which suggests the erotic rather than the maternal aspect of the mother, having a 'sprightly, tricky air,' is similarly disappointing. Underneath the sprightly surface is a void: 'It had ... no viscera behind its glistening ribs, and its bosom resembled a strong wire bird-cage ... she never fooled St Peter' (p. 19).

St Peter has been disappointed by women in life as well, for they inevitably fail to satisfy his needs. His wife and daughter Rosamund, like the first mannequin, are described as 'hard'; their interest in material possessions disturbs him, but their real sin is their failure to be as emotionally giving as he would like. At the end of the novel, as the professor becomes increasingly enamored of his own childhood self, his 'original ego,' he associates women with the sexual urges that destroyed his inviolate childhood self in adolescence (p. 265). Although St Peter feels that he is returning to his 'first nature' in resurrecting the inviolate childhood self free from reliance on women for sexual or emotional gratification, Cather shows us through his continued barnaclelike attachment to his attic room that he is not inviolate and independent, but increasingly passive and dependent (p. 267). His needs for nurturance are disguised rather than eradicated. The professor is rescued from the death to which his regressive needs lead by the sewing woman Augusta, and Edel interprets this to mean that 'a mother-figure has once more appeared upon the scene for the professor, who thus hangs on to his fixation even though it has brought him an immense threat. The book ends with the professor's problem unresolved.'[58] My view differs. Just as Cather survived the loss of Isabelle, moving on in adult life despite its disappointments, so the professor commits himself to continuing. After his rescue, he realises he must live without all the gratifications the child within would like. His savior Augusta is far from an indulgent maternal figure; she represents reality, not wish fulfillment ('She wasn't at all afraid to say things that were heavily, drearily true' [p. 280].) She represents the 'bloomless side of life' that he had always 'run away from,' but now that he must face it, he 'found it wasn't altogether repugnant' (p. 280). At the end of the novel, having accepted that adults at times have to live 'without delight,' St Peter finally faces the future rather than the past.

Even more than *O Pioneers!* and *My Ántonia* with their archetypal female figures, *The Professor's House* could trouble a feminist reader. Once again Cather portrays women as seen in terms of male desires and fears; in addition, the professor's happiest human bond is with a male companion, Tom Outland, rather than with his wife. At first it seems we are in the classic masculine wilderness of the American novel, reading a text by Twain, Fitzgerald, or Hemingway that denigrates women and celebrates male bonding; at times it seems that the professor's deepest yearning is to light out for the territory with Tom Outland. But as I have been arguing, when we add a biographical and psychological component to the analysis, the assumption that Cather was either unthinkingly reflecting male views of women or strategically employing male themes in order to gain critical esteem must be challenged. As we have seen, by the time she wrote this novel,

Cather had long abandoned her contempt for women. Her choice of male characters to explore sexual and emotional drives was necessitated by cultural and perhaps personal pressures to camouflage her own 'unnatural' attachments, and perhaps also by an inner need to place the barrier of gender between herself and the female force she found so compelling. The fact that her portrayals of women at times parallel those created by male writers suggests that those archetypes are compelling and persistent in those people whose emotional and erotic needs remain directed toward women after childhood. Hence, I would argue, Cather's use of such recurring female images reflects her continuing emotional investment in women more than her indoctrination by patriarchal literature and culture.

The professor's idyllic bond with Tom Outland, which a feminist reader may find even more offensive than the images of women in this novel, is more difficult to explain satisfactorily. Why would Willa Cather celebrate male bonding? Since Tom gradually comes to represent the professor's 'original ego,' it seems that Cather was forced to create this masculine pairing by her original choice to cast St Peter as male. And in fact St Peter's friendship with Tom is only a mask for his deeper yearning to return to childhood and the maternal presence symbolised by his attic room.

In the next few years, Willa Cather became increasingly acquainted with the bloomless side of life. She and Edith Lewis were forced to leave their comfortable apartment when the building was torn down, and Cather—who hated rootlessness—was forced to live in a hotel for several years until the couple resettled. Her father died in 1927, a blow she found devastating; then her mother suffered a stroke which left her paralysed until her death in 1931. The fiction Cather wrote during this period—*My Mortal Enemy* (1926), *Death Comes for the Archbishop* (1927), *Shadows on the Rock* (1931)—shows a turning away from human relationships and emotional turmoil for the calm, eternal consolations of religion, which provides her characters with the self-transcendence the land had offered Alexandra Bergson. Although these novels do not draw heavily on the themes discussed here, it is interesting to note that Cather's vision of Catholicism centers on the image of the Virgin, the eternally caring Mother who will not fail her human children. The solitary, aging archbishop finds his loneliness dissipated and 'sense of loss . . . replaced by a sense of restoration' by her Presence, which offers his soul not life's bloomless side but a 'perpetual flowering.'[59]

Evidently the impersonal consolations of religion and the Virgin did not satisfy, for in her last works, Willa Cather turned more directly to her personal past for inspiration than she ever had before, drawing on memories of her own family and childhood rather than on acquaintances like Annie Sadilek or Mrs Garber. The mother/daughter configuration is central in this late fiction, dominating 'Old Mrs Harris' and *Sapphira and the Slave Girl* (1940). But it appears in a new form here. Cather is no longer exploring a male persona's attachment to an idealised mother. In this fiction she throws away the masks: the daughter is female, not a disguised male; both daughter and mother are clear visions of Willa Cather and Virginia Cather; and the mother is now a complex human being with strengths and weaknesses, not the 'good' or the 'bad' mother of early childhood.[60] Cather's new interest in exploring her bond with her mother overtly as well as her ability to view her mother more objectively was connected with Virginia Cather's illness and death. As Edith Lewis observes, 'the long illness of Mrs Cather ... had a profound effect on Willa Cather, and I think on her work as well.'[61] The role reversal Cather experienced as she sat by her mother's bedside, mothering her weakened and helpless mother, enabled her to discard previous views of her mother which related to herself. She was now separate enough both to see her mother as a person and to acknowledge their similarities. Instead of fearing they shared the same identity, Cather could manage sympathetic identification with her mother: 'She realized with complete imagination what it meant for a proud woman like her mother to lie month after month quite helpless.'[62] Cather's new understanding coupled with the feelings of guilt, love, and loss roused by her mother's death prompted her to re-examine the mother/daughter relationship from a more objective perspective in the late fiction.

The beautifully crafted 'Old Mrs Harris' is her most autobiographical work (it could have been titled 'Family Portraits,' Edith Lewis commented).[63] The story explores the tensions and misunderstandings linking three women in the same household—the grandmother Mrs Harris, her daughter Victoria Templeton, and her granddaughter Vicki, the three corresponding to Rachel Boak, Virginia Cather, and the adolescent Willa. Only the self-forgetful grandmother can transcend her own ego to sympathise with the other two, for both Victoria and Vicki are too self-absorbed to see or respond to others' needs. Grandma Harris's fatal illness they at first interpret only in terms of themselves until they are shocked by the old woman's uncomplaining death. The triumph of the story is Willa Cather's handling of point of view. Although the author judges Vicki and Victoria for their self-absorption, she understands the reasons for it; each woman is given a complex and many-sided portrayal. When Victoria Templeton withdraws to her bedroom and lies there with camphor-soaked handkerchief around her head, the omniscient author offers the sympathetic insight into her predicament that Vicki—or her own adolescent self—does not possess. Victoria's seemingly self-indulgent withdrawal from the family conceals her despair at an unwanted pregnancy. But Vicki, concerned only with herself and her imminent break from the family, is not privy to this insight that only comes with age. The story's moving portrayal of generational conflicts suggests that Cather's ability to achieve compassionate understanding of her mother came too late for life but not for art.

In her last novel, Cather returned even further into the past for creative inspiration, tapping memories of her Virginia childhood in *Sapphira and the*

Slave Girl. The novel dramatises the separation and eventual reconciliation between three pairs of mothers and daughters: the tyrannical Sapphira and her daughter Rachel, the Negro slave Old Till and her daughter Nancy, and Willa Cather and her own mother, whose reconciliation inspired the novel and is reflected in the other mother/daughter reunions. In her previous fiction, Cather had shown the daughter/artist drawing strength and inspiration from symbolic or distant mothers—Alexandra from the land, Thea from her womb/cave and the Indian women—and in interviews she acknowledged her creative debt to the pioneer mothers whose stories fired her imagination.[64] It is fitting that in her last novel, Cather acknowledges her own mother's contribution to her creative imagination, for the book's unusual structure—novel followed by an autobiographical epilogue in which the center of consciousness is the five-year-old Willa—reveals that Virginia Cather provided her daughter with her last novel.

The fictional portion of the book, which is set in Virginia in the 1850s, had its origin in Cather's most intense and enduring childhood memory: the reunion of Old Till and her daughter Nancy, whose return from Canada the young child had witnessed. Sapphira Colbert, a strong, tyrannical southern lady, is the central character. Becoming unreasonably jealous of the slave girl Nancy Till whom she thinks her husband desires, Sapphira torments and persecutes the innocent girl; eventually she invites her husband's nephew for a visit in hopes that he will seduce—even rape—the slave girl. Her own daughter Rachel Blake then opposes her mother's plan and helps Nancy escape to Canada. The vengeful Sapphira breaks all ties with her daughter, but the two women are finally reconciled when Rachel's own daughter dies and Sapphira is jolted from her self-absorbed pride by compassion. The novel suggests the harm women's erotic attachment to men brings to mother/daughter relationships, since it is Sapphira's possessive feelings about her husband that prompt her to throw Nancy in the path of her would-be rapist; she is Ceres abandoning Persephone to Pluto instead of searching for her. By contrast, the reunion is solely a mother/daughter affair, with one daughter being sacrificed so that the mother and grandmother can be reconciled. The fictional portion of the novel ends with Sapphira asking Rachel and her daughter to spend the winter with her.

Then Cather attaches the curious Epilogue in which the distinction between fiction and fact, art and life, is erased. Set in Back Creek twenty-five years later, the Epilogue describes Nancy Till's poignant reunion with her aging mother Old Till. Cather often added codas to her novels that take place years later, but this is the only one that purports to be factual. Nancy and Old Till, fictional characters in the novel proper, now become real people Willa Cather knew as a child. Of course, an autobiographical fragment like the Epilogue is a type of fiction, since the view of the past is filtered through memory and shaped by imagination. But significantly, in letters to friends, Cather insisted that the Epilogue was literally true.[65]

The Epilogue's imaginative center is the powerful memory that had endured in her mind for over sixty years:

> Till had already risen; when the stranger followed my mother into the room, she took a few uncertain steps forward. She fell meekly into the arms of a tall, gold-skinned woman who drew the little old darky to her breast and held her there, bending her face down over the head scantily covered with grey wool. Neither spoke a word. There was something Scriptural in that meeting, like the pictures in our old Bible.[66]

The person responsible both for the child's interest in the two women and for her witnessing this dramatic reunion was Virginia Cather. She had first stimulated Willa's imagination by telling her stories about the escaped slave. 'Ever since I could remember anything, I had heard about Nancy. My mother used to sing me to sleep with: *Down by de cane brake, close by de mill, Dar lived a yaller gal, her name was Nancy Till*' (p. 281). Virginia Cather continues to minister to her child's needs as the memory is unrolled. On the day Nancy is to return to Back Creek, Willa is sick with a cold, but her mother persuades the two women to stage their reunion at the Cather farmhouse so that the child can be included in the unfolding drama. Then she puts Willa in her own bed so that she can watch the road from a good vantage point and see Nancy as soon as the stage arrives. When that moment comes, Virginia arranges a front-row view for her daughter:

> Suddenly my mother hurried into the room. Without a word she wrapped me in a blanket, carried me to the curved lounge by the window, and put me down on the high head-rest, where I could look out. There it came, the stage, with a trunk on top, and sixteen hoofs trotting briskly round the curve where the milestone was. [p. 281-82]

So, the Epilogue suggests, Virginia Cather's maternal concern for her daughter's emotional and imaginative needs gave Cather the dramatic memory from which she fashioned her last novel. The Epilogue thus both ends the novel and, in a way, begins it. Set in the 1870s, it completes the story of Sapphira and Rachel, Nancy and Old Till. But it also begins the story by showing the psychological and emotional source for the novel the adult woman would write in 1940. The insight Cather reveals into the sources of her creativity, linked here with the mother/daughter relationship, is startling and somehow very satisfying. *Sapphira's* Epilogue is the right ending not only for Willa Cather's last novel but also for her entire literary career.

Notes

1. Judith Fetterley, *The Resisting Reader: A Feminist Approach to American Fiction* (Bloomington: Indiana University Press, 1978), p. viii.
2. For an example of this type of criticism pertaining to American fiction, see Judith Fryer, *The Faces of Eve: Women in the Nineteenth-Century American Novel* (New York: Oxford University Press, 1976).

3. Cheri Register, 'Literary Criticism,' *Signs: Journal of Women in Culture and Society* 6, no. 2 (Winter 1980): 268-82.
4. Sandra Gilbert and Susan Gubar, *The Madwoman in the Attic: The Woman Writer and the Nineteenth-Century Literary Imagination* (New Haven: Yale University Press, 1979), pp. 45-92.
5. Gilbert and Gubar, *Madwoman*, pp. xi, 84.
6. Register, 'Literary Criticism,' p. 277.
7. David Stouck, *Willa Cather's Imagination* (Lincoln: University of Nebraska Press, 1975), p. 208.
8. For two brief discussions of the connection between Willa Cather's relationship with her mother and her fiction, see Jane Lilienfeld, 'Reentering Paradise: Cather, Colette, Woolf and Their Mothers,' in *The Lost Tradition: Mothers and Daughters in Literature*, ed. Cathy N. Davidson and E.M. Broner (New York: Ungar, 1980), pp. 160-75; and G.B. Stewart, 'Mother, Daughter and the Birth of the Female Artist,' *Women's Studies* 6, no. 2 (1979): 127-45.
9. Quoted in Mildred Bennett, *The World of Willa Cather* (Lincoln: University of Nebraska Press, 1951; rpt. University of Nebraska Press, Bison 1961), p. 168.
10. The major sources for biographical information on Willa Cather and Virginia Cather are E.K. Brown, *Willa Cather* (completed by Leon Edel) (New York: Knopf, 1953); James Woodress, *Willa Cather: Her Life and Art* (New York: Pegasus, 1970); Edith Lewis, *Willa Cather Living* (Lincoln: University of Nebraska Press, 1953); Elizabeth Sergeant, *Willa Cather: A Memoir* (New York: Lippincott, 1953); and Bennett, *World of Willa Cather*.
11. Lewis, *Willa Cather Living*, p. 6.
12. Nancy Chodorow, *The Reproduction of Mothering: Psychoanalysis and the Sociology of Gender* (Berkeley: University of California Press, 1978), pp. 67-129 in particular; and Jane Flax, 'The Conflict between Nurturance and Autonomy in Mother-Daughter Relationships and within Feminism,' *Feminist Studies* 4, no. 2 (June 1978): 171-91. Register describes the impact Chodorow's book has had on feminist literary criticism in her review essay.
13. I have discussed the cultural sources for her William Cather period more extensively in 'Tomboyism and Adolescent Conflict: Three Nineteenth-Century Case Studies,' in *Woman's Being, Woman's Place: Female Identity and Vocation in American History*, ed. Mary Kelley (Boston: G.K. Hall, 1979), pp. 351-72.
14. Lewis, *Willa Cather Living*, p. 13.
15. For some startling photographs of Cather during this period, see Bennett, *World of Willa Cather*.
16. Chodorow, *Reproduction of Mothering*, pp. 130-40.
17. A full discussion of Cather's early views of art and artists can be found in Bernice Slote's comprehensive introductory essays in Slote, ed., *The Kingdom of Art: Willa Cather's First Principles and Critical Statements 1893-1896* (Lincoln: University of Nebraska Press, 1966), pp. 3-114, hereafter referred to as *KA*.
18. *KA*, p. 423.
19. *KA*, pp. 158, 70.
20. William M. Curtin, ed., *The World and the Parish: Willa Cather's Articles and Reviews, 1893-1902*, 2 vols. (Lincoln: University of Nebraska Press, 1970), I:276-77.
21. A discussion of Willa Cather's college years that includes uncollected short fiction as well as views of classmates can be found in James Shively, *Writings from Willa Cather's Campus Years* (Lincoln: University of Nebraska Press, 1950).
22. The Pound letters are in the Manuscript Department, Perkins Library, Duke University. Because of testamentary restrictions, Willa Cather's letters cannot be quoted directly, so I am forced to resort to paraphrase and summary.
23. Carroll Smith-Rosenberg. 'The Female World of Love and Ritual: Relationships between Women in Nineteenth-Century America,' *Signs: Journal of Women in Culture and Society* 1, no. 1 (Autumn 1975): 1-29.
24. Lillian Faderman, *Surpassing the Love of Men: Romantic Friendship and Love between Women from the Renaissance to the Present* (New York: Wm. Morrow, 1981), pp. 273-353.
25. Willa Cather to Louise Pound, 15 June 1892.
26. All quotations are from stories available in Virginia Faulkner, ed., *Collected Short Fiction, 1892-1912* (Lincoln: University of Nebraska Press, 1965).
27. *KA*, pp. 437-41.
28. Willa Cather, *Not under Forty* (New York: Knopf, 1936), p. 85.

29. Quoted in Cather's Preface to *Alexander's Bridge* (Boston: Houghton Mifflin, 1922), p. vii.
30. Sergeant, *Willa Cather*, p. 60.
31. See both the Preface to the 1922 edition of *Alexander's Bridge* and 'My First Novels: There Were Two,' in *Willa Cather on Writing* (New York: Knopf, 1932).
32. *O Pioneers!* (Boston: Houghton Mifflin, 1913; rpt. 1941), p. 65. All future references in the text will be to this edition.
33. Bennett, *World of Willa Cather*, p. 208.
34. Sergeant, *Willa Cather*, p. 86.
35. 'The Unity of Willa Cather's "Two-Part Pastoral": Passion in *O Pioneers!*', *Studies in American Fiction* (Fall 1978):157-71.
36. Lewis, *Willa Cather Living*, p. 78.
37. Sergeant, *Willa Cather*, p. 215.
38. See her continuing use of this imagery in 'Katherine Mansfield' in *Not under Forty*, pp. 123-47.
39. Bennett, *World of Willa Cather*, p. 195.
40. Ibid., p. 212; Sergeant, *Willa Cather*, p. 137.
41. Lewis, *Willa Cather Living*, p. 81.
42. *The Song of the Lark* (1915; reprint ed., University of Nebraska Press, 1978), p. 48. All future references in the text will be to this edition.
43. Ellen Moers, *Literary Women* (New York: Doubleday, 1976), p. 258.
44. Gilbert and Gubar, *Madwoman*, discuss the connections between women's use of the cave image and feminine oppression and creativity. Although often symbolising female constriction and confinement, the womb/cave can also be 'the place of female power' to which the woman artist retreats 'to retrieve what has been lost,' her creative power and matrilineal heritage (pp. 95, 99); Cather uses the womb/cave in the positive sense they describe in 'The Parables of the Cave,' pp. 93-104.
45. Adrienne Rich discusses the traditional association of femininity, creativity and pottery making in *Of Woman Born: Motherhood as Experience and Institution* (New York: Norton, 1976), pp. 96-102.
46. *My Ántonia* (Boston: Houghton Mifflin, 1918; rpt. Houghton Mifflin, Sentry), p. 339. All future references in the text will be to this edition.
47. Blanche Gelfant, 'The Forgotten Reaping-Hook: Sex in *My Ántonia*,' *American Literature* 43 (March 1971):63-64.
48. In an unpublished paper '*My Ántonia*, Jim Burden, and the Dilemma of the Lesbian Writer,' Judith Fetterley argues that 'Jim Burden is Willa Cather's cover for her own lesbian sensibility' because she 'wants to disguise . . . the fact of love between women.'
49. Gelfant, *Reaping-Hook*, p. 64.
50. Ibid., p. 63.
51. *A Lost Lady* (New York: Knopf, 1923; rpt. Knopf, Vintage, 1972). All future references in text will be to this edition.
52. Bennett, *World of Willa Cather*, p. 69.
53. Prefatory Note to *Not Under Forty*.
54. Kathleen L. Nichols offers a perceptive analysis of the unconscious forces that distort Niel's vision in 'The Celibate Male in *A Lost Lady*: The Unreliable Center of Consciousness,' *Regionalism and the Female Imagination* 4, no. 1 (Spring 1978): 13-23.
55. Leon Edel, *Literary Biography* (Toronto: Univ. of Toronto Press, 1957), p. 70.
56. Ibid., p. 68.
57. *The Professor's House* (New York: Knopf, 1925; rpt. Vintage ed., 1973), p. 18. All future references in the text will be to this edition.
58. Edel, *Literary Biography*, p. 70.
59. *Death Comes for the Archbishop* (New York: Knopf, 1927; rpt. Knopf, Vintage, 1971), p. 256.
60. The terms refer to the young child's 'splitting' of the actual mother, who is at times both nurturant and rejecting, into an all-giving 'good' mother and a cold 'bad' mother. The split is reflected in the fairy-tale pattern of the fairy godmother and the witch. See Bruno Bettelheim, *The Uses of Enchantment: The Meaning and Importance of Fairy Tales* (New York: Vintage Books, 1977), pp. 66-73.
61. Lewis, *Willa Cather Living*, p. 156.
62. Ibid., p. 156.

63. Ibid., p. 6.

64. 'I have never found any intellectual excitement any more intense than I used to feel when I spent a morning with one of those old women at her baking or butter making. I used to ride home in the most unreasonable state of excitement,' Cather said in a 1913 interview (*KA*, p. 449).

65. Willa Cather to Dorothy Canfield Fisher, 14 October 1940 (Guy Bailey Memorial Library, University of Vermont).

66. *Sapphira and the Slave Girl* (New York: Knopf, 1940; rpt. Knopf, Vintage, 1975), p. 283. All future references in the text are to this edition.

176
To Write 'Like a Woman': Transformations of Identity in the Work of Willa Cather

◆

JOANNA RUSS

How is a lesbian to write? Or to put the question more accurately, how can a lesbian novelist use her experiences and feelings, especially her sexual ones, in an era which doesn't permit her to be open about them?

Although Willa Cather's biographer, James Woodress, does not state openly that his subject was homosexual, her early life, as he describes it, very much resembled the lives of Alice Mitchell and Alberta Lucille Hart, who appear in Jonathan Katz's *Gay American History*.[1] By the age of 15, Cather had cut her hair 'shorter than most boys' and was signing her name 'William Cather, Jr.' She had always played male roles in amateur theatricals, and even in college was 'trying her best not to be a girl.' She also still signed herself 'William Cather,' had a 'masculine' voice, and made her entire elementary Greek class laugh when she first appeared in the college classroom because she looked like a boy from the waist up but was skirted from the waist down.[2] In adult life she was 'obsessed with the desire for privacy'[3] — not surprising for a woman who 'had no need for heterosexual relationships' (Woodress goes this far only to add 'She was married to her art'), whose romances were with other women, and who called the death of one of her intimates, Isabelle McClung, 'a thunderbolt.' After McClung's death, according to Woodress, Cather hardly knew how to go on living, was in a comatose state, and was unable to feel anything. She also declared that all her novels had been written to Isabelle McClung.[4]

SOURCE   Joanna Russ, 'To Write "Like a Woman": Transformations of Identity in the Work of Willa Cather', *Historical, Literary and Erotic Aspects of Lesbianism*, ed. Monika Kehoe, New York: Harrington Park Press/Haworth Press, 1986, pp. 77–87

Even Cather's literary mentor, Sarah Orne Jewett, criticised her for adopting a man's point of view in her fiction, calling it a masquerade.[5] Woodress himself complains about Cather's 'masquerades,' as does the critic Mary Ellmann.[6] According to Woodress, Cather also received a great deal of criticism on the publication of her novel *One of Ours*, a novel in which the central consciousness is that of a young man, Claude Wheeler, and in 1921 she told a reviewer, in Woodress's words, that she 'always felt it presumptuous and silly for a woman to write about a male character.'[7] However emphatic such a declaration was, I believe it to have been placatory and very likely insincere, since the 'presumption' was one the novelist insisted upon in most of her work, including the novels *A Lost Lady*, *The Professor's House*, 'Tom Outland's Story' (a self-contained part of *The Professor's House*), *Death Comes to the Archbishop*, *O Pioneers!*, *My Ántonia*, and *One of Ours*, and short stories such as 'Coming, Aphrodite,' 'Paul's Case,' 'A Wagner Matinee,' 'A Death in the Desert,' and the marvelous 'The Enchanted Bluff.' If Willa Cather was masquerading, it was a masquerade she returned to again and again, despite Jewett's advice, despite reviewers' possible reactions, and despite her own belief, spoken if not felt, that such a masquerade was silly and presumptuous. What had been common, respectable behavior between women during most of Sarah Orne Jewett's lifetime—'romantic friendship,' 'the development of affection between friends to the point where it becomes indistinguishable from love,' women's love poems written to women, and 'a model "Boston marriage" [to Annie Fields] which lasted for almost three decades'[8]—such was by Cather's time simply perversion. Lillian Faderman traces this change of social climate in the last two decades of the 19th century. Krafft-Ebings's *Psychopathia Sexualis*,[9] first published in 1882, when Willa Cather was nine years old, was the first widely influential text to establish the idea of female 'inversion' as both morbid and a medical entity, and by the time Cather was in her early 20s any intellectual who had missed *Psychopathia Sexualis* in translation could find the same ideas in Havelock Ellis's also very influential *Studies in the Psychology of Sex* (1897).[10] The innocent rightness in feelings of love for and attraction to women which Jewett and her contemporaries enjoyed was not possible to Cather's generation; the social invention of the morbid, unhealthy, criminal lesbian had intervened. Indeed, when Annie Fields wanted to bring out a volume of Jewett's letters after Jewett's death, Mark DeWolfe Howe, Fields's friend and biographer, suggested that she omit four-fifths of the indications of the women's affection for each other lest readers misinterpret it.[11] This event is very reminiscent of the recent publication of Eleanor Roosevelt's letters to Lorena Hickok, after which the excuse/complaint the executor of the estate offered was that what seems to be so clear in the letters of course isn't, that readers just don't understand Roosevelt's effusive, old-fashioned style.[12] In view of the changed social climate in the early 20th century (American popular concern with lesbianism's morbidity began in the 1920s, but any au courant intellectual must have known about such matters much earlier), Willa Cather's 'masquerade' was a necessity. Following Jewett's advice, specifically about an early story, 'On the Gull's Road,' and changing her heroes to heroines (Jewett wrote 'a woman could love her—in the same protecting way—a woman could even care enough to—take her away from such a life'[13]) would have meant personal and professional disaster.

Cather's novels show distinct traces of this masquerade. In an earlier version of this paper I wrote that Cather's novels depict a world in which heterosexual relationships are impossible, but this is not really the case. Such relationships can appear in her work if they are described from a distance; they are impossible only to those of Cather's heroes who are at the center of the story's consciousness. And described over and over again is that these loves are not so much frustrating, enraging, or embittering as they are simply hopeless.

One of the things James Woodress chooses to find ridiculous in *One of Ours* is Claude Wheeler's wedding night, when his wife, Enid, literally locks him out of their train compartment, breaking Claude's heart. What is missing, says Woodress, is sexual frustration.[14] This is true. But there's more missing than that. What's missing is a whole complex of feelings which a real young man would feel under those circumstances, both in our day and in the era in which the novel occurs.

From literature, consciousness-raising groups, and psychotherapy groups, and from what men have told me, I have surmised what such a man would feel. First of all, he might not feel sexually frustrated in that particular scene for Claude, after all, is a virgin and can easily be thought of as rather frightened. But as the situation evolves, Cather makes it clear that Enid remains distant and disgusted, however physically available she may be, Claude would most certainly feel first of all angry, and the anger would be born of a feeling of entitlement. After all, he might well think, what did she get married for? What did she think marriage was about? A sensitive man, Claude would also feel the guilt that exists on the other side of the entitlement, that he was a cad for forcing himself on Enid, that he is bestial, that, given the era in which the novel is set, women really are more pure than men, and so on. What Cather creates instead is a kind of absolute heartbreak at the sheer untouchability of the woman and her rejection of Claude. In fact, one gets a very strong impression from the book that Enid might as well lock her bedroom door at night. They're married people living in the same house, and yet there's absolutely no sense of physical contact between them, not even in the negative forms of anger, bitterness, or frustration.

Even in *O Pioneers!*, where there is a tangible obstacle between the young couple—the young woman, Marie, is married to someone else—there are elements that simply do not make sense. Again, I doubt that a male writer would imagine the situation as Cather does, nor would a real man live it the same way. For one thing, Emil is not only in love with Marie, but remains so, monogamously and hopelessly, for several years, not even thinking of another woman during that entire time. (He certainly doesn't go and visit the local whorehouse, as he might very likely do in, say, a Hemingway story.) Again, it's not the specific physical frustration that's emphasised, but the emotional deprivation, the impossibility and hopelessness of the situation. Moreover, although she makes it clear that she will not become his lover, the woman responds with a great deal of affection. The two young people are surprisingly intimate, in an unchaperoned way, which strikes me as extraordinary for that time and place, although it would certainly not be strange for such a friendship to develop between two young women, a relationship in which one of them could feel at once extremely affectionate while also totally secure from any sexual problems or sexual advances.

In *The Professor's House*, no tangible obstacle separates the couple since the professor and his wife have been married for some years, and yet they clearly have not really spoken with or touched each other in a long time. There is no open anger, only resolute detachment on his side and chilliness on hers. In this novel occurs the absolutely astonishing imagery that Ellen Moers points out in *Literary Women*: the dress dummies in the professor's study, intensely seductive and soft to the eye, yet which when touched astonish and repel by the extremely unpleasant hardness of their texture.[15] (One might note here that the professor's study is a converted sewing room in the attic of the family house and that Cather's own study, in which she wrote *O Pioneers!*, was a converted sewing room in the attic of the McClung family house). Moers, in her passages on Cather's work, is very coy about naming the 'ancient very female view of the nature of love' expressed by Cather, but there is no doubt that the love in question is lesbian, as the other writers she discusses in this connection make clear, including Woolf, Stein, and Colette. Nor is Tom Outland, who appears in the middle of *The Professor's House*, more sexual than the Professor, indeed, he is about as non-sexual a young man as one can find in literature – not unsexed, but in some strange way set apart from the possibility of any sexual act or occasion. The atmosphere of his stay on the mesa is so intensely, so transcendentally imaginative that the preserved female corpse found there, which he, his friend, and the priest who is his teacher call 'Mother Eve,' is a shock. Even more shocking is the priest's rather risqué hint that this ancient Indian woman may have been killed for adultery. The event, its unexpectedness and its surprising ugliness, parallels the shock of touching those seemingly generous and lovely dress dummies, only to find them extremely unpleasant.

The longer one looks at these stories, the less the feelings of the characters seem to match the novelistic situations. The Professor, although his detachment from his wife is matched by his detachment from life itself as expressed finally by his almost-suicide, has no specifically sexual memories of the past, just as Marie in *O Pioneers!* feels only sadness that she must remain married to a man she no longer loves. She's afraid of him, yet Cather gives us no memory or fearful anticipation of his making sexual demands of her. Again, what Cather emphasises is the impossibility of the whole situation, well expressed by Emil's desire for one look of love from Marie's eyes and nothing more. The prohibition against adultery is not enough to explain a love that can be satisfied only in death. Rather, in one of the strongest scenes in the book, love is made identical with death; only in death can anything happen between the two women. In *The Professor's House*, the Professor's 'original nature' returns to him at middle age after 'his nature as modified by sex'[16] has somehow disappeared. The misogyny he expresses throughout the rest of the book results in an absolute lack of interest in family life, his children, and 'especially' his wife, whose presence he cannot stand any longer and whom he describes as 'chiselled . . . a stamp upon which he could not be beaten out any longer . . . a hand holding flaming arrows,' that is, something unbearable.[17]

Death, impossibility, monogamy, heartbreak, untouchableness, loneliness, inevitable frustration—through these Cather is making the very strong statement that the desire for women, the love of women, is impossible to her protagonists. Other men may be entitled to it, as in Emil's case in *O Pioneers!*, or achieve it, as in *A Lost Lady*, but never is it accessible to the male character at the center of the story. In *The Professor's House*, the Professor simply gives it up. Never explicitly described in her fiction but probably very real to Cather was the experience of living outside a lesbian circle in an essentially heterosexual world, where information about lesbianism did not exist, where she was the only one of her kind (or thought she was), and where the only women she could be attracted to were heterosexual women who would respond with friendship, with a great deal of affection and concern, even perhaps with the considerable non-sexual touching permitted between women, but with absolutely nothing more. In the face of such total deprivation, the sense of specific genital frustration Woodress complains of as missing in *One of Ours* simply gets lost in the general starvation, and the appropriate response becomes that of Claude Wheeler: heartbreak, hopelessness, and helplessness.

If one goes back and translates the situations in Cather's novels into lesbian situations, the fiction often makes clearer sense. If Claude and Enid were women setting up house together, one of them affectionate, the other passionate, then the horror of the affectionate one at the passionate one's passion and the consequent distance between them make perfect sense, as do the passionate one's helplessness and hopelessness. The impossibility of Marie and Emil's love and his extraordinary monogamy make sense. (Emil's showing off his Mexican costume to all the town girls in one scene in the book recalls young Cather's taking male roles in local dramatic productions. The costumes and roles are possible; the reality is not.) The bitterness of the young man who finds out that the heroine in *A Lost Lady* is having an adulterous love affair also makes more sense. The lady is available, all right, *but to men*. Moers calls the novel 'an Electra story, raw and barbarous.'[18]

Willa Cather grew up in an extremely deprived situation, one that did not end with the 19th century, a truth to which much contemporary writing by openly lesbian artists attests. Like most lesbian artists, she did not have the protection of (for example) Natalie Barney's money. Apparently she did not find an openly lesbian circle in which, for example, Renee Vivien could write openly of lesbian passion. She did not or could not risk her respectability. Such a situation is mitigated only somewhat by finding a partner; Jill Johnston has written very well of the 'fearfully tenacious dependent isolated ... declasse, illegal and paranoid marriage'[19] in which one clings desperately to the other precisely because there is no assurance that either of them will ever be able to find another partner, and even if one does, she will never be socially entitled to her. As Johnston convincingly shows, everyone and everything conspire to separate lesbian lovers, from the isolation forced on them by society to deliberate attempts by parents, friends, institutions, or merely heterosexual men who feel challenged, to break the couple up. In short, the sexual psychology depicted in so much of Cather's work is that of the lesbian in love with the heterosexual woman because she believes there is nobody else to be in love with. Lesbian writers who moved in a predominantly and openly lesbian society, like Radclyffe Hall or Djuna Barnes, did not seem to exhibit this psychology. (The misery of *The Well of Loneliness* was special pleading; Hall's *The Unlit Lamp* has no such deferring to prejudices.) I suspect many such writers face other phenomena such as Renee Vivien's guilt or the ghetto problem since their community, rejected by the larger society, is far too closed in; however, deprivation per se is not the same kind of problem. It is, however, a problem for writers who live, or have lived, in the same social context as Cather—for example, Carson McCullers. Again, in McCullers' work one finds the emphasis on imaginary rather than real satisfactions, and the presentation of mutual love as inherently impossible. And in May Sarton's *Mrs Stevens Hears the Mermaids Singing*, there is something of the same feeling, that loving a woman is somehow transcendentally wonderful but always transitory, in some sense unspeakable if not actually impossible. The difference is always one of social context, of the possibility of honesty, and of the availability of sexual partners. Does this kind of ambiguous material in Cather make the work worse? I think not. If her male characters were in accord with either real male experiences or the literary traditions governing such things, we would merely have an addition (observed at second hand at that) to material which is in very long supply. Descriptions of female sexuality are rare, however, and rarer still are descriptions of lesbian sexuality. Nor does the 'masquerade,' the existence of lesbian feeling in Cather's work, seem to lessen the value of the work. Quite to the contrary, it was possible for Cather, in masquerade, to speak more completely, more clearly, and less self-consciously than could, for example, Djuna Barnes in *Nightwood*. The sense of alienation and the grotesque, which Bertha Harris finds admirable in lesbian literature,[20] is precisely what is missing in Cather. The male mask enabled her to remain 'normal,' American, public, and *also* lesbian. Even now, any openly lesbian writer is almost forced to be a self-conscious rebel, a position congenial to some, but one that can be constricting nonetheless; such a role Cather simply did not take or need.

I would suggest that, as an example, the character of Claude Wheeler is not one of Cather's greatest failures, as she and her biographer seem to think, but rather one of her greatest successes. The scene in which Claude imagines himself to be one of the world's 'moon children' and his wife, Enid, to be one of the world's 'sun children,' is echoed in many fairly recent lesbian novels in which the protagonists feel themselves to be members of a world of darkness, not of the daily world of heterosexual social life. Yet how many of these characters have been able to do this kind of musing while lying on their backs under the moonlight on a Nebraska farm—and so un-self-consciously, so innocently, while so unaware of the presence of the moon in Western literature as a female symbol?

The innocence, of course, had to go. If the next stage can be called guilty self-consciousness, and the stage after that self-conscious rebellion, no matter what aesthetic advantages they offer (and I believe they offer many not available to Cather, honesty being one of them), they do not have the same advantages as Cather's masquerade; they cannot possibly create the aesthetic completeness and richness of Cather's work. Under whatever disguise, Tom Outland, Claude Wheeler, and so many of the other male personae of the books Cather gave us are, in a very precious and irreplaceable way, records not of male but of female experience, indeed of lesbian experience. In a sense not thought of by contemporary reviewers, and even possibly by Cather herself, Claude Wheeler and many other nominally male characters in Cather's work are, for lesbians, truly *One of Ours*.

Notes

1. Katz, J. (1978). *Gay American history: Lesbians and gay men in the U.S.A.* New York: Avon Books. (pp. 390–414).
2. Woodress, J.E. (1970). *Willa Cather: Her life and art.* New York: Pegasus. (pp. 45, 53).
3. *Ibid.*, p. xi.
4. *Ibid.*, p. 173.
5. *Ibid.*, p. 132.
6. Ellmann, M. (1968). *Thinking about women.* New York: Harcourt, Brace & Jovanovich. Ellman speaks of Cather's 'bluff, middy-blouse suspicions of . . . sexuality' (p. 114) and calls Claude Wheeler in *One of Ours* an aspirant to the feminine in spirit (p. 192). Ellman appears to be annoyed at Cather's attributing 'male' virtues to her female characters, and 'female' virtues to her male characters. I believe homophobia to have been at work here.
7. Woodress, p. 194.
8. Faderman, L. (1981). *Surpassing the love of men: Romantic friendship and love between women from the renaissance to the present.* New York: William Morrow. (pp. 197–199).
9. Kraft-Ebing, R. von. (1925). *Psychopathia sexualis.* (— —, Trans.). New York: Surgeon's Book. (Original work published 1886.)

10. Ellis, H. (1911). *Studies in the psychology of sex: Sexual inversion.* Philadelphia: F.A. Davis. (Original work published 1897.)
11. Faderman, p. 197.
12. 'Was Eleanor a lesbian?' *Seattle Gay News*, November 23, 1979.
13. Faderman, p. 202.
14. Woodress, p. 194.
15. Moers, W. (1977). *Literary women: The great writers.* Garden City, NJ: Anchor Books. (p. 359).
16. Cather, W. (1973). *The Professor's House.* New York: Vintage. (p. 267).
17. *Ibid.*, p. 274.
18. Moers, p. 363.
19. Johnston, J. (1973). *Lesbian nation: The feminist solution.* New York: Simon & Schuster. (p. 157).
20. Harris, B. (1977, Fall). What we mean to say: Notes toward defining the nature of lesbian literature. *Heresies 3: Lesbian art and artists* (pp. 5–8).

177
My Gay Ántonia: The Politics of Willa Cather's Lesbianism

TIMOTHY DOW ADAMS

After years of critical comment that avoided the issue of Willa Cather's homosexuality, or only hinted about it, in 1975 Jane Rule publicly identified Cather as a lesbian by devoting a chapter to her in *Lesbian Images*, although failing to see any traces of lesbianism in Cather's fiction. Lillian Faderman, in *Surpassing the Love of Men*, her book-length study of love and romantic friendship between women, refers to Cather's forty-year relationship with Edith Lewis as a 'Boston Marriage,' a late nineteenth century term encompassing life-long friendship between women, with or without sexual relations. But like Rule, Faderman sees 'absolutely no suggestion of same-sex love in Cather's fiction.'[1] Because of the political consequences of writing openly about lesbianism in the time that Cather came of age, according to Faderman, 'perhaps she felt the need to be more reticent about love between women than even some of her patently heterosexual contemporaries because she bore a burden of guilt for what came to be labeled perversion.'[2]

While it would certainly have been possible for Cather to live a discreet lesbian life without showing any traces of homosexuality in her writing, it is more likely that her sexual preferences are present in her literature, whether consciously or unconsciously, and that an analysis of her work, particularly *My Ántonia*, in terms of homosexual images can add a new dimension to Elizabeth Sergeant's contention that 'her books, provided one does not take them too literally, are a better guide to Willa Cather's life than any biographical dictionary.'[3]

Sexual tension is never absent in Cather's books. As Blanche Gelfant notes in an article on sex in *My Ántonia*:

SOURCE Timothy Dow Adams, 'My Gay Ántonia: The Politics of Willa Cather's Lesbianism', *Historical, Literary and Erotic Aspects of Lesbianism*, ed. Monika Kehoe, New York: Harrington Park Press/Haworth Press, 1986, pp. 89–98

> Once we redefine his [Jim's] role, *My Ántonia* begins to resonate to new and rather shocking meanings which implicate us all. We may lose our chief affirmative novel, only to find one far more exciting—complex, subtle, aberrant.
>
> Jim Burden belongs to a remarkable gallery of characters for whom Cather consistently invalidates sex. Her priests, pioneers, and artists invest all energy elsewhere. Her idealistic young men die prematurely; her bachelors, children, and old folk remain 'neutral' observers. Since she wrote within a prohibitive genteel tradition, this reluctance to portray sexuality is hardly surprising. What should intrigue us is the strange involuted nature of her avoidance. She masks sexual ambivalence by certainty of manner, and displays sexual disturbance, even the macabre, with peculiar insouciance. Though the tenor of her writing is normality, normal sex stands barred from her fictional world. Her characters avoid sexual union with significant and sometimes bizarre ingenuity, or achieve it only in dreams. Alexandra Bergson, the heroine of *O Pioneers!*, finds in recurrent reveries the strong transporting arms of a lover; and Jim Burden in *My Ántonia* allows a half-nude woman to smother him with kisses only in unguarded moments of fantasy. Their dreams suggest the typical solipsism of Cather's heroes, who yield to a lover when they are most solitary, most inverted, encaptured by their own imaginations.[4]

Despite the use of such suggestive words as 'aberrant,' 'involuted,' 'sexual disturbance,' 'macabre,' 'bizarre,' and 'inverted,' in reference to Willa Cather's portrayal of sexuality in her characters in general, and particularly in Jim Burden, Blanche Gelfant sees these characters as merely afraid of sexual and emotional contact with each other, thus echoing Marcus Klein's thesis that 'It is the struggle to get beyond the necessity of human relationships that is the secret history of all Willa Cather's novels.'[5]

Although Jim and Ántonia do transcend or avoid the necessity of expected human relationships—every reader has probably wondered why they did not marry when Jim returned to Black Hawk after Ántonia had been deserted by Larry Donovan—the story, cast as it is in the form of a fictional combination of Jim's autobiography and Ántonia's biography, is centered around the long-lasting and deep human relationship between the dual protagonists. And it is the confusing nature of that relationship that causes 'emptiness where the strongest emotion might have been expected.'[6] Jim Burden's autobiography focuses too much on Ántonia to explain a normal friendship. A way out of these confusions lies in the realisation that both Jim and Ántonia were imagined by Willa Cather as homosexuals. Their attraction to each other is as deep as it is, not because they are failed lovers, but because their friendship is reinforced by the realisation that their 'aberrant,' 'inverted,' sexual disturbance is basically homosexual. It is not surprising that Willa Cather's lesbianism is reflected in both Jim and Ántonia when we consider that Elizabeth Sergeant calls Jim 'Ántonia's twin-sister.'[7] At one point Jim says to Ántonia, 'I'd have liked to have you for a sweetheart, or a wife, or my mother or my sister—anything that a woman can be to a man.'[8] One of the things that a woman can be to a man when both are homosexuals is a confidante, a cover to shield one's sexual preferences from others. As Frank Caprio writes, 'It is not uncommon for lesbians to establish friendly relations with male homosexuals. One reason is that the relationship is apt to be a platonic one and consequently they have no need to fear being seduced, particularly if they harbor antipathy toward men in general.'[9] Homosexual men and women are attracted to each other out of a common feeling of separation from societal norms and a common desire for non-sexual friendship, the kind of friendship that exists between heterosexual men or women.

Although Ántonia and Jim chose each other as playmates, they never seem to feel the slightest sexual interest in each other, even in experimentation. At an age when boys typically show their incipient affection for girls by pulling their hair, chasing them, or affectionate indifference, Jim and Ántonia instead go for sleigh rides where they 'burrowed down in the straw and curled up close together' (p. 52).

At first, Jim and Ántonia seem to be acting out the standard male/female roles in the episode with the snake at the prairie dog village: Ántonia as the screaming, frightened female, Jim as the calm, brave male. But in actuality the situation is only, as Jim later realises, 'a mock adventure' (p. 49), both in the sense that the snake is not really so dangerous as it appears and in the mutual realisation that Jim and Ántonia are only acting out their respective roles in a pretense of normality. Although some critics see the snake-killing episode as an authentic test of courage and initiation into manhood,[10] it is clearly a false test, and both Jim and Ántonia realise that fact immediately. It is Ántonia who alertly spots the snake and her screams, unfortunately delivered in Bohemian, are a warning rather than a cry of fright. Jim's reaction to the snake is hardly masculine:

> His abominable muscularity, his loathsome, fluid motion somehow made me sick. He was as thick as my leg, and looked as if millstones couldn't crush the disgusting vitality out of him. (p. 45)

Jim stands up to the snake only because he was too scared to think of running, while Ántonia approaches the snake fearlessly, even though barefooted. The scene ends with Ántonia calmly wiping Jim's sickened face. According to Blanche Gelfant's interpretation of this scene, which she feels has implicit sexual connotations, 'as Jim accepts Ántonia's praise, his tone becomes wry and ironic, communicating a unique awareness of the duplicity in which he is involved.'[11] While Gelfant sees duplicity only in terms of the snake's oldness and the fact that the contest was 'fixed by chance' (p. 50), Jim remembers the incident as a conscious agreement between Ántonia and himself to mask their growing awareness of their sexual differences and 'to confront deeply repressed images, to acknowledge for the only time the effect of 'horrible unconscious memories.'[12] 'The ancient, eldest Evil' (p. 47) seen in the snake and in Jim's symbolic cutting of it, represents on one level another version of Adam and Eve's awareness of evil, and on another Jim's and Ántonia's recognition of their latent homosexuality. Seeing his homosexuality as an ancient evil and remembering his first admission of it as a 'horrible, unconscious memory,' reflects Jim's sense, recalled years afterward, of the 'guilt at the core' of homosexuality which 'begins long before a sexual experience, with just the feeling of being different.'[13]

As they mature, Jim and Ántonia's sexual differences become more apparent. In Black Hawk, Jim shows little interest in Mr Harling or in boys his own age, including Charley Harling, who live around him. Instead, Jim prefers the company of 'Sally, the tomboy with short hair,' (p. 149), who 'always dressed like a boy' (p. 175), or the adult Frances, who replaces Charley in Mr Harling's eyes as a son, father, and daughter walking 'home together in the evening, talking about grain-cars and cattle, like two men' (p. 150). David Stouck sees that 'The specific conflict that arises for Jim in Book III is sexual,' and notes that 'the best times for Jim occur when men are absent — when grandfather is at church and Mr Harling is away on business — leaving the carefree world of happy children presided over by the indulgent Mrs Harling, the older daughter Frances, and Ántonia.'[14]

Ántonia, meanwhile, has become even more masculine in appearance and occupation. Calling herself Tony, as Willa Cather called herself Willy, Ántonia, whom Gelfant refers to as an 'ultimately strange bisexual,'[15] takes pride in her maleness. With perspiration on her lip 'like a little moustache' (p. 130), Ántonia says joyfully, 'I like to be like a man' (p. 138), while asking Jim 'to feel the muscles swell in her brown arm' (p. 138). While in town, Ántonia temporarily adopts a more feminine appearance, although her voice is now 'deep and a little husky' (p. 176). Although Ántonia is presented in this section in more feminine terms, her basic lack of interest in the opposite sex is still obvious. She does go happily to dances, but she is just as glad to dance with the other girls, as she does in the scene where she waltzes with Mary Dusak, knowing 'there's a roomful of lonesome men on the other side of the partition' (p. 190). Some young men begin to notice Ántonia at the Vannis' tent dances, but Jim never mentions her being interested in any of them. Her love of dancing is presented, not as romantic desire, but as a love of physical activity common to the strong immigrant girls whose 'out-of-door work had given them a vigour' (p. 198) which is reflected in their dancing ability. Ántonia goes to the dances, not as a shy young farm girl, but by breaking 'into a run, like a boy' (p. 205). Although Ántonia is popular with the town boys, the only sexual incident with them involves Ántonia slapping young Harry Paine for kissing her.

Jim's lack of sexual interest in girls begins to cause questions about his masculinity:

> Anna knew that whispers were going about that I was a sly one. People said there must be something queer about a boy who showed no interest in girls of his own age, but who could be lively enough when he was with Tony and Lena or the three Marys. (p. 216)

To forestall these rumors, Jim attempts to kiss Ántonia in a sexual way. Ántonia responds with surprise and indignation. Having failed again at a heterosexual relationship, Jim bolsters his pride by imagining that he 'knew where the real women were, though [he] was only a boy; and [he] would not be afraid of them, either' (p. 225). At this point in his remembrance of his sexual development, Jim recalls a pleasant recurring dream about Lina Lingard in a short skirt, flushed and 'carrying a curved reaping-hook in her hand' (p. 225). The castration image of the curved reaping-hook and cut wheat reinforces the earlier image of the snake and the spade. Significantly, even though he wants to, Jim is never able to have 'this flattering dream' (p. 226) about Ántonia.

Later, Jim and Ántonia are involved in what Stouck calls 'a sublimated erotic dalliance'[16] during a July picnic in the country. Ántonia and Jim's mock-erotic game is broken up by the appearance of Lena, looking 'almost as flushed as she had been' (p. 238) in Jim's dream.

Although Ántonia is banished from the Harlings to work for the evil Wick Cutter because of her supposed sexual encounters with boys, she actually dreads the thought of a heterosexual experience. Cutter's sexual history and his preparation to rape Ántonia cause her to suggest that Jim take her place, symbolically sleeping in her bed. Although Cutter's attempted rape of Jim seems obvious, Jim's latent homosexuality drives him deliberately to put himself in the position of substituting for Ántonia in a sexual encounter with a man. Jim must have been aware of Cutter's plans to seduce Ántonia, yet he pretends to be asleep when he hears Cutter's steps outside his room:

> The next thing I knew, I felt someone sit down on the edge of the bed. I was only half awake, but I decided that he might take the Cutter's silver, whoever he was. Perhaps if I did not move, he would find it and get out without troubling me. I held my breath and lay absolutely still. A hand closed softly on my shoulder, and at the same moment I felt something hairy and cologne-scented brushing my face. (p. 248)

Jim's reaction to Cutter, who is earlier described as 'a peculiar combination of old-maidishness and licentiousness' (p. 211), is as excessive as his revulsion of the snake, and includes the same tone of disgust and sickness. 'Vile as the Cutter incident is—and it's also highly farcical—Jim's nausea seems an overreaction, intensified by his shrill rhetoric and unmodulated tone.'[17] Jim's awareness of his homosexual desires and his disgust at the nature of his encounter with another male combine to produce an outraged tone of over-protestation that only emphasises his sexual fears. As Clyde Fox notes, 'I have never been reconciled to the feeling about the "disgustedness" that Miss Cather gives Jim after he has been lewdly pawed over by Mr Cutter. It would seem more natural to me for a boy to smother in a burst of anger whatever anti-homosexual emotions he might feel about it.'[18]

Jim's homosexuality becomes more apparent by Book III. While at the University of Nebraska, he never dates or even talks to young women except for Lena Lingard, who reappears as in his dream still teasingly flirtatious. Although Jim and Lena frequently go to plays and dinners, their relationship is clearly asexual. Lena is at this point more nearly in Jim's social sphere; she seems to suggest a closer relationship, but Jim resists and they part with 'a soft, slow renunciatory kiss' (p. 293). When the narrator of the introduction to *My Ántonia* describes Jim, she says that he still has 'the romantic disposition which often made him seem very funny as a boy' (p. ii). This view of Jim as a funny boy is echoed by Lena who says to Jim just before they part—their 'renunciatory kiss' sealing forever the chance of a sexual relation—that 'You aren't sorry I came to see you that time? It seemed so natural. I used to think I'd like to be your first sweetheart. You were such a funny kid' (p. 293). Lena's statement, which seems similar to Jim's later remark to Ántonia about having any relationship a man and woman can, supports the image of Jim Burden as a funny boy suggested by the narrator in the introduction. These repeated statements seem odd in light of the Jim Burden revealed in *My Ántonia*, one who never seems humorous. Perhaps the two people who see Jim as funny mean that he is funny in the sense of being odd in the role of a boy.

While Jim is at the university, Ántonia deliberately enters a mock-heterosexual relationship with Larry Donovan, whose reputation as a scoundrel could hardly have escaped her notice. Her lesbianism being in conflict with her maternal instincts results in a deliberate attempt to live with Donovan so that she could become a mother without the worry that a traditional marriage would be expected. Even before she has her child, Ántonia has returned to her mannish ways, wearing 'a man's long overcoat and boots, and a man's felt hat with a wide brim' (p. 316). Jim and Ántonia meet, and it is at this juncture in their lives that most critics feel they should have married each other.

Because Jim and Ántonia understand each other's sexual preferences, they both feel the difficulty and sorrow of their individual attempts at solving the homosexual's dilemma in a heterosexual world. When Jim and Ántonia meet again after 20 years, they have both solved that dilemma by contracting marriages of convenience that serve as masks for their sexual variance. Jim's wife is described by the narrator of the introduction, in the revised 1926 version, as 'handsome, energetic, executive . . . unimpressionable and temperamentally incapable of enthusiasm . . . She has her own fortune and lives her own life. For some reason, she wishes to remain Mrs James Burden' (p. ii). Jim's sterile, childless marriage is contrasted with Ántonia's fruitful marriage to Anton Cuzak, but Ántonia and Cuzak relate to each other more as friends than as lovers. As Alexandra Bergson says in *O Pioneers!*, 'I think when friends marry they are safe.'[19]

When Jim and Ántonia are reunited at the book's end, they walk along the familiar roads of the divide. Thinking about their mutual homosexuality, Jim reflects that

For Ántonia and for me, this had been the Road of Destiny; had taken us to those early accidents of fortune which predetermined for us all that we can ever be. (p. 372)

The early accidents of fortune had caused each of them to leave the main road of heterosexual life for their personal destiny as homosexuals. For Jim and for Ántonia, deep friendship based on mutual homosexuality was all they could ever share.

Notes

1. Faderman, L. *Surpassing the love of men: Romantic friendship and love between women from the renaissance to the present*, (New York: Morrow, 1981), p. 21. For a discussion of historical and biographical evidence for Cather's lesbianism and her need to conceal her sexuality, see Sharon O'Brien's (1984) '"The Thing Not Named": Willa Cather as a Lesbian Writer', *Signs, 9*, 576–599, which was published too late to be incorporated into this essay.
2. Faderman, p. 201
3. Cited in Slote, B., 'Willa Cather,' *Sixteen modern American authors*, ed. by Jackson Bryer (New York: Norton, 1973), p. 38.
4. Gelfant, B. 'The forgotten reaping-hook: Sex in *My Ántonia*,' *American Literature, 43*, (1971), p. 61.
5. Klein, M., Introduction, *My Mortal Enemy* (New York: Vintage Books, 1926), p. 59.
6. Brown, E.K., & Edel, L. *Willa Cather: A Critical Biography*, (New York: Knopf, 1953), p. 202.
7. Cited by Lewis, E., *Willa Cather Living* (New York: Knopf, 1953), p. 149.
8. Cather, W., *My Ántonia*, (Boston: Houghton, Mifflin, Sentry Edition, 1946), p. 321. Further references are to this edition.
9. Caprio, F., *Female Homosexuality*, (New York: Citadel Press, 1954), p. 87.
10. See for example Miller, J.E., '*My Ántonia*: A frontier drama of time,' *American Quarterly, 9* (1958), p. 482.
11. Gelfant, p. 64.
12. Gelfant, p. 70.
13. Abbott, S., & Love, B., *Sappho was a Right-on Woman* (New York: Stein & Day, 1972), p. 20.
14. Stouck, D. *Willa Cather's Imagination* (Lincoln: University of Nebraska Press, 1975), p. 51.
15. Gelfant, p. 73.
16. Stouck, p. 52.
17. Gelfant, p. 73.
18. Fox, C., 'Revelation of character in five Cather novels,' Dissertation. University of Colorado 1963, p. 211.
19. Cather, W., *O Pioneers!* (Boston: Houghton, Mifflin, Sentry Edition, 1913), p. 308.

178
From Lighting Out for the Territories

SANDRA GILBERT and SUSAN GUBAR

[. . .] The woods of Arcady were to come alive for Willa Cather when she excavated a past and produced a pastoral which could provide an adventure story for women. In doing so, she had to come to terms with scholarly and literary myths of the frontier that presented an image of women's misery in the wilderness. For writers from Alexis de Tocqueville to D.H. Lawrence, after all, the frontier woman was a tired wife and wretched mother. Tocqueville's frontier woman is 'prematurely pale' with 'shrunken limbs,' a 'frail creature' who has 'already found herself exposed to unbelievable miseries.' Although a 'profound sadness' marks her features, although she has 'exhausted herself' giving birth to her children, 'she does not regret what they have cost her.'[1] In a similar vein, as G.J. Barker-Benfield has pointed out, Hamlin Garlin claimed that 'the wives of the American farmers fill our insane asylums,' while Lawrence imagined the homesteader's mate as a 'poor haggard drudge, like a ghost walking in the wilderness.'[2] But perhaps the privations of the pioneer women were most brilliantly described by the critic Thomas Beer. Considering 'women stately as great cows, and grammarless, before whose eyes the legend of the West had been erected,' Beer recognised how their experiences had been erased and hoped that 'the forgotten kindness of their hands may raise them up a chronicler, else they are lost who were not ladies.'[3]

Both *O Pioneers!* and *My Ántonia* question the view that pioneer women were shrunken, frail, maddened, or—for that matter—'stately as great cows, and grammarless.' Yet both novels do provide a chronicle to reclaim those 'who were not ladies' from historical and imaginative oblivion. For even while Cather revised myths of pioneer women's misery, she also implicitly rejected legends of the west that denied women's existence. As R.W.B. Lewis's analysis of the American Adam 'poised at the start of a new history'

SOURCE Sandra Gilbert and Susan Gubar, from 'Lighting Out for the Territories', *No Man's Land*, Vol II, *Sex Changes*, New Hanen: Yale U.P., 1989, pp. 182-97, 409-11

and 'undefiled by . . . family' suggests, and as Leslie Fiedler's account of 'the pure marriage of males' with each other and 'their union with the wilderness itself' documents, the literary tradition of the frontier from Cooper to Twain uses both male bonding and masculine escape from civilisation to characterise a quest that provides what Fiedler terms 'an innocent substitute for adulterous passion and marriage alike.'[4] Lewis and Fiedler show that the heroes of frontier novels exert 'strenuous efforts to stay outside' society—to remain inside 'a lost childhood and a vanished Eden'—an effort inextricably related to their authors' protests against the feminisation of American culture and those same authors' creation, in Fiedler's words, of a 'mythic America [which] is boyhood.'[5] But, of course, for such writers as Stevenson and Kipling in works like *Treasure Island* and *Kim*, the adventure story, with its setting in unexplored territory and its celebration of male bonding, also functions to mythologise boyhood.

As Henry Nash Smith and Marcus Cunliffe have observed, moreover, diction quite similar to that of the literature of adventure informs the arguments of the foremost turn-of-the-century historian of the American frontier, Frederick Jackson Turner. In his famous 1893 essay 'The Significance of the Frontier in American History' and in a number of other influential articles, Turner claimed that the settlement of successive areas of free land fostered economic, political, and social equality in American society. Like the novelists, Turner identified the virgin land as a female: 'this great American West took [European man] to her bosom,' and 'she opened new provinces, and dowered new democracies.'[6] Turner's ideal of rugged individualism was not unrelated to his admiration for Tennyson's 'Ulysses,' who aspires 'To sail beyond the sunset and the baths / Of all the western stars,' and for Kipling's 'Explorer,' who seeks to 'blaze a nation's way, with hatchet and with brand, / Till on his last-won wilderness an empire's bulwarks stand.'[7] Praising the heroic ideals—'grim energy and self-reliance'—of the pioneer who is always assumed to be male,[8] Turner's essay functions as a gloss on the imaginative vision established in 'The Leather-stocking Tales' and *Huckleberry Finn* and in the Whitman poem whose title Cather uses in *O Pioneers!*, as well as by the figure of Robinson Crusoe that Carl Linstrum draws at the beginning of *O Pioneers!* and the pages of *The Life of Jessie James* that Jim Burden brings with him to Nebraska at the beginning of *My Ántonia*.[9]

Cather's first two versions of pastoral invoke the adventure tales 'the boy in us' loved but reject their masculinist ideology by drawing upon a regionalist perspective even while they resist the limitations imposed by that perspective. As Richard Brodhead has recently argued, regionalism functioned 'to open up isolated native regions to public knowledge and to figure a new population of foreigners; to dramatise the pluralism of contemporary American culture and to put such pluralism under the sway of a culture more concerned than ever to maintain its rule.'[10] Cather, who praised the local color writings of Eliot, Jewett, and Mansfield, struggled to use and yet extend a genre whose apparent modesty had been particularly congenial for women like Mary E. Wilkins Freeman, Rose Terry Cooke, Constance Woolson, Grace King, and Kate Chopin.

Not merely recording 'sketches' about backwater customs in remote countries and counties, Cather nevertheless brought the muse of the regionalists to the frontier in order to undermine the identification of assertive strength (the west) with masculinity and of effete gentility (the east) with women. The injunction 'Go West, young man' becomes ironic in her works because when male characters like Carl Linstrum and Jim Burden go west, they encounter not male freedom but female primacy. In other words, for Cather, the American frontier functions in a manner similar to that of the colonised country or remote outpost in the works of Olive Schreiner and Charlotte Perkins Gilman. Specifically, in both *O Pioneers!* and *My Ántonia*, Cather creates a mythic America which is girlhood, for she tells the story of the gender dislocation fostered by immigration into the wilderness, a dislocation that results in the death of the father, the diminution of the son, and the empowerment of the daughter with the concomitant centrality of female work. That shades of the prisonhouse of culture inevitably threaten to obscure this centrality serves only to emphasise Cather's darkening vision of the 'boundless freedom' she celebrated in Kipling's books, a 'freedom that delights because we have it not' (*WP* 1, 138).

'The wilderness masters the colonist,' Turner wrote, going on to declare, as Cooper did in a different way, that 'It strips off the garments of civilization and arrays him in the hunting shirt and moccasins'; but Cather is haunted by the realisation that initially the frontier environment is, as Turner mentions, 'too strong for the man.'[11] At the beginning of *O Pioneers!*, 'The great fact [of] the land itself, which seemed to overwhelm the little beginnings of human society that struggled on its sombre wastes,' makes the wild land a waste land for the boys and men who believe 'that men were too weak to make any mark here, that the land wanted to be let alone, to preserve its own fierce strength, its peculiar, savage kind of beauty, its uninterrupted mournfulness.'[12] Even the plow only leaves imprints likened to 'feeble scratches on stone left by prehistoric races, so indeterminate' that they seem more like glacial 'markings' than a human 'record' (19-20).

Precisely this indeterminacy convinces John Bergson that the 'Genius' of the Divide is 'unfriendly to man' (20). On his deathbed, Mr Bergson commands his sons Otto and Lou to 'be guided' by their older sister, Alexandra (27). Because these young men 'were meant to follow in paths already marked out for them, not to break trails in a new country' (48), they submit to their sister's directions (albeit with petulance) after trying unsuccessfully to convince her to sell the farm. Otto works 'like an insect, always doing the same thing over in the same way' (55), and such mindlessness is also evident in Lou, who is 'fussy and flighty,' often getting 'only the least important things done' (56). Though the third son, Emil, is sent by Alexandra to the university, Otto and Lou are ruled by her determination to keep and enlarge their farm, but all three recognise that 'the struggle in which [their] sister was destined to succeed while so many men broke their hearts and died' (78) somehow excludes or belittles them.

The frontier is therefore a virtual no man's land, as two other male characters demonstrate. First, Alexandra's childhood companion Carl — whose family has 'depended so' on her (52) — leaves the land because his sensitivity and artistic aspirations make him 'a fool' (53) there, and when he briefly returns looking 'stooped' and 'pale,' he explains to Alexandra that he is 'a failure,' with no ties, no family, and no property: 'It is your fate,' he tells her, 'to be always surrounded by little men' (181). Second, Ivar — a religious recluse and a self-taught veterinarian who forbids the killing of wild creatures — is presented as 'a man [who] is different' (93), a kind of misfit: subject to spells, unable or unwilling to speak English, he is 'a queerly shaped old man, with a thick, powerful body set on short bow-legs' (36–37). Although he begins in a 'wild homestead' where 'his Bible seemed truer to him' (38), this 'little man' is a no-man who brings his knowledge of nature to Alexandra, whom he calls 'Mistress' and to whom he devotes his services. By the end of the novel, moreover, both Carl and Ivar have become inhabitants of Alexandra's house and instruments of her pioneering idealism.

If anything, the portrait of the frontier as a no man's land is extended in *My Ántonia*, for this more complex novel begins with a meditation on the land's resistance to men's strivings and on the father whose death and burial mark the sacrifice exacted by the wild. When the young Jim Burden arrives at the place where 'the world ended' (16), he feels himself to be 'outside man's jurisdiction' (7). Not only 'erased' (8) by a landscape which is 'not a country at all, but the material out of which countries are made' (7), he is all but dissolved by the 'rough, shaggy, red grass' which 'was the country, as the water is the sea' (14–15). No wonder, then, that the resonant scene in which Jim kills a snake in the garden and thereby supposedly saves Ántonia, the damsel-in-distress, while proving himself the 'equal' to the 'great land,' turns out to be 'in reality . . . a mock adventure' (49). Although Ántonia claims Jim is 'a big fellow' (46), she has in fact constructed a fiction of Jim's masculinity, for the rattler was old, torpid, with 'not much fight in him' (49). In addition, as a number of critics have noted, what is probably most clearly revealed in this fall in the garden is Jim's nausea at the phallic snake's 'abominable muscularity, his loathsome, fluid motion' (45).[13]

But the first in a succession of figures who will become Jim's male mentors is an even more crucial sign that the frontier is a no man's land. Mr Shimerda, 'the old man [who] had come to believe that peace and order had vanished from the earth' (86), cannot endure the dislocation and homesickness of immigration. Having lost his trade as a weaver, his art as a fiddler, and his youthful friendship with another musician, Mr Shimerda retains only remnants of his old world culture, specifically the gun and fiddle which he wants to bequeath to Jim and Ántonia respectively. Unable to provide for his family during the harsh frontier winter, he shaves, washes, dons clean clothes, then lies down on the bunk bed next to the ox stall, puts the end of his gun barrel in his mouth, and pulls the trigger with his big toe. Coming during the Christmas festivities of the Burden household, the tragedy at the Shimerdas' is described in devastating detail: the farmhand who relates the story to Jim and his grandmother explains, '"When we found him, everything was decent except"—Fuchs wrinkled his brow and hesitated—"except what he couldn't nowise foresee"' (96).

Frozen in a pool of blood and excrement, this dead father—who is strikingly similar to the central character in Cather's first published story, 'Peter' (1892)—is literally buried at the crossroads. Many years later, his grave, dug by axes chopping out the frozen earth, becomes an unmowed 'little island' of tall red grass, a relic of the frontier saved by the curve of two roads around it, for Mr Shimerda's buried life almost seems to represent the paternal absence—the sacrifice—that becomes a signifier of the wilderness. In any case, the suicidal father represents the settlers' bewilderment at the impermanence of human signification on the frontier. His refinement makes him unfit to tame a land that here, as in *O Pioneers!*, seems to 'overwhelm the little beginnings of human society that struggled in its sombre wastes' (15). As in the earlier novel, the surviving sons are inadequate to the world in which they find themselves: like Otto and Lou, Ambrosch, although the favorite of Mrs Shimerda, is described as almost stupidly surly, while Marek, like Ivar, seems a strangely primitive creature, for he has webbed fingers and barks like a dog or crows like a rooster. As in *O Pioneers!*, then, the death of the father means the end of the old world's patrilineage. John Bergson sees in his daughter 'the strength of will' that comes from his father and that he 'would much rather, of course, have seen . . . in one of his sons' (24), and Mr Shimerda recognises in Ántonia the survivor who inherits his father's strength so it is she who literally steps into the dead man's shoes.

Cather was as fascinated as other mythologists of the American west by the idea that originatory moments—the beginning of culture itself—recurred over and over again on the frontier. An Italian economist quoted by Turner argues that 'America has the key to the historical enigma which England has sought for centuries in vain, and the land which has no history reveals luminously the course of universal history.'[14] As Eudora Welty has shown, Cather was inspired by 'the absence of history as far as she could see around her,' a blank that 'only made her look further, gave her the clues to discover a deeper past.'[15] But in particular Cather can be said to be uncovering the 'universal history' of gender in those works that examine the primacy of the female in the context of the 'historical enigma' of the development of patriarchy. For her, the west is a place in which women at least briefly experienced an exhilarating autonomy. According to one contemporary historian, this freedom, which meant that '"women's work" soon came to mean whatever had to be done,' helps explain why the first suffrage laws in America were passed by western states.[16] Far from being a waste land to the inheriting daughters of *O Pioneers!* and *My Ántonia*, the frontier is a blank page on which Cather inscribes 'women's work.' Indeed, the wild land is a kind of wild zone between what Turner called 'savagery and civilization,'[17] a liminal space in which Alexandra Bergson and Ántonia Shimerda can exercise their powers.

Wearing 'a man's long ulster,' which she carries as if it 'belonged' to her and as if she were 'a young soldier' (6), Alexandra exhibits an 'Amazonian fierceness' (8) that from the very beginning of *O Pioneers!* extends far beyond her physical vitality, for she reads the papers, follows the markets, and learns the agricultural innovations that allow her to make the family's fortunes. Although Cather explains that the 'history of every country begins in the heart of a man or a woman,' it is the face of Alexandra which, 'For the first time, perhaps, since that land emerged from the waters of geologic ages,' is 'set toward it with love and yearning' (65). Not a particularly 'clever' person, Alexandra discovers that her chief source of joy comes from contemplating 'the great operations of nature' and 'the law that lay behind them' (70–71).

The orchards, fields, and beehives of her farm, soon the richest on the Divide, therefore contrast oddly with her 'curiously unfinished' and oddly furnished house because her real home is 'the big out-of-doors' (83–84). The 'fiery ends' of curls escaping from her braids 'make her head look like one of the big double sunflowers' in her vegetable garden, and, although her face is tanned, the rest of her skin has the smoothness, whiteness, and freshness 'of the snow itself' (88). To Carl, remembering her in 'the milky light' of dawn (126), Alexandra looks 'as if she had walked straight out of the morning itself' (126). With her soul reflected in the cultivation of the soil, Alexandra has no trouble defending herself against Otto's and Lou's later efforts to assert their claim that 'the property of a family really belongs to the men of the family' (196). Indeed, when she invokes the laws of culture to state her faith in her own entitlement—'Go to the county clerk and ask him who owns my land' (168)—her farm becomes a luminous image, although quite different from Charlotte Perkins Gilman's, of Herland. For unlike that of Gilman's Herlanders, Alexandra's inheritance is not merely the result of a lucky strike, but, like theirs, it recalls the 'morn by men unseen'—the 'different dawn'—that Emily Dickinson envisioned in her poem about a 'mystic green' (J. 24).

Besides the patrilineal 'strength of will' Alexandra has inherited, at least part of her resilience comes from exactly the sort of gardening that Annette Kolodny identifies with women's mythologising of the wilderness. Rejecting male metaphors of 'either erotic mastery or infantile regression,' women writers, according to Kolodny, replace the forest with rolling fields and log cabins, the woodsman or the hunter with the gardener.[18] But, of course,

Cather could also have drawn upon the domestic artistry celebrated in *The Country of the Pointed Firs*, as her dedication to Jewett makes clear.[19] Just as in that book Mrs Todd's herbal concoctions produce comforting medicines, Mrs Bergson's 'unremitting efforts to repeat the routine of her old life among new surroundings' (28) result (when the family first moves to the Divide) in the construction of a log—instead of a sod—house, and in a garden that allows her to preserve and pickle to her heart's content. Similarly, as in Jewett's Dunnett Landing, where gardening and gossiping knit together the community, in *O Pioneers!* preserving—which 'was almost a mania with Mrs Bergson' (29)—is a metaphor for the preservation of life women accomplish through their work.

Although in its depiction of the extremity of the daughter's situation and in its disparaging of the maternal inheritance, *My Ántonia* offers a more qualified vision, it nonetheless still hints at the 'Amazonian fierceness' of its heroine. Terence Martin, who finds Ántonia 'a bit too muscular for conventional romantic purposes,'[20] inadvertently points to the physical vitality of this heroine who, four years older than Jim, refuses to submit to his sentimental impulses. Initially, to be sure, Jim's childhood companion experiences even greater deprivation than he does on their entrance into the wilderness. As a foreigner who is considered contaminating, as a Bohemian with no knowledge of English, Ántonia lives in a house 'no better than a badger hole' (20) which is far more primitive than Jim's home: a cave made out of earth, her sod house in the significantly named Squaw Creek resembles the tunneled nests in the 'prairie dog town' where the earth-owls live a 'degraded' life (30). Underdressed in cotton, sharing a single overcoat with her siblings, Ántonia knows that 'Things will be easy for [Jim]. but they will be hard for us' (140). As if contrasting Jim's and Ántonia's situations so as to meditate on the historic poverty of daughters, Cather nevertheless attributes her heroine's resiliency at least in part to her youthful dispossession.

Soon after arriving on the Divide, Ántonia manages to escape with her sister and Jim for a series of adventures in the 'great fresh open' that 'made them behave like wild things' (64). But even in the context of her family, Ántonia is immediately singled out as the Shimerda interpreter, the one who is to learn English. Quick to name the new country with the new words Jim supplies, she is 'the only one of his family who could rouse the old man from the torpor' of his misery (41). At least in part, this is because Ántonia is the repository of the family's communicable past. She tells Jim stories about the Old World, but she also translates Mr Shimerda's stories about his sense of loss in the New World, even as she relates the 'mock adventure' of Jim's induction into masculinity. Just as significantly, she recounts in English a story told by yet another man dying in the wilderness. Pavel's tale about the sleigh ride of a Russian wedding party pursued by hundreds of hungry wolves culminates in his confession that he decided to lighten the load by throwing the bride overboard. That Ántonia's retelling of this legend gives her and Jim 'a painful and peculiar pleasure' (61) testifies to their freedom as children in the New World, for this story of brutality seems to suggest that in the world of the past all brides were on their wedding night at least metaphorically thrown to the wolves they married.

After the deaths of both Pavel and her father, Ántonia—now 'Tony'— appears to acquire the physical freedom of a man. Working the land and aged beyond her fifteen years by her labor, she displays 'arms and throat [that] were burned as brown as a sailor's' (122). Because she cannot be spared from the farm, she condescends with seeming bravado to Jim when he begins his education: although she 'always wanted to go to school' (230), she declares, ' "I ain't got time to learn. I can work like mans now. . . . School is all right for little boys. I help make this land one good farm' (123). Eating 'noisily now, like a man' (125), she disgusts Jim, who feels that there are 'some chores a girl ought not to do' (126). Indeed, after he sees her 'come up the furrow, shouting to her beasts, sunburned, sweaty, her dress open at the neck, and her throat and chest dust-plastered' (126), Jim snobbishly thinks of her as a peasant. But she defends herself and defies his censorious notion that 'work out-of-doors' is indecorous: 'I like to be like a man' (138). That Ántonia's sexchange has less to do with biology than it does with farm work becomes clear when she returns to both ploughing and male clothing during her first pregnancy.

At the same time, however, Ántonia also excells in the kitchen, for she learns all of the arts of her own mother and of Jim's grandmother: cooking, baking, preserving, and pickling.[21] Empowered by both their paternal and their maternal inheritances and pictured amid 'the feathered stalks [which] stood so juicy and green' in the 'world's cornfields' (137), both Alexandra and Ántonia recall popular pictures of Columbia, imagined as a sort of Demeter figure offering cornsheaves or a cornucopia. Like the woman Mary Beard sees on 'the horizon of dawning society' in a passage we have used as an epigraph here, both illuminate Margaret Mead's more recent characterisation of the girls 'willing to come to America': 'they weren't afraid of facing new conditions; they weren't afraid of hardship; they weren't afraid that they might be left alone.'[22] Given Cather's success at imagining what Fiedler calls 'an innocent substitute for adulterous passion and marriage alike,' these figures might seem (at least from their author's point of view) significantly different from, say, Lyndall, petulantly railing against her lover's strength, or Edna Pontellier, pursuing an affair with one man when she desires another, or Lily Bart, languishing on the marriage market.

Because Cather's heroines are older, wiser, and stronger than the male characters—brothers and brother surrogates—to whom they are implicitly compared, this writer sets her analyses of sex roles against any biological explanation of gender asymmetries within a patriarchal culture. If anything, those traits that distinguish the girls of *O Pioneers!* and *My Ántonia* demonstrate their superiority to boys. But actually, Carl and Alexandra, like

Jim and Ántonia, have 'always felt alike about things . . . we've liked the same things and we've liked them together' (52), for the fluid boundaries between male and female roles on the frontier resemble those on the sexual 'frontier' Havelock Ellis identified with modern society. Yet both of Cather's novels go on to document the social construction of rigid gender demarcations at the turn of the century, not as a result of biological essentialism but as a consequence of surplus value and, ironically, a surplus value that women's work helps to produce. Inevitably, then, first in *O Pioneers!* and then even more definitively in *My Ántonia*, the emergence of a mercantile economy leads to a sexual division of labor. Like Anne Finch, who saw women as 'Education's, more than Nature's fools,' Cather views sex roles as the result of an education 'dessigned' to alienate her characters from the Divide of Nebraska, which becomes symbolic of a widening divide that separates men from women.

In the world of *O Pioneers!*, the very different desires Lyndall, Edna, and Lily express for male lovers or protectors reappear as an index of a process of feminisation that would be inconceivable in an agrarian economy. To begin with, the contrast between the first two parts of this novel—'The Wild Land' of 1883 and the 'Neighboring Fields' of 1899—highlights a process of cultivation that has brought the Bergsons the comforts of new riches as well as the crudities of the nouveau riche. Even Alexandra is 'willing to be governed by the general conviction that the more useless and utterly unusable objects were, the greater their virtue as ornament' (97). And Cather's satire against Lou's family comes close to Wharton's attack on the female as ornament and on conspicuous leisure because the 'reassuring emblems of prosperity' Alexandra only produces for her guests' approbation have totally compromised her brother's wife.

Wearing 'her yellow hair in a high pompadour,' Annie Lee—Lou's spouse—'is bedecked with rings and chains and "beauty pins"' (99). Preoccupied not only with her own 'high-heeled shoes [which] give her an awkward walk' (99) but also with a hat that 'look[s] like the model of a battleship' (113), she plans to 'move into town as soon as [her] girls are old enough to go out into company' (111) so that instead of running about the country as she herself used to do, they will—like her oldest daughter—attain such lady like accomplishments as piano playing and, of all things, pyrography ('That's burnt wood, you know' [110]). Despite her blustering husband's warning that the 'West is going to make itself heard' (112), he and his wife have assimilated eastern values, and they therefore make Annie's mother feel humiliated about her immigrant ways.[23]

As the youngest brother, Emil, realises, 'Lou and Oscar would be better off if they were poor,' for 'it gets worse as it goes on' (238-39). But Emil is another example of the destructiveness of surplus value. 'I want you to be independent,' Alexandra confides to Otto and Lou at the beginning of the novel, 'and Emil to go to school' (68). Although Emil's adventures in the world outside the farm reconcile Alexandra to the hardness of her fate, his upward mobility—his college education, traveling, and plans to attend law school—may, in fact, have 'ruined him,' as Lou and Oscar suppose (302), for, having become a person 'fit to cope with the world' (213), Emil 'scarcely remember[s]' (78) the wild country of his childhood when, at twenty-one years of age, he returns to the farm after college.

Many critics have noted the way in which Alexandra's story is yoked by violence to the tale of the far more conventional triangle that joins Alexandra's neighbor Marie Shabata and Marie's husband, Frank, to Emil.[24] When Emil realises that he is too old to 'play' with Marie 'like a little boy' (156) and when he goes off to Mexico because of his scruples about desiring a married woman, the familiarity of Cather's plot appears to be almost deliberately uncovered, for the story of this doomed romance echoes the plot of Kate Chopin's *The Awakening*. Just as Robert Lebrun flees from Edna Pontellier, Emil hopes to find a vocation in Mexico that will save him from adultery. Like Edna, Marie reads the letters her lover has purportedly written to another person, letters really meant for her eyes. Like Edna, who is jealous of the women with whom Robert might have flirted, Marie wonders if Emil brought his guitar to serenade 'all those Spanish girls' (193). And evoking Chopin's major metaphor, the narrator of *O Pioneers!* likens the lovers' first embrace to a sigh, 'as if each were afraid of *wakening* something in the other' (225; emphasis ours). But, of course, Marie does not decide to leave her husband. Instead, when Emil and Marie finally consummate their desire, they are accidentally discovered by her husband and murdered. Cather's swerve from Chopin's plot demonstrates her belief that the 'overvaluation of love' which fuels her precursor's tale must precipitate an expulsion from paradise that can only elicit the mournful verdict of the wise healer Ivar when he discovers the dead bodies of the lovers in the Shabatas' orchard: 'it has fallen! Sin and death for the young ones!' (271).

The unhappy marriage of the Shabatas that at least partially contributes to the love and death of Emil and Marie is itself a reflection of a fatal fall into gender. Even as a 'city child' (11) visiting the Divide, Marie Tovesky was an exceptionally 'pretty and carefully nurtured' (12) coquette who was offered 'bribes' of candy by her uncle's friends, men who wanted to become her 'sweetheart' (12). Her later elopement with Frank Shabata is presented not only in terms of the construction of her ornamental femininity, but also in relation to Frank's almost parodic masculine posturing. For, according to Cather, the femme fatale meets her match in the figure of the *homme fatal*. '[T]all and fair, with splendid teeth and close-cropped yellow curls' (143), Frank exhibits an expression of discontent as well as a cambric handkerchief and a yellow cane, all of which endow him with a 'melancholy and romantic' charm (144). But the narcissism that leads him to give his fiancée photographs of himself, 'taken in a dozen different love-lorn attitudes' (146), eventually causes him to resent in his wife what attracted him during his courtship, namely Marie's vivacity and friendliness. Like a working-class version of the speaker in Browning's 'My Last Duchess,' Frank becomes a jealous braggart who bullies Marie, and, although she begins as 'his slave,' she eventually experiences what Browning's duchess must have endured:

> always the same yearning, the same pulling at the chain—until the instinct to live had torn itself and bled and weakened for the last time, until the chain secured a dead woman, who might cautiously be released. (248)

That Marie's analysis of her incompatability with Frank is superficial, however, is clarified by uncanny similarities which connect the man she dislikes to the man she desires. Like Frank, Emil becomes jealous of Marie's high spirits on more than one occasion.[25] In addition, if Marie fell in love with the almost comically Byronic posturings of Frank (whom her father recognised immediately as a 'stuffed shirt' [144]), she grants her first kiss to Emil when he is costumed in a black velvet coat with real silver buttons, a silk sash, and a tall Mexican hat. At a church fair where young women sell their embroidery to their suitors, Marie becomes angry that Emil offered his shirt studs to the highest bidder and so she is delighted when he enters her fortune-telling tent to bestow a handful of uncut turquoises, an event that recalls the 'bribes' of candy she had received as a child. In addition, the fair held at the Church of Sainte-Agnes—besides evoking the romanticism of Keats's 'Eve of St Agnes' in the context of a sexual auction[26]—takes on an ominous centrality because of the fate of a couple married there.

From the moment one of Emil's friends becomes a bridegroom, he is inexplicably doomed, as if Cather wanted to italicise not her indictment of adultery but her sense of the fatality of heterosexuality. At first, the death and funeral of this 'good boy' (252) teach Emil a way to convert his destructive erotic desire into 'a kind of rapture in which he could love forever without faltering and without sin' (255). But the 'equivocal revelation' (256) that leads both Emil and Marie to believe that they can relinquish each other and yet still 'live a new life of perfect love' (249) fails to disentangle love from desire. Paradoxically, at the very moment when they meet to renounce each other and dedicate themselves to an ideal that transcends sexuality, Emil and Marie embrace, and both are made 'to pay with their blood for the fine ideals of the poets' (*WP* 2 689).

Toward the realm of gold that is the moonlit orchard of romance in which Marie dreams, Emil is driven 'wild with joy,' like 'an arrow shot from the bow' (258). The embracing lovers lying next to the resplendently white mulberry tree, the suspicious husband parting the leaves to peer in on shadowy figures, the gun that springs to his shoulder, the moaning of a mutilated woman who leaves a trail of blood on the orchard grass and on the white mulberries in her effort to drag herself back to her lover's corpse: Cather's primal scene of sex is a version of sex war. But, as Sharon O'Brien has noted, this scene also brings together all the images in *O Pioneers!* that draw upon Sarah Orne Jewett's now classic story 'A White Heron' (1886).[27]

A tale about the young girl Sylvia's attraction to a handsome hunter who is searching for a rare white bird, 'The White Heron' records the sylvan girl's decision not to give away the secret of a heron's nest. Her silent refusal implicitly rejects an alliance with the hunter and explicitly protests against birds 'dropping silently to the ground, their songs hushed and their pretty feathers stained and wet with blood.'[28] Cather links the scene in the orchard to Jewett's story through an earlier episode in *O Pioneers!* during which Emil shoots down five birds and Marie lifts one of them out of her apron, 'a rumpled ball of feathers with the blood dripping slowly from its mouth' (128). Although Marie goes on to prohibit the killing of 'wild things' (128), as a result of the secret logic that has connected husband to lover, a gun—which Jewett associated with the hunter and Cather originally identifies with Emil—appears in Frank's hands, and the blood of Jewett's heron transforms itself into the blood of Cather's heroine. For while Jewett seems to acquiesce in the necessity of the renunciation of (female) desire, Cather questions the possibility of such renunciation.

Far from being tacked on, in Cather's 'two-part pastoral' Marie's story tells us what Alexandra's fate would be, if she had been constructed as a feminine ornament. Like Marie, Alexandra agrees with Ivar that 'wild things' must not be killed. Ivar makes this point initially about a 'big white bird. . . . she was in trouble of some sort, but I could not understand her' (40). And Alexandra soon feels 'as if her heart were hiding down' in the long grass of the Divide, 'somewhere, with the quail and the plover and all the little wild things . . .' (71). Stirred for a bird, Alexandra also treasures an image of a wild duck—'a kind of enchanted bird that did not know age or change' (205) —as one of her happiest recollections. Through the death of Marie, however, Cather questions the efficacy of Alexandra's identification with nature, for *O Pioneers!* swerves from what Louis A. Renza sees as Jewett's faith that 'women can reclaim a gender-exclusive relation to the origins of life or the Edenic Garden.'[29] With far deeper pessimism than Jewett, who presents the bond between women and nature as a viable alternative to the culture of death represented by a man and his gun—a hunter-taxonomist who threatens to kill the heron/heroine into art—Cather envisions female centrality in the natural realm as an empowerment qualified by the inescapable advent of a culture that depends on private property and that links ownership to the possession of women.

For this reason, even Alexandra's potency is interrogated as the Nebraskan Divide moves from savagery to civilisation. Besides serving as a patron to Emil, Alexandra is inexplicably insensitive to the affair brewing between him and her closest friend. More malevolently, the Swedish girls whom she has 'broken in' as domestic servants and whom she marries off (often to 'men they were afraid of' [228]) testify to 'the impervious calm of

[this] fatalist,' a calm that is 'disconcerting' (226). After the death of the lovers, moreover, Alexandra's final assertion that 'the people who love [the land] and understand it are the people who own it' (308) illustrates her massive repression, for it ignores the fate not only of Marie but also of two no-men. Frank Shabata—turned into the number 1037 in prison—is 'not altogether human' (294) so he wants to go back home to enlist his mother's protection; Carl—back on the farm that is Alexandra's home—disregards the evidence of Frank's and Emil's guilt and instead echoes her blaming of Marie for the tragedy in the orchard: 'There are women who spread ruin around them through no fault of theirs, just by being too beautiful, too full of life and love' (304).[30]

Because her own personal life is 'almost a subconscious existence' (203), Alexandra exhibits a lack of imagination that reflects the limits of her capacity for experiencing 'in her own body the joyous germination in the soil' (204):

> Her mind was a white book, with clear writing about weather and beasts and growing things. Not many people would have cared to read it; only a happy few. She had never been in love, she had never indulged in sentimental reveries. Even as a girl she had looked upon men as work-fellows. She had grown up in serious times. [205]

Of course, there seems to be one crucial exception to the 'white book' of Alexandra's blankness, namely her recurrent fantasy of union with the Genius of the Divide. 'It was a man, certainly, who carried her, but he was like no man she knew.' Large, strong, and swift, he bears her 'as easily as if she were a sheaf of wheat,' although it is he who—'yellow like the sunlight' —emanates the smell of cornfields. That Alexandra 'prosecutes her bath with vigor' after this dream and that later in life the 'old sensation of being lifted' (206-07) occurs when she is fatigued suggest that this is a compensatory sexual fantasy appropriately imagined as a kind of union with the fertile wilderness incarnate. Later, when grief over Emil's death causes her to long 'to be free from her own body,' she again receives 'the old illusion of her girlhood, of being lifted and carried lightly by some one very strong.' But this time she sees her Genius clearly and realises that his arm was 'of the mightiest of all lovers' (282-83). Finally, after Alexandra's emotional crisis manages to convince Carl to overcome his anxieties that union with her would turn him into an exploitative dependent, she sees her impending marriage as an alternative to the obliteration her phantom suitor offered.

Yet this dream sequence, mentioned first directly after the description of Alexandra's mental 'white book,' is introduced not as an exception to but as an instance of the 'clear writing about weather and beasts and growing things': 'There was one fancy indeed, which persisted through her girlhood' (205). Neither a love story nor a sentimental reverie, the fantasy about the Genius of the Divide is associated with the price exacted by Alexandra's renunciation of desire. Therefore, if Marie's story demonstrates that love leads to death, Alexandra's recurrent dream hints that thanatos is the only alternative to eros. Half in love with an easeful death that would release her from the gravity of her autonomy, Alexandra represents all those characters in Cather's later novels who seek an earlier, lighter, childhood self—stripped of social baggage—that will carry them back to an impersonality which is both unsayable and unlivable. In this context, Carl's view that on the Divide 'the old story has begun to write itself over' takes on an ominous ring: 'there are only two or three human stories,' Carl had told Alexandra earlier in the book in a passage that now fatalistically hints at the deadliness of romance and the romance of death, 'and they go on repeating themselves as fiercely as if they had never happened before' (119).

The old stories of love and death may be written—as Alexandra insists at the end of *O Pioneers!*—'with the best we have' (307), but Carl is not wrong to recall the grandeur of 'this country when it was a wild old beast' (118), for the 'safe' marriage between mature friends (308), and even the milk and honey of their farm are not due recompense for earlier splendors in the grass. 'Wo bist du, wo bist du, mein geliebtest Land'' (118) is the old German song that haunts not only Carl but also Cather, who wrote about the 'fierce necessity' and 'sharp desire' at the beginning of life in her introductory poem to the novel, a poem in which both necessity and desire are 'Singing and singing, / Out of the lips of silence, / Out of the earthy dusk.' Although Cather dedicated *O Pioneers!* to Sarah Orne Jewett because 'in this book I tried to tell the story of the people as truthfully and simply as if I were telling it to her by word of mouth' (*KA* 448), the evocative phrase 'the lips of silence' intimates that this novel about a heroine 'who could not write much' or 'very freely' (286) would give way as inevitably as would the mother tongue to a kind of paternal or patriarchal speech.

Notes

1. Tocqueville, 'Fortnight in the Wilderness,' in George Wilson Pierson, *Tocqueville and Beaumont in America* (New York: Oxford University Press, 1938), p. 245.
2. See Barker-Benfield, *The Horrors of the Half-Known Life*, p. 6, for a discussion of Lawrence's *Studies in Classic American Literature* and Garland's *Other Main Travelled Roads*.
3. Beer, *The Mauve Decade: American Life at the End of the 19th Century* (New York: Alfred A. Knopf, 1926), pp. 93-94.
4. Lewis, *The American Adam: Innocence, Tragedy and Tradition in the Nineteenth Century* (Chicago: University of Chicago Press, 1955), pp. 1 and 5; Fiedler, *Love and Death in the American Novel* (New York: Stein and Day, 1966), pp. 211, 210, and 339.
5. Lewis, *American Adam*, pp. 101 and 129; Fielder, 'Come Back to the Raft Ag'in, Huck Honey!' in Fielder, *An End to Innocence: Essays on Culture and Politics* (Boston: The Beacon Press, 1955), p. 144.
6. Smith, *Virgin Land: The American West as Symbol and Myth* (Cambridge: Harvard University Press, 1950), p. 254.
7. Cunliffe, 'The Two or More Worlds of Willa Cather,' in *The Art of Willa Cather*, ed. Slote and Faulkner, especially pp. 33-34.
8. Smith, p. 260.

9. For a discussion of the similarity of Cather's and Cooper's response to the American frontier, see John J. Murphy, 'Cooper, Cather, and the Downward Path to Progress,' *Prairie Schooner* 55:1-2 (Spring-Summer 1981): 168-84.

10. We are grateful to Richard Brodhead for sharing part of an essay on regionalism that will appear in the *Cambridge History of American Literature*, ed. Sacvan Bercovitch, p. 24 of the typescript. For a discussion of the centrality of women writers in the regionalist tradition, see Josephine Donovan's examination of the works of Annie Fields, Harriet Beecher Stowe, Rose Terry Cooke, Elizabeth Stuart Phelps, Sarah Orne Jewett, and Mary E. Wilkins Freeman in Donovan, *New England Local Color Literature: A Woman's Tradition* (New York: Frederick Ungar, 1983).

11. Turner, 'The Significance of the Frontier in American History,' in Turner, *The Frontier in American History*, with a foreword by Ray Allen Billington (Huntington, N.Y.: Robert E. Krieger, 1976), p. 4

12. Cather, *O Pioneers!* (Boston: Houghton Mifflin, 1941), p. 15. Further references will be to this edition, and page numbers will appear in the text, preceded by the citation *OP* when necessary.

13. Jim also tries to see the Burden's farmhands as desperado cowboys and similarly fails to keep himself from realising that they are, in fact, 'the sort of men who never get on, somehow, or do anything but work hard for a dollar or two a day' (p. 68).

14. Turner, p. 11.

15. Welty, 'The House of Willa Cather,' in *The Eye of the Story: Selected Essays and Reviews* (New York: Vintage Books, 1979), p. 47. Also see Dorothy Van Ghent, *Willa Cather* (Minneapolis: University of Minnesota Press, 1964), especially pp. 8-9.

16. Cathy Luchetti in collaboration with Carol Olwell, *Women of the West* (St George, Utah: Antelope Island Press, 1982), pp. 31 and 35. See also the description of the 'more equal footing' of pioneer spouses in Joanna L. Stratton, *Pioneer Women: Voices from the Kansas Frontier*, intro. by Arthur M. Schlesinger, Jr. (New York: Simon and Schuster, 1981), p. 57.

17. Turner, p. 3.

18. Kolodny, *The Land Before Her: Fantasy and Experience of the American Frontiers, 1630-1860* (Chapel Hill: University of North Carolina Press, 1984), pp. 8-9.

19. See Cather's preface to *The Best Stories of Sarah Orne Jewett*, reprinted in *OW*, pp. 47-59. For further analyses of Jewett's vision of women's artistry, see Josephine Donovan, *Sarah Orne Jewett* (New York: Frederick Ungar, 1980), especially pp. 99-121 on *The Country of the Pointed Firs*; and Elizabeth Ammons, 'Jewett's Witches,' in *Critical Essays on Sarah Orne Jewett*, ed. Gwen L. Nagel (Boston: G.K. Hall, 1984), pp. 165-84.

20. Martin, 'The Drama of Memory in *My Ántonia*, *PMLA* 84 (March 1969): 304-11.

21. Although Mrs Shimerda is presented by Jim as a garrulous troublemaker and miserable housekeeper, at the end of the first book she is as shrewd as she is shrewish, triumphing in arduous circumstances by imposing a legal fine on a farmhand who beat up Ambrosch and by appropriating one of Mr Burden's cows. In addition, Jim's disdain of her sour-dough bread and dried mushrooms merely reflects his own provincialism.

22. For the Mead quotation we are indebted to Shoshana David, who brought it to to our attention.

23. Like Lou's spouse, Oscar's wife refuses to allow Swedish to be spoken at home, in her case because she is 'ashamed of marrying a foreigner' (p. 99).

24. For a discussion of the critics who view the book as 'split' between 'Alexandra' and 'The White Mulberry Tree,' see Woodress, pp. 231 and 247.

25. Emil asks himself, 'Why did she like so many people . . .?' (p. 179) and later admonishes her, 'Sometimes I think one boy does just as well as another for you' (pp. 229-30). In addition, Marie's discussion of 'Frank's other wife' (p. 198) — the woman whom he would desire but whom she could never become — suggests that perhaps Emil is her 'other' husband.

26. John J. Murphy suggests a relationship between Keats's 'The Eve of St Agnes' and *O Pioneers!* in 'A Comprehensive View of Cather's *O Pioneers!*,' *Critical Essays on Willa Cather*, ed. Murphy (Boston: G.K. Hall, 1984), p. 124.

27. O'Brien, p. 442.

28. Jewett, 'A White Heron,' reprinted in Jewett, *The Country of the Pointed Firs and Other Stories*, ed. Mary Ellen Chase, with an introduction by Marjorie Pryse (New York: W.W. Norton, 1981), p. 239. Cather's language also evokes Tennyson's 'She took the speckled partridge flecked with blood' and Hopkins's 'The Windhover.'

29. See Renza's analysis of Jewett's allusions to a 'sexual-biblical war' in Renza 'A White Heron' and the Question of Minor Literature (Madison: University of Wisconsin Press, 1984), p. 83.

30. What both Alexandra's and Carl's explanation does not take into account when they construct a stereotypical portrait of Marie as a destructive Eve or femme fatale is Frank's own admission of his guilt, his realisation that 'he was to blame. For three years he had been trying to break her spirit' (p. 266).

Writing Against Silences: Female Adolescent Development in the Novels of Willa Cather

SUSAN J. ROSOWSKI

Adolescence is one of the most important subjects of Willa Cather's fiction, one she treated far more extensively than she did subjects with which she is most identified. She wrote about pioneers, for example, in only three of her twelve novels, while she wrote of adolescence in eleven. In doing so, she provided as full and complex an exploration of adolescence, and particularly of female development, as we have in American literature. As so often, the writer has anticipated the theoretician, for questions psychologists are now asking about development as distinctly female run through Cather's canon and are the subject of two novels, *The Song of the Lark* and *Lucy Gayheart*.

First—definitions. Though Cather ordinarily used the term 'youth' rather than 'adolescence,' she provided marker events that define adolescence as beginning with puberty at twelve or thirteen and as lasting until her character has 'assumed a full adult role in society,' the general criterion Patricia Meyer Spacks suggests as an ending for adolescence.[1] In Cather's fiction, late adolescence ordinarily lasts until the mid-or even late twenties.

Second—her general idea of adolescence. Cather writes of this period as one in which gender differences shape lives. Male development proceeds by linear, sequential stages, one replacing the other: childhood is followed by adolescence, and after that adulthood. Among these stages, adolescence is a time of disruption. Bartley Alexander, Jim Burden, Claude Wheeler, Niel Herbert, Godfrey St Peter—all left their 'original selves' behind when as adolescents they were distracted by work, success, love, and public expecta-

SOURCE Susan J. Rosowski, 'Writing Against Silences: Female Adolescent Development in the Novels of Willa Cather', *Studies in the Novel*, 21, 1989, pp. 60–77

tions. For the male, passage from adolescence to adult life is so complete, the stages so separate, that Cather describes it by metaphors of death. Claude Wheeler and Tom Outland actually die, but had they lived, Cather suggests, they would have joined her other middle-aged men in regretting their lost youth, perhaps realising as the singer Clement Sebastian in *Lucy Gayheart* does, 'that when people spoke of their dead youth they were not using a figure of speech.'[2]

Cather's fiction of female development is another matter altogether, not by sequential movement from one discrete stage to another but by transformations. Continuity lies beneath apparent changes as her female characters age, and instead of metaphors of death, Cather uses ones of reconfigurations. She compares her female adolescent to a plant, by which development occurs through continuous, ongoing transformations— from seed to seedling, and from that to flowering plant, which in its turn produces the seed. She writes of her female adolescent's development too by metaphors of female reproduction, by which gestation, birth, and mothering are not separate stages but ongoing, simultaneous aspects of female life. Her girls contain within themselves the women they will become, and her adult women remain in touch with the children they once were.

The two patterns of development have to do with two ideas of creativity, since Freud interpreted narrowly, by sexuality. Unlike a Freudian view that girls and women suffer anxiety from the absence of outward signs of creative (i.e., sexual) activity (visible genitalia made more visible by erections and emissions of sperm), Cather described girls and women as enjoying the security of knowing they carry within themselves that which they need to be creative. The idea of possession is central to her descriptions of adolescence, again with significant gender differences. While to grow up male is to be dispossessed of childhood in adolescence and then of adolescence in adulthood, to grow up female concerns claiming that which is within, then giving it form.

Not surprisingly, in Cather's fiction a sojourn in the cliff dwellings of the Southwest Mesa Verde is one thing for a female adolescent and quite another for a male. Cather used the setting first in *The Song of the Lark*, making it a metaphorically female, interior landscape. Within a crack in the earth and within that a cave, Thea Kronborg learns about her own potential to serve as a receptacle. She takes nothing tangible from the canyon, no trinkets or artifacts; instead, she leaves with the realisation that she has inherited a female legacy to make 'a vessel' of herself.[3] When in *The Professor's House* Cather used the setting a second time for another adolescent story, it is with significant gender differences. Tom Outland's story is set primarily on top of the Mesa, from which he makes forays into the canyon. When Tom does enter the canyon, it is not to inhabit so much as to explore, excavate, then to bring others to 'dig out all its secrets.'[4] Like Thea, Tom seeks to claim a heritage, but his method is secondhand, by reading Virgil and gathering artifacts which he plans to preserve in a museum. The artifacts are as engendered as his quest, for they depict female experience and mystery that cannot be possessed by such a method. The mummy Tom names Mother Eve remains behind when his partner attempts to remove her, for her box is too wide for the narrow trail leading from the canyon, and the burro carrying it falls to its depths. The highly symbolic action suggests a would-be delivery, with Mother Eve a female experience too profound to be contained and forcibly removed from its womb-like resting place. A water vessel, another classically female artifact, represents a second futile attempt to claim a surrogate mother, for Tom eventually falls from the favor of the woman he gives it to, Mrs Godfrey St Peter.

Gender differences illustrated by these two stories characterise the roles Cather gives her characters throughout her canon. The nostalgia so often associated with Cather's fiction appears exclusively in her male characters: there is no female character even remotely comparable to Jim Burden in his return to childhood memories with Ántonia. At the same time, Cather's functioning artists are exclusively female, which by her idea of art includes the pioneer Alexandra Bergson, the earth mother Ántonia Shimerda, and the domestic Cécile Auclair, who creates 'a climate within a climate.'[5]

Cather's first major female adolescent was Alexandra Bergson, who transformed the land by loving it. As Sharon O'Brien has argued, by writing Alexandra's story in *O Pioneers!* Cather celebrated female love as the creative principle of the American westering myth. The novel is important because Cather 'heard her own voice emerge' in it.[6] But *O Pioneers!* is important also because in it Cather so clearly presented problems she associated with female growth and success. Even as she celebrated female creativity in Alexandra Bergson, she made her character unaware of her own power, as if modesty were another aspect of her femininity. Far from acknowledging her impact, Alexandra denies it. She didn't transform the land, she says; the country did it by itself, and she got rich just by sitting there. Her unconsciousness of her effect upon the land is similar to her passivity in human relationships, which disintegrate in direct proportion to her success: 'I wonder why I have been permitted to prosper, if it is only to take my friends away from me,' she says in her middle years when she is estranged from her older brother and their families, separated from her younger brother, and aware that the man she loves, Carl Linstrum, will not marry her because she is more successful than he.[7] Once she had created a powerful woman, in other words, Cather had the dilemma of what to do with her. In the final scenes of *O Pioneers!*, Cather returned Carl to Alexandra, but only when she had suffered such grief that she now needed him. We last see Alexandra leaning heavily upon Carl's shoulder, murmuring 'I am tired . . . I have been very lonely, Carl,' then going with him into the house, 'leaving the Divide behind them' (p. 309).

Cather had broken through one set of conventions for girls—those that would limit their growth—only to encounter another set that, following a male paradigm for advancement as isolating, would associate success with severed human relationships. Did success by whatever method, even by the female one of loving, mean sacrificing the personal relationships by which women identify themselves? Cather's response was her most important novel of female development, *The Song of the Lark*. Imaginatively recasting details from her own and the singer Olive Fremstad's lives, Cather wrote an empowering tale of a girl's growth, an apparently realistic fiction with the magical possibilities of a fairy tale. For her setting, Cather transformed her childhood town of Red Cloud into Moonstone, by its name as well as by the moon that shines upon key scenes evoking ancient Dianian myths of female mystery and power. For the central character Cather similarly transformed historical prototypes, naming her Thea (or 'female divinity') and describing her 'as if some fairy godmother had caressed her . . . and left a cryptic promise' (p. 10). By the end of the novel, a childhood friend reflects that Thea's life has seemed 'a fairy tale,' and even as Thea responded 'we don't get fairy tales in this world,' snowflakes 'fell and disappeared [about her] with magical rapidity' (p. 468, p. 466; see also p. 360).

Like a fairy godmother who bestows gifts upon a favored child, Cather broke gender conventions to tell of Thea's growth into the diva, Kronborg. She gave to Thea qualities ordinarily reserved for men—fierce independence, ambition, discipline, and hard headedness. At the same time, she gave to supporting male characters roles ordinarily granted to women, of serving as instruments in the central character's advancement. Finally, she granted to Thea public life and success in terms conventionally associated with male achievement: the last section is titled 'Kronborg' and tells of Thea as a world-renowned soprano, at the pinnacle of her profession.[8]

Yet Cather didn't simply cast her female character in a male role. In *The Song of the Lark* she revised the terms of development and changed the metaphor for describing it, making both female. Cather began with the promise that the young Thea Kronborg contains creativity within herself, and she then set her character on a quest to claim her own creativity. The territory she would take possession of is not Alexandra Bergson's unbroken land stretching before her, but instead herself as a creative being. Metaphors of growth are female ones of gestation, birth, and mothering.

> Every artist makes himself born. It is very much harder than the other time, and longer. Your mother did not bring anything into the world to play piano. That you must bring into the world yourself,

her teacher tells her (pp. 175-76).

This nurturing of her own secret self, this making herself reborn, occurs most obviously by Thea's creating private spaces.[9] When she is twelve, she makes for herself an attic bedroom in her family home; when she is nineteen, she claims a second 'sunny cave' (the same description as for her attic bedroom), this time in an ancient cliff dwelling of the Southwest; later, when she is almost thirty, she returns imaginatively to her childhood home, which 'stands in [her] mind, every stick and timber' (p. 458). An attic bedroom, a cliff dwelling cave, and a memory of such places—all are metaphors of female creativity, and the awakening of Thea's artistic consciousness consists of her making them hers. In Panther Canyon, that 'deep crack in the earth' that Ellen Moers described as 'the most thoroughly elaborated female landscape in literature' (p. 258), Thea stretches herself out in her cave and realises that 'she could become a . . . receptacle' (p. 300); there also she sees pottery sherds and realises they are from water vessels made by Indian women, expressions of their desire; bathing in a pool, she fuses the intuitions to realise that art is 'an effort to make a sheath, a mould in which to imprison for a moment the shining, elusive element which is life itself . . . In singing, one made a vessel of one's throat and nostrils and held it on one's breath' (p. 304). Thus Thea comes to understand that she is such a vessel, and by doing so she claims her legacy from the Indian woman who in pottery making modeled 'not simply vessels, but images of herself, the vessel of life'[10] and, more generally, 'of magical action.'[11]

Throughout Cather describes Thea's growth in terms of claiming that which is for her, of 'possession'—the phrase runs like a motif through the book as Thea makes hers a bedroom, an ancient cave, and an idea of art. And thus Cather describes the climax of Thea's growth, her triumphant performance, not as her producing art but of her taking possession of her own self:

> That afternoon nothing new came to Thea Kronborg . . . She merely came into full possession of things she had been refining and perfecting for so long. Her inhibitions chanced to be fewer than usual, and, within herself, she entered into the inheritance that she herself had laid up. (p. 477)

Other aspects of Thea's story are especially interesting because they so directly anticipate recent theories of female development. 'The secrets of the female adolescent pertain to the silencing of her own voice,' Carol Gilligan wrote in *In A Different Voice*, 'a silencing enforced by the wish not to hurt others but also by the fear that, in speaking, her voice will not be heard.'[12] *The Song of the Lark* is an affirmation of the silences by which Thea protects her 'secret voice' that, more than anything else, is who she is. The most important times of Thea's adolescence are those in which she is inactive and silent. Her 'creative hour' in Panther Canyon, for example, occurs when she is 'out of the stream of meaningless activity and undirected effort' and is 'singing very little': she simply lies quietly for hours at a time, 'holding pleasant and incomplete conceptions in her mind.' At such times she makes experiences hers, holding them within herself to later remember them 'as if they had once been part of herself' (p. 299, p. 301).

In writing so fully of the silences of Thea Kronborg, Cather wrote of the silences of women in general, against which she had railed in her early essays. Why aren't there great women writers, she had asked, anticipating Tillie Olsen's question generations later.[13] Thea's protecting her voice is so basic to her story as a singer that we easily overlook its broad implications: her knowledge that her voice is a secret she must protect describes the adolescent girl's primary challenge, 'her struggle to disentangle her voice from the voices of others and to find a language that represents her experience of relationships and her sense of herself' (Gilligan, p. 51). In this regard, Thea Kronborg is similar to Cather's other female adolescents, none of whom is naturally articulate. All the successful ones find alternate means of expressing themselves: Alexandra Bergson through the land, Thea Kronborg by performing, Ántonia Shimerda Cuzak through her children, Cécile Auclair through domestic ritual.

Cather validates silences, then, by writing of them as positive. In Thea's life, early silences serve as a protective cloak that grants invisibility, enabling its wearer to proceed safely on her quest. For Thea, that quest is to find the speech she needs for her individual voice. When she is young, she is curiously 'inept in speech,' seldom talking in school and, often, speaking awkwardly even with family and friends (p. 16). Her growth involves getting 'a new speech, full of shades and color like [her] voice . . . like [her] mind.' It is 'almost like being born again,' she is told; with it she will transform herself into her daughter (p. 378). As if drawing that cloak around herself, Thea at twelve and thirteen is remarkable for refusing to talk: 'Why do you ask me questions,' she says to her Moonstone teacher; 'it spoils things to talk about them' (p. 78). Later she tells her Chicago teacher that she can't talk about her voice, that secret she has kept from him. Each confidant respects her silence, Wunsch bowing slightly to her, Harsanyi saying 'you need n't tell me. I know. Every artist knows' (p. 211).

Most importantly, Mrs Kronborg protects her daughter's silences as firmly as she protects her privacy in her attic bedroom. Repeatedly, Mrs Kronborg 'speaks up' for Thea: when Thea's voice quavers as she tries to defend her Moonstone music teacher against criticism, Mrs Kronborg calls from the next room, saying 'he's a good teacher' (p. 16). When she hears that townspeople are critical of Thea for playing secular music on the Sabbath, she says to send them to her, for she will talk with them about composers; when she hears gossip of Thea's going to a Mexican festival, she says she'll speak her mind about that too. Throughout Mrs Kronborg uses language in an exceptionally generous way, deflecting criticism and imparting understanding. When Mr Kronborg calls his daughter impertinent, she says 'Thea's all right,' then talks with him until he repeats her words, 'Thea's all right' (p. 101). In one example of the reproduction of mothering (the term is Nancy Chodorow's)[14] that runs through the novel, the young Thea, inept as she is with speech, is like her mother—sensitive and generous with language. When her foolish Aunt Tillie 'struck the shallows' in talking, Thea 'was usually prompt in turning the conversation' (p. 21).

By the novel's end Cather *tells* us that Thea has come into 'full possession' of her singing voice, but she *shows* us that Thea has claimed possession of her language through speech. Whereas the child Thea seldom spoke and almost never explained herself, the woman Thea explains her life with extended discussions worthy of a novel by George Eliot.

Cather uses those discussions to redefine success. As 'Kronborg' Thea has reached the top of her field, a position psychologists now recognise as particularly threatening to a woman because it presents a fear of being stranded from the personal relationships so important to her.[15] Again, Cather anticipated recent theories by making the central tension of the last section precisely this—whether the girl Thea has been lost in the public figure, 'Kronborg.' For this tension Cather relied heavily on the point of view of Dr Archie, Thea's childhood doctor who, in coming to New York to hear her sing for the first time, fears that he has lost his friend in the star. There are, indeed, changes—changes so great that he doesn't at first recognise Thea. Yet what ensues is her affirming that the friendship continues: in her seeing Dr Archie after a performance, despite the fact that she is drained from it; in her desiring 'to be the person her old friend expected her to be' (p. 427); most importantly, in their conversations. As they talk, Thea weaves together memories, explanations, and allusions, until she creates a tapestry of her consciousness. That consciousness is one of continuing relationships: for certain roles Thea wears her hair as her mother did hers; she calms herself by returning in memory to her childhood home; she continues to measure life by Moonstone standards. References to people and experiences tie together the conversations and the performances until we realise that they are of a piece. The form of these relationships has changed: Mrs Kronborg has died and Thea no longer visits Moonstone; yet continuities are there in phrases that echo from childhood conversations and memories that live. 'After all, Thea, —in spite of all, I still know you,' Dr Archie comes to say (p. 429).

In this final section Cather defies logic of the plot (at least by expectations of a novel, though not of a fairy tale) to bring to New York for her triumphant performance virtually all Thea's living childhood friends—even the singer Spanish Johnny, who 'happened to be there because a Mexican band was to be a feature of Barnum and Bailey's circus that year' (p. 478). She went to extraordinary lengths, in other words, to maintain relationships for her character, so that even as she granted to Thea great success she redefined that success, describing it by continuities. When the middle-aged Thea says 'We travel in circles,' she announces the circular movement begun by this last section (p. 441). The childhood friends assembled in the audience serve not so much to applaud Thea (though they do applaud, each in his or her own way) as to enable Thea to give back to them in the most generous, spontaneous way she knows—by performing (p. 442).

As if that were not enough, Cather affirms continuities further in an epilogue, closing the circle by returning to Moonstone. Though Thea doesn't appear directly, Cather establishes that she has remained true to those values so closely identified with women, a morality of responsibility and care (Gilligan, pp. 64-105). Thea continues her friendship with Fred Ottenburg (now in marriage) and maintains responsibility for her Aunt Tillie both emotionally and financially. Furthermore, Cather describes Thea's professional life not by public acclaim but by Moonstone standards: as tides refresh waters of a quiet lagoon, so news of Thea Kronborg and the broader world refreshes persons in her hometown, inviting the youth there to dream. Most important, the epilogue as a whole serves as a reminder of continuities, a loving description of Moonstone, where life remains very much as it was when Thea lived there as a girl.

I have no personal life, Thea had told Dr Archie in the final section: 'Your work becomes your personal life . . . It's like being woven into a big web. You can't pull away, because all your little tendrils are woven into the picture' (pp. 455-56). Ironically, this passage, which so often has been read as describing the sacrifice of the woman to the artist, is actually Cather's describing the artist *as* woman. We need only substitute 'family' for 'work' and we recognise immediately its female values: 'Your family becomes your personal life . . . It's like being woven into a big web.' Indeed, Carol Gilligan could have been writing of the 1915 *Song of the Lark* when, 67 years later, she described the different voice of female development:

> Illuminating life as a web rather than a succession of relationships, women portray autonomy rather than attachment as the illusory and dangerous quest. In this way, women's development points toward a different history of human attachment, stressing continuity and change in configuration, rather than replacement and separation, elucidating a different response to loss, and changing the metaphor of growth. (p. 48)

Following *The Song of the Lark* Cather continued to write of adolescents. In her next novel, *My Ántonia*, Cather had her character face what Patricia Meyer Spacks described as the two threats to which young women are traditionally most vulnerable—seduction and social rejection (pp. 98-101). She then gave to Ántonia the strength to defy those threats and to create from herself a new world. Again Cather rewrote our national myth and placed female creativity at its center; this time, however, she did so with a character who, like Thea Kronborg, is in full possession of her own creativity. As 'a rich mine of life'[16] Ántonia is a classic figure of woman as receptacle; significantly, she has fulfilled her mission independently from society's judgments. She defies, for example, her first employer's demand that she stop dancing, her second employer's desire to make her a sexual object, and her brother's rejection of her baby. Just as interesting, she defies her narrator's expectations, with which Cather again included the threat that female voices will be silenced. At the outset Ántonia seems dependent upon Jim Burden, first to teach her the language of a new country and later to tell her story. Eventually, however, Jim moves aside from story teller to recorder when he reports the Widow Steavens' account of Ántonia's first pregnancy—a woman's account of a woman's experience. In the final section Jim seems in many ways irrelevant, for Ántonia's scenes are so powerful that she breaks through his narrative, and thus through his attempts to possess her by writing of her. There is simply Ántonia herself, 'speaking' for herself through the children she has given birth to, the orchard she has nurtured, and the home she has created.

In other novels of female development Cather gave increasing importance to mother-daughter relationships. *Shadows on the Rock* tells of the year in which Cécile Auclair celebrates her thirteenth birthday and comes to realise that the domestic duties she performs are as much for herself as in memory of her mother. A girl's development takes yet another form in 'Old Mrs Harris,' where Cather extended her story of adolescence to three generations of women: the grandmother who is dying even as her daughter learns that she is yet again pregnant with new life; and the adolescent granddaughter who prepares to leave home, carrying with her a female legacy she will claim as she grows closer to the women before her.

In her last two novels, *Lucy Gayheart* and *Sapphira and the Slave Girl*, Cather wrote of the tragic silences of girls who enter an adolescence for which they are unprepared. Far from the continuities central to Cather's earlier stories of female development, her final ones begin with broken mother-daughter relationships, then explore the painful consequences of separation. Lucy Gayheart's mother died when Lucy was six; the slave girl Nancy Till is doubly betrayed by two mothers—the surrogate one who owned her and favored her until Nancy entered adolescence, at which time she plotted for the girl to be raped; and the biological mother, who remained wilfully blind to Nancy's danger.

Of these late novels, *Lucy Gayheart* is particularly interesting as the other side of the coin from *The Song of the Lark*. While *The Song of the Lark* was Cather's fantasy of healthy female development, *Lucy Gayheart* is her nightmare of adolescence, as if she had returned to the idea of the early novel and explored it again, this time to probe its dark possibilities. Similarities between the two novels are striking. Like Thea, Lucy spends her early adolescence in a small town (as was Moonstone, so is Haverford based on Cather's Red Cloud); as did Thea, so Lucy too goes to Chicago to study piano, where she too falls in love and awakens to art. But Lucy's story ends tragically: after the singer she loves drowns, she suffers a breakdown and returns to her hometown, where she drowns also.

Thea Kronborg's strength was that she broke with conventions limiting a girl's development; Lucy Gayheart's weakness is that she remains imprisoned within those conventions, Cather's version of the feminine mystique long before Betty Friedan coined the phrase.[17] Cather's indictment of conventional femininity is as painful and as damning as Friedan's, for Lucy is attractive for precisely those qualities that limit her growth—for her 'irrepressible light-heartedness' (p. 4), which reminds others of the 'singular brightness of young beauty' (p. 5); for the fact that she is 'talented, but too careless and light-hearted to take herself very seriously,' and as a result 'never dreamed of a "career"' (pp. 4-5), or, as we learn later, of an independent life at all. All this makes Lucy so lovely that Harry Gordon, the most eligible bachelor in Haverford, 'picked her out' when she was thirteen; when the novel opens eight years later, he is deciding to marry Lucy despite her lack of social position and money (pp. 20-23).

As is evident from even so brief a summary, Lucy's story begins as the stuff of women's magazines, and so it continues.[18] In Chicago Lucy has fallen in love with a soul-weary singer, for whom she gratefully plays as an accompanist on the piano and, more importantly, as a child giving to him new interest in life. It is the situation of Jane Eyre and the countless romance heroines who are her literary cousins. But Cather turns the screw in the plot to probe its implications: the artist dies and leaves Lucy alone. As restricted to others' scripts in her death as in her life, Lucy dies in action that mirrors Sebastian's, drowning just as she thought she had returned to life.

Drownings image the instability that lies at the heart of *Lucy Gayheart*, a novel of female development that produces powerlessness and psychic annihilation. Lucy Gayheart is unable to take responsibility for her world, her language, and her self. Fearing spaces she cannot possess and rooms she cannot fill, she feels threatened by so simple a thing as being momentarily solitary. When Sebastian leaves his studio to fill a kettle for tea, Lucy finds herself 'alone in a room which she seemed unable to enter. The piano and the book-shelves were far away, out of reach; and she was far away from herself. She felt as if everything were on the point of vanishing' (p. 87). Instead of making space hers, she inhabits that possessed by others, and then only temporarily. In Chicago she sleeps in a series of rented rooms, practices in her teacher's studio between his lessons, and spends her days in Sebastian's apartment after he has moved on. When she returns to Haverford, she feels defenseless in her bedroom, for its walls are thin and her sister on their other side can hear her every move. Even her own bed, that place of such restful dreams for Thea Kronborg, holds the terror of nightmares for Lucy.

From her teacher's Chicago studio to her childhood bedroom—and within that her bed—the spaces identified with Lucy become increasingly interior and psychological, for it is her self that she never claims as her own. Most tellingly, Lucy seems alien within that most personal of spaces, her own body. Again, comparison with Thea Kronborg is illuminating. Thea Kronborg was remarkably active—climbing, walking, stretching, bathing. She felt comfortable with her body, and she affirmed her developing womanliness as specifically and positively physical. When at seventeen she was at home on vacation, her mother felt her developing breasts, commented that she was filling out nicely, and advised her to leave off her buttons. In Chicago she rejoiced in the freedom of singing in a dress that allows her body free movement; and in Panther Canyon she flourished in a sexual relationship with Fred. When she was middle-aged as when she was younger, she liked the sight of her body while bathing. At first glance Lucy seems similar to Thea, for she too is always in motion—skating, dancing, walking. But unlike the intense physicality of Thea, Lucy seems curiously detached from her body, moving so lightly that she seems hardly corporeal. There is no time at which she revels in her body as an extension of herself; instead, when she is aware of it at all, it is most often as a burden that she yearns to be rid of:

> if only one could lose one's life and one's body and be nothing but one's desire; if the rest could melt away, and that could float with the gulls, out yonder where the blue and green were changing! (p. 102)

As in *The Song of the Lark*, so again silences surround an adolescent girl, but here they threaten that she will become invisible rather than provide to her a protective cloak of invisibility. There is no suggestion of Lucy's carrying within her a 'secret voice'; instead, she seems to lack any voice of her own, secret or otherwise. She seldom speaks, and when she does, it is usually to mutter that she feels afraid or is tired. Her few extended conversations end in rupture. When Harry Gordon reveals his plans to marry her, Lucy stops him by 'clubbing' him with a lie about her relationship with Sebastian; when her music teacher asks about her future, Lucy feels depressed and resolves not to visit him again; when her sister inquires about her past, Lucy runs away.

It is no wonder that Lucy fears speech, for its language is as second-hand and impersonal as the rooms she rents. Harry Gordon weighs his marriage prospects in a vocabulary of business; Clement Sebastian considers Lucy in images of his own youth; Pauline voices her concern in tones of Haverford gossip. Whatever individual emotion each feels is debased by convention, what Cather described in *The Song of the Lark* as Moonstone speech, that could be applied to any occasion. When Harry Gordon resorts to adolescent circumlocution to ask about Lucy's love for Sebastian ('how far has this nonsense gone?'), and Lucy responds with similar circumlocution ('all the way'), misunderstanding is inevitable (p. 111). Similarly, when after Sebastian's death Lucy reaches an apparently liberating epiphany, she does so in such melodramatically conventional language that she seems simply to transfer her romantic script from the dead singer to Life:

> What if—what if Life itself were the sweetheart? It was like a lover waiting for her in distant cities—across the sea; drawing her, enticing her, weaving a spell over her . . . She crouched closer to the window and stretched out her arms to

the storm, to whatever might lie behind it. Let it come! Let it all come back to her again! Let it betray her and mock her and break her heart, she must have it. (pp. 184–85)

As surely as conventional language obscures personal feelings, society's corporate voice drowns out individual speech, particularly of a young woman. When Lucy tries to talk with Sebastian's valet, they 'could scarcely hear each other speak for the clatter of truck wheels on the dirty pavements' (p. 116); when she attempts to listen to Sebastian's plans for her, she is distracted by his agent and accompanist, 'who were talking very loud, as if they wished everything they said to be heard' (pp. 123–24). As if in a flood of words, others are 'talking to her, about her, around her. Sometimes she listened and sometimes she did not' (p. 118). With words so emptied of meaning, body language becomes especially important, and it too suggests a violent impersonality. Others speak to Lucy carelessly, turning their backs to her, addressing her over their shoulders, interrupting her and cutting her short.

What Cather was describing, we now realise, is characteristic of a dominant culture's treatment of women. In her depiction of Lucy's response, she described classic symptoms of powerlessness, passivity, and victimisation, a modern version of patient Griselda. 'It was strange, to feel everything slipping away from one and to have no power to struggle, no right to complain. One had to sit with folded hands and see it all go,' Lucy feels upon learning that Sebastian is leaving Chicago (pp. 117–18). Here as elsewhere she draws back, cringing in a chair or couch, hiding her face, averting her eyes. Thea Kronborg had railed against such passivity whenever she encountered it — in the sad acceptance of Mrs Tellmanetez over her husband's 'craziness' or in the apologetic cough of a girl who, dying of consumption, is afraid of men: 'there is nothing so sad in the world as that kind of patience and resignation . . . People had no right to be so passive and resigned' (p. 44). Yet it is precisely this passivity that makes Lucy so attractive to the two men who love her, for both seek to live their own lives through her. Harry Gordon says the only life he wants is her life (p. 109), and Sebastian selects Lucy because of her 'elasticity' in adapting to him (p. 41). The idea of possession is as central here as in *The Song of the Lark*, but in *Lucy Gayheart* it is of a parasitic variety. Lucy's relationship with Sebastian and, to a lesser extent, Gordon, reveals a gothic threat by which a soul-weary man can live only by drawing life from a young woman. It is Cather's version of the classic story of possession, *Dracula*, told from Lucy's point of view, and it illuminates gender questions of power and powerlessness, dominance and subordination, so basic to this novel.[19]

Cather extends silencing to courtship, that ritual long granted a pivotal place in female development. Again, *Lucy Gayheart* seems the reverse of *The Song of the Lark*, for Harry Gordon and Clement Sebastian are altogether different from the suitor she provided for Thea Kronborg. Fred Ottenburg provided an alternative to the usual courtship, a point significant enough that he explains it, saying he values Thea's talent, her independence, her fierceness, and most of all her direction: 'most fellows would n't, you know. I'm unusual,' he tells Thea. 'Jolly fellows have no imagination. They want to be the animating force. When they are not around, they want a girl to be — extinct' (pp. 316-17).

By such terms, to be extinct is the opposite of Thea's self possession. For Thea what was important was

> waking up every morning with the feeling that your life is your own, and your strength is your own, and your talent is your own; that you're all there, and there's no sag in you. (p. 317)

For Lucy, however, being herself is a burden, and she is happiest when she is enveloped by another. Embraced by Sebastian, she presses her face against his shoulder,

> lying there she felt herself drifting again into his breathing, into his heart-beats. She knew this could not last; in a moment she must gather herself up and be herself again. (p. 89)

With a central character who wishes to disappear, *Lucy Gayheart* is a novel of slippages, of apparent stabilities that yield to instabilities and of a text that contradicts its own laws. Indeed, its central image is that of clinging briefly over an abyss: Clement Sebastian clings to Lucy as the youth that will save him from despair; his accompanist clings to him after their boat collapses; Lucy clings to Sebastian's memory as later, when the ice upon which she is skating gives way, she clings momentarily to a section of it.

Interestingly, Cather's novel of conventional female adolescence seems a fictional form of current theories of deconstruction, for we see Lucy posing before the yawning abyss of indeterminacy and realise that she is herself such an abyss. Lucy is a character so insubstantial that we ask, finally, where she is in her own story. The question leads to the layering effect of a Chinese box, each apparently closed box containing another, until we reach the innermost box and, opening it, find emptiness. For this most feminine of Cather's characters consists of negatives and silences. Others plan her life, talk for her, pack her clothes; in doing so, they see not her but aspects of themselves. Harry Gordon views her as his sentimental nature, Sebastian as his youth, Auerbach as his charming student, her father as his pretty daughter, and her sister as an ornament to herself. What is true for Pauline is true for the others: 'everything that was most individual and characteristic in Lucy she resented' (p. 168). As when Lucy happens to glance into a mirror to see reflected there not herself but Mockford (p. 63), so when she looks about her she sees no confirmation that she exists.

'For women . . . being oneself — authenticity — was hardly spoken of seriously until recently' (Miller, p. 98), except, we might add, by novelists. As if writing a case study for psychologists fifty years later, Cather made Lucy subordinate by gender and training, then revealed authenticity and subordination as incompatible. Lucy's dilemma becomes dramatically clear when, struggling to recover from a breakdown after Sebastian died, she feels that she can return to life if only someone with imagination and strength will 'look directly into her eyes' and 'speak kindly when they happened to meet' (pp. 174–75). It is what she has needed through her life—someone to look at and speak with *her*. Yet as earlier others had been unable or unwilling to see Lucy, so now Harry Gordon refuses to acknowledge her need, adhering instead to a morality of rights and justice characteristic of male responses (Gilligan, pp. 64–105). 'She deserved to be punished,' he feels, giving yet one more example of the silencing Lucy has encountered throughout her life (p. 216).

There are thus no mirrors for Lucy, no reflections of who she was, is, and might become. Most importantly, there is no mother, an absence that may be the single most significant factor in Lucy's development. Lucy Gayheart is Cather's first female orphan, her novel the first in which there is no female presence at the center of a home. Because mother-daughter relationships figured so prominently in Cather's writing, and particularly in those works immediately preceding this one (*Shadows on the Rock* and 'Old Mrs Harris'), their absence is particularly striking in *Lucy Gayheart*. Unlike the earlier fiction, *Lucy Gayheart* is about separation, according to Carol Gilligan that most basic threat to female gender identity. The song, 'When We Two Parted,' runs like a motif through Lucy's story as the 'evil omen' under which she suffers (p. 32).[20] Sung by Sebastian, the song announces the multiple separations that mark Lucy's life, beginning with the death of her mother when she was six and continuing to her own death. Tellingly, what Lucy seeks with Sebastian is not a lover but attachment, and her comfort in his embraces seems that of a child, even a fetus, to its mother: lying there in the dark, 'she felt herself drifting again into his breathing, into his heart-beats' (p. 89).

The narrative proceeds inexorably to Lucy's death, and as it does so Lucy's characterisation unravels by a regressive movement, both geographically and psychologically. Following Sebastian's death, Lucy returns to her childhood home of Haverford to rest and, by doing so, to recover her self upon which she might build a new life. Return reveals the emptiness of her childhood, however. Members of the Gayheart family are familiar from Cather's other fiction: the good-natured but ineffectual father, the officious older sister, the more talented and headstrong younger one. What is different is that there is no female presence to knit them into a family, to maintain communal order and protect individual freedom. The result is the desperate loneliness of furtive lives. The house is ruled by Pauline, 'always walking behind herself,' pushing before her a 'mannikin' of normalcy (pp. 168–69). Other Gayhearts seem alien from their own home: Mr Gayheart embraces Lucy secretively in an upstairs hallway, but mainly he retreats to his shop where he ignores customers to play chess by telephone, and Lucy hides in her room or flees to a neglected orchard.

As the sound of a pin dropping makes silence dramatic, so a neighbor, Mrs Ramsay, makes dramatic the void in the Gayheart house. Whether or not Cather modelled her character upon *To the Lighthouse* (she was requesting fiction by Woolf in 1926), she included in her Mrs Ramsay an idea of woman that is reminiscent of Woolf's.[21] The Haverford Mrs Ramsay appears in two brief scenes. In the first, she sits looking out her window, her adult daughter working in the room behind her. The scene provides a physical image of the continuity between mother and daughter that is the point of their exchange. Seeing Lucy pass, Mrs Ramsay sighs and says simply, 'Whatever it was, I wish it hadn't happened. Poor little Lucy!' (p. 147).

> Mrs Norwall glanced up from her work, almost startled by something beautiful in her mother's voice. It was not the quick, passionate sympathy that used to be there for a sick child or a friend in trouble. No, it was less personal, more ethereal. More like the Divine compassion. And her mother used to be so stormy, *so* personal. If growing old did that to one's voice and one's understanding, one need not dread it so much, the daughter was thinking. (pp. 147–48)

The second scene is slightly longer. In it Mrs Ramsay invites Lucy to talk with her and, when Lucy cannot, tells her to trust to time. As much as her words, it is her house that is important, for we glimpse in it the home that Lucy does not have. As a girl Lucy had loved to come to this house, with its comfortable order. Now as a young woman she felt that

> there was something in the air of it that one was glad to come back to. The house had some reality, had colour and warmth, because the woman who made it and ruled it had those things in her nature. (p. 163)

Mrs Ramsay reinforces the tragic dimensions of Lucy's story, for as the mother Lucy doesn't have and the woman she might have become, she reminds us of a female legacy that might have saved Lucy.

Lucy's life ends with the last of the slippages that run through the book. Breaking through a surface she assumed was solid while skating on a river she didn't realise had changed its course, Lucy clings briefly to a section of ice: 'as soon as she touched bottom she could manage,' she thinks, 'groping cautiously with her feet when she felt herself gripped underneath. Her skate had caught in the fork of a submerged tree, half-buried in sand by the spring flood. The ice cake slipped from under her arms and let her down' (p. 199). While arbitrary and contrived in terms of 'real world' action, the scene works psychologically, as a nightmare makes sense not by the logic of its plot but by the validity of the feelings it reveals. Lacking any sense of who she was, Lucy had been gripped from underneath throughout her adolescence; her death is an extension of her life, even a fulfillment of her most ardent desire in it, to lose her body with its threatening changes that announce an adult life she is unable to assume.

Again, Cather provides an epilogue, but this time to tell of discontinuities. The last scene is of Mr Gayheart's burial, and with him the family's passing into 'complete oblivion' (p. 207). Lucy survives in memory of only a few, most deeply in that of Lucy's hometown suitor, now a middle-aged man. But in his mind, too, Lucy is vanishing; he scarcely remembers the young woman Cather wrote about, and we last see him pausing before footprints of the thirteen-year-old Lucy, preserved in cement, forever barred from moving into adolescence.

Alexandra Bergson, Thea Kronborg, Ántonia Shimerda, Nellie Birdseye, Cécile Auclair, Vickie Templeton, Lucy Gayheart, Nancy Till—Cather created a gallery of adolescents whose voices combine to tell a story of female development. *The Song of the Lark* provides a vocabulary for that story. It changes the metaphor of growth from passages to transformations; it respects silences as one means by which girls protect their individual selves until they acquire the personal speech they need; it devises strategies of reconfigurations to affirm relationships and maintain continuities, and it enables a girl to come into 'full possession' of those things that were for her (p. 477). Cather explores ideas from *The Song of the Lark* more fully in her subsequent books, giving particular attention to mother-daughter relationships. Finally, in her last books Cather writes of adolescent development thwarted and female voices silenced.

Notes

1. Patricia Meyer Spacks, *The Adolescent Idea: Myths of Youth and the Adult Imagination* (New York: Basic Books, 1981), p. 7.
2. Willa Cather, *Lucy Gayheart* (1935: New York: Random House. Vintage Books, 1976), p. 77.
3. Willa Cather, *The Song of the Lark* (Boston: Houghton Mifflin. 1915). p. 304.
4. Willa Cather, *The Professor's House* (1925; New York: Random House, Vintage Books, 1973), p. 224.
5. Willa Cather, *Shadows on the Rock* (1931; New York: Random House, Vintage Books, 1971), p. 198.
6. Sharon O'Brien, *Willa Cather: The Emerging Voice* (New York: Oxford Univ. Press. 1987), p. 447.
7. Willa Cather, *O Pioneers!* (1913; Boston: Houghton Mifflin, Sentry Edition, 1962), p. 182. See Warren Motley, 'The Unfinished Self: Willa Cather's *O Pioneers!* and the Psychic Cost of a Woman's Success,' for an argument 'that patriarchal culture repays Alexandra's trespass [against the male prerogatives of power and autonomy] by isolating her and thus injuring her ability to express her emotions and her sexuality.' in *Women's Studies* 12 (1986): 149–65.
8. See Susan J. Rosowski. 'The Novel of Awakening,' *Genre* 7 (1979): 313–32: rpt. in *The Voyage In: Fictions of Female Development*, ed. Elizabeth Abel, Marianne Hirsch, Elizabeth Langland (Hanover, NH: Univ. Press of New England, 1983), pp. 49–68; Linda Huf, *A Portrait of the Artist as a Young Woman* (New York: Frederick Unger, 1983).
9. Changes in views of Cather's symbolic use of space are worth noting. Early critics viewed Cather's creation of enclosed spaces as signaling her insecurities and her desire to escape or retreat; this approach is represented by Leon Edel's essay, first published as 'Willa Cather's *The Professor's House*: An Inquiry into the Use of Psychology in Literary Criticism.' *Literature and*

Psychology 4 (1954): 66–79; revised and reprinted most recently as 'A Cave of One's Own.' in *Stuff of Sleep and Dreams: Experiments in Literary Psychology* (New York: Harper & Row, 1982), pp. 216–40. A quite different approach interprets positively a woman's creation of metaphoric or symbolic spaces that mirror the female body. This approach was articulated by Ellen Moers, who argues that women writers in general, and Cather in particular, evoke often sexually explicit female landscapes 'for the . . . purpose of solitary, feminine assertion,' *Literary Women* (Garden City, NY: Doubleday & Company, 1976), p. 259. In this tradition of recognising that women writers may engender experience by the ways they describe landscapes, Judith Fryer interprets the enclosed spaces Cather created as positive, in *The Song of the Lark* enabling 'the ingathering of the creative person.' *Felicitous Space: The Imaginative Structures of Edith Wharton and Willa Cather* (Chapel Hill: The Univ. of North Carolina Press, 1986), p. 301.

10. Adrienne Rich, *Of Woman Born: Motherhood as Experience and Institution* (New York: W.W. Norton, 1976), p. 96.

11. Erich Neumann, *The Great Mother: An Analysis of the Archetype*. Trans. by Ralph Manheim (New York: Pantheon Books. 1955), p. 136.

12. Carol Gilligan, *In A Different Voice: Psychological Theory and Women's Development* (Cambridge, MA: Harvard Univ. Press, 1982), p. 51.

13. In 1895–96, for example, Cather asked 'whether any woman ever really had the art instinct, the art necessity,' posed as 'a very grave question whether women have any place in poetry at all,' and lamented that 'they are so few, the ones who really did anything worth while,' in *The Kingdom of Art: Willa Cather's First Principles and Critical Statements, 1893-1896*, ed. Bernice Slote (Lincoln: Univ. of Nebraska Press, 1966), pp. 158, 348, 409.

14. Nancy Chodorow, *The Reproduction of Mothering: Psychoanalysis and the Sociology of Gender* (Berkeley: Univ. of California Press, 1978).

15. See Jean Baker Miller, *Toward a New Psychology of Women* (Boston: Beacon Press, 1976), and Carol Gilligan, *In a Different Voice*.

16. Willa Cather, *My Ántonia* (1918; Boston: Houghton Mifflin, Sentry Edition, 1961), p. 353.

17. Betty Friedan, *The Feminine Mystique* (New York: W.W. Norton, 1963).

18. I wish to note another approach to Cather's use of convention here. Blanche H. Gelfant has argued that Cather used the conventional love story 'as a pre-text for *Lucy Gayheart*' in an effort to turn 'the popular romance into an allegory of Romantic desire,' 'Movement and Melody: The Disembodiment of *Lucy Gayheart*,' in *Women Writing in America: Voices in Collage* (Hanover, NH: Univ. Press of New England, 1984), pp. 117–143.

19. Susan J. Rosowski, *The Voyage Perilous: Willa Cather's Romanticism* (Lincoln: Univ. of Nebraska Press, 1986), pp. 223–31.

20. Beginning in 1927, Cather suffered a series of losses: there was her forced move from her Bank Street apartment in 1927, the death of her father and the paralytic stroke of her mother in 1928, the mortal illness of her friend Isabelle McClung beginning in 1931, the death of her mother in 1931. James Woodress writes of Mrs Cather's death that Cather felt 'relief to have the long ordeal over, but the pain of parting was nonetheless agonising,' and notes that 'Cather was almost totally unproductive in 1932.' When Cather did write again, it was *Lucy Gayheart*, a novel about 'the pain of parting,' *Willa Cather: A Literary Life* (Lincoln: Univ. of Nebraska Press, 1987), pp. 435–36.

21. See two letters from Willa Cather to Blanche Knopf, requesting a copy of *The Voyage Out*, October 7 and October 18, 1926. Humanities Research Center, The Univ. of Texas at Austin.

180
My Ántonia, Jim Burden, and the Dilemma of the Lesbian Writer

◆

JUDITH FETTERLEY

In 'To Write "Like a Woman": Transformations of Identity in Willa Cather,' Joanna Russ claims Cather as a lesbian writer and essays to understand the central situation in many of her novels and stories as an indirect expression of a lesbian sensibility. In *Lesbian Images*, Jane Rule explicitly decries a lesbian approach to Cather's work, suggesting that it violates Cather's sense of herself as an artist and a person and fulfills Cather's worst fears of the critical act as merely an effort to 'reduce great artists to psychological cripples, explaining away their gifts and visions in neuroses and childhood traumas' (74). Rule shares Cather's fears about the motives of critics; she presents a series of 'readings' which she labels 'grossly inaccurate' and which she claims 'can only be explained by a desire of each of these men to imply that Willa Cather's "basic psychology," "personal failure," or "temperament" negatively influenced her vision' (75, 76). Obviously Rule has reason to assume that masculinist critics will seek to find in Cather's lesbianism the 'flaw' that explains what is 'wrong' with her work. While Rule's anxiety to protect Cather against the masculinist misreadings that result from patriarchal homophobia is both understandable and commendable, her solution is problematic. Reciting the biographical evidence for viewing Cather as a lesbian, she nevertheless severs the life from the work, evidently *unable* to imagine the possibility that Cather's lesbianism might have influenced her art. Labeling *My Ántonia* Cather's 'most serene and loving book,' she thus demonstrates that, while Cather was emotionally devastated by Isabelle McClung's marriage to Jan Hambourg, her personal torment as a lesbian did not interfere with her ability to write a classic of heterosexual love. While

SOURCE   Judith Fetterley, '*My Ántonia*, Jim Burden and the Dilemma of the Lesbian Writer', *Lesbian Texts and Contexts*, eds Karla Jay and Joanne Glasgow, New York: NY University Press, 1990, pp. 145-63

this reading supports her theory, it seems rather out of touch with the text under consideration. Indeed, Rule's theory would appear to require a renunciation of the text Cather actually wrote.

Like many of Cather's readers, I have long thought *My Ántonia* both a remarkably powerful and a remarkably contradictory text and have long suspected that its power was connected with its contradictions.[1] Recently, I have come to suspect that these contradictions are intimately connected to Cather's lesbianism. Seeking like Russ to claim Cather as a lesbian writer and to understand her art in the context of her life, I propose the following reading of *My Ántonia*.[2] As Deborah Lambert has demonstrated, *My Ántonia* was a watershed book for Cather, marking the transition between her ability to write as a woman about women and her decision to write as a 'man' about men. In *My Ántonia*, the transition and transformation are still in process and the process is incomplete. What marks *My Ántonia*, then, as a central, if not *the* central Cather text, is not so much the evidence it contains of Cather's capitulation to convention, but rather the evidence it contains of her deep-seated resistance to such capitulation. As such, it defines the nature of Cather's situation as an American writer who was also a lesbian writer and it defines the nature of her solution to the inherent contradiction between American and lesbian.

In Book IV, the Widow Steavens informs Jim of the fate of their Ántonia:

> My Ántonia, that had so much good in her, had come home disgraced. And that Lena Lingard, that was always a bad one, say what you will, had turned out so well, and was coming home every summer in her silks and her satins, and doing so much for her mother. I give credit where credit is due, but you know well enough, Jim Burden, that there is a great difference in the principles of those two girls. And here it was the good one that had come to grief![3]

One might well inquire as to the source of the Widow's certainties, the principles that determine the comfortable clarity of her moral universe. How is she enabled to distinguish so easily the good woman from the bad one? And one might well assume that, for the Widow Steavens, Ántonia's definitive goodness derives from her conventionality; she is all that one could ask for in the way of a traditionally defined woman. She is smart as a whip, but will never attend school; eager and quick to learn the language of her new country, she will always speak broken English with an accent that marks her as foreign and eventually she will speak no English at all; nurturant in the extreme, she saves even the insects, making a nest in her hair for the protection of the sole surviving cricket. Above all, she identifies with men and against women. Passionately devoted to her father, she ennobles him, in a moment of extraordinary disclosure, for having married her mother when he could have bought her off. Since Ántonia herself will recapitulate her mother's experience, her idealisation of her father and denigration of her mother are as painful as they are predictable. She pads about after Charley

Harling, 'fairly panting with eagerness to please him' (155); and she equally 'pants' after Jim and his approval, hoping that 'maybe I be the kind of girl you like better, now I come to town' (154). With Lena she is cold and distant because Lena 'was kind of talked about, out there' (164). Tony is not one to give a sister the same uncritical support she gives men.

In Book II, we learn that Tony is all heart and that this is the source of her power. In Book IV, we learn the limitations of the power of heart: 'The trouble with me was,' she later explains to Jim, 'I never could believe harm of anybody I loved' (344). This radical severance of head from heart leads her directly into the arms of Larry Donovan, for whom she performs the conventional female function of becoming the mirror in which one is seen as large. Against her better judgment, she participates in the mythology of the transforming power of women's love: 'I thought if he saw how well I could do for him, he'd want to stay with me' (313). The arms of Larry Donovan open directly onto the realm of the seduced and abandoned and 'my' Ántonia is 'poor' Ántonia now. Though Jim professes anger at this convention, there is a direct connection between the qualities he values in Ántonia and her abandoned state, between being 'good' and being 'poor.' At the end of Book I, Jim murmurs, 'Why aren't you always nice like this, Tony?' (104) Previously, she has not been so nice: 'Ántonia ate so noisily now, like a man' (125) and 'like a man' she works, competing daily with Ambrosch and boasting of her strength. From the 'fate' of acting like a man and losing 'all her nice ways,' Grandmother Burden 'saves' her, getting Ántonia a job in town serving the Harlings. Tony's salvatory tenure at the Harlings is abruptly terminated, however, by another incursion of not-niceness. Forced to choose between working for the Harlings and going dancing, Tony 'set[s] her jaw' and leaves. To which Jim responds, 'Tony, what's come over you?' (208).

But Jim needn't worry, for Tony's badness is merely a temporary deviation from her path to apotheosis as an earth mother. Book V, fittingly titled 'Cuzak's Boys,' delivers her to us in this role. Defined not simply as the mother of sons but as the mother of the sons of her husband, Ántonia admits: 'That Leo; he's the worst of all. . . . And I love him the best' (335). Obviously, for Ántonia, in boys badness is goodness. Though 'a rich mine of life' to others, Ántonia herself appears depleted. A battered woman, her grizzled hair, flat chest, and few remaining teeth reflect the toll exacted of one who plays the role of earth mother.

This is a role that Lena, 'coming home here every summer in her silks and satins, and doing so much for her mother,' has firmly refused, eliciting thereby the Widow's denunciation of her as 'bad.' From the moment she first appears at the Harlings' back door, Lena presents a marked contrast to Ántonia. While Tony pants after approval in broken English, Lena moves through the world with perfect composure and perfect English. Unlike Tony, Lena likes town because she sees it as the way up and out, and up and out Lena intends to get.

Through with the farm, with family life, and with marriage, Lena wants to be economically and personally independent; she has come to town to learn a profession. Lena puts her clear head in the service of her own self-interest and while she 'gave her heart away when she felt like it . . . she kept her head for her business and had got on in the world' (298). Though Lena's success is in itself sufficient to draw the Widow's ire, her definition of 'good' requiring an element of failure in which head is submerged in heart and self is deferred to other, perhaps equally upsetting is Lena's desire to extend her success to her mother. To Ántonia's male-identification and glowing commitment to father-right and brother-right, Lena opposes the image of a woman-identified-woman whose hidden agenda is to rescue her mother. Lena resists marriage because she sees it as bad for women—too much work, too many children, too little help, too much danger of physical abuse from cross or sullen husbands. At the same moment that Tony builds a shrine to her father for actually having married a girl he seduced, Lena reveals her hidden agenda: 'I'm going to get my mother out of that old sod house where she's lived so many years. The men will never do it' (241). The handkerchiefs Lena wants to buy for her mother carry the letter 'B' for Berthe, not 'M' for mother.

Though the moral universe of the Widow Steavens is simple, that of the text of *My Ántonia* is not. At several points and in several ways, *My Ántonia* fails to confirm or ratify the Widow's easy differentiation. Indeed, *My Ántonia* visibly confronts the reader with a series of contradictions that force one to raise questions. One such question emerges from Jim's final apotheistic tribute to Ántonia: 'It was no wonder that her sons stood tall and straight. She was a rich mine of life, like the founders of early races' (353). But where are these sons? Look at the men in *My Ántonia*—weak, insubstantial, self-destructive. Emblematic is the nameless tramp whose story Tony recounts in Book II. Arriving out of nowhere, he offers to run the threshing machine and minutes later jumps into it head first. Tony's response emphasises the peculiar maleness of this behavior: 'What would anybody want to kill themselves in summer for? In threshing time, too! It's nice everywhere then.' And besides, she adds, 'the machine ain't never worked right since' (179, 178). Bewildered Tony may well be as to the cause of this behavior but hardly as to its existence; her own father, in an act which anticipates the demise of Wick Cutter, has blown his head off because life is simply too much for him. He becomes daily less substantial until there remains only enough energy to mark the fact of his existence by the violence of its termination. Are we then to assume that Ántonia herself comprises an entire category, no other earth mother existing, all these other men being the sons of women who are something other than earth mothers? Yet whom has Ántonia nourished? Not her father certainly. Cuzak?—'a crumpled little man' who lifts 'one shoulder higher than the other . . . under the burdens of life' (356). Jim, who seems to have no life at all? Where are Ántonia's tall, straight sons?

If there is no evidence of nourishment, there is evidence of poison. Wick Cutter's viciousness, which culminates in his wife's murder and his own suicide, runs on the energy generated by Mrs Cutter's outrage. Mrs Harling feeds Mr Harling, but the result of his feasting is an arrogant imperialism that stops life: 'We had jolly evenings at the Harlings' when the father was away' (156). And what are the consequences of Ántonia's whipping up cakes for 'Charley'? Charley/Larry doesn't seem to have benefited from her hot lunches. He is last seen disappearing toward Mexico where he may get rich 'collecting half-fares off the natives and robbing the company' and where he may just as easily get killed. And Charley/Jim? The most intricate exposure of the problematic nature of female nourishment occurs in a scene that involves Jim, architect of the earth mother image. In Book I, Jim kills a snake, and Ántonia sings the praises of his courage; single-handedly she creates monster and hero, dragon and George, feeding Jim's ego until 'I began to think that I had longed for this opportunity, and had hailed it with joy . . . Her exultation was contagious. The great land had never looked to me so big and free. If the red grass were full of rattlers, I was equal to them all' (47–48). Back at the ranch, Otto, the cowboy, succinctly punctures Ántonia's windy distortion. Later Jim learns how lucky he really was:

> A snake of his size, in fighting trim, would be more than any boy could handle. So in reality it was a mock adventure; the game was fixed for me by chance, as it probably was for many a dragon-slayer. I had been adequately armed by Russian Peter; the snake was old and lazy; and I had Ántonia beside me, to appreciate and admire. (49–50)

But what if there were no Otto? What if Ántonia's were the only voice Jim heard? Might he not, thus stuffed with heroic imagery, have set off on other adventures where, not so lucky, he would return on his shield rather than with it?

I do not mean to suggest here that *My Ántonia* is an antifeminist text designed to demonstrate how bad women are for men, a position implicit if not explicit in Blanche Gelfant's provocative and insightful essay and a position that finally reinforces the apotheosis of the earth mother. Rather, I wish to suggest that the text of *My Ántonia* radically undercuts the premises of the figure that occupies its center; thus, it calls into question the value of the very conventions it seems to assert. Women are not under attack here for failing to be earth mothers. Nor are earth mothers under attack for failing to fulfill their promises or, more insidiously, for masquerading as nourishers while actually emasculating those they nurture. Rather, it is the apotheosis of the earth mother figure itself that is under seige. The pressure the text resists is the pressure embodied in the voice of the Widow Steavens with her easy assurance of good and bad, and it resists this pressure by undermining the system that supports the earth mother figure. Like a body responding to the implantation of a foreign object, *My Ántonia* surrounds Ántonia with antistories.

One such antistory features Russian Peter and Pavel who, for heroically daring to act out a powerful and radical vision, have suffered banishment and stigmatisation. For the Widow Steavens, Lena's badness directly connects to her resistance to marriage; yet *My Ántonia* supports Lena's badness more than Tony's goodness. The significance of the Russians' story may be taken, as Gelfant suggests, from its mode of presentation.[4] Like any highly explosive material, it is carefully contained. Dying, Pavel tells his story to Mr Shimerda; Ántonia overhears it and, translating first from Russian to Bohemian and then from Bohemian to English, she repeats it to Jim who tells it to us. This highly explosive tale contains a hatred of marriage as pure as the snow onto which the bride and bridegroom are thrown and as intense as the hunger of the wolves who consume them. Pavel's and Peter's priorities are ratified by a text whose hostility to marriage would be hard to exceed. Examples of destructive marriages abound: Cutters, Shimerdas, Harlings, Crazy Mary and just as crazy Ole, Jim and the woman who 'for some reason' wishes to remain Mrs Burden. Good marriages appear only when their absence would be so notable as to turn the antistory into the story — for example, the marriage of Jim's grandparents and that of Ántonia and Cuzak. Yet even the latter instance proposes a vision of marriage as a structure of mutually conflicting interests:

> It did rather seem to me that Cuzak had been made the instrument of Ántonia's special mission. This was a fine life, certainly, but it wasn't the kind of life he had wanted to live. I wondered whether the life that was right for one was ever right for two. (345)

The hatred of marriage embedded in the antistory carries with it an equally negative attitude toward heterosexuality. The positive assertion of Ántonia's extraordinary fecundity finds neither resonance nor reinforcement in a text whose sexual emblems are Crazy Mary, Wick Cutter, and Lena with the reaping hook. The act required to support the 'rich mine of life' motif is fraught with danger and repugnance. Mr Shimerda's dalliance with the servant girl who comes to work for his mother terminates in the gruesome scene in a Nebraska barn with a frozen corpse on the floor and hair stuck to the roof. Like her father's, Ántonia's brief moments of eroticism, those nightly trips to the dancing tent, find an equally painful conclusion in the house attached to the barn. Haunting the landscape of heterosexual passion is the figure of Crazy Mary, whose jealousy of Lena reduces her to a caricature with a corn knife in danger of being recommitted. The pathetic object of her passions has little better luck with his own sexual longing; having married his Mary to keep him steady, he finds the remedy insufficient and himself wandering the prairies looking for Lena.

Though heterosexual desire dooms men as well as women in *My Ántonia*, a loathing of male, not female, sexuality informs the negative context. Emblematic here is Wick Cutter, whose name reveals at once his phallic identity and the narrative attitude toward it. In Wick, male sexuality emerges as unrestrained, unrestrainable, and rapacious, preying on those women who must serve him to survive. He articulates the hidden and shameful sexual history of Black Hawk, a history of exploitation and abuse which spawns an endless series of pregnant 'Marys,' some of whom return to town after being 'forced to retire from the world for a short time' and some of whom do not return but move on to Omaha and Denver where they are 'established in the business' for which they have been 'fitted' (203, 210). Though less obvious than the abuse of the hired girls, the anemia, paralysis, and unlived lives of the 'white,' middle-class town girls must also be laid in part at the door of a sexuality which requires 'purity' in wives and mothers and vents its lust on the bodies of servants. Yet *My Ántonia* contains a loathing of male sexuality that transcends the presumably political. The disgust that Wick Cutter's flesh elicits, 'his pink, bald head, and his yellow whiskers, always soft and glistening' (210), is adumbrated in the nausea elicited by the extraordinarily phallic snake of Book I:

> His abominable masculinity, his loathsome, fluid motion, somehow made me sick. He was as thick as my leg, and looked as if millstones couldn't crush the disgusting vitality out of him. . . . He seemed like the ancient, eldest Evil. (45–47)

Still, even phallic loathing, however much combined with sexual politics, while richly informative of the attitude toward marriage, seems inadequate to explain the aura of fear that encircles sexual experience in *My Ántonia* and creates a radical contradiction within the conventional story between the romanticisation of earth mother fecundity and the attribution of 'goodness' to her stance of asexuality. Indeed, we must now consider the fact of contradiction within both story and antistory as well as the fact of contradiction between them, and we must consider as well the possibility that the two stories do not simply coexist but coincide, both necessarily present because dynamically related.

The key here rests with the figure of Lena Lingard, whose 'badness' is related to her sexuality and whose sexuality reveals the erotic asymmetry at the heart of the novel. If Wick Cutter's flesh elicits loathing and disgust, Lena's elicits desire—in crazy Ole; in the Polish musician who lives across the hall; in old Colonel Raleigh, her landlord; in Jim himself; and in the narrative voice that describes her. The fear Lena arouses can only be understood as a response to the desire she has also and first aroused. And Lena does arouse fear. The landscape of Ántonia's 'rich mine of life,' the fruit cave whose explosion of life dizzies Jim temporarily, finds no complement in the erotic landscape of Jim's dream life. Rather this landscape is bare, cut and full of shocks. In the dream Jim dreams again and again, Lena appears to him as the grim reaper, armed with the hook that he, at least, never forgets. Though Jim says he wishes he could have this 'flattering' dream about Ántonia, it seems clear that his ability to idealise Ántonia, like the Widow's ability to define her as 'good,' stems directly from her refusal to appear to him as sexual and from her willingness to serve him as an agent of sexual repression and prohibition, reinforcing that part of him which needs to set the erotic in the context of dream and fear. Shortly before Jim tells us about his dream, he records an equally significant exchange between himself and Ántonia. Attempting to kiss Tony as 'Lena Lingard lets me kiss her,' Jim experiences a sharp rebuff (224). Tony gasps with indignation and snarls protectively, 'If she's up to any of her nonsense with you, I'll scratch her eyes out' (224). Looking back on the incident, Jim responded with an outburst of pride in Ántonia and avowed that he now knew 'where the real women were, though I was only a boy; and I would not be afraid of them, either!' (225)

It would be quite a job to unravel the contradictions and confusions of this particular bit of textual sequence. But it would be irresponsible to fail to note their existence or to fail to observe that this excessive confusion coincides, precisely with the most overtly sexual moment in the text. Surely, if not answers, questions are being forced upon us. Why is Jim's pride in Ántonia tied to her protecting him from Lena? How can an earth mother, the real woman, be idealised at once for her fecundity and her asexuality? And behind these and all the other questions one might raise is the overriding issue of the source of the imperative against responding to female sexuality. Why can't Jim have erotic dreams about Tony or see Lena without her reaping hook?

In Book III, Jim, accompanied by Lena, attends the theater and on one particular afternoon encounters for the first time the transcendent power of art. *Camille*, the initiating play, has as its theme renunciation. Why is Jim so transfixed by the drama of renunciation and why does this drama enable him to grasp the meaning and function of art? What is being renounced here and who is doing the renouncing?

Jim Burden has presented a problem to many readers of *My Ántonia*. Indeed, Cather's own uneasiness on the subject of her point of view is apparent, not simply in her various explanations/rationalisations of her narrative choice, but also within the text itself.[5] How else can one understand the 'Introduction' save as an effort to substantiate Jim Burden, explain his relation to story and character, and make him credible as a narrator? 'Unlike the rest of the book,' Brown tells us, Cather found the introduction 'a labor to write' (Brown and Edel 153). Her difficulty may well suggest something false in the nature of the task, an inability to say what needs to be said, an unwillingness to explain where explanation is essential. Her discomfort was such that for the 1926 reissue of *My Ántonia* she revised the introduction, improving the effect, according to Brown, and most particularly by removing from 'the reader's mind a question that could do the book no good—whether in fact it would not have been better told by another woman, the query Miss Jewett had raised about "On the Gull's Road"' (Brown and Edel 153). Cather's revisions may indeed have improved the introduction, but not because they solved its problems. Rather, her revisions refocus the questions which the introduction will inevitably raise so as to more accurately reflect and engage these problems. The ultimate effect of the revised introduction is to focus the reader's attention on the problematic nature of the narrative voice in the text, for instead of explaining Jim Burden the introduction leaves us wondering who has made the attempt. The 'I' who introduces our 'eye' is not now Willa Cather who, as a 'little girl,' had watched Ántonia 'come and go' and who has made a feeble attempt to write Ántonia's story herself. Instead, it is a nameless faceless, sexless voice. Three pages into the story, and we itch for definition, crave knowledge of whom we hear. Neither itch nor craving is satisfied here or later and this, I would propose, is precisely the point of Cather's excisions and final 'solution.' While putatively existing to solve a problem, the introduction in fact serves to identify a problem and to indicate that the problem is the point. Indirect in its strategy, the introduction further reveals that the inability to speak directly is the heart of the problem which is the point.

In revising the introduction, Cather removed all references to herself. Dramatised in the act of revision and embedded thus in the revision itself, palimpsest subtext informing the superimposed surface text, is the renunciation of Cather's own point of view and of the story that could be told from that point of view. To return to the motif of *Camille*, I would suggest that the renunciation at issue is Cather's own. In *My Ántonia* Cather renounces the possibility of writing directly in her own voice, telling her own story, and imagining herself in the pages of her text. Obviously autobiographical, the obvious narrator for *My Ántonia* would have been Cather herself. Yet for Cather to write in a female voice about Ántonia as an object of emotional desire would, in the context of early twentieth-century awareness of sexual 'deviance' and thus of the potentially sexual content of 'female friendships,'[6] have required her to acknowledge a lesbian sensibility and to feel comfortable with such a self-presentation—a task only slightly easier to do now than then.[7] Indeed, in this context, Jewett's directive to Cather to avoid the 'masquerade' of masculine impersonation and write openly in her own voice of women's love for women—('a woman could love her in that same protecting way—a woman could even care enough to wish to take her away from such a life, by some means or other')—seems faintly specious (Fields 247). In fact, it was not 'safer' for Cather to write 'about him as you did about the others, and not try to be he!' (Fields 246). Her 'safety' lay precisely in her masquerade.

Yet *My Ántonia* is not simply 'safe.' Choosing to transpose her own experience into a masculine key, Cather nonetheless confronts us with a transposition radically incomplete. At the end of Book IV, Jim confesses to

Ántonia, 'I'd have liked to have you for a sweetheart, or a wife, or my mother or my sister—anything that a woman can be to a man' (321). Why, then, does he not so have her? Cather makes no attempt to answer this question for the contradiction between speech and act cracks open the text and reveals the story within the story, the story that can't be told directly, the essence of whose meaning is the fact that it can't be told.

Though nominally male, Jim behaves in ways that mark him as female. On the farm, he rarely leaves the kitchen; he inhabits women's space: 'When grandmother and I went into the Shimerdas' house, we found the women-folk alone. . . . The cold drove the women into the cave-house, and it was soon crowded' (114, 115). Yet Cather can't have him doing women's work; thus Jim does virtually nothing, a fact which at once contributes to his insubstantiality and provides a context for understanding its source. Jim's most active moment comes, not surprisingly, when he is left alone. With no one to observe him and with reponsibility for all tasks of both sexes, he throws himself into housework and barn work with equal vigor. A point in Book II similarly defines his ambiguity. Realising he is about to leave Black Hawk, Jim delivers a reminiscent tribute to his life as a Black Hawk boy:

> For the first time it occurred to me that I should be homesick for that river after I left it. The sandbars, with their clean white beaches and their little groves of willows and cottonwood seedlings, were a sort of no-man's-land, little newly created worlds that belonged to the Black Hawk boys. Charley Harling and I had hunted through these woods, fished from the fallen logs, until I knew every inch of the river shores and had a friendly feeling for every bar and shallow. (233)

To which we can only murmur, 'Really?' For we have seen no part of this boys' world. Instead, we have seen Jim hanging out at the Harlings, participating in female-centered family life; Jim playing with the hired girls and getting a reputation for being 'sly' and 'queer'; Jim studying his books at home alone; Jim walking the streets at night and sneering at the cowardice and hypocrisy of these very Black Hawk boys who are supposedly his fishing and hunting buddies.

Nor does Jim identify with Black Hawk men. How are we to explain Jim's hatred of Mr Harling, a figure who presumably represents Jim's own possibilities for future gratification? Significantly, Jim's hostility attaches precisely to those features of Mr Harling's life that most reflect patriarchal privilege—the subservience of his wife and children, their complete catering to his every whim, his ownership of time and space; in short, his 'autocratic' and 'imperial' ways, the ways of a man 'who felt that he had power' (157). Jim's hostility, reminiscent of his earlier contempt for the arbitrary predominance accorded Ambrosch, though unintelligible in a male, makes perfect sense in a female who recognises in patriarchal privilege both her own future as the object of personal tyranny and a possibility of power from which she is excluded.

Jim's sexual self-presentation equally reveals his gender ambiguity. With Harry Paine, the town boy who loses Tony her job by forcing her to kiss him on the Harlings's back porch, as the Black Hawk norm for adolescent male sexuality, Jim's behavior stands out as 'queer' indeed. Attempting to kiss Tony himself and meeting with a similar rebuff, he responds not with force but with petulance and then support. 'Lena Lingard lets me kiss her,' he weakly asserts, rhetorically disclosing his essential sexual passivity and foreshadowing the postures of his erotic dream. After listening to Tony's lecture on the dangers of playing with Lena, Jim capitulates completely, submerging his dissent in a rush of pride at the 'true heart' of his Ántonia. Jim's sympathy for Tony's position, based on her own experience of the dangers of sexuality for women, is worthy of a mother or a sister or a friend, but not of a suitor whose sexual self-interest lies in undermining her perceptions and making her ashamed of her resistance.

Two scenes in *My Ántonia*, both explicitly about sex and gender, unmistakably define the essential femaleness of Jim Burden. In Book I Jim tells us of an incident that made a change in his relationship with Ántonia, a change he claims to have welcomed and enjoyed. By virtue of this experience Ántonia presumably learns that gender means more than age; thus taught, she abandons her tone of superiority and assumes her appropriately subservient place:

> Much as I liked Ántonia, I hated a superior tone that she sometimes took with me. She was four years older than I, to be sure, and had seen more of the world; but I was a boy and she was a girl, and I resented her protecting manner. Before the autumn was over, she began to treat me more like an equal and to defer to me in other things than reading lessons. This change came about from an adventure we had together. (43)

Jim's sexism here, so unlike anything we know of him before or after, can of course be understood as Cather's attempt to give her 'boy' masculine colors. Yet even a cursory glance at the snake episode reveals an agenda very different from the one Jim claims for it, indicating once again Cather's unwillingness to cover the tracks of her narrative transposition and renunciation. Not masculine superiority and the validity of masculine privilege but the fraudulence of male heroics and hence of the feminine worship that accompanies and inspires it are the subjects of this episode. Jim responds to the sudden appearance of the snake with sheer terror, and he kills it by sheer luck. From his experience he learns that a stacked deck makes heroes and a chorus of female praise obscures the sleight of hand. The aura of the impostor colors the scene and explains the absence of any sequel to it. For Jim's experience is far more intelligible as that of a girl, who, while temporarily acting a boy's part, discovers the fraudulence of the premises that support the system of sexism and thus comes to see all men as impostors; but who nevertheless recognises that, though she may play male roles and sign herself William Cather, her signature is a masquerade and her identity a fake.

The second scene occurs in Book II when Tony, made nervous by the more than usually bizarre behavior of her employer, Wick Cutter, asks Jim to take her place. In theory, Ántonia's request ought to provide Jim with a golden opportunity, a chance to demonstrate that masculine superiority which is the putative lesson of the earlier scene by protecting the woman whom he continually tells us he loves. Further, since Cutter's intention is rape and since the whole town loathes the man, the situation carries with it the additional possibility of becoming a local hero. Knight in shining armor, defender of fair womanhood, Black Hawk avenger—Tom Sawyer would jump at it. Jim Burden turns and runs, straight home to grandmother where he puts his face to the wall and begs, 'as I had never begged for anything before,' that she allow no one else to see him, not even the doctor (249). To her reiterated note of thankfulness 'that I had been there instead of Ántonia,' Jim responds with pure hatred: 'I felt that I never wanted to see her again. I hated her almost as much as I hated Cutter. She had let me in for all this disgustingness' (250). Surely Jim has literally taken Ántonia's place and experienced the rape intended for her. The physical repulsion, awareness of sexual vulnerability, sense of shame so profound as to demand total isolation—all are intelligible as responses to rape. Jim's identity as 'girl' structures the scene, undermining his pretense to masculinity and maleness. Is it not obvious why Jim can't marry Ántonia?

At the end of his story, Jim returns to the landscape of his youth. Setting out, north of town, into 'pastures where the land was so rough that it had never been ploughed up,' Jim has

> the good luck to stumble upon a bit of the first road that went from Black Hawk out to the north country; to my grandfather's farm, then on to the Shimerdas' and to the Norwegian settlement. Everywhere else it had been ploughed under when the highways were surveyed; this half-mile or so within the pasture fence was all that was left of that old road which used to run like a child across the open prairie, clinging to the high places and circling and doubling like a rabbit before the hounds. (369, 370–71)

Formless, unploughed, and unsurveyed, with possibilities for wildness, this landscape, so steeped in nostalgia for childhood, reflects a longing for a time before definition, before roads have been marked and set and territories rigidly identified. By the end of the book Jim has returned to a psychological state parallel to that of his beloved landscape. Reunited at last with Ántonia, he is also reunited with a past before the domination of sexual definition when one might be a tomboy and love one's Ántonia to one's heart's content. Not surprisingly, the spirit attendant upon the longing for gender ambiguity is a profound fear like that of a rabbit before hounds. At those moments when gender crossing actually occurs—for example, when Ántonia begins to dress and act like a man and Grandmother Burden determines to 'save' her—the text exudes a profound uneasiness. So it is that the tension between impulse and repression, desire and renunciation determines the circlings and doublings described by the text of *My Ántonia*.

Indeed, the text as a whole recapitulates the burden of narrative choice — a transposition only partially completed; a story, a sensibility, an eroticism only partially renounced. Emblematic of the eroticism Cather can not bring herself to renounce completely is the character of Lena Lingard. If the idealisation of Ántonia in 'the pioneer woman's story' requires the steady denial of her sexuality,[8] Lena remains convincingly sexual. And significantly, her sexuality is neither conventionally female nor conventionally male but rather identifies an erotic potential possible only outside the patriarchal, heterosexual territory of rigid definitions and polar oppositions. Characterised by a diffused sensuality rooted in a sense of self and neither particularly aggressive nor particularly passive, Lena represents one model of lesbian sexuality. Her presence in the text as a symbol of desire, felt as desirable and allowed to be desired, 'flushed like the dawn with a kind of luminous rosiness all about her' (226), provides occasional moments of pure sensual pleasure and indicates the strength of Cather's resistance to renouncing her lesbian sensibility.

In the foreword to his biography of Willa Cather, James Woodress writes: 'Although Willa Cather wrote an old friend in 1945 that she never had any ambitions, the truth was just the opposite. Her entire career down to the publication of *O Pioneers!*, her first important book, shows a very ambitious young woman from the provinces, determined to make good' (13). Certainly that determination to make good must have played a large role in Cather's decision to renounce her own point of view, masquerade as a male, and tell a story that is not her own. As critics from Leslie Fiedler to Carolyn Heilbrun to Nina Baym have demonstrated, American literature as defined by the literary establishment whom Cather intended to impress, is a male preserve; the woman who would make her mark in that territory must perforce write like a man. The pressure that converted Willa Cather into Jim Burden was not simply homophobic; equally powerful was the pressure exerted by the definition of the American 'I' as male and the paradigm of American experience as masculine. Yet perhaps the ultimate irony of Cather's career lies in the fact that we remember her best, not for her impersonations of male experience, her masculine masquerades, but rather for the strategies she evolved to maintain her own point of view and tell her own story within the masquerade. In a word, we remember her less for the consequences of her renunciation than for the results of her resistance.

In *My Ántonia*, Cather reveals the face of that ambition which she later declared the book to have satisfied: 'The best thing I've done is *My Ántonia*. I feel I've made a contribution to American letters with that book' (Bennett 203). It is not surprising that the book in which Cather reveals her artistic ambitions should be her most powerful work. Nor are we surprised to find this book marked by the theme of renunciation and defined by the tension between the pressure to renounce and the equally imperative need to resist this pressure. Nor finally is it surprising that here in this text Cather works out the terms of her compromise with her context—the context of an ambitious American writer who is also female and lesbian.

At the opening of Book III, Jim sits musing on the lines from Virgil's *Georgics*: '"*Primus ego in patriam mecum . . . deducam Musas*"; "for I shall be the first, if I live, to bring the Muse into my country"' (264). He remembers that his teacher, Gaston Cleric, had explained 'that "patria" here meant, not a nation or even a province, but the little rural neighborhood on the Mincio where the poet was born,' and he wonders whether 'that particular rocky strip of New England coast about which he had so often told me was Cleric's *patria*' (264, 265). Surely Jim's musings illustrate Cather's ambition—to be, like Virgil, the first to bring the muse into her own country. But if Virgil's country is a *patria*, Cather's Nebraska is ardently female, envisioned and embodied in a lavishly feminine imagery, metaphor, and analogy, that culminates in the identification of the Bohemian girl with the American land.

Equally female is Cather's muse. A knock at the door and the entrance of Lena Lingard interrupts Jim's musings on poets and poetry. After she leaves, 'it came to me, as it had never done before, the relation between girls like those and the poetry of Virgil. If there were no girls like them in the world, there would be no poetry' (270). It would be hard to overestimate the significance of this moment for the career of Willa Cather or for the history of the woman artist in America. Locating the source of poetic inspiration in the figure of Lena Lingard—the unconventional, the erotic, the lesbian self retained against all odds—instead of in the figure of Ántonia—the conventional, the desexed, the self distanced and defined as Other (for Ántonia, unlike Lena, could never have written *My Ántonia*), the location one would expect if one read the entire text as 'The Pioneer Woman's Story,' Cather reverses the transposition that produced Jim Burden, drops her masquerade, defines a woman's love for women as the governing impulse of her art, and places lesbian eroticism at the heart of her concept of artistic creation. Moreover, if muse and country are both female, and if the function of the writer is to bring muse and country together, then in this formulation the textual act itself is equally lesbian. Yet in what sense really does *My Ántonia* bear out this theory of Cather's poetics? Beyond eroticising Lena Lingard and refusing to make Jim Burden convincingly male, has Cather done anything else in *My Ántonia* to reveal that lesbian eroticism is the governing impulse of her art?

In the introduction to *My Ántonia*, we hear a voice marked neither as male nor female. This voice recurs throughout the text. Often we forget that we are listening to Jim Burden—his maleness, as suggested above, has been made easy to forget—and we assume instead that we are hearing the voice of Willa Cather. This slippage occurs most frequently and most easily when the subject of contemplation is the landscape. A woman's voice making love to a feminine landscape — here, I would suggest, is the key to Cather's genius and achievement. Unable to write directly of her own experience and to tell her own story in her own voice, and thus baffled and inhibited in the development of character and plot, Cather turned her attention elsewhere, bringing the force of her talent to bear on the creation of the land, her country, her *matria*. In the land, Cather created a female figure of heroic proportions, proportions adequate to both her lived experience as woman and to her imaginative reach as a woman writer. In the land, Cather successfully imagined herself; in the land, she imagined a woman who could be safely eroticised and safely loved. Thus the story she could not tell in terms of her characters is told in terms of narrator and country, and the flattening and foreshortening of personality that is the consequence of her renunciation of her own voice has as its corollary a complementary lengthening and enriching of landscape. Cather made her mark in the territory of American literature with her landscape; we remember her *matria* long after we have forgotten her masquerade. Though she may have sold her birthright, the price she got for it was gold.

Notes

1. See, for example, Brown and Edel, 152–59; Gelfant, 60–82; Stuckey, 473–83.
2. This essay was written before the publication in 1987 of Sharon O'Brien's monumental study of Cather as a lesbian writer, *Willa Cather: The Emerging Voice*. Obviously, O'Brien's book supports my interpretation of *My Ántonia* as the work of a lesbian writer. While reading O'Brien has not materially altered my interpretation of *My Ántonia*, were I to write this essay today I would incorporate O'Brien's perception that Cather's need to separate the maternal and the erotic derived from her complex relationship as a lesbian daughter to her mother. Thus donning a male masquerade protected Cather not only from overtly identifying her erotic sensibility as lesbian; it equally protected her from confronting directly her attraction to a mother at once feared and desired.
3. Willa Cather, *My Ántonia* (Boston: Houghton, 1918; rev. 1926; pb. rpt. 1980), 313. All subsequent references are to the paperback edition and will be included parenthetically within the text.
4. See Gelfant, 74. Gelfant must be credited with first according this scene the attention it deserves. It is, however, interesting that in her interpretation of it as a 'grisly acting out of male aversion' to women, she overlooks the fact that the groom as well as the bride gets eaten.
5. See Woodress, 176: 'She felt obliged to defend her use of a male point of view, however, when she wrote her old friend and editor Will Jones. Because her knowledge of Annie came mostly from men, she explained, she had to use the male narrator, and then she rationalized that she felt competent to do this because of her experience in writing McClure's autobiography.' Or Bennett, 46–47:

> One of the people who interested me most as a child was the Bohemian hired girl of one of our neighbors, who was so good to me. She was one of the truest artists I ever knew in the keenness and sensitiveness of her enjoyment, in her love of people and in her willingness to take pains. I did not realize all this as a child, but Annie fascinated me and I always had it in mind to write a story about her. But from what point of view should I write it up? I might give her a lover and write from his standpoint. However, I thought my Ántonia deserved something better than the *Saturday Evening Post* sort of stuff in her book. Finally, I concluded that I would write from the point of a detached observer,

because that was what I had always been. Then I noticed that much of what I knew about Annie came from the talks I had with young men. She had a fascination for them, and they used to be with her whenever they could. They had to manage it on the sly, because she was only a hired girl. But they respected and admired her, and she meant a good deal to some of them. So I decided to make my observer a young man.

6. For a discussion of the emergence of this self-consciousness and of the loss of 'innocence' attendant on it, see Faderman, 297-331.

7. For a fuller exploration and discussion of the issues involved in such a decision, see Lambert, 676ff.

8. See Lambert for a detailed analysis of the stages by which Ántonia is 'reduced to an uttterly conventional and asexual character.'

Works Cited

Bennett, Mildred, *The World of Willa Cather*, Lincoln: Nebraska Univ. Press, 1961.

Brown, E.K., and Leon Edel, *Willa Cather: A Critical Biography*, 1953. Rpt. New York: Avon, 1980.

Cather, Willa, *My Ántonia*, 1918, Rev. 1926. Rpt. Boston: Houghton, 1980.

Faderman, Lillian, *Surpassing the Love of Men: Romantic Friendship and Love between Women from the Renaissance to the Present*, New York: Morrow, 1981.

Fields, Annie, ed., *The Letters of Sarah Orne Jewett*, Boston: Houghton, 1911.

Gelfant, Blanche, 'The Forgotten Reaping Hook: Sex in *My Ántonia*', *American Literature*, 43, (1971): 60-82.

Lambert, Deborah, 'The Defeat of a Hero: Autonomy and Sexuality in *My Ántonia*', *American Literature*, 53, (1982): 676-90.

O'Brien, Sharon, *Willa Cather: The Emerging Voice*, New York: Oxford Univ. Press, 1987.

Rule, Jane, *Lesbian Images*, Garden City, N.Y.: Doubleday, 1975.

Russ, Joanna, 'To Write "Like A Woman": Transformations of Identity in the Work of Willa Cather', *Journal of Homosexuality*, 12, (1986): 77-87. Reprinted in *Aspects of Lesbianism*, ed. Monika Kehoe, New York: Hawthorne, 1986.

Stuckey, William J., '*My Ántonia*: A Rose for Miss Cather', *Studies in the Novel* 4, (1972): 473-83.

Woodress, James, *Willa Cather: Her Life and Art*, Lincoln: Nebraska Univ. Press 1970.

181
From Displacing Homosexuality: The Use of Ethnicity in Willa Cather's *My Ántonia*

KATRINA IRVING

[. . .] Why should Cather, in a novel that has been characterised as a paean to the beauty of the plains and to the innocence of childhood, deal with the plight of East-European immigrants? I believe that Cather's concern to point out the ethnocentric assumptions of this midwest community stems from an attempt to displace and hence work through a series of splits within herself, splits arising from her role as female author within what she saw as a predominantly male profession, and her position as lesbian within a heterosexual society. The problem of ethnicity displaces that of homosexuality.

Ellen Moers has pointed out that with Cather's childhood move to Red Cloud, Nebraska, from Virginia, Cather was positioned ambivalently among a series of discourses concerning ethnic roles:

> As she [Cather] was very well aware, she herself came from 'old' people, that is, good, solid, Eastern-seaboard Virginian stock. And the 'new' people she encountered were crude, poor, not well spoken, servant people who had illegitimate children and were dirty people. . . . I think this is very much in the books as much as there is the sense that the cultivated world is the European world. (62)

Here a web of conflicting discourses emerges: Europeans as cultured, yet unclean: Europeans as providing the vital imaginative input to America, yet positioned by that culture as alien. If, in this context, Cather is nearer to Jim in being of 'solid' white stock, surely a sense of her subordinate status as woman and her 'monstrous' position as lesbian allowed her to appreciate a

SOURCE   Katrina Irving, from 'Displacing Homosexuality: The Use of Ethnicity in Willa Cather's *My Ántonia*', *Modern Fiction Studies*, 36, 1990, pp. 92–102

similar exclusion operating at the expense of ethnically marginal groups. By displacing themes of 'deviant' sexuality onto those of gender and ethnic marginality, Cather is able to include in her art, despite societal and psychological strictures, 'the socially forbidden — and hence unnameable — desires and emotions'; she is enabled both to 'express and repress, disclose and conceal' (O'Brien 6). The figure of Ántonia as outsider allows Cather — as we shall see — to gesture toward themes of homosexuality because, as Sharon O'Brien puts it, Cather 'is the lesbian writer forced to disguise or to conceal the unnameable emotional source of her fiction, reassuring herself that the reader fills the absence in the text by intuiting the written subtext' (127).

But ethnicity serves as more than a displacement of the *theme* of homosexuality. In this novel Cather also transposes her *ambivalence* about her gender and sexuality. Cather was, as many critics have pointed out, acutely aware of the contradictions of her own position: as woman and as lesbian, subordinate and marginal; as an intellectual and a middleclass white, able to escape some of the negative positioning arising from her gender and sexuality. With regard to gender, critics have observed that Cather, faced with a dominant culture that valorised the male intellectual and writer at the expense of women, initially responded by disavowing her own femininity. This led to a deep split within her. As O'Brien states: 'At the same time that she was describing fiction as a manly art and literary talent as a "ghastly joke God played on women," Cather aspired to the "solemn and terrible" act of writing fiction in which most women were exposed as frauds, liars or sentimental fools' (197).[2] A similar conflict emerges concerning sexuality. Deborah Lambert points out that 'Cather was a lesbian who could not, or did not, acknowledge her homosexuality and who, in her fiction, transformed her emotional life and experiences into acceptable, heterosexual forms and guises' (676).

I read Jim's oscillating attitude to Ántonia as a repetition of Cather's own uneasiness with her female and lesbian self. In the figure of Ántonia is played out the part of Cather that approves both of her own femininity and of the forging of a new gender role that would seem to eschew a passive, ineffectual femininity. Ántonia's refusal of Jim's attempt to coerce her into being his reflection plays out Cather's own attempt to reject those psychological and social strictures against both the feminine and the transgressive feminine in which she herself was implicated. Her anxiety as a 'closeted' lesbian about the reaction of society to such a redefinition of female sexuality and her attempt to escape the cultural aspersions associated with such sexuality and to assume the male role in order to gain male privilege and power are associated with Jim. His attempt to coerce Ántonia into a more acceptable role is indicative of her own dilemma, torn as she was between love of and identification with women and a violent disavowal of the limitations of femininity in order to claim the privileges of the dominant order. By casting the splits in her own psyche in the form of two characters, Cather is able to dramatise and play out a personal conflict while at the same time raising larger issues. For, if part of the animus against homosexuality derives from its abrogation of the 'responsibility' of procreation, thus placing itself outside and as a threat to the heterosexual economy of productivity, this also is the concern that emerges with the figure of the 'ethnic' other. Thus, Cather's displacement of sexual 'deviance' onto ethnicity enables her to raise a whole series of sociocultural and economic issues.

Many critics elide these issues, however, by identifying Cather with either Jim or Ántonia, and thus they attempt to retrieve the novel for a dominant reading. Seduced by the nostalgic overtones with which Jim endows his retrospective narrative of childhood on the frontier, some critics (James E. Miller being the preeminent example) have identified Cather with Jim and have seen him as the archetypal hero or as a representative of 'universal man' (112). His growth toward adulthood comprises an inevitable and progressive estrangement from a time of innocence, an estrangement Cather experienced in her move from the plains to New York City. Jim's disillusionment with time's depredations becomes an expression of Cather's romanticism, whereas Jim's estrangement from an invigorating frontier life is symbolised by his increasing distance from the elusive figure of Ántonia, a character whom he endows with mythic dimensions. By reading Jim as a reliable narrator who fully embodies the author's intentionality, the critics thus reproduce and collude in Jim's coercion of Ántonia, a move which necessitates a repression of Ántonia as an independent figure.[3] If we insist on reading the novel as Jim's—and by extension, America's—tragedy, then we must elide the experience of the Shimerdas as Bohemian immigrants and repress the issues of ethnocentrism and gender roles that erupt continually into the surface of the narrative.

But it is not only traditional critics who elide the tension in the book. Some feminist critics have recently started to view *Ántonia* as Cather's surrogate, and this is equally an attempt to smooth out the conflicts in the text. As Robert F. Nelson puts it, it is to move from a phallocentric interpretation of the text to a vaginocentric one (142). These critics bring to a consideration of the novel the possibility that Cather is *foregrounding*, rather than endorsing, the representation of Ántonia by Burden as his muse and symbol of a dream and exposing the consequent denial of subjectivity to Ántonia herself. In other words, they emphasise the absolute distance between Cather and Burden.[4] Ántonia ends the novel as the wellspring of life to which the jaded city man, Jim, returns again and again for renewal. These feminist critics maintain that the novel is feminist because it holds up Ántonia as the creative center of the book, but this is merely a reversal of the binary opposition that characterises the phallocentric structure: as Nelson points out, 'It shows Cather paradoxically riveted to the phallocentric order with its own binary oppositions concerning male and female social behaviors' (143). To deny that Burden is partly an expression of Cather's own personality is to ignore the extent to which Cather did indeed wish to repress those parts of her position as female and lesbian that prevented her from 'engaging in outward action,' from being subject rather than object.

What needs to be added to these feminist readings of *My Ántonia* is a perspective that takes into account Ántonia's status as immigrant and hence as 'other' to the midwest community in which she finds herself *and* Cather's own ambivalent relationship to her heroine's marginal status.[5] On the one hand, we can see in *My Ántonia* an attempt to work through Cather's disavowal of the marginal parts of herself, a disavowal located in the figure of Burden, whose normalising narrative and attempt to mold Ántonia figures her own molding of herself as a 'male' intellectual somehow above the foibles of femininity. Similarly the problems of Ántonia, her ostracisation by the community for her various transgressive acts and style, are a metaphor for Cather's continued fear about what would happen if she were to announce her sexuality publicly and expose herself as female and hence, by definition, ineffectual. By rejecting that marginality she is enabled to claim, to some extent, the privileges of the dominant white, male order. On the other hand, if, as I argue, Jim wavers between treating Ántonia like himself (when she cooperates in reflecting back to Jim a flattering portrait,) and placing her with her siblings as irredeemably alien, then by dramatising this polarised response Cather manages to exemplify her own intermittent desire to lay claim to the feminine and marginal part of herself.

As some feminist critics have pointed out, it is clear that Cather's primary method of undercutting Jim's narrative is through the use of the 'frame' device. This is the means by which she achieves a dual perspective: the first three pages that contextualise Jim's narrative provide an external perspective on his narration. Judith Fryer points out that 'The American pastoral is more representative for (white and middle-class) men than for women, and this I think is the reason for the frame story — to remind us that Jim Burden's pastoral romance is a fiction' (380 n6). Similarly, Cather foregrounds the denigration of the values of the marginal group by the dominant culture through a device illustrated best in the scene depicting Jim's grandmother's treatment of the Shimerdas' gift of dried mushrooms: 'We could not determine whether they were animal or vegetable. . . . She threw the package into the stove' (52). In this instance, as in many others, Jim's silence, his failure to condemn this action and his concurrence in his grandmother's wisdom serve to recall us to another point of view by its very absence.

Jim is, in many ways representative of the ideology of the frontier and a spokesperson for its values. Parentless, in love with open spaces, and fiercely independent ('I told [his grandmother] that I was used to taking my bath without help,' [9]), his narrative starts with his own fresh beginning: his arrival from Virginia. He fights shy of all connection: 'I had almost forgotten that I had a grandmother' (12). Despite these traits, he is prone to a malaise that seems to affect many native or naturalised Americans in this novel: an apathy and lack of enthusiasm demonstrated by his repeated desire to merge with nature: 'I was something that lay under the sun and felt it, like the pumpkins, and I did not want to be anything more' (14). The arrival of the immigrant, Ántonia, always associated with energy and light, provides him with his one fascination.

His constant attraction to her, to all that he is not, is tempered, however, by his fastidiousness and his disgust at her 'otherness,' for, like his grandmother, he is 'exceedingly desirous that everything should go with due order and decorum' (10). His attempts to control her difference provide the impetus for the narrative, from Ántonia's father's first injunction to him to 'te-e-ach, te-e-ach my Ántonia' (20) to the actual writing of the narrative itself. The extent to which Ántonia is under the sway of her brother or of Jim indicates the extent to which the coercion is succeeding, especially in the first section where Jim takes Ántonia and Yulka away on picnics and teaches both of them English. At this stage of the book Ántonia and her little sister Yulka are constantly split off from the rest of the family; the shrewish mother, retarded Malek, and sullen Ambrosch are associated with their burrow and bestiality: with their inalienable foreignness they are not assimilable to American culture. They can never make the move to the town that Ántonia accomplishes. Jim signifies his revulsion from them with the proliferation of animal imagery. Malek is the epitome of the family's bestiality: his 'fingers... were webbed to the first knuckle, like a duck's foot.... he began to crow delightedly, "Hoo, hoo-hoo, hoo-hoo!" like a rooster' (18). The whole family lives in a 'badger hole' (16), and Mrs Shimerda is described thus: 'her narrow eyes snapping at us' (87). Jim's grandfather wonders 'If [Mrs Shimerda] wouldn't have scratched a little if we'd laid hold of that lariat rope' (87). The fact that both associate Mrs Shimerda with animals signals the extent to which they are both informed by the same ideology.

Toward the end of the first section, Jim asks Ántonia, when she is in one of her more amenable moods, 'Why aren't you always nice like this, Tony?.... Just like this; like yourself' (90). Here, Jim tries to construct the 'real' Ántonia: being 'like yourself' implies conforming to his wishes, to a certain style of passive femininity (they are both lying quietly on the roof looking at the stars) and to a certain American code of behavior, both of which are defined in opposition to Ambrosch: 'Why do you all the time try to be like Ambrosch?' (90). (Later in the book, Ántonia will be contrasted with that embodiment of female passivity, Lena, of whom Jim says: 'How I loved to hear her laugh again! It was so soft and unexcited and *appreciative*' [173, my emphasis].)

Once Jim loses control over Ántonia's behavior, his sole method of coercion is through his control of her representation. Subjecting Ántonia to his coercive gaze, he comments: 'Her arms and throat were burned as brown as a sailor's.... One sees that draught-horse neck among the peasant women in all old countries' (79). Again and again, Jim focuses in minute and cruel close-up on Ántonia's physical traits: 'I remember how ... beads of perspiration used to gather on her upper lip like a little moustache' (89). Luce

Irigaray's comments on the gaze illuminate Jim's operation: 'Investment in the look is not privileged in women as in men. More than the other senses, the eye objectifies and masters. It sets at a distance, maintains the distance' (quoted in Heath 50). Jim's objectifying gaze ('that draught-horse neck') sets him over Ántonia, guarantees his power.

After the death of her father, Ántonia diverges increasingly from the required submissive role, and Jim therefore associates her more and more with Ambrosch. Her masculinity is seen as working in tandem with her foreignness, accentuating her repulsive difference: 'Ántonia and Ambrosch were talking in Bohemian; disputing about which of them had done more ploughing that day. Mrs Shimerda egged them on, chuckling while she gobbled her food' (80). Similarly, at the end of this first section, Ántonia is associated by Jim with her mother, an association he has hitherto rejected: 'They [Ántonia and her mother] came on, screaming and clawing the air' (83). Jake draws the moral of the tale for Jim: 'These foreigners ain't the same. You can't trust 'em. . . . You heard how the women turned on you' (84). Here, the foreigners are set off as a race apart, inherently and irrecoverably other: their cultural difference extends to a moral question regarding their inherent deceitfulness. Jim's relation to Ántonia here exemplifies what Abdul JanMohamed calls the 'economy of Manichean Allegory,' which is based on the 'transformation of racial difference into moral and even metaphysical difference' (61).[6] Jim immediately accepts Jake's view, and decides: 'I'll never be friends with them again. . . . I believe they are all like Krajiek and Ambrosch underneath' (84). Ántonia's refusal of Jim's values leads him to classify her—along with all her race—as monstrous and even as sexually transgressive ('sailor/moustache'). The significance of Jim's second name, 'Burden,' inheres then not as some critics have supposed in Jim's career as artist but in his coercion of the foreigner: his is indeed the 'white man's burden.'[7]

As already indicated, Cather's foregrounding of the hegemonising effects of dominant white culture can be read as an implicit admission by her of the extent to which her frequent early condemnations of the female sensibility, as evidenced in her reviews and articles, and her elision of her own lesbianism constitute an identification with the dominant order at the expense of a marginal culture to which, however much she disliked it, she belonged. Eve Kosofsky Sedgwick has indicated how Cather's virulent attack on Oscar Wilde during his trial was part of a paranoid counter-investment and disavowal of her homosexuality (63). Similarly, O'Brien writes that, 'Judging from Cather's letters and her fiction, she wanted to be viewed as a woman but not as a lesbian. Her love for women was a source of great strength and imaginative power to her, but she feared misunderstanding and repudiation if this love were to be publicly named' (6). The question is largely, however, displaced onto questions of androcentrism and ethnicity. Cather's fear is still too great to let lesbianism as such surface in the novel.

There is, however, one part of the novel where the pressure of this subtext becomes too great and the issue of homosexuality forces its way through. This is the story of Peter and Pavel. David Daiches remarks of this tale that, 'It is a remarkable little inset story, but its relation to the novel as a whole is somewhat uncertain' (9). But this tale of the throwing of the bride and bridegroom to the wolves is a clear allegory for the adoption of homosexuality. The two men are disowned by their mothers for 'feeding the bride to the wolves,' and this incident haunts them from village to village: 'They had been alone ever since' (40). Peter and Pavel are 'batches,' but they share a bed, and they are a perfectly complementary couple: the one is fat and feminine, associated with the laundry and ripe watermelons, the other, 'Said to be an anarchist. . . . Must once have been a very strong man' (24). Jim describes their house thus: '[there] was a wide double bed built against the wall, properly made up with blue gingham sheets and pillows' (25). Although Cather cannot explicitly introduce the theme of homosexuality into her novel, this incident is a clear metaphor for it and thus suggests the anxieties she associated with an open avowal of her own homosexuality. Peter and Pavel have no luck, no friends, are ostracised. Far from being an irrelevant part of the narrative, as Daiches would have it, it is integral to Cather's theme: the pressures on Ántonia to conform are emphasised, whereas Cather's own need to take refuge in the persona of a male narrator, thus eliding her own 'deviant' sexuality, is elucidated.

Just as homosexuality is constructed as 'deviant' partly because it stands outside the heterosexual economy of productivity, so too the discursive construction of the ethnic 'other' is intimately tied up with economic considerations.[8] JanMohamed has pointed out that the (colonial) text as discursive field is overdetermined by economic and political imperatives: the colonised are 'written' so that their economic exploitation can proceed apace (62). In *My Ántonia* Cather foregrounds the economic imperatives of the appropriation of the foreign female: the continued wellbeing of the community is based on the repeated admission of outside sources of energy. The novel shows how American culture manages to efface the threatening difference of European culture and to harness its energy to the cause of American prosperity and material values. In the course of the narrative, Ántonia—with her foreign and female difference—moves from the position of menace to the community to that of vital prop for the culture of materiality: despite her clinging to vestiges of marginality, she becomes the term on which society predicates itself.

Behind Jim stand many figures colluding with his coercion of Ántonia. Chief among them are Jim's grandparents and the Harlings. The image of the acculturating process at work is Ántonia in the kitchens of these families.[9] At the Burdens' she is 'So gay and responsive that one did not mind her heavy, running step, or her clattery way with pans' (89). In town, however, Ántonia does resist the acculturation process somewhat. The figure against whom we measure her shortcomings is Lena: likewise a 'country-girl,' she conforms much more readily than Ántonia. Lena is 'quietly conventionalised by city-clothes' (170), although the fact that she appears in Jim's wet dreams indicates the extent to which she has effaced some of her threatening difference. Jim explicitly compares the two: 'Ántonia had never talked like the people about her. Even after she learned to speak English readily, there was always something impulsive and foreign in her speech. But Lena had picked up all the conventional expressions she heard' (180). Lena's assimilation to American values is too complete, however: she, like Jim, is lethargic, she has a 'sleepy smile' (109) and a 'lazy, good-natured laugh' (108). She too ends up childless: it is as if acceptance of the ethos of money-making precludes fertility.

Similarly, another of the country-girls, Tiny Soderball, becomes one 'in whom the faculty of becoming interested is worn out' (194). In this, of course, she recalls Jim's wife, who is 'temperamentally incapable of enthusiasm' (1). It is as if the total effacing of difference effaces also the vitality and energy that is the necessary contribution of the immigrants to the new world. By contrast, Jim describes the mien of these immigrants — the country girls — before their acculturation as follows:

> Physically they were almost a race apart, and out-of-door work had given them a vigour which, when they got over . . . shyness, . . . developed into a positive carriage and freedom of movement, and made them conspicuous among Black Hawk women. (127)

By contrast, the well-to-do town girls had 'bodies [which] never moved inside their clothes; their muscles seemed to ask but one thing — not to be disturbed' (128).

Why Ántonia's difference is tolerated is made most clear by Jim's grandfather. He is the very image of the benevolent patriarch; only he refuses to feud with the Shimerdas: 'When we complained of her, he only smiled and said, "She will help some fellow get ahead in the world"' (81). He can see the historic and economic implications that underlie the squabbles over ethnic values:

> It took a clear, meditative eye like my Grandfather's to see that they would enlarge and multiply until they would be, not the Shimerdas' cornfields . . . but the world's cornfields; that their yield would be one of the great economic facts, like the wheat crop of Russia, which underlie all the activities of men. (88)

In the sterility of the Burdens' world, where Jim has no siblings, no parents, no children, and may in fact be the last of his line, Ántonia's fecundity and energy are the flip-side of her otherness and must be accommodated to help the community survive. Thus, although 'The country girls were considered a menace to the social order' (129), by the end of the novel, they all end up as staunch pillars of the community. As Jim puts it, because of their hard work, 'The girls who once worked in Black Hawk kitchens are to-day managing big farms ... their children are better off than the children of the town women they used to serve' (128).

Although Ántonia continually resists the meanings and constructions of Jim throughout the novel, her inability to deny them is demonstrated by the fact that Cather gives Jim narrative power: he ultimately 'writes' Ántonia, despite the fact that she has continually 'disappointed' him in her failure to conform. In this respect, Ántonia's move back to the country at the end of the novel must be seen as profoundly ambivalent. On the one hand, she reverts to foreign customs and languages, signaling her escape from convention: ' "And, then, I've forgotten my English so". . . . The little ones could not speak English at all' (216). Her move back to the country, seen in the book as a kind of half-way house between 'otherness' and conformity, equally signals her resistance to societal strictures. On the other hand, her accession to a productive motherhood and wifehood fulfills Grandfather Burden's predictions. Situated on the edge of culture, Ántonia becomes repository of all those values inimical to a money-grubbing urban society — motherhood, love, and fecundity — which Jim, Lena, Tiny, and others reject but which are equally necessary to the community's survival. Thus, Miller, accepting Jim's version of things, says that 'At the end of *My Ántonia*, a weary, disillusioned Jim Burden returns from his successful but emotionally empty life in the East to find Ántonia on the prairie, full of vitality and total commitment to experience, surrounded by the explosive life of her large family' (135). Her foreignness is mitigated by her accession to a 'normal' femininity: the threat of her difference is effaced. As Lambert points out, Cather 'Retreats into the safety of convention by ensconcing Ántonia in marriage and rendering her apotheosis as earth-mother' (684). This effacing is redoubled by Jim's narration of her life: her final cooptation is signaled by the fact that her story is narrated by a representative of all she has ostensibly rejected. The ending of the novel must be seen as profoundly ambivalent, as Ántonia retreats with her family to the prairie, forming an enclave of 'European-ness' that is still set amid, and serves, the economic and cultural imperatives of the American culture.

In terms of the sexual dynamic, the ending of the book is equally uncertain. Although Jim and Ántonia are finally reconciled, they remain at a difference geographically and politically. Ántonia casts off her masculine bearing and seems elevated in these closing pages to the position of earth mother, but her image is a curiously ambiguous one: mother of many children, she remains curiously asexual — flatchested and toothless. One must agree, therefore, with the position of Nelson, who refutes O'Brien's view that Cather, by the time she came to write *My Ántonia*, had resolved the gender conflicts arising from her positioning among discourses which valorised the male as writer and denigrated the woman and the lesbian. He writes: 'I have found a less successful break than O'Brien and others with the phallocentric hegemony under which the writer began and continued to write throughout her life' (142). Cather was not able, given her positioning within a phallocentric and heterosexist hegemony, to resolve her warring identities, but by the time of *My Ántonia* she was able to externalise this conflict in a transmuted form and to probe and explore it.

Notes

1. See the early chapters of Sharon O'Brien's biography, *Willa Cather*.
2. For O'Brien, however, Cather's development as an artist was contingent on her movement away from that position, and she sees Cather as finally able to resolve the conflict by acknowledging the 'feminine' as an important part of her art. Linda Pannill follows this view: 'She arrived at a conception of the woman artist which reconciled the conflict because she . . . conceived of the woman artist in distinctly "womanly" terms' (230).
3. Such readings are clearly overdetermined by both the conventions of the novel in general and by literature about women in the West and Plains in particular, which, as June O. Underwood points out, views 'women as "the other"—not creatures who grow, learn, and expand to heroism—but as vehicles for enlarging the male hero's sense of the challenge and terror of the land' (3).
4. One of the most important of these critics is Susan J. Rosowski. She points out that the book deconstructs male mythology: 'Cather was acutely aware that our culture assigns to men the position of subject and to women that of object, and she incorporates these assumptions into her novel. Jim Burden expresses conventionally male attitudes: he assumes the subject position, moves outward, engages in change and progress, and writes possessively about *his* Ántonia as the archetypal woman who provides an anchorage for his travels and a muse for his imagination. Through Jim, Cather presents myths of male transcendence, of man as a liberating hero; . . . of women to be rescued, loved, and transformed into art' (88). Rosowski suggests that the undercutting of Jim's myths occurs primarily through a contrast between these and the 'reality' of Jim and Ántonia's lives. Thus Jim's predilection for quest myths has led to a wandering and empty life, a childless and unhappy marriage, whereas Ántonia, formerly a passive mirror to his self-projection, emerges as the source of meaning and vitality in the novel. However, such a reading requires a radical change of direction for the critic. Although Rosowski has read Burden's earlier mythologising of Ántonia 'against the grain,' she concurs with his final construction of Ántonia—as earth mother and source of life. But there is no reason why this mythologising should be seen as any less coercive than the first, especially given its clichéd nature.
5. John J. Murphy is one of the few critics who recognises the importance of Ántonia's status as immigrant. He states that Jim is representative of the dominant culture as opposed to foreigners like Ántonia who are seen as inferior by virtue of that foreignness. Ántonia achieves her apotheosis despite the dominant culture, and the fact that she is 'rescued' by a non-American, Cuzak, is extremely pertinent (173). He sees Ántonia as retreating, in the final section of the book, from the American culture which has rejected her as inferior and 'identifying with the differences that have limited her' (176). Cather sees Ántonia's European culture as something richer and superior to the American culture of materiality and holds the two civilisations up against each other. Ántonia represents a 'counterculture in the west, . . . poverty rather than riches, family rather than town society, and spiritual rather than material prosperity' (177). However, it is not enough to say that Cather holds one culture up over the other. Rather, the immigrants' hardships that Jim's narrative romanticises are in fact a device for exposing his mythologising to the reader as coercive and partial.
6. Jim's relation to Ántonia is governed by the same impulse that, argues JanMohamed, informs much colonial literature, namely, the operation of the 'imaginary.' In such a relation, the self either identifies with or rejects absolutely the Other. Once the latter occurs, the absolute separation between self and other becomes manifest in a whole series of binary oppositions: 'White and black, good and evil, superiority and inferiority, civilization and savagery, intelligence and emotion, rationality and sensuality, self and Other, subject and object' (63).
7. I am indebted to Poonam Arora for providing me with this detail.

8. See John Higham for an account of the impact of economic considerations on the reception of the immigrant in the early part of the twentieth century.

9. A major symbol in the novel for this acculturating process is the piano-playing negro: Cather's satirical portrait of the wild negro whose 'barbarity' is harnessed to provide dance music for the town.

Works Cited

Cather, Willa, *My Ántonia*, (1918), Boston: Houghton, 1988.

Daiches, David, 'Decline of the West', *Willa Cather's 'My Ántonia': Modern Critical Interpretations*, ed. Harold Bloom, New York: Chelsea, 1985, pp. 7-21.

Fryer, Judith, *Felicitous Space: The Imaginative Structures of Edith Wharton and Willa Cather*, Chapel Hill: U of North Carolina P, 1988.

Heath, Stephen, 'Difference', *Screen*, 9.3, 1978: pp. 51-112.

Higham, John, *Strangers in the Land: Patterns of American Nativism, 1860-1925*, New York: Atheneum, 1975.

JanMohamed, Abdul R., 'The Economy of Manichean Allegory: The Function of Racial Difference in Colonialist Literature', *Critical Inquiry* 12, 1985: pp. 59-87.

Lambert, Deborah, 'The Defeat of a Hero: Autonomy and Sexuality in *My Ántonia*.' *American Literature* 53 (1982): 676-690.

Miller, James E., '*My Ántonia* and the American Dream', *Prairie Schooner*, 48.2, 1974: pp. 112-124.

Moers, Ellen, 'Comment.' *The Art of Willa Cather*, eds Bernice Slote and Virginia Faulkner, Lincoln: U of Nebraska P, 1974, pp. 62-64.

Murphy, John J., 'The Virginia and Ántonia Shimerda: Different Sides of the Same Coin', Stauffer and Rosowski, pp. 162-179.

Nelson, Robert J., *Willa Cather and France: In Search of the Lost Language*, Chicago: U of Illinois P, 1988.

O'Brien, Sharon, *Willa Cather: The Emerging Voice*, New York: Oxford UP, 1987.

Pannill, Linda, 'Willa Cather's Artist Heroines', *Women's Studies*, 11, 1984: pp. 223-232.

Rosowski, Susan J., *The Voyage Perilous: Willa Cather's Romanticism*, Lincoln: U of Nebraska P, 1986.

Sedgwick, Eve Kosofsky, 'Across Gender, Across Sexuality: Willa Cather and Others', *South Atlantic Quarterly*, 88, 1989: pp. 53-71.

Stauffer, Helen Winter, and Susan J. Rosowski, eds, *Women and Western American Literature*, Troy: Whitson, 1982.

Underwood, June O., 'The Civilizers: Women's Organisations and Western American Literature', Stauffer and Rosowski, 3-16.

182
Female Sexuality in Willa Cather's *O Pioneers!* and the Era of Scientific Sexology: A Dialogue Between Frontiers

C. SUSAN WIESENTHAL

Perhaps the most critical issue which immediately confronts any discussion of Willa Cather's fictional portrayal of sexuality is the nature of the relationship between the author's life and her work, between biography and art. For it is primarily on biographical bases such as Cather's adolescent rejection of femininity—her masquerade as the short-haired, boyishly-dressed 'William Cather Jr'—and her adult relationships with women such as Louise Pound, Isabelle McClung, and Edith Lewis, that an increasing number of critics have been led to consider her as a 'lesbian writer.' Although no evidence exists to indicate that any of Cather's relationships with women involved an erotic dimension, many scholars agree that, at the very least, her life may be regarded as 'lesbian' in the sense of Adrienne Rich's extensive definition of the term. Briefly, Rich conceives of a broad 'lesbian continuum' which 'includes a range . . . of woman-indentified experience,' embracing any extra-sexual or emotional form of 'primary intensity between women,' and 'not simply the fact that a woman has had or [has] consciously desired genital experience with another woman' (648).

Almost invariably, however, when critics turn to Cather's novels, it is precisely the absence of any 'lesbian' sensibility which they emphasise. Thus, Jane Rule, the first writer to situate Cather specifically within a lesbian lit-

SOURCE   C. Susan Wiesenthal, 'Female Sexuality in Willa Cather *O Pioneers!* and the Era of Scientific Sexology: a Dialogue Between Frontiers', *Ariel*, 21, 1990, pp. 41–63

erary tradition along with Radclyffe Hall, Gertrude Stein, and others, sharply reproves readers who attempt to find a homoerotic sensibility in Cather's art, claiming that if the author's private 'sexual tastes' manifest themselves in the fiction at all, it is only in her 'capacity to transcend the conventions of what is masculine and feminine' (87, 80). More recently, Phyllis Robinson has flatly asserted that 'the loving relationships with women that were so important in [Cather's] personal life are no where reflected in her fiction' (158). In *Willa Cather: The Emerging Voice*, Sharon O'Brien concurs, stating that '[c]ertainly the most prominent absence and the most unspoken love in her work are the emotional bonds between women that were central to her life' (127). O'Brien does not insist on wholly divorcing author and text, however, and argues instead that Cather's fiction works to both disclose and conceal a lesbian psyche. Nevertheless, in '"The Thing Not Named": Willa Cather as a Lesbian Writer,' she concentrates on the latter aspect of her thesis—on those 'literary strategies' whereby Cather is able to 'disguise' or 'camouflage' the 'emotional source of her fiction.' For O'Brien, Cather's 'lesbian' sensibility represents 'the unwritten text' of the novels ('The Thing Not Named' 577, 593-94, 577).

The object of this essay is not to determine whether the authorial sensibility manifest in Cather's fiction is or is not a specifically 'lesbian' one. Rather, it is to reverse the prevailing critical preoccupation with the 'absent' and 'unwritten,' and to explore the possible ways in which an authorial attitude towards a broader concept of 'deviant' female sexuality, in general, does disclose itself in the written text. In the written text of *O Pioneers!*, in particular, this authorial attitude may be perceived to inhere implicitly in the hermaphroditic, heterosexual, and same-sex relationships Cather does portray. In this novel, for example, the heroine, Alexandra Bergson, is depicted as a character who embodies a seemingly hermaphroditic sexual nature which is viewed positively, as a potentially self-fulfilling value, while the more unambiguously heterosexual natures of other characters, on the contrary, are seen to result exclusively in unhappy and debilitating 'love' relationships. This dichotomous portrayal seems to suggest an authorial sensibility, which, while it is not specifically sympathetic to a homosexual nature, is certainly sensitive to the potential gratification which unconventional forms of sexuality may yield.

In order to grasp the full significance of Cather's portrayal of sexuality in *O Pioneers!* it is necessary to consider not only the dialectic between life and art, but the dynamic relationship between text and context as well. For as the 'golden age of scientific determinism, Social Darwinism, and eugenics' (Smith-Rosenberg 267), Cather's contemporary milieu represented, in fact, a stridently heterosexual era especially obsessed with what it perceived as the 'unnatural' or 'inverted' (that is, lesbian) nature of virtually all manifestations of female sexuality or eroticism beyond heterosexual marriage (Smith-Rosenberg 53-76, 245-96; Faderman 147-277). The extent to which

O Pioneers! courageously challenges dominant medical and cultural assumptions about female sexuality can be gauged only when the text is considered in a dialogic relation to this larger historic discourse. For indeed, Cather's positive delineation of the sexually unorthodox Alexandra, and, conversely, her negative or critical depiction of conventional heterosexuality, actually work together to controvert systematically a number of contemporary tenets about the nature of the sexually 'inverted' woman. In this way, Cather's novel of pioneer life indirectly addresses the issue of the 'New Scientific Discourse' (Smith-Rosenberg 265) being promulgated by such influential and widely popularised theorists as Richard von Krafft-Ebing and Havelock Ellis. And in so far as these late nineteenth- and early twentieth-century 'sexologists' also self-consciously beheld themselves as 'pioneers' in a hitherto unexplored psychosexual 'borderland' (Ellis 2 : 219), the subtle interplay between text and context may be regarded as a form of dialogue between two disparate sorts of frontiers.[1]

Ultimately, however, the crucial limits of the challenge implicit in Cather's treatment of sexuality in *O Pioneers!* must be also firmly acknowledged. For although she repeatedly re-inverts, as it were, contemporary convictions about the perversity of female 'inversion,' her novel also reflects an element of self-conscious restraint which expresses itself most clearly in her highly circumspect handling of close female friendship—an integral thematic and structural component of the novel, which is deftly and gingerly developed by Cather, only to be rather abruptly abandoned when she is brought to deploy a somewhat disappointing, conventional romance closure, an ending both marked and marred, as one critic suggests, by the purely 'token marriage' of the heroine (Bailey 396).[2] Whether this novelistic outcome may be ultimately ascribed, as critics such as Sharon O'Brien would contend, to 'the lesbian writer's need to conceal the socially unacceptable' ('The Thing Not Named' 592) must remain, perhaps, a moot point. A close reading of *O Pioneers!*, however, does, at least, appear to substantiate the more general claim that internalised cultural strictures governing the 'socially unacceptable' in the realm of sexuality do indeed exert a profound force upon Cather's artistic impulse, and, consequently, upon the shape of this novel as a whole.

Through a comprehensive examination of contemporary women's diaries and letters, as well as medical literature and fiction, feminist historians such as Lillian Faderman and Carroll Smith-Rosenberg have been able to trace the critical late nineteenth-century shifts in the theoretic conceptualisation and social experience of female homosexuality throughout the Western world. Unlike male homosexuality, that is, which had long been perceived as a punishable offence against scriptural and secular order, lesbianism had not only been 'generally ignored by the law' until this point, but did not even constitute a conceptual category of deviance until the 1880s and 1890s (Faderman, 'The Morbidification of Love' 77, 75; Smith-Rosenberg 266). Indeed, in the earlier decades of the Victorian century, passionate homosocial bonds between women—physically uninhibited as well as emotionally intense relationships—were 'casually accepted in American society' as forms of romantic love 'both socially acceptable and fully compatible with heterosexual marriage' (Smith-Rosenberg 53, 50).[3] Such 'legitimate' romantic friendships between women, however, came to be stigmatised by medical authorities and educators as 'morbid' and 'unnatural' during the final decades of the century, because it was at this point that such alliances first became an economically feasible alternative to heterosexual marriage for a small, but growing, group of autonomous, college-educated New Women. 'For the first time,' as Lillian Faderman remarks, 'love between women became threatening to the social structure,' posing truly portentous consequences, not only for the institutional nucleus of the social fabric, the family, but—as eugenicists and imperialists alike pointed out—for the already 'dangerously low' birth-rate of the American Republic as well (Faderman 238).[4]

As steadily increasing numbers of New Women, like Willa Cather herself, began to eschew marriage and motherhood for higher education and professional livelihoods, one form which the simultaneously escalating anti-feminist reaction took was in the widespread expression of fear and repugnance of an 'intermediate sex': an appalling type of 'semi-woman' whose behaviour and physical appearance 'violated normal gender categories' (Smith-Rosenberg 265, 271). To accommodate such freaks of nature, the leading European neurologist, Richard von Krafft-Ebing, promptly created in his *Psychopathia Sexualis* (1886) the new 'medico-sexual category' of the 'Mannish Lesbian': a nosological classification in which, as Smith-Rosenberg observes, 'women's rejection of traditional gender roles and their demands for social and economic equality' were linked directly to 'cross-dressing, sexual perversion, and borderline hermaphroditism' (272). More influential yet in Britain and America, however, were the theories of Havelock Ellis. It was his 1901 work, *Sexual Inversion*, which most powerfully contributed to the 'morbidification' of the formerly innocent 'female world of love and intimacy,' because in it, Ellis re-defined the close friendships of college-aged and adult New Women 'as both actively sexual and as actively perverted' (Smith-Rosenberg 269, 275).[5] Thus, forms of affection between women which had long been regarded with equanimity or indifference suddenly came to be viewed with suspicion and alarm as subversive and abnormal affairs.

If the theories and beliefs of Krafft-Ebing, Ellis, and others were a matter of 'common knowledge' by the turn-of-the-century, as Faderman contends (*Surpassing the Love of Men* 238), then by 1910–1920, the decade during which *O Pioneers!* was written, medical tropes of the 'Mannish Lesbian' or the 'unsexed' woman had been so pervasively disseminated throughout the cultural imagination—via newspaper caricatures, anti-feminist tracts, and sensational as well as 'high' literature—that they had begun to have a substantial impact upon the marital and educational standards of young women, as statistical evidence of the period clearly shows (Smith-Rosenberg 281).

That Cather herself would have been fully conscious of the contemporary medico-cultural discourse of deviant female sexuality, then, seems almost inevitable on historical bases alone. More specifically, however, biographical details further support this assumption. Cather's work as an editor for *McClure's Magazine*, for example, led her to regularly read the columns of the rival *Ladies' Home Journal*, in which articles admonishing women 'against forming exclusive romantic bonds with women' often appeared (O'Brien, *Willa Cather* 133). More importantly, despite the fact that Cather and Edith Lewis destroyed the vast majority of Cather's personal correspondence, some of the letters she wrote during her two-year obsession with Louise Pound — 'the most serious romantic attachment of [her] college life' — have indeed survived. Unfortunately, testamentary restrictions prevent scholars and biographers with access to these letters from quoting them directly (Robinson 58).[6] According to Sharon O'Brien, however, Cather states in one of these epistles that 'it is so unfair that female friendships should be unnatural,' before she goes on to accede that, nevertheless, 'they are.' As O'Brien suggests, Cather's self-conscious, if grudging, awareness of the fact that female friendships are 'unnatural,' reflects the extent to which she internalised the sexual norms of her age, and recognised the nature of her intense attachment to Louise as a 'special category not sanctioned by the dominant culture' (O'Brien, *Willa Cather* 131-32).[7]

If critics' descriptions of Cather's 'turbulent' and 'passionate' 'love letters' (O'Brien, 'The Thing Not Named' 583) are accurate, her college 'crush' on Louise Pound represents precisely the sort of 'flame,' 'rave,' or 'spoon' relationship which so gravely concerned sexologists and educators of the period. Ellis, for instance, devotes a lengthy appendix in his book to documenting such unsavoury 'School-Friendships of Girls,' in which he cites the cautionary words of one 'American correspondent': 'Love of the same sex ... though [it] is not generally known, is very common; it is not mere friendship; the love is strong, real, and passionate' — sometimes, indeed, as he has been informed, it is 'insane, intense love.'[8] Speculating on the explosive end of the Cather-Pound alliance, one biographer has even suggested that Pound's older brother may have intervened because he interpreted their relationship apprehensively in this current context:

> Perhaps he called the friendship unnatural and his sister's friend perverse. He may have even used the term 'lesbian' to describe her. We do not know. We do know, however, that losing Louise caused Willa the most intense suffering she had ever known. (Robinson 60-61)[9]

In any case, whether or not the widespread cultural anxieties of deviant female sexuality, fanned by the 'New Scientific Discourse' of the sexologists, actually affected Cather's personal life with such painful immediacy, it remains plausible to assume, at the very least, that a sharp awareness of such medico-cultural censures must have impinged uncomfortably upon her conscious mind at one time or another.

It is with such biographical and contextual background in mind that one may, perhaps, most fruitfully approach the question of sexuality in *O Pioneers!* For as Annette Kolodny has argued, whether one speaks of critics 'reading' texts or writers 'reading' the world, one 'call[s] attention to interpretive strategies that are learned, historically determined, and thereby necessarily gender-inflected' (47). In this sense, Cather's fictional portrayal of sexuality represents a cultural construct shaped largely by the lived experiences of her gender. And because she experienced and observed, or 'read,' female sexuality in an age in which traditional sexual roles and distinctions were being rapidly erased and eroded, sparking feelings of confusion, fear, and guilt, it is relatively unsurprising that her fictional treatment of the subject should embody an element of the conflict which marked both her life and her times.

Set on a wild, windswept prairie frontier, *O Pioneers!* initially appears far removed indeed from Cather's controversial modern era. And yet the profound extent to which her novel is informed by the milieu in which it was produced is apparent even in the central character of Alexandra Bergson: a heroine who incorporates many definitive features of the New Woman upon whom the contemporary debate of the 'intermediate sex' centred. In so far as the New Woman of the age 'constituted a revolutionary demographic and political phenomenon' (Smith-Roseberg 245), of course, Alexandra eludes the historical paradigm: unlike Cather herself, she is neither part of a novel, homogeneous group of college-educated women, nor does she self-consciously resist traditional gender roles on intellectual or ideological grounds. Practical circumstances, as she angrily informs her brothers, have dicated the nature of her pioneering career: 'Maybe I would never have been very soft, anyhow; but I certainly didn't choose to be the kind of girl I was' (Cather, *O Pioneers!* 171). On the other hand, there are also strong suggestions in the text that the intellectually gifted Alexandra would have made a fine student, and that had she in fact had a choice in the matter, she would not have remained on the outside of the State University's 'long iron fence' curiously 'looking through,' and observing campus life from a distance (287).

At any rate, beyond these few fundamental differences, Cather's heroine embodies the majority of qualities typical of the late nineteenth-century New Woman: she is single, economically autonomous, and quite ready to assert her legal and social equality, defiantly maintaining her right to 'do exactly as [she] please[s] with her land' (167). Moreover, with her innovative silos and pig-breeding schemes, Alexandra is the owner of 'one of the richest farms on the Divide' (83), and as such, assumes the position of a community leader. In these respects, she corresponds closely to Smith-Rosenberg's description of the quintessential New Woman:

> Eschewing marriage, she fought for professional visibility, espoused innovative, often radical, economic and social reforms, and wielded real political power. At

the same time, as a member of the affluent new bourgeoisie, most frequently a child of small-town America, she felt herself part of the grass roots of her country. (245)

It is also interesting to note that although Alexandra presents a new type of heroine in the tradition of American frontier fiction, she is by no means an anomaly in a historical context; indeed, by the late nineteenth century, many women had begun to take advantage of the Homestead Act to acquire property in the West—some of them single, adventurous New Women who 'exploited their claims to earn money for other ventures' like college tuition (Myers 258-59). The conceptual distance between the modern era of the New Woman and that of Cather's farming pioneer, then, is not so great as it may first appear to be.

The affinities between the New Woman of Cather's period and the heroine of *O Pioneers!* extend to the portrayal of Alexandra as a representative of a type of 'intermediate sex': a vaguely intimidating sort of 'mannish' woman who appears to combine certain traditional aspects of masculinity and femininity in one. This trait is immediately apparent in Cather's initial description of Alexandra as 'a tall, strong girl' who

> walked rapidly and resolutely, as if she knew exactly where she was going and what she was going to do next. She wore a man's long ulster (not as if it were an affliction, but as if it were very comfortable and belonged to her; carried it like a young soldier), and a round plush cap, tied down with a veil. She had a serious, thoughtful face, and her clear, deep blue eyes were fixed intently on the distance. (6)

Krafft-Ebing, who believed, as Smith-Rosenberg states, that 'only the abnormal woman would challenge gender distinctions—and by her dress you would know her' (272)—would have likely recognised his 'Mannish Lesbian' here, on the basis of Alexandra's manly ulster alone. Ellis, too, would have detected an element of perversity in the 'comfortable' confidence with which Alexandra 'carries' her masculine garb, since he maintained that the 'very pronounced tendency among sexually inverted women to adopt male attire when practicable' could be 'chiefly' accounted for by the fact that 'the wearer feels more at home in them' (245). Moreover, the heroine's rapid and resolute gait and the 'Amazonian fierceness' with which she cows the 'little drummer' who dares ogle her (8) also reflect the sort of 'brusque, energetic movements' and 'masculine straightforwardness and sense of honour . . . free from any suggestion of either shyness or audacity,' which, according to a 'keen observer' like Ellis, betrayed an 'underlying psychic abnormality' (250). As a heroine of epic proportions, in fact, Alexandra corresponds strikingly to one sexologist's profile of the typical female 'invert,' whom he held to be

> more full of life, of enterprise, of practical energy, more aggressive, more heroic, more apt for adventure, than either the heterosexual woman or the homosexual man.
>
> (Magnus Hirschfeld, qtd. in Ellis 251)

Endowed with a greatness of stature which dwarfs the 'little men' who surround her (181), as well as a 'direct[ness]' of manner which often makes men 'wince' (121), Alexandra is indeed the most enterprising, energetic, and heroic character in Cather's novel.

Importantly, however, this positive vision of the heroic 'manly woman' appears to constitute the exception rather than the rule in medical literature of the period. For while early nineteenth-century commentators could still gloat contemptuously that 'Amazonian' types were 'their own executioners' and presented no danger of 'perpetuating their race,' since they had 'unsexed themselves in public estimation,'[10] most of the sexologists of Cather's era were much less confident — for by then it was clear that the ranks of the 'intermediate sex' were indeed continuing to swell. Such women were thus viewed collectively with a good deal of trepidation as the 'ultimate symbol of social disorder' (Smith-Rosenberg 181).

This understandable though fallacious perception of the 'deviant' woman as an emblem of social disruption emerges as the first issue implicitly addressed and refuted by Cather in *O Pioneers!* For having once established her heroine as an 'Amazonian' or 'manly woman,' Cather proceeds to depict her not as a harbinger of chaos, but as precisely the opposite: as a preeminent symbol of order and a bedrock of stability. Under Alexandra's creative and loving will, for example, the natural world is gradually though steadily transformed from a hostile 'wild land' to a productive and geometrically neat farm, noteworthy for its 'most unusual trimness and care for detail' (83). Hence, there is an

> order and fine arrangement manifest all over [Alexandra's] great farm; in the fencing and hedging, in the windbreaks and sheds, [and] in the symmetrical pasture ponds. (84)

'Not unlike a tiny village' (83), Alexandra's farming homestead also represents a contained microcosm of fair but efficient social and domestic order. When she has no 'visitors' and dines with 'her men,' for instance, Cather's heroine sits 'at the head of the long table,' and the place to her left is routinely reserved for old Ivar, her trusted advisor (85-86). With a democratic spirit, Alexandra 'encourage[s] her men to talk' during these meals, to voice their opinions and concerns over the business affairs of the farm, but throughout the novel there is never a doubt that she retains an absolutely firm control over the hierarchical structure she has created. 'As long as there is one house there must be one head,' John Bergson declares before his death, and it is a maxim by which his 'dotter' unswervingly abides (25-26).

Cather's affirmative portrayal of the 'manly woman' also works in a similar fashion to subvert or re-invert the prevailing medical and cultural conception of the sexually inverted woman as a physiologically 'morbid' or diseased, mutant being. For not only were such women of 'intermediate sex' judged to be 'unnatural' in the sense of being quirkily unconventional in dress and behaviour, but, as the 'visible symptom[s] of a diseased society,' they were also held to be innately sick—organically degenerative and neurotic as well as morally contaminating. Because contemporary authorities habitually transposed social and political evils into physiological terms, medical discourses of the sexually deviant woman abound in metaphors of morbidity and pathology (Smith-Rosenberg 245, 261-62). Krafft-Ebing, for example, believed that lesbianism was the sign of 'an inherited diseased condition of the central nervous system,' which he referred to as a form of 'taint.'[11] Similarly, Ellis, although ostensibly aware that 'the study of the abnormal is perfectly distinct from the study of the morbid,' still claimed that female sexual inversion was a type of 'germ' fostered by the feminist movement (319, 262).[12]

The Amazonian Alexandra may assume manly attire, but she is not, as the narrator notes, in any sense 'afflicted' by it; quite the contrary, in fact, she is depicted by Cather as the epitome of health and wholesomeness. Her body, so 'tall and strong' that 'no man on the Divide could have carried it very far,' is also a 'gleaming white body' (206), consistently associated with images of both vigour and purity. While Cather thus likens her heroine's sunkissed face to 'one of the big double sunflowers' in the garden, she also emphasises the contrasting 'smoothness and whiteness' of the delicate skin beneath her shirt collar and sleeves: it is skin which 'none but Swedish women ever possess; skin with the freshness of the snow itself' (88). Just as Jim Burden, in *My Ántonia*, thinks 'with pride that Ántonia, like Snow White in the fairy tale, is still the fairest of them all' (215), so in this novel does Carl Lindstrum remember admiringly how the fair Alexandra used to appear at dawn with her milking pails, 'looking as if she had walked straight out' of the 'milky light' 'of the morning itself' (126). Even as an older, successfully established farming businesswoman, the pristine aura of the dairymaid still suffuses Alexandra, who blandly admits that people find her 'clean and healthy-looking' appearance pleasant (132).

At once robust and delicate, fusing conventional attributes of male and female within herself, the heroine's healthy, hermaphroditic nature also facilitates a vital, erotically fulfilling relationship with the land—virtually the only salutary relationship offered by Cather in *O Pioneers!* Indeed, the Nebraskan prairie is charged with 'the same tonic, puissant quality' characteristic of Alexandra herself (77). Like her tanned face and white body, 'the brown earth' is yet so clean and pure that it rolls from the shear of the plow without 'even dimming the brightness of the metal' (76). And like Alexandra, too, the land is presented as a hermaphroditic entity. Thus, it both 'yield[s] itself eagerly' to her active and yearning 'human will' (76, 65), and 'stir[s]' beneath her like a giant leviathan, eliciting, in turn, a sensual responsiveness or 'yielding' in the heroine herself:

> Alexandra remembered . . . days when she was close to the flat, fallow world about her, and felt, as it were, in her own body the joyous germination in the soil. (204)

As a sexually animated presence within the text, however, the land may constitute not so much an autonomous entity in its own right as it does a specular reflection of the heroine's own hermaphroditic nature. For it is, in fact, Alexandra who sublimates her sexual energies into the land—who sets her face 'toward it with love and yearning' (65)—and it is also her perception and sense of it that are invariably conveyed to the reader, who sees only the way the land 'seem[s]' to her or the way she 'remember[s]' it (65, 204).

What Cather actually appears to present, then, is a type of autoerotic, onanistic relationship of the heroine with a part of her hermaphroditic sexual self which has been displaced onto the 'Other' of the land. In this respect, her portrayal of sexuality in *O Pioneers!* is comparable to that of Martha Ostenso's in the Canadian prairie novel *Wild Geese* (1925), in which the heroine, Judith, lies upon the 'damp ground' nude and feels that 'here was something forbiddenly beautiful;' something as 'secret as one's own body' (67). Seemingly complete in herself, Cather's heroine may be perhaps best likened, though, to the 'single wild duck' she so fondly recalls in her memory: the 'solitary bird' which 'take[s] its pleasure' quite alone, and which strikes Alexandra as more 'beautiful' than any 'living thing had ever seemed to [her]' (204–05). A subtle celebration of the hermaphroditic and perhaps even bisexual sensibility, the portrayal of Alexandra's fulfilling erotic life suggests that she may not be as lonely in her unmarried state as the narrator would sometimes have us believe.

By presenting her 'manly woman' as a fresh and vital human being whose hermaphroditic attributes constitute the source of positive erotic gratification, Cather's novel works to break down the contemporary myth of the diseased and degenerative woman of 'intermediate sex.' Significantly, however, her artistic response to the large, pseudo-scientific discourse of sexuality does not end at this point, for Cather also proceeds to challenge her culture's yet more fundamental assumption of the intrinsic desirability and 'normalcy' of heterosexuality itself. In *O Pioneers!*, indeed, it is not the seemingly 'deviant' but the socially acceptable heterosexual impulse which is portrayed as 'morbid' and unhealthy. Thus, when Alexandra does indulge in one of her rare heterosexual fantasies, she is apt to experience it as a form of profoundly sordid 'reverie': literally, an unclean impulse which she immediately attempts to wash away, via a penitential ritual of Spartan ablution, with 'buckets of cold well-water' (206). And the one and only time that Alexandra does envisage a heterosexual embrace as a positive desire to be unresisted, it is rather alarmingly associated with the hooded figure of Death, 'the mightiest of all lovers' (283).

Similarly, Cather also consistently links the major heterosexual relationship within her novel—the love of Emil and Marie—to images of decay, sickness, and pain. Emil's passion, for example, is compared to a defective grain of corn which will never shoot up 'joyfully into the light' but is destined instead to rot and fester in the dark, damp earth (164). The essential morbidity of his relationship with Marie is further conveyed by the nature of the three gifts he drops into the lap of his beloved over the course of the novel: the uncut turquoises are pretty, but must, like the grain of corn, remain concealed in dark secrecy (224-25); the branch full of 'sweet, insipid fruit' is already overripe and on the verge of decay (153); and, in stark contrast to Alexandra's sportive and contented solitary duck, the birds associated with the two young lovers are dead and dripping with blood (127-28). Gone for both Emil and Marie are those 'germless days' of childhood (216), for their experience of adult heterosexuality is indeed like a type of 'affliction,' a perverse sort of malaise in the grip of which they 'cannot feel that the heart lives at all' unless 'its strings can scream to the touch of pain' (226).

Neatly reversing her society's binary equation of deviant sexuality with disease and heterosexuality with health, Cather also continues to turn contemporary medical theory upon its head by attributing to the nature of heterosexuality a number of other specific aberrations which sexologists typically ascribed to the sexual 'invert.' By the early twentieth century, for instance, the notion of 'sexual inversion' was commonly associated not only with physical disease, but with all manner of tragedy, insanity, and criminality as well. 'Inverted women,' as Ellis asserts in his work, 'present a favourable soil for the seeds of passional crime,' and to illustrate his point, he promptly proceeds to recount, in gruesome detail, several cases of lesbian homicides and suicides, deeming one particularly sensational 1892 murder of a young Memphis woman by her female lover as quite 'typical' (201). The sexual nature of the 'inverted' person, moreover, was thought to 'constitute as well a specific atavistic response, a sudden throwback to a primitive bisexuality, a tragic freak of nature' (Smith-Rosenberg 269). '[F]rom a eugenic standpoint' such as Ellis's, therefore, 'the tendency to sexual inversion' could be regarded as 'merely . . . nature's merciful method of winding up a concern which, from her point of view, has ceased to be profitable' (335).

In Cather's novel, conversely, it is heterosexuality which is presented as the direct cause of such grievous afflictions and processes. While the component of tragedy is, of course, most dramatically evident in the violent and premature deaths of Marie and Emil, almost all of the heterosexual alliances in the text are presented as unhappy or pathetic. Hence, John Bergson is 'warped' by his marriage, which is described as a mere 'infatuation' on his part: 'the despairing folly of a powerful man who [could] not bear to grow old' (23). Similarly, the snug security of Angélique's happy little family is blighted by the sudden death of Amédée; the confused young Signa is afraid of her bullish husband even before he forces her to plod home with the cows on their wedding day; and 'young farmers' like Lou betray a measure of embarrassed discomfort in their spousal relations in that they can seldom bring themselves to address their wives by name (111). And, unlike Alexandra's orderly household, the Shabata home is frequently the scene of domestic crises and violence, for Frank is a rash and volatile man whose unleashed temper has 'more than once' compelled Marie to struggle with him over a loaded gun (265-66). Uniting themselves in relationships which all too often result in animosity, violence, divorce (148), or death, the majority of heterosexual characters in this novel are to some degree culpable, like Marie, of 'spread[ing] ruin around' (304), and as such, they are viewed collectively by the author not only as a tragic lot but, indeed, as the 'ultimate symbol' of what the sexual invert was supposed to represent: utter social and domestic chaos.

It is also Frank Shabata, the most aggressively heterosexual character in the novel, who emerges from Cather's perspective as the 'most favourable soil for the seeds of passional crime,' as well as madness and degeneration. After his passionate jealousy has resulted in the murders of Emil and Marie, he regresses in prison to an atavistic creature, a grey, unshaven, and stooped figure who appears 'not altogether human.' Left to ponder his guilt in a wretched cell, the now pathetic Frank depicts a dismal future for himself; as he confesses to Alexandra when she visits him, 'I guess I go crazy sure 'nough' (294). The implicit but clear message in Cather's text, then, is that the heterosexual nature, far from embodying an unambiguously 'normal' or healthy appetite, may manifest itself as 'unnatural' and 'morbid' in precisely the same ways as those of 'inverted' or 'deviant' sexual tendencies were thought to. Or, considered from an obverse angle, Cather's novel is one whose sexually unorthodox but sane, vigorous, and prosperous heroine serves as a timely reminder to those, who, like Ellis, tended to forget that what may be perceived as 'abnormal' need not necessarily be 'morbid.'

Through her own process of conceptual 'inversion,' then, Cather may be seen to respond in a creative and challenging way to dominant contemporary theories of sexuality, quietly establishing, in *O Pioneers!*, her own alternate paradigms of human sexuality. And yet it is, perhaps, an authorial consciousness of implicitly engaging—and controverting—this larger medico-cultural ethos which may also be seen to constitute the source of an inhibiting force in Cather's art. In *O Pioneers!*, this aspect of the narrative is best illustrated by Cather's treatment of the relations between women. For indeed, contrary to the pervasive critical over-generalisation that Cather 'never' deals in her fiction with the homosocial emotions and bonds which filled and fuelled her own life, a very complex and subtle relationship does unfold in this novel between Alexandra and Marie, which, to the best extent of my knowledge, has not been extensively or adequately examined. And it is important that it should be, for it suggests that within this novel of pioneer life, Cather begins to explore a second sort of 'frontier': not a historical and geographical one, but a psychic 'frontier between friendship and love' (M. Tarde, qtd. in Ellis 75). This is not to argue that Cather depicts the friendship between her heroine and Marie as one which moves toward incipient lesbianism. Rather, it is to suggest that, along with its nostalgia for the heroic cultural and geographical Nebraskan frontier of the past, Cather's text also quietly but perceptibly mourns the passing of that older world of passionate yet innocent female love, so well documented by Smith-Rosenberg, into a modern era of 'morbidified' relations.

Perhaps because of the disparity of their respective ages, the affection Alexandra feels for Marie clearly manifests itself on one level as a type of maternal love. 'Sit down like a good girl, Marie,' Alexandra says in her best matronly manner, for example, 'and I'll tell you a story' (137). Marie, that 'crazy child' who married at eighteen (119), seems in this respect to present a surrogate daughter-figure for Alexandra, just as she thinks of her younger brother, Emil, as her 'boy.' On the other hand, however, the friendship between the two women is marked by both a degree of intensity and a dimension of sensuality which makes it a far more 'romantic' relationship than, in fact, Alexandra's ostensibly 'real' romance with Carl Lindstrum. Indeed, when Cather's heroine reflects on the 'pretty lonely life' she has led, the primacy of her bond with the young Bohemian girl is indicated by the order in which she names her two closest companions: 'Besides Marie, Carl is the only friend I have ever had' (177). Unlike Carl, who drifts in and out of Alexandra's life between long intervals, Marie is woven closely into the fabric of her daily existence. 'It is not often,' therefore, that Alexandra 'let[s] three days go by without seeing Marie'—and when Carl does reappear at one point, and Alexandra postpones her regular visit, she frets guiltily that her younger friend will think she has 'forsaken her' (130). Later, of course, it is Alexandra herself who feels woefully 'forsaken' when she learns of Marie's affair with Emil:

> Could you believe that of Marie Tovesky? I would have been cut to pieces, little by little, before I would have betrayed her trust in me! (303)

Not only is it revealing that Alexandra apparently does not recognise Marie 'Tovesky' as Frank Shabata's wife, but her emphatic language and words of 'betrayal' and 'forsaken' anguish also clearly echo the 'romantic rhetoric' of 'emotional intensity' which Smith-Rosenberg notes as characteristic of close female friendships before the late nineteenth century (59).

Furthermore, while Alexandra's relationship with Carl remains a fairly dispassionate affair throughout—arrested, in fact, at the stage of hand-holding until a light kiss at the very end of the novel is offered as a prelude to a marriage of 'friends' (308-09)—her relationship with Marie allows for a great measure of uninhibited physical contact. At one point, for example, Marie runs up to her friend 'painting,' throws 'her arms about Alexandra,' and then gives her arm an affectionate 'little squeeze' as they begin to walk together (134). And Alexandra similarly expresses her sentiments by 'pinch[ing] Marie's cheek playfully' when they meet (192). The two women have an acute and joyful sense of each other's physical proximity as well; hence, Alexandra confides that she is 'glad' to have Marie living 'so near' her, while Marie delights in the delicate scent of rosemary on Alexandra's dress (119, 134).

Like Cather herself, who so ardently admired female beauty that she sometimes strapped herself financially by loaning money to attractive actresses whose plays she reviewed (Woodress 105; O'Brien, *Willa Cather* 134), Alexandra responds to Marie with pleasure and admiration on an aesthetic level. Of course, almost every character in the novel does, for Marie's spectacular 'tiger eyes' (11) are irresistibly captivating. Indeed, at the risk of pressing a fine (but in this context, relevant) point too closely, Marie's striking eyes may reflect a subtle authorial allusion to Balzac's sensational lesbian novel, *The Girl With the Golden Eyes*—particularly since that novel is believed to have been inspired by the real-life relationship of George Sand (Cather's avowed role-model) and a woman named Marie Dorval.[13] At any rate, Alexandra is especially drawn by the unique blend of exoticism and innocence in Marie, comparing her to both a 'queer foreign kind of doll' and a 'little brown rabbit' (192, 133). Carl's observation of Marie's sensuously 'full' and 'parted' lips, and of the 'points of yellow light dancing in her eyes' (135) reinforces Alexandra's perception of her friend as an attractively animated yet vulnerable young woman who is 'too young and pretty for this sort of life' (121).

With Marie, Alexandra thus enjoys an emotional and physical intimacy which is a source of innocent pleasure to them both. The crucial point, however, is how others perceive their relationship. Through the perspective of Carl Lindstrum, Cather subtly but deftly probes the perverse interpretations apt to be construed from such close homosocial bonds in the new era of 'scientific' sexology. When Alexandra explains to Carl how 'nice' it has felt for her to have 'a friend' at 'the other end' of the path between the Bergson-Shabata homesteads since he has lived there, for instance, Carl responds with a rueful 'smile': 'All the same, I hope it has n't [*sic*] been *quite* the same' (130). It is an odd remark, laden with an innuendo that makes Alexandra look at Carl 'with surprise,' and respond defensively:

> Why no, of course not. Not the same. She could not very well take your place, if that's what you mean. I'm friendly with all my neighbors, I hope. But Marie is really a companion, someone I can talk to quite frankly. You would n't want me to be more lonely than I have been would you? (130)

To this, Carl laughs nervously, fusses with his hair, and replies uncertainly:

> Of course I don't. I ought to be thankful that this path has n't been worn by— well, by friends with more pressing errands than your little Bohemian is likely to have. (131)

Carl realises that he 'ought' to be thankful that Alexandra's female 'friend' is not 'likely' to pose a serious rival for her affections, but his hesitant manner and doubtful language suggest that his suspicions are obviously not allayed. When he does, therefore, have an opportunity to scrutinise the type of relationship the two women share, he carefully 'watch[es]' them from 'a little distance' (135). That they make a 'pretty picture' together is his first thought, but after observing Marie's intense and delighted absorption in Alexandra for a time, Carl goes on to reflect: 'What a waste . . . she ought to be doing all that for a sweetheart. How awkwardly things come about!' (136).

Significantly, it is not long after Carl's reappearance on the Divide that the pleasant state of affairs between Cather's heroine and the attractive young immigrant girl begin to alter. Indeed, the shift in Alexandra and Marie's friendship, the point at which each woman first begins to distance herself warily from the other, occurs as issues of their respective heterosexual relationships begin to impinge upon their lives. When it comes to the subject of Carl and her differences with her brothers over him, for example, Alexandra 'instinctive[ly]' feels that 'about such things she and Marie would not understand one another' (188). Suddenly, when the topic is Alexandra's relationship with a male, Marie no longer appears to represent the 'real' 'companion' she 'can talk to quite frankly' (130). It is a blind 'instinct' which Alexandra follows without testing when she has the opportunity. For when during one of their last intimate moments together, Marie begins to speak 'frankly' about her own unhappy union with Frank, Alexandra withdraws guardedly from the conversation, abruptly recalling Marie to the 'crochet patterns' for which they have been searching: 'no good,' she rationalises, can ever come 'from talking about such things' (198).

Immediately after this incident, a reciprocal process of withdrawal takes place on Marie's part. As the narrator observes:

> After that day the younger woman seemed to shrink more and more into herself. When she was with Alexandra she was not spontaneous and frank as she used to be. She seemed to be brooding over something, and holding something back. (200–01)

The pain, confusion, or guilt which each woman experiences over her respective relationship—or relationships—with men is the one thing they cannot share with each other directly, and it is as a stave which wedges them further and further apart. Finally, when Alexandra places her hand tenderly on the arm of a pale and tired-looking Marie, just after Emil has drained the blood from her cheeks with an electrifying kiss, she can feel her young friend 'shiver': 'Marie stiffened under that kind, calm hand. Alexandra drew back, perplexed and hurt' (226).

Cather's novel thus clearly traces the steady disintegration of a formerly intimate female friendship to the point of physical recoil and abiding resentment. But what happened? Certainly, in so far that the 'pretty picture' which consists of Alexandra and Marie becomes 'awkward' only when men enter into it, it may be argued that Cather's depiction of a loving female relationship is intended as an illustration of the sad consequences of social pressures which compel women (and men) to erect psychic barriers between one another in an obsessively heterocentric culture—lest their affection, that is, be construed by the Carls of the world as suspiciously 'unnatural.' If this is what Cather attempted, however, she does not wholly accomplish her goal. For although she does begin to critique the contemporary attitude toward, and perception of, innocently romantic female friendships, she eventually abandons this daring impulse in what seems a silent submission to the established sexual prejudices and stereotypes of her day, a submission which sharply reinforces O'Brien's contention that Cather never fully 'freed herself from male constructs of femininity' ('The Thing Not Named' 596; *Willa Cather* 124-25). Because indeed, the whole tragic point of the devolution of Alexandra and Marie's relationship is undermined by Cather's ultimate reliance upon the archetypal paradigm of the fallen Eve for Marie, and by her apparently unqualified endorsement of a conventional marriage for Alexandra—an authorial enthusiasm which is nevertheless unconvincing because it purports to applaud a heterosexual alliance which has been portrayed from the beginning as tepid and watery, at best.

Ultimately, then, Cather's careful dissolution and final destruction of the poignant bond first established between her women represent an authorial retreat into literary convention and rather insipid romanticism. It is a retreat which is in itself tragic. For as the character of Carl suggests, Cather was at some point while writing her novel obviously aware of just how 'awkwardly' her portrayal of an artless and genuine female friendship might appear to her modern audience. Whether unconsciously or with a painful memory of her own past friendship with Louise Pound, Cather therefore defuses the potentially scandalous subject she has begun to probe, before it becomes too overt an issue within the text. The simple beauty of a loving friendship between women was the one central aspect of the contemporary discourse of sexuality which Cather could not fully address, because it involved not merely an indirect, artistic inversion of her culture's metaphors, myths, and theories, but entailed, rather, a direct and necessarily polemical authorial entry into the heartland of the sexologists' 'frontier' territory, that twilight and controversial no-woman's land separating socially acceptable female companionship from illicit same-sex love. And for all the dramatic adolescent rejection of frocks and frills and curls; for all the aggressively outspoken, critical target-shooting of youth; for all the steadfast, personal commitments to other women in her maturity, this was something the adult 'Billy Cather, Jr' was not rebel enough to risk.

Notes

1. Ellis uses terms such as 'frontier,' 'pioneer,' and 'borderland' quite extensively throughout.

2. For a differing interpretation of the marriage of Carl and Alexandra, see O'Brien, *Willa Cather* 444-46.

3. This chapter of Smith-Rosenberg's book, entitled 'The Female World of Love and Ritual: Relations Between Women in Nineteenth Century America,' appeared originally in the first issue of *Signs* (1975).

4. Smith-Rosenberg also explores the potentially revolutionary social implications which a strong network of homosocial female bonds posed in the context of the feminist movement, and makes a similar point; see *Disorderly Conduct* 277–82.

5. The term 'morbidification,' however, is taken from Faderman.

6. On Cather's destruction of her letters and the legal provisions of her will, see Robinson 33–34 and 274; Brown xxiii; Woodress xiii–xiv.

7. See 127–37 for the most compelling and comprehensive account, to date, of Cather's complex and contradictory sense of lesbian self-identity.

8. E.G. Lancaster, qtd. in Ellis, *Sexual Inversion* 382. The colloquial terms 'flame,' 'rave,' and 'spoon' also appear in Ellis's appendix, 368–84 *passim*.

9. It should be noted, however, that subsequent biographers have dismissed Robinson's suggestion as 'pure speculation' (Woodress 87).

10. Anon., 'Female Orators,' *The Mother's Magazine*, VI (1838): 27, qtd. in Faderman, *Surpassing the Love of Men* 235.

11. Krafft-Ebing, qtd. in Faderman, 'The Morbidification of Love' 77. Faderman points out that Krafft-Ebing later changed his stance on homosexuality as a disease, but that this was announced only shortly before his death in 1902 and had 'minimal' impact 'on popular notions regarding homosexuals' (77–78, n. 6).

12. In fairness, it must be noted that Ellis also uses the word 'germ' elsewhere in *Sexual Inversion* in a purely organic sense. In language very appropriate to the context of Cather's novel, in fact, he describes human sexuality in terms of a 'soil' which at conception is 'sown' with an equal amount of masculine and feminine 'seeds' or 'germs.' In bisexuals and homosexuals, he maintains, the 'normal' process whereby the 'seeds' of one sex come to 'kill off' most of those of the other sex has somehow dysfunctioned, a phenomenon, he says, that can only be attributed to an inherent abnormality 'in the soil' (309–11).

13. On the relevance of Balzac's novel in the context of late nineteenth-century French aesthetic-decadent literature, see Faderman, *Surpassing the Love of Men* 254, 267. Cather was known to be a fan of such literature, which strengthens the possibility that she had indeed come across Balzac's book; see O'Brien, *Willa Cather* 134–35; Woodress 119; and Brown 98, 103.

Works Cited

Bailey, Jennifer, 'The Dangers of Femininity in Willa Cather's Fiction.' *Journal of American Studies*, 16.3, 1982: pp. 391–406.

Brown, E.K., *Willa Cather: A Critical Biography*, completed by Leon Edel, New York: Knopf, 1953.

Cather, Willa, *O Pioneers!* (1913), Boston: Houghton, 1941.

—, *My Ántonia*, (1918), Cambridge, Mass.: Riverside P, 1926.

Ellis, Havelock, *Sexual Inversion*, Vol. 2 of *Studies in the Psychology of Sex*, 6 vols., 3rd ed, Philadelphia: Davis, 1918.

Faderman, Lillian, *Surpassing the Love of Men: Romantic Friendship and Love Between Women from the Renaissance to the Present*, New York: William Morrow, 1981.

—, 'The Morbidification of Love Between Women by Nineteenth-Century Sexologists,' *Journal of Homosexuality*, 4.1, 1978: pp. 73–90.

Kolodny, Annette, 'A Map for Rereading: Gender and the Interpretation of Literary Texts,' *The New Feminist Criticism: Essays on Women, Literature, and Theory*, ed. Elaine Showalter, New York: Pantheon, 1985, pp. 46–62.

Myers, Sandra L., *Westering Women and the Frontier Experience, 1800-1915*, Albuquerque: U of New Mexico P, 1982.

O'Brien, Sharon, *Willa Cather: The Emerging Voice*, New York: OUP, 1987.
—, '"The Thing Not Named": Willa Cather as a Lesbian Writer,' *Signs* 9.4 1984: pp. 576–99.
Ostenso, Martha, *Wild Geese*, Toronto: McClelland & Stewart, 1925.
Rich, Adrienne, 'Compulsive Heterosexuality and Lesbian Existence,' *Signs*, 5.4, 1980: pp. 631–61.
Robinson, Phyllis, *Willa: The Life of Willa Cather*, Garden City, New York: Doubleday, 1983.
Rule, Jane, *Lesbian Images*, Garden City, New York: Doubleday, 1975.
Smith-Rosenberg, Carroll, *Disorderly Conduct: Visions of Gender in Victorian America*, New York: Knopf, 1985.
Woodress, James, *Willa Cather: A Literary Life*, Lincoln: U of Nebraska P, 1987.

183
Thea Kronborg's Vocal Transvestism: Willa Cather and the 'Voz Contralto'

JOHN H. FLANNIGAN

Willa Cather's *The Song of the Lark* (1915) may be, as John Dizikes has called it, 'the finest American novel about art and the artist' (277). Ironically, however, Cather's third novel may also be her least appreciated work (277). Its excessive length (nearly 500 pages in its original edition) probably discourages many general readers. But even sympathetic critics of Cather's fiction such as David Stouck have regretted a more serious flaw, namely the novel's hollow center. 'On the surface it is a success story . . . but the incontrovertible truth of every such story is that art is achieved at the expense of life' (184).

Cather herself realised that Thea Kronborg's rise from naive child of Moonstone, Colorado into world-renowned Wagnerian diva necessitated a depletion of the very energy that had made Thea interesting to readers. In an introduction written for the novel's re-issue in 1932, Cather compared its dramatic arc to that of Wilde's *The Picture of Dorian Gray*: 'As the gallery of [Thea's] musical impersonations grows in number and beauty, as that perplexing thing called "style" (which is a singer's very self) becomes more direct and simple and noble, the Thea Kronborg who is behind the imperishable daughters of music becomes somewhat dry and preoccupied' (*The Song of the Lark*, [1938] vii–viii).[1] Thea's life was in fact 'the reverse of Wilde's story.' Unlike Dorian Gray, the musical artist 'comes and goes, subject to colds, brokers, dressmakers, managers,' while the 'free creature, who retains her youth and beauty and warm imagination, is kept shut up in the closet along with the scores and wigs' (Preface, viii).

SOURCE   John H. Flannigan, 'Thea Kronborg's Vocal Transvestism: Willa Cather and the "Voz Contralto"', *Modern Fiction Studies*, 40, 1994, pp. 737–63.

Thea's artistic struggles likewise have their physical counterparts à la Dorian Gray. According to Susan J. Rosowski, these struggles involve Thea's incarnation of romantic desires for an imaginative existence, 'a secret or second self' whose 'gestation, birth, and passion' are charted throughout the novel (*Voyage Perilous* 63). In a letter to Elizabeth Shepley Sergeant, Cather wrote that when Thea achieved vocal maturity near the novel's middle, she (Cather) could almost feel Thea's burgeoning body within her own flesh (7 Dec. 1915). Yet Sharon O'Brien sees the full-blooded Thea Kronborg as Cather's last experiment with a strong female character before succumbing to 'romantic women and male perceivers in later novels,' a move that O'Brien explains in terms of Cather's disillusionment with her lesbian attachment to Isabelle McClung following the latter's marriage to Jan Hambourg in 1916 ('The Thing Not Named' 596).

I believe that all of the above readings are valid and highlight important aspects of Thea's character. But I would like to add to the discussion about Thea's artistic development some ideas about two vital *physical* aspects of her character: the voice itself; and the music it produces. Of particular interest to me are Cather's curious choice of range for the young Thea—a contralto—and her use of musical texts that amplify Thea's struggle for artistic freedom by linking it to her struggle for physical maturity.

Thea's passage through puberty and adolescence to adulthood resembles her search for the right voice and musical texts. Her early use of the contralto voice represents her vocal, physical, and social confusion—her 'working-out' of competing impulses that define her as a daugher, an artist, and a woman. Thus Thea's 'imaginative rebirth' (in Rosowski's terminology) also has a profoundly physical component illustrated by her search for a particular vocal range and the musical texts appropriate to it in charting her progress toward sexual awareness and professional success.

The Song of the Lark contains various references to musical texts that underline the transgressive and transvestite possibilities of the contralto voice. Cather's allusions sometimes make only oblique reference to a transvestite context, but elsewhere Thea performs with the approximation of a masculine voice and point-of-view. Such examples not only complicate a reader's assessment of this feminine *Künstlerroman* (David Stouck's label) but also suggest a new way of hearing the musical texts utilised by Cather as themselves producing gendered conflict.

The fact that music can express or create 'gendered conflict' has been admitted only in recent years. Musicologists and critics are now beginning to ask new questions that challenge accepted notions of music as an ungendered, 'transcendent' language. Susan McClary notes that feminist criticism, for example, has had little to do with musical analysis: 'Music has been and continues to be almost entirely excepted from criticism as it is practiced within other humanities disciplines. . . . Meaning is not inherent in music, but neither is it in language; both are activities that are kept afloat only because communities of people invest in them, agree collectively that their signs serve as valid currency' (20–21). If, as I believe to be the case, Cather carefully documented in her fiction the power of music as she herself had experienced it, then her writing furnishes important evidence for McClary's ideas. And if, as John Shepherd argues, audiences negotiate 'the politically personal . . . from within the internal processes of music,' then music, instead of being an autonomous 'speech of the soul' as Cather once called it, is susceptible to the same immense variety of interpretive approaches that enables literary texts to disclose new meaning to readers interested in fictional representations of gender, sexual, and political roles (Shepherd 172; *World and the Parish* 1: 657).

The relationship between music and Thea's growth to womanhood has unfortunately received little critical attention. Richard Giannone's groundbreaking study, *Music in Willa Cather's Fiction* (1968), remains one of the most insightful and valuable works dealing with Cather's oeuvre. Yet the current trend in Cather criticism seems to be away from investigations of the apparent 'harmony between man and his place and his time' that Giannone detected as the musical underpinnings of her work and toward a reassessment of Cather's sophisticated narrative techniques and her use of autobiography (Giannone 13).[2] In place of harmony, critics such as O'Brien and Hermione Lee have found dissonances and jarring notes.[3] In particular, Blanche Gelfant's ground-breaking study of *My Ántonia* spotlights how Cather 'masks sexual ambivalence by certainty of manner, and displays sexual disturbance, even the macabre, with peculiar insouciance' (104). It seems appropriate, then, to reassess the vital role music plays in Cather's fiction, particularly *The Song of the Lark*, her most 'musical' novel, in the light of these studies. Such a reassessment may not entirely fill the 'hollow core' of the novel, but it may illustrate how Cather's treatment of the tension between Thea's visceral and intellectual struggles is far more sophisticated than has been previously acknowledged.

Coincidentally, this essay discusses some of the same issues as another essay that appeared as I was revising my work for publication. Elizabeth Wood's excellent article 'Sapphonics' examines *The Song of the Lark*, fiction by Gertrude Atherton and Marcia Davenport, and literary and musical figures such as Natalie Barney and Ethel Smyth. Wood explores the female voice as 'a mode of articulation, a way of describing a space of lesbian possibility, for a range of erotic and emotional relationships among women who sing and women who listen' (27). 'Sapphonics' has important implications for Cather studies as well as for studies of other literary figures, and it speaks eloquently to the larger issue of the importance of literary characters in examining socially and historically constructed musical vocabularies expressing gender difference.

Although I agree with Wood's position that Cather's dependence on Olive Fremstad in shaping Thea Kronborg's character 'invites the reader to participate aurally in the landscape of lesbian operatic life and listening,' I am more concerned in this essay with describing the musical evidence of Thea's *transvestism* (Wood 39); Wood discusses only Gluck's *Orfeo* in this connection. Wood also uses the figure of Dr Archie to argue that 'men experience [Thea's] voice as exclusion, an acoustic barrier between the singer and men who desire her,' but this reading does not account for the responses of other male characters in the novel such as Andor Harsanyi, Fred Ottenburg, Professor Wunsch, Mr Kohler, Spanish Johnny, Mr Nathanmeyer, and even Ray Kennedy, all of whom find Thea and her voice strongly attractive (Wood 34).

Thea's possible lesbianism and Cather's sexuality-charged experience of Fremstad's voice and personality are surely linked as Wood maintains, but Cather's wide range of musical allusions demonstrates that there is more going on in the novel than Thea's supplying a substitute for the author's sexual object. In the early chapters of the novel, Thea is consistently identified with masculinised visual and musical images; in fact Thea's growth to womanhood, as charted *musically*, parallels her discovery of other, more obviously heterosexual desires. Cather surely inhabited the aural 'landscape of lesbian operatic life,' to use Wood's phrase, but I believe this landscape, at least as it is depicted in *The Song of the Lark*, is also composed of heterosexual operatic characters such as Donizetti's Lucia, heterosexual male singers (Schumann's *Dichterliebe*), and effeminate, possibly gay men such as Cather's friend Julio.

Thea's teacher Professor Wunsch notes that, as a child, Thea reserves her contralto voice for reading verse. Yet Wunsch also asks Thea, during her piano lessons, to try out certain vocal texts that are normally identified with male singers, requiring her to adopt a male persona and vocal range. Schumann's song cycle *Dichterliebe* and Gluck's opera *Orfeo ed Euridice*, both of which are strongly gendered works in terms of their texts, vocal demands, and performance histories, become working exercises for Thea's joint exploration of vocal limits and gender identities. As she grows older, Thea associates herself with musical texts that stimulate her curiosity about how her body can be harnessed to unusual narratives expressing her own yearning for sexual maturity.

A vivid display of this harnessing of sexual and musical energies is found in Jonathan Demme's recent film *Philadelphia*. The character Andrew Becket (Tom Hanks) furnishes a memorable example of how what I call 'vocal transvestism' can be used to challenge taboos and conventions surrounding questions of gendered identity. When Becket plays for his attorney, Joe Miller (Denzel Washington), Maria Callas' recording of the aria 'La mamma morta' from Umberto Giordano's opera *Andrea Chenier* (1896), the audience witnesses a non-drag transvestite performance created by joining a woman's voice to a man's body. Of course, Becket doesn't sing at all, but he declaims the words of the text, explicating the soprano's words and expressing through his face and gestures the character Maddalena de Coigny's transcendent suffering. The spectacle of Becket, connected to his I–V unit, reenacting for his dumbfounded attorney the operatic scene with Callas' electrifying voice, practically merges his character with the soprano's. It is, as Wayne Koestenbaum suggested in a recent National Public Radio interview, as if the audience had been admitted into the opera house of Becket's mind.

Callas' voice and Giordano's music take on a new narrative power through the linking of a male body with a woman's musical text and a woman's performance as a way of highlighting Becket's struggle to achieve a gendered identity defying conventional binary divisions. For Koestenbaum, the attraction that Callas, who died in 1977, still has for gay male opera lovers is in her ability to elude strictly enforced demarcations: 'she was a mess *and* she was a goddess. Her voice gave evidence of long attempts to domesticate the unacceptable' (*Queen's Throat* 136).

Cather also appreciated the struggle undertaken by some singers to explore vocal ranges beyond their own physical limits. She was particularly impressed by the expressive qualities of the contralto voice, and significantly both Thea and her model Olive Fremstad (1871–1951) experimented with contralto parts before achieving success with roles such as Sieglinde and Isolde requiring a higher range.[4] Because the contralto is the lowest female voice, lying below the mezzo-soprano and soprano ranges, it represents the point at which a singer approaches a 'gender barrier,' for the next lowest range, the male tenor voice, is outside the usual boundaries of the female singer. But the contralto voice also embodies a certain quality of sound or timbre exclusive of its pitch that, in John Shepherd's study of music and male hegemony, can serve the stereotypes either of woman-as-nurturer or of male usurper (Shepherd 166–170).

The contralto voice thus *merges* male and female so as to create, if not a third sex, a third voice that defies easy categorisation according to gender. This vocal blending of genders is described in a curious poem that makes a brief appearance in Wilde's *The Picture of Dorian Gray*. Théophile Gautier's 'Contralto' (1853) describes the imaginative transformation of a statue of an androgynous figure into a contralto voice.

> *Que tu me plais, ômbre étrange!*
> *Son double, homme et femme à la fois,*
> *Contralto, bizarre mélange,*
> *Hermaphrodite de la voix!* (37-40)
> [*'How you please me, strange shadow!*
> *Its double, both man and woman,*
> *Contralto, bizarre blending,*
> *The voice's hermaphrodite!'*] [my translation]

Gautier's poem proceeds to enumerate the contralto's operatic successes portraying men and women ('C'est Roméo, c'est Juliette') (41), as well as the distinctly masculine roles of Arsace in Rossini's opera *Semiramide* and the title character in the same composer's *Tancredi*.

Significantly, operatic representations of gender switches were important in Cather's own life and in her fictional worlds. Sharon O'Brien has noted how the opera house provided Cather with a particularly effective forum for gender experiments that were otherwise taboo:

> The artifice of a performance of an opera like [Beethoven's] *Fidelio* visually offers the possibility for transformation and inversion of gender and sexuality: when a woman dons male attire and becomes the object of another woman's love, the lines between heterosexual and homosexual, sexual and nonsexual, male and female—fixed in the social world—become blurred upon the stage. Yet the potentially disruptive passion is contained: the listener's emotional release is made pleasurable by the 'four walls' of the theater as well as by the 'laws' of musical composition. (*The Emerging Voice* 171)

Judith Butler has also noted how 'the sight of a transvestite onstage can compel pleasure and applause while the sight of the same transvestite on the seat next to us on the bus can compel fear, rage, even violence' (527). It is hardly accidental that some of Cather's earliest experiments with gender switching were conducted on the amateur stage (Woodress 57). As Cather gained recognition as a writer, the world of fiction may have provided her with a vicarious substitute for the real-life gender play she was forced to give up while a student in Lincoln (Woodress 69–70).

But the question of how gender divisions are articulated in the first place is, according to Butler, best examined in terms of a theatrical metaphor: 'The acts by which gender is constituted bear similarities to performative acts within theatrical contexts . . . One is not simply a body, but, in some very key sense, one does one's body and, indeed, one does one's body differently from one's contemporaries and from one's embodied predecessors and successors as well' (521). Butler contends that gender is not invented by an individual, nor is it the expression of an essential physical and psychological chemistry that predates an individual's social interaction. Rather, 'gender is an act which has been rehearsed, much as a script survives the particular actors who make use of it, but which requires individual actors in order to be actualized and reproduced as reality once again' (526).

Hence, the portrayal of blurred gender divisions on the stage or screen is in effect the *re-enactment* of other, off-stage portrayals of gendered scripts. These scripts subvert or reaffirm conventional binary divisions that in turn provoke audiences to re-examine their own scripted lives. Wayne Koestenbaum's description of his own youthful sexual confusion is, I think, pertinent to Thea Kronborg's predicament as a girl in search of her womanhood: 'I spent much of childhood trying to distinguish identification from desire, asking myself, "Am I in love with Julie Andrews, or do I think I *am* Julie Andrews?" I knew that to love Julie Andrews placed me, however vaguely, in heterosexuality's domain; but to identify with Julie Andrews, to want to be the star of *Star!*, placed me under suspicion' (*Queen's Throat* 18). Perhaps because of similar anxieties, some female singers have successfully violated gender boundaries on the opera stage by resorting to scripts that actually take advantage of their physical attributes. Olive Fremstad was proud of her ability to play male roles on the opera stage, and her interests in the part of the adolescent boy Octavian in Richard Strauss's opera *Der Rosenkavalier* (1911) were both musical and physical.[5] This is not offered as conclusive evidence that Olive Fremstad was a lesbian, nor that Cather's habitual adoption of masculine attire in her youth and a male persona in her fiction *proves* anything about her sexuality. But it seems logical to accept Fremstad and Cather's individual experiments with violating discrete gender roles as evidence of their awareness that gender codes, given certain circumstances, could be broken with impunity.

My analysis of Thea Kronborg's character in the light of the musical choices she makes likewise does not attempt to settle the issue of Thea's sexual orientation, but rather to *unsettle* the notion that she accepts blindly the gender identities endorsed by Moonstone, Colorado. There is abundant evidence that Cather wished to dramatise Thea's gradual achievement of artistic success as inseparable from her struggle to reach sexual maturity, and that this struggle takes place in dramatic situations in which Thea is able to see her own femininity as a sexual 'other.' Susan Rosowski argues that 'Cather broke gender conventions to tell of Thea's growth into the diva, Kronborg. She gave to Thea qualities ordinarily reserved for men—fierce independence, ambition, discipline, and hard headedness' ('Writing Against Silences' 63). It seems plausible that Thea has learned some of her hard headedness by creating, in Wunsch's phrase, 'a Phantasie' surrounding her self-image, and that she has been able to usurp masculine power for her own uses through shrewd observations of the ways in which this power is employed in the straitlaced world of Moonstone and the worlds of music and musical drama.

Early in the novel, Thea discovers Orfeo's lament 'Che farò senza Euridice' in its German translation, 'Ach, ich habe sie verloren,' from Gluck's *Orfeo ed Euridice*, and this music returns throughout the novel as a refrain recalling her student days with the alcoholic Professor Wunsch. But as with other musical selections, Orfeo's lament does more than merely supply an alternative textual voice that tells the reader what he or she already knows from reading the novel. Thea makes strategic *musical* use of the lament to showcase her voice. Moreover, because Gluck's opera has had a long and fascinating performance history, not the least interesting part of which is the continuing debate about whether a man or a woman should sing the role of Orfeo, Thea thus enters into the gender drama written into the music itself.

As Wunsch describes his own memories of Gluck's opera *Orfeo ed Euridice*, Thea learns that the role was written for a contralto voice, and that there was only one singer who could do justice to the role, the great Spanish contralto Pauline Viardot-Garcia. But Wunsch's retelling of *Orfeo's* performance history is only partially correct; Christoph Willobald Gluck (1714-1787) wrote the part of Orfeo not for a contralto but for a castrated male's soprano voice. Because papal edicts barring women from appearing on the stage were not officially repealed until 1798, operatic roles male and female alike were taken by male singers throughout most European opera houses. At the first performance of *Orfeo ed Euridice* in Vienna in 1762, the role of Orfeo was sung by the great castrato Gaetano Guadagni, a fact which probably gave to the character of Orfeo a mythical, other-worldly quality appropriate to the opera's story (Heriot 25; Barsham 93). The role became associated with contraltos and mezzo-sopranos only after Viardot-Garcia's triumphant performances using Hector Berlioz's 1859 revisions of Gluck's score (Barsham 93-94).

Like many contemporary listeners, Cather was untroubled by the appropriation by women singers of Orfeo's character. At the same time she was beginning to write *The Song of the Lark*, Cather wrote the essay 'Three American Singers' for the December 1913 issue of *McClure's*. In the essay, Cather praises contralto Louise Homer for her portrayal of Orfeo during the Metropolitan Opera's 1909-10 season, a role that contains 'perhaps the most beautiful music ever written for the contralto voice' (36). Yet Cather must have known that Gluck's music actually had been *rewritten* so as to accommodate the contralto voice, for the same essay goes on to discuss Viardot-Garcia's career as well as Henry Chorley's *Thirty Years' Musical Recollections*, the most enthusiastic pages of which give an account of how Viardot-Garcia rescued Gluck's opera from the obscurity caused by its association with the *castrati* and made it the crowning achievement in her illustrious career (Chorley 237).[6]

I do not wish to argue in favor of or against any one casting scheme for Gluck's opera. I merely want to stress that the sexual attractions and interests of Gluck's Orfeo, like those of the mythological figure on whom he/she is based, are at best ambiguous and are the product of various scripts and interpretive styles. Thea tells Wunsch that she is already familiar with the story of Orpheus, so she is probably aware from her reading of Ovid that the singer, after his final loss of Eurydice, took comfort in young boys and introduced homosexual love to the Thracians, and that the Ciconian women, humiliated by Orpheus' preference for male lovers, tore him apart. Thea's early introduction to Ovid gives her an opportunity to use her childhood reading when she participates in a reenactment of the passions of Ovid's mythological figures. It is of little importance, I think, that Thea may be only dimly aware of the ambiguous expressions of heterosexual love in the opera. After all, how many women undertaking the role of Orpheus are conscious of the private joke that Gluck and his librettist Ranieri Calzabigi might have enjoyed by giving lines such as 'I have lost my Eurydice' to a castrated man, whose vocal register spoke ringingly of another, more personal, loss?

In any event, Thea is made an unsuspecting participant in the on-going struggle to settle the issue of Orfeo's gender at the same time that her own sexual innocence is being challenged. *Orfeo's* history coincides with Thea's coming to terms with her own female body and her search for suitable models. When she finds these models, she does not hesitate to incorporate them into her personal history. She later appropriates Gluck's music for her own use — as Viardot-Garcia had done thirty years before — and by stretching her voice downward makes her first conquest of her piano teacher Andor Harsanyi while simultaneously challenging the performance tradition of Orfeo's lament. This improvised concert takes place not on the stage but in the Harsanyi parlor, with no artifice or costume, for Thea is dressed in her street clothing and makes no effort to conceal the fact that she is singing a man's words about the loss of his wife.

No one seems discomforted, however, by Thea's challenging of the notion that a man's body, voice, and dress are necessary elements of the character she is trying to create for the Harsanyi family. Certainly, the music lesson or audition is itself a convention that has its own traditions and codes that help conceal Thea's 'subversive' behavior. Thea's transvestite performance of Orpheus' song without any visible attempt to disguise her own femininity is consequently understandable in the context of the novel, even if some male audiences would find it intolerable if she *did* put on a man's costume for the sake of dramatic verisimilitude (Wood 30).

If Thea resembles an innocent cog in Wunsch's machinery when she is introduced to *Orfeo ed Euridice*, she becomes considerably more her own master several months later. After attending a music lesson on her thirteenth birthday during which she learns Robert Schumann's setting of Heine's 'Im Leuchtenden Sommermorgen,' Thea behaves as if she were fully aware that her usurpation of the song as a feminine narrative is hardly as innocent as it appears. In fact, it is downright startling, for there are practically no historical links between the work and any female performers. In his notes to a critical edition of the score of the *cycle Dichterliebe* ('Poet's Love') from which 'Im Leuchtenden Sommermorgen' is drawn, Arthur Komar warns that 'only performances by tenors — women rarely sing the role in public because of its poetic content — can be expected to conform to the original keys' of *Dichterliebe* (93).

Even though Schumann's song is both musically and emotionally 'out of reach' for most women, Thea learns it and apparently performs it for her teacher. Afterwards, she

> wandered for a long while about the sand ridge, picking up crystals and looking into the yellow prickly-pear blossoms with their thousand stamens. She looked at the sand hills until she wished she *were* a sand hill. And yet she knew that she was going to leave them all behind some day. (79)

Her encounter with Schumann's song has given her an awareness of male desire that she had never grasped before. She seems to notice for the first time the 'prickly-pear blossoms with their thousand stamens' rudely asserting their masculine potency. This awareness of threats to her feminine sexuality seems to be triggered by her having played the role of the male for the song's duration.

> From that day on, she felt there was a secret between her and Wunsch. Together they had lifted a lid, pulled out a drawer, and looked at something. They hid it away and never spoke of what they had seen; but neither of them forgot it (79).

The discovery of sexual difference as dramatised in this scene suggests something more profound than a mere grasping for the forbidden fruit. Cather implies that Thea experiences an awareness of physical nakedness, a recognition of genital difference that forever alters her relations with Wunsch. (Wunsch has grilled Thea about the masculine perspective necessary to perform the song.) Not only has sex become a deeply attractive secret that Thea will guard jealously until maturity forces her to share it with others; it is equated with a kind of stolen merchandise, as if Thea were aware of the gendered male world only after she had been forced to recognise her own role in nearly recreating a physically complete male through the voicing of masculine desire in the Schumann song.

In both the Gluck and Schumann examples, Thea seems at first to stumble inadvertently into questions about her own sexual identity. She plays the part of Trilby to Wunsch's benign Svengali, who furnishes the material through which Thea articulates a response to her own sexually immature longing. Yet Thea also knows neither guilt nor embarrassment because of her dangerous adoption of a male persona. Instead, Wunsch gives her space in which to experiment with the musical tools at hand, and no one in the novel, least of all Cather herself, seems troubled by Thea's appropriation of a masculine identity. It should be stressed again that Thea's experiments with gender play are normalised because she resorts to a *musical* script that, unlike that used in Demme's film *Philadelphia*, possesses enough of a middle range—the contralto voice—to enable a singer to enjoy free passage above and below the shifting musical dividing line between male and female performers.

Thea is fortunate in that she possesses the musical vocabulary necessary to normalise her assaults on the gender code, because she seems to envision even stranger transformations than those made possible by her musical expertise. After her thirteenth birthday, 'she looked at the sand hills until she wished she *were* a sand hill' (79). Her desire for an Ovidian metamorphosis into a sand hill resembles other strange desires expressed later in the novel. During the restorative summer at Panther Canyon, Thea muses,

> she could become a mere receptacle for heat, or become a color, like the bright lizards that darted about on the hot stones outside her door; or she could become a continuous repetition of sound, like the cicadas. (300)

Curiously enough, Thea's adoption of different identities is less an exercise of the imagination, as Rosowski suggests, than it is a physical accomplishment.

When Wunsch leaves Moonstone after his final disgrace, he watches Thea wave to him from the station platform. He muses about her 'imagination and ... stubborn will, curiously balancing and interpenetrating each other.' He suddenly realises that she has become 'the yellow prickly-pear blossoms that open there in the desert; thornier and sturdier than the maiden flowers he remembered; not so sweet, but wonderful' (96). Thus, by an independent route, Wunsch comes to the same conclusion Thea reached on her thirteenth birthday. Thea is effectively masculinised in Wunsch's memory, just as the girl herself once discovered something about her innermost secrets as she wandered the sand hills full of Heine's poem and Schumann's music. In contrast to Gelfant's detection of an 'aversion to sex' expressed by the 'enigmatic gestures' of characters in *My Ántonia*, Thea's gestures, her very demeanor and appearance, evoke an adolescent who is intensely and unashamedly sexual.

Once her desire for gender transformations can be articulated, Thea is no longer bound by *any* conventions, not even — if we recall the references to sand hills, lizards, and cicadas — the natural laws governing the integrity of the human species. This breakdown of categories, while exhilarating, is more deeply subversive of accepted codes of behavior than are Thea's musically-based gender roles, and shows that Cather, once she had charted such a radical course for Thea, necessarily had to retreat from it in order to get on with the story she was trying to tell. Unfortunately, as I argue at the end of this essay, Cather also retreated from Thea's gender breakthroughs as well, so that much of the drama and promise of Thea's thirteenth birthday is canceled by the end of the novel.

Before this disillusioning abandonment, however, Cather continued to explore Thea's approaching womanhood in terms of musical texts. After a disappointing year of studying voice in Chicago, Thea accepts Spanish Johnny's invitation to a Mexican ball in Moonstone, and asks him to teach her the Mexican serenade 'Rosa de Noche.' Johnny is doubtful about the propriety of such a song; not only is it for a low voice ('voz contralto') as opposed to Thea's now higher one, it is only to be sung by 'married ladies': '"They sing it for husbands — or somebody else, may-bee." Johnny's eyes twinkled and he apologised gracefully with his shoulders' (226).

But Thea is adamant about learning the *serenata*, and Johnny writes down the words for her. At the ball, she sings the *serenata* not once but twice, and Cather's description of her audience's involvement is particularly striking.

> For the moment they cared about nothing in the world but what she was doing. Their faces confronted her, open, eager, unprotected. She felt as if all these warm-blooded people débouched into her. Mrs Tellamantez's fateful resignation, Johnny's madness, the adoration of the boy who lay still in the sand; in an instant these things seemed to be within her instead of without, as if they had come from her in the first place. (232)

The growth in sophistication that separates Thea's discoveries of *Orfeo* and Schumann's song from the sexually-charged performance at the ball is significant. In the latter, Thea's voice becomes an embodiment of her sexuality — Cather felt the ball corresponded to the flowering of Thea's femininity — and by synechdochical extension it comes to represent her gradually maturing body's development as a conquering instrument (Letter, 7 Dec. 1915).

But the *serenata* 'Rosa de Noche,' like Gluck's *Orfeo*, has a complex performance history, most of which is available only through Cather's letters to Elizabeth Shepley Sergeant describing her first trip to the Southwest. During a visit to Winslow, Arizona in April–May 1912, Cather's brother Douglass introduced her to a musical trio composed of a Mexican bartender and two section hands on the railroad who played for her. The trio brought with them an uncommonly handsome youth named Julio who sang for Cather the *serenata* 'Rosa de Noche' that Thea performs at the ball. Cather fell under Julio's spell, and references to his beauty and mystery abound in her letters. But she was also so struck by his song that she made an English translation of it and included it at the end of a rhapsodic letter to Sergeant describing her own experiences as the only white person in attendance at a Mexican ball in Winslow.[7]

Critics have wrestled with the questions surrounding Cather's infatuation with Julio. Her biographer James Woodress includes an extended description of the journey to the Southwest as the introduction to his biography, but although he acknowledges the importance of the trip in understanding Cather's later career, he makes little of her relationship with the enigmatic youth. Loretta Wasserman, on the other hand, argues that 'the intensity felt wherever Cather treats the Southwest or Mexico in her fiction derives from Julio' (353).

Cather's own descriptions of Julio are curiously ambiguous. In fact, he might have stepped out of Gautier's poem as a re-working of the contralto's 'bizarre mélange.' Cather wrote to Sergeant that he resembled statues of Antinous in the Naples Museum, that his beauty was unearthly, that he was not soft or sunny but that he carried his great beauty with consummate grace and lightness (Letters, 12 May 1912; 21 May 1912; 15 June 1912). Cather carefully avoids any description of Julio's *machismo*, and by comparing him to Antinous, the Emperor Hadrian's homosexual lover who drowned while crossing the Nile and who was later deified by Hadrian, suggests the image of a man who was sexually attractive to both men and women.[8]

Julio's ambiguous gender is emphasised by the description Cather gave Sergeant of his musical performances. His *serenata*, she wrote, is to be sung in a 'voz contralto,' and is to be sung only by a married lady to her husband or her lover. Cather nowhere describes the quality of Julio's voice, but her transcription of the song's text and her specification of the appropriate voice and audience make it clear that Julio must have adopted a feminine persona and vocal register as necessary elements of a transvestite performance. The reversal of gender roles that Julio under took in order to perform the song is made more intriguing by the fact that Julio apparently sang the song to Cather during an intimate serenade and not at a public performance. Was Julio having a private joke at a *gringa's* expense by identifying himself with the woman-subject and Cather with the male-object, the woman's husband or lover? Or was Cather fully aware of her own identity as the masculinised audience and proud of Julio's insight into her character? Or was this confusion of gender and sexuality merely the necessary by product of a performance, the very artificiality of which made it so memorable for Cather?

It is impossible to choose between these readings of Cather's 'readings' of Julio and his music, but it is clear that when she used the episode in *The Song of the Lark*, she took care to purge it of its obvious transvestite trappings, without, however, excluding an important erotic component that emphasises Thea's burgeoning femininity.[9] Unlike Julio, Thea is of course a *woman* possessing a contralto voice; she tells Spanish Johnny 'I can do more with my low voice than I used to' (226). But her voice nonetheless crosses a gender boundary in that it achieves a kind of masculine conquest of her audience. Thea is still a virgin at this point of the novel, so her adoption of the persona of a sexually aware woman seeking to seduce a man through her song signifies a daring attempt to achieve sexual knowledge both figuratively (through the song's text) and literally (by singing to the men at her feet). Her conquest is complete, as shown by the quasi-post-coital exhaustion of the Mexican men around her: 'The men began hunting feverishly for cigarettes . . . Johnny dropped on his elbow, wiping his face and neck and hands with his handkerchief. "If you sing like that once in the City of Mexico, they just-a go crazy"' (232–233).

Thea's audience's fervor can be seen as evidence of her *masculine* potency; she seizes the attention of her 'unprotected' audience with something approaching sexual violence and leaves it ravished by her attack. But she also maintains her femininity by *retrieving* the men and women around her into her very body ('these warm-blooded people débouched into her'). In Rosowski's words, Thea reabsorbs the external world through 'metaphors of female reproduction, by which gestation, birth, and mothering are not separate stages but ongoing, simultaneous aspects of female life' ('Writing Against Silences' 61). Notably, she accomplishes this reabsorption by employing a voice that, like Julio's, is not strictly female. Instead, it hovers at the region in which male and female voices share a common timbre and musical territory, thereby enabling her to vocalise simultaneously masculine and feminine desires.

Thea's performance may be more persuasive as an actual tool of seduction than Julio's, but it seems Cather was simply trying to portray in her novel what she had felt herself while listening to the young man in the Arizona desert. Her great care in preparing a translation of 'Rosa de Noche' —that, because it enigmatically concludes an unsigned letter to Sergeant, practically constitutes a love song to Sergeant herself—reflects her desire to preserve an experience that was deeply important to her. Cather's encounter with the androgynous youth who gave her this song also helps to enlarge a reader's understanding of Thea who, although not obviously androgynous herself, first senses the flowering of her femininity at the moment she adopts Julio's pseudo-masculine musical text.

So far, Thea's musical adventures have been of a more or less intimate nature. Her lessons with Wunsch, her church singing, and even the Mexican ball, are relatively private affairs. But at the ball's end, as Thea undertakes the role of Lucia in the sextet from *Lucia di Lammermoor*, Cather enlarges her narrative focus to bring in Thea's friends, the Kohlers, who hear the girl's incandescent voice from the other side of Moonstone. At the same time that Thea 'lets out' her voice and finds unsuspected power in her highest notes, her audience is correspondingly broadened to include the entire town, presaging how Thea's voice will one day travel the world through her recordings. 'Gender' becomes a public performance that discloses for her 'the possiblity of a different sort of repeating, in the breaking or subversive repetition of that style' (Butler 520). Thea thus begins her movement toward scripts and musical texts, such as Wagner's operas, that will disclose her femininity, rather than her sexual ambiguity, to audiences.

The sextet from Act II of *Lucia di Lammermoor* is especially important because it provides a setting for Thea's dramatisation of her uneasy relationship with her family and her past. Donizetti's ensemble, a tour-de-force of great musical ingenuity and originality, is a complicated piece weaving disparate musical and emotional narratives into a marvelously coherent musical fabric. In the opera, Lucia has been humiliated by her lover's confrontation with her fiancé, and these two rivals for her affection join vocal forces with Lucia's brother and her friend Raimondo to describe the simultaneous fury and restraint that paralyzes them. Meanwhile, Lucia and her maid Alicia grieve over the humiliating scene and pray for deliverance from the inevitable horrors of Act III.

Yet as Paul Robinson has recognised, a listener does not actually 'hear' the words of the sextet: 'Once past the solo tenor introduction, very little [of the sextet] can be understood, although incomprehensibility is hardly its dramatic point. This wonderful piece works its effect on us in spite of our not understanding what is being said, and it does so almost entirely through musical means' (339). These musical means involve a near erasure of the text's intelligibility so that, according to Robinson, 'the words are simply liquified in a sea of operatic tone' (337). The asymmetrical apportionment of vocal forces—two tenors, two sopranos, a baritone and a bass—creates the aural impression of a predominantly masculine vocal fabric challenged, and ultimately conquered, by the repeated high B-flats of Lucia's vocal line. Thus the sextet is a veritable case study of how gendered musical voices seek mastery over each other not only to serve the dramatic requirements of an opera plot about the oppression of a woman but also to create sexual tension solely by musical means (Clément 88–90).

Cather's description of Thea's triumphant performance makes no mention of the words she is singing but nonetheless emphasises its musically-grounded gender divisions:

> There was silence for a few moments. Then the guitar sounded fiercely, and several male voices began the sextette from 'Lucia.' Johnny's reedy tenor they knew well, and the bricklayer's big, opaque barytone; the others might be anybody over there — just Mexican voices. Then at the appointed, at the acute, moment, the soprano voice, like a fountain jet, shot up into the light. (235)

The condescension expressed by reference to the vague identity of the other voices of the sextet — 'just Mexican voices' — is appropriate to the racial stereotyping that infiltrates the Kronborg family council when it reprimands Thea the following morning, but it also provides telling evidence of the unique quality of Thea's voice, brilliantly highlighted by its contrast with the 'dusky' voices of the men. Just as Lucia vocally — if not literally — conquers the family and social forces that imprison her at the end of Act II, so Thea's impromptu performance at the ball signals her achievement of congruence between her vocal, professional, and sexual longings. For she now shows her mastery of a wide vocal range. By moving from a convincing delivery of the *serenata* in a contralto voice to the subsequent thrilling performance of Lucia's high soprano music, she confirms her awakening to the unabashedly feminine timbre of her vocal cords.

But Thea pays a price for her performance. The morning after the ball she discovers that most of her family is embarrassed by her behavior. Her sister Anna is appalled. 'Everybody at Sunday-School was talking about you going over there and singing with the Mexicans all night, when you won't sing for the church' (237). The taboos invoked against Thea have distinct racial and religious overtones, but it seems that Thea's *vocalisation* of the sexual desires in the text of the *serenata* and her choice of secular music like Donizetti's *Lucia* have been so dangerously subversive that, at least among the more conservative citizens of Moonstone, she is already a ruined woman. For them, singing about sin is equivalent to committing it.

After retreating to her stifling room upstairs, Thea resolves to cut the last ties to her family: 'Nothing that she would ever do in the world would seem important to them, and nothing they would ever do would seem important to her' (240). Thea now sees herself and her family in an entirely new light. She takes a giant leap toward artistic maturity with the self-assurance gained from this impromptu performance; she is determined to continue her musical studies in Chicago and someday in Europe: 'She was going away to fight, and she was going away forever' (246).

The irony of the moment is that by adopting for apparently the first time in her career a traditionally feminine operatic role like Lucia, Thea has also come closest to expressing, as Lucia had, her frustration with the conventional world of family and town. Yet this awakening, or in Rosowski's term, this 'transformation,' depends on an essentially virile seizing of the dramatic moment;

Thea's singing is in fact expressed as a kind of male ejaculation in prose rhythms that imitate the concert's accumulated sexual tension 'at the appointed, at the acute, moment, the soprano voice, like a fountain jet, shot up into the light.' Across town, the Kohlers are mesmerised by the performance; Thea's voice 'leaped from among those dusky male voices! How it played in and about and around them and over them' (235). Donizetti's shaping of the sextet calls for the sudden release of feminine vocal energy at the very moment when women's voices seem to have been deliberately excluded. Significantly, the reworking of her own gender, family, and vocal tensions with those of the fictious Lucia Ashton represents Thea's first conquest of the world of audiences.

Her defense of her attendance at the ball—the Mexicans 'know something about what I'm doing. They're a talented people' (238)—also shows that Thea is now sure of the kind of audience she wants to pursue. Her admirers will not be found in the churches in Moonstone or Chicago where she has done most of her singing, nor will they be the kind likely to enjoy the pious hymns and oratorio selections she has come to loathe. The sextet furnishes a dramatic situation in which Thea can sing about her own boring life in Moonstone, her growing awareness of a powerful sexual identity, and her desire for an audience susceptible to her powers. She has not abandoned any of the vocal expertise she learned as a child, but she no longer depends solely on the transvestite 'voz contralto' to perform her gendered identity.

Nonetheless, the 'voz contralto' returns toward the end of the novel to highlight Thea's indecision about leaving New York to undertake voice studies in Germany. As Thea is packing her belongings in a New York hotel room, her erstwhile lover Fred Ottenburg, having misled Thea about his intention to marry, stumbles upon her score of Gluck's *Orfeo*. Wunsch had bequeathed the score to her and written on the inside page the words 'Einst, O Wunder,' the tragic refrain from Beethoven's song *Adelaïde*, ('Soon, o marvel!'), describing the tenor's wish for death so that on his grave may bloom a flower in memory of his beloved. Ottenburg senses the dramatic rightness of Wunsch's inscription, and he begins to sing the Beethoven song as if to tell Thea that she has taken yet another male victim in the course of her musical and sexual struggles.[10]

Ottenburg then suggests that Thea's singing career has so far been a kind of apprenticeship, and he predicts Thea's eventual triumph as he runs through Beethoven's song. Voice and womanhood become synonymous: 'You'll get a new speech full of shades and color like your voice; alive, like your mind. It will be almost like being born again, Thea' (378). This rebirth is an example of one of the ongoing processes of gestation and birth described by Rosowski; it also represents the conclusion of a sexual apprenticeship, because Fred hopes that Thea will, upon her return, accept his offer of a sexual relationship outside marriage.

But Thea is uneasy about the consequences of her imminent trip to Europe. She has one last moment of doubt and looks into the abyss:

> She could still hear [Wunsch] playing in the snowstorm, '*Ach, ich habe sie verloren!*' That melody was released in her like a passion of longing. Every nerve in her body thrilled to it. It brought her to her feet, carried her somehow to bed and into troubled sleep. (381)

Gluck's melody triggers memories of the stifling, conventional world of Moonstone to which, only a few moments before, she was willing to capitulate. It may be that her awareness of her own, once-unwitting challenge to the rigidly enforced gender boundaries enforced by musical texts gives her new energy to resist forever the attractions of the conventional world. Moreover, the parallel to the aftermath of the Mexican ball is dramatically right: Thea takes stock of her present predicament and cuts her ties to familiar people and places. It seems hardly accidental that these difficult decisions are made against an elaborate backdrop of musical allusions that remind Thea of who she is and who she can become.

But there is also a tragic quality to Thea's recollection. For a brief, crucial moment, her voice and that of the long-vanished Wunsch overlap in the reference to Orfeo's lament. She realises that Wunsch, too, was called to do great things but ended his life a broken, disillusioned, despairing wreck of a man. His 'Phantasie,' defined in Thea's mind by his own singing of Orfeo's lament, stands as a symbol for the ultimate 'bad' transvestite performance. For Wunsch is a performer without any singing voice at all, without, indeed, any power to create an illusion. He is measured in terms of his losses—of students, of respectability, of his symbolic Eurydice. Thea understands through her recollection of Wunsch's tragic performance that her own 'Phantasie' must be lived as well as sung—that her singing career is co-extensive with her identity as a woman, and that this realisation is essentially, even perhaps dangerously, liberating.[11] Thus Thea later decides against returning to Moonstone to visit her dying mother because her engagement by the Dresden Opera to sing Elizabeth in Wagner's *Tannhäuser* is the chance of a lifetime. Once the decision to become an artist has been made, there is no possibility for compromise. Even her oldest friendships and family ties must be sacrificed.

In fact, all of Thea's models—from her parents, to her teachers, to her lovers, to the very musical texts she chooses to showcase her voice—are ultimately disposable. 'She is very much interested in herself—as she should be,' Mrs Nathanmeyer tells Ottenburg (278). Thea's legacy, if she leaves one at all, is hardly musical, but it is surely political. She instructs readers, artists, opera singers, to leave behind family, friendship, teachers, students. And it is surely not accidental that Thea's rebelliousness has its roots in her earliest studies with Wunsch, with her questioning of, in Marjorie Garber's phrase, 'the categories of "female" and "male," whether they are considered essential or constructed, biological or cultural' (10).

David Stouck is correct when he lumps together Thea's circle of friends—Wunsch, Ray Kennedy, Spanish Johnny, Aunt Tillie—and calls them failures whose 'frustrations sometimes find an outlet in bizarre and pathetic gestures' (188). And because she is surrounded by such useless models, Thea resembles a reversal of Wilde's Dorian Gray different from the one Cather wrote about in the novel's preface. For unlike the earlier novel, *The Song of the Lark* begins in chaos and ambiguity—the Kronborgs' disorganised family life, Thea's childhood illness, delirium, and her later sexual confusion—and moves toward a sense of order and certainty. By contrast, when Dorian reflects on Gautier's poem 'Contralto' the morning after he has murdered the painter Basil Hallward, he seems to wallow in the mystifying ambiguities portrayed in the poem as expressive of his own moral collapse. Thea's growth from contralto to Wagnerian soprano echoes—perhaps even constitutes—her escape from 'a vague, easy-going world into a life of disciplined endeavor' (480).

In the novel's epilogue, Cather unfortunately 'shaves off' the rough edges of Thea's sexuality by having her climb the heights of musical greatness as the wife of Fred Ottenburg after the complex issues of bigamy and deception have been quietly disposed of. Cather recognised in her 1932 preface that this plot-turn was a necessary if ineffective device: 'The life of a successful artist in the full tide of achievement is not so interesting as the life of a talented young girl "fighting her way," as we say' (vii). Thea's life as Mrs Fred Ottenburg somehow represents a capitulation to the very conventions that Thea had so vigorously opposed throughout the earlier parts of the novel.[12]

The book's concluding line—

> So, into all the little settlements of quiet people, tidings of what their boys and girls are doing in the world bring real refreshment; bring to the old, memories, and to the young, dreams (490)

in fact sounds as hollow as the distant echo of Thea's voice through the gramophone horn. Cather's *Künstlerroman* ultimately turns its back on Thea's struggle to forge an identity challenging traditional notions of feminine happiness outside heterosexual marriage. Thea's model Olive Fremstad was not so easily tempted by conventionality, but Cather apparently felt the need to fictionalise at this point rather than adhere to the narrative agenda that Thea's rebelliousness prescribed.

Perhaps Cather suspected that Thea's musical accomplishments, after all, were not enough for happiness, and she therefore sought a romantic alternative to the artist's lonely world of unrealised (presumed) heterosexual love. But Cather's purported reversal of Dorian Gray's story to illustrate how the 'artistic life is the only one in which [the opera diva] is happy, or free, or even very real,' while the artist's real life is composed of 'exacting engagements and dull business detail,' rests on the very idea—the separation of the artistic life from a physical one—that Thea's story ultimately *disproves* (Preface, viii). Artist and woman are, for Thea at least, overlapping, mutually defining, and inextricably bound together.

On the other hand, it may be that Cather's need to sentimentalise grew out of a premonition that Olive Fremstad's actual 'epilogue,' could it have been disclosed, would have been intolerably lonely and sad. Confined to a nursing home toward the end of her life, Fremstad was visited by her devoted companion Mary Watkins Cushing, or 'Tinka' as Fremstad called her, in a real-life 'epilogue' to the diva's career. In *The Rainbow Bridge*, Cushing movingly recounts how the two women sat listening to the Saturday afternoon Metropolitan Opera radio broadcast of soprano Ljuba Welitsch in Richard Strauss's *Salome*, an opera that had received its scandalous American premiere at the Met in 1907 with Fremstad in the title role. As the music reached 'its noisiest climax, the aged prima donna reached out her crippled hand and switched off the whole thing. "My God, Tinka!" she exclaimed, regarding me with deep dismay, "for that I once shed my heart's blood!"' (49). The thought that Thea Kronborg's epilogue—a life devoted only to music and fictionalised identities—could end up resembling Fremstad's is certainly a sobering thought.

Nonetheless, despite O'Brien's complaint that after writing *The Song of the Lark*, Cather lapsed into a world of 'romantic women and male perceivers.' Cather learned from the experience. In subsequent novels, particularly *My Ántonia* (1918) and *The Professor's House* (1925), she offered interesting alternatives to the anticipated final reconciliations of such characters as Jim Burden with Lena Lingard or Ántonia Shimerda, and Godfrey St Peter with his wife Lillian. I would argue that it is no accident that both of these later novels also include important musical episodes—Jim and Lena's attendance at a performance of Reginald De Koven's opera *Robin Hood*, and Godfrey and Lillian's enjoyment of Ambroise Thomas' opera *Mignon* during their visit to Chicago. Nor is it accidental that both De Koven's and Thomas' works depend on the vocal transvestism of significant characters to tell their convoluted stories—the contralto/male role of Allan-a-Dale in *Robin Hood*, and the cross-dressed mezzo-soprano Mignon herself.

The subversion of conventional gender roles through the use of what Judith Butler calls performative gender identities or scripts in these two musical allusions is repeated in the fictional narratives in which Cather has situated them. By including such intriguing musical references, Cather signified her increasing sensitivity to the power of dramatic depictions of gender identities that violate traditional binary divisons, and also her diminishing vulnerability to the attraction of conventional—and illusory—happy endings for her characters. Such a reading of Cather's career also lends greater substance and depth to the memories and dreams that Thea Kronborg's voice unleashes at the end of *The Song of the Lark*—dreams that go a long way toward challenging the surface tranquility of towns like Moonstone, Colorado.